FOUNDATIONS AND PERSPECTIVES OF INTERNATIONAL TRADE LAW

AUSTRALIA
LBC Information Services
Sydney

CANADA AND USA
Carswell
Toronto

NEW ZEALAND
Brooker's
Auckland

SINGAPORE AND MALAYSIA
Sweet and Maxwell Asia
Singapore and Kuala Lumpur

FOUNDATIONS AND PERSPECTIVES OF INTERNATIONAL TRADE LAW

Edited by

PROFESSOR IAN FLETCHER
DR LOUKAS MISTELIS
PROFESSOR MARISE CREMONA

LONDON
SWEET & MAXWELL
2001

Published in 2001
by Sweet and Maxwell Limited
of 100 Avenue Road, Swiss Cottage
London NW3 3PF.
(http://www.sweetandmaxwell.co.uk)
Typeset by J&L Composition Ltd, Filey, North Yorkshire.
Printed in Great Britain by MPG Books Ltd, Bodmin, Cornwall

No natural forests were destroyed to make this product; only farmed
timber was used and replanted.

A CIP catalogue record for this book is available from the British Library.

ISBN 0-421-741-007

The editors wish to dedicate this book to the memory of their friend and colleague, Anna Mörner, who died tragically on November 3, 2000.

CONTENTS

PART ONE

THE FUTURE OF HARMONISATION AND FORMULATING AGENCIES

1. IS HARMONISATION A NECESSARY EVIL? THE FUTURE OF HARMONISATION AND NEW SOURCES OF INTERNATIONAL TRADE LAW BY DR LOUKAS MISTELIS

2. THE ROLE OF UNCITRAL BY DR GEROLD HERRMANN

3. HARMONISING COMMERCIAL LAW: KEEPING PACE WITH BUSINESS BY MARIA LIVANOS CATTAUI

PART TWO

REGULATION AND DEREGULATION OF INTERNATIONAL TRADE

10. THE RISE AND FALL OF THE MULTILATERAL AGREEMENT FOR INVESTMENT: LES-
SONS FOR THE REGULATION OF INTERNATIONAL BUSINESS BY PROFESSOR PETER T.
MUCHLINSKI

11. MULTILATERAL AND BILATERAL APPROACHES TO THE INTERNATIONALISATION
OF COMPETITION LAW: AN EU PERSPECTIVE BY PROFESSOR MARISE CREMONA

PART THREE

MODERN TRENDS IN CONFLICT LAWS

12. PLEADING ACTIONS AND DEFENCES UNDER FOREIGN LAW BY PROFESSOR DR
OSKAR HARTWIEG

13. RENVOI: A NECESSARY EVIL OR IS IT POSSIBLE TO ABOLISH IT BY STATUTE? BY
PROFESSOR KURT SIEHR

PART FOUR

CURRENT ISSUES IN INTERNATIONAL COMMERCIAL ARBITRATION

PART FIVE

INTERNATIONAL CONTRACTS—HARMONISATION OF SALES CONTRACTS AND E-COMMERCE

23. Revisiting the autonomous contract—transitional contract "law",
trends and supportive structures by Ralph Amissah

24. Principles of contract law in electronic commerce by Professor
Raymond T. Nimmer

PART SIX

FINANCE OF INTERNATIONAL TRADE IN THE 21ST CENTURY

25. The curious dynamics of free trade in the western hemisphere:
Prospects for the FTAA by Professor Joseph J. Norton

26. FINANCING TRADE WITHIN A REGIONAL FRAMEWORK – LEGISLATIVE OPTIONS: CLIVE M. SCHMITHOFF ON THE UNIFICATION OF THE LAW OF INTERNATIONAL TRADE REVISITED BY ANNA MÖRNER

27. CROSS-BORDER TRADE IN FINANCIAL SERVICES BY DR. ROSA MARIA LASTRA

28. PAYMENT SYSTEMS IN THE 21ST CENTURY BY DR. ROBERT C. EFFROS

29. RECENT TRENDS IN EC PAYMENT SYSTEMS BY PROFESSOR DR. NORBERT HORN

PART SEVEN

RE-SHAPING THE INTERNATIONAL INSOLVENCY PROCESS

30. MANAGING DEFAULTING MULTINATIONALS WITHIN NAFTA BY PROFESSOR JAY LAURENCE WESTBROOK

31. UNCITRAL PROJECTS; INSOL INTERNATIONAL BY RON W. MARMER

32. INTERNATIONAL INSOLVENCY AT THE CROSSROADS – A CRITICAL APPRAISAL OF CURRENT TRENDS BY PROFESSOR IAN F. FLETCHER

PART EIGHT

TRADE RELATED ISSUES OF INTELLECTUAL PROPERTY

33. GLOBAL HARMONISATION OF INTELLECTUAL PROPERTY BY RICHARD C. WILDER

34. INTELLECTUAL PROPERTY IN THE MILLENIUM ROUND – THE TRIPS AGREEMENT AFTER SEATTLE BY PROFESSOR MICHAEL BLAKENEY

SUMMARY TABLE OF CONTENTS

PART ONE

THE FUTURE OF HARMONISATION AND FORMULATING AGENCIES

PART TWO

REGULATION AND DEREGULATION OF INTERNATIONAL TRADE

PART THREE

MODERN TRENDS IN CONFLICT LAWS

PART FOUR

CURRENT ISSUES IN INTERNATIONAL ARBITRATION

PART FIVE

INTERNATIONAL CONTRACTS-HARMONISATION OF
SALES CONTRACTS AND E-COMMERCE

PART SIX

FINANCE OF INTERNATIONAL TRADE IN THE 21ST CENTURY

PART SEVEN

RE-SHAPING THE INTERNATIONAL INSOLVENCY PROCESS

PART EIGHT

TRADE RELATED ISSUES OF INTELLECTUAL PROPERTY

LIST OF CONTRIBUTORS

Ralph Amissah — Ralph Amissah is a Fellow of Pace University, Institute for International Commercial Law (http://www.cisg.law.pace.edu/). He built the first website related to international trade law, now known as lexmercatoria.org and described as "an (international/transnational) commercial law and e-commerce infrastructure monitor". (http://lexmercatoria.org). He works with the law firm Amissahs. Ralph@Amissah.com.

Camilla Baasch Andersen — Camilla Baasch Anderson is a Research Fellow at the University of Copenhagen Law School. Her research project focus on the unification objective of the Vienna International Sales Convention.

Dr Joanna Benjamin — Joanna Benjamin is Senior Lecturer at the Centre for Commercial Law Studies, Queen, Mary University of London and Consultant to Clifford Chance, London.

Professor Dr Klaus Peter Berger — Klaus Peter Berger is Professor for Civil, Commercial, Comparative and Private International Law; Director, Institute for International Business Law and Center for Transnational Law (CENTRAL), Münster University, Germany.

Professor Michael Blakeney — Michael Blakeney is Herchel Smith Professor of Intellectual Property at Queen Mary, University of London and Director of the Queen Mary Intellectual Property Research Institute. This Institute, together with CEIPI, the University of Alicante and the Swiss Technological University at Zurich form the European Intellectual Property Institutes Network (EIPIN).

Professor Michael Joachim Bonell — Professor of Law at the University of Rome I "La Sapienza"; Consultant — the International Institute for the Unification of Private Law (UNIDROIT); member of the Italian Delegation at the 1980 Vienna Diplomatic Conference for the adoption of the United Nations Convention on Contracts for the International Sale of Goods (CISG); Chairman of the Working Group for the Preparation of the UNIDROIT Principles of International Commercial Contracts.

Maria Livanos Cattaui — Maria Livanos Cattaui is Secretary-General of the International Chamber of Commerce. From 1977 to 1996 Maria Cattaui was with the World Economic Forum in Geneva, with responsibility to develop the Annual Meeting in Davos into a "global summit". Mrs Cattaui, who is of Swiss nationality and Greek origin, was educated in the United States. She is an Honours graduate of Harvard University.

Professor Marise Cremona — Marise Cremona is Professor of European Commercial Law, Head of the European Commercial Law Unit and Deputy Director of the Centre for Commercial Law Studies.

Dr Robert Effros — Robert Effros, A.B., LL.B., Harvard University; LL.M. Georgetown University Law Center, is a consultant on banking and financial law. Formerly Assistant General Counsel (Legislation), International Monetary Fund.

Professor Ian F. Fletcher — Ian Fletcher is Professor of Commercial Law and Director of the Centre for Commercial Law Studies, Queen Mary, University of London. He was called to the Bar by Lincoln's Inn in 1971, and currently practises from 3/4 South Square, Gray's Inn. He is a member of the American Law Institute, of the National Bankruptcy Conference (USA), and of the Insolvency Lawyers' Association (U.K.). As of January 2001 Ian Fletcher moved to University College London, as the Herbert Smith Professor of International Commercial Law.

Professor Alejandro Garro — Alejandro M. Garro is Adjunct Professor of Law at Columbia University and Senior Research Scholar of the Parker School of Foreign and Comparative Law. He was born and educated in Argentina, where he received his law degree (*abogado*) and practised law. He then pursued graduate legal studies in the United States, where he has been teaching since 1981. Professor Garro received the LL.M degree by Louisiana State University School of Law and the degree of Doctor of Laws (J.S.D.) by Columbia University. He is admitted to practice in Buenos Aires, Madrid and New York.

Ron W. Harmer — Ron W. Harmer is an Australian lawyer with wide experience in the practice and reform of insolvency law. He was in charge of the work of the Australian Law Reform Commission on insolvency law reform (1984–87). He is a consultant to the Asian Development Bank on insolvency law projects in a number of Asian jurisdictions, and has recently completed a major comparative study of insolvency laws and related practices in eleven Asian jurisdictions. He is a Senior Visiting Fellow at Queen Mary, University of London.

Professor Dr Oskar Hartwieg — Oskar Hartwieg is Professor of International Business Law and Private International Law at the University of Hanover, Germany. He has been visiting professor in England, the United States and Japan.

Dr. Gerold Herrmann — Dr. Gerold Herrmann is, since 1991, Secretary of the United Nations Commission on International Trade Law (UNCITRAL) and Chief, International Trade Law Branch, Office of Legal Affairs, United Nations. Dr. Herrmann holds law degrees from the Universities of Cologne in Germany and the University of California at Berkeley in the United States of America. He is an Honorary Professor of the University of Vienna, where he also serves as a part-time lecturer.

Professor Dr Norbert Horn — Norbert Horn is Professor of Private and Commercial Law, Banking and International Business Law and Legal Philosophy at the University of Cologne. He is Director of the Banking Law Institute and of the Law Centre for European and International Co-operation (R.I.Z.) at the University of Cologne.

Professor John Jackson — Professor Jackson joined the Georgetown faculty after a distinguished career as Hessel E. Yntema Professor of Law at the University of Michigan. He has been a visiting faculty member at the University of Delhi, India and the University of Brussels, Belgium, a Consultant on Legal Education to the Ford Foundation, a Research Scholar at the headquarters of General Agreement on Tariffs and Trade (GATT) in Geneva, Switzerland, and a Rockefeller Foundation Fellow in Brussels, Belgium. He has served as Associate Vice President for Academic Affairs at the University of Michigan and as General Counsel for the Office of the President's Special Representative for Trade in the U.S. Executive Office of the President in Washington, D.C.

Professor Dr Drres hc Konstantin D. Kerameus — Professor of Civil Procedure at Athens University School of Law (since 1982) and Director of the Hellenic Institute of International and Foreign Law (since 1990). Visiting professor at Berlin University, Hamburg University, Université de Paris II, Louisiana State University, Ohio State University, Tulane University, Chuo University. In July 1997 he taught at the Hague Academy of International Law ("Enforcement in the International Context"). Since 1993 the Board of the International Association of Legal Science and since 1994 a member of the Academia Europaea (London). Since 1998 President of the International Academy of Comparative Law.

Professor Catherine Kessedjian — Professor, University of Paris II Panthéon—Assas, Former Deputy Secretary-General, Hague Conference on Private International Law.

Professor Dr Herbert Kronke — Herbert Kronke is Secretary-General, International Institute for the Unification of Private Law (UNIDROIT), Rome (Italy). Professor of Law and Director, Institute of Foreign and International Private and Commercial Law, University of Heidelberg (Germany) (on leave).

Dr Rosa Maria Lastra — Rosa Lastra is a Senior Lecture in International Financial and Monetary Law at the Centre for Commercial Law Studies, Queen Mary, University of London. She is also an Associate Member of the Financial Markets Group of the London School of Economics and Political Science, an Affiliated Scholar of the Centre for the Study of Central Banks at New York University School of Law and a member of the European Shadow Financial Regulatory Committee.

Dr Julian D.M. Lew — Dr Lew is a partner of the international law firm Herbert Smith. He practices, teaches and researches international commercial law and international commercial arbitration. He is also the Head of the School of International Arbitration and visiting Professor at the Centre for Commercial Law Studies at Queen Mary, University of London.

Dr Loukas Mistelis — Loukas Mistelis is the Clive M. Schmitthoff Lecturer in International Commercial Law, Centre for Commercial Law Studies,

Queen Mary, University of London. Teaching and research in international commercial law, conflict of laws, international commercial arbitration, and emerging markets law reform. Member of the Vienna International Sales Convention Interpretative Council.

Anna Mörner — Anna Mörner (1964–2000) was a Research and Teaching Fellow in Central and Eastern European Financial Law at the Centre for Commercial Law Studies, Queen Mary, University of London, until her sudden and tragic death in November 2000. This paper formed the basis of her presentation at the Symposium in honour of Clive M. Schmitthoff held at CCLS in June 2000, and was revised for publication by Anna before her death.

Professor Peter Muchlinski — Peter Muchlinski is the Professor of Law and International Business, Kent Law School, University of Kent at Canterbury. Until April 2001 he was the Drapers' Professor of Law in the Law Department of Queen Mary, University of London. He specialises in international and European business law, competition law and commercial regulation. In 1990 he qualified as a barrister in the field of commercial law and is a door tenant at Brick Court Chambers, London. He acts as a principal adviser to UNCTAD on their major issues papers series concerning international investment agreements.

Professor Raymond Nimmer — Raymond T. Nimmer is the Leonard H. Childs Professor and Director, Information Law Program. Houston. Counsel, Weil, Gotshal & Manges, Houston, since 1991. Subjects: Commercial Law; Commercial Paper; Creditors' Rights; Patents, Copyrights. Member: Law & Society Association; ALI. Consultant, NSF, since 1978; Reporter, National Conference on Uniform Laws, since 1991. His teaching and research interests include Commercial Law, Information Law and Intellectual Property.

Professor Joseph J. Norton — Joseph Norton is the Sir John Lubbock Professor of Banking Law (CCLS, Queen Mary, University of London); James L. Walsh Distinguished Faculty Fellow in Financial Institutions Law, Professor of Law and Director of the Law Institute of the Americas (Dedman School of Law, SMU, Dallas, Texas); and Editor-in-Chief of *The International Lawyer* and *NAFTA: Law and Business in the Americas*.

Professor William W. Park — William (Rusty) Park is Professor of Law at Boston University, Counsel to Ropes & Gray, and a Vice-President of the London Court of International Arbitration. His publications include International Chamber of Commerce Arbitration. Educated at Yale and Columbia, he now serves as arbitrator on the Claims Resolution Tribunal for Dormant Swiss Bank Accounts.

Professor Dr Ernst-Ulrich Petersmann — Professor of law at the University of Geneva and its Graduate Institute of International Studies. Former lecturer/professor of law at the Universities of Hamburg, Heidelberg, Saarland,

St. Gallen, Fribourg and Lausanne; former legal adviser in the German Ministry of Economic Affairs (1978–81) GATT (1981–1995) and the WTO (1995–2000). Chairman of the International Trade Law Committee of the International Law Association.

Professor Dr Kurt Siehr — Kurt Siehr holds a Chair of Private Law, Private International Law, and Comparative Law at the University of Zürich (since 1980). Professor of Law, University of Geneva, 1985/86 and 1996/97. Formerly, Research Fellow, Member of the Max-Planck-Institute for Foreign and Private International Law 1970–1990; Lecturer, University of Hamburg 1971–73, University of Zürich 1977–78. Guest Professor at the Universities of Oslo, Southampton, Rome, Ferrara, Budapest and Tel Aviv, Asser Institute Den Haag, Dubrovnik Centre.

Dr Geert van Calster — Dr Geert Van Calster, LL.M. (Bruges), Ph.D. (Leuven) is a senior research fellow at the IMER—Collegium Falconis, K.U.Leuven. He was a Chevening Scholar at Oxford University in 1997–98. He is a member of the Brussels Bar, now with Caestecker & Partners/Andersen Legal. He practices and teaches trade law and environmental law, and is a regular speaker at conferences in both domains. He publishes extensively in the areas of EC and international trade and environmental law.

Hans van Loon — Johannes Hendrik Albert (Hans) van Loon studied at the Universities of Utrecht and of Leyden, and at the Graduate Institute of International Studies, Geneva. Secretary (since 1978), First Secretary (since 1988), Secretary General (since June 30, 1996) at the Permanent Bureau of the Hague Conference on Private International Law.

Professor Stephen Weatherill — Stephen Weatherill is the Jacques Delors Professor of European Community Law, University of Oxford; Associate Director of the Institute of European and Comparative Law, Faculty of Law, University of Oxford; Fellow of Somerville College.

Professor Jay Laurence Westbrook — Benno C. Schmidt Chair of Business Law, The University of Texas School of Law. Private practice, Washington, D.C. 1969–80 (Associate and Partner, Surrey & Morse). Visiting Professor, Harvard Law School, 1991–92; Visiting Professor, University of London, 1990. Reporter, American Law Institute Transnational Insolvency Project. Co-chair, U.S. Delegation to UNICITRAL Conference on Transnational Insolvency. Senior Advisor, National Bankruptcy Review Commission.

Richard C. Wilder — Mr. Wilder is currently Director, Global Intellectual Property Issues Division and Director-Advisor, Office of Legal and Organization Affairs in the World Intellectual Property Organization, Geneva, Switzerland. In those capacities he is responsible for programs and activities in respect of life sciences issues, including biotechnology and access to health care, the protection of bio-diversity, traditional knowledge (including folklore), and relations between WIPO and the private sector and non-governmental organisations.

FOREWORD

The twentieth century has seen a consolidation of the status of international trade law, and a significant increase in its scope. It has evolved to become a legal domain derived from national commercial law codification, international conventions, and well-established trade usages. This combination of sources has influenced the character and development both of the law itself, and of the areas of debate within the discipline. International trade law has thus become a focus for the interchange between public and private law, as well as between domestic and international law. Within this domain, the conflict of interests between freedom of contract and mandatory rules, between party autonomy and public policy, has been articulated.

The evolution of the law applicable to international commercial transactions in the twentieth century has been marked by an ever increasing internationalisation and regulation: the protection of intellectual property rights, developments in telecommunications and transport, the emergence of electronic commerce and paperless transactions and the role of both national and international regulators were significant features of the last century and are likely to remain so. Although the merits of harmonisation, regulation and self-regulation continue to be debated, we are entering an era of international trade law in which State interference in regulation is a reality, often exercised collectively by more than one State at a regional or international level. Legal professionals and the business community have attempted to reduce legal risk by drafting their own codes of conduct and by deciding to resolve their disputes in a non-judicial setting. The international trade law landscape is at present complicated by ever more layers of rules, both state and private. This is a meta-modern, or a post-harmonisation era for international trade.

The Centre for Commercial Law Studies (CCLS) at Queen Mary, University of London, celebrating its twentieth anniversary and launching the activities of the Clive M. Schmitthoff Foundation decided to look into the future. Not only was international trade law at the centre of Clive Schmitthoff's extraordinarily wide range of interests, it was the discipline pioneered by him through his work with the CCLS in its early years. It also represents particularly well the combination of the scholarly and the highly practical which has characterised the mission of the CCLS since its beginning, as Professor Ian Fletcher demonstrates in his brief introduction to the CCLS, setting the context for this work.

This volume is a distillation of ideas discussed in a three-day symposium held in London in June 2000. A wide array of specialist contributors undertook the task of taking a fresh look at international trade and demonstrated over the three days not only the increasing breadth and scope of the subject, but also the way in which many of its themes and issues cross legal and disciplinary boundaries and pose questions as to the future of law in an internationalised world. The outcome manifests the fact that international trade law forms a junction of national, international and conflicts laws, public and private law and substantive and procedural law, within which particular disciplines, including the law relating to electronic commerce, insolvency and intellectual property play a fundamental—and often interrelated—role.

The book includes a toast to the late Professor Clive Schmitthoff, as the scholar who defined modern international trade law. The toast is proposed by Gerold Herrmann, Secretary General of the United National Commission on International Trade Law (UNCITRAL). The main body of the book consists of 34 chapters arranged in eight parts. These parts are grouped in two sections. The focus of Parts one to four is on institutional and regulatory issues and that of Parts five to eight on substantive law issues, although the substance of many papers in each part demonstrates the ultimate artificiality of such distinctions.

The *first part* explores the future of harmonisation and the challenges faced by formulating agencies. Loukas Mistelis contextualises the debate about harmonisation and sources of law in presenting the relevant historical and doctrinal dimensions. The Secretaries General of UNCITRAL (Gerold Herrmann), ICC (Maria Cattaui Livanos), UNIDROIT (Herbert Kronke), and the Hague Conference (Hans van Loon) give an account of the work of their institutions and take a look into the future and the function formulating agencies may have in an era of globalisation. Stephen Weatherill discusses the increasingly dominant role of European Community law in the conduct of business.

The *second part* is dedicated to the issue of regulation and deregulation of international trade. John Jackson offers a distinctive view of the role of the World Trade Organisation and its dynamic character, while Ernst-Ulrich Petersmann looks in particular at the potential of modern human rights law as applied to international trade issues, and need for democratic reform of the integration law of the World Trade Organisation. Geert van Calster focuses on the interaction between, and management of, different levels of regulation in the trade and environment context and in particular the role of the WTO and of industry. Peter Muchlinski, taking as an example the failure of the negotiations of multilateral investment rules, draws a number of lessons for the regulation of international business. Marise Cremona explores bilateral, multilateral and plurilateral approaches to the internationalisation of competition policy and law, mainly from an EU perspective but also discussing the interplay between EU and WTO initiatives.

The *third part* is dedicated to modern trends in conflict of laws. Oskar Hartwieg follows the thread from Roman law remedies to their modern incarnations as actions and defences and highlights the private international law implications of their split. Kurt Siehr discusses the pervasive issue of renvoi and assesses recent efforts to abolish renvoi by statute. Joanna Benjamin looks at property rights in the securities markets and explores the impact of computerisation on the theory and practice of conflict of laws. Catherine Kessedjian presents the Hague Conference Global Jurisdiction and Judgments Preliminary Draft Convention while Konstantinos Kerameus focuses on modern perspectives of international jurisdiction, both in the context of litigation and arbitration.

The *fourth part* looks at current procedural issues in international commercial arbitration. Julian Lew assesses the arbitrator's control of tactical and procedural issues, highlights tactical issues and suggests the determination of adequate procedural rules by agreement. William (Rusty) Park discusses abuse of process by the parties and gives examples of arbitrators' discontents. Klaus Peter Berger focuses on the power of arbitrators to fill gaps and revise contracts.

The *fifth part* covers aspects of modern international contracts, looking in particular at the harmonisation of sales contracts and electronic commerce. Camilla Baasch Andersen questions the degree of uniformity in the Vienna Convention on Contracts for the International Sale of Goods by looking at the case law from the first decade of its application. Michael Joachim Bonell establishes the role of the UNIDROIT Principles of International Commercial Contracts in the harmonisation of international sales. Alejandro Garro revisits the issue of private rule-setting, using the example of standardisation of international sales contracts. Ralph Amissah explores the potential of an autonomous contract, emerging transnational contract law, relevant trends and supportive structures. Raymond Nimmer gives an overview of the principles of contract law pertaining to electronic commerce looking, in particular, at the U.S. and the EU.

The *sixth part* explores current issues relating to the finance of international trade, encompassing regional economic integration, the commoditisation of financial services and development of payment systems. Joe Norton examines the curious dynamics of free trade in the western hemisphere by assessing the prospects for a free trade area for the Americas. Anna Mörner discusses how Clive Schmitthoff's model for the unification of international trade law can work within a regional framework of economic integration. Rosa Maria Lastra looks at cross-border trade in financial services and mechanisms for reconciling the competing goals of prudential supervision and trade liberalisation. Robert Effros puts the development of payment systems in the twenty-first century in a historical context while Norbert Horn highlights recent trends in EC payment systems and the need for global solutions.

The *seventh part* provides an account of the reshaping of the international insolvency process. Jay Westbrook examines the American Law Institute's *Principles* for managing defaulting multinationals within the NAFTA. Ron Harmer look at recent projects and law reform under the auspices of UNCITRAL and INSOL International. Ian Fletcher in his comparative appraisal also looks at the recent (2000) EU Regulation on Insolvency.

The *final part* looks at trade related issues of intellectual property. Richard Wilder discusses the global period in the protection of intellectual property rights as a result of TRIPS and developments in WIPO, focusing in particular on biotechnology and biological diversity. Michael Blakeney examines the future of the TRIPS agreement after Seattle in the light of the TRIPS' own built-in review and reform agenda, and surveys the principal reform and interpretative issues, in particular the protection of plant varieties, geographical indications, non-violation complaints and dispute settlement.

The evolution of international trade law may be seen not as a revolution, but rather as an organic transformation. While this book indicates the richness and diversity of the field, the main ingredients of harmonisation and regulation of international trade law as defined and discussed by Clive M. Schmitthoff are ever present. Their function is safeguarded and promoted by international legal co-operation at the level of formulating agencies, professional associations and international legal scholarship. The

Centre of Commercial Law Studies wishes to thank all contributors who so enthusiastically agreed to discuss the foundation and perspectives of international trade law with us and to share their views with the readership of this publication. We also want to thank our publishers at Sweet and Maxwell, for their efficient editorial work and their efforts to produce this book promptly. On November 3, 2000, our colleague Anna Mörner, a contributor to the symposium and to this book, died after a tragic accident. In many ways, Anna, while young and at the start of her career, epitomized in her work the ethos of the CCLS and a central theme of the symposium and this book: the value of working across boundaries, whether professional, academic or national.

January 2001

A TOAST IN HONOUR OF PROFESSOR CLIVE SCHMITTHOFF

BY GEROLD HERRMANN*

With tonight's reception and dinner, the Schmitthoff Symposium 2000 has finally become a true symposium, a "Get-and-drink together". In this spirit I should like to invite you to join me in a toast . . . . wait . . . not yet . . . . now is the invitation, the actual toasting comes later.

First you need to know to whom and for what the toast will be proposed . . . yet, I cannot present all the merits of the candidate since that would easily take us beyond midnight.

In fact, you were given a lot of hints, so many signs with the letters CCLS . . . yes, this stands for Clive Commercial Law Schmitthoff. Commercial law was really his life, which began in 1903 in Berlin as a child of a well-known family of lawyers.

First we salute the *brilliant student*: he graduated from the "Gymnasium" as the first in his grade. He studied law in Freiburg and Berlin and excelled with equal success in the Assessor exam (second state exam). Much to the astonishment of his great teacher Martin Wolff, he finished in record time his doctoral thesis with the extremely difficult topic of shares controlled by management of public limited companies.

We salute the *pragmatic lawyer*, first Rechtsanwalt, then Barrister: poised for an academic career in Germany, the adverse political conditions and threats in the twenties forced him to forego that dream; instead he became a successful Rechtsanwalt (and a competent legislative adviser). The rise of the dictator in 1933 forced him to emigrate under extremely difficult circumstances; he soon became a student at the London School of Economics and completed his exams at Gray's Inn within 18 months (but not all his "dinners". . . . obviously, fast food was not yet in vogue then). Later he practised in Sir Valentine Holmes Q.C.'s Chambers, acting in landmark cases like *The Barcelona Traction*.

We salute the *born comparatist* and *substantive private international lawyer*, as my own teacher Professor Gerhard Kegel praised him in his seminal "Crisis of the Conflict of Laws". Like various other emigrants, Clive M. Schmitthoff shaped comparative law and, clearly more than others, the art of applied comparative law . . . and thus the road to unification.

We salute the *judicial adviser*, the highly respected *authority*: At a lecture in Vienna, Lord Wilberforce named him as one of three exceptions to the rule that English judges, especially in the House of Lords, do not cite scholars or other writers (the others were F.A. Mann and S. Holland).

* Dr.jur. (Cologne); LL.M. (Berkeley, Cal.); Honorary Professor (Vienna); Secretary of UNCITRAL (until January 31, 2001; the views expressed in this paper are personal ones and do not necessarily reflect the views of the Organisation); Member of ICCA, LCIA Court, Presiding Council of International Arbitration Court of Austrian Economic Chamber, Consultative Commission of WIPO Arbitration Center, Board of ACICA, and International Academy of Commercial and Consumer Law.

We salute the *encyclopedically knowledgeable commentator* and *scholarly writer*: following the tradition of his two famous commentator uncles (Goldman), he wrote superb commentaries on the Sale of Goods Act and Company Law, scholarly treatises on Mercantile Law and was, in the words of Professor Chia-Jui Cheng, a "pioneer in formulating material parts of the developing international trade law"; his most prominent and influential opus "The Export Trade" was translated into many languages and made that topic teachable.

We salute the *didactic genius*, a *fascinating teacher* of many student generations: he could explain a most difficult theory by juggling three oranges in his hands. I must reveal to have attended his famous summer course twice . . . . . not because I failed the first one, but because of an irresistible personal fascination which makes me thank him belatedly for the liquid gold flowing abundantly from his mouth (I learned a great deal from him, not only that the words "irrespective of weather", written on an invitation to his and Twinkie's hospitable home at Blenheim Road, did not provide an exception to *force majeure* along the following lines: No excuse in case of hail or snowstorm).

We salute the *analytical, pragmatic thinker* with *common sense*: His expert opinions and considerations were never *"l'art pour l'art"* (as much as he adored real art and music). An example of his pragmatic and innovative approach was the determination of the late Helena Rubinstein's domicile by selecting, out of five equally equipped and evenly used apartments, the one where she kept her family pictures. Such commonsense seems particularly refreshing in our times where dot-com seems to connote more often commonplace than commonsense.

We salute the *insightful diagnostic* (since we meet here in a hospital) and the *bold visionary*: In the words of Professor John Honnold, the second Secretary of UNCITRAL, his writings had helped to produce the climate of opinion that made the creation of UNCITRAL by the General Assembly possible. His scholarship has shown that international trade had once enjoyed a legal regime unencumbered by nationalism; his boldness of mind had permitted him to envisage the possibility that modern trade could again be freed from many of the embarrassments of conflicting national rules.

We salute the *realistic therapist* and *e-volutionary*, who drew the consequences from his analytical comparison between the medieval *lex mercatoria* and the modern law merchant: the old one made in practice by merchants themselves, while the new one is deliberately created by formulating agencies, and the old one subject to no other order than the merchant's order (although a recent analysis of a thirteenth century treatise entitled *"Lex mercatoria* and Legal Pluralism" found no evidence), while new international trade law is, in his words, 'applied by the tolerance of the sovereign", "with the leave and license of all national sovereigns".

His upright international trade law is a far cry from the creeping *lex mercatoria* or, more correctly, *leges mercatoriae* or variations on the theme, promoted as a totally new approach to international trade law (or is it trade law marketing when we see the non-legislative preparation of a model law?). He would be quite surprised, or even astonished about the apparent misunderstanding of the term "law merchant" as meaning trader in law, a *lex mercatoria* marketeer (as if commercial law consists primarily of law commercials) We have indeed gone far away from the Law of Trade Fairs (starting 1133 here in Smithfield) to the often Unfair Trade of Laws, putting down traditional "Conventional" methods and promoting "*Super lex mercatoria*", "*Lexmex*" and regional, transnational or global principles under the Madison Avenue theme "start spreading your *léx mércatoriá*".

Thus, at the Schmitthoff Symposium 2010, the Hague Convention Center will propose a draft Convention on the *droit dominant*, the *lex superior* in case of conflict between *leges mercatoriae*. In turn, the observer of UNIDROIT will object to this for lack of need since all *leges mercatoriae* were complementary and the UNIDROIT Principles on International Commercial Contracts (UPICC) were designed as an aid to the interpretation of any other texts. He will, however, clearly disapprove of marketing techniques such as Frequent Applier Programmes with prizes like: appointment as arbitrator in a million dollar case or free entrance to the "True Magic Show of Filling Non-Existent Gaps". He will finally make it clear that, contrary to popular belief and despite the constant reminder of the link with the League of Nations, UNIDROIT is not a UN Organization and its acronym does not stand for : "United Nations Institute for the Determination of Rights and Obligations in International Trade".

Ten years later, at the Schmitthoff Symposium 2020, the Executive Directors of UNCITRAL, UNIDROIT, the Hague Convention Centre, International Chamber of Commerce and other formulating agencies will announce the completion of Clive Schmitthoff's dream, the Global Code of Communication and other Conduct (GCCC). Sir Ian Fletcher, World Insolvency Warden, will present the last chapter, the one on insolvency. Based on a project of the year 2000 between UNCITRAL and the World Bank, now part of the Universal Finance Organisation (UFO), the final breakthrough will have been achieved in close co-operation with the World Zoological Society, realising that the human factor in insolvency is heavily shaped by animalistic behaviour. Zoologists are useful experts on pecking orders and feeding chains, they know best the flight patterns of hovering vultures (after all, "creditor" rhymes with "predator") and can best judge different attacks, telling a mock charge from a floating charge and a simple debtor in possession of a Master Card.

The Insolvency Chapter will be added to the Health Chapter under the Book title "Ailment". You should know that the GCCC will have a book for each human activity or problem sector. Other book titles are: entertainment, nourishment, movement, environment, investment, payment, settlement and abatement . . . . no, sorry, I misread; the title is "*bâtiment*"(one French term was included upon special request by OHADA, the Organisation pour l'harmonisation en Afrique du droit des affaires).

Finally, all books of the GCCC will become binding in all Free Trade Areas and the few remaining national jurisdictions in the world, by virtue of René David's finally adopted proposal to reverse the burden of inertia, by bringing into force any uniform law unless objected to by a jurisdiction within six months of its promulgation.

In the light of this development, the topic of the Schmitthoff Symposium of 2030 will be: Is there any future for formulating agencies? Since not many participants are expected to come, the meeting will be held online and without drinks.

Today, we are in a much better position: now, please grab your glasses for the proposed toast in which we include (Twinkie) Ilse Schmitthoff, the lawyer and personalised kindness at Clive's side, the generosity in person which brings us together here today; we salute Clive M. Schmitthoff, who with his many visionary thoughts and suggestions is still very much alive: TO CLIVE!

INTRODUCTION

The Centre for Commercial Law Studies

Professor Ian F. Fletcher, LLD
Director, 1994–2000

The Centre for Commercial Law Studies owes its existence to the unique vision and unparalleled energy of its founding Director, Professor (now Sir) Roy Goode. Having entered academic life directly from legal practice, when in 1971 he was invited to occupy a newly vacant Chair at what was then Queen Mary College in the University of London, Professor Goode embarked upon a lifelong mission to create a dynamic environment in which commercial law could be studied, taught and developed through an active fusion between academics and practitioners, meeting in an atmosphere of mutual respect and shared goals. The opportunity to give these innovative ideals an institutional form came in the late 1970s with the proposal from Dr Herchel Smith to endow a Chair in Intellectual Property Law within a university law school in Britain. By conceiving an exciting and original proposal for a Centre for Commercial Law Studies, to provide a reinforcing context within which the endowed chair could function, Roy Goode ensured that the Herchel Smith Chair was established at Queen Mary, and by 1980 the Centre was formally in existence.

The early phase of the Centre's development was inevitably marked by a dependence on the ability of hope and enthusiasm to triumph over adversity, often in the shape of bureaucratic inertia to which British universities, then as now, are all too prone. Professor Goode himself has written of the exhilarating experience of embarking on the quest for funding, sponsorship, accommodation—and above all students to bring the entire vision to life—at a time when the Centre consisted of just two professors, one secretary, and some newly minted note paper proudly proclaiming its existence! The moral that might be drawn from the Centre's formative period is: "Never underestimate the power of headed stationery!"

During the first decade of the Centre's life, its growth and success were truly breathtaking. Postgraduate courses, diploma courses, evening lectures, weekend conferences, summer schools, supervised research, a growing list of outstanding and influential publications—the range and intensity of activity in the field of commercial law far outstripped anything hitherto attempted in any British law school, regardless of age or size. All this was characterised with an unswerving dedication to the maintenance of the highest possible standards of scholarly inquiry and intellectual debate. The Centre's mission, proudly affirmed in its prospectus from the outset, has been ". . . to promote the systematic study and research of national and international commercial law and its social and economic implications, and to develop a body of knowledge, information and skills that can be placed at the service of government, public bodies, overseas institutions, the legal profession, industry and commerce". Throughout its existence, the Centre's aim has been "to identify legal problems of the future" and to act as "a forum for the testing of new ideas".

These ideas, and the vigorous way in which they were being pursued from the Centre's base in the Mile End Road, attracted a steadily growing galaxy of eminent and gifted scholars to become involved in its activities. Among the earliest was Professor Clive Schmitthoff, then approaching his mid-eighties, who was instrumental in introducing the International Trade Law course into the LLM programme and who co-taught it with Professor Goode during the initial sessions. Professor Schmitthoff's widow, Twinkie, subsequently gave the writer a moving account of her late husband's immense pleasure, during those final years of his life, in being able to share in the creation of a spiritual home for the study of commercial law, to which his own long and illustrious career had been dedicated. It was to honour Clive's stated wishes that Twinkie subsequently bequeathed the bulk of her considerable estate to enable the Centre to establish the Clive M. Schmitthoff Foundation, thereby helping to ensure the continuation of the Centre's work in the areas of international trade and commercial law.

Within a decade of its inception, the Centre for Commercial Law Studies could fairly claim to be the foremost institution of its kind anywhere in the world. Such had been the impact of its distinctive working philosophy— the very antithesis of the "ivory tower" concept of the Academy—that by the end of 1987 no less than five Chairs, and three research fellowships, had been funded with the aid of endowments from the private sector. In addition to the original Chair in Intellectual Property Law, there were further Chairs, and associated research units consisting of a mixture of permanent and visiting lecturers and scholars, in Banking Law, International Tax Law, Information Technology Law, and Comparative Law. The Centre had also established its School of International Arbitration whose cycle of courses and events was sustained through the unstinting labours of Dr. Julian Lew in somehow combining a full-time, international legal practice with the role of Visiting Professor. Thus, by the time of Professor Goode's departure in 1990 to take up the Norton Rose Chair of English Law at Oxford University, the Centre had attained the requisite critical mass, and vigorous diversity, to ensure its ability to continue its development under sucessive Directors, even during a period of attrition and retrenchment across the university sector in general. Thanks to the sustained faith of the private sector in the value of the Centre's work, and thanks also to the equally vital support of the College, the Centre has succeeded during its second decade in not merely maintaining the historic numbers of its staff and students, and the quality and intensity of its research output, but indeed it has pursued a sustained programme of growth and development on all fronts. While continuing to honour the ideas and objectives on which it was founded, the Centre for Commercial Law Studies enters a new millenium with confidence in its ability to address fresh challenges in a resourceful and innovative way.

PART ONE

THE FUTURE OF HARMONISATION AND FORMULATING
AGENCIES

CHAPTER 1

IS HARMONISATION A NECESSARY EVIL?
THE FUTURE OF HARMONISATION AND NEW
SOURCES OF INTERNATIONAL TRADE LAW

DR LOUKAS MISTELIS
CLIVE M SCHMITTHOFF LECTURER IN INTERNATIONAL COMMERCIAL
LAW, CCLS

1. Introduction: recent legal history and legal futurology

It is now official: The twentieth century can be characterised as the "century   **1-001**
of transition". One can observe five distinct significant legal transitions in
the twentieth century.

First, as a result of two major world wars, two 'worlds' were formed and a
third joined them in the de–colonisation decades of the 1960s and 1970s. The
membership of the United Nations increased from 50 states in the 1950s to
188 states in the late 1990s. The established world order with the 'east–west'
and 'north–south' divides entered a period of transition in the 1990s with
the collapse of the Soviet Union. A number of emerging markets are now
in place with their legal systems in transition. In this legal (r)evolution,
law reform projects draw upon existing domestic law, existing foreign
laws, and law harmonised by various formulating agencies.[1] A great deal of
'harmonised law' was negotiated and drafted without participation of the

---

[1] See Loukas Mistelis, "Regulatory Aspects: Globalization, Harmonization, Legal Transplants
and Law Reform. Some Fundamental Observations", in Lastra (ed.). *The Reform of the
International Financial Architecture*, London *et al.* (Kluwer) 2000, pp.153–173, 163–165 = 34 (3)
The International Lawyer 1055–1069 (Fall 2000).

1–002   majority of emerging markets, or at least, before the majority of these States (in the former Soviet Union and the large number of ex–colonies) assumed legal personality in public international law.

Secondly, after a period of nationalisation of legal systems in the first half of the 20th century—which was manifested, in particular, in civil law countries, with the introduction of national civil and/or commercial codes—in the second half of the century we have experienced a desire for harmonisation of law. Against this background, conflict of laws adequately served national legal interests,[2] and 'localisation of issues' and 'localisation of disputes' were the main objectives of (private) international law.[3] With the emergence of more instruments harmonising commercial law there is a need for a new conflict of laws system which may resolve conflict of conventions or conflict of harmonising instruments.[4]

1–003   Thirdly, in the final decade of the twentieth century, harmonisation of law entered a new era. Newly independent states or emerging economies are in the process of rewriting their laws. While national identity is important, an effort is also made to the effect that internationally recognised standards or harmonised law forms the bulk of this modern legislation. Accordingly we have a symbiosis of convergence of legal systems and the creation of more (not purely arithmetically) diversified national legal systems. Modern harmonisation has often taken the shape of legal transplants, of exports of legal concepts and rules, from industrialised nations to emerging economies.[5] Such 'harmonisation' results in regional groupings and considerable, albeit justified, diversification. More than ever before, it becomes evident that harmonisation is by no means synonymous with unification; harmonisation is a process which may result in unification of law subject to a number of (often utopian) conditions being fulfilled, such as, for example, wide or universal geographical acceptance of harmonising instruments, and with wide scope of harmonising instruments which effectively substitute all pre-existing law. To the extent that harmonisation of law is sporadic and incomplete, in practice, most harmonising laws are designed to work within and with existing laws.

1–004   Fourthly, an additional characteristic of this second half of the twentieth century can be seen in the process of regional economic integration and the

---

[2] See Gerhard Kegel, "Fundamental Approaches", in *International Encyclopaedia of Comparative Law*, Vol. III, Chapter 3, Tübingen *et al.* (Mohr) 1987, at paras 3–8 to 3–13, in particular, para. 3–13 (pragmatists).

[3] See Friedrich Carl von Savigny, *System des heutigen Römischen Rechts*, Vol. VIII, Berlin 1849, at p. 28 and 108 and Kegel, *ibid.*, at pp. 3–8.

[4] For the methodological challenges of modern conflict of laws see Loukas Mistelis, *Charakterisierungen und Qualifikation im internationalen Privatrecht*, Tübingen 1999 (Mohr), pp. 16–19, 201–208. See also Henri Batiffol, "Le pluralisme en droit international privé", RCADI 139 (1973–II), pp. 75–148; Erik Jayme, "Identité culturelle et intégration: le droit international privé postmoderne—Cours général de droit international privé", RCADI 251 (1995), pp. 9–268; Friedrich Juenger, *Choice of Law and Multistate Justice*, Dordrecht *et al.* (Kluwer) 1993, pp. 143–146; Gerhard Kegel, "The Crisis of Conflict of Laws", RCADI 112 (1964–II), 95–263; Klaus Schurig, *Kollisionsnorm und Sachrecht - Zu Struktur, Standort und Methode des internationalen Privatrechts*, Berlin 1981.

[5] See Loukas Mistelis, *supra* n. 1, 34(3) *International Lawyer* pp. 1065–1067 (2000). See also Alan Watson, "Legal Transplants and European Private Law", 4.4. *Electronic Journal of Comparative Law* (December 2000), available at http://law.kub.nl/ejcl/44/44–2.html. Watson initiated the discussion about legal transplants with his book *Legal Transplants*, (1st ed., Edinburgh, 1974, 2nd ed., Athens, Ga., 1993). This book has been often criticized, more recently by Pierre Legrand,

delegation of law-making to regional international organisations. Consequently, regulation which is often understood to be of a public law nature enters the domain of commercial transactions which is traditionally referred to as private law. Similarly, private law self-regulation touches upon public law. Regulation of economic activity by way of legislation is linked with inherent problems. While regulation normally denotes state interference in the organisation of trade and is more often used for the 'public law aspects' of commerce, in the second half of the twentieth century trade regulation became a matter of international concern with the introduction of GATT and more recently of the World Trade Organisation and GATS. This international concern is also expressed by regional international organisations. While regulation is not synonymous with harmonisation, some experiences from regulatory attempts can help us to draw useful conclusions for the harmonisation process and vice versa. International commercial transactions are the interchange between public and private law,[6] between domestic and international law.

Finally, international arbitration has emerged as the preferred method for settlement of disputes in international business transactions.[7] The application of a national substantive law or a non-legal standard by the arbitral tribunal is far more complicated than the application of national law by the judges. The arbitrators may have no connection with or access to the applicable national law, unlike the national judges who normally apply the law they have been trained in for years. This is no defect of arbitration as a settlement of disputes mechanism. Arbitration deals preponderantly with international trade disputes while national courts deal predominately with national cases for which national law and state interests are often called upon. Thus, when selecting the standard to apply, parties or arbitrators may denationalise or internationalise the dispute. If there is an international convention relevant to the dispute, it should be given preference over the application of a national law. Further, where the dispute can most easily be resolved be resorting to the customs and usages of the particular trade or industry, such customs or usages should be the standard applied. Trade standards, which comprise the law of international trade, should be applied in preference and often in deference to the rules of national law.[8] Accordingly for a considerable number of

1–005

"The Impossibility of 'Legal Transplants'", 4 *Maastricht Journal of European and Comparative Law* 111 *et seq.* (1997).

[6] Some of the theoretical background in: John A. Spanogle, "The Arrival of Private International Law", 25 *Geo. Wash. J. Int'l L. & Eco.* pp. 477–522 (1991). Ralph G. Steinhardt, "The Privatization of Public Law", 25 *Geo. Wash. J. Int'l L. & Eco.* pp. 523–553 (1991). Steinhardt states in the context of the public/private distinction in international law that "the distinction ... can no longer be defended because the concerns, the actors and the processes of "public" international law have been expanded—"privatized"—in this century. Conflicts law and international business transactions have become a staple of state-to-state relations, and non-state or private actors have taken an increasing role in the articulation and enforcement of international standards". *ibid.* at 543.

[7] In London alone there are annually more than 4,500 arbitration and ADR proceedings. See Judith Gill, Lord Hacking, Arthur Marriott, Geoff Prevett and Peter Rees (eds.) *Delivering Results - Dispute Resolution in London* (2000), at 5.

[8] See Julian D. M. Lew, *Applicable Law in International Commercial Arbitration*, Oceana 1978, para. 443, at pp. 582–83. For further references regarding the law applicable to the merits of international arbitration disputes see Julian D. M. Lew, Loukas Mistelis and Stefan Kröll, *Comparative International Commercial Arbitration*, London (Kluwer) 2001, Chap. 17.

international trade disputes a new transnational legal order has emerged,[9] which is, if not detached from existing legal systems, more liberal in its application than existing substantive law. It seems that there may soon be a movement in national courts which will follow non-judicial settlement of disputes methods by applying anational and extra-legal and standards.[10]

1–006   The twentieth century was the century of transition and emerging globalisation. Globalisation is rather a western economic concept with significant legal connotations. 'Western' lawyers observed that this is an era of globalisation of law which will inevitably accompany the globalisation of economy.[11] Globalisation is foremost an economic process.[12] It is also a political event,[13] as evidenced by the spread of rule of law and human rights among nations; many human rights violations are no longer treated as domestic affairs. 'Globalisation is causing, and being reinforced by, a world-wide convergence of economic and political values that portend a possible, though distant, future world in which human beings will look upon themselves as part of a single humane civilisation comprised of a single human race."[14] Law has been important in managing the global economy and may gain importance with respect to political globalisation.[15]

---

[9] See Yves Dezalay and Bryant Garth, *Dealing in Virtue — International Commercial Arbitration and the Construction of a Transnational Legal Order*, Chicago & London (University of Chicago Press), 1996.

[10] See to the same effect Gunther Teubner (ed.), *Global Law Without a State* (Aldershot, Dartmouth 1997); Klaus-Peter Berger, "The New Law Merchant and the Global Market Place: A 21st Century View of Transnational Commercial Law", [2000] Int.A.L.R. 91–102, 100–102. See also *Channel Tunnel Group v. Balfour Beatty Ltd* [1993] 1 All E.R. 664 at 673.

[11] See John A. Spanogle, Jr., "American Attorneys' Use of International and Comparative Legal Analysis in Everyday Practice", 28 *Wake Forest L. Rev.* 1–5, at p. 1 (1993): "Any business person can tell you that the Global Economy is here. The necessity to produce wherever it is most advantageous, and then to market and compete all over the world, is hardly news to them. It does still seem to be news to much of the legal profession, however, and to many in legal education."

[12] The origins of globalisation can be traced back to the writings of Wendell Wilkie and the Club of Rome. These early formulations, however, occurred prior to the collapse of Bretton Woods and the development of the new global communication technology. See Gordon Walker & Mark Fox, "Globalisation: An Analytical Framework", 3 *Ind.J. Global Legal Stud.* (1995/96): http://www.law.indiana.edu/glsj/vol3/no2/walker.html. "Globalisation" should be distinguished from "internationalization", the guiding force of the twentieth century, see Jost Delbrück, "Globalisation of Law, Politics, and Markets - Implications for Domestic Law: A European Perspective", 1 *Ind. J. Global Legal Stud.* (Fall 1993): http://www.law.indiana.edu/glsj/vol1/delbruck.html.

[13] In response to "fears of globalisation" many nations have taken to defending their culture against foreign influence. Regarding such fears see "The New Trade War", *The Economist*, December 4, 1999 and letters to the editor, *The Economist*, December 18, 1999.

[14] Alex Y. Seita, "Globalisation and the Convergence of Values", 30 *Cornell Int'l L.J.* 429–491, at 429 (1997).

[15] See *ibid.*, at pp. 479–484 with accompanying footnotes. The focus is on rule of law, human rights and the regulation of international trade. See Martin Shapiro, The "Globalization of Law", 1 *Ind. J. Global Legal Stud.* (Fall 1993): http://www.law.indiana.edu/glsj/vol1/shapiro.html; The Symposium "The Rule of Law in the Era of Globalization" published in 6 *Ind. J. Global Legal Stud.* (Spring 1999) and in particular, David P. Fidler, "Introduction", *id.*, pp. 421–424; Bruce A. Markell, "A View from the Field: Some Observations on the Effect of International Commercial Law Reform Efforts on the Rule of Law", *id.*, pp. 497–510. For all major aspects of globalisation of law see Eric Loquin and Catherine Kessedjian, *La mondalisation du droit* (Litec 2000); Jürgen Basedow and Toshiyuki Kono (eds.), *Legal Aspects of Globalisation - Conflict of Laws, Internet, Capital Markets and Insolvency in a Global Economy* (Kluwer, 2000). See further Ernst-Joachim Mestmäcker, "Rechtsfragen einer Ordnung der Weltwirtschaft", in Holl / Klinke (eds.) *Internationales Privatrecht — Internationales Wirtschaftsrecht*, Köln et al. 1985, pp. 25–36; Klaus-Peter Berger, "Einheitliche Rechtsstrukturen durch außergesetzliche Rechtsvereinheitlichung", *Juristen-Zeitung* 369–377 (1999); Jarrod Wiener, *Globalization and the Harmonization of Law* (London and New York, Pinter 1999).

This is not the first era of globalisation of law. Medieval *lex mercatoria*   **1–007**
and *ius commune (europae)* were genuine global legal rules.[16] The same view
was expressed several times about 40 years ago by Clive Schmitthoff.[17]
Although globalisation of markets is a process, which appears to be unstoppable, as seen, for example, in the recent increase in mergers and acquisitions,
there are a number of good reasons why globalisation of law (*i.e.* an introduction of a legal system binding all over the world) is problematic. The
main question linked with such a potential development is who will dictate
authoritatively what 'best law' is? If an international organisation, which?
There are also matters of democratic accountability associated with the legislative process and the different levels of power and influence of the negotiating states as well as national or regional interests. It may be the case that
for a certain transitional period the interest of a state is to have a protective
or liberal policy.

Undoubtedly, with the increasing globalisation of economy, we will experience   **1–008**
more cross-border activities, and, with the emergence of electronic
commerce, lawyers will be faced with transactions which cannot be easily
localised. To the extent that the modern economy is a natural development,
regulators should not interfere in anticipation of problems. Technology is
faster than legislative procedures and legislators should interfere only to 'correct' or amend insufficient existing laws.

In this new era of a globalising economy it remains to be seen what the   **1–009**
reaction of global capital markets to continuing differences in commercial
law systems will be. It appears that the notorious phenomenon of forum
shopping has been welcomed in several circumstances.[18] Currently, it appears
that a similar 'capital market shopping' and the risk taking relating to that
have been beneficial to some global players. However, the need for certainty
and predictability, or indeed uniformity is topical. Convergence of legal systems or harmonisation of commercial law will, in the long run, stabilise and
strengthen national economies and will create a healthy competition
environment. This is expected to be a lengthy process as in the interim both

---

[16] See Rudolf Meyer, *Bona fides and lex mercatoria in der europäischen Rechtstradition*,
Göttingen 1993 (Wallstein). See also Berger, *supra* n. 10, at 92 *et seq.* See also Watson, in EJCL
2000, *supra* n. 5, sections III and VIII.

[17] Clive M. Schmitthoff, "The Law of International Trade, Its Growth, Formulation and
Operation", in Clive M. Schmitthoff (ed.), *The Sources of the Law of International Trade with
special reference to East-West Trade* (London, 1964) pp. 3–38 = Chia-Jui Cheng (ed.), *Clive M
Schmitthoff's Select Essays on International Trade Law*, Dordrecht *et al.* (Kluwer, 1988) pp.
137–169; Clive M. Schmitthoff, The Unification of the Law of International Trade, JBL 1968 pp.
105–119 = Cheng, *id.*, 206–218; Clive M. Schmitthoff, "The Codification of the Law of
International Trade", JBL 1985, pp. 34–44 = Cheng, *id.*, 243–251; Clive M. Schmitthoff, "Nature
and Evolution of the Transnational Law of Commercial Transactions", in Norbert Horn and
Clive M. Schmitthoff (eds.), *The Transnational Law of International Commercial Transactions*,
Deventer 1982, pp. 19–31 = Cheng, *id.*, pp. 231–242; Clive M. Schmitthoff, "International
Business law: A New Law Merchant", II *Current Law and Social Problems* 129 (1961) = Cheng,
id., pp. 20–37.

[18] See Kurt Siehr, "Forum Shopping" im internationalen Rechtsverkehr", *Zeitschrift für
Rechtsvergleichung* 1984, pp. 124–144; X., "Forum Shopping Reconsidered", 103 *Harv. L. Rev.*
1677–1696 (1990); Friedrich Juenger, "What's Wrong with Forum Shopping?", 16 *Sydney L. Rev.*
5–13 (1994); Brian R. Opeskin, "The Price of Forum Shopping: A Reply To Professor Juenger",
16 *Sydney L. Rev.* 14–27 (1994); Friedrich Juenger, "Forum Shopping: A Rejoinder", 16 *Sydney
L. Rev.* 28–31 (1994); Oskar Hartwieg, "Forum Shopping zwischen Forum Non Conveniens und
"hinreichendem Inlandsbezug" - Ein realer Fall-Vergleich", 51 *Juristen-Zeitung* 109–118 (1996).

legislators and the business community will have to cope with the increased regulatory competition.

1–010   What does it leave for the twenty-first century? Has the twentieth century succeeded in harmonisation? The choice is whether we will opt for a globalisation of commercial and financial law, a gradual convergence of legal regimes through legal and institutional transplants or an international harmonisation though hard or soft law. What are the objectives of harmonisation in the twenty-first century?[19] And what is the agenda of the formulating agencies?[20] Is it possible to develop a new corpus of legal provisions which is tailor-made for international commercial transactions? The purpose of this chapter is to revisit relevant writings of Clive Schmitthoff. We will look at the way the law of international trade has developed in the last century (see section 2); then we will briefly discuss the concept, the advantages and pitfalls of harmonisation (see section 3). In the final part we will focus on the chances of developing new sources of law applicable to international transactions, in the manner of the old *jus gentium* (see section 4).

2. The law of international trade, its growth, formulation and operation

1–011   The law of international trade has grown and shaped up significantly in the twentieth century. Clive Schmitthoff has effectively delimited international trade law in its modern proportions and supported its harmonisation (see section 2.1), clarified the relevant sources of law (see section 2.2) and asserted the relevance and importance of the various fora in which the law is applied (see section 2.3).

2.1. Schmitthoff and international trade law

1–012   The law of international trade in its modern perception has been largely defined by Clive Schmitthoff. His standpoint is of paramount importance. 'It is a remarkable fact—as remarkable as the world-wide acceptance of the rule of law and the universal acceptance of corporateness—that the law of international trade shows a striking similarity in all national legal systems".[21] Two remarks can be added here. First, Schmitthoff highlights similarity not uniformity. It may be argued that it is the similarity and the functional comparison that should be addressed by legal scholars and practitioners and not the issue of uniformity, which is as difficult to achieve as it is desired. Similarity and a functional comparative approach[22] can lead to convergence which in most cases will be synonymous to uniformity. Second, the law of international trade is applied in every municipal jurisdiction only by leave

---

[19] See *infra*, chap. 2–6 where the role of UNCITRAL, ICC, EU, UNIDROIT, and the Hague Conference with respect to harmonisation of law is discussed by Gerold Herrmann, Maria Cattaui Livanos, Stephen Weatherill, Herbert Kronke and Hans van Loon, respectively.
[20] See *id*.
[21] Clive M. Schmitthoff, "The Law of International Trade, Its Growth, Formulation and Operation", in Clive Schmitthoff (ed.), *The Sources of the Law of International Trade with special reference to East-West Trade*, London 1964, pp. 3–38, at 3.
[22] On comparative concepts see C.J.P. van Laer, "The Applicability of Comparative Concepts", 2.2 *Electronic Journal of Comparative Law* (1998), and van Laer, *Het nut van comparatieve begrippen*, Antwerp/Groningen (Intersentia) 1987.

and license of the sovereign. According to Schmitthoff international uniform or domestic international trade law rules are applicable as a result of conflict of laws. It is implied that international comity[23] and sophisticated conflict of laws systems will allow for application of foreign law, at least if the parties have exercised their autonomy and made an effective choice of law in their contract or subsequently.[24]

Schmitthoff provided a delimitation of international trade law. Accordingly,

"... the law of international trade covers an unusually wide spectrum of business activity. [It includes] ... The International Sale of Goods; Marketing Organisation Abroad; Finance of Exports; Insurance of Exports; Transportation of Exports; International Commercial Dispute Settlement; Construction and Long Term Contracts; and Customs Law".[25]

In a more conceptual manner he added:

"International trade transactions relate to the exportation of goods or services from one country to another ... These transactions are referred to ... as *export transactions*. The conduct of export transactions can be divided into two categories: transactions founded on the contract for the international sale of goods and those having as their object the supply of services abroad, such as the construction of works and installations in another country."[26]

Schmitthoff clearly saw the emergence of international trade law as a sepa-   **1–013**
rate body of legal rules, as one of the outstanding features of the legal development of the twentieth century and contributed significantly to its current shaping. The development of international trade led to a division of the traditional commercial law into two branches, the law applying to domestic transactions and that applying to international business transactions.

The emergence of special rules governing international commercial trans-   **1–014**
actions was also the result of the intensification of trade in the post Second World War era and the development of modern telecommunications.[27] Another significant development is illustrated in the different levels of international economic integration and incrementally significant regulation. While domestic transactions are firmly embedded in national law, in the law of international trade a growing tendency can be observed to move away from the fetters of national law and to establish a common international

---

[23] See for example Joel Paul, "Comity in International Law (Private International Law)", (1991) *Harv. J. Int'l. L.* 1–79; P. Dane, "Vested Rights, 'Vestedness' and Choice of Law", 96 *Yale L. J.* 1191–1275 (1987).
[24] In some legal systems, also if pleaded and proven by the parties. According to Richard Fentiman, *Foreign Law in English Courts, Pleading, Proof and Choice of Law*, Oxford 1998, at 21: "It is commonly supposed, ..., that all choice of law rules are optional, in the sense that the application of foreign law can always be prevented if neither party pleads it." She also Chapter 12 by Oskar Hartwieg.
[25] See Clive Schmitthoff, *Schmitthoff's Export Trade. The Law and Practice of International Trade* (9th ed. Stevens & Sons/ Sweet & Maxwell, London, 1990), p. vii.
[26] *Ibid.*, p. 3; 10th ed. by Leo D'Arcy, Carole Murray and Barbara Cleave, London (Sweet & Maxwell) 2000, at para. 1–001.
[27] Clive Schmitthoff already in the 1980s was aware of the issues of dematerialisation of trade instruments and the emergence of electronic commerce. See Clive M. Schitthoff and Roy M. Goode (eds.), *International carriage of goods: some legal problems and possible solutions*, London (CCLS) 1988.

consensus.[28] It is observed[29] that the legal techniques of carrying on international trade are the same irrespective of the political, ideological or economic orientation of the countries in question. The universal acceptance of the legal techniques of international trade has led to a new conception of international trade law which includes along with statutory, customary, and case law, voluntary law and the lex mercatoria.[30]

1–015   Against this background there has been an increasing movement away from the purely domestic law of international trade and towards what has become known as transnational commercial law, *i.e.* the corpus of law resulting from the harmonisation or convergence of national laws, whether by international convention, conscious or unconscious judicial parallelism, uniform rules for specified types of contract and, more recently, international restatements of principles of contract law.[31]

1–016   All these aspects are examined in this book[32] and are also considered in the discussion of harmonisation in this chapter. Consequently, the notion of international trade law *lato sensu* is adopted.

2.2. Two meanings of 'sources of law'—fontes juris

1–017   The modern character of the law of international trade is derived from many sources. The international business community itself supported by international agencies and trade associations, formulates international commercial custom in terms intended to have international currency.[33] Hence, the next step after the delimitation of the subject matter of international trade is to determine the sources of this law. In this process it is essential to distinguish the two meanings of 'sources of law'—*fontes juris*.

1–018   The term 'source of law' denotes not only the sovereign authority by which a legal rule is applied and the origin of such rules but also the manifestations and substance of the principles and rules of law. The analysis of the term includes both substantive sources—what the law is, what the regulation is— and formal sources, e.g. statute, custom, convention. It is essential in that context to assert the internationality of the relevant sources, or at least their suitability for international transactions. Consequently, we cannot overemphasise the role of party autonomy in establishing an autonomous international commercial law founded on universally accepted standards of business conduct. Again, the criterion of similarity, and not that of uniformity, should be adopted.

---

[28] See Clive Schmitthoff, *Commercial Law in a Changing Economic Climate* (2nd ed., Sweet & Maxwell, London, 1981), p.18.
[29] A. Goldštajin, "The New Law Merchant Reconsidered", in *Law and International Trade, Festschrift for Clive M. Schmitthoff*, Frankfurt 1973, p. 171, 174.
[30] See Schmitthoff, *Commercial Law in a Changing Economic Climate, supra* n. 28, at 1 *et seq.*, 19 *et seq.*
[31] See Roy Goode, *Commercial Law in the Next Millennium*, (Sweet & Maxwell, London, 1998), p. 88.
[32] See chapters 6 (by van Loon), 7–11 (by Jackson, Petersmann, Muchlinski, van Calster and Cremona), 25–26 (Norton, Mörner) and 23–24 (by Amissah and Nimmer).
[33] See Clive Schmitthoff, "The New Sources of the International Trade Law", XV *International Social Science Journal* 2 (1962) = Chia-Jui Cheng (ed.), *Clive M. Schmitthoff's Select Essays on International Trade Law*, Dordrecht *et al.* (Kluwer) 1988, 131–136, 131.

Schmitthoff, who believed in the spontaneous growth and development of the law of international trade, especially in the shape of lex mercatoria, was, however, aware of the fact that legal certainty could not rest in spontaneity. Accordingly in the late 1950s and the early 1960s a number of meetings were convened by the International Association of Legal Sciences with the support of UNESCO.[34] There, Clive Schmitthoff, looking at all the organisations that were formulating uniform law texts at the time, concluded that there was a lack of purposeful co-operation and co-ordination between these agencies and that an international agency of the highest order, possibly on the level of the United Nations, was needed. The General Assembly of the United Nations with its Resolution 2205 (XXI) of December 17, 1966 accepted the proposal and created UNCITRAL. **1–019**

2.3. Sources of law and their application by the various fora

Schmitthoff was also aware of the fact that the law of international trade, whatever its origin, is applied in a domestic jurisdiction only by leave and licence of the sovereign. This was particularly relevant in jurisdictions of planned economy.[35] In his 1968 Travers lecture he stated that 'one of the major problems of our time is the need to reconcile the demands of the national state with the ideal on international co-operation. This problem constitutes a challenge not only to governments but to the conscience of each of us . . . members of the society. The present world order is still founded on the traditional concept of the national state . . . but we cannot disregard the growing trend towards internationalism which, despite occasional failings, has developed new forms of global and regional organisation".[36] **1–020**

This problem is, however, not simply a political or ideological one. In litigation, courts have to apply the law in making decisions. Most national courts are reluctant to apply foreign law, more so if the foreign or international rule can only be found in a trade usage. Most national laws acknowledge customary rules as a source of law. The problem with customary rules and trade usages relates to their crystallisation. There is uncertainty until the parties have pleaded and the court has found and crystallised the custom. **1–021**

In addition it must be pointed out that while the parties are free to regulate their transactions as they see fit, this freedom is restrained once the transaction has effects outside the parties' contractual sphere, their micro-cosmos. In the 'outside world' freedom of contract may be restrained by public policy considerations and/or relevant mandatory rules. **1–022**

With the growth of non-judicial settlement of disputes, the landscape has changed significantly. International commercial arbitration with its liberal **1–023**

---

[34] The London 1962 Conference resulted in a famous publication: Clive M. Schmitthoff (ed.), *The Sources of the Law of International Trade with special reference to East-West Trade*, London (Stevens & Sons) 1964.
[35] Clive M. Schmitthoff, *ibid*, p. 4.
[36] Clive M. Schmitthoff, The Unification of the Law of International Trade, JBL 1968 105–119, at 105 = Cheng, *op. cit.*, 206–218, at 206. See to the same effect Ernst-Joachim Mestmäcker, Rechtsfragen einer Ordnung der Weltwirtschaft, in Holl/Klinke (eds.), *Internationales Privatrecht Internationales Wirtschaftsrecht*, Köln et al 1985, 25–36; Uwe Blaurock, "Übernationales Recht des Internationalen Handels", *Zeitschrift für Europäisches Privatrecht* 247–267, at 248 (1993).

and international approach contrasts favourably with the nationalist conceptions of many national courts.[37] Arbitration is normally a tailor-made procedure for international trade disputes. Extra-legal standards, trade usages, and
other trade standards, which are part of the law of international trade, may
be applied in preference and often in deference to the rules of national law.[38]
Accordingly for a considerable number of international trade disputes a new
transnational legal order has emerged,[39] which is a new law merchant for the
global marketplace,[40] a *lex arbitralis materialis*.

1–024   Further, alternative disputes resolution proceedings may well result in a
decision without the strict application of law, or even without any reference
to law. However, ADR decisions are binding on the parties and are deemed
to be a legal (but non-judicial) settlement of the dispute.

3. Concept and pitfalls of traditional harmonisation

1–025   There is no doubt that during the past 50 years there has been a remarkable
degree of harmonisation among nations in the law applied to international
commercial transactions. A considerable number of different harmonising
instruments has been employed in the realisation of this goal. Often harmonisation has occurred and will occur for reasons exogenous to the law.[41] Is
harmonisation an ideal and how this ideal can be best achieved? What are the
means of harmonisation and how can they be classified (see section 3.1)?
Which groups of formulating agencies are involved in the process of harmonisation of law (see section 3.2)? What are the advantages and the disadvantages (see section 3.3) of traditional harmonisation of law?

3.1. Means of harmonisation/sources of international trade law

1–026   There are several classifications of the means of harmonisation of law. Most
of them do not consider the theoretical discussion about sources of international trade law. Often, lex mercatoria is included as a distinct source of law.
We will first look at the various classifications before suggesting a *via media*.
An appropriate classification will also delimit the nature and evolution of
transnational commercial law.

1–027   Schmitthoff makes the distinction between "international legislation" and
"international commercial custom":

---

[37] Judge Lagergen, cited in Schmitthoff, in Cheng (ed.), *Clive M. Schmitthoff's Select Essays on International Trade Law*, Dordrecht *et al.* (Kluwer) 1988, pp. 137–169, 157.
[38] See, for example, Julian D. M. Lew, *Applicable Law in International Commercial Arbitration*, para. 443, pp. 582–83.
[39] For further references regarding to the law applicable to the merits of international arbitration disputes see Julian Lew, Loukas Mistelis and Stefan Kröll, *Comparative International Commercial Arbitration*, London *et al.* 2001, Chapter 17. See also Article 28 UNCITRAL Model Law on International Commercial Arbitration; section 46 English Arbitration Act; Article 1496 New French Code of Civil Procedure; section 1051 German Code of Civil Procedure; Article 187 Swiss Private International Law Act.
[40] See Berger, *supra* n. 10, at 93–97, and Klaus Peter Berger, "The CENTRAL Enquiry on the Use of Transnational Law in International Contract Law and Arbitration", 15(9) *Mealey's International Arbitration Report* (2000).
[41] See Arthur Rosett, "Unification, Harmonization, Codification, and Reform in International Commercial Law", 40 *The American Journal of Comparative Law* 683–697, at 684 (1992).

- '*International legislation*', a convenient term but also a misnomer, indicates normative regulations devised internationally and then introduced into national law by national legislation or a mere ratification act. International legislation includes international conventions and model laws;[42] as examples one can mention the 1958 New York Convention on the Recognition and Enforcement of Foreign Arbitral Awards, the 1980 United Nations (Vienna) Convention on Contracts for the International Sale of Goods, the 1985 UNCITRAL Model Law on International Commercial Arbitration. International legislation as a harmonising instrument is used by UNCITRAL,[43] UNIDROIT,[44] the Hague Conference,[45] the European Union,[46] and other intergovernmental international organisations.

- *International commercial custom* which consists of commercial practices, usages or standards that have been formulated by international agencies such as the International Chamber of Commerce (ICC), or international trade associations. International commercial custom may be codified or uncodified. Codified or formulated commercial customs have acquired a more permanent form.[47] Examples of codified or formulated customs by the ICC are INCOTERMS and Uniform Customs and Practice for Documentary Credits (UCP 500).[48] Other examples of codified international commercial customs with some 'legislative–regulatory' interference are the standard forms[49] in commodities trade, *e.g.* GAFTA,[50] or in the construction industry, *e.g.* FIDIC.[51]

Schmitthoff's distinction does not prima facie accommodate *international (scholarly) restatements of law*, although, arguably in most cases, these may well fall under the scope of international commercial custom, formulated not by international agencies but by professional groups. Examples of such international restatements are the 1994 UNIDROIT Principles of International Commercial Contracts,[52] the 1994/1999 Principles of European Contract   **1–028**

---

[42] Schmitthoff, *Commercial Law in a Changing Economic Climate* (2nd ed., London 1981) pp. 22–3.
[43] See *infra* Chapter 2 by Gerold Herrmann and http://www.uncitral.org for list of conventions and model laws.
[44] See *infra* Chapter 5 by Herbert Kronke and http.//www.unidroit.org for list of conventions.
[45] See *infra* Chapter 6 by Hans van Loon and http://www.hcch.net for list of conventions.
[46] *e.g.* the 1980 Rome Convention on the Law to Applicable to Contractual Obligations.
[47] Schmitthoff, *supra* n. 42, p. 23.
[48] See *infra* Chapter 3 by Maria Cattaui Livanos and http://www.iccwbo.org for list of ICC instruments of international commercial law harmonisation.
[49] For standard contract see *infra*, Chapter 22 by Alejandro Garro and Clive M. Schmitthoff, "The Unification or Harmonisation of Law By Means of Standard Contracts and General Conditions", 17 ICLQ 551 (1968), Chia-Jui Cheng, ed., *Clive M. Schmitthoff's Select Essays on International Trade Law*, Dordrecht *et al.* pp. 1988, pp. 188–205.
[50] Grain and Feed Trade Association. See also http://www.gafta.com for further information.
[51] International Federation of Consulting Engineers. See also http://www.fidic.org for further information.
[52] See, for example, *infra* Chapter 21 by Michael Joachim Bonell and Michael Joachim Bonell, "The UNIDROIT Principles of International Commercial Contracts Prepared by the Institute for the Unification of Private Law (UNIDROIT)", in Center for Transnational Law (ed.), *Transnational Law in Commercial Legal Practice*, (Münster 1999), pp. 7–44.

Law,[53] the 1999 CENTRAL List of Principles, Rules and Standards of Lex Mercatoria[54] and the 1999 IBA Rules of Evidence in International Commercial Arbitration.[55]

Spanogle focuses on four harmonising techniques:[56]

(1)   Uniform substantive law

(2)   Uniform choice of law rules

(3)   Lex mercatoria

(4)   Standard form contracts

1–029   Spanogle's list emphasises rightly the importance of conflict of laws. The techniques are neither mutually exclusive nor incompatible. Only the first two may be characterised as sources of law *stricto sensu*. Nevertheless formulating agencies may elaborate any of the four.

1–030   Goode suggests that there are at least nine methods by which harmonisation may be either effected or induced, namely:[57]

(1)   a multilateral convention without a uniform law as such;

(2)   a multilateral convention embodying a uniform law;

(3)   a set of bilateral treaties;

(4)   [European] Community legislation—typically, a directive;

(5)   a model law;

(6)   a codification of custom and usage promulgated by an international non-governmental organisation;

(7)   international trade terms promulgated by an international non-governmental organisation;

(8)   model contracts and general contractual conditions;

(9)   restatements by scholars and other experts.[58]

---

[53] See, for example, Ole Lando, "Principles of European Contract Law in the Third Millennium", in Center for Transnational Law (ed.), *Transnational Law in Commercial Legal Practice* (Münster 1999) pp. 73–84.
[54] Klaus Peter Berger, "The CENTRAL-List of Principles, Rules and Standards of the Lex Mercatoria", in Center for Transnational Law (ed.), *Transnational Law in Commercial Legal Practice* (Münster 1999), pp. 121–145.
[55] See, for example, V.V. Veeder, "Evidential Rules in International Commercial Arbitration: From the Tower of London to the New 1999 IBA Rules", *Arbitration* 291–301 (November 1999).
[56] See Spanogle, *supra* n. 6, at pp. 486–494 (1991).
[57] See Roy Goode, "Reflections on the Harmonization of Commercial Law", in Ross Cranston and Roy Goode (eds.), *Commercial and Consumer Law. National and International Dimensions*, Oxford (Clarendon) 1993, 3–27, pp. 6–7.
[58] For discussion of harmonising instruments see *ibid*, pp. 7–9. Similar views are expressed by Louis F. Del Duca, "Developing Transnational Harmonization Procedures for the Twenty-first Century", in Ross Cranston and Roy Goode (eds.), *Commercial and Consumer Law. National and International Dimensions*, Oxford (Clarendon) 1993, pp. 28–40. He discusses, in particular, conventions (pp. 31–32), model laws (p. 32), guidelines (p. 32), voluntary contractual applicability texts (pp. 32–33) and the special case of EC law (pp. 34–37).

According to Goode, only the first four can be seen as sources of law, subject   **1–031**
to such constitutional acts as may be necessary to give them force of law in
a given jurisdiction. The last four instruments 'depend for the[ir] efficacy
upon incorporation into contracts, though a codification of custom and
usage could perhaps be relied on as the best evidence of custom and usage
and as such be imported by implication into a contract."[59] Goode here
excludes uncodified trade usages because of their diffuse and variegated
character. However, a few years later he focused on trade usages[60] and commented:

> ". . . At the time of its making a convention is not law at all; at most its existence signi-
> fies that States are contemplating its adoption. By contrast an international trade usage
> has normative force through the conjunction of *usus* and *opinio juris*."[61]

Goode's classification is inclusive and takes account of the doctrinal hierar-   **1–032**
chy of norms. It does not, however, consider the fact that contractual parties
often want to regulate their transactions without any reference to a state law.

Van Houtte highlights the classification of the harmonising instrument in   **1–033**
the origin and hierarchy of sources of law. Accordingly, three main groups
can identified with several sub-groups:[62]

I.   International law
    1. Treaties (bilateral treaties; multilateral treaties; international
       standards)
    2. Customary law
    3. Other sources (resolutions of international organisations; soft law;
       state contracts)
    4. Economic sanctions and boycott

II.   National law
    1. Public law
    2. Private law (Private international law; uniform substantive law)

III. Lex Mercatoria.

The above classification has merits in that it sheds light on the multiplicity of   **1–034**
sources of international trade law. The pitfalls of this classification are the
emphasis on state-made law and the support for so-called hard law provisions. It implies a certain hierarchy of international trade law norms which
favours international conventions and mandatory national rules over contractual stipulations and trade usages.

A number of different means are employed for the harmonisation or   **1–035**

---

[59] Goode, *supra* n. 57, at 7.
[60] Roy Goode, "Usage and its Reception in Transnational Commercial Law", in Jacob S. Ziegel
(ed.), *New Developments in International Commercial and Consumer Law*—Proceedings of the
8th Biennial Conference of the International Academy of Commercial and Consumer Law,
Oxford (Hart) 1998, 3–36, at 9–28 (nature, normative effect, position in international commercial law, etc.).
[61] *ibid*, p. 6.
[62] See Hans van Houtte, *The Law of International Trade*, (Sweet & Maxwell, London, 1995),
paras. 1.01–1.34.

international regulation of commercial law. An alternative to the previous classifications may be found in a distinction which will accommodate both the mandatory or optional nature of rules and proximity of the rules to the parties. According to this categorisation a distinction can be made between hard law, soft law[63] and softer law or extra-legal standards. A collateral distinction for harmonisation purposes can be made between 'hard law' or law harmonised by (inter-)governmental agencies and 'private harmonisation' or 'soft law".

1–036 • *Hard law* consists of international conventions, national statutory law and regional or international customary law. Only a small proportion of hard law rules will be of mandatory nature and they will normally be national legal system specific. Their 'hardness' is due to the fact that when parties make an effective choice of substantive law they will have to take the law as they find it; they cannot modify it, but they may amend it with their contractual stipulations. Only rarely are conventions or laws drafted with an express possibility for the parties to opt out of the application of a number of provisions or the entire legal text.[64] The parties' freedom to amend the law will be even more restricted when it comes to the choice of procedural law. The universal principle that all procedural matters are governed by the lex fori, limits, if it does not extinguish, party autonomy. Party autonomy exists with regard to substantive law or for a grey zone of issues which may be characterised procedural or substantive,[65] *e.g.* quantification of damages. Party autonomy is also extensive in the context of international commercial arbitration where the parties are free to choose applicable procedural law as well.

Typical examples of hard law include the 1980 United Nations Convention on Contracts for the International Sale of Goods, the UNIDROIT Factoring Convention, the 1958 New York Convention for the Recognition and Enforcement of Foreign Arbitral Awards, the UCP 500 (Uniform Customs and Practice for Documentary Credits), the English Sale of Goods Act, the customary (universal) choice of law rule for proprietary rights, *lex rei sitae.*

---

[63] Please note that in this chapter the concept of soft law is different from the concept of soft law to be found in van Houtte, *ibid.*, para. 1.13, and quite different from the term used in Harald Koch, " Private International Law: A 'Soft' Alternative to the Harmonisation of Private Law?", 3 *European Review of Private Law* (1995) 329–342.

[64] See, for example, Article 6 of the 1980 United Nations (Vienna) Convention on Contracts for the International Sale of Goods ('CISG'): " The parties may exclude the application of this Convention or, subject to article 12, derogate from or vary the effect of any of its provisions."

[65] See *Dicey & Morris on Conflict of Laws*, 13th ed. by Lawrence Collins, London (Sweet & Maxwell) 2000, pp. 157–181; *Cheshire and North's Private International Law*, 13th ed. by P. M. North and J. J. Fawcett, London (Butterworths) 1999, pp. 67–98; *Morris, The Conflict of Laws*, 5th ed. by David McClean, London (Sweet & Maxwell) 2000, pp. 471–489; Symeon C. Symeonides, Wendy Collins Perdue and Arthur T. von Mehren, *Conflict of Laws: American, Comparative, International*, St. Paul, Minn. (West) 1998, pp. 55–66; Edgar H. Ailes, "Substance and Procedure in the Conflict of Laws", 39 *Michigan L. Rev.* 392–418 (1941); Walter Wheeler Cook, "'Substance' and 'Procedure' in the Conflict of Laws", 42 *Yale L. J.* 333–358 (1941/42); Albrecht Mendelssohn Bartholdy, "Delimitation of Right and Remedy in the Cases of Conflict of Laws", 16 B.Yb.I.L. 20–41 (1935); Erwin Spiro, "Forum regit processum (Procedure is governed by the lex fori)", 18 ICLQ 949–960 (1969). See also Chapter 12 by Oskar Hartwieg.

- *Soft law*[66] consists of provisions embodied in model laws (but not   **1–037**
  incorporated in the national law), principles to be found in legal guides,
  and in scholarly restatements of international commercial law. Contractual stipulations agreed upon by the parties which do not conflict
  with relevant mandatory rules or public policy principles also belong to
  soft law. All these rules and principles are not legally binding and
  enforceable unless the parties to a commercial transaction decide otherwise. It follows, soft law is capable of having or developing legal effects.
  This is true also in cases where the parties have not expressly incorporated soft law provisions in their contract: soft law often gives guidance
  for the conduct of the parties, the interpretation of the agreement of the
  parties or an international convention.[67] Soft law may even create a
  framework for the expectation of the parties,[68] or provide the basis for
  negotiations. It is often the recommended harmonisation method.[69]

  Typical examples of soft law are the 1985 UNCITRAL Model Law
  on International Commercial Arbitration, the 1996 UNCITRAL
  Notes on Organising Arbitral Proceedings, the 1994 UNIDROIT Prin-
  ciples of International Commercial Contracts, the UNCITRAL Legal
  Guide on International Countertrade Transactions, the 1992 UNC-
  TAD/ICC Rules for multi–modal transport documents, the 1998 ICC
  Guidelines on Advertising and Marketing on the Internet.

- *Softer or Non Law* consists of any non- or extra-legal standards which   **1–038**
  are relevant for the assessment of legal questions. Quality of goods or
  packaging, for example, is normally assessed by the use of standards
  which are not legal in origin. Lawyers often tend to overlook that the
  business community has elaborated sets of rules to be used for their
  own trade. Such rules and standards are of paramount importance for
  the trade in question and are followed by the parties involved in it. The
  established common practice has the effect of harmonisation.

This tripartite distinction of harmonising instruments reflects also the origin   **1–039**
of authority of the various sources of international commercial law. Hard

---

[66] The term was first used in the context of public international law in order to describe state
obligations which derive from a midway between hard law (treaty or custom) and sheer political
engagement, *i.e.* gentlemen's agreement or recommended codes of conduct. See A. Aust, "The
theory and practice of informal international instrument", 35 ICLQ 787 (1986); C. Chinkin,
"The challenges of soft law: development and change in international law", 38 ICLQ 850 (1989);
Emmanuel Roucounas, "Engagements parallèles et contradictoires" RCADI 206 (1987–VI) at
176–178. In the EU context, soft law is sometimes used to describe a non-binding instrument
which may nevertheless be a guide to the way in which an institution or other agency will exercise its discretion within the framework of hard law rules. I am indebted to Marise Cremona for
pointing out this aspect of EU law.
[67] See, for example, CISG Articles 6, 7, 8 and 9.
[68] With regard to the UNIDROIT principles see *infra*, chapter 21 by Bonell, and Michael
Joachim Bonell, "The UNIDROIT Principles of International Commercial contracts—Nature,
Purposes and First Experiences in Practice", available at http://www.unidroit.org/english/princi-
ples/pr-exper.html.
[69] See Berger, "Einheitliche Rechtsstrukturen durch außergesetzliche Rechtsvereinheitlichung",
54 *Juristen Zeitung* 369–377 (1999); Oskar Hartwieg and Jens Grunert, "Bedarf und
Möglichkeiten provisorischer Eilverfügungen im E-Commerce - The mareva injunction at the
very edge of what is permissable", in 21 ZIP 721–732 (2000).

law is normally made be the state (statutory law or international conventions) or at least endorsed by the state (international custom codified or crystallised). Soft law is normally approved and given legal effect by private parties, although often states are involved in its formulation.

3.2. Formulating agencies

1–040   Under the term 'formulating agencies' we understand all agencies or organisations, national, regional or international, which are entrusted, delegated with or merely involved in the formulation of trade policy or rules for the conduct of international commercial transactions. The term 'formulating agencies'[70] precisely describes one aspect of the activities of international organisations but suitably covers all 'new international law-making' organisations. A significant number of formulating agencies have emerged in the last 100 years.[71] Most of them claim to be international standard setters in that they possess either acquired expertise in legislative drafting or have international experience by virtue of their membership or may even export in modified form successful domestic legislation.

Schmitthoff has recommended a distinction between:

- Intergovernmental agencies and

- Non–governmental agencies.[72]

1–041   This distinction was adequate for its time. In this chapter our differentiation goes further and is the result of the ever increasing number of formulating agencies. We are looking at the following groups:

- First, international (intergovernmental) organisation entrusted with the harmonisation of law;

- Secondly, regional (intergovernmental or supranational) organisations pursuing economic integration;

- Thirdly, non-governmental organisations; and

- Fourthly, international (intergovernmental) organisations which are not normally entrusted with harmonisation of law.

1–042   A few international organisations are entrusted with the task of harmonising aspects of commercial law and they actually use both hard and soft law means. These organisations are the United Nations Commission on International Trade Law (UNCITRAL),[73] the International Institute for the Unification of Private Law (UNIDROIT),[74] and the Hague Conference on Private

---

[70] The term was introduced by Schmitthoff, *supra* n. 42, at 24. (Note that 1st edition in 1977).
[71] See the links of the web site of the European Commercial Law Unit, Centre for Commercial Law Studies, Queen Mary, University of London http://www.ccls.edu/eclu/links.html and the international commercial/trade law monitor web site: http://www.lexmercatoria.net.
[72] Schmitthoff, *supra* n. 47, at 24.
[73] See http://www.uncitral.org and *infra*, Chapter 2 by Gerold Herrmann.
[74] See http://www.unidroit.org and *infra*, Chapter 5 by Herbert Kronke.

International Law.[75] Recently, the World Trade Organisation (WTO)[76] joined this group.

Most regional international economic integration organisations entail an element of harmonisation of law: ASEAN,[77] EC/EU,[78] MERCOSUR,[79] North American Free Trade Association (NAFTA),[80] Organisation of American States (OAS)[81] and the Organisation for African Unity (OAU).[82] In the case of the EC approximation of laws covers the lengthy list of aspirant member states. Regional organisations use again both private and public means.   **1-043**

Further, a number of non-governmental international mercantile organisations or professional associations attempt to unify and harmonise commercial law. Among them most prominently and successfully, the International Chamber of Commerce (ICC),[83] the International Law Association (ILA),[84] the International Bar Association (IBA),[85] and the Comité Maritime International (CMI). Non-governmental organisations or professional associations often promulgate model laws, model rules, standard contracts or draft conventions, in short, they most often employ soft law. Occasionally they co-operate with intergovernmental organisation in the formulation of hard law instruments, in particular, international conventions.[86]   **1-044**

Finally, several other international organisations, such as the World Bank,[87] the European Bank for Reconstruction and Development (EBRD),[88] the International Monetary Fund (IMF)[89] have demonstrated in a number of endeavours their interest in being involved in the lawmaking process or at least in standard-setting. In principle, neither the World Bank nor the EBRD nor the IMF have any power to legislate and hence standard–setting is the appropriate form of involvement.   **1-045**

Inevitably there are at least two competing strategies in the harmonisation of international commercial law on a world-wide basis: the competition is between the 'global' conventions proposed by international organisations and the regional agreements drafted by regional organisations. The goals of such regional conventions often derive from quite different motivations, but often produce agreements that concern the same subject matter as the global conventions.[90] In principle, the conflict between harmonisation initiated by intergovernmental organisations and non-governmental organisations may not be as acute, provided that lobbyists from one side and state functionaries   **1-046**

---

[75] See http://www.hcch.net and *infra*, Chapter 6 by Hans van Loon.
[76] See http://www.wto.org.
[77] See Association of Southeast Asian Nations at http://www.aseansec.org.
[78] See http://europa.eu.int. Harmonisation of private law (*e.g.* contract law) is only recently on the EU agenda. See *e.g.* new Article 65 EC and *infra*, Chapter 4 by Stephen Weatherill.
[79] See http://embassy.org/uruguay/econ/mercosur/.
[80] See http://www.nafta-sec-alena.org/english/nafta/. See also *infra*, Chapter 25 by Joe Norton.
[81] See http://www.oas.org/.
[82] See http://www.undp.org/popin/oau/oauhome.htm.
[83] See http://www.iccwbo.org and *infra*, Chapter 3 by Maria Cattaui Livanos.
[84] See http://www.ila-hq.org .
[85] See http://www.ibanet.org.
[86] For examples see *infra*, Chapters 2 and 3.
[87] See http://www.worldbank.org.
[88] See http://www.ebrd.org. See also the journal of the EBRD entitled Law in Transition.
[89] See http://www.imf.org.
[90] See Spanogle, *supra* n. 6, pp. 483–486.

on the other side communicate clearly the interests they represent and the necessary compromises are made. It is in any event essential that formulating agencies co-operate closely, both in terms of selecting projects, agreeing on organisations to undertake the drafting work and deciding the appropriate means of harmonisation.[91] Actually, it is undoubted that 'there are horses for courses', *i.e.* some agencies have more experience and expertise in dealing with some issues and formulating a specific type of instrument, others specialise in different types of harmonising technique. In any event the professional associations and the commercial community must be involved in the law–making process, as the intended or ultimate beneficiaries often have clearer and more concrete views as to potential solutions.

3.3. Advantages and drawbacks of traditional harmonisation

1–047 Harmonising instruments, irrespective of their origin, have two major permissive and not mutually exclusive objectives. First, they aim at unification of law, where there is disparity. Secondly, they aim at law reform when the existing law cannot cope with evolving commercial practices. In either case the ultimate objective is the development of a legal framework and the setting of international standards (often as a result of crystallisation of existing trade usages). Against these two objectives the advantages of harmonisation of law seem to be self-evident. However, the business community is very reluctant to embrace any change in law. The same applies for both the practising lawyers and legislators. 'Why mend what is not broken?' is a question often asked by legislators when law reform is recommended. Accordingly it is often very hard to convince the business community or national legislators even to take an interest in proposals for harmonisation, still less to give the proposal their support.[92] A typical example is the ongoing reluctance of the United Kingdom with respect to the CISG.[93]

It is essential to restate some of the advantages of harmonisation:

- First, it facilitates commerce with the lifting of barriers resulting from the complexities of different legal regimes.

- Secondly, harmonisation of international commercial law creates a legal framework tailor-made for international transactions, disregarding differences in the regulation of domestic transactions.

- Thirdly, harmonisation normally produces neutral law, *e.g.* the CISG is a system of international sales law which is compatible with both civil and common law.[94]

---

[91] See the discussion in Goode, *supra* n. 57, pp. 5–6 (selecting the field) and pp. 9–11 (which organisation?).

[92] Goode, *supra* n. 57, at 24 and discussion in 25–27.

[93] See, for example, Barry Nicholas, "The Vienna Convention on International Sales Law", 105 LQR 201 (1989); Hobhouse, "International Conventions and Commercial Law: The Pursuit of Uniformity", 106 LQR 539 (1990); Derek Wheatley, "Why I Oppose the Winds of Change", *The Times*, March 27, 1990; Roy Goode, "Why Compromise Makes Sense", *The Times*, May 22, 1990; Barry Nicholas, "The United Kingdom and the Vienna Sales Convention: Another Case of Splendid Isolation?", *Saggi, conferenze e seminari n° 9*, Centro di studi e ricerche di diritto comparato e straniero, Rome 1993 = http://www.cnr.it/CRDCS/nicholas.html.

[94] See, for example, Peter Winship, "Formation of International Sales Contracts under the 1980 Vienna Convention", 17 *International Lawyer* 1–14 (1983); Alejandro Garro, "Reconciliation of

- Fourthly, harmonisation often fills a legal vacuum by providing rules in a field where national law was previously non-existent, *e.g.* UNCITRAL Model Law on Electronic Commerce, or obscure, *e.g.* the draft UNIDROIT Convention of Security Rights in Mobile Equipment.

- Fifthly, *effective* harmonisation substitutes a single law for a proliferation of national laws and thus within the given field dispenses with the need to resort to conflict of laws rules and the opportunity these give for forum shopping. Ineffective harmonisation, on the other hand, results in increased conflict of laws and wider possibilities for forum shopping.[95]

- Sixthly, harmonisation of law with the collateral reduced conflict of laws results in significant reduction of transactional costs.

- Seventhly, in a field of law where conflict of laws has little or no role to play, there is increased predictability and legal certainty and consequent reduction of legal risk.

- Finally, for a number of legal systems harmonisation of law bears fruits of law reform. While in some countries law reform is a complicated and thorny issue, reforms can more easily be achieved once a provision has been adopted at international level.

The attribute "effective" was added to the advantages relating to conflict of laws. Unfortunately, as harmonisation does not usually result in wholesale unification, conflict of laws remains relevant and significant.[96] There are two reasons why harmonisation does not normally result in unification or uniformity: (a) normally the harmonising measure has limited scope (*e.g.* formation of contracts of sales only) and (b) not every state in the world adopts the harmonising measure. In addition, there are two reasons why harmonisation instruments are not successful: (a) often the wrong type of harmonising instrument is chosen and (b) there is lack of political will or support in implementing the harmonising instrument into national law. All of the above four reasons assume that the harmonisation effort was adequately negotiated and drafted and that it undisputedly has merits.　　**1–048**

The main pitfalls of traditional international harmonisation of commercial law or indeed co-ordination of trade regulation relate to international conventions. Here are the major drawbacks of harmonisation by international conventions:　　**1–049**

- The negotiation and drafting of international conventions is normally a lengthy and costly process. This is also true for all amendments and updates.

Legal Traditions in the UN Convention on Contracts for the International Sale of Goods", 23 International Lawyer 443–483 (1989).

[95] See *supra* n. 18.

[96] See, for example, Jan Kropholler, *Internationales Einheitsrecht*, Tübingen (Mohr) 1975, at 167 *et seq.*; Christian von Bar, *Internationales Privatrecht*, Vol. I, Munich (Beck) 1987, paras 83–99, 65–74, 66; Henri Batiffol and Paul Lagarde, *Droit International Privé*, Vol. I, 8th ed., Paris 1993, paras 30–35 and 343; 43–50 and 561.

- Because of the participation of states with different legal traditions and different expectations, the degree of unification may be excessively restricted and the differences may be irreconcilable.[97] Irreconcilable differences often result in unacceptable compromises. Conventions reflect the common denominator and this is often very small; *i.e.* a convention may produce minimum rather than maximum unification of law.

- It has been observed that on occasions states do not negotiate such treaties as equal partners and issues of sovereignty may arise in the context of international trade regulation.[98] In any event, a new international law has emerged and questions of legitimacy, accountability, authority, and freedom in this new global legal order may arise.[99]

- International conventions normally operate through a national act of positive law (ratification or implementing act). Delays in ratification result in conventions coming into force after many years. In any event, positive law is more predictable and creates legal certainty. However, statutory law is subject to interpretation by the courts or administrative authorities often to the effect that law in action has little in common with law in books. There is no guarantee that harmonised law will be interpreted in a harmonised manner.

1–049 Alternative means of soft harmonisation of commercial law, such as codification of customary law or trade usages, in most cases avoid the pitfalls of international conventions. Soft harmonisation is open-ended and provides for a flexible and effective convergence of different legal systems. In any event, both trade regulation and international harmonisation of commercial law are manifestations of the need for comparative law studies.[1] Modern comparative law is functional and, if properly used, produces remarkable results. One problem that needs to be addressed is that traditional and modern harmonisation alike ignores aspects of public and procedural law.

---

[97] See for balanced accounts of harmonisation: Rosett, *supra* n. 41, 683–697; Goode, *supra* n. 57, at 24–27; Spanogle, *supra* n. 6, at 510–516. For a critical and stimulating account of harmonization see Uriel Procaccia, "The Case Against Lex Mercatoria", in Jacob S. Ziegel (ed.), *New Developments in International Commercial Law*, Oxford (Hart) 1998, pp. 87–95.

[98] See the fascinating historical note Gary N. Horlick, "Sovereignty and International Trade Regulation", 20 *Can.-U.S. L.J.* 57–65 (1994). Discussing NAFTA and looking at historical treaties such as the Westphalia Treaty of 1648 he points outs that "when you look into the future, the question is not whether there will be more of this international "cessation of sovereignty", rather the question is how." *Id.* at 65. He further quotes Lord Wilbeforce's observation in the English Westinghouse case in 1978, in connection with the traditional (since 1945 in Alcoa) U.S. attempts to extend its sovereignty in antitrust areas, that frequently the policies being attacked are precisely the ones the host country is determined to defend.

[99] See the stimulating essay by Paul B. Stephan, "The New International Law - Legitimacy, Accountability, Authority, and Freedom in the New Global Order", 70 *U. Colo. L.Rev.* 1555–1587 (1999).

[1] Mathias Reimann, "Stepping Out of the European Shadow: Why Comparative Law in the United States Must Develop its Own Agenda", 46 *Am. J. Comp. L.* 637 (1998). Mathias Reimann, "The End of Comparative Law as an Autonomous Subject", 11 *Tul. Eur. &. Civ. L. F.* 49 (1996).

4. Concluding remarks: the new legal era—new sources of law?

Five sets of conclusions can be drawn from the exposition above and some   **1–050**
forecasts will also be attempted.

First, when policymakers and scholars think of global trade lawmaking, they generally think of treaties and declarations of states. The 'public' or 'hard law' model based on state rights and obligations has predominated. But alongside that effort, little remarked on by activists or academics, a system of 'private' or 'soft' standards and obligations is developing. This soft or private law model is initiated by and applicable to producers of goods and providers of services rather than to states. 'It appears that globalisation may not erode state power but may merely re–channel it".[2] In fact, we experience the emergence of a new international law. International law, once the province of specialists concerned mostly with traditional public international law (how national governments deal with each other or with international organisations), 'has become an important body of regulatory and commercial law directly affecting private lives and commercial transactions. Our legal culture, however, has not caught up with this transformation."[3] The emergence of a new body of rules has proceeded in parallel to the continued development of what we traditionally have thought of as international law. The 'new international law' is stemming from a collection of very different international agencies, such as the International Monetary Fund and the organs of the EU, or private self-constituting, and ad hoc, such as the working groups of the International Chamber of Commerce.[4] All these formulating agencies employ many different processes in promulgating (negotiating and drafting) rules and standards that constrain individual actors more or less directly. This body of new international law is relatively permanent and independent of individual states, in that it is not subject to any ratification.

Secondly, the merits and drawbacks of international harmonisation   **1–051**
through hard and soft law, have been discussed extensively in the last 20 years. In addition, *lex mercatoria*[5] is an effort to standardise commercial

---

[2] See Aseem Prakash, Book Review, 4 *Ind. J. Global Legal Stud.* 575–591 at 575 (1997).

[3] Stephan, *supra,* n. 99, at 1555. See also *supra,* n. 6 (para. 1–004).

[4] *ibid.* at 1563. See also Spanogle and Steinhardt, *supra,* n. 6 (para. 1–004).

[5] See, for example, Gesa Baron, "Do the UNIDROIT Principles Form a New Lex Mercatoria?" 15 *Arb. Int.* 115 (1999) = http://www.cisg.law.pace.edu/biblio/baron.html; Klaus Peter Berger, *The Creeping Codification of Lex mercatoria* (Kluwer) 1999; Berger, *supra* n. 10 (para. 1–005); Blaurock, *supra* n. 36 (para. 1–020); Michael Joachim Bonell, "Das autonome Recht des Welthandels", 42 *RabelsZ* 485 (1978); Patrick J. Borchers, "The Triumph of Substance over Rules of Choice in International Commercial Transactions: From the Modern Lex Mercatoria to Modern Standards", in Raish and Schaffer (eds.), *Introduction to Transnational Legal Transactions*, New York *et al.* (Oceana) 1995, 139–158; Thomas Carbonneau (ed.), *Lex Mercatoria and Arbitration: a Discussion of the New Law Merchant* revised edition 1998 (Kluwer and Juris Publishing); Felix Dasser, *Internationale Schiedsgerichtsbarkeit und lex mercatoria*, Zürich, 1989; Filip De Ly, *International Business Law and Lex Mercatoria* (1992); Freeman, "Lex mercatoria: its emergence and acceptance as a legal basis for the resolution of international disputes", IX ADRLJ (1997) 289–300; Berthold Goldman "The applicable law: general principles of law", in Julian Lew (ed.), *Contemporary Problems in International Arbitration*, London (Kluwer) 1986, 113; Berthold Goldman, "Le lex mercatoria dans les contrats et l'arbitrage internationaux; réalités et perspectives", *Clunet* 1979, 475; Berthold Goldman, "Lex Mercatoria", 3 *Forum Internationale* 194 (1983); Aleksandar Goldstájn, "The New Law Merchant, JBL 1961, 11; Aleksandar Goldstájn, "The New Law Merchant Reconsidered", in *Law and International*

1–052   terms and practices across international borders. It brings more certainty to cross–border transactions and helps increase international economic activity that benefits the economies involved. It is incomplete, as it covers only areas, where businesspersons feel there is a need for uniformity, and is virtually global. This soft law harmonisation is arguably more effective than other models and functional when needed.

Thirdly it appears that all harmonisation methods have their supporters. However, as far as sources of law are concerned, we move towards substantive international private law, international choice-of-law rules and more lex mercatoria,[6] or *leges mercatoriae*. Here a threefold prognosis may be outlined:

- The use of substantive international private law can be seen in the elaboration and formulation of substantive rules applicable to international transactions, *e.g.* the CISG or the UCP 500. This new dualism (different sets of rules for domestic and international transactions) has long–term effects, as it will gradually denationalise commercial law applicable in international context. Common interpretation and uniform application of substantive international private law will remain the major problem.

- The increased denationalisation of regulation of international business together with the widespread of uniform law will reduce the effect or at least will change the function of conflict of laws rules. Denationalisation may, however, be successfully challenged when legal systems declare a set of their rules to be mandatory. In such cases mandatory rules prevail over party autonomy. The use of mandatory rules, *inter alia*, performs the task of safeguarding the undistorted well-being and promotion of national interests. On a number of issues conflict of laws rules have already assumed this new role of co-ordinating choice law

---

Trade, Festschrift für Clive M. Schmitthoff, F. Fabricius (ed.), 1973, 171; Aleksandar Goldstájn, "Reflections on the Structure of the Modern International Trade", in Petar Šaršević. (ed.), *International Contracts and Conflict of Laws*, London 1990, pp. 14–35; Goode, *supra*, n. 60 (para. 1–031); Martin Hunter, "Publication of Arbitration Awards and Lex Mercatoria", 54 *Arbitration* 55 (1988); Ole Lando, "The Lex Mercatoria in International Commercial Arbitration", 34 ICLQ 747 (1985); Eugen Langen, *Transnational Commercial Law*, 1973; Andreas F. Lowenfeld, "Lex Mercatoria: An Arbitrator's View" 6 *Arb. Int*.133 (1990); Abdul Maniruzzaman, "The Lex Mercatoria and International Contracts: A Challenge for International Commercial Arbitration", 14 *Am. U. Int'l L. Rev.* 657 (1999); Pierre Mayer, "Mandatory rules of laws in international arbitration", 2 *Arb. Int.* 274 (1986); Meyer, *supra,* n. 16 (para. 1–007); Michael Mustill, "Contemporary Problems in International Commercial Arbitration: A Response", 17 *Int'l Bus Law* 161 (1989); Lord Mustill, "The New Lex Mercatoria—the First Twenty-five Years" in Bos & Brownlie (ed.), *Liber Amicorum for Lord Wilberforce*, Oxford 1987, pp. 149–183 and 2 *Arb. Int.* 86 (1988); Luke Nottage, "The Vicissitudes of Transnational Commercial Arbitration and the Lex Mercatoria: A View from the Periphery", 16 *Arb. Int.* pp. 53–78 (2000); Jan Paulsson, "Le lex mercatoria dans l'arbitrage CCI", *RevA*.1990 55; David Rivkin, "Enforceability of Arbitral Awards based on Lex Mercatoria", 9 *Arb. Int.* 67 (1993); Clive M. Schmitthoff, "International Trade Law and Private International Law", in: *Vom deutschen zum europäischen Recht, Festschrift für Hans Dölle* II, 1963, 264; Clive M. Schmitthoff, "Das neue Recht des Welthandels, 28 *RabelsZ* 47 (1964); Rolf A. Schütze, "The Precedential Effect of Arbitration Decisions", 11 *J. Int. Arb.* 69 (1994); Ursula Stein, *Lex mercatoria - Realität und Theorie*, Frankfurt am Main 1995; Christoph W. O. Stoecker, "The Lex Mercatoria": To What Extent does it Exist?" 7 *J. Int. Arb* 101 (1990); Vanessa L. D. Wilkinson "The New Lex Mercatoria - Reality or Academic Fantasy?" 12 *J. Int. Arb.* 103 (1995).

[6] See Spanogle, *supra*, n. 6 (para. 1–004), at 520.

between national interests and positivism on the one hand and inter-nationalisation and emergence of transnational rules on the other hand. Many choice of law rules are nowadays unilateral rules. In the commercial law context there is an emerging trend in favour of har-monisation which is reflected at all three levels of conflict of laws rules: jurisdiction, choice of law, recognition and enforcement of foreign judgments. Accordingly, the majority of conflict of laws rules can be found in international conventions, *e.g.* party autonomy in interna-tional contracts, or international custom, *e.g. lex rei sitae*. (Positive or negative) conflict of conflict of laws rules and conflicts of conventions will remain present and problematic. The same applies to the pervasive problems of conflict of laws: characterisation, renvoi, public policy, pre-liminary questions, mandatory rules (*lois de police, Eingriffsnormen*).

- New lex mercatoria is quite different from its medieval counterpart. Not only professional associations but also legal scholars are working for the codification of lex mercatoria.[7] The implication is that effec-tively we have more than one lex mercatoria, we actually have several *leges mercatoriae*. A number of *leges mercatoriae* are compatible with one another. This is by-and-large the case for the UNIDROIT Princi-ples of International Commercial Contracts, the Principles of Euro-pean Contract Law and the CENTRAL List of Principles, Rules and Standards of Lex Mercatoria. On the other hand, as lex mercatoria can now be derived from several sources, it has built-in ambiguities. In short, we are going to have conflicts of *leges mercatoriae*. As an opti-mistic note, it may be emphasised that arbitral tribunals have little or no difficulty with the application of lex mercatoria.[8] National courts will have to follow.

Fourthly, a triumph of substance over procedure has been observed.[9] This statement may be given two different interpretations and further implications: **1–053**

---

[7] See *supra*, n (para. 1–005). 52–55.
[8] See Lew, *supra*, n. 8 (para. 1–005), paras 366–372, at 465–474; Berger, *supra*, n. 10, passim; Lew, Mistelis and Kröll, *supra*, n. 8 (para. 1–005), chapter 17. See, for example, Paris Chamber of Arbitration Award in case no. 9246 of March 8, 1996, *Austrian Agent v. Egyptian Principal*, ICCA YBCA XXII, 1997, 28–34; ICC Award no. 5485, 1987, *Bermudian Company v. Spanish Company*, YBCA XIV, 1989, 156; ICC Award no 3540, 1980, *French Contractor v. Yugoslav Sub-contractor*, YBCA VII, 1982, 124; ICC Award no 2321, 1974, *Two Israeli Companies v The Government of an African State*, YBCA I, 1976, 133; ICSID Award in case no. ARB/81/1, *Amco Asia Corp. v. Republic of Indonesia*, 21 ILM 1022, 134 (1985); *Sapphire Award*, ILR 1967, at 136; Interim Awards and Final Award of 1983, 1984 and 1986 in ICC case no. 4145, *Establishment of Middle East country v. South Asian construction company*, 112 Clunet 985 (1985), YBCA XII, 1987, 97–110; Iran-US Claims Tribunal Award in Case No. 59 (191–59–1) of 25 September 1985, *Questech, Inc. v. The Ministry of National Defence of the Islamic Republic of Iran*, YBCA XI, 1986, 283–289; ad hoc Award of July 6 1983, *Hungarian State Enterprise v. Jugoslavenski Naftovod* (Yugoslav Crude Oil Pipeline), YBCA IX, 1984, 69–70
[9] See Borchers, *supra*, n. 5 (para. 1–051) and Francis A. Gabor, "Stepchild of the New Lex Mercatoria: Private International Law form the United States Perspective", 8 *Nw. J. Int'l L. & Bus.* 538–560 (1988); Willis Reese, "Commentary on Professor Gabor's *Stepchild of the New Lex Mercatoria*", 8 *Nw. J. Int'l L. & Bus.* 570–573 (1988).

- The first implication is a rather unintentional and indirect result of the observation: While a great deal has been accomplished in terms of harmonisation of substantive law very little has been achieved in procedural unification. This is due largely to wide acceptance of party autonomy in substantive law while most of the procedural law is labelled public or mandatory law.[10] Differences in procedural law encourage forum shopping.[11] International commercial arbitration has gladly stepped in to accommodate the needs of the business community. Arbitration has soft procedural rules, with the exception of procedural fairness, and emphasises the settlement of dispute as a matter of substantive justice.

- The second implication directly relates to the statement and to the previous comment concerning the re-orientation of conflict of laws. Modern conflict of laws will focus on the application of specialised substantive rules.[12] This was an expression of the old lex mercatoria but it is also reflected in the modern lex mercatoria, in modern lex mercatoria codifications and, last but not least, in the modern contract drafting culture, according to which parties make a self-regulatory contract.

1–054 Finally, a paramount consideration of everyone involved in the harmonisation of international commercial law is the establishment of a legal framework which will facilitate cross-border trade. This will depend on two factors: predictability and availability of familiar legal or non–legal standards.[13]

- Predictability reduces transactional costs; it assists the parties to assess risks related to their prospective transaction and has impact on contract drafting. Predictability also has effects on the potential dispute settlement.

- Availability of familiar legal or extra-legal standards assists the parties with regard to choice of applicable law. In particular, when parties decide to opt for a neutral law, the availability of such a familiar standard is essential.

The emergence of lex mercatoria and soft law along with traditional sources of law brings to mind Roman law and *ius gentium*. In Roman law there was a distinct law applicable for international cases. Both the very essence of lex mercatoria and the emergence of a new dualism (national law for domestic transactions, substantive international private law for international transactions) are descriptive of the past and prescriptive for the future. Given the potential for further genetically modified conflict of laws, Schmitthoff's call for a world commercial code[14] remains intact. This is the beginning of third generation of harmonisation of international trade law. The new dualism is

---

[10] See *supra*, n. 65 (para. 1–036).
[11] See *supra*, n. 18 (para. 1–009).
[12] See Borchers, *supra*, n. 5 (para. 1–051), p. 141.
[13] See Borchers, *supra*, n. 5 (para. 1–051), p. 156.
[14] See Schmitthoff, *supra*, n. 28 (para. 1–014), pp. 29–31.

no absolute virtue. Often the success of the current regulatory web lies in the interaction between different sources of law and when a good framework is elaborated this should be applicable for both domestic and international transactions. A world commercial code could be formulated for international transactions first with the expectation to be applicable for domestic transactions too at a later stage. Schmitthoff wanted UNCITRAL to be entrusted with the magnus opus, for which UNCITRAL should co-operate with other formulating agencies. 'When—and not if—this task is accomplished our time will have what it needs: a transnational code of international trade law of world-wide application.'[15] Let us hope that this symposium and this book may lay a modest foundation stone.

---

[15] See *ibid.*, p. 31.

Chapter 2

THE ROLE OF UNCITRAL

by Gerold Herrmann[1]

1. Introduction

2–001 Under the heading "Law, International Commerce and the Formulating Agencies—The Future of Harmonisation and Formulating Agencies", I am supposed to address the role of UNCITRAL. From that I would conclude that I should talk about not only the current but also the future role of UNCITRAL.

2–002 It might be a good idea to approach this in a concrete, empirical fashion and try to learn from the past. Let us look at what we have done, where we have come from and where we are going. Let us then see whether there is anything that could and should be improved.

---

[1] Dr.jur. (Cologne); LL.M. (Berkeley, Cal.); Honorary Professor (Vienna); Secretary of UNCITRAL (until January 31, 2001; the views expressed in this paper are personal ones and do not necessarily reflect the views of the Organisation); Member of: ICCA, LCIA Court, Presiding Council of International Arbitration Court of Austrian Economic Chamber, Consultative Commission of WIPO Arbitration Center, Board of ACICA, and International Academy of Commercial and Consumer Law.

As the representative of the youngest of all the formulating agencies 2–003
present here, but personally the oldest warrior in the unification camp, having
started 25 years ago, I think as UNCITRAL Secretariat we are very lucky. We
are very lucky because of the one person to whom this symposium is dedicated: Professor Clive M. Schmitthoff. We are indebted to him for his foresight
and vision, about which I make more extensive reference in the formal toast.[2]

Loukas Mistelis has already referred to some of the meetings that were 2–004
convened by the International Association of Legal Sciences with the support
of UNESCO in the late fifties and early sixties.[3] There, Clive Schmitthoff,
when looking at all the organisations that were formulating uniform law texts
at the time, concluded that there was a lack of purposeful co-operation and
co-ordination between these agencies and that an international agency of the
highest order, possibly on the level of the United Nations, was needed. The rest
is history: General Assembly resolution 2205 (XXI) of December 17, 1966,
which created UNCITRAL. The Commission began its work in 1968 at a
session where one of the contributors of this symposium was present: Robert
Effros,[4] who already at that time represented the IMF.

2. Global commerce (whether e-commerce or other trade) needs global uniform law, best elaborated by a world body

Why do I say we were lucky? I think the way the Commission was conceived 2–005
and how it approached its work really boded well for meeting the new challenges of globalisation. Global commerce, whether e-commerce or not,
requires global law. We talk about the global marketplace, the global village,
but what a funny village: every house still has its own laws, sometimes different streets in the village have different traffic rules. This cannot work, certainly not on the Internet, and it cannot work well in the rest of commerce.

UNCITRAL's major strength, which is there almost by virtue of it being 2–006
a United Nations body, is its truly universal participation. The idea was not
simply, as some believe, to have negotiations between North and South, but
to have truly universal representation of countries from all regions and different economic and legal systems, whether or not they have a well developed
commercial law. While some countries have more expertise and experience to
share than others, all certainly have needs or aspirations and can tell us the
conditions under which they could accept certain texts. There are many
examples where this has proven to be the guarantee of acceptability. It may
be tempting to have three of the top professors prepare an excellent text,
maybe the best text possible (however you measure the quality of such a
text), but if it is not accepted, it does not further the unification of law.

A similar factor is the preparation of texts in six world languages, that is: 2–007
parallel preparations, with every oral or written portion of the preparatory
work in six languages and an accompanying consistent review in a drafting
group of commercial law experts and linguists. This is clearly superior to

---

[2] See *supra*, p. xxvii.
[3] See *supra*, chapter 1.
[4] See *infra*, chapter 28.

preparing a text in only one language and later translating it into many others. Another plus is the pragmatic, technical, non-politicised consensus approach which we have in UNCITRAL (not in all bodies of the United Nations as you know). Of considerable value is also what one may call private/public partnership. The main example is our close cooperation with the ICC which was already mentioned, and we have been doing this with many other organisations.[5] It helps us to get the balance right, not be taken in by the industry to rubber stamp a certain text, but also not having exclusively ministry officials agree on a text which affects business without listening to business in the first place. After all, those interested non-governmental international organisations tend to represent the practitioners, merchants, bankers and other commercial people who are the ultimate consumers and beneficiaries of the text.[6]

2–008   Seeing Professor Jay Westbrook as one of the contributors to this volume,[6] I am reminded of the joint venture with INSOL International and the IBA Committee J, which led to the UNCITRAL Model Law on Cross-Border Insolvency (1997). That was a really good joint venture, even better than the old prototype, where two partners come together, one has the knowledge and the other one has the money, and two years later it is the other way around.

3. Main objectives of UNCITRAL's work (with primary examples of its uniform texts)

2–009   Let us now look at the main objectives of our Commission: we are mandated to further the progressive harmonisation or unification of the law of international trade. I think we have furthered and achieved quite a number of different objectives of harmonisation, and I will give you some of the pertinent examples.

3.1. Harmonisation to overcome disparity of laws or otherwise disruptive borders

2–010   The first is harmonisation in general or "equalisation", that is, to have the same law in different countries. In this learned circle, I need not explain the practical value of having the same law apply to all of your imports or exports, namely the United Nations Sales Convention. With 57 member countries[7] that account for about two thirds of world trade, this is truly a world sales law (which applies unless parties agree otherwise).

2–011   This Convention was based on very solid research and on the very good work of UNIDROIT that led to the Hague Uniform Laws 1964. The crucial value added by UNCITRAL was the universal representation. Apart from

---

[5] *e.g.* ICCA, CMI, INSOL, IBA, UIA, IABA, EBF, CFA, FCI, PASA.
[6] See *infra*, chapter 30.
[7] Argentina, Australia, Austria, Belarus, Belgium, Bosnia & Herzegovina, Bulgaria, Burundi, Canada, Chile, P.R. China, Croatia, Cuba, Czech Republic, Denmark, Ecuador, Egypt, Estonia, Finland, France, Georgia, Germany, Greece, Guinea, Hungary, Iraq, Italy, Kyrgystan, Latvia, Lesotho, Lithuania, Luxembourg, Mauritania, Mexico, Moldova, Mongolia, Netherlands, New Zealand, Norway, Peru, Poland, Romania, Russian Federation, Singapore, Slovakia, Slovenia, Spain, Sweden, Switzerland, Syrian Arab Republic, Uganda, Ukraine, USA, Uruguay, Uzbekistan, Yugoslavia and Zambia.

substantive improvements of the text, it was clearly the participation and involvement of 62 states at the 1980 Vienna Conference that led to the wide adherence. The objective of overcoming disruptive borders underlies clearly the Model Law on Cross-Border Insolvency[8] (like any other UNCITRAL text with commentary available or downloadable from our website: www.uncitral.org). Another such "trans-national" example is the UNCITRAL Bills and Notes Convention.[9] If chosen by the parties, you have the legal system travel with the negotiable instrument.

Equalisation is in essence simplification (which translates into reduction of transaction costs). It is the same law that applies, irrespective of where you go. Equalisation in itself does not depend on content, it simply says it is the same. That reminds me of the person who once told his friend: "I will be very rich soon, I invented a nail-cutting machine". When the other one asked, "how does it work?" the response was, "It's like a vending machine, you put in two German Marks (or one Euro, that drops so easily) and then put in your fingers and it cuts your nails". When the other one said, "This can never work", he asked, "why not?" and got the reply, "Well, because fingers are of different lengths!" His replique was, "Oh, that is only *before* the treatment".   **2–012**

3.2. Specialisation to accommodate special needs and features of international transactions and disputes

2–013

While equalisation is a worthwhile objective, you have to look at content too. One of the substantive purposes is to cater for special needs or features of international transactions. The Sales Convention has quite a number of such features. For example, preservation of contract and preservation of goods are given more emphasis than typically in domestic sales laws. Another good example is the Convention on Independent Guarantees and Stand-by Letters of Credit which entered into force on January 1, 2000.[10] It provides the legal framework for the expanded use and inter-operability of instruments hitherto known only in certain regions. The UNCITRAL Model Arbitration Law[11] is another text catering for specific features of international transactions and disputes.   **2–014**

Such orientation has been our mandate (as clearly expressed in the name United Nations Commission on *International* Trade Law). Yet, the interesting experience is that quite a number of countries have taken the Model Arbitration Law immediately also for domestic transactions, or they used it first only for international cases and, once they were more familiar with it, also for domestic ones. International orientation often means essentially a more liberal system which, once one is more familiar with it, will be regarded as quite suitable for domestic cases. Moreover, it might be wrong to

---

[8] UNCITRAL Model Law on Cross-Border Insolvency 1997 with Guide to Enactment.
[9] United Nations Convention on International Bills of Exchange and International Promissory Notes (New York, 1988).
[10] United Nations Convention on Independent Guarantees and Stand-by Letters of Credit (New York, 1995).
[11] UNCITRAL Model Law on International Commercial Arbitration (1985).

distinguish in the future between international and domestic transactions, something we cannot do in e-commerce anyway. That is why we no longer have this distinction in our Model Law on Electronic Commerce.[12]

3.3. *Modernisation to take into account changes in values, in technology or in financial or commercial practices*

2–015   Modernisation should take into account relevant changes in value, in attitude, in technology, in commercial or financial practice. A typical example is the Hamburg Rules,[13] which, compared with the still prevailing Hague system, provide considerably more fairness in the allocation of risk, and more consistency with the rules in other modes of transport. The same applies to the Terminal Operators Convention,[14] establishing rules for transported goods when not moving, but stationary (although, in fact, they may be moving more than one wants, we call that pilferage or loss by theft; more than 50 per cent of the damage to cargo in international transport occurs this way).

2–016   A very important and current example is our Draft Convention on Assignment of Receivables in International Trade. It embraces novel financing practices and constitutes an equally good example of the next objective, "barrier demolition".

3.4. *"Preventive unification" or other facilitation to remove legal obstacles to novel modes of finance, commerce or communication*

2–017   Apart from harmonising the rather disparate laws, especially as regards perfection of security interests, that Convention will remove obstacles to modern financing practices (including securitisation, forfaiting, project finance, factoring) such as absolutely effective no-assignment clauses or prohibitions of assignments of future receivables or in bulk.

2–018   The removal function is most apparent in the field of electronic commerce, including electronic funds transfers, and relates primarily to paper-based requirements or obstacles. Here we did what I call "preventive unification", something which we will have to do more in the future. This is not to revise traditional laws, to update them, to adjust them to modern technologies, but it is to create something new where no laws exist in the first place. When we did the Model Laws on Credit Transfers[15] and on Electronic Commerce,[16] there was not one country in the world which had a specific law on the respective topic. The idea here is totally different from the past, where we said: there is disparity between laws which creates problems or costs, let us unify them. The new idea is to get the experts of the world together in one room, if there is some novel area requiring legislation, and let us try to find a uniform solution before every nation does its own home cooking.

---

[12] UNCITRAL Model Law on Electronic Commerce (1996).

[13] United Nations Convention on the Carriage of Goods by Sea, 1978.

[14] United Nations Convention of the Liability of Operators of Transport Terminals in International Trade, 1991.

[15] UNCITRAL Model Law on International Credit Transfers (1992).

[16] See *supra*, n. 11.

3.5. Creation or enhancement of confidence and legal certainty

Pursuit of the aforementioned objectives contributes to the attainment of confidence and legal certainty which, however, may well be regarded as a goal in itself because of its pre-eminence in various uniform law texts. A splendid example is the Model Arbitration Law[17] which has been the first successful model law ever on the universal level, with enacting jurisdictions covering more than one third of the world's territory. Being by far the most widely and best known arbitration law in the world, it provides (with this "hi-fi factor") confidence and certainty to potential users, which is of particular interest to foreign investors or traders.   2–019

Two other good examples are our Model Law on Procurement of Goods, Construction and Services[18] as well as, though below the level of unification, our recently adopted Legislative Guide for Privately Financed Infrastructure Projects. In both fields, the effect of "certainisation" instils confidence into would-be-investors and either encourages them to participate in that economically important activity or, at least, to reduce their prices.   2–020

4. Information, training and technical assistance

Of the various UNCITRAL publications and means of disseminating international trade law information, let me particularly mention our case law collection system ("CLOUT"). Of course, there are quite a number of other such systems; the only reason why we maintain CLOUT is again the six languages. You will find the Sales Convention and most cases thereon 50 times on the Internet these days. But do you find Chinese case abstracts, do you find them in French or in Arabic? Unfortunately that language point is often underestimated (although recently it was predicted that in ten years the majority of websites will be in Chinese and not in English).   2–021

Probably the most important UNCITRAL activity other than preparing uniform law texts is the holding of regional or national seminars, briefing missions, training courses and, more recently, judicial colloquia, often jointly with other organisations. Unfortunately, scarcity of financial and human resources prevents the Secretariat from meeting the demand therefor which has been increasing exponentially with the increasing number of uniform law texts and the countries adopting them.   2–022

Law reform assistance is a related activity which suffers from the same defect. The Secretariat's lack of resources is a particularly disappointing feature here, for two reasons: First, the preparation of a uniform law is an extremely expensive affair (the Sales Convention cost the United Nations alone an estimated 6 million U.S. dollars) which would mean a considerable waste if, for lack of a comparatively minute amount, the text will not be made known to the relevant people. The second reason is what I would call "tax-payer funded disunification of law": international financial institutions   2–023

---

[17] See *supra*, n. 10.
[18] UNCITRAL Model Law on Procurement of Goods, Construction and Services (1994) with Guide to Enactment.

and other development agencies often send out experts who either do not know uniform law texts, and I am not talking only of UNCITRAL texts, it applies to texts of UNIDROIT and others as well, or they know these texts but think: "It is a bit cheapish to collect 100,000 and simply say: use the Model Law", or they think "let me draft my own law", or "what is reasonable is what I learned at school and that is my national law', or they even go there with a fairly clear (thinly concealed) mandate, "let me bring my own law to that country".

5. Co-ordination and co-operation between formulating agencies

2–024   The next area is co-ordination and co-operation, which, remember, was the main purpose of establishing UNCITRAL. We employ a number of means, including general or specialised reports on current activities of other formulating agencies, at times endorsing or recommending texts of others, frequent consultations with the secretariats of other formulating agencies and participation in their meetings.

2–025   Unfortunately, co-ordination efforts meet increasingly with limited success. I think I know what I am saying here having been involved both on stage and behind the scenes for quite some time. That deterioration is due to a number of reasons: organisations have to justify their existence to those who pay, our times are characterised by an individualistic competitive spirit, everyone is the "centre of excellence", whether the capacity or competence is there or not. We have particular problems with regional commissions in the United Nations which want to go global, applying the well-known Peter Principle and creating disparity of laws, duplication of efforts and, particularly undesirable in a global economy, fragmentation of what should be universal efforts. There is a lot of marketing out there: we have more law commercials than commercial laws these days.

6. Future focus

2–026   The future focus therefore shall be first: UNCITRAL will continue to formulate uniform law texts, where UNCITRAL's special strengths are required, *i.e.* its universal representation, its working methods, experience and competence, or where others are not prepared or willing to take on a special project whose desirability and feasibility has been determined.

2–027   Secondly, we should provide interpretive guidance on texts, like the Sales Convention. We will start with the Model Arbitration Law and the 1958 New York Convention. Rather than using the method of an amending protocol, the UNCITRAL Working Group on Arbitration will prepare a declaration for the General Assembly itself as to how certain provisions should be interpreted. We know that this is not binding on any judge or arbitrator; but it will come with a certain persuasive force, backed by the reputation of UNCITRAL.

2–028   Thirdly, we should more closely co-operate with multi- and bilateral development agencies involved in legislative assistance programmes. With a view to reducing the earlier described "tax-payer funded disunification of law", we should try to ensure that consultants active in law reform countries are at least aware of pertinent uniform law texts.

Fourthly, we should assist as a think tank which can assess global accept- 2–029
ability in devising truly de-localised solutions for de-localised borderless
commerce, especially, but not exclusively, e-commerce or m-commerce. Let
me give you three examples. If you have a "de-localised" sales transaction
and you do not know where the parties are, or at least where the seller is
located, the chances today are already two out of three that the United
Nations Sales Convention applies. It would be a simple conflicts rule, though
not of the traditional type, that says: let us top up the last third. Obviously I
chose an example where we have a high uniformity factor. Whenever we
achieve this in other areas too, I think we should use the same e-volutionary
approach.

As far as dispute settlement is concerned, the de-localised solution is 2–030
online mediation or arbitration, whether via cable or wireless. By the way, the
technological/commercial controversy "cable versus wireless" has been
settled at a recent archaeology congress where one excavator reported about
the find of a wire in 2000-year-old soil, concluding therefrom that his
country already then used cable telephony, whereupon a professor from
another country asserted that, having found no wire in 5000-year-old soil, his
country already then used wireless communication.

Even enforcement could be done over the Internet. For example, you 2–031
can have a bank guarantee mechanism, with the guarantee issued (and
payment of the award effected) electronically. This can validly be done
under our Guarantee and Standby Convention, providing another example
of UNCITRAL's forward-looking spirit.

Fifthly, much more needs to be done to improve the co-operation and 2–032
co-ordination between formulating agencies, at least those that are globally
active. I am not primarily thinking of the Secretariats because we tend to be
in close contact. The main key lies with the governments. At UNCITRAL we
have representation by all governments of the world, and all the other
formulating agencies have at least some of those. Yet, often there is no
co-ordination between the individuals representing the very country,
directly or indirectly, and that is the main reason for the low level of
co-ordination.

Finally, I would suggest as a new focus, which would also help to improve 2–033
co-ordination, to "unite" people towards one big project, like in a religious
order: the project would be to develop a universal code of international trade
law, following a similar proposal by Clive Schmitthoff 15 years ago.

The expected benefits of a global commercial code would be a compact 2–034
package deal providing a coherent and consistent body of commercial law,
certainising the rights and obligations of parties to commercial and similar
transactions by providing a single global reference law (rather than the 50
leges mercatoriae which are likely to be developed by various professorial
groups). It would be an ideal opportunity for reviewing alternative competing texts in the light of modern trends, especially the use of electronic communications. It should help to reduce the otherwise increasing trends of the
disunification by purposeful co-operation, recommended and monitored by
a Code Co-ordination Council.

Finally, we could thereby clarify and utilise the often confused distinction 2–035
between international legislation with a long term perspective focussing on

the abstract eternal principles to avoid the risk of solidification, and the much more flexible, frequently revised contractual system rules for uniform practices as prepared particularly by the ICC, the true law merchant (made by merchants). These Uniform Rules or Practices could be incorporated, or referred to, in an annex to the future Global Commercial Code based on an endorsement by UNCITRAL or the Code Coordination Council, which should comprise representatives of all interested global formulating agencies and of all sectors concerned and which will keep all of us busy for a number of decades.

CHAPTER 3

HARMONISING COMMERCIAL LAW: KEEPING PACE WITH BUSINESS

ADDRESS BY MARIA LIVANOS CATTAUI
SECRETARY-GENERAL OF ICC

1. Introduction: Business Development and Harmonisation of Commercial Law

ICC is honoured to be present at the Schmitthoff Conference, particularly in view of Professor Schmitthoff's contributions to ICC work.

3–001

As you all know, we work closely with the several formulating agencies, including, in particular, the institutions represented here: UNCITRAL, UNIDROIT, the European Union and the Hague Conference. I agree with Gerold Herrmann that the global economy needs global rules and that there needs to be some co-ordination among those agencies formulating such rules.[1]

3–002

The question for us from the business world is—to what purpose? Our purpose in business is to create wealth, value, jobs—to serve clients, customers, employees and our investors and shareholders. The purpose of any harmonisation of commercial law should be to sustain and facilitate this process. If legal systems, if harmonisation of law, ends up being too static and constraining, they will be bypassed in this era of swift global economic movements. Business moves so fast it often works beyond and outside the "legislative" frameworks (which do not even exist in the case of much of e-commerce). Business cannot and will not wait. It will continue to operate in areas that are beyond those known to the legal sector, often because such frameworks are not relevant. In many cases, business goes out and creates

3–003

---

[1] See *supra*, chapters 2 by Gerold Herrmann and 1 by Dr Loukas Mistelis.

rules and standards long before these are consecrated inside legal systems. This is a self-regulation of business activity that ICC has traditionally welcomed and endorsed.

2. ICC and the harmonisation of commercial law

3–004   Since its creation in the early years of the last century, ICC has been a leading organisation in the harmonisation of rules and practices governing international trade. The harmonisation of trade terms incorporated in international sales contracts is one of the reasons for ICC's foundation.[2]

2.1. ICC harmonising instruments: contract method and recommendations

3–005   ICC contributes to the harmonisation of commercial law through several channels elaborating self-regulatory instruments:

- codes,[3]

- guidelines,[4]

- rules,[5]

- model contracts[6] and

- model clauses,[7] etc.

3–006   ICC's approach is mainly a contractual one, although some other instruments, such as position papers and other types of recommendations made by ICC on specific subjects contribute actively to the harmonisation of international trade. In this latter case, harmonisation is not direct (an instrument

---

[2] INCOTERMS 2000 are the most recent edition of the ICC Rules for the interpretation of the most commonly used trade terms. They were first published in 1936 and they have since been revised several times. See also *infra*, Chapter 22 by Alejanaro M. Garro.

[3] See, for example, ICC International Code of Direct Selling (1999), ICC International Code of Direct Marketing (1998, currently under revision), ICC International Code of Advertising Practice (1997), ICC/ESOMAR International Code of Marketing and Social Research Practice (1995), ICC International Code on Sponsoring (1992), ICC Code of Environmental Advertising (1991, currently under revision), ICC International Code of Sales Promotion (1987).

[4] See, for example, ICC Guidelines on Advertising and Marketing on the Internet (1998, currently under revision).

[5] See, for example, ICC International Court of Arbitration Rules (1998), Uniform Customs and Practice for Documentary Credits - UCP 500 (1993), Uniform Rules for Demand Guarantees - URDG (1992), Uniform Rules for Collections - URC 522, International Standby Practices - ISP (1999), ICC Uniform Rules for Contract Bonds - URCB (1994), ICC Uniform Rules of Conduct of Interchange of Data by Tele-transmission (1988), UNCTAD/ICC Rules for multimodal transport documents (1992). See also *infra*, Chapter 22 by Alejandro M. Garro.

[6] See, for example, ICC Model International Franchising Contract (2000), ICC Model Occasional Intermediary Contract (Non-circumvention and non-disclosure agreement) (1999), ICC Model Sale Contract (Manufactured goods intended for resale) (1997) which has been used as a model by UNCTAD/WTO, ICC Model Commercial Agency Contract (1991); ICC Model Distributorship Contract (1993). ICC Model Mergers & Acquisitions Contract and an ICC Model Turnkey Contract are currently being elaborated.

[7] See, for example, ICC Force Majeure Clause.

being proposed for adoption by users) but is indirect—governments and businesses being asked either not to take any decision that would be inconsistent with a definite practice, or to follow some guiding principles to achieve a certain uniformity of commercial practice.

Use of these instruments is purely voluntary, though their worldwide acceptance incites business to follow these global standards. For example, the use of INCOTERMS is recommended by UNCITRAL and by the European Commission for statistics about the movement of goods. INCOTERMS are also referred to in the 1999 model sales contract for perishable goods recently released by the International Trade Centre (a joint UNCTAD/WTO organisation that promotes international trade in developing countries).[8] The ICC International Code of Advertising Practice[9] has been fixing the rules governing such an activity since 1937.

3–007

Some of the ICC instruments such as INCOTERMS, all model contracts, the advertising and marketing codes and guidelines can be adopted in their entirety, adapted to local or sectoral requirements, or used as a basis for ideas by parties to international transactions, national legislators, etc.

3–008

2.2. ICC formulating process: rules by users for users

INCOTERMS

Compared to national or supra-national legislators, private formulating agencies such as ICC allow direct consultation of all parties interested in international trade transactions. Users of the harmonised rules are those who have elaborated the rules, including lawyers and business experts.

3–009

Elaboration of INCOTERMS or ICC codes, guidelines and position papers on advertising and marketing are good examples of this extremely broad consultation process. These ICC instruments are the result of comprehensive international surveys. Based on the information collected by ICC National Committees and observer organisations, several draft documents have been elaborated by working parties, each of these documents being commented on and amended by ICC members. ICC chapters all over the world are also requested to comment on the drafts before a final text is sent to the relevant ICC commission for approval and then to the ICC Executive Board.

3–010

This democratic process ensures that all business sectors, and also consumers and governmental authorities, are duly consulted. This guarantees a perfect adequacy to the needs of all parties involved in international trade.[10]

3–011

3. A new era of private-sector-driven harmonisation: justification and pitfalls

Harmonisation through self-regulation by private agencies is efficient and cost effective. It is elaborated by users, for users. The rules are elaborated

3–012

---

[8] This model sales contract is further influenced by the ICC Model Sale Contract (1997).
[9] The ICC Marketing Codes has been in existence since 1937 and have been adopted by most European countries as well as many emerging markets (Hungary, Poland, Slovenia, Russia and Uzbekistan).
[10] See *infra*, Chapter 22 by Alejandro M. Garro.

because they respond to a business need and this need constitutes a powerful incentive to create rules that would be immediately applicable by users. Furthermore, no public funding is required to launch preliminary studies or to finance any step of the rules-elaboration process. This process and the release of a self-regulatory instrument does not depend on any financial or policy decision of a public authority.

3–013   A potential problem is that formulating agencies may not work closely enough to ensure that their respective fields of work are consistent and do not unnecessarily duplicate. ICC's response to this waste of resources—which may discredit and delay harmonisation of commercial law and commercial practice—is to liase continuously with other formulating agencies, many of whom are represented here today.

3–014   As all of you know, these efforts towards harmonisation in commercial law, particularly for informational transactions, are not new. A paper that Professor Roy Goode delivered in 1990 emphasises this.

> "... The rules and trade terms promulgated by the International Chamber of Commerce, demonstrate how much can be achieved by the contractual approach to the harmonisation of commercial law and practise ... The International Chamber of Commerce promotes non-law instruments which depend for their effect upon contractual incorporation. The advantages of the contract route are becoming increasingly appreciated. Since governments are not involved, the role of lawyers is reduced and the procedure is more flexible and informal, proposals can be implemented more rapidly, and rules found to cause difficulty can be changed more readily. The utility of contract rules increases as their use expands. The most striking example is provided by the Uniform Customs and Practise of the International Chamber of Commerce, which has been adopted by banks throughout the world. The beauty of the UCP is that since all relevant contracts involve a bank there is a ready mechanism for ensuring that all contracts are governed by the UCP. The result is to connect up a network of contracts by a uniform set of rules and thus give them multilateral force."[11]

Equally important, especially today, is speed. Professor Goode again states:

> "In general, a minimum of ten years is required to bring to fruition an initial proposal for an International Convention, though there are exceptions. Very often the period is much longer and securing the requisite number of ratifications may take a decade more, if, indeed, this is achieved at all. Projects of the International Chamber of Commerce can usually be completed much more quickly, since not only are they less formal but they are not legal instruments in themselves, simply rules or trade terms incorporated by contract, so that the legal issues are de-emphasized and, indeed, the product is primarily the work of non-lawyers."[12]

4. Digression: issues for further consideration

3–015   I would like to leave you with five points for consideration in the future, from the point of view of world business.

1.   The first involves the role of all "agencies", which changes with the evolving concept of "harmonisation" and changing marketplace needs. Too few governmental and business organisations are prepared for the

---

[11] Unpublished. See, to the same effect, most recently Roy Goode, *Commercial Law in the Next Millennium*, (Sweet & Maxwell) London 1998, p. 90.
[12] *ibid.*

new business environment, in which (following today's "race to the top" that will develop from an Internet phenomenon to a general business trend) many basic services and goods will increasingly be "commoditised" due to the use of ever more efficient information and communications tools, and where innovative customer-friendliness and the ability to adapt will be the key competitive factors in many business sectors.

2.   What does this mean for the development of business rules and practices and for the institutions that are traditionally responsible for it? We at ICC are in the privileged position of having direct feedback from the marketplace, but even we often see a development with major impact on our role only after it hits us. We are only now getting used to the fact that even very few people in the business community can anticipate tomorrow's trends, and we're learning how to find these people and work with them to stay on the cutting edge of rule-making.

3.   There will be tremendous pressures on all "agencies" to network and co-ordinate among themselves. Isolationist tendencies or antiquated membership philosophies will be penalised by the marketplace, and those who cannot adapt to this will disappear or become irrelevant.

4.   We also have to learn that certain assumptions about the need for harmonisation will need to be revised if we do not want to run the risk of distorting rather than promoting business efficiency. In some areas there will be a need where previously there wasn't, but more often we will be faced with marketplace resistance that many of us cannot understand from a traditional harmonisation perspective. Here, a word of advice: the moment you find yourself in that position or are puzzled at resistance in your membership to action that seemed logical to you and your staff, you know that your organisation is in great danger of being overtaken by events. By the way, that doesn't mean that you should give in to pressures for any kind of regulatory or disciplinary action to be halted in favour of market forces—in many cases there will be a need for some form of intervention or regulation, but it will very often not take the same form it would have taken five years ago.

5.   We at ICC are not only experimenting with new ways of encouraging sufficient understanding among businesses without locking them into rules that stand in the way of innovation, we are also working on new ways to bring such rules and guidelines to the business community. Examples include instruments that are labelled "living documents", which are posted on the Internet and adapted in new ways using the Internet. We believe that in the future it will no longer be sufficient to issue a rule or guideline, or any other harmonising instrument, without attention to the ways in which such instruments can be integrated into existing IT-based business platforms and practices. This is why we're working on a suite of mixed rules/applications-based services that allow businesses to create customised contracts within parameters set by legal experts in our membership.

3–016   The message we are receiving from the broad constituencies we either interact with or represent is the following:

> The acceleration of new business processes and the entry of new kinds of "non-professional" voices in legal issues is causing all of us to question what we mean by harmonisation, what objectives it fulfils today and to what extent (and in what ways) it is really beneficial. Above all, we are reconsidering what kinds of new alliances among old and new formulating agencies are needed to achieve appropriate and relevant international harmonisation.

CHAPTER 4

THE ROLE OF THE EUROPEAN COMMUNITY

PROFESSOR STEPHEN WEATHERILL[1]

1. Abstract/Introduction

This paper traces the development of the European Community's harmoni-   **4–001**
sation programme, with special emphasis on its impact on national private
law. It will be possible to extract some of the themes of this paper as a basis
for comparison and contrast with the regimes that are the subject of the
other papers comprising this section of the book, although the author has
not attempted in a comprehensive fashion to make explicit those potential
connections. This paper takes as its dominant theme the perception that
the EC's harmonisation programme has implications that extend far
beyond the technical matter of hammering out common rules. Instead it
insists on the constitutional dimension that necessarily accompanies any
appraisal of the scope and intensity of the EC's activities in the field today.
This paper examines current constitutional sensitivities arising out of EC
initiatives to harmonise laws and shows that these tensions are liable to
increase as the geographical and functional expansion that has characterised
the European integration movement over the last 15 years continues to
develop. In so far as this theme may be connected with other arenas for harmonisation discussed in other papers in this collection, the lesson suggested
by the EC's experience in this field is that (for good or ill) harmonisation
activity tends to "spill over", exerting an impact on ever wider areas of regulatory activity and carrying ever more sensitive implications for the shaping

---

[1] Jacques Delors Professor of European Community Law, University of Oxford; Director of the
Institute of European and Comparative Law, Faculty of Law, University of Oxford; Fellow of
Somerville College.

of constitutional arrangements governing the relationship between the several national and transnational entities engaged in the harmonisation process. In fact, harmonisation of laws offers a window on that teasingly ambiguous debate: in so far as the growth of transnational rule-making responding to economic trends loosely labelled "globalisation" risks by-passing established national systems of supervision and accountability, is it right to revert to emphasis on national-level governance or instead to strengthen credible transnational institutional mechanisms of oversight.

2. Rationales for harmonisation in the EC

4-002   Why does the European Community possess a competence to harmonise laws? An orthodox answer holds that the EC possesses a competence to harmonise laws as an element in the process of achieving market integration.

4-003   It is first useful to recall that laws may be harmonised "negatively". This occurs when a court finds that a national measure conflicts with the treaty rules governing the free movement of goods and services. This is "negative harmonisation" in the sense that a national impediment to cross-border trade is disapplied, removing an element of regulatory diversity between the Member States. The impact of the Community on the national market is in such circumstances deregulatory. It promotes integration and consumer choice. This is the familiar territory famously claimed by the court for the treaty rules governing free movement of goods in the *Cassis de Dijon* case, which supplies a classic illustration of the capacity of EC trade law to set aside public choices about national market regulation in favour of the private autonomy of traders and consumers[2]. The court's expectations of consumer competence act as a lever in favour of integration, by eliminating national preferences to "over-protect" consumers. So, for example, the court insisted on the existence of a "reasonably circumspect consumer" in *Mars* as it indicated that German restrictions on marketing devices used by Mars across Europe could not be justified because they went beyond what the European Court was willing to regard as permissible intervention to protect such a benchmark consumer.[3] It should however be appreciated that the interest in integration does not always prevail. The Court concedes that "the fact that one Member State imposes less strict rules than another Member State does not mean that the latter's rules are disproportionate and hence incompatible with Community law".[4] Accordingly negative harmonisation has its limits, for the court is willing to accept that justifications may be advanced for trade-restrictive national measures. Regulatory pluralism among the Member States is not excluded under the court's approach to the treaty provisions governing free movement of goods and services even where impediments to trade integration have been identified. Nevertheless, it should be admitted

---

[2] Case 120/78 [1979] E.C.R. 649; [1979]3 C.M.L.R. 494. See generally S. Weatherill and P. Beaumont, *EC Law* (3rd ed., 1999), Chapter 17 (goods), Chapter 19 (services).
[3] Case C-470/93 [1995] E.C.R. I-1923. See S. Weatherill, *EC Consumer Law and Policy* (1997), Chapter 2.
[4] *E.g.* Case C-3/95 *Reisebüro Broede v. Gerd Sandker* [1996] E.C.R. I-6511; [1997] 1 C.M.L.R. 224.

that the court's track record in casc law arising under the treaty articles dealing with free movement suggests that the party seeking to defend trade-restrictive rules has an uphill task. In part this is explicable by the location of the burden of proof, which must be discharged by the regulator rather than by the proponent of market freedoms.[5] In part it is the consequence of the availability of EC law to challenge the deadwood of centuries of regulatory eccentricities in the Member States which would not otherwise have been likely to undergo renovation because of deficiencies in local constitutional arrangements which under-represent the interest in integration shared by in-state consumers and out-of-state producers.[6]

The limited capacity of "negative harmonisation" to level the commercial playing field in the EC leaves room for a need for a supplementary "positive" contribution by the Community to harmonise laws. This involves legislative act rather than judicial decision. It is this form of harmonisation that forms the dominant concern of this paper. Legislative harmonisation is, like judicial harmonisation, deregulatory in the sense that, on the simplest model, 15 diverse (national) rules are reduced to one (Community) rule in order to establish a common rule as the platform for a common market. If the task were merely to set a common rule, its content would be of no concern. All that would matter would be that it should apply in common. But this is also re–regulation (at EC level). The Community has to make a choice about the level at which that uniform rule shall be pitched. In fact, since harmonisation is an attempt to provide a "Europeanised" framework within which to cope with the complex pattern of diverse regulatory choices made over time within the Member States, and given that, moreover, the "Community" is not an entity wholly divorced from its Member States and is therefore influenced by their anxieties, it is inevitable that close attention must be paid to the quality of the chosen harmonised standard. Harmonisation is more than merely a technical process of eliminating barriers to trade. It is a classic example of the way in which trade integration "spills over" to confront ever more complex areas of regulatory policy. So, for example, if the Community harmonises national laws of consumer protection, it does so ostensibly because of the need to establish common rules in the area in order to promote the integration of the market. But the effect of such a reactive policy is to create a form of Community consumer law. Choices have to be made about the quality of the harmonised regime. The same observation may be directed at the harmonisation of environmental laws and social policy.

4–004

The relevant legal bases for harmonisation in the treaty are Articles 94 and 95 EC, which in comparable though not identical form were Articles 100 and 100a, respectively, before the entry into force of the Treaty of Amsterdam. The provisions are distinguishable in practice most significantly by the applicable voting rule in Council, unanimity under Article 94, qualified majority ("QMV") under Article 95. Neither supplies carte blanche to

4–005

---

[5] Case 227/82 *Van Bennekom* [1983] E.C.R. 3883; [1985] 2 C.M.L.R.
[6] For an important discussion of the law in this area from a constitutional perspective, see M. Poiares Maduro, *We, the Court* (1998).

harmonise laws. Rather, the terms of the relevant provisions stipulate that legislative harmonisation by the Community is confined to a process with a given end—market-building. So Article 95, the key provision in practice in the development of the Community's harmonisation programme in recent years, states that acting in accordance with the co-decision procedure, the council and parliament may "adopt the measures for the approximation of the provisions laid down by law, regulation or administrative action in Member States which have as their object the establishment and functioning of the internal market".

4–006   The inevitable link between harmonisation as a technical process and the quality of the harmonised regime has been clear at a constitutional level since the amendments to the EC Treaty made by the Single European Act (which entered into force in 1987). This association is now reflected in Article 95(3):

> "The Commission, in its proposals envisaged in paragraph 1 concerning health, safety, environmental protection and consumer protection, will take as a base a high level of protection, taking account in particular of any new development based on scientific facts. Within their respective powers, the European Parliament and the Council will also seek to achieve this objective."

4–007   The intertwining of harmonisation policy as a basis for market integration and choices about the quality of the harmonised regime is given further confirmation in the EC Treaty by the "horizontal" provision in Article 153(2) EC. This dictates that consumer protection requirements shall be taken into account in defining and implementing other Community policies and activities, including, no doubt, market-building listed in Article 3 EC and elaborated in, *inter alia*, Article 14 EC Environmental protection has similar horizontal effect by virtue of Article 6 EC

4–008   Articles 95(4)–(10) EC demonstrate the anxiety that harmonisation in pursuit of integration may damage local preferences for stricter rules. A managed opt–out is available, although the scope of derogation permitted under this notorious procedure is to be interpreted narrowly.[7] This procedure hints at the general trend of recent years towards "flexibility" in EU law[8] and serves as a different kind of illustration of the inevitably tense association between market building and the anxiety to defend patterns of regulatory intervention selected over time in the Member States.

3. Some EC Measures of harmonisation

4–009   The European Community's harmonisation activity in the field of private law embraces a wide range of measures. Among the more prominent are the following:

---

[7] See, pre-Amsterdam, Case C-41/93 *France v. Commission* [1994] E.C.R. I-1829; [1995] 3 C.M.L.R 733 and Case C-319/97, *Antoine Kortas* judgment of June 1, 1999, though the significance of the latter decision is reduced by the Amsterdam amendments.
[8] For a collection of relevant essays, see G. De Burca and J. Scott, *Constitutional Change in the EU: From Uniformity to Flexibility?* (2000).

Dealing chiefly with formation of contracts

- Directive 85/577 on the protection of the consumer in respect of contracts negotiated away from business premises (Doorstep Selling), [1985] O.J. L372/71;

- Directive 90/314 on package travel, package holidays and package tours, [1990] O.J. L158/59;

- Directive 94/47 on protection of purchasers in respect of certain aspects of contracts relating to the utilisation of immovable property on a timeshare basis, [1994] O.J. L280/83;

- Directive 87/102, [1987] O.J. L42/48, amended by Directive 90/88, [1990] O.J. L61/14, on consumer credit

- Directive 97/7 on distance contracts, [1997] O.J. L144/19;

- Directive 97/5 on cross-border credit transfers, [1997] O.J. L43/25.

Dealing with the content of contracts

- Directive 93/13 on unfair terms in consumer contracts, [1993] O.J. L95/29;

- Directive 99/44 on certain aspects of the sale of consumer goods and associated guarantees, [1999] O.J. L171/12.

Tort law

- Directive 85/374 on the approximation of laws concerning liability for defective products, [1985] O.J. L210/29, "the Product Liability Directive".

4–010 This is a rather mixed bag. The Directives affect some contracts, predominantly consumer contracts, but not all. The dominant regulatory technique is mandatory information disclosure designed to improve the quality of the environment in which the bargain is struck combined with opportunities to withdraw from a contract for a defined period after agreement, although direct checks on the content of the bargain form a small part of the package, most strikingly via Directive 93/13. EC law adds a rather jumbled overlay to existing national private law.[9] In part, this patchwork character is attributable to the constitutional and institutional focus of the harmonisation programme on market-building.

4–011 The community had no explicit competence in the field of consumer protection until the entry into force of the Maastricht Treaty in 1993 and even then the competence conferred was carefully confined, a matter considered further below. Private lawmaking is not a competence conferred on the

---

[9] On the challenge of absorption, see *e.g.* W. Heusel (ed.), *New European Contract Law and Consumer Protection* (1999); H. Schulte-Noelke and R. Schulze (eds), *Europäische Rechtsangleichung und nationale Privatrechte* (1999).

Community by its Treaty. All these Directives were adopted on the basis of Articles 94 or 95, Article 100 or 100a as were, and all are in formal terms measures of harmonisation, the subject matter of which happens to touch private law. In this sense, a species of EC private law has evolved, but it has not been planned as such. It is ad hoc: it is EC private law only indirectly. A similar story may be told of EC labour law and environmental law, for example, where treaty bases that are not directly connected to those spheres of activity have nevertheless been used as the basis for legislation which has exerted an indirect influence on labour and environmental law.

4–012   There are inevitable limitations to depiction of these legislative packages as anything so grand or coherent as "EC consumer law" or "EC private law" or "EC environmental law" or "EC labour law", but the accretion of material under the cover of a broadly conceived harmonisation programme has made it possible to devise intellectual frameworks for examining the intensity, scope and purpose of the EC's role in such realms. For EC consumer policy, for example, it is possible to draw out underpinning themes such as the promotion of social justice, the protection of legitimate expectations, tackling information assymetries, the role of the well-informed consumer and the quest to build consumer confidence in the viability of the internal market.[10] Harmonisation creates its own academic sub-disciplines.

4–013   It is also significant that many of the Directives listed above are pitched as minimum measures of harmonisation only. The minimum formula implies variation between states even in areas supposedly harmonised, in so far as states choose to set stricter rules. The Community does not occupy the field entirely, to the exclusion of Member State choice, but rather both rule-makers remain active in the field. So the "Doorstep Selling" Directive stipulates in Article 8 that the Directive "shall not prevent Member States from adopting or maintaining more favourable provisions to protect consumers in the field which it covers." Stricter controls are not excluded by the Directive, although they must not violate primary treaty provisions such as those governing the free movement of goods.[11] The price may be loss of the level playing field, but harmonisation has been achieved, albeit only at a minimum level, and appreciation of diversity has been given expression. On the other hand, of course, minimum harmonisation implies that there can be no *systematic* EC private law. It is not like a national system. And it does not typically *replace* national private law, it adds to it. In the area of private law at least, "Europeanisation" under EC law is a process of influence and cross-fertilisation, not conquest.[12] In so far as this induces jurists to engage with a

---

[10] See, *e.g.*, H.-W. Micklitz, "Principles of Social Justice in European Private Law: the role of Private Law" *Yearbook of European Law*, forthcoming; S. Weatherill, "The Evolution of European Consumer Law and Policy: From Well Informed Consumer to Confident Consumer?" *in Rechtseinheit oder Rechtsvielfalt in Europa? Rolle und Funktion des Verbraucherrechts in der EG und den MOE-Staaten* (H.-W. Micklitz ed., 1996), Chapter 25; J. Stuyck, "European Consumer Law after the Treaty of Amsterdam: Consumer Policy in or beyond the Internal Market?" (2000) 37 C.M.L.Rev. 367; L. Kramer, H.-W. Micklitz and K. Tonner (eds), *Law and diffuse interests in the European legal order: Liber Amicorum Norbert Reich* (1997); H. Schulte-Noelke and R. Schulze, n. 8 above; and more generally N. Reich, *Europäisches Verbraucherrecht* (1996).

[11] See Case C-382/87 *Buet v. Ministère Public* [1989] E.C.R. 1235; [1993]3 C.M.L.R. 659.

world beyond their own legal borders, it is submitted that it presents an appealing prospect.

This history demonstrates the rupture of any supposed divide between the Community as the motor of integration and the Member States as the entities responsible for choices about market regulation. The pattern of harmonisation has led to a much more complex allocation of responsibilities in the EC. In its quest to build a market, the EC reacts to choices made about regulatory preferences within the Member States and finds itself seeking to provide a European-level re-regulatory framework within which to address the anxieties underpinning those pre-existing national choices.

4-014

4. The future of harmonisation

There are some reasons to suspect that the harmonisation programme of the EC will be less ambitious in future. The Commission has changed its focus since the expiry of its deadline under Article 14 EC for the completion of the internal market at the end of 1992. It is overtly concerned to pursue "better lawmaking"—fewer laws, simplified laws, better laws, better enforcement. This approach has been captured in a series of policy documents issued by the Commission since the groundbreaking "Sutherland Report" of late 1992, which first concentrated minds on the new post-1992 challenges of market maintenance and market management, a world beyond market building.[13] The internal market is to be made real on the ground as well as on the statute book.

4-015

At a more constitutional level, one may anticipate greater scepticism about the role of harmonisation in future. It is not immediately apparent why some of the measures mentioned above fall within EC competence. For example, the Directive on "Doorstep Selling", Directive 85/577, contains in its Preamble the statement that the practice of doorstep selling is the subject of different rules in different Member States, and that "any disparity between such legislation may directly affect the functioning of the common market". The case for harmonisation is treated as made without more. But is this really convincing? No supporting evidence is given for this less than plausible claim that such disparity may directly affect the market in this way. The language of (what was then) Article 100 EC has been borrowed and EC competence to act has simply been asserted with no noticeable attempt to demonstrate that the constitutional pre-conditions for harmonisation have really been

4-016

---

[12] *Quaere* the role of a European Civil Code, which might, depending on one's reading of this history, be treated as essential (in order to improve coherence) or as wholly misconceived. *Cf.* A. Hartkamp *et al.* (eds.), *Towards a European Civil Code* (2nd ed., 1998). See also the result of the work of a private working group, the Lando Commission Principles of European Contract Law: Ole Lando and Hugh Beale (eds.), *The Principles of European Contract Law, Part I and II combined and revised*, The Hague / London / Boston, 2000. The principles may form the basis of a European Civil Code.

[13] See on "Better lawmaking" COM (97) 626, COM (98) 715, COM (99) 562; also Council Resolution on legislative and administrative simplification in the internal market, [1996] O.J. C224/5 and subsequently COM (99) 88, COM (00) 56. *Cf.* C. Timmermans, "How can one improve the quality of Community legislation?" (1997) 34 C.M.L.Rev. 1229; S. Weatherill, "New Strategies for Managing the EC's Internal Market" in *Current Legal Problems* (M. Freeman ed., 2000).

met. The reason for action in the field was that the member states were unanimously agreed that such consumer policymaking was desirable and, given the absence at the time of any explicit EC competence in the field of consumer protection, they grabbed the harmonisation legal base in the treaty in order to realise their ambitions to add to the Community's legislative track record in the field. In this sense, the council, acting unanimously, was prepared to treat itself as equipped with *carte blanche* to issue measures of harmonisation. At least, legislative initiatives such as the 1985 Directive on "doorstep selling" suggest few political scruples about asserting that the treaty pre-conditions for harmonisation are met while neglecting serious efforts to provide convincing reasons. Political expediency prevailed over constitutionally rigorous inspection of the limits of Community competence.

4–017   The same could happen today. Directive 99/44 on certain aspects of the sale of consumer goods and associated guarantees was adopted under Article 95 (*ex Article 100a*) EC and may be thought to raise rather more awkward (though not unanswerable: see section 5.2) questions about the Community's competence than are revealed in the measure's recitals. It seems that there was an adequate political will in both council and parliament to see the measure adopted. There was no serious wrangling about the scope of EC competence. But as a general observation it is altogether more likely today that proposed harmonisation initiatives will generate opposition. Harmonisation is a more overtly contested process. One point is simply that there are more Member States. Admittedly, dissentients can be outvoted in council when measures are adopted under Article 95. This has been the case since the Single European Act entered into force in 1987. But the price paid for the abandonment of the political veto has been greater sensitivity to the proper definition of the limits of Community competence. This may manifest itself in several forms. The following section identifies three dimensions of the constitutional sensitivity which has come to surround the process of harmonisation of laws in the European Community. The general lesson is that harmonisation of laws spills over not simply in the sense that it comes to affect an ever wider range of forms of regulatory activity but also in that its spread causes it to assume the character of a constitutional issue.

5. The constitutional sensitivity of harmonisation

5.1 Choice of legal base

4–018   The availability of specific legal bases governing specific areas, rather than general mandates such as that for harmonisation, is now more common in the EC Treaty as a result of its periodic revision. For consumer protection, for example, the Community is competent under Article 153 (a Maastricht innovation, in force since November 1, 1993) to:

> "contribute to protecting the health, safety and economic interests of consumers, as well as to promoting their right to information, education and to organise themselves in order to safeguard their interests . . . through: (a) measures adopted pursuant to Article 95 in the context of the completion of the internal market; (b) measures which support, supplement and monitor the policy pursued by the member states."

The Community's competence to act in the field of consumer protection is **4–019** now put beyond question. But the measures envisaged in clause (b) are based on a carefully confined competence, which stands in marked contrast to the more familiar relatively open terrain of Article 95 EC, which is the subject of cross-reference in clause (a).

How to demarcate the two routes to consumer policymaking referred to in **4–020** Article 153(3)? It is in principle important to do so. Consumer-related legislation is permissibly advanced under Article 95. This is plain from practice, but as a constitutional matter it is also plain that the fact that a harmonisation measure involves choices about consumer protection does not debar use of Article 95 provided only that the main aim of the measure is market-building and the impact on consumer protection incidental. This can be deduced from Article 95(3) and from Article 153(1)–(3) EC. The Court has moreover frequently asserted the other side of the coin, namely that recourse to Article 95 (*ex Article 100a*) is not justified where the measure has only the incidental effect of harmonising market conditions within the Community.[14]

It bears repetition that practice shows that debate about the true purpose of **4–021** a measure of harmonisation does not tend typically to exercise the Community's institutions provided there is unanimous support for the adoption of the relevant measure. But—in principle—if a measure is properly treated as concerned predominantly with matters of consumer protection falling out with the ambit of Article 95 then the chosen legal base must be Article 153, and the limitations on the form of Community action stipulated by Article 153(3)(b) must then be taken seriously. In fact, although Article 153(3)(b), a Maastricht innovation embroidered at Amsterdam, is at one level a breakthrough, in that it confers competence on the Community in the field of consumer protection *per se*, it is simultaneously striking for the limits it carefully places on the Community's role in the consumer policymaking field. The Community is placed in a role subordinate to that of the Member States. Harmonisation of laws is not contemplated. Strictly, Article 95 is not available for harmonisation as a mere cover for consumer policy (strictly, of course, it never was!), while Article 153 is not available for harmonisation at all. This is part of the complex bargain struck at Maastricht. More EC competences were absorbed into the treaty, but a tighter definition of the manner in which they may be exercised was imposed.

To complete the picture of closer modern scrutiny of the scope of Community competence, the Court's insistence that a specific legal base should be **4–022** used where available in preference to a general legal base[15] means also that the existence of, and limits within, Article 153 EC (and other similarly structured provisions such as Article 152 on public health) reduce the viability of recourse to Article 308, which has in the past been used in some areas with remarkably tenuous links to the objectives of the Community (albeit only with unanimous support in the Council).[16]

---

[14] *E.g.* Case C-70/88 *Parliament v. Council* [1991] E.C.R. I-4529; [1992] 1 C.M.L.R. 91; Case C-155/91 *Commission v. Council* [1993] E.C.R. I-939; Case C-209/97 *Commission v. Council* judgment of November 18, 1999.
[15] *E.g.* Case 45/86 *Commission v. Council* [1987] E.C.R. 1493; [1998] 2 C.M.L.R. 131.
[16] See, *e.g.* J. Usher, "The Continuing Development of Law and Institutions" *in Collected Courses of the Academy of European Law Volume II* (Academy of European Law ed., 1992).

4–023   These are complex matters. In particular, it is no easy task to isolate objectively the true purpose of a measure from its incidental effects. In the mixed economy, regulatory intervention is inevitably multi-functional. And admittedly the issue frequently lacks practical significance. Using harmonisation as a cover for consumer policymaking is not today off the agenda. But the terrain is more contested today. Tracing the limits of Community competence is a more vivid and politically sensitive process today than 15 or more years ago. The key political point is that exactly this debate is the price that is paid for swapping a practice of unanimous voting in Council for one based on Qualified Majority Voting ("QMV").[17] QMV, of course, gets things done. Veto rights no longer obstruct the process. Yet the possibility of dissentients in the legislative process sharpens sensitivity to the definition of EC competence. A state that loses the political battle in Council may well be tempted to translate its opposition into a judicial forum. It may argue that the matter on which the EC has legislated lies in any event beyond its competence. An opponent to consumer policy allegedly dressed up as harmonisation may be outvoted under Article 95 but may return to battle not in Council but before the court, submitting that Article 95 was wrongly used (for the measure was allegedly not predominantly concerned to build the internal market), that Article 153 is not capable of providing a legally valid base for harmonisation and that the measure is therefore liable to be annulled.

4–024   Constitutional anxieties of this nature, spilling over into applications for judicial review of Community legislation, are submerged by a unanimity voting rule, for a simple vote against a proposal performs the function of stopping an unwanted initiative more cleanly than a legal debate about competence. The injection of QMV has in this sense wakened the dragon of attributed competence after the pre-Single European Act years (in particular) in which Preambles to Directives merely trotted out the wording of the treaty as rationales for harmonisation, paying bland but, crucially, unanimous lip service to the constraints of attributed competence. Much will depend on the intensity of the Court's review function in such cases. It was noticeably soft (and therefore pro–majority in Council) in *United Kingdom v. Council* ("Working Time"),[18] a case concerned with social policy not consumer policy but which raised analogous questions about the court's readiness to review choice of legal base with implications for the validity of a measure. The court will have the opportunity to examine again the scope of its review function (including other intriguing matters such as the significance of a measure's legislative history in judging its aim when finally adopted) in the pending "Tobacco Advertising" cases in which the validity of Directive 98/34 is under challenge,[19] decision in which is expected in 2000. This litigation fits perfectly into the pattern of the State outvoted in Council willing to resume the battle before the European Court,

---

There is evidence that the Court is today alert to the risk that Art. 308 may be over-stretched; see Opinion 2/94 *Accession of the EC to the ECHR* [1996] E.C.R. I-1759.

[17]   Article 205(2) EC

[18]   Case C-84/94 [1996] E.C.R. I-5755; [1996] 3 C.M.L.R. 671.

[19]   Directive 98/43 [1998] O.J. L213/9; see case C-376/98 *Germany v. Council and Parliament*, October 5, 2000, decided too late for analysis in this paper.

arguing that the majority has no sufficient legal basis for action purportedly taken pursuant to the treaty.

5.2 Keck and Mithouard

The court's ruling in *Keck and Mithouard*[20] raises unresolved questions in the debate about the proper scope to be allowed today to harmonisation legislation based on Article 95 of the EC Treaty. The controversial *Keck* ruling, in short, asserts a less extensive interpretation of Article 28 (*ex Article 30*) EC than had been previous European Court practice, with the result that some national measures of market regulation that might previously have been required to run the gauntlet of justification according to standards recognised by community law are now treated as lying beyond challenge based on Article 28 (*ex Article 30*). Rules requiring the closing of shops for stipulated periods on Sunday would now, after *Keck* but not before it,[21] be regarded as unaffected by the Treaty provisions governing the free movement of goods, for any impact on the volume of goods sold would be entirely divorced from *cross-border* trade patterns.   **4–025**

It is not settled how adjustment of the scope of Article 28 (*ex Article 30*) EC affects the scope of harmonisation under Articles 94 and 95 (*ex Article 100 and 100a*) EC. If, say, a national rule restricting doorstep selling is beyond the reach of Article 28 (which, post- but not pre-*Keck*, it probably is), the question arises whether that means it is also incapable of forming the subject matter of harmonisation under Article 95. The point is far from clear. Such a submission, if accepted, would seem apt to allow a challenge to the validity of adoption under Articles 95–100a as was—of key measures such as Directive 93/13 on unfair terms in consumer contracts. Moreover, and at a more general level, it is an argument that tends towards separating out trade integration as an EC concern from local market regulation, a national concern. This runs contrary to the well-documented patterns of "spillover" explained above and yet exactly this type of anxiety has found its way on to the agenda as the expanding harmonisation programme has gathered its sceptics.   **4–026**

It is submitted that it is not necessarily the case that limits placed on Article 28 should be considered automatically to exert a parallel limitation to Article 95. The wording of Article 95 EC, combined with Article 14 EC, points towards something broader than a market which is merely shorn of quantitative restrictions and measures. The relevant treaty provisions are more narrowly worded than to allow the Community *carte blanche* to harmonise laws, but a dynamic notion of market-building is envisaged which, in my submission, allows the use of Article 95 to establish harmonised rules designed to foster integration even in areas where the relevant national rules would escape challenge against the standards laid down by Article 28.   **4–027**

This invites a need to identify what the function of harmonisation policy

---

[20] Joined Cases C-267/91, C-268/91 [1993] E.C.R. I-6097; [1995] 1 C.M.L.R. 101.
[21] *Cf.* pre-*Keck* Case 145/88 *Torfaen BC v. B & Q plc* [1989] E.C.R. 765; [1990] 1 C.M.L.R. 337; Case C-169/91 *Stoke-on-Trent BC v B & Q plc* [1992] E.C.R. I-6457; and, post-*Keck*, Cases C-401 & C-402/92 *Tankstation 't Heukste vof and J.B.E. Boermans* [1994] E.C.R. I-2199.

4–028 in the area of consumer protection may be, in so far as it extends beyond knocking down trade barriers falling within the scope of Article 28 as currently interpreted by the Court. It is here that the significance of the quest to reveal linking and guiding themes in the pattern of existing EC legislative activity may be appreciated.[22] A more positive strain may be advanced: the desire to promote consumer confidence in the viability of the market as a legitimate objective of law-making under Article 95. This candidate paradigm of "consumer confidence" is already apparent in the Preamble to Directive 93/13 on unfair terms:

> "Whereas, generally speaking, consumers do not know the rules of law which, in Member States other than their own, govern contracts for the sale of goods or services; whereas this lack of awareness may deter them from direct transactions for the purchase of goods or services in another Member State;
> "Whereas, in order to facilitate the establishment of the internal market and to safeguard the citizen in his role as consumer when acquiring goods and services under contracts which are governed by the laws of Member States other than his own, it is essential to remove unfair terms from those contracts . . ."

4–029 This envisages a consumer who is active in the market, not simply a consumer who passively awaits the economic advantages of integration. That activity will be induced only where the consumer has sufficient confidence to treat the European market as border-free. A system of market access based on mutual recognition of national laws and competition between national regulators would seem insufficient to generate this necessary consumer confidence. Something more is needed. One may naturally question how compelling the need to promote the active cross-border shopper really is in building and maintaining a European market. It is a perspective that is perhaps less immediately convincing to the British than to inhabitants of other Member States. Geographical isolation is one factor in that disparity, reduced awareness of the imminence of a single currency another. However, while one may expect lively debate, even healthy scepticism, about the cogency of the "confident consumer" as a paradigm (and by no means only from the British perspective), it is plainly a notion that is finding its way into EC policymaking. This consumer confidence is engendered only where the crossing of a border has no detrimental impact on the consumer's minimum level of legal protection. The same perspective (which, it may be noted in passing, is regrettably undermined by the court's enduring refusal to accept the capacity of Directives to exert horizontal direct effect) emerges from the Preamble to Directive 99/44 on the sale of consumer goods and associated guarantees, adopted under Article 95 EC. The following reasons are given:

> "Whereas the laws of the Member States concerning the sale of consumer goods are somewhat disparate, with the result that national consumer goods markets differ from one another and that competition between sellers may be distorted . . . .
> "Whereas consumers who are keen to benefit from the large market by purchasing goods in Member States other than their State of residence play a fundamental role in the completion of the internal market ....
> "Whereas the creation of a common set of minimum rules of consumer law, valid no

---

[22] See *supra* n. 10.

matter where goods are purchased within the Community, will strengthen consumer confidence and enable consumers to make the most of the internal market ..."

This approach connects with, *inter alia*, the *Action Plan for the Single Market*[23] in which the Commission insists that "The Single Market stands or falls on confidence". This was endorsed by the European Council in Amsterdam in June 1997 and has retained its place in subsequent Commission thinking on the management of the internal market, including the November 1999 strategy for the Internal Market to cover the next five years.[24] Confidence relates to both commercial and consumer perspectives. This discloses a wider notion of the dynamics of constructing an internal market than merely eliminating trade barriers falling within Article 28. This might in turn help in the identification of distinct roles for the two routes to consumer policymaking referred to in paragraphs 3(a) and 3(b) of Article 153 EC Building "consumer confidence" in the integrating market involves the establishment of harmonised consumer rights under Article 95 (via Article 153(3)(a) and Article 153(2)). But, as in any system of effective consumer protection, legal rights on paper are but part of the battle. Article 153(3)(b) is reserved for activities which support areas in which the Member States hold principal competence such as consumer education and better access to justice, in respect of which tentative support has lately begun to be shaped at Community level.[25] This concern for better law enforcement is part of the wider anxiety of the Commission to do less, but to do it better. For the consumer sphere in particular this is revealed in the Consumer Action Plan for 1999–2001.[26]

5.3 Subsidiarity

Subsidiarity has attracted a vast literature. This paper contents itself with the brief observation that subsidiarity will, of course, continue to form part of the breezy and often unilluminating political debate about the division of competence between the Community and its Member States, a debate in which the shape of harmonisation policy is but part. The more specifically legal issue is whether, beyond chatter inside or outside the Council, the subsidiarity principle is capable of informing the evolving constitutional approach to fixing the limits of harmonisation.

    4–031

The Amsterdam Treaty adds to the EC Treaty a protocol on the application of the principles of subsidiarity and proportionality. This is designed to give fuller shape to the notoriously woolly notion of subsidiarity. Among the guidelines are the instruction that:

"Subsidiarity is a dynamic concept and should be applied in the light of the objectives set out in the Treaty. It allows Community action within the limits of its powers to be

---

[23] Action Plan for the Single Market, Communication of the Commission to the European Council, CSE(97)1, final, 4 June 1997.
[24] COM (99) 642. See also references at n. 12 above.
[25] *e.g.* Recommendation 98/257 on the principles applicable to the bodies responsible for out-of-court settlement of consumer disputes, [1998] O.J. L115/31.
[26] COM (98) 696. *cf.* n. 12 above.

expanded where circumstances so require, and conversely, to be restricted or discontinued where it is no longer justified."

4-032   This offers a reminder that subsidiarity is not a one-way street, directing communautaire traffic back to national capitals. Subsidiarity initiates the debate about how and where to regulate.[27] For example when recommendation 90/109 on the transparency of banking conditions relating to cross-border financial transactions was shown to be inadequate to bring about the desired improvement in the working of the market, Directive 97/5 on cross-border credit transfers was adopted.[28] The shift from soft to hard law was fully in accordance with the dictates of subsidiarity because of the failure of the soft law, unharmonised route. In its first annual report on the subsidiarity principle the Commission wryly observed that "one cannot help observing that principle and practice are often far apart with Member States meeting within the Council often adopting positions on individual cases at variance with their respect in principle for Article [5 *ex Article 3b*]"[29] and in the light of the complex variation between actors and sectors in the patterns of demand for Community legislative intervention[30] one should not be at all surprised that the magic word subsidiarity has not miraculously dispelled the need to take a hard look on a case-by-case basis at how and why the EC acts. Subsidiarity, then, does not remove harmonisation of laws from the agenda, though it might operate in order to induce the fuller articulation of rationales for harmonisation. The Amsterdam Protocol adds that:

> "For any proposed Community legislation, the reasons on which it is based shall be stated with a view to justifying its compliance with the principles of subsidiarity and proportionality; the reasons for concluding that a Community objective can be better achieved by the Community must be substantiated by qualitative or, wherever possible, quantitative indicators."

4-033   This instruction would be intriguing were it to be considered today by the Court in a legal challenge to a Directive as laconically reasoned as the Doorstep Selling Directive was in 1985. In *Germany v. Council and Parliament*[31] the Court declined to annul a Directive for inadequate reasoning in circumstances where it considered that explanation of compliance with the demands of subsidiarity could be discovered from the Preamble even though explicit reference to subsidiarity was absent from the Preamble. This was a pre-Amsterdam decision and even post-Amsterdam the protocol does not go so far as to insist formally on reasoning being explicitly directed at the impact of subsidiarity. However, it seems highly probable that such reasoning will normally be provided and that in its absence a challenge to the validity of a measure as inadequately reasoned can be pursued with some

---

[27] *cf.* in a different area, J. Wouters, "European Company Law: Quo Vadis?" (2000) 37 C.M.L.Rev. 257, especially at pp.278 et seq.
[28] [1990] O.J. L67/39, [1997] O.J. L43/25, respectively.
[29] COM (94) 533.
[30] See, *e.g.*, F. Scharpf (ed.), "Special Issue: Governance in the Internal Market", (1997) 4 J.E.P.P. Issue 4.
[31] Case C-233/94 [1997] E.C.R. I-2304.

optimism. Therefore one may expect to see in future more overt discussion of why harmonisation, rather than market competition between national regulators fed by mobile consumers of state regulation (and/ or readiness to leave the field to other extra-EU harmonising agencies such as UNCI-TRAL), is truly needed to build the internal market.[32] More generally, the deployment of the subsidiarity principle as a basis for challenge to the validity of Community acts looks set to become a growth industry.[33] Here too much will hinge on the intensity of the review performed by the Court in such cases.

6. Conclusion—Harmonisation's constitutional dimension

There are anxieties in some quarters that harmonisation has gone too far or at least that it is treading on the toes of other, more specific EC competences. This is a political matter but it is also a legal matter. Harmonisation has become an area of deepening constitutional sensitivity. The constitutional rule that the EC possesses only the competence attributed to it by its treaty, for so long the subject of mere lip service in Council, a trend of which some of the Directives harmonising consumer law offer a good example, becomes a matter of real practical importance.　　　　　　　　　　　　　　　　　**4–034**

This is above all the consequence of the rise of QMV in Council. The ability of the Council to fix and potentially to stretch the limits of Community competence in practice by unanimous vote was never something that should have been accepted placidly; it risked a leakage of power from national to Community level in areas unforeseen by the treaty and thereby threatened subversion of domestic constitutional controls. The prospect of such stealthy transfer by QMV in Council may be reckoned still more alarming, but a counterweight of sorts is provided by the likely existence of whistle-blowers in the shape of dissentient states willing and able to contest the matter. Harmonisation thus obtains an enhanced profile as a constitutionally significant process, demanding attention to the type of issues raised in section 5.3.　　　　　　　　　　　　　　　　　**4–035**

It is not only politicians who are alert to the contested constitutional dimension of the EC's harmonisation programme. Laws L.J., in another of the "tobacco advertising" cases decided recently by the English Court of Appeal, expressed concern about possible "damage to the rule of law" resulting from (alleged) abuse of the harmonisation programme.[34] In his examination of the constitutional consequences of the EC legislature's readiness to use Article 100a, now 95, to impose severe restrictions on the circumstances in which tobacco products may be sold, he made plain his inability on the evidence presented to see any valid basis in EC law for the EC's 1998 harmonisation Directive in the light of that measure's perceived predominant concern to pursue public health policy. He did not, however, suggest that he would refuse to apply　　　　　　　　　　**4–036**

---

[32] This speculation is subject to the unresolved question whether Art. 95 ring-fences an area of exclusive Community competence and that subsidiarity therefore has no role to play.
[33] See D. Wyatt, "Subsidiarity and Judicial Review", Chapter 32 in *Judicial Review in European Union Law: Liber Amicorum Gordon Slynn* (D. O'Keeffe and A. Bavasso eds., 2000).
[34] *R v. Secretary of State for Health, ex parte Imperial Tobacco Ltd* [2000] 1 All E.R. 572, 606.

the Directive as a valid legislative act were he subsequently instructed so to do by the European Court in Luxembourg. Nor would one imagine that such a step might be taken by an English judge applying the European Communities Act 1972 according to the orthodox understanding. But that dramatic step might be taken in some other Member States, where different constitutional traditions prevail. The *Bundesverfassungsgericht's* famous 1993 Maastricht ruling operates on several levels,[35] but a key element of the judgment is to the effect that the Community institutions should think hard about the possible consequences for the integrity of the Community legal order if consensus is not maintained on the question of fixing the limits to the scope of EC competence. The German court seems ready to refuse the valid application of measures of the EC institutions on German territory if it, the *Bundesverfassungsgericht*, concludes that the treaty provides no adequate legal basis for the acts in question. This might in exceptional circumstances involve defiance of the European Court's reading of the validity of the relevant act. In 1998 the Danish *Hofsteret* has ruled in similar vein, in a careful judgment plainly inspired in part by the views of their judicial counterparts in Karlsruhe.[36] Although it must be stated that the German

4–037   and Danish courts are as yet only bark not bite, and that their threat to deny the European Court the exclusive competence to decide on the scope of the EC's competence is certainly not intended to be executed lightly, if at all, nonetheless it is clear that these apparently technical questions about the scope of harmonisation go to the heart of the identification of the appropriate level of governance for the market of Europe and the shaping of the European polity. Who bears the competence and the responsibility for market regulation? And who will rule on whether the correct levels of control are being exercised? The European Court's imminent ruling in the "Tobacco Advertising" case will command intense interest for its explanation of some of these constitutional questions,[36a] and it should be appreciated that, in delivering that judgment on the shape of the Community's contested competence and, by necessary implication, on the scope of residual national competence and, moreover, in thereby disclosing further information about the strength of its own resolve to police the ambitions of the Community legislature, the Court will be fully aware that its addressees, direct and indirect, include not only the Community institutions and the governments of the Member States but also the judicial watchdogs testing their chains in the national courts of the Member States.[37] In this sense, the evolution of the harmonisation programme has led the Community into ever wider fields of regulatory activity, slicing deeper into national competence, up to the point where not simply its functional necessity but also its very constitutional legitimacy has been called into question. This is spillover with a vengeance.

---

[35] *Brunner* [1994] 1 C.M.L.R. 57.
[36] See H. Rasmussen, "Confrontation or Peaceful Co-Existence? On the Danish Supreme Court's Maastricht Ratification Judgment", Chapter 24 in D. O'Keeffe and A. Bavasso, n. 32 above.
[36a] Case C-376/98 n. 19 above was decided on October 5, 2000, but too late for analysis in this paper.
[37] See, generally, on variation in attitudes among national supreme courts, A.-M. Slaughter, A. Stone Sweet and J. Weiler, *The European Courts and National Courts* (1998). For an overview of the approach of the European Court in advance of the "Tobacco Advertising" decision, see J. Mischo, "The Contribution of the Court of Justice to the Protection of the Federal Balance in the European Community" in D. O'Keeffe and A. Bavasso, n. 32 above.

CHAPTER 5

THE FUTURE OF HARMONISATION AND FORMULATING AGENCIES: THE ROLE OF UNIDROIT

PROFESSOR HERBERT KRONKE[1]

1. Do we need intergovernmental organisations and uniform law conventions?

1.1 Intergovernmental organisations

Having grown up in the commercial environment and the merchant society **5–001** of a port city, my answer to the question "do we need a government?" a number of years ago would have been "no—the chamber of commerce is quite enough". And in this perspective, mention of intergovernmental bodies might have led to even more eye-brow raising. But then, I knew of the International Maritime Organisation (IMO) and later, during my law studies, I learnt of UNIDROIT and its preparation of the Uniform Sales Laws, of the Hague Conference and, later still, of UNCITRAL and its brilliant idea to baptise the modernised set of rules on carriage of goods by sea "Hamburg"-Rules. That, of course, was the place where I lived and doubts as to the legitimacy of intergovernmental organisations subsided.

Thirty years later, and not only because I receive now my salary from such **5–002** an entity, I am even more convinced of the intergovernmental organisations'

---

[1] Secretary General, International Institute for the Unification of Private Law (UNIDROIT), Rome (Italy). Professor of Law and Director, Institute of Foreign and International Private and Commercial Law, University of Heidelberg (Germany) (on leave).

usefulness. While governments cannot guarantee, let alone enforce, successful harmonisation of private and commercial law they can certainly slow that
process down and even prevent it, in particular as far as certain areas of the
law and certain types of instrument are concerned. Now, as governments for
good reasons prefer organised and administered consultation processes
amongst themselves intergovernmental organisations are in fact needed. The
leaner government agencies are the more the organisations may serve as a
device for outsourcing preparation of the legal framework for international
economic relations.

1.2 Conventions and other types of instruments

1.2.1 Objectives—old and new

5–003   In the early days, *i.e.* in the 1920s, the moral aspects of harmonising the legal
environment of international trade were emphasised: only significantly
improved conditions for more commercial exchange between nations would
lay reliable foundations for a better understanding between peoples. Today,
moral considerations are confined to the discussion of private-international-
law or, conflict-of-laws instruments (*e.g.* child abduction) whereas harmonisation
of substantive law does not seem to direct our thoughts towards the basics.
There is, of course, one exception, namely the UNIDROIT Convention on
the Restitution of Stolen or Illegally Exported Cultural Objects[2] which lends
itself to be discussed—even violently as I may say from experience—in terms
of morality.

5–004   Apart from this, the recurring themes are reduction of transaction costs
through less cumbersome ascertainment of the rules governing a given transaction, assisting nations and regions in developing certain industries and
attracting investment and, lastly, either the establishment of level playing
fields for competitors or, on the contrary, getting a competitive edge over
other geographical areas.

However, there are also two novelties to be noted:

- First, uniform or harmonised law is much less geared at eliminating
  the recourse to private-international-law (conflict-of-laws) operations.
  Both the bar and the bench have become either bolder or more
  knowledgeable in this once professorial fief of legal analysis and
  method.

- Secondly, it is more harmonised *modernisation*, i.e. development of new
  solutions for new problems rather than harmonisation or unification in the
  sense of making the law of Malaysia a little more Austrian or Chilean law
  a little more English which governments and business are expecting from
  us.

---

[2] Diplomatic Conference for the Adoption of the Draft UNIDROIT Convention on the
International Return of Stolen or Illegally Exported Cultural Objects, Rome, June 24, 1995, Acts
and Proceedings.

1.2.2 Classic and post-modern Approaches—subjects and examples

Unlike an individual scholar or an academic institution, an intergovernmental organisation moves within its institutional framework. Article 1 of the UNIDROIT Statute[3] reads *inter alia* as follows:

> *"The purposes . . . are to examine ways of harmonising and co-ordinating the private law of States and of groups of States, and to prepare gradually for the adoption by the various States of uniform rules of private law."*
> This, albeit incomplete, is useful; in particular the rather open wording "ways of harmonising and co-ordinating", less so the reference only to the "law of States".
> *Paragraph 2 then goes on to state that:*
> *"To this end the Institute shall:*
> *(a) prepare drafts of laws and Conventions with the object of establishing uniform internal law;*
> *(b) prepare drafts of agreements with a view to facilitating international relations in the field of private law;*
> *[(c)—(e) omitted]."*

5–005

While the mandate to prepare "drafts of laws and Conventions" is clear, not open to interpretation, and—seen from the general viewpoint of this volume—undoubtedly too narrow, the somewhat ambiguous reference to "agreements . . . facilitating international relations", in our view, injects the required measure of flexibility.

5–006

The UNIDROTT Governing Council, at its 73rd session in 1994,[4] took note of a Secretariat memorandum stating:

5–007

> *"Attempts to realise those [i.e. the statutory] aims ... have assumed two principal forms, on the one hand the preparation of uniform laws, a term which should be understood in a broad sense and therefore as encompassing for example the Principles of International Commercial Contracts, and on the other, dissemination of information concerning uniform law coupled with study of the methodology of the unification process so as to ensure that the benefits It is capable of offering to the international community as a whole can be maximised to the best possible advantage."*

The Secretariat regards this formula as essential.

Notwithstanding the success that not only the UNIDROIT Principles,[5] but also even "softer" instruments are enjoying, the choice of type and form does pose institutional questions. On the one hand, the organisation is accountable to governments. On the other hand governments, just as any other body, corporate or indeed individual, tend to entertain more interest in matters in which they are actively involved and which are or will shortly be of immediate concern to them.

5–008

How important *intergovernmental* exchange on the objectives and content of uniform or harmonised law is—and such exchange occurs primarily in the

5–009

---

[3] Statute incorporating the amendment to Art. 6 (1) which came into force on March 26, 1993, Rome 1993.
[4] Governing Council, 73rd Session, Rome, May 9–14, 1994, Agenda Item 9, Secretariat Memorandum, UNIDROIT, c.d. (73) 9 (Original: English), p. 1.
[5] Principles of International Commercial Contracts, Rome (1994). The UNIDROIT Principles have since been published in all five official UNIDROIT languages (English, French, German, Italian and Spanish) as well as in nine other languages, most recently (2000) in Arabic, Portuguese and Vietnamese.

preparation of Conventions—is reflected by the fact that the United States of America acceded to the UNIDROIT Statute barely a month before the diplomatic Conference leading to the Hague Sales Laws,[6] and that since the Conference and in the run-up to Vienna, Ottawa[7] and Rome[8] no fewer than 20 states from all continents have acceded or re-acceded to the Institute.[9]

5–010   How do we know whether the classical form of harmonising or unifying private law, *i.e.* the Convention, is suitable for tackling a given issue, problem area or type of transaction? A large number of ratifications, a rapidly growing body of case law from many countries which succeeds in maintaining uniformity, no calls for revision enable us, with hindsight, to dub "advantageous" those Conventions that succeed in eliciting such a response.

5–011   As we now know, there were plenty of advantages which might have been cited when the Vienna Sales Convention (CISG)[10] was being drafted if only someone had, first, put the question and, second, if a viable alternative had been in sight. But CISG is hardly your average uniform law Convention. No matter how many ratifications and `accessions it collected, the sponsors of an instrument would still be dissatisfied if, despite its intrinsic technical qualities, traders regularly excluded its application to their transactions.

5–012   By the same token, there is no evidence whatsoever that those Conventions which, though praised sky-high, have been blessed with few or no ratifications would have known a different fate had a different form been preferred.

5–013   And again, does the ascertainable success of a Convention—*e.g.* the CMR[11]—in one region of the world necessarily mean that it might be a good idea to "export" it to other regions? While some might regard this as advantageous compared to the *status quo*,[12] others will disagree and cite advantages, *in terms of uniformity*, of the Convention-less situation.[13]

5–014   In the abstract, the disadvantages of the treaty form are numerous and they have been discussed many times. In particular, drumming up support for the UNIDROIT Principles of International Commercial Contracts required some stark language. As Professor Sir Roy Goode, member of the UNIDROIT Governing Council, put it:

> *"the treaty collections are littered with Conventions that have never come into force, for want of the number of required ratifications, or have been eschewed by the major trading States. There are several reasons for this: failure to establish from potential interest groups at the outset that there is a serious problem which the proposed Convention will help to*

[6] On March 13, 1964. See M. Matteucci, "The Activities of the International Institute for the Unification of Private Law (1963–64)", *L'unif. dr. / Unif. L. Yearbook* 1964, 21.

[7] Diplomatic Conference for the adoption of the draft UNIDROIT Conventions on International Factoring and International Financial Leasing, May 9–28, 1988.

[8] Diplomatic Conference for the adoption of the draft UNIDROIT Convention on the International Return of Stolen or Illegally Exported Cultural Objects, June 7–24, 1995.

[9] See Secretariat Memorandum, *supra* n. 2 at 3.

[10] Reproduced in *Unif. L. Rev.* (1980–81), 60.

[11] Convention on the Contract for the International Carriage of Goods by Road, signed at Geneva on May 16, 1956, reproduced in *L'unif. dr. / Unif. L. Yearbook* 1956, 116.

[12] Basedow, in: *Münchener Kommentar, Handelsgesetzbuch, VII, Transportrecht* (München, 1997), Einleitung CMR, No. 52; Larsen, "International Carriage of Goods by Road in the Americas: Time to Revise the Inter-American Convention?", *Unif. L. Rev.* (1999), 33.

[13] Fresnedo de aguirre / Aguirre ramirez, "International Carriage of Goods by Road in the Americas: Looking at Policy Aspects of a Revised Inter-American Convention", *Unif. L. Rev.* (1999), 50.

resolve; hostility from powerful pressure groups; lack of sufficient interest of, or pressure on, Governments to induce them to burden still further an already over-crowded legislative timetable; mutual hold-backs, each State waiting to see what others will do, so that in the end none of them does anything."[14]

However, most of this, except for the packed legislative agendas and the hold-back games between states regarding ratifications, could apply to other instruments as well. So, much depends on the structure of the elaboration process.   **5–015**

As far as the number of ratifications is concerned, there is bad news and good news. First the bad news. The United Kingdom, according to a senior Department of Trade and Industry official, will ratify the Vienna Sales Convention as soon as "angry masses take to the streets, marching through the City of London and waving banners with the outcry "we demand ratification of the CISG'." The good news: the two UNIDROIT Conventions signed in Ottawa in 1988 have prompted some governments, among them the United States, henceforth to advocate the limitation, in appropriate cases, of the number of ratifications needed for a Convention to enter into force to three or five.   **5–016**

As far as the elaboration process is concerned, I shall limit myself to three observations: **5–017**

- The *choice of subject* is the first step, and it is this step where in the past most mistakes have been made and where we are likely to make mistakes in the future. Traditionally, the subject was chosen by academics and/or intellectual leaders in decision-making centres such as governments and international organisations. In some instances—we need but think of the Sales and Carriage-of-Goods Conventions—the choice was obviously good but subsequently parameters changed. A thoughtful initial choice, therefore, is still no guarantee for sustainable harmonisation for many reasons we cannot discuss here. Some projects were either too broadly or too narrowly tailored. Some tackled problems which commercial circles did not see at all or which were not felt to be really serious. Uncertain support from such quarters should in any event be an orange, if not a red traffic light for law-makers. More specifically, if the result envisaged by the sponsoring states or organisation, on average, is not clearly a win-win situation for both parties to the transaction envisaged (carrier/shipper, creditor/debtor, bank/client, seller/buyer), the chances of wide-spread acceptance recede.

- Another pitfall is when *participating governments are not sufficiently committed* to the Convention and/or when the latter is not connected with adjacent work. For example, in one important UNIDROIT member state the official in charge not only of relations with the Organisation as such but dealing also with the substance of its most important current work, in the light of the other international and

[14] Goode, "International Restatements of Contract and English Contract Law", *Unif. L. Rev.* (1997), 231 at 232.

purely domestic tasks assigned to his unit is able to allot barely one twelfth of his time to the Institute's work. Again, only four out of roughly, 40 states participating contemporaneously in an UNIDROIT and an UNCITRAL project with one rather tricky interface manage to provide for some form of tangible co-ordination between the two delegations.

•   Lastly, governmental delegations to expert committees or diplomatic Conferences still often seem to have trouble viewing issues raised in negotiating *private* law Conventions from a strictly economic, technical or legal perspective; instead, they perceive their own private law solutions as forming part of their national sovereignty.

5–018 Now, the intergovernmental organisations have learnt their lesson. After the Convention we saw alternative forms of instruments, first the model-law technique, then Principles, best-practice guides, etc.

5–019   In some instances, the impact of our work on domestic law reform is greater, and arguably more important, than the harmonisation proper. Moreover, new negotiation structures and features such as audit and monitoring-committees as well as quite novel fast-track accession and revision procedures are under consideration. However, it would be a misconception to envisage a future of harmonisation and unification of commercial law solely driven by the market operators and loosely framed by soft law instruments. A situation where one would hardly ever rely on soft law is the law of property in general and delicate issues such as the acquisition of title from a non-owner in particular. The UNIDROIT Convention on the Return of Stolen or Illegally Exported Cultural Objects[15] may serve as further illustration.

5–020   On the other hand, areas deeply rooted in legal and cultural tradition and everywhere moulded down to the finest details and levelled to become coherent systems resembling mathematics or philosophy, such as civil procedure or general theories of contract, are unlikely to lend themselves to successful harmonisation through Conventions. The Principles of International Commercial Contracts acquired *their* cloak because there was no hope whatsoever—as had been discussed at an earlier stage—of a Convention emerging that would contain the general part of the UNIDROIT Conventions dealing with contractual transactions that had entered into force over the years. And the dismal failure successfully to unify civil procedure in certain areas through the Hague Conventions on the Service Abroad of Judicial and Extra-judicial Documents in Civil or Commercial Matters[16] and the Taking of Evidence Abroad in Civil or Commercial Matters[17] is one of the germs out of which it is hoped that the UNIDROIT/American Law Institute (ALI)

---

[15] Adopted in Rome on June 24, 1995 and reproduced in *Unif. L. Rev.* (1996), 110.
[16] Convention on the Service Abroad of Judicial and Extra-judicial Documents in Civil or Commercial Matters of November 15, 1965, *Actes et Documents de la Dixième Session*, octobre 7–28, 1964, Tome III, Conférence de La Haye de droit international privé.
[17] Convention on the Taking of Evidence Abroad in Civil or Commercial Matters of 18 March 1970, *Actes et Documents de la Onzième Session*, octobre 7–26, 1968, Tome IV, Conférence de La Haye de droit international privé.

joint venture on Principles and Rules of Transnational Civil Procedure[18] will grow.

2. The current UNIDROIT work programme

2.1 Contracts

There are three current projects in the area of contract law:
    5–021

- A new working group is currently busy drafting Part II of the UNIDROIT Principles of International Commercial Contracts dealing with agency, assignment, third parties" rights, set-off, limitation of actions and waiver. At the end of that process we shall have an almost complete general part of rules regarding contractual obligations.

- A model law on disclosure and the consequences of insufficient disclosure in franchising[19] will pass from the study group to the governmental consultation process later this year.

- UNIDROIT, in its capacity of the CMR's "mother" has been approached to act as adviser in the ECE's current revision process with regard to that Convention, in particular its adaptation to electronic communication and electronic documentation.

2.2 Protection of cultural heritage

The 1995 UNIDROIT Convention on the Restitution of Stolen and Illegally   **5–022** Exported Cultural Objects is experiencing great success in some countries and encounters bitter opposition from certain quarters (both "loosing countries" and advocates of unlimited freedom for art commerce). Further promotion efforts will be crucial.

2.3 Civil Procedure

UNIDROIT and the American Law Institute have joined forces in elaborat-   **5–023** ing principles and rules which cater for the atypical but increasingly frequent situation of transnational litigation, involving parties from jurisdictions other than the forum.[20] The working group has just concluded its first session.

2.4 Credit, finance, capital markets

The two 1988 UNIDROIT Conventions on Financial Leasing and Factor-   **5–024** ing are in force and have been ratified by major trading countries. More

---

[18] See UNIDROIT 1999, Study LXXVI—Doc. 4, *Transnational Rules of Civil Procedure*, Feasibility Study prepared by Rolf Stürner, Professor of Law, University of Freiburg (Germany).
[19] See UNIDROIT 2000, C.D. (79) 7, Item 7, *Model Law on Franchising.*
[20] It is estimated that in about half the cases heard in the English High Court involve no British party. See *The Times*, November 8, 2000—Law Supplement at p. 3.

ratifications of the Leasing Convention as well as its use for domestic law
reform are expected in the near future.

5–025   Currently the most ambitious and time-consuming project is the draft
Convention on International Interests in Mobile Equipment[21] (in commercial circles dubbed the asset-backed finance convention), providing for a
new international regime of secured transactions geared at reducing credit
costs for high-value mobile infrastructure such as aircraft, space objects and
railway rolling stock.

5–026   As soon as this centre piece of a broader effort to modernise the law of
asset-based finance, which was given priority by governments, will be in place
work on a model law on secured transactions will resume.

5–027   In the medium and long-term perspective the law of transactions on
transnational capital markets will be the centre of gravity of our activities.
The problem areas have been identified and range from cross-border
takeovers to regulation of connected-market transaction to clearing and
settlement rules. Currently, consultations with stock exchanges, regulators
and the financial intermediaries" community are being held.

3. Conclusions

5–028   There is no time to be wasted. UNIDROIT, as our sister organisations, is
underfunded and understaffed. But its role is obvious, its work programme is
loaded like never before in its history, the business community's expectations
are high and we are looking forward to co-operating with the international
business and scientific communities in setting sail for new shores.

---

[21] Third Joint Session, March 20–31, 2000, Report (Original: English/French). See numerous
articles and an earlier version of the text in *Unif. L. Rev.* 1999, pp. 237–586.

CHAPTER 6

LAW, INTERNATIONAL COMMERCE AND THE FORMULATING AGENCIES—THE FUTURE OF HARMONISATION AND FORMULATING AGENCIES— A PERSPECTIVE FROM THE HAGUE CONFERENCE

HANS VAN LOON, SECRETARY-GENERAL
OF THE HAGUE CONFERENCE ON PRIVATE INTERNATIONAL LAW

It is no exaggeration to say that the future is already upon the Hague **6–001** Conference on Private International Law. Three major recent developments are at the root of this. The first is globalisation, the growing interconnectedness, world-wide, of individuals, societies, legal systems and economies (1); the second is regional integration, in particular within the European Union (2); and the third is the exponential growth of electronic data interchange, the Internet and electronic commerce (3). Together these three interrelated developments have already started to transform the Organisation, its working methods and its Agenda, and in all likelihood they will continue to do so for years to come.

1. Globalisation

The effects of globalisation are, as far as the Hague Conference is concerned, **6–002** reflected in the sharp increase in countries linked to the Organisation, whether as Member States or as States Parties to one or more Hague Conventions. Ten years ago they numbered 57. Today they are 107, from all continents. These effects are also reflected in the steady rise of the number of visits to our website,[1] which is now in its second year: the website now receives more than 5,000 hits per day, and there is also an increasing flow of requests for assistance and information, again from all parts of the world.

Current projects such as the negotiations on a world-wide Convention on **6–003** jurisdiction and recognition and enforcement of judgments in civil and commercial matters, and the forthcoming negotiations on a Convention on the law applicable to securities held through intermediaries, are intended to

---

[1] See http://www.hcch.net.

produce a result which will be acceptable world-wide, that is far beyond the circle of the present 49 Member States. The world-wide interest in these projects, as well as in other topics on our Agenda such as the Internet, environmental damage, or maintenance obligations, clearly shows that the Hague Conference has an increasingly world-wide vocation. In fact, the Organisation is now actively expanding its membership more rapidly than in the past. Over the past year or so, Ukraine, Peru, South Africa, Jordan and Belarus have been admitted as Member States. Lithuania and Georgia have applied for membership. Brazil has accepted and become the 49th member state.

6–004   Increasing participation of new countries with little experience in private international law poses new challenges to the organisation. More preparation and more, very basic, "after sale" activity of the "products" of the Conference, its multilateral Conventions (now 34 in number)[2] and of its "services"—advice and assistance concerning their practical operation—will be necessary in respect of these countries. The traditional voting procedures which have so far been considered as essential for the formulation of precise, highly informative and technical texts are coming under pressure because experts participating for the first time in the proceedings may have difficulties understanding what the vote is about. Political and cultural sensitivities may creep in unexpectedly.

6–005   Increasingly, we are faced with the paradox that while the number of legal conflicts involving cross-border elements is growing exponentially as a result of the impact of globalisation, at the same time the capacity to deal adequately with these conflicts by legislators, administrations and the court systems in many developing countries in particular remains limited both at present and in the foreseeable future. What, then, may we expect?

(i)   Harmonisation by establishing channels of communication and co-operation *between* legal systems—as opposed to harmonisation by requiring major modifications of those legal systems themselves—will continue to expand. Recently, we have been witnessing impressive expansion of the use of the Hague Conventions on judicial and administrative co-operation, such as those on the abolition of legalisation, on service of documents and on taking of evidence abroad, as well as on international child abduction and intercountry adoption in the family law area. All of these Hague Conventions can, in many instances (there are exceptions of course) be ratified without major reforms to the existing legal systems of the ratifying States and they are clearly potentially applicable world-wide. The implementation and monitoring of these Conventions and their review and revision (see *infra*, section 3) will remain high on the Agenda of the Conference.

(ii)   The current project on jurisdiction and recognition and enforcement of judgments in civil and commercial matters,[3] which is to be completed late 2001 or early 2002, will need to be supplemented sooner

---

[2] See the website of the Hague Conference on Private International Law: http://www.hcch.net
[3] See chapter 15 by Catherine Kessedjian.

rather than later by some sort of system of uniform interpretation. We remain convinced that, for the time being, the most realistic option would be the creation of a system allowing for panels of experts in international litigation which would be at the disposal of courts or parties to provide non-binding advisory opinions on questions of interpretation. This would be an innovation and require considerable thought. At the same time alternative dispute resolution (ADR), especially in the context of e-commerce, will require our full attention. The Special Commission on general affairs and policy of the Conference, which met in May 2000 at The Hague, recommended that this item be specifically included in our Agenda for future work.

(iii) Globalisation, its dissolving impact on the Nation State, and the emerging role of the individual and other entities in the world economy, will lead to an ever-growing role for *party autonomy*. In a more diversified world economy, it becomes more difficult to define specific classes of weaker parties: special rules for consumers and workers will come under pressure. On the other hand, in fields where global interests are to be protected, such as the environment, we may well see evolution towards a wider choice available of applicable law for the (potentially) damaged party.

(iv) Is there then no future for work in the field of applicable law? Certainly there is, but more probably in a specific field of urgency and often in combination with attempts to unify substantive law. Recent examples include our work on the law applicable to receivables financing, in the context of the more extensive work by UNCITRAL on unification of the substantive law on that topic.[4] Another example is the decision of the Special Commission on general affairs and policy of the Conference, held in May 2000, to give immediate priority to the question of the law applicable to collateral securities.

2. Regional integration

The second development which is likely to have a profound effect on private international law and on the Hague Conference, is the effect of regional integration. This is not a phenomenon limited to Europe; we also see it in MERCOSUR, for example. However, its effect is undoubtedly greatest in Europe and, since the Hague Conference traditionally comprises the EU countries as a core, increasing communitarisation is bound to have a profound effect on the Hague Conference and its work. Let me just mention four aspects: 6–006

(i) The first is the effect of increased consultation among the 15 EU States. Obviously, in an organisation of 47 Member States, of which all 15 current EU States and all the candidate EU States are members, a strict co-ordination of positions among the 15 could make or break the negotiations. Depending on the degree and effect of consultations, our traditional working methods may have to be reviewed. This should however be done in such a way as to have no detrimental effect on the product—texts which are precise and clear and which provide predictability, certainty and fairness.

(ii)   The exact effect of the external competence of the European Community, which follows from the internal competence attributed to it by Article 65 of the Amsterdam Treaty, is still rather unclear. In any event, the Community as such is not yet a Member of the Hague Conference. It must, therefore, express its views through the EU Member States, but this will have an impact on the negotiations. It is likely that the future Convention on jurisdiction and recognition and enforcement of judgments in civil and commercial matters will contain a clause allowing the European Community to sign and ratify the Convention. Such a clause may well have a multiplying effect on the scale of adherence to the Convention.

(iii)   As to the effect on *existing* Hague Conventions, one would have thought that the only rational position here would be that Member States of the EU, even where a Community instrument would deal in whole or in part with a matter covered by existing Hague Conventions, would remain free to accept treaty obligations in respect of third States such as Switzerland, Israel or Canada. This would seem obvious in the case where the Community instrument declares itself to prevail over earlier Conventions and/or where the existing Hague Convention contains a so-called disconnection clause to the effect that future community instruments will not be affected, as will be the case in the future judgments Convention. However, it should not be different where such clauses do not exist, if only because otherwise the net effect would be to block further development of the existing corpus of Hague Conventions—an effect not in the interest of citizens world-wide, thus including those of the EU.

(iv)   A further logical development would be the accession by the Community to the Hague Conference. Pending accession, practical ways should be found to enable the Community to participate in the negotiations. There is certainly a role for the Community as a new motor for world-wide activities within the Hague Conference. One could imagine here, for example, a future EU initiative for a world-wide Convention on the law applicable to contractual obligations. Indeed, in the long run it would not be satisfactory to have in place in the EU a set of choice of law rules on contracts (and torts) which would apply irrespective of any connection between that contract (or tort) and the EU. It would be preferable to aim at a set of rules applicable world-wide so as to avoid conflicts of choice of law regimes.

3. The exponential growth of electronic data interchange, the Internet and electronic commerce

6–007   While "problems of private international law raised by electronic data interchange" and "by protecting privacy in connection with transboundary data flows" had been on the Agenda of the Conference since 1993, until recently the focus of the Conference was on following up the work of other international organisations, such as UNCITRAL and the Council of Europe. It was only in 1997 that the Conference started its own review of the new, and manifold, questions of private international law raised by the Internet and by electronic commerce. A Colloquium organised in collaboration with the University of Utrecht (September 1997), a Round table for governmental experts in collaboration with the University of Geneva (September 1999), and an Expert Group meeting in Ottawa (February/March 2000) helped to define and analyse a number of important issues further to be developed in a joint meeting with OECD and ICC in the fall of this year. It is clear, however, that while areas of consensus on some of these issues are emerging, much is still in debate—which means that work remains for years, if not decades ahead. Four aspects may be mentioned in particular:

(i)   Several issues arise in the context of the ongoing negotiations on the Convention on jurisdiction and recognition and enforcement of judgments.   **6–008**

    a   As yet unresolved is the question of how to harmonise the needs of consumer protection on the one hand and those of the electronic commerce industry on the other. The very notion of "consumer" is already changing in the e-commerce context, and it is not at all obvious that the principles of the Brussels and Lugano Conventions would be acceptable on a world-wide scale. A default rule of jurisdiction in favour of the consumer in cases where ADR would not be available or not be effective may be the ultimate solution, but is certainly not generally accepted yet. The solution has not only to be good; like justice, it has to be *seen* to be good, *i.e.* by all the interested parties.

    b   A further complication of business to consumer contracts is created by choice of court clauses. If the consumer is habitually resident in a jurisdiction which prohibits such clauses, may he or she then expect such a prohibition to be respected by a business operating in a jurisdiction which does not declare such clauses as valid?

    c   A general problem is that of localisation and identification of a party to a contract. Again, solutions are available here but the question is whether one can count on their general acceptance.
The challenge in the next year or so is to build a wide consensus on solutions to these and other questions.

(ii)   The Hague Conventions on service abroad, taking of evidence abroad, access to justice and legalisation, to mention just a few relevant to commercial law, are all undergoing the effects of electronic communication. To a large extent, it would seem, the method   **6–009** of the functional equivalent may provide the answer: the *ratio* of the legal requirements to habitual forms of communication, for the serving of process or the taking of evidence, also generally applies in an electronic environment.

Particular safeguards such as crypted sites may be needed, however, to protect the authenticity, confidentiality and integrity of documents or communications transmitted through the Internet. The Conference will be studying this and other questions in the near future, and this may well lead to further work on a review of the 1965 and 1970 Conventions. Moreover, it seems probable that, as a parallel instrument to the popular 1961 Convention on the abolishment of legalisation, there may be a need for a new instrument providing for electronic service of electronic public documents.

6–010 (iii)   As I mentioned (see *supra* section 1, (iv)), the study of online ADR mechanisms has now been specifically included in the Agenda of the Conference. Electronic on-line means of dispute resolution are particularly well-suited to the likely increase in the number of disputes in the context of electronic commerce, and especially between consumers and businesses. The challenge will be to ensure that fundamental principles of independence, impartiality and transparency, of equal arms and access to justice are respected.

6–011 (iv)   Further ahead lie questions of applicable law in the field of on-line contracts and torts (should the victim have a choice between the law of the country where the injurious act took place and the law of the country where the injury was sustained?). The question of the law applicable to data protection also requires further study. Party autonomy in this, as in other fields (see *supra*, section 1(iii)) is likely to feature strongly.

6–012   Globalisation, regionalisation, Internet and e-commerce will continue to transform the Conference. For more topics than in the past, it is likely that co-operation with other international organisations will be necessary— changing partnerships, so to speak, depending on the subject. The future of commercial law is one of co-operation due to the inherently global and increasingly omnipresent nature of the subject matter.

PART TWO

REGULATION AND DEREGULATION OF INTERNATIONAL TRADE

CHAPTER 7

REGULATION AND DEREGULATION OF INTERNATIONAL TRADE: INTRODUCTORY REMARKS

SESSION CHAIRMAN'S REMARKS BY
PROFESSOR JOHN H. JACKSON[*]

The title of Part Two is *Regulation and De-Regulation of International Trade.*   **7–001**
As you are probably well aware, regulation can mean many different things,
it can mean regulation at a national level, or an international level. In some
sense, the function of regulation at the international level, at least part of the
historical tradition of the GATT (now WTO) institutions, is to regulate what
governments can regulate. In other words, to impose restraints on how
governments regulate matters such as trade across borders. In this, the last
panel and chapter of this symposium, we will examine many of the regulatory concepts considered in the context of the multilateral treaty system,
including that of the WTO. I will use this introduction to present some
thoughts as to how these concepts relate to the very rich material that is
contained in the rest of this volume, and I will suggest some general themes
for the remaining contributions in this volume.

This symposium has included an intensive look at private law affecting   **7–002**
matters or transactions that cross borders. One interesting idea mentioned by
one of the authors,[1] and to some extent, although not always explicitly, continued through the rest of the contributions, is the degree to which activity
towards harmonising or unifying the different types of national laws that
bear on these private transactions has an important implication for a world
trading system, or for the globalising economy. To the extent that such
harmonising or co-operative mechanisms can be relatively effective, they
can indeed reduce transaction costs and can reduce the temptation to use a
variety of factors in such legal schemes that are really designed for protectionist purposes or other kinds of non-market-oriented distortion motivations that can come with interest groups at the national level (as well as with
some at the international level).

It is interesting to contemplate then, the degree to which nations, at the   **7–003**
government to government level, should be paying attention to this question
of private law. I think we encountered in some of the contributions some
antagonism to the notion that governments should be "sticking their noses"
in these affairs. The rubric or phrase defining this antagonism is "party
autonomy." On the other hand, there may be some situations where party

---

[*] Georgetown University Law Centre.
[1] See Anna Mörner, "Financing Trade Within a Regional Framework: Legislative Options: Clive
M. Schmitthoff on the Unification of International Trade Law Revisited', chap. 26.

autonomy needs to yield to governmental attention. That point raises some important fundamental and philosophical economic questions, raised by many economists in the last several decades, although certainly the history of these questions goes way back. I am thinking of Nobel Laureates such as Ronald Coase and Douglas North,[2] who make the very strong point that markets, as effective as they may be for creating the kind of life that many people want to live, nevertheless depend on institutions, on human institutions. They declare that markets cannot be viable and will not perform effectively and efficiently unless there are human institutions of a variety of kinds that form the framework for those markets. A large part of those human institutions is law. Indeed, in Douglas North's very profound book, he writes about many of the things that sound very familiar to lawyers, but without using the words *law* or *lawyers,* or at least very rarely using them. Thus human institutions, I think, are part of what the international system is about.

7–004   Most of you, I think, are familiar with the rather profound directions that the international multilateral trading system has taken in the last five to six years. The Uruguay Round, finishing in April 1994, was indeed the most extensive trade Round ever; certainly, as the eighth and last of the GATT Rounds, it was quite formidable. Many people at Punta del Esta in September 1986 (when the Round was launched) felt that if the Round agenda declared there were even half fulfilled, it would be the largest Round ever held in the context of the GATT. In fact, after delays and impasses and all the usual diplomatic furor, it came out much better than half. If you want to pull a number out of the air, there was probably an 80 per cent fulfilment. It was really quite remarkable.

7–005   But now we are beginning to see the consequences of that fulfilment. First of all, we have new institutions put in place. The new WTO (World Trade Organisation) was the first true international organisation for trade, since the GATT itself was never intended to be such, and never was such explicitly (although *de facto* over years of practice, it did eventually become such an organisation). We also now have a dispute settlement system that is remarkable and unique in international law terms. Part of that uniqueness is the development of an Appellate Body, an appeal procedure. After a dispute is handled by a first level panel (usually of three persons-ad hoc and discharged after its report) that panel report can be sent to an appellate division consisting of three persons drawn from a permanent roster of seven. We now have about 35 reports from that system, including 27 or 28 reports from the Appellate Body itself. That jurisprudence is quite remarkable. If you have not had a chance to look at these reports, they are all very accessible on the World Wide Web.[3] You will find very profound minds struggling with some of the issues that I will only be able to touch on in this introduction, issues that we have to face in a globalising world economy. To put it another way, some of the activity of governments in the last few years can be called "catch up ball." They are catching up with developments that have outstripped the governments and the national government capacities

[2] Ronald Coase, *The Firm, the Market and the Law,* chap. 5. See also Douglas C. North, *Institutions, Institutional Change and Economic Performance* (1990).
[3] See the web site of the World Trade Organisation at http://www.wto.org.

to regulate. If the governments don't face these developments, they are going to find themselves behind the "eight ball."

One such development is the tension arising from the key fundamental or **7–006** systemic question of where certain kinds of decisions should be made. In a very broad brush, this is often discussed under the rubric "national sovereignty." "We must protect national sovereignty," say some of the politicians, including some whom I have encountered when testifying before Congress in Washington DC. On the other hand, there are those who say that we must have a greater role for international institutions. I think this is a persistent tension throughout this subject matter, and I think that tension is part of a current running throughout this symposium, in somewhat different contexts. In a very broad landscape view of this, you could ask, "do you want certain decisions to be made in Geneva or Washington or Sacramento, California, or Berkeley, California, or in the neighbourhood of a Berkeley, California?" There is a whole hierarchy of sovereignty that is very close to what many in Europe call "subsidiarity." This is a core question with which the trade system is struggling.

Indeed, the new jurisprudence and the dispute settlement system are having **7–007** a profound effect on diplomacy. When you talk to the diplomats in Geneva, you begin to see this. Some of them are very uneasy about what is happening because the dispute settlement system is now basically a set of procedures that create a binding report automatically. There is no real diplomatic second-guessing anymore (as there used to be under the GATT) where the Council would approve dispute reports but the reports could be blocked by any member, including the "losing party." There is a Dispute Settlement Body (DSB) that approves the reports, but that approval is automatic after a certain number of days, unless there is a reverse consensus (which has never happened, and never will happen, in most people's minds). The diplomats are encountering a different landscape on which they must perform. It is much less a matter of dickering over nice, three-star restaurant meals and more having to tolerate young, whipper-snapper lawyers that come in with very sharp-edged arguments in these dispute settlement processes. It has become much more like a tribunal or even, an arbitration (although those words are never used in the treaties).

This developing jurisprudence has many attributes so far, but I will only **7–008** mention three. First of all, the Appellate Body has pushed the system further than was even the case in GATT, toward a "textual" approach to interpreting the treaties. This is based on general principles of international law, and particularly, Articles 31 and 32 of the Vienna Convention on the Law of Treaties that relate to Treaty Interpretation. Those principles urge the international system to be very textual, to pay a lot of attention to the specific words of the treaty. We are hearing some diplomats saying, "But I was there, I was in that negotiation, that's not what we meant." But of course, it is what the words say in the minds of the Appellate Body or first level panels, coloured by context, object, and purpose, that is what counts.

The Appellate Body has enormous power, it is not second-guessed and **7–009** there is some fear about that. Part of the reason for this is that we do not have a comparable institution at the WTO that would be analogous to the legislature of a nation-state. We do have decision making and we do have potential negotiations for new rules and rule making, but in the WTO Charter, the nation-states expressly constrained the organisation with heavy requirements of super-majority and full consensus exactly because they did not want the organisation infringing too much on their "sovereign authority." That constraint means it is quite difficult to have the equivalent of legislation, or rule making.

7–010   Thus there is a recipe for impasse, to some extent. That, I think, is becoming a relatively serious problem.[4] One of the great manifestations of that problem was the attempt to select a new Director-General for the WTO during the last year. But there are other indicia of that problem. If that problem is indeed serious, as I think it is, then we have another category of difficulty, a sort of constitutional problem. Because, in the text of a treaty this size (26,000 pages, about 1,000 pages of it being dense treaty text, the rest schedules) resulting from 120 nations negotiating for a decade or so, there are bound to be gaps and ambiguities. A key question is, how do you resolve those? If you do not have an effective decision making process, with negotiation or quasi-legislative opportunities to fill these gaps, the temptation is to throw the problem at the "judiciary," in other words, at the dispute settlement process of the WTO. There is going to be (and already is) some temptation to do that, and that could put the dispute settlement process in the very difficult position of having to make decisions that they probably ought not to make, in the sense that they would be law-making, rather than law-applying.

7–011   How do these problems relate to the topics of this symposium? Here are just a few examples. A very interesting conference contribution here took up the question of insolvency, how governments create insolvency procedures, and how some harmonisation or unification can be achieved. There is a problem in the GATT/WTO that could relate to these rules of insolvency, namely, it is argued that if certain kinds of insolvency procedures are too lenient, if too much of a "bail-out" atmosphere is created by governments, this could be a "subsidy" that could violate the text of the WTO regarding subsidisation.

7–012   There are similar topics embedded in the WTO texts throughout. In fact, sub-federal state governments in the United States have just begun to wake up to some of the risks involved in what they do to attract industry to their territories.

7–013   When you look at the Services Agreement (GATS), for instance, you find embedded in it many different things. In particular, there is an article that explicitly requires quite a bit of transparency and also requires governments to provide the opportunity to go to an impartial judiciary to handle some of the regulatory issues. Article VI of this agreement seems to authorise the Services Council of the WTO to bring into force measures of good governance (I'm paraphrasing now, not using the text of the Treaty) and minimum standards of how governments could go about regulating, almost like an Administrative Procedure Act, but at the international level. That has not been done yet, I must quickly say, and maybe it will not be done, but when you read that text, as well as a number of other texts, you begin to see that there are some significant, longer term implications of this system. As we shall see, the following symposium contributions reveal a variety of opinions on these issues.

---

[4] See Jackson, John H. "Dispute Settlement and the WTO: Emerging Problems." *Journal of International Economic Law* 1 (1998): 329–51

CHAPTER 8

HUMAN RIGHTS, COSMOPOLITAN DEMOCRACY AND THE LAW OF THE WORLD TRADE ORGANISATION

PROFESSOR DR. ERNST-ULRICH PETERSMANN[1]

[1] Professor of law at the University of Geneva and its Graduate Institute of International Studies. Former lecturer/professor of law at the Universities of Hamburg, Heidelberg, Saarland, St. Gallen, Fribourg and Lausanne; former legal adviser in the German Ministry of Economic

8–001   As a former student of Professor Clive Schmitthoff and admirer of his cosmopolitan efforts at reforming international commercial and economic law
for the benefit of the citizens, it is a great pleasure for me to contribute to this
Schmitthoff Symposium. Due to his encyclopaedic knowledge of national and
international private and public law, Clive Schmitthoff could speak on almost
any subject of national and international law. He would certainly have appreciated the political importance and legal difficulties of the vast subject of my
contribution: the modern human rights revolution and the need for democratic reforms of the integration law of the World Trade Organisation (WTO).

1. Human rights and WTO law: paradigm changes in international law

8–002   From a citizen perspective, classical public international law was a state-
centred and power-oriented system that never succeeded in protecting human
rights and democratic peace effectively. Since the fall of the Berlin wall in
1989, human rights have become universally recognised also as part of
general international law and require interpreting the law of worldwide
organisations in conformity with universally recognised human rights.[2] Yet,
international lawyers, politicians and human rights activists have hardly
begun to examine the legal consequences of human rights for the law of
worldwide economic organisations like the Bretton Woods institutions and
the WTO. There is neither a convincing legal theory nor a political strategy
for integrating human rights more effectively into the agreements establishing the WTO, the International Monetary Fund (IMF) and the World Bank.
One pre-condition for developing such strategies is to overcome the "splendid isolation" and separation of human rights law and international
economic law, for instance the one-sided focus of most international
organisations on states and the inadequate protection of economic liberties
and disregard of property rights in UN human rights covenants.

8–003   In contrast to the explicit incorporation of human rights into the treaty
establishing the European Union (*e.g.* Article 6) and the limitation of EU
membership to democracies (*cf.* Articles 7,49 EU Treaty), the law of most
worldwide organisations continues to focus on the rights and duties of
governments rather than on the human rights of their citizens. The WTO, the
Food and Agricultural Organisation (FAO) and the UN Seabed Authority
remain the only worldwide institutions so far whose constitutive agreements
admit membership also of regional organisations like the EU. The now regular street protests at the annual conferences of the Bretton Woods institutions
and of the WTO are useful reminders for governments that non-transparent
rule-making in worldwide institutions behind closed doors without regard to
human rights is hardly compatible with democratic governance.

Affairs (1978–81) GATT (1981–95) and the WTO (1995–2000). Chairman of the International
Trade Law Committee of the International Law Association.

[2] This follows also from the general international rules on treaty interpretation which require
international treaties to be construed "in good faith in accordance with the ordinary meaning to
be given to the terms of the treaty in their context and in the light of its object and purpose",
including "any relevant rules of international law applicable in the relations between the parties"
(*cf.* Art. 31 of the 1969 Vienna Convention on the Law of Treaties which is widely recognised as
reflecting customary rules of treaty interpretation).

Human rights law requires adjusting international law and international   **8-004**
organisations so that they protect human rights more effectively.[3] The WTO
Agreement is the first worldwide agreement in the history of mankind that
protects freedom, property rights and rule of law across frontiers by means of
compulsory national and international adjudication.[4] The WTO objective of
a global division of labour offers unprecedented opportunities for economic
and social development. Yet, WTO law protects transnational freedom of
trade only as *obligations of governments* rather than as *individual rights* of
citizens; human rights and social policies to deal with the adjustment problems of global competition are left by WTO law to domestic policy discretion
(*e.g.* to adopt safeguard measures and grant financial adjustment assistance)
and to the jurisdiction of other international organisations (like the UN
human rights bodies, the World Bank, IMF and International Labour Organisation). Unfortunately, both human rights treaties and worldwide economic
treaties often ignore that the human rights objective of promoting "human
dignity" and individual self-government cannot be achieved without more
effective protection of *economic liberties* and *property rights* as *individual
rights* across frontiers so as to enable and induce citizens to save, invest and
participate in the international division of labour and, thereby, increase their
real income, freedom of choice and access to goods, services and employment
opportunities.

The sad fact that more than a billion people still have to live with one   **8-005**
dollar per day, appears largely due to the persistent "government failure" to
protect human rights and peaceful economic co-operation among citizens
more effectively across frontiers.[5] Human rights and the *paradox of liberty—*
i.e. the inherent tendency of political and economic liberties to destroy themselves by abuses of public and private power unless liberty is legally protected
by national as well as international constitutional rules and competition
law—require the limitation of abuses of power through local, national and
international constitutional rules and guarantees of human rights wherever
power is being exercised and risks being abused.[6]

2. A human rights agenda for transforming state-centred WTO rules into citizen-centred global integration rules

The conceptualisation of human rights as moral, constitutional and legal   **8-006**
"birth rights" of every human being has important consequences for the
necessary restructuring of international law. The universal recognition of

---

[3] See *e.g.* Art. 28 of the 1948 Universal Declaration of Human Rights: "Everyone is entitled to
a social and international order in which the rights and freedoms set forth in this Declaration can
be fully realised."
[4] *cf.* E.U. Petersmann, From the Hobbesian International Law of Coexistence to Modern
Integration Law: The WTO Dispute Settlement System, in: *Journal of International Economic
Law* 1 (1998), 175–198.
[5] The *Human Development Report 2000* (UNDP, 2000) and Nobel Prize economist A.Sen,
Development as Freedom, 1999, have convincingly argued that human rights and democracy are
not only moral and legal values, but also constitutive of the very process of development and
instrumental for economic and social welfare.
[6] *cf.* E.U. Petersmann, How to Constitutionalize International Law and Foreign Policy for the
Benefit of Civil Society? in: *Michigan Journal of International Law* 20 (1998), pp. 1–30.

human rights as part of modern general international law requires also the construction of WTO rules in conformity with universally recognised human rights. Just as the value of governments derives from promoting human rights and individual self-development and democratic self-governance, so also *international organisations* derive their democratic value from enhancing human rights. What are the consequences of a human rights approach for the global integration law of the WTO, for examples for the interpretation of WTO guarantees of freedom, non-discrimination and property rights, the numerous "public interest" and safeguard clauses in WTO law, the treatment of individuals in WTO law and for the two-thirds-majority of less-developed WTO member countries? How to induce WTO member states to adjust the WTO legal and institutional system in a way which recognises legitimate claims for democratic participation and protection of human rights? How to integrate human rights into relations between democracies and non-democracies?

2.1 The manifold functions of human rights

8–007   The needed clarification of the interrelationships between human rights and international economic law must take into account the diverse functions of human rights for protecting equal individual freedoms, self-government, democratic legitimacy and "justice" of legal systems.

2.1.1 Human rights as moral rights

8–008   As *moral rights*, human rights derive from "human dignity", *i.e.* the rational and moral autonomy of human beings to think for themselves and to live and develop their personalities in accordance with self-imposed rules which respect equal rights and human self-development for all others. Moral and legal theories of "justice" require governments to promote and protect maximum equal liberties of all citizens across frontiers.[7] From a human rights perspective, the GATT and WTO guarantees of freedom, non-discrimination and rule of law serve human rights values by reinforcing and extending national human rights guarantees of freedom, non-discrimination and rule of law across frontiers. The numerous exceptions and safeguard clauses in WTO law (*e.g.* GATT Articles XX and XXI) give clear priority to non-economic values if departures from WTO rules should prove necessary for the protection of human rights or of other "public interests".

2.1.2 Human rights as constitutional rights and government obligations

8–009   As *inalienable constitutional citizen rights* and corresponding *legal obligations of governments* that are explicitly recognised in many national constitutions

---

[7] According to Kantian moral and legal theory, for instance, the "justice" of national and international law depends on a "constitution allowing the greatest possible human freedom in accordance with laws which ensure that the freedom of each can coexist with the freedom of all others" (*cf.* H.Reiss, ed., *Kant—Political Writings*, 1991, at 23). For Kant, "the state has three principal functions and obligations: a duty of justice to ensure a condition of maximum law-governed freedom; a duty of benevolence to provide for the needs of its subjects; and a teleological responsibility to create the framework within which all forms of human rationality

and international treaties, human rights constitutionally limit public and private power and commit governments to the promotion of human rights as constitutive elements of "justice". Their inalienable character and recognition as constitutional rights "retained by the people"[8] makes clear that human rights precede the constitution of government powers and are not conferred by governments. Human rights tend to be of a defensive ("negative"), procedural (*e.g.* participatory) or re-distributive ("positive") nature, including rights of access to courts and judicial protection against abuses of/power.

The GATT and WTO guarantees tend to focus on "negative freedoms" **8–010** (*e.g.* freedom from welfare-reducing tariffs and non-tariff trade restrictions) and on procedural guarantees (*e.g.* of individual access to domestic courts) that go far beyond what tends to be explicitly provided for in national constitutions and human rights law. By empowering individuals to increase their real income and freedom of choice through trade, WTO rules also promote economic welfare and poverty alleviation.[9] However, WTO law and its numerous safeguard clauses (*e.g.* GATT Article XX, GATS Article XIV, TRIPS Article 8) treat human rights, protection of the environment, poverty alleviation and redistribution of income within countries as matters of *national* regulation and of international human rights law, environmental law and social law to be regulated *outside* the WTO in other, more qualified international organisations.

2.1.3 Legislative rules with "human rights functions"

The WTO guarantees of freedom and non-discrimination thus illustrate that **8–011** there are numerous national and international *"rules with human rights functions"* which, even if not mentioned in traditional human rights instruments, protect individual freedom, non-discrimination and rule of law across national frontiers. The interpretation of human rights guarantees of liberty in conformity with national and international guarantees of liberal trade derives moral legitimacy from the explicit references in human rights law to "human dignity" and to its requirement of maximising equal liberties of the citizens under the rule of law.[10] For example, the judicial recognition, by the EC Court of Justice, of freedom of trade as a fundamental individual right illustrates how human rights guarantees of liberty can dynamically evolve

---

can flourish" (A.D. Rosen, *Kant's Theory of Justice*, 1993, at 218). J. Rawls, *A Theory of Justice*, 1973, proceeds from a similar "first principle of justice": "each person is to have an equal right to the most extensive basic liberty compatible with a similar liberty for others" (at 60).

[8] *cf.* the Ninth Amendment to the U.S. Constitution and e.g.: W.D.Moore, *Constitutional Rights and Powers of the People*, 1998.

[9] See the empirical study by Ben-David, Nordstrom and Winters, *Trade, Income Disparity and Poverty*, WTO 1999, which shows that trade tends to contribute to the economic growth of nations and to the alleviation of poverty (which is often due to inadequate protection by governments of human rights, education and health as well as to government failures to promote efficient use of resources by liberalising trade and finance and protecting individual rights and legal security).

[10] According to C.B. Macpherson, *The Life and Times of Liberal Democracy*, 1977, in "most of the English-speaking world and most of Western Europe there is general acceptance of a principle of maximum individual freedom consistent with equal freedom for others" (at p. 7).

through legal and judicial protection of individual freedom across frontiers in conformity with liberal international trade rules.[11]

2.1.4 Human Rights as Political Claims

8–012   "Bills of Rights" (*e.g.* 1689 in England), Declarations of the "Rights of Man and of the Citizen" (*e.g.* 1789 in France) and other historical human rights instruments emerged from revolutionary struggles for constitutional democracy. They reflect *political claims* that later became recognised in legal texts focusing on the particular political priorities of a given historical moment (*e.g.* freedom of religion in England during the seventeenth century, civil and political liberties in the USA during the eighteenth century, economic and social rights in modern EC law).[12] From a policy perspective, the progressive realisation of the human rights objectives of maximum equal liberties and "justice" in all fields of national and international law remains a never ending challenge which can be realised only progressively to the extent individuals, governments and courts defend human rights. This dynamic function of human rights justifies "functional" legal and judicial interpretations rather than merely "historical" and "textual" interpretations of human rights instruments.[13] For example, the guarantees of individual liberty in German and Swiss constitutional law, as well as in the EC. Treaty, have been construed by German, Swiss and EC courts as also protecting individual "freedom of trade as a fundamental right" across national frontiers even though such "functional" interpretations were not explicitly mandated by the wording of the constitutional provisions concerned and were politically opposed by protectionist governments.[14]

2.1.5 Human rights as instruments for personal and economic development

8–013   Modern economic theory rightly emphasises the *instrumental role of human rights* for economic and personal development, *e.g.* as incentives for savings and investments, as legal preconditions of professional freedom and transfer of property rights in an exchange economy, and as defensive rights promoting the "internalisation of external effects" through contractual agreements or court litigation: "Freedoms are not only the primary ends of development, they are also among its principal means . . . Freedoms of different kinds can strengthen one another."[15] Hence, "Rights make human beings better economic actors. You cannot legislate good health and jobs. You need an economy strong

---

[11] *c.f.* E.U. Petersmann, *National Constitutions and International Economic Law*, in: Hilf/Petersmann (eds.), National Constitutions and International Economic Law, 1993, 3, at pp. 17–28.

[12] On the incoherent historical development of human rights instruments see *e.g.* J. Gordon, The Concept of Human Rights: The History and Meaning of its Politicization, in: *Brooklyn Journal of International Law* 23 (1998), 689.

[13] On the importance of functional, teleological interpretations in the jurisprudence of the E.C. Court of Justice see *e.g.* H.G. Schermers/D.Waelbroeck, *Judicial Protection in the European Communities*, 5th ed. 1992, pp. 18–26.

[14] For references to the case-law see Petersmann, *Constitutional Functions and Constitutional Problems of International Economic Law*, 1991, chap. VIII.

[15] A. Sen, *Development as Freedom*, 1999, at pp. 10–11.

enough to provide them—and for that you need people economically engaged. People will work because they enjoy the fruits of their labour: fair pay, education and health care for their families and so forth. So, economic and social rights are both the incentive for, and the reward of, a strong economy."[16] Recognition of human rights, such as freedom of producers and consumers, gives rise to market competition and calls for legal rules enabling and facilitating mutually agreed market transactions (*e.g.* liberty rights, contract law, property rights), limiting abuses of market power (*e.g.* by means of consumer protection law), and promoting monetary stability and undistorted competition (*e.g.* by means of monetary, securities and competition laws).

2.1.6 Need for mutual balancing of human rights through democratic legislation

All human rights need to be mutually balanced and reconciled through dem- **8–014** ocratic legislation. For instance, while intellectual property rights may be necessary incentives for private investments in the development and financing of pharmaceutical products, the WTO Agreement on Intellectual Property Rights (TRIPS) includes numerous safeguard clauses recognising the need for limiting abuses of intellectual property rights and for protecting public interests (*e.g.* in socially acceptable pharmaceutical prices). The mutual delimitation and progressive development of human rights by means of democratic legislation and international treaties differ from country to country depending on the political circumstances concerned. All constitutional democracies recognize the principle that human rights may be restricted by governments only on the basis of public legislation and only to the extent necessary for the protection of other human rights. GATT and WTO rules (*e.g.* in GATT Article XX and GATS Article XIV) reflect these human rights principles by making restrictions of liberal trade subject to requirements of necessity and non-discrimination.

2.2 Should freedom of trade be protected as a human right?

Does the human right to self-development include freedom of trade across **8–015** frontiers? Or do human rights guarantees of "liberty" end at national borders? It is characteristic of the nationalist bias of human rights instruments and of the confusing "bundling" of private and state-centred rights in the UN resolutions on the "right to development" as a human right that individual freedom to co-operate across frontiers through mutually welfare-increasing division of labour is not mentioned in the politicised UN resolution[17] nor in most national human rights instruments.

---

[16] Human Development Report 2000, UNDP 2000, at pp. iii and 57.
[17] The UN General Assembly Declaration 41/128 of December 4, 1986 on the "Right to Development", for instance, refers also (*e.g.* in Article 4) to collective obligations of states, and to the need for "legislative and other measures at the national and international levels" (Art. 10), to protect and promote the "right to development" as an "inalienable human right by virtue of which every human person and all peoples are entitled to participate in, contribute to, and enjoy economic, social, cultural and political development, in which all human rights and fundamental freedoms can be fully realised" (Art. 1). Numerous follow-up reports on this UN Declaration

8–016   If the moral and legal purpose of human rights is to empower citizens by protecting maximum equal liberty (including positive rights to satisfy basic human needs) for the development of their human potential, then billions of citizens demonstrate day by day that their access to foreign markets (*e.g.* to imports of food, books and medicines, foreign education and work opportunities abroad, foreign technology, information systems, tourism, development assistance) is highly valued by citizens, including the millions of poor people whose well-being depends on food aid, financial aid and medical assistance from abroad. There is worldwide consensus today also among economists that division of labour through liberal trade and through worldwide communication and information networks increase real income and consumer welfare, and that trade restrictions are hardly ever an optimal policy instrument for promoting public interests. Political scientists also emphasise certain political values of mutually beneficial trade co-operation across frontiers, such as its contribution to non-discrimination of foreigners and "positive peace".

8–017   If moral, legal, economic and political theories support the view that individual freedom to import and export should be protected as an individual right unless governmental restrictions are necessary for the protection of other, more important human rights values: Has it not become anachronistic today that trade politicians and most judges outside the EC interpret constitutional guarantees of liberty as protecting freedom of trade only among *domestic citizens* but not with *foreigners* across frontiers?[18] Would it not be more consistent with the "categorical imperative" of promoting "human dignity" (*e.g.* in the Kantian sense of maximum equal liberties of citizens) if human rights guarantees of liberty were construed by national judges in conformity with self-imposed international guarantees of freedom of trade across frontiers? Do WTO dispute settlement rules and procedures offer an adequate legal basis for the interpretation and application of the often vague human rights concepts (such as the "right to food" and the "right to development" proclaimed in numerous UN resolutions) by WTO dispute settlement bodies? Are the GATT and WTO prohibitions (*e.g.* in GATT Article XX) of "unnecessary" and "discriminatory" trade restrictions a legal reflection of the human rights principle that governmental restrictions of individual freedom must not go beyond what is necessary for the promotion of other human rights and must be non-discriminatory and proportionate? Is it inappropriate for WTO law to focus one-sidedly on protection of freedom of trade and of traditional intellectual property rights without *e.g.* WTO legal guarantees of social and cultural human rights and without effective WTO protection of the traditional knowledge of indigenous peoples and local communities? Or do the economic arguments in favour of "separation of policy instruments" justify the WTO approach of leaving the

---

have called upon international organisations to incorporate human rights into their policies and promote participation of civil society organisations in the work of international organisations (*cf. e.g.* the Report of the Intergovernmental Group of Experts on the Right to Development, UN doc. E/CN.4/1998/29 of November 7, 1997).

[18] For a detailed comparative analysis of constitutional protection of freedom of trade see Petersmann (n. 14).

regulation of economic, social and cultural human rights to Member States and to other international organisations with more expertise in human rights and social policy problems?

2.3 Need for more effective protection of the human rights objective of maximum equal freedom of citizens across frontiers

The secrecy and producer-driven agenda of the Uruguay Round negotiations resulted in one-sided protection of *producer interests*: For instance, GATT and WTO law, and domestic implementing legislation in many WTO member countries, provide for "producer rights to import protection" (*e.g.* in anti-dumping and safeguards legislation) without corresponding "rights to import" by traders and consumers. Also the TRIPS Agreement focuses one-sidedly on the rights of intellectual property holders with few safeguard clauses protecting broader social and consumer interests. **8–018**

The "protectionist biases" in WTO rules indicate that the self-interests of producers and trade bureaucracies in discretionary import protection may conflict with the human rights interests of consumers in maximum equal liberty and open markets. For instance, both the EC and U.S. legislation on the domestic implementation of the Uruguay Round Agreements prevent individual citizens from invoking WTO rules before domestic courts in order to hold domestic governments accountable for their frequent violations of the WTO guarantees of freedom and non-discrimination.[19] As a result of such bureaucratic self-interest in "rights of governments" rather than "rights of citizens", the guarantees of intellectual property rights in the TRIPS Agreement—unlike the corresponding guarantees in WIPO conventions which used to be protected by domestic courts in Europe as "directly applicable individual rights"—may therefore be no longer directly applicable by domestic courts and by the citizens concerned. Treating one's own citizens as mere objects rather than legal subjects of WTO rules is hardly consistent with the human rights ideal of maximum liberty, equal rights and self-determination of citizens. **8–019**

The large number of more than 200 intergovernmental WTO dispute settlement proceedings since 1995 reflect the determination of some WTO governments to clarify and further develop WTO law through quasi-automatic judicial interpretations and "case-law" rather than by recourse to the rigid WTO rules for "authoritative interpretations" and by amendments of WTO law to be ratified by national parliaments (*cf.* Articles IX and X of the WTO Agreement). Again, there is legitimate and increasing concern that the lack of transparency, one-sided trade-orientation and state-centred design of WTO dispute settlement proceedings may be inconsistent with the requirements of transparent, democratic rule-making and public judicial review in constitutional democracies. Both multilateral rule-making and dispute settlement proceedings in the WTO require more transparency and more effective democratic "checks and balances". WTO dispute settlement rules and procedures offer few incentives for WTO judges to interpret WTO **8–020**

---

[19] *cf.* E.U. Petersmann, The GATT/WTO Dispute Settlement System, 1997, at pp. 18–22.

rules in conformity with human rights law for the benefit of individual citizens.

2.4 The need to protect freedom of trade also against private restraints of competition

8–021   The GATT guarantees of freedom, non-discrimination and rule-of-law contributed to preventing a recurrence of a world-wide economic crisis as in the 1930s when the U.S. *Smoot-Hawley Tariff Act* triggered a spiral of protectionist countermeasures by other trading countries resulting in a breakdown of the international trading and payments system. Yet, the "paradox of freedom" is characteristic also for *private* markets and *private* restraints of competition: Without competition safeguards, economic markets risk destroying themselves through abuses of private market power (such as economic cartels and monopolies) and through other "market failures".

8–022   "Constitutional economics" and "*ordo*-liberalism"[20] emphasise the need for protecting market economies by means of an "economic constitution" based on a coherent set of "constituent principles" (such as monetary stability, open markets, private ownership, freedom of contract, liability, policy coherence) and "regulative principles" (e.g. independence of monetary and competition authorities *vis-à-vis* "rent-seeking" interest group pressures). According to the U.S. Supreme Court, "antitrust laws ... are the Magna Carta of free enterprise. They are as important to the preservation of economic freedom and our free enterprise system as the Bill of Rights is to the protection of our fundamental freedoms".[21] The historical experience with the comprehensive EC Treaty guarantees of "a system ensuring that competition in the internal market is not distorted" (Articles 3(g), 81 *et seq.*) confirms that the economic objective of maximising consumer welfare and competition through liberal trade cannot be achieved without competition laws and institutions protecting individual freedom of competition and consumers against anti-competitive restraints.

8–023   It is characteristic of the "producer bias" of GATT and WTO rules that the long-standing proposals for multilateral competition rules—*e.g.* in the 1948 Havana Charter, in GATT and WTO negotiations—continue to be resisted by many trade politicians.[22] Trade negotiators have strong self-interests in their power to negotiate market-sharing agreements (e.g. for textiles, maritime and air transports) and other trade restrictions by which they can distribute "protection rents" to their trade "clientèles". For decades, they have circumvented liberal GATT rules through protectionist "voluntary export restraints" and "orderly marketing arrangements", thereby distribut-

---

[20] *cf.* E.U. Petersmann (n. 14), pp. 61–72; D.J. Gerber, *Law and Competition in Twentieth Century Europe*, 1998, chap. VII.
[21] *United States v. TOPCO Assoc. Inc.*, 405 U.S. 596, 610 (1972).
[22] *cf.* E.U. Petersmann, Competition-oriented Reforms of the WTO World Trade System—Proposals and Policy Options, in: R. Zäch (ed.), *Towards WTO Competition Rules*, 1999, pp. 43–71; *idem*, Legal, Economic and Political Objectives of National and International Competition Policies: Constitutional Functions of WTO "Linking Principles" for Trade and Competition, in: *New England Law Review* 34 (1999), pp. 145–162.

ing billions of dollars to rent-seeking lobbies, often without transparent democratic discussion, without legislative authorisation and without parliamentary and judicial control.

Even though many sectors of international trade are subject to international cartelisation (*e.g.* by "shipping conferences"), monopolies (*e.g.* for telephone and other telecommunications, railway services) and bilateral market-sharing agreements (*e.g.* for air and maritime transports), GATT and the General Agreement on Trade in Services (GATS) do not include effective competition rules. The TRIPS Agreement acknowledges that "appropriate measures may be needed to prevent the abuse of intellectual property rights by right holders or the resort to practices which unreasonably restrain trade or adversely affect the international transfer of technology" (Article 8). Yet, even though "nothing in the agreement shall prevent members from specifying in their legislation licensing practices or conditions that may in particular cases constitute an abuse of intellectual property rights having an adverse effect on competition in the relevant market" (Article 40), the WTO offers no effective help to the numerous WTO member countries without national competition laws to introduce such laws against the protectionist resistance by powerful industries and to protect consumers against anti-competitive restraints of competition. In July 2000, the worldwide International Law Association has adopted detailed proposals for introducing competition rules into WTO law and for liberalising "parallel imports" that are often prevented by private holders of intellectual property rights to the detriment of domestic consumers.[23] Yet, such recommendations from non-governmental organisations are unlikely to be taken up in the WTO as long as WTO bodies focus so one-sidedly on the interests of producers and trade bureaucracies.[24]

8–024

3. Need for democratic reforms of WTO law

The 1948 Universal Declaration of Human Rights protects not only "freedom of thought" (Article 18), "freedom of opinion and expression" (Article 19) and "freedom of peaceful assembly and association" (Article 20). According to Article 21:

8–025

> "(1) Everyone has the right to take part in the government of his country, directly or through freely chosen representatives.
> (2) Everyone has the right of equal access to public service in his country.
> (3) The will of the people shall be the basis of the authority of government; this will shall be expressed in periodic and genuine elections which shall be by universal and equal suffrage and shall be held by secret vote or by equivalent free voting procedures."

The 1966 UN Covenant on Civil and Political Rights confirms these and additional "democratic rights", for instance in Article 25:

8–026

---

[23] The text of these ILA resolutions adopted on July 29, 2000 can be visited at the ILA web site: http://www.ila-hq.org.
[24] For further discussion, see Cremona, "Multilateral and Bilateral Approaches to the Internationalisation of Competition Law: An E.U. Perspective", chap. 11 of this volume.

"Every citizen shall have the right and the opportunity, without any of the distinctions mentioned in Article 2 and without unreasonable restrictions:
(a)   To take part in the conduct of public affairs, directly or through freely chosen representatives;
(b)   To vote and to be elected at genuine periodic elections which shall be by universal and equal suffrage and shall be held by secret ballot, guaranteeing the free expression of the will of the electors;
(c)   To have access, on general terms of equality, to public service in his country."

3.1 Three basic functions of the emerging "right to democracy"

8–027   The "right to democracy",[25] regardless of particular cultures and history, has been recognised not only in numerous subsequent UN human rights instruments, such as the 1993 Vienna Declaration on Human Rights:

"Democracy, development and respect for human rights and fundamental freedoms are interdependent and mutually reinforcing. Democracy is based on the freely expressed will of the people to determine their own political, economic, social and cultural systems and their full participation in all aspects of their lives."[26]

There are also an increasing number of multilateral and bilateral international treaties (notably by the EC) that include "democracy clauses" and authorise suspension of treaty provisions in case of violation of human rights and "democratic principles".[27] The "right to democracy" is increasingly recognised as a human right and effective means of promoting "democratic peace" not only among democracies but also *vis-à-vis* non-democratic governments (*e.g.* so as to prevent internal armed conflict and external intervention in support of human rights struggles). Just as market economies are the only form of economic regime compatible with respect for human rights, democracy is the only political form of government respecting the human right to individual self-determination and collective self-government.

8–028   Since the Athenian paradigm of direct democracy during the time of *Pericles*, numerous different kinds of direct and representative forms of democratic self-government have developed at national and international levels. There are also different concepts of the relationship between human rights and democracy depending on whether democracies focus on "parliamentary sovereignty" (as in England), "popular sovereignty" (as in the U.S.) or "individual sovereignty" protected by inalienable human rights even against abuses of power by parliaments and "We the People" (as in Germany). Yet, all constitutional democracies appear to recognise at least three basic functions of democracy:

• *First*, to legitimise "government of the people" on the basis of popular sovereignty and equal human rights that require a "government for the people".

---

[25] See Resolution 1999/57 on "Promotion of the Right to Democracy" adopted by the UN Commission on Human Rights in 1999 (UN Doc. E/CN.4/1999.SR 57). *cf.* also: T.M. Franck, The Emerging Right to Democratic Governance, American Journal of International Law 86 (1992), 46.

[26] Section 8 of the 1993 Vienna Declaration adopted by more than 170 states at the UN World Conference on Human Rights, *cf.*: The United Nations and Human Rights, 1995, at 449.

[27] For an overview of this treaty practice see: P. Alston (ed.),*The E.U. and Human Rights*, 1999.

- *Second*, to constitute and limit "government by the people" through democratic institutions (*e.g.* political parties, representative parliaments) and procedures (*e.g.* popular referenda, parliamentary elections, majority votes, public legislation).

- *Third*, to promote *participatory democracy* based on public discourse in an informed civil society and active citizen participation in public policy-making as well as in private market economies accommodating private demand and supply.

3.2 Need for promoting "cosmopolitan democracy" also at the international level in worldwide international organisations

The more government powers are collectively exercised in international organisations, the more civil society claims to democratic participation and to more effective protection of human rights in international organisations are likely to increase. If values can be derived only from individuals and from their human rights, and if the end of states and of international law is to serve individuals by protecting their human rights, then individuals and their human rights—rather than states, "nations" or "people" (*demos*) whose collective rights are merely derivative of the human rights of their citizens— should be recognised as primary normative units also in international law and international organisations.[28] The increase in the number of democratic states must be accompanied by democratic reforms of international organisations leading to mutually complementary forms of "cosmopolitan democracy" at national and international levels.[29]

8–029

This need for democratic politics also at the international level calls for democratic reforms of international law and international organisations so as to give citizens, non-governmental organisations (NGOs), and the "nascent global civil society"[30] more voice and input, more effective political representation in international affairs, and also more effective human rights and legal remedies to hold national and international decision-makers accountable. Even though NGO representatives may not be democratically elected and may not always express "public interests", they can enrich international decision-making processes by offering additional information, perspectives, arguments, criticism and support by "We the People". The idea of limiting NGO participation to the state level is inconsistent with the history of federalism and of international organisations[31] and with the need for "cosmopolitan democracy". Both at national and international levels, public opinion and criticism by NGOs offer important democratic "checks

8–030

---

[28] If human dignity, as the central concept of human rights law, is interpreted in conformity with Kant's categorical imperative (see Reiss, above n. 7, at p. 18), then respect for the dignity of persons and for the effectiveness of human rights law call for treating individuals as subjects rather than mere objects also of international law.

[29] *cf. e.g.* D. Archibugi/D. Held (eds.), *Cosmopolitan Democracy*, 1995; D. Held, *Democracy and the Global Order*, 1995.

[30] *cf.* R. Falk, The World Order between Inter-State Law and the Law of Humanity: the Role of Civil Society Institutions, in: Archibugi/Held (n. 29), pp. 163–179.

[31] *cf. e.g.* S.Charnovitz, Two Centuries of Participation: NGOs and International Governance, in: *Michigan Journal of International Law 18* (1997), 183.

and balances" against secretive policy-making processes and abuses of public power. Just as judicial protection of individual rights has predated parliamentary democracy in many countries and in the EC, constitutional reforms of international law and of international organisations are easier to achieve through legal and judicial protection of human rights and of spontaneous co-operation among citizens across frontiers ("democratisation and globalisation from below") than through premature initiatives for worldwide parliamentary and other democratic institutions without adequate "democratic infrastructure".

3.3 From "negative" to "positive" integration in the WTO: need for better democratic legitimisation of WTO rule-making procedures

8–031   The 1944 Bretton Woods Agreements, the 1945 UN Charter and the 1948 Havana Charter for an International Trade Organisation (ITO) pursued not only economic but also political objectives, such as the prevention of another worldwide economic and political crisis (as in the 1930s) and the creation of "conditions of stability and well-being which are necessary for peaceful and friendly relations among nations" (Article 1, Havana Charter). The preamble of the GATT 1947 referred exclusively to *economic* objectives. The numerous safeguard clauses in the General Agreement gave, however, clear priority to national sovereignty to pursue *non-economic* policies, for instance so as to prevent "serious injury to domestic producers" (Article XIX), to protect "public morals" (Article XX, a) and "human, animal or plant life or health" (Article XX, b), "conservation of exhaustible natural resources" (Article XX, g), or national security (Article XXI).

8–032   The 1994 Uruguay Round Agreements were ratified by national parliaments in most WTO member countries without thorough examination of the more than 25,000 pages of treaty text and without real possibility of modifying the treaty provisions agreed among trade experts from 124 countries and the EC.[32] Also during the eight years of multilateral trade negotiations, most national parliaments (with the exception of the U.S. Congress) exercised little, if any, political influence on the contents of the Uruguay Round negotiations. As long as GATT negotiations focused on reciprocal tariff liberalisation, subsequent parliamentary ratification of mutually beneficial GATT agreements was considered as conferring sufficient democratic legitimacy. The "positive integration law" of the WTO, however, goes far beyond the trade liberalisation rules of GATT 1947.[33] In contrast to GATT 1947, WTO law:

●   liberalises and regulates the various kinds of division of labour (e.g. trade in goods and services, licensing of know-how, foreign investments) in a much more comprehensive manner;

---

[32] See the comparative country studies in J. Jackson/A. Sykes (eds.), *Implementing the Uruguay Round*, 1997.
[33] For a detailed analysis see: E.U. Petersmann, From "Negative" to "Positive Integration" in the WTO: Time for Mainstreaming Human Rights into WTO Law? in: *Common Market Law Review*, December 2000 pp. 1363–1382.

- requires far-reaching legislative, administrative and judicial measures for the implementation of WTO rules in domestic laws;

- prescribes substantive and procedural individual rights (notably intellectual property rights) and their protection by domestic courts; and

- has introduced far-reaching new limitations on national sovereignty over non-discriminatory internal regulations (as protected under GATT Article III) and national safeguard measures (as protected *e.g.* by GATT Articles XIX–XX), for instance by new WTO legal requirements of "necessity"; "sufficient scientific evidence"; "harmonisation" of national measures on the basis of "international standards"; "agreements on recognition of the equivalence of specified sanitary or phytosanitary measures"; "assessment of risk and determination of the appropriate level of sanitary or phytosanitary protection"; "consistency in the application of the concept of appropriate level of sanitary or phytosanitary protection"; participation in "appropriate international standardising bodies of international standards"; requirements *e.g.* for the preparation, adoption and application of technical regulations by central, local and non-governmental bodies, or for government procurement procedures by central and sub-central government entities.[34]

In the context of the old GATT 1947, the U.S. and other GATT member countries had introduced special "fast-track legislation" facilitating reciprocal tariff liberalisation agreements in GATT and their speedy incorporation into national implementing legislation. The main political motivation for these special legislative procedures had been the traumatic U.S. experience with the Smoot-Hawley-Tariff Act of 1930 by which protectionist interest groups and political "log-rolling" had prompted Congress to introduce the highest tariffs in U.S. history, triggering retaliatory trade and payments restrictions by other countries leading to a worldwide economic crisis and finally the second world war. Rather than "circumventing democracy", such special legislative and political procedures for reciprocal tariff liberalisation have proven to be effective "pre-commitments" for protecting the general citizen interest in transnational legal freedom, liberal trade and welfare-increasing legislation.[35] **8–033**

The Uruguay Round Agreements suggest, by contrast, that the special national and international rule-making procedures for reciprocal tariff-liberalisation are hardly appropriate for legislation in fields such as sanitary and phytosanitary standards, technical regulations, investment rules, environmental rules and intellectual property rights. GATT negotiations used to be politically driven by export industries interested in access to foreign markets. WTO rule-making requires more active involvement by national parliaments and a much broader democratic representation and balancing of **8–034**

---

[34] The quotations are illustrations from the WTO Agreements on Sanitary and Phytosanitary Measures, Technical Barriers to Trade, and Government Procurement.
[35] See: R.E. Hudec, Circumventing Democracy: The Political Morality of Trade Negotiations, in: R.E. Hudec, Essays on the Nature of International Trade, 1999, pp. 215–225.

all interests involved, for instance because industries may have no self-interest in negotiations or effective competition and environmental rules.

4. Need for advisory parliamentary and civil society institutions in the WTO so as to promote better representation of citizen interests

8–035   International law assumes (*e.g.* in Article 7 of the Vienna Convention on the Law of Treaties) that ministers of trade and ambassadors, if they present appropriate full powers, are representing a state for the purpose of adopting an international treaty, regardless of whether the government concerned has democratic legitimacy. Also GATT and WTO have never scrutinised the agency relationship between governments and citizens. In most worldwide organisations, there are no effective guarantees that government representatives respect human rights and take into account all national and private interests involved.

4.1 Need for promoting more "participatory democracy" in the WTO

8–036   Constitutionalism and democracy require to control power wherever it is exercised, and to offer all citizens affected by governmental decisions the possibility of voicing their concerns, participating in the exercise of government powers, and seeking judicial protection against violations of their human rights. How to deal with the "democratic deficit" of international organisations which allocate one vote to each state regardless of its population and do not afford citizens adequate possibilities for "democratic participation" in, and democratic control of, secretive international negotiations on collective international rule-making? How to overcome the resistance to protecting human rights, including the "right to democracy" more effectively in WTO law and practice?

8–037   Democracy aims at national and international self-government based on transparent discussion and public scrutiny; democratic legislation by representative parliamentary bodies maximising the human rights of the citizens; and democratic procedures and accountability based on respect for principles of "inclusiveness",[36] transparent policy-making and public access to judicial proceedings. "International legislation" through worldwide treaties involves a delegation of rule-making powers to government executives which are rarely effectively supervised by national parliaments and by public opinion, for example, due to the confidentiality, length and complexity of worldwide negotiations and the frequent, practical impossibility of reopening negotiations after the final text has been approved at the international level. The Uruguay Agreements illustrate how democratic principles can easily be circumvented through confidential negotiations among more than 120 government representatives. For instance, between the signing

---

[36] On the "principle of democratic inclusion" and accountability to those affected by government activities see *e.g.*: S. Marks, The Riddle of All Constitutions, 2000, at pp. 88–92, 109 *et seq*: "'democratic inclusion" is used to refer to the idea that all should have a right to a say in decision-making which affects them, and that systematic barriers to the exercise of that right should be acknowledged and removed" (p.119).

of the agreements in April 1994 and their entry into force on January 1, 1995, there remained so little time for translating the 25,000 pages of treaty text that some national parliaments (*e.g.* in Germany) had to discuss the agreements without a complete translation of the texts into their national language, and this within only a few days which did not enable parliaments to really understand, evaluate, discuss or criticise such complex and important "international legislation".

4.2 Proposals for advisory WTO bodies representing civil society interests

In order to enhance information on and transparency of international rule- **8–038**
making in international organisations, an increasing number of international
organisations provide for advisory parliamentary assemblies (*e.g.* in the
Council of Europe) and advisory "Economic and Social Committees" (*e.g.*
in the EC) consisting of "representatives of the various categories of economic and social activity, in particular, representatives of producers, farmers,
carriers, workers, dealers, craftsmen, professional occupations and representatives of the general public" (Article 257 EC Treaty). Proposals for the
establishment of similar advisory bodies in the WTO have been made long
since in order to strengthen parliamentary and private participation in WTO
activities and, by requiring special interests to balance their views among
each other, to contain one-sided protectionist pressures.[37] In July 2000, the
International Law Association has recommended that "WTO members
should strengthen the rule of law in international trade by enhancing the
legitimacy and acceptance of WTO rules by, in particular:

(a)   Improving the transparency of the WTO rule making process *i.e.* by
        increasing the participation of national representatives of the eco-
        nomic and social activities in the work of the WTO, for instance by cre-
        ation of an Advisory Economic and Social Committee or an advisory
        parliamentary body of the WTO to be consulted regularly by the
        WTO organs.

(b)   Opening the WTO dispute settlement system for observers represent-
        ing legitimate interests in the respective procedures, and promoting
        full transparency of WTO dispute settlement proceedings.

(c)   Allowing individual parties, both natural and corporate, an advisory
        locus standi in those dispute settlement procedures where their own
        rights and interests are affected."[38]

Unlike the UN and many other worldwide organisations, the WTO has so **8–039**
far made only inadequate use of its authority to "make appropriate
arrangements for consultation and co-operation with non-governmental
organisations concerned with matters related to those of the WTO" (Article

---

[37] *cf.* E.U. Petersmann, Trade and the Protection of the Environment after the Uruguay Round, in: R. Wolfrum (ed.), Enforcing Environmental Standards: Economic Mechanisms as Viable Means?, 1996, 165–197, at p. 189.
[38] See *supra*, n. 23.

V:2 WTO Agreement).[39] Whereas the annual meetings of the Bretton Woods institutions and of the International Labor Organisation and World Intellectual Property Organisation benefit from the presence and expertise of NGOs, the WTO's "public relations policy" appears comparatively underdeveloped. Past WTO initiatives for meetings and symposia with environmental and developmental NGOs have enhanced public understanding and transparency of WTO activities. Such sporadic and selective meetings are, however, no substitute for institutionalising civil society representatives as an advisory body with access to WTO documents and with the right to submit recommendations to all WTO bodies subject to procedures which ensure more accountability and representativeness of NGOs and check their democratic legitimacy.[40] There are also no convincing reasons why meetings of WTO bodies should not be open for the public, including meetings of WTO dispute settlement bodies. For, "justice should not only be done, but should manifestly and undoubtedly be seen to be done."[41]

5. Conclusion

8–040   The universal recognition of human rights calls for the interpretation of WTO provisions in conformity with universally recognised human rights and requires democratic reforms of the WTO, for instance the establishment of an advisory parliamentary WTO body and an advisory WTO Civil Society Committee institutionalising active, yet more representative and more responsible participation of NGOs in the WTO. Meetings of the WTO Council and of WTO dispute settlement bodies should, as a matter of principle, be open to the public. In order to promote "participatory democracy" and protect human rights more effectively, precise and unconditional WTO guarantees of freedom and non-discrimination should be protected by domestic laws and judges as individual rights. The numerous "public interest clauses" and safeguard clauses of WTO law grant governments ample opportunities to apply WTO rules with due regard to social and other human rights.

---

[39] On the 1996 WTO Guidelines for Arrangements on Relations with NGOs, the improved transparency of WTO documents, and for other changes in the public relations policy of the WTO see: G. Marceau/ P.N. Pedersen, Is the WTO Open and Transparent?, in: *Journal of World Trade 33* (1999–1), pp. 5–49; W. Benedek, Developing the Constitutional Order of The WTO—The Role of NGOs, in: Benedek, Isak and Kicker (eds.), Developing and Development of International and European Law, 1999, pp. 313–335; D. Esty, Non-Governmental Organisations and the WTO, in: *JIEL 1* (1998), pp. 123–148.
[40] See n. 39 and J. Scholte, R. O'Brien and M. Williams, The WTO and Civil Society, in: *Journal of World Trade 33* (1999–1), pp. 107–123.
[41] Dictum of Lord Hewart C.J. in *R v. Sussex Justices ex parte McCarthy* (1924) 1 KB 256.

CHAPTER 9

THE MANAGEMENT OF ENVIRONMENTAL REGULATIONS BY INTERNATIONAL ORGANISATIONS

Dr Geert Van Calster[1]

This contribution looks at how international institutions manage the multitude of national regulatory regimes in the environment and public health sector. It considers some of the issues which are part of what has been phrased the Trade and Environment conundrum: how to ensure that ever-increasing global free trade does not counter environmental protection.[2]   **9–001**

The World Trade Organisation (WTO) is the global organisation with the highest profile in international trade. As a result, much of the Trade and Environment debate has been geared towards providing the WTO with a framework for tackling the identified challenges. In the pursuit of such framework, reference has been made to the European Community ("EC") and to its experience in dealing with many of the issues that coincide with a variety in national regulatory regimes, both in the environment and in the public health sphere. Indeed some of other contributions of this volume touch upon this issue. In the relevant heading below, this author shall   **9–002**

---

[1] LL.M., Ph.D.; Senior research fellow, IMER—Collegium Falconis, K.U. Leuven; Member of the Brussels Bar, Caestecker & Partners/Andersen Legal; e-mail:geert.vancalster@law.kuleuven.ac.be.

[2] Geert Van Calster, *International and EU trade law—The environmental challenge*, London, Cameron May, 2000.

highlight some of the weaknesses of the EC's Trade and Environment "solutions".

9–003   The contribution also considers what role, if any, the WTO can play in international harmonisation efforts, and looks at the position of the organisation's dispute settlement system in this respect.

9–004   The efforts to align international eco-management systems are taken as an example of the challenges ahead. Finally, the author looks into the role of industry, focusing on negotiated agreements with authorities, and on corporate good governance.

1. The broad lines of (il)legality of trade-related environmental measures

9–005   Trade and Environment disputes, where barriers to trade are erected in the name of environmental protection, are of course not merely the result of diverging regulatory responses to environmental problems. What's more to the point, is that members of the WTO do not always regard the regulatory regime of others to be sufficiently efficient in tackling environmental problems, and/or that such dissatisfaction may in fact amount to disguised protectionism.

9–006   Trade and environment issues arise where goods are physically prevented from being marketed and used in an importing state, where mechanisms such as eco-labels are employed to steer consumers towards consumption of "preferred" goods, where subsidies are granted to one's domestic industry in order to produce more eco-friendly, where environmental taxes which are levied domestically are re-imbursed at the border, and/or imposed on imported goods, etc.

9–007   Where the environmental problem at issue is confined to the territory of the exporting state, the latter justifiably may invoke the territoriality principle to substantiate a claim of illegality under international law of the importing State's measure. Where the environment concerned is part of the so-called "global commons", allegations of extraterritoriality may be more cumbersome.[3]

9–008   Whether a state's trade barriers based on alleged environmental protection are lawful under international law, depends very much on a more or less complex set of circumstances. Should the goods concerned possess intrinsic physical qualities, which render them hazardous and/or harmful for the environment of the "receiving" State, WTO- and GATT-legality is more or less guaranteed. This is especially so where the measures which target the imported goods, are equally applied to national production. The legal analysis becomes more blurred when it comes to measures based on so-called "PPMs", *i.e.* production processes and methods.

9–009   Both unilateral trade-related environmental measures ("TREMs"), and TREMs based on multilateral environmental agreements ("MEAs"), have led to controversy where they target the PPMs used in manufacturing the product concerned, rather than the very physical properties of the products.

---

[3] The issue of extraterritoriality falls outside the scope of this contribution.

2. WTO Members' domestic policy autonomy

GATT and/or current WTO dispute settlement (not necessarily the texts of **9–010** the WTO Agreement[4]), has rejected the compatibility of a range of TREMs with the basic GATT obligations, in particular with GATT Article III and XI. This effectively forces the vast majority of trade and environment disputes into an assessment of GATT's Article XX.

The purpose of Article XX is to ensure that the commitments under **9–011** GATT do not hinder the pursuit of policies aimed at realising the goals which have been set out in the article. Article XX is not designed generally to re-install national sovereignty in those areas where such sovereignty has been limited by the relevant provisions of the GATT. GATT Article XX is not the only protection of national sovereignty. GATT Parties have only limited their regulatory sovereignty to the extent foreseen in the Agreement. This is generally referred to as the GATT principle of domestic policy autonomy. "The GATT principle of 'national sovereignty' protects diverging domestic policies, experimentation and competition among rules",[5] and is an important determinant of the comparative advantage of countries.

This author, after having carefully analysed the issue, personally believes **9–012** that much of the Trade and Environment debate should be taken out off the application of GATT Article XX, and may be solved by a different interpretation of GATT's basic obligations, in particular of Article III. Meanwhile, however, the recent application of Article XX by the WTO Appellate Body, bears the wholemark of a teleological, consistent approach of the WTO's domestic policy autonomy.[6]

3. The EU: A shining example?

There is a lot of merit in examining the EU's approach of Trade and **9–013** Environment issues. Wherever comparisons are made between regional arrangements such as the EU, and the international trade system spearheaded by the WTO, a word of caution is appropriate. Each of these systems of course operates within its own context. The EU's trade policy is embedded in the overall goals of the Union. Even though Internal Market principles, including the "four freedoms", stood at the cradle of the European Communities, the treaties have always aimed for more than merely economic objectives. One of the challenges of the GATT/WTO today, is precisely the identification of its agenda. These agreements are fundamentally pure trade agreements, and the integration of values such as environmental and social protection obliges them to assess their "mission".

Some of the provisions of the original treaty establishing the European **9–014** Economic Community were almost literally copied from the GATT

---

[4] This is exactly the point made by the author in the book referred to in n. 2 above.
[5] E.-U. Petersmann, *International and European Trade and Environmental Law after the Uruguay Round*, London, Kluwer, 1995, p.17.
[6] See the author's relief expressed in "The WTO Appellate Body Report in Shrimp/Turtle: Picking up the pieces', *European Environmental Law Review*, 1999, pp.111–115, after the rather disputable interpretation of the Panel "The WTO Shrimp/Turtle Panel Report: *Marine conservation v. GATT conservatism?*", *European Environmental Law Review*, 1998, pp. 307–314.

Agreement. GATT Article III:4 and 5 prohibit protectionism in the application of internal regulatory measures; GATT Article XI prohibits quantitative restrictions. Articles 23, 25, 28 and 29 EC.[7] prohibit tariffs, quantitative restrictions, and other measures which directly or indirectly, actually or potentially, hinder trade.

9–015   GATT Article XX secures domestic policy autonomy, provided national measures do not involve arbitrary discrimination, are no disguised restrictions to trade, and meet the specific conditions of the subparagraphs. Article 30 EC secures domestic policy autonomy, provided the measures concerned further the policy goals enumerated in that article, do not involve arbitrary discrimination or disguised restrictions to trade, and meet the conditions of the proportionality test (including necessity).

9–016   Whilst the texts may be similar or, in places, even identical, little is to be learnt from merely comparing the application of these texts by the European Court of Justice and the WTO dispute settlement institutions, respectively. One also has to study the mechanisms behind the analysis. This is not the place for a complete assessment of the EC's Trade and Environment debate; here, this author would merely like to emphasise that not all that glitters is gold. The EC is often represented as some kind of a model for striking a balance between trade and environmental interests. Yet, quite a number of issues remain unresolved even in the EC, and the balance that has been struck has not always received praise.

9–017   For instance, up until a few years ago, the ECJ has not had to deal with cases involving product distinctions based on PPMs. In the recent cases where it has, in particular *Lomas*[8] and *Compassion*[9] (but also in *Dusseldorp*),[10] it has based its judgment on the basis of exhaustive harmonisation. The E.C.J. has effectively avoided having to tackle the PPM-issue, by confining the analysis, in its relevant judgments, to the rather complex theory behind pre-emption and harmonisation.[11] The judgments concerned provoked controversy, and led to scepticism among the environmental community, just as the two *Tuna/Dolphin* cases did within the context of the GATT.

9–018   Furthermore, the ECJ has not unequivocally indicated whether it sees itself fit to judge the very level of environmental protection sought by the Member States. Most judgments would seem to indicate that it does not, but the debate is open (see, for instance, the Opinion of the AG in *Danish Bottles*[12]).

9–019   Moreover, the ECJ has likewise not decided whether Member States may take unilateral initiatives to protect the environment in other Member States.

---

[7] Previously Art 9, 12, 30 and 34 EC The Treaty of Amsterdam has led to a general renumbering of the EC Treaty.
[8] Case C-5/94, *The Queen v Ministry of Agriculture, Fisheries and Food, ex parte Hedley Lomas (Ireland) Ltd*, [1996] E.C.R. I-2553; [1996] 2 C.M.L.R. 391.
[9] Case C-1/96, *The Queen v. Minister of Agriculture, Fisheries and Food, ex parte Compassion in World Farming Limited*, [1998] E.C.R. I-1251.
[10] Case C-203/96, *Chemische Afvalstoffen Dusseldorp and Others v. VROM*, [1998] E.C.R. I-4075.
[11] See the author's analysis in "Export restrictions – A watershed for Article 30", *European Law Review*, 2000, pp. 335–352.
[12] Case 302/86, *Commission v. Denmark*, [1988] E.C.R 4607.

This "extraterritoriality" issue has been at the centre of a majority of the trade and environment discussions in the WTO: it was debated in *Tuna/Dolphin*, references to it were made in *Shrimp/Turtle*, and if for instance the EC's Leghold Trap Regulation[13] were ever to be brought before the WTO, it would be crucial again. The European Court has not addressed the issue in either *Scottish* Grouse,[14] *Lomas*, *Compassion*, or *Dusseldorp*, even though all these could be taken to involve some degree of extraterritoriality.

Finally, the EC's harmonising legislation, which could be typified as an **9–020** attempt to tackle trade and environment issues head on, is often said to have failed in its pursuit. Both legislation based on Article 95 EC (previously Article 100A), and on Article 176 EC (previously Article 130T), allow for stricter unilateral measures by Member States (the Treaty of Amsterdam has however tightened the conditions for the former). It should be noted, however, that this route is hardly ever used by the more environmentally proactive Member States. Additionally, harmonising legislation now sometimes includes in its provisions itself, differing standards for the various Member States. The packaging and packaging waste Directive is a case in point.[15] This is sometimes phrased as a solution for tensions (Member States explicitly recognise each others' differing standards and do not let it hamper free trade). Others however describe it as an indication of failure.

Despite the inherent difficulty of having to compare two substantially **9–021** different sets of international law, and notwithstanding the caution expressed above, the experience of the EC is a useful reference for the WTO. Clearly, if trade and environment issues are to be resolved successfully, a great deal of co-operation will have to be realised between the trade and the environmental community. The EC is "lucky" in that its agenda includes both trade and the environment. The WTO clearly has no environmental agenda. This obliges it, with the international environmental community, to broker a successful partnership on trade and environmental issues.

Three arguments figure strongly in commentators' caution in comparing **9–022** the EC and the GATT 1947 set-up.[16] First, the GATT 1947 was far more limited *ratione materiae*. GATT had set trade liberalisation as its goal, whilst in the EC, social cohesion and regional re-distribution of wealth, among others, have figured alongside economic development as the Communities' purpose, even if no express reference was made to environmental protection as one of the initial objectives of the Community.[17] Secondly, GATT's institutional structure, and in particular the weaknesses of its dispute settlement provisions, prevented "creative law-making".[18] And finally, the homogeneity among EC Member States is far greater than among GATT Members.

---

[13] Regulation 3254/91 of November 4, 1991, [1991] O.J. L308/1.
[14] Case C-169/89, *Criminal proceedings against Gourmetterie Van den Burg*, [1990] E.C.R. I-2143.
[15] Directive 94/62 of December 20, 1994, [1994] O.J. L365/10.
[16] See e.g. P. Demaret, "TREMs, Multilateralism and the GATT", in J. Cameron, P. Demaret, and D. Geradin, (eds.), *Trade and the Environment: The Search for Balance*, London, Cameron May, 1994, (pp. 52–68) p. 65.
[17] E-U. Petersmann, *op.cit.*, n. 5 *supra*, p. 53.
[18] *Ibidem*.

9–023   In the WTO, the first two arguments may have altered. First, even though such issues as environmental protection and social cohesion are not amongst the WTO's aims, the Agreement nevertheless has recognised the need for these considerations to be taken into account in the further liberalisation of international trade. Secondly, the dispute settlement provisions of the WTO are of course far more advanced than those of the GATT, including the provision that Panel and AB Reports are deemed to be accepted, unless rejected by unanimity.

9–024   However, the third argument reflects a reality which is still in place. For instance, one of the elements of the ECJ's "mutual recognition" jurisprudence,[19] is the requirement that Member States recognise each other's measures which serve the protection of the interest concerned, when adopting stricter rules, or in the absence of Community harmonisation. This includes, for instance, the existence of adequate health and sanitary inspections in the exporting Member State. This represents an application of good faith, mutual confidence and quasi-federal loyalty, which is not justified in the WTO (see also below, *re* judicial activism).

9–025   One crucial characteristic of the EC, a precondition for making its harmonisation programme a success, is its supranational nature. Through the doctrine of the supremacy of Community law, and the direct effect of some of its provisions, Community law penetrates directly into the legal regimes of the Member States. The WTO remains a classic instrument of international diplomacy, without an equivalent of the direct effect doctrine.

4. "Negative harmonisation"— the role of WTO dispute settlement

4.1 The WTO and judicial activism

9–026   Is the WTO dispute settlement mechanism equipped to play the brokering role which the ECJ has played? The role of the ECJ in addressing trade and environment concerns in the EC, has been crucial. The ECJ has not confined itself to a textual interpretation of Community law. It has followed a proactive approach, moving the issues forward in what it perceived as being the best interest of the Community.

9–027   GATT and WTO dispute settlement panels and the WTO Appellate Body have formed the so called "negative harmonisation" tier of the trade and environment debate within the WTO.[20] GATT Panels have traditionally stuck to a literal and textual interpretation of the Agreement. Even if this may have pushed the trade and environment debate into a certain direction, it cannot be interpreted as "judicial activism". The latter arguably requires

---

[19] Which, subject to exceptions, foresees that Member States are obliged to allow the marketing, on their territory, of products manufactured in accordance with the laws and regulations of the "home" Member State.

[20] "Positive harmonisation" refers to the alignment of national regulatory systems through explicit legislative or inter-governmental action, whether it be in the context of formal legislation (such as by the EC Institutions), international Treaties or otherwise. "Negative" harmonisation refers to the dismantling of regulatory barriers to trade, by reason of them falling foul of existing trade agreements; the finding of incompatibility takes place within some kind of judicial body.

some sort of a stout approach which has so far been absent in GATT and WTO dispute settlement practice.

Contrasting the debate on "green" Border Tax Adjustment, both within the EC and in the GATT/WTO, may serve as a good example.

Article 90 EC, which regulates Member States"internal taxation regime   **9–028** where it has an effect on Community trade, much as GATT's Article III, is rigid in its conception. However, in the light of the overall slow progress in Community tax harmonisation, and the sensitivity of national fiscal legislation, the ECJ has allowed Member States considerable leeway under Article 90. It has held that Community law does not restrict the freedom of each Member State to lay down tax arrangements which differentiate between certain products on the basis of objective criteria, such as the nature of the raw materials used or the production processes employed. Such differentiation is compatible with Community law if it is based on objective criteria, such as the nature of the raw materials used or the production processes employed; if it pursues economic or social policy objectives which are themselves compatible with the requirements of the Treaty and secondary law; and if it avoids any form of discrimination, direct or indirect, in regard to imports from other Member States or any form of protection of domestic products.

This jurisprudence-based exception extends to products which are "simi-   **9–029** lar" within the meaning of Article 90 EC.

The Court's emphasis on the absence of any discrimination, direct or   **9–030** indirect, of imported produce, or any form of protection of domestic products, is its guarantee against abuse. It is noteworthy that in recent jurisprudence, a strict reading of the non-discrimination requirement, with particular emphasis on the need for a total absence of even *de facto* discrimination, in effect makes the ECJ's concession in Article 90 rather hollow, in particular for environmental taxes.[21]

Whatever the impact of the ECJ's strict approach of the non-discrimination   **9–031** requirement, this example of judicial activism remains in stark contrast to a similar debate in the WTO/GATT, namely that of "like products". The 1992 Panel on *US Alcoholic and Malt Beverages*[22] held the view that GATT Article III should not prevent members from differentiating between different product categories for policy purposes unrelated to the protection of domestic production. This led the panel to conclude that in determining the likeness of two products subject to different treatment, it is necessary, within the meaning of Article III, to consider whether such product differentiation is made so as to afford protection to domestic production.

This Panel's approach of the issue mirrors the view of the ECJ under   **9–032** Article 90 EC, which allows fiscal differentiation, where there is no discrimination or protectionism. It was also adopted by the 1994 unadopted Panel on *US—Taxes on Automobiles*,[23] but rejected by the WTO Panel on *Japan—*

---

[21] See the author's analysis "Greening the EC's State Aid and Tax regimes', *European Competition Law Review*, 2000, pp.294–314.
[22] Report of Panel on United States—Measures affecting alcoholic and malt beverages, BISD 39S/206 (1992), at 5.25.
[23] Report of Panel on United States—Taxes on automobiles, (1994, unadopted), at 5.10, reprinted in 33 ILM (1994), 1399.

Taxes on Alcoholic Beverages[24] and by the practice of the WTO Appellate Body.

9–033   The blow dealt by the AB's rejection of this like products approach to environmental regulation in particular, is considerable. The "aims and effect"approach of the like products issue could have opened the door for product distinction based on *inter alia* non-incorporated PPMs, but has now very clearly been rejected, based on the AB's wish to adhere strictly to textual interpretations. It would seem that by sticking to a legalistic interpretation of the GATT and other WTO Agreements, the AB wishes to protect itself from charges of over-zealous judicial interference.

9–034   The like product issue is not the only area where judicial activism is possible in the GATT/WTO. The renewed emphasis on the Headnote of GATT's Article XX in particular, could well increase the role of the dispute settlement panels, and lead them from a purely textual interpretation of the Agreement, to a more teleological approach. The Appellate Body report in *Shrimp/Turtle* has often been quoted for its "evolutionary" approach (it stated in particular that the interpretation of the term "exhaustible natural resources" is not static but evolutionary); however, it is as yet unclear whether this one occurrence of the term indicates a trend in the Body's line of reasoning.[25]

9–035   For instance, the inclusion of the element "arbitrary" in the Headnote, could imply some Panel discretion in reviewing the national measures concerned. The test of arbitrariness could be read as including a *de facto* proportionality test of the type sometimes advocated for the ECJ. In such a reading, the severity of the impact of the measure on trade flows, would be contrasted with the environmental benefit sought.[26] However, the AB's application of the Headnote in *Shrimp Turtle*, indicates that it prefers to take the procedural approach, rather than to assess the contents of a particular measure.

9–036   Deeper integration of trade and environment interests could to some extent be realised through dispute settlement. This therefore requires judicial activism. Is the WTO dispute settlement mechanism prepared to take up such a role, and if it is, should it play such a role?

9–037   A variety of panels, as well as the AB, have added an "environment obiter" to their conclusions in environment-related disputes.

9–038   The first *Tuna-Dolphin* panel set the scene. It reasoned that "if the contracting parties were to permit import restrictions in response to differences in environmental policies under the General Agreement, they would need to impose limits on the range of policy differences justifying such responses and to develop criteria to prevent abuse. If the contracting parties were to decide to permit trade measures of this type in particular circumstances it would therefore be preferable for them to do so not by interpreting Article XX, but by amending or supplementing the provisions of the General Agreement or

---

[24] Report of Panel on Japan—Taxes on alcoholic beverages, WT/DS8-10-11/R (1996).
[25] Neither is it always received enthusiastically; see e.g. A.E. Appleton, "*Shrimp/Turtle*: Untangling the nets', *Journal of International Economic Law*, 1999, (477–496) 481–482.
[26] See J.H. Mathis, "Trade Related Environmental Measures in the GATT", *Legal Issues of European Integration*, 1991, (37–67) 49.

waiving obligations thereunder. Such an approach would enable the contracting parties to impose such limits and develop such criteria."[27]

This panel clearly did not consider it the panels' responsibility to force a breakthrough. It points to the main advantage of a positive intervention by the WTO Members (at that time the GATT Contracting Parties), namely that they would enjoy the kind of authority needed to qualify the integration of environmental concerns in the GATT, through providing for terms and conditions.　　　　　　　　　　　　　　　　　　　　　　　　**9–039**

One understandable concern with judicial activism in the WTO, is the "slippery slope" argument.[28] If the WTO dispute settlement mechanism were to take a proactive stance in the trade and environment issue, this could have ramifications, for instance, for the debate on social clauses.　　**9–040**

Thus, even if the GATT may be able to cope with an important part of the trade and environment issues through the normal application of non-discrimination rules, so much so that Article XX need not even be invoked,[29] extending GATT rules and concepts beyond product characteristics "might open the risk of GATT allowing potential import restrictions based on thousands of societal and economic characteristics of the exporting" and indeed the importing nation. In other words, the argument goes that after decades of trade liberalisation, states would be allowed to once again retire into national values.　　　　　　　　　　　　　　　　　　　　　　　　**9–041**

Thus, the accommodation of environmental values into GATT, is to some extent possible through the application and interpretation of the existing rules, in other words, at the initiative of the panels and the AB. Nevertheless, a direct intervention of the WTO members, through an interpretative decision, authoritative statement or otherwise, would seem necessary in order not to subject international trade to a floodgate of protectionism. However, even after such intervention, the role of the panels and of the AB will remain crucial, as no such general statement, waiver, or other type of intervention, will be able to cope with all ins and outs of further tensions.　　**9–042**

For the moment, however, WTO members are leaving a "policy vacuum that the DSB is now having to fill on a case-by-case basis."[30] Indeed, the Committee on Trade and Environment, which would seem to be the natural forum for such move, has so far failed to draft a set of principles on which all delegates agree, let alone having these principles somehow accepted by the General Council of the WTO.　　　　　　　　　　　　　　　　　**9–043**

---

[27] Report of Panel on United States – Restrictions on imports of tuna (unadopted), reproduced in 30 ILM 1594 (1991), at 6.3.

[28] For example. the "difficulty of a quasi 'judicial' body consisting of three experts making an interpretation which could have extensive ramifications (by the operation of informal precedent and analogy) beyond the specific environmental cases.": J. Jackson, "Greening the GATT: Trade rules and environmental policy', in J. Cameron, P. Demaret, and D. Geradin, (eds.), *Trade and the Environment: The Search for Balance*, London, Cameron May, 1994, (pp.39–51) p.43 (prior to the installation of the WTO's DSB).

[29] J. Jackson, "Greening the Gatt: Trade rules and environmental policy', in J. Cameron, P, Demaret, and D. Geradin, (eds.), *Trade and the Environment: The Search for Balance*, London, Cameron May, 1994, (pp. 39–51) pp. 43–44.

[30] J. Cameron, and K. Campbell, "Challenging the boundaries of the DSU through trade and environment disputes", *in idem* (eds.), *Dispute Resolution in the World Trade Organisation*, London, Cameron May, 1998, (pp.204–231) pp. 204.

4.2 A victim of its own success

9–044   Certain features of the WTO dispute settlement mechanism attract environment-related disputes. Even if a conflict includes States which are all Parties
to a MEA, for instance, they still seem to prefer taking recourse to the WTO
dispute settlement system.[31] Outside the MEA context, one alternative would
be the International Court of Justice, which has created a special chamber for
international environmental disputes in 1993.

9–045   The WTO dispute settlement presents considerable attractions to quar-
relling states which are well reported.[32] First, the WTO Agreements, including GATT 1994, result in a comprehensive set of altogether rather clear rules.
Most MEAs by contrast lay down framework obligations only, the precise
content of which is moulded during Conferences of the Parties. The framework character of such MEAs has become particularly prevalent in the
treaties that arose out of the 1992 Rio process. Furthermore and crucially,
WTO dispute settlement proceedings are fast, subject to a clear set of rules,
and enforceable. Although sometimes criticised by politicians, they are
graced with an aura of effectiveness, including the loyalty of the world's
largest trading nations. Moreover, through the working of public international law, WTO dispute settlement now takes binding international environmental law more or less fully into account.

9–046   The importance of GATT and WTO abandoning legal isolationism, has
been emphasised throughout the agreements and in dispute settlement practice. WTO dispute settlement panels, and the AB, have emphasised that the
WTO Dispute Settlement Understanding obliges them to apply any binding
rule of public international law between the members. The DSU and the
Vienna Convention on the Law of Treaties, enable WTO members to adhere
to a variety of international environmental agreements, whether bi- or
multilateral. Through this mechanism, MEAs in particular may "serve functions in the context of GATT/WTO law similar to those of secondary EC
environmental law in the context of EC law."[33] GATT Panels in particular
have been accused of deciding conflicts in splendid isolation, using the
GATT as the only parameter and leaving aside all other relevant rules of
public international law. The WTO's DSU underlines the need for the WTO
to operate in the context of the complete set of public international law. This
is in line with the Vienna Convention on the Law of Treaties, and, in particular, its Article 31.

9–047   Crucially, the further elaboration and clarification of international environmental law would serve the settlement of environment-related disputes in
the GATT/WTO. This is, in particular, the case for such unclear principles as
the precautionary principle, or indeed the status of the global commons.

---

[31] See also S. Ohloff, and H.L. Schloemann, "Rational allocation of disputes and 'constitution-
alisation': Forum choice as an issue of competence", in J. Cameron, and K. Campbell, (eds,),
op.cit., n. 30 above, pp.302–329. See also the consideration by James Cameron in "Dispute
settlement and conflicting trade and environment regimes", in A. Fijalkowski., and J. Cameron,
(eds,), *Trade and Environment: Bridging the gap*, London, Cameron May, 1998, (pp.16–26) in
particular p. 18 *et seq.*
[32] See E.-U Petersmann, *op.cit.*, n. 5 *supra*, p. 78 *et seq.*
[33] *Ibidem*, p. 62.

Rebus sic stantibus, states would seem to prefer the WTO as the most   **9–048**
appropriate forum for addressing conflicts with a trade angle, even if other
organisations would have been an option. The WTO in the author's view
should take up this role and give it enhanced credibility, by providing for
appropriate mechanisms to integrate the developments in the other fora.

The "negative harmonisation" pillar of the WTO integration process is   **9–049**
clearly at cruise speed. Dispute settlement such as in *Shrimp/Turtle* helps to
bring consistency in the application of Article XX, for instance. The CTE
has noted that it should act, for instance through issuing a (proposal for) a
statement on the interaction between MEA and WTO rules. Idle words?
Maybe the CTE will once again end up over-analysing, without expressing
policy options. However, one could also give it the benefit of the doubt. After
all, European Community Institutions took 6 years to issue a quasi-
legislative answer to the ECJ's ground-breaking decision in *Cassis de Dijon*
(which brought about the mutual recognition rule).[34]

Only the future will tell whether the international environmental develop-   **9–050**
ments which the WTO should accommodate, will include the creation of
some kind of Global Environmental Organisation. This would at any rate do
away with the criticism that the WTO lacks the expertise needed to judge the
environmental issues at stake. In our view, in the meantime, one has to guarantee at any rate that the GATT/WTO is able to accommodate justifiable
environmental concerns. Moreover, even if one were to create a Global
Environmental Organisation, environmental measures with a clear trade
impact, will arguably stay within the remit of GATT and should not be
moved away from it.

If such a Global Environmental Organisation is created, there will be a   **9–051**
need for a Protocol delineating the respective competencies of the WTO and
the new organisation. It is not inconceivable that the International Court of
Justice would be entrusted with the application of such Protocol, should it be
agreed (some argue that the ICJ itself should continue to deal with Trade and
Environment cases).

5. The room for "positive harmonisation" within the WTO

The introduction of common minimum standards within the WTO frame-   **9–052**
work is not untested. The TRIPS Agreement, for instance, has introduced
comprehensive obligations for the protection of private property rights by
requiring substantive minimum standards for the availability, scope, use and
protection of intellectual property rights.[35] At the time the Uruguay Round

---

[34] The *Cassis de Dijon* Case was decided in 1979; the Commission adopted its Communication
on the "New Approach" in Community harmonisation, focusing on mutual recognition, in 1985
[Commission Communication to the Council in relation to the New Approach under
Community harmonisation, COM(85) 19, and the Council Resolution of May 7, 1985 endorsing
it, [1985] O.J. C136/1.
[35] E.-U. Petersmann, *op.cit.*, n. 5 *supra*, p.94; *see* also M.C.E.J. Bronckers, "The impact of TRIPs:
Intellectual property protection in developing countries', *Common Market Law Review*, 1994,
1245–1281; and W. Lesser, *Institutional mechanisms supporting trade in genetic materials: Issues
under the Biodiversity Convention and GATT/TRIPs*, UNEP Trade and Environment Series #4,
Geneva, 1994.

Agreements were signed, ministers recognised that the TRIPs Agreement could serve as an approach that could also be used to harmonise domestic policy in other areas.

9–053   The WTO Agreement itself, in Article III states that "the WTO shall provide the forum for the negotiations among its members concerning their multilateral trade relations in matters dealt with under the [WTO Agreements]. The WTO may also provide a forum for further negotiations among its members concerning their multilateral trade relations, and a framework for the implementation of the results of these negotiations, as may be decided by the Ministerial Conference." Thus, there is arguably a brief for the WTO to step into a wide range of issues with a trade impact, including the co-ordination of environmental harmonisation efforts.

9–054   Of course, to the extent that harmonisation be realised, this will not *ipso facto* entail that all environmental unilateralism will be ruled out and that no more disputes will arise. For instance, even if international harmonisation will be realised, the SPS Agreement expressly authorises members to maintain higher standards (linked to a set of appropriate conditions). The preamble to the Agreement furthermore expressly notes that harmonisation is to be furthered, without however, requiring members to change their appropriate level of protection of human, animal, or plant life or health.

9–055   Harmonisation techniques are plentiful. The most basic distinction is between "mutual recognition", whereby States accept each other's standards in a given area as being equivalent, as opposed to some form of true "harmonisation", *i.e.* alignment, of the different national standards. Some specific environmental issues are the subject of a growing consensus in international environmental policy. This consensus may well lead to true harmonisation for those few, specific single issues, such as some ozone-depleting substances, and dangerous substances. Harmonisation in these few, well-defines areas, could exceed the procedural and methodological level.[36]

9–056   The improvement of transparency procedures could serve as an interim solution for part of the tensions caused by the development of national, regional and multilateral TREMs.

9–057   It should also be noted that mutual recognition must not only be seen as the only option, failing full harmonisation, but indeed as the most appropriate way forward for a number of environmental issues. For instance, in the context of eco-labelling, the positive role which mutual recognition could play is undisputed. This will require mutual recognition of environmental criteria, certification agencies, evaluation and auditing procedures. Work is underway in a variety of international organisations, to broker mutual recognition. True harmonisation of the eco-label criteria themselves, is not always the preferred option, given the differing national conditions and priorities.

9–058   International efforts to streamline eco-labels could serve as a practice area for the wider issue of harmonisation. What role could international harmonisation realistically be expected to play?[37] Ideally, harmonisation should

---

[36] Along those lines, see also A.E. Appleton, *op.cit.*, n. 25 *supra*, p.24.
[37] See *inter alia* the revealing study by M. Lehtonen, *Criteria in environmental labelling: A comparative analysis of environmental criteria in selected labelling schemes*, UNEP Series on Environment and Trade, No.13, 1997.

tackle the very diversity in national eco-labelling schemes and develop international eco-labels. However, environmental and geographic conditions of states differ to such extent, that the transposition of national eco-labelling schemes to a variety of states might damage the environment more than it would protect it. Therefore, apart from a number of key commodities such as timber and timber products, the use of and the potential for harmonisation and mutual recognition of the *criteria* and *methodologies* used to award eco-labels is greater. In this context, there is a good argument to be made that one should not over-emphasise the room for international harmonisation of LCAs themselves, precisely because the characteristics of various eco systems ought to be reflected in the very LCAs.[38] Again, the focus should be on procedural and methodological harmonisation.

It is clear that if positive harmonisation is to form part of solving the Trade and Environment debate at the GATT/WTO level, it will *not* be realised by the WTO itself. Rather should the WTO take proper account of the developments in other international fora, including UNEP, the ISO, the FAO, etc. The provisions of the TBT Agreement could in this respect serve as an example. The creation of one global super-environmental forum, where the gradual co-ordination and harmonisation of environmental policies would take place, is neither feasible, nor warranted. A realistic alternative is the establishment of a set of international agreements, for specific environmental topics. The co-ordination between these would be ensured by a set of common environmental norms.[39]

9–059

6. Taking EMAS and ISO 14401 as an example

Reconciling key differences between the EC's eco-management scheme, and the International Standardisation Organisation's (ISO) 14000 series of environmental standards, may serve as a good example of the work ahead. From the outset, it should be emphasised that in this instance, the EC and ISO did not sit down to try and hammer out a common scheme which both parties could agree on. Rather did the Commission, in the face of little interest in the European scheme, do its utmost to realise a link between the two schemes, without compromising the core contents of the European version.

9–060

Regulation 1836/93 of June 29, 1993, the "EMAS Regulation", entered into force on April 10, 1995.[40] The system is voluntary. It relies on consumer and peer pressure to expand its popularity. State intervention is however not absent. It is the Community legislator which has drafted the criteria which lead to EMAS recognition. Member States are to set up the necessary certification bodies which verify compliance with the criteria.

9–061

Verification under EMAS did not run smoothly. The installation of the national certification bodies took its time. The scheme also experiences heavy competition from existing national schemes, and from initiatives within ISO.

9–062

---

[38] See S. Shaltegger, "Economics of Life Cycle Assessment: Inefficiency of the present approach", *Business Strategy and the Environment*, 1997, Vol. 6, pp.1–8.
[39] H. Verbruggen, and O. Kuik, "Environmental standards in international trade", in P. Van Dijck, and G. Faber, (eds.), *Challenges to the New World Trade Organisation*, The Hague, Kluwer, 1996, (pp.265–290) pp.274.
[40] [1993] O.J. L168.

6.1 The main differences between EMAS and ISO 14001

9–063   The main differences between EMAS and ISO 14001, concern the management issues which are to be considered when drafting the environmental
analysis of a given location, and when setting the guidelines for the environmental management thereof; the identification, under EMAS, of the continuous improvement of the environmental performance of the location, as one
of the central obligations; the clear obligation under EMAS to draft a new
analysis for new projects; Regulation 1836/93 provides for third-party verification, whilst ISO 14001 defines the completion and the communication of
the environmental audit as a responsibility for the organisation itself; and
publication of the audit and of the results of the environmental analysis are
crucial under EMAS (ISO 14001 merely obliges companies to "consider"
publication).

6.2 Ensuring compatibility

9–064   Given that a lot of firms preferred not to go through two certification
processes, and that the global activities of most involved made them opt for
ISO rather than EMAS, the Commission had to find a way to link the two,
without compromising EMAS' specificities. It eventually legislated so as to
render the two schemes partially compatible. The main Decision enumerates
those EMAS requirements which correspond to equivalent ISO 14001 provisions (Decision 97/265, [1997] O.J. L140/37). This allows EMAS verification
bodies to concentrate on those issues which are not covered by ISO 14001.
The second Decision concerns the audit procedure of ISO 14010, 14011 and
14012 (Decision 97/264, [1997] O.J. L104/35). Where ISO accreditation has
been given through any of three recognised procedures, the site concerned
meets the EMAS audit requirements. The only exception to this equivalency,
is the frequency with which the audit is to be performed. EMAS accreditation bodies are to ensure that the internal audit is completed at least once
every three years, as required by EMAS.

9–065   The Commission has also issued a guidance which is to help the accreditation bodies to judge whether a site which has already been registered under
ISO 14001, meets the requirements of EMAS [Commission of the European
Communities, July 1, 1997: Community eco-management and audit
scheme—EMAS Guidance to Verifiers where a certificate of compliance to
ISO14001/EN already exists for the site to be verified]. The attention of these
bodies should focus on the environmental audit, and on the public statement.

9–066   CEN, the European standardisation body, was also kept under pressure by
the national standardisation bodies. Some of them already certified under
the ISO standard even before this was formally approved. Most of the
enquiries from national bodies to CEN, concerned the equivalence between
national standards and ISO 14001, and between EMAS and ISO 14001. For
some time, it looked as though CEN might have voted against the ISO standard, within the international organisation. Eventually, however, CEN
agreed with ISO 14001, in September 1996. A CEN "Comparison Document"
was issued, which includes a table pointing at the various differences between
ISO 14001 and EMAS. A Report was approved by the Governing Board of

CEN, the so-called "bridging document". This document is to help accreditation bodies.

By way of conclusion, it is noteworthy that the "solution" in the case of the differing eco-management systems, was for the "less successful" party to accept the equivalence with its standards of the other's regime, albeit within certain limits. Commercial pressure was very much a driving factor in this case. Of course, when it comes to more hard core environmental regulations, States/regional groupings may be less inclined to "give in" in this way. **9–067**

7. The role of industry–corporate good governance and voluntary agreements

Companies' internal organisation is the subject of a great deal of myth, which we shall not aim to unravel here. Suffice to say that companies do of course have to operate within the regulatory constraints of the states in which they operate and that it would seem fair to say that mainstream business is not in a position to mould environmental law to its specific needs. **9–068**

Industry and trade associations have nevertheless been identified as an ally in tackling some of the most pressing environmental concerns. **9–069**

Voluntary agreements are one of the means which are perceived as offering great potential in addressing environmental concerns. Both in the United States, and in the EU, their appeal and modes of operation are being pondered, and, whilst it is as yet uncertain whether these agreements may yield the benefits that were expected from them in the early nineties, they nevertheless would seem to harbour good prospects for a limited number of sectors. Crucially, the effectiveness of voluntary agreements requires consolidated partners on both sides. In the EU, it is the Commission which negotiates these agreements (of which they are very few examples to date, at least of EU-wide agreements), acting upon a mandate by the Council. Member States constantly look over the Commission's shoulder and no such agreement receives the green light unless Member States agree. **9–070**

In the EC, the use of voluntary agreements forms the subject of a Commissions Communication[41] which is cautiously optimistic as to the use of such agreements at the national policy level, but much less so with respect to their use at the Community level. Generally, comparing voluntary agreements with regulatory action has to be done with caution. One has a tendency to over-simplify and/or over-idealise both. The advantages of the actual regulatory system are rarely as good as those of the model. Likewise, of course, for voluntary agreements. **9–071**

Industry and some academics have opposed the preponderant reliance of the EC's environmental policy on standard regulatory action, claiming that one cannot improve our environment if one of the principal actors, industry, does not go along voluntarily. Looking at the policy documents issued by the Commission, and, exception made arguably for the waste sector, at its reluctance to even consider letting the Member States implement EC environmental legislation via voluntary agreements, it is clear that the EU institutions do not put such agreements forward as a major tool of environmental **9–072**

---

[41] COM (96) 561, [1996] O.J. L333/69.

policy in the EU. The Council is at most lukewarm towards the use of agreements in most sectors; the EP is outrightly hostile.

9–073   From looking at the policy documents of the European Commission and the Council of Ministers, there are strong indications that the EC policy on voluntary agreements has not met with plenty of enthusiasm. First and foremost, the 1996 Communication does not indicate any kind of rhetoric *pro* such agreements.

9–074   Furthermore, within the EC's legal framework, there are a number of pitfalls, legal obstacles obstructing the widespread use of voluntary agreements both at the national and at the EC level. For agreements at the national level, these can first of all not be used to implement Community legislation, where that legislation confers rights and obligations upon individuals and the use of voluntary agreements as an implementation measure has not been specifically authorised. Furthermore, Articles 81 (competition), 87 (State Aid) and 28–30 (free movement of goods) impose a number of limitations to such agreements, requiring the input of specialised lawyers to check against EC compatibility. For agreements at the EC level, the industry requires EC representativeness before the Commission will be prepared to sit down with it and start negotiations. The subsidiarity principle could harbour further limitations for the future.

9–075   In summary, it would seem unlikely that EU-wide voluntary agreements will become widespread in future. On the other hand, industry's participation in shaping EC environmental policy is very considerable and arguably counters many of the disadvantages of classic regulation.[42] The Commission and Member States have made it a top priority to engage industry in close cooperation in the development of environmental standards.

9–076   At the international level, industry's influence is mostly felt via briefings and lobbying of national representatives. However, at key international conferences, such as in the area of climate change, delegations of key industry actors do play a direct role themselves in the negotiating process. This has raised the issue of representativeness, not just as to whether environmental interests are equally represented, but also as to whether the "global" industry necessarily reflects the interests of industry as a whole (in particular SMEs).

9–077   With respect to corporate good governance, the current amount of initiatives is unprecedented. One of the most visible efforts is being made within the framework of the OECD. The OECD guidelines for multinational enterprises, were recently updated. They include an environmental chapter (which was inserted in 1991), and issue a set of minimum corporate governance standards. The overall emphasis of such approaches is not necessarily altruistic. For instance, the Advisory Group on Corporate Governance considers that improved corporate governance is vital for the survival and prosperity of corporations, since it allows them to be more competitive in their endeavour to achieve access to global capital and product markets.[43] If there is indeed a

---

[42] The increasing involvement of Europe's industry in moulding actual environmental legislation, raises the important question of whether the environmental and consumer lobby is involved to a similar degree.
[43] A. Dignam, and M. Galanis, "Governing the world: The development of the OECD's corporate governance principles", *European Business Law Review*, 1999, (396–407) 396.

synergy between corporate good governance and commercial success, in other words, if it pays to produce environmentally-friendly (even where it does not produce direct cost benefits), and to promote labour standards, then these would truly be areas where trade/environment—trade/labour standards, etc. would be mutually supportive. However, both among economists and political activists, this is subject to debate.

8. Conclusion

It is very much this author's view that blaming the Trade and Environment conundrum on the lack of room within the GATT/WTO for environmental considerations, is all too easy ànd wrong. Much of the current malaise is caused by the lack of unity among the international environmental community when it comes to dealing with some of the even most pressing environmental problems. This is not to be understood as an accusation, but rather as an observation. **9–078**

Thus the management of states' differing environmental regulations is of utmost importance. This will have to be tackled by some degree of harmonisation, whether via the principle of mutual recognition, or some degree of "true" harmonisation. It is the author's view that, apart from the issue of the global commons (the definition of which is as yet unclear), national sovereignty and international co-operation based on the recognition of each other's sovereignty, remains the best possible adjudicator for dealing with environmental disputes. This in effect means that unilateral environmental activities to protect the environment outside one's territory, should be rejected. **9–079**

CHAPTER 10

THE RISE AND FALL OF THE MULTILATERAL AGREEMENT ON INVESTMENT: LESSONS FOR THE REGULATION OF INTERNATIONAL BUSINESS

PETER T. MUCHLINSKI[1]

10–001   Clive Schmitthoff was a scholar of immense range within the field of commercial law. Among his many achievements he is recognised, perhaps above all, as a pioneer in the study of international trade law. However, he also numbers among the earliest legal writers on questions relating to the regulation of multinational enterprises (MNEs).[2] Indeed, he was among the first to see the law relating to international trade and foreign investment law as two parts of a single continuum.[3] It is, therefore, fitting that a symposium on law

---

[1] Professor of law and International Business, Kent Law School, University of Kent and Canterbury. Formerly Drapers Professor of Law, Queen Mary, University of London.

[2] See, for example, *Schmitthoff's Export Trade* (London, Stevens, 9th ed., 1990, 10th ed., 2000,). part Two; "Multinationals in Court" [1972] JBL 103; "The Multinational Enterprise in the United Kingdom" in H.R. Hahlo, J. Graham South and Richard W. Wright (Eds) *Nationalism and the Multinational Enterprise* (Leiden, Sijthoff, 1977) chap. 4; "The Wholly Owned and Controlled Subsidiary" [1978] JBL 218.

[3] Foreign direct investment by MNEs can be seen as an alternative to export sales by such firms in the supply of an overseas market. Equally about one third of all international sales transactions are now carried out between affiliates of the same multinational group. See generally

and trade named for Professor Schmitthoff should also contain within it a dimension concerned with the regulation of MNEs. Accordingly, it is the aim of the present paper to offer a contribution that addresses some of the main contemporary issues in this area. These have become particularly prominent in recent times at the multilateral level, with the rise and fall of the draft Multilateral Agreement on Investment (MAI), negotiated unsuccessfully under the auspices of the OECD, and with the opposition to the adoption of multilateral investment rules on the part of the developing countries and civil society groups at the WTO Seattle Ministerial in November 1999.[4] Despite the failure of the Seattle Ministerial, the British Government and the European Commission continue to favour the adoption of multilateral investment rules by the WTO, as part of a comprehensive round of negotiations that would not only consider trade and investment but also include competition policy, government purchasing, industrial tariffs, labour rights and the environment.[5] However, even if investment does not appear on any future negotiating agenda, the issues raised by the MAI will continue to influence developments in bilateral and regional investment negotiations. Therefore, an understanding of its shortcomings is useful in a more general context.

In the course of the conference on which this volume is based, certain central themes had emerged. These concerned, first, the harmonisation of private law through international agreements; secondly, how proper institutions for the regulation of international business could be built, so that they could act as "human" institutions that have a relevance and sensitivity to the concerns of all stakeholders in the global economy and not only to narrow commercial and corporate interests; thirdly, the rise of the WTO as a new institution and the direction in which it should be developing; and, finally, the continued significance of the conflict of principles between national sovereignty and the transfer of regulatory powers to international economic institutions. These themes emerged mainly in relation to discussions concerning the regulation/deregulation of international trade, as is reflected in other papers in this volume. However, it would be wrong to assume that they are confined to this sphere of international business regulation. The field of foreign direct investment (FDI) regulation encounters similar issues, as the present paper hopes to demonstrate. The story of the rise and fall of the MAI is one in which all of the above–mentioned themes have played a greater or lesser part. Each theme will now be considered in turn.

10–002

1. Harmonisation of private law

This theme is the one in which the divergence between trade and investment is the greatest. The majority of international trade agreements deal with the

10–003

J.H.Dunning *Multinational Enterprises and the Global Economy* (London, Addison-Wesley, 1993) Chapters 2, 3 and 14; UNCTAD *World Investment Report 1996* Part Two.

[4] On which see John Vidal "secret world of WTO deal makers" *The Guardian* December 3, 1999 pp.1–2.

[5] See Clare Short "Lifting One Billion People out of Poverty: The Role of Trade and Investment" a speech given at UNCTAD X Bangkok, February 16, 2000 (DFID); EC Commission "EC Approach to Trade and Investment" April 2000, http://www.europa.eu.int/comm/trade/miti/invest_en.htm.

harmonisation of private contractual rules so as to put in place a genuinely transnational specialised private law by which trade transactions can be governed. This may occur through the adoption of existing customs and practices, that may already be enshrined in standard form contracts, or through the development of new norms.[6] This is not an aim shared by International Investment Agreements (IIAs). Such treaties do not seek to harmonise private law relationships. Their focus is on the harmonisation of standards of treatment for foreign investors and their investments and on the creation of an international legal obligation on the part of the contracting states to pay heed to those standards in the future development of national regulation. IIAs are concerned, therefore, more with public regulatory law than with private law.

10–004   On the other hand, there is a broader similarity between trade agreements and IIAs in that, through the creation of a more uniform and predictable legal order for the conduct of international business, both types of agreements seek to reduce transaction costs for business. In this sense both private and public law regimes may require a degree of harmonisation across national legal systems. Furthermore, it would be wrong to assume that all international trade agreements deal with private law issues alone. A public law element in the field of international trade regulation clearly arises from, for example, the GATT, the General Agreement on Trade in Services or the North American Free Trade Agreement (NAFTA). Indeed, the regulation of international trade by such agreements materially affects the conduct of FDI, given the close economic relationship between these forms of international business activity. Thus, while the specific subject matter of harmonisation agreements in international trade and in IIAs may not coincide, they do form complementary parts of an integrated system for the effective regulation of international business, a phenomenon that straddles private law and public law, contract and corporation. The MAI would have contributed to this type of harmonisation if it had been adopted. This remains a significant reason why the idea of a future multilateral agreement on investment has not been laid to rest.

2. Development of "human" international economic institutions

10–005   This theme embodies a major issue underlying the story of the MAI. The building of an institutional system for the harmonious regulation of FDI has proved to be highly problematic. The failure of the MAI is only the latest episode in a much longer process. Demands for international business protection, and also for its regulation in the public interest, are far older than might be imagined.[7] The starting point for discussion is the concept of

---

[6] See Roy Goode "Usage and its Reception in Transnational Commercial Law" 46 ICLQ 1 (1997); P.T. Muchlinski "Global Bukowina" Examined: Viewing the Multinational Enterprise as a Transnational Law-making Community" in Gunther Teubner (ed.) *Global Law Without a State* (Aldershot, Dartmouth Publishing Company, 1997) p.79 at pp. 86–87, John Braithwaite and Peter Drahos *Global Business Regulation* (Cambridge, Cambridge University Press, 2000) chap. 7.
[7] See further P.T. Muchlinski "A Brief History of Regulation" in Sol Picciotto and Ruth Mayne (eds.) *Regulating International Business: Beyond Liberalisation* (London, Macmillan Press/Oxfam, 1999) p. 47.

international minimum standards of treatment for aliens and their property, developed in the nineteenth century by the major Western European powers and the United States.[8] Two principles in particular stand out: first, the property of foreigners could not be taken without due process of law and without prompt, full and effective compensation; secondly, contractual relations entered into between host states and private foreign investors were to be accorded the utmost respect, requiring the preservation of the bargain even where its terms proved to be disadvantageous to the host state.

These principles were challenged by a number of political and associated legal developments. Thus, the independence movement in Latin America in the nineteenth century gave rise to the Calvo doctrine. This influenced Latin American resistance to international minimum standards in the late nineteenth and much of the twentieth centuries, on the basis that foreign investors were entitled to treatment no better than that accorded to domestic investors. Secondly, the rise of socialism and its delegitimation of private property rights helped to undermine the accepted Western views of the sanctity of contract and property. Thirdly, the decolonisation movement in Europe after the First World War and Africa and Asia after the Second World War, led to greater demands for economic self-determination and, with it, a reinforcement of the state's sovereign right to regulate national economic policy within its borders. The result of these challenges was to generate uncertainty as to the content of customary international law in the field of foreign investment. This uncertainty was reinforced in the early 1970s by the demands for greater control over national economic policy made by the developing countries under the New International Economic Order. However, one area has remained certain, in that all states have accepted the right to control the entry and establishment of foreign investors into the territory of the receiving state unless the latter is bound by treaty to accord such rights to investors.[9]

                                     10–006

Amid such growing uncertainty attempts have been made, since the late 1920s to develop an agreed international code for the regulation of foreign investor/host state relations.[10] These can be divided between attempts to conclude a binding international investor protection convention, and attempts to reconcile the interests of investors for protection and the interests of states to control investors in the national interest.

                                     10–007

In the first category, there were numerous unsuccessful initiatives undertaken by the League of Nations between 1929 and 1930. However, the most influential initiative came from private sector interests in the United Kingdom and Germany which led, in 1959, to the conclusion of the "Abs-Shawcross" draft convention. This convention was taken up by the then Organisation for European Economic Cooperation (OEEC now OECD) for consideration. It led to the OECD Draft Convention on the Protection of

                                     10–008

---

[8] See C. Lipson *Standing Guard: Protecting Foreign Capital in the Nineteenth and Twentieth Centuries* (Berkeley, University of California Press, 1985).
[9] See further UNCTAD *Admission and Establishment* UNCTAD Series on issues in international investment agreements (New York and Geneva, United Nations, 1999) pp. 7–14.
[10] For examples see Muchlinski *op.cit.* n. 7 *supra* or P.T. Muchlinski *Multinational Enterprises and the Law* (Oxford, Blackwell Publishers, 1999, Revised Paperback Edition) pp. 573–75.

Foreign Property of 1962.[11] However, this draft was never adopted, due to opposition from the less developed South European member countries. In 1967 the Council of the OECD, by a resolution adopted on October 12, 1967, commended the draft convention to Member States as a model for bilateral investment protection treaties and as a basis for ensuring the observance of the principles of international law which it contained. Such bilateral treaties—of which there are in excess of 1,300—have been highly influential in the development of investor protection standards, and may be regarded as a significant source of such standards for the MAI.[12] Alongside the abortive attempt to adopt the Convention, the OECD also initiated a policy on the progressive liberalisation of capital flows under the Codes of Liberalisation of Capital Movements and Current Invisible Operations of 1961.[13] These instruments committed the members to the progressive removal of barriers to the conduct of cross-border capital transactions as specified in the Liberalisation Lists appended to each Code. Of particular importance to the future development of the MAI was the introduction, in 1984, of a right of establishment into the Code on Capital Movements.[14] This was based on a prohibition against the maintenance or introduction of regulations or practices in relation to the granting of licences, concessions or similar authorisations, including conditions or requirements attached to such authorisations, which would affect the operations of enterprises by raising special barriers or limitations with respect to non-resident as compared to resident investors, and which had the intent or effect of preventing or significantly impeding inward direct investment by non-residents.

10–009   More recent developments that have also played a part in providing sources for MAI provisions include the NAFTA, which exemplifies the North American model of investor promotion and protection, with its distinctive feature of including pre-entry as well as post-entry protection for foreign investors, the 1994 Energy Charter Treaty (ECT), an experiment in multilateral standard setting for trade and investment in a specific industrial sector and the 1994 WTO Agreements dealing with investment related issues, namely, the General Agreement on Trade in Services (GATS), the Agreement on Trade Related Aspects of Intellectual Property Rights (TRIPs) and the agreement on Trade Related Investment Measures (TRIMs). In addition, there have been some notable institutional developments aimed at furthering the protection of investors adopted under the auspices of the World Bank. These include the 1965 Washington Convention on the Settlement of Investment Disputes Between States and Nationals of Other States, which provided a model for the dispute settlement provisions of the MAI, and the 1985 Multilateral Investment Guarantee Agency Convention.

10–010   In the second category, the most significant historical example is the

---

[11] 1-2 ILM 241 (1962–63).

[12] See further UNCTAD *Bilateral Investment Treaties in the Mid-1990s* (New York and Geneva, United Nations, 1998).

[13] Code on the Liberalisation of Current Invisible Operations OECD/C(61)95; Code on the Liberalisation of Capital Movements OECD/C(61)96, periodically re-issued with updated country schedules.

[14] *ibid.* Annex A.

Charter of the International Trade Organisation, Havana, Cuba, of March 24, 1948.[15] The Charter contained a number of provisions relevant to the regulation of foreign investment by corporations, including proposals for the control of restrictive business practices, provisions protecting the security of foreign investments and an assertion of the right of capital importing states to control the conditions of entry and establishment for inward investment. This caused widespread opposition to the Havana Charter among business interests and led to its demise when the United States and other signatory states did not ratify it.[16]

More recently, in the 1970s, numerous negotiations commenced for the adoption of codes of conduct for MNEs. International organisations began to accept the legitimacy of claims by capital-importing states for greater control over the conditions of entry and establishment and over the subsequent conduct of foreign investors within their territory. The balancing of the interests of private foreign investors and those of the host state, first attempted in the abortive Havana Charter, became the basis for these new codes of conduct for MNEs. The most significant initiative was the UN Draft Code of Conduct on Transnational Corporations.[17] It was never adopted. Nonetheless its contents continue to inform the debate on how corporate responsibility issues should be formulated in IIAs.[18] More successful was the ILO initiative which led to the adoption, in 1977 of the ILO Tripartite Declaration of Principles Concerning Multinational Enterprises and Social Policy.[19] Equally, in 1976 the OECD Guidelines for Multinational Enterprises were adopted. These contain the most comprehensive set of responsibilities for MNEs but are not legally binding. They should be read alongside the OECD Declaration on International Investment and Multinational Enterprises which contains references to national treatment and international law. These guidelines have recently been revised.[20] Finally, mention should be made of the 1992 World Bank Guidelines on the Treatment of Foreign Investment. These guidelines are aimed at investor protection but, significantly, they accept the right of host states to control the entry and establishment of foreign investors.[21]   **10–011**

The history of discussions regarding the rights of investors and their protection has raised a number of hitherto unresolved issues concerning multilateral investment rules: should these tend towards investor protection alone, or towards a balance between protection and regulation; should they be binding or voluntary; should investors be offered privileged treatment based   **10–012**

---

[15] The investment related provisions of the Charter are reproduced in UNCTAD *International Investment Instruments: a Compendium Vol.I.* (New York and Geneva, United Nations, 1996) pp.3–13 (hereafter "Compendium").
[16] See Lipson *op.cit.* n. 8 at pp. 86–87.
[17] See UNCTAD *Compendium Vol.I. op.cit.* n. 15 at pp. 161–80.
[18] See for example WTO *1998 Report of the Working Group on the Relationship Between Trade and Investment to the General Council* WTO Doc.WT/WGTI/2 December 8, 1998 especially at pp. 51–62 paras 191–225.
[19] See UNCTAD *Compendium Vol.I. op.cit.* n. 15 at pp. 89–103. See too the ILO *Declaration on Fundamental Principles and Rights at Work* (Geneva, ILO, 1998).
[20] See OECD *Guidelines for Multinational Enterprises* June 27, 2000, http:// www.oecd.org/daf/investment/guidelines/newtext.htm.
[21] See UNCTAD *Compendium Vol.I. op.cit.* n. 15 at pp. 247–255.

on international minimum standards or only the same treatment as national investors? It has been argued that these debates have been overcome by events, in that the contemporary environment is more suited to the successful creation of a new multilateral regime for investor protection, as a result of shifts towards liberalisation, privatisation and the recognition of the utility of inward direct investment by transnational corporations as a source of capital and technology.[22] The MAI is undoubtedly a product of this conviction.[23] According to the Report of the Committee on International Investment and Multinational Enterprises and the Committee on Capital Movements and Invisible Transactions:

> "The MAI would build on the achievements of the present OECD instruments, consolidating and strengthening existing commitments under the Codes of Liberalisation and the 1976 Declaration and Decisions on International Investment and Multinational Enterprises. The aim of the negotiations is to conclude an agreement incorporating rollback, standstill, national treatment and non-discrimination/most favoured nation (MFN) as well as new disciplines to improve market access and to strengthen the basis of mutual confidence between enterprises and states. The liberalization obligations would be complemented by provisions on investment protection. The obligations under the agreement would need to be reinforced by effective dispute settlement procedures ... The agreement would be comprehensive in scope, covering all sectors under a broad definition of investment focusing mainly on [foreign direct investment]. The MAI would aim to raise the level of existing liberalisation based on a "top-down" approach under which the only exceptions permitted are those listed when adhering to the agreement and which are subject to progressive liberalisation."[24]

10–013   Thus, the draft MAI was based on earlier models of binding investor protection standards leading it to be crafted as an investor and investment protection and promotion agreement, similar in type to the first category of agreements and instruments mentioned above. Although the OECD Guidelines for Multinational Enterprises were to be included as a non-binding Annex, thereby offering some indication of what types of obligations MNEs had towards the states in which they operated, this essential quality of the MAI could not be disputed. It would prove to be a major cause of the failure of the negotiations.

10–014   At the outset, significant obstacles to the successful conclusion of such an instrument were identified.[25] Of the many obstacles encountered in the negotiating process the following are worthy of highlighting: the negotiating environment, the contents of the draft MAI and other "deal breakers" that were added to the negotiations as they progressed. These introduce, in turn, aspects of the third and fourth themes identified at the beginning of the paper. Thus the problem of the negotiating environment is linked to the wider issue of the WTO as an emerging regulatory institution. Indeed, the fact that the OECD was chosen over the WTO as the forum for the MAI negotiations

---

[22] See Thomas Waelde, "Requiem for the New International Economic Order: The Rise and Fall of Paradigms in International Economic Law" in N.Al. Nauimi and R. Meese (Eds) *International Legal Issues Arising Under the United Nations Decade of International Law* (The Hague, Kluwer, 1995) p. 1301.

[23] See OECD *Towards Multilateral Investment Rules* (Paris, OECD, 1996) at p. 9. and *ibid.* William Witherill "Towards an International Set of Rules for Investment" at pp.17–30.

[24] *ibid.* at pp.10–11.

[25] See Guy de Jonquieres, "Rocky road to liberalisation" *Financial Times* April 10, 1995 p. 17.

offers significant insights into the perceived problems of using the WTO as a location for the pursuit of multilateral investment rules. Furthermore, the disagreements over the contents of the MAI, and over the other "deal breakers", shed light on how the conflict of principles between national sovereignty and the development of multilateral rules, that aim to constrain such sovereignty, is no nearer resolution than in earlier times.

3. The WTO as an emerging institution and the negotiating environment of the MAI in the OECD

The origins of the OECD negotiations can be traced back to United States initiatives in 1991 which called for the OECD to engage in the discussion of a wider investment instrument. This was supported by the Business and Industry Advisory Committee to the OECD in 1992. The United States wanted the OECD to adopt a "state-of-the-art" investment agreement with high standards of liberalisation, investor protection and dispute settlement procedures.[26] Equally, calls for the institution of negotiations for a multilateral agreement on investment came from the European Commission which, in 1995, argued for the establishment of a "level playing field" for direct investment.[27] The then EU Trade Commissioner, Sir Leon Brittan, also gave weight to such a programme. He favoured a binding code which would be negotiated in, and subsequently administered by, the WTO.[28] The attraction of the WTO was threefold: first, it covered a large number of states, including developing countries; secondly, it possessed a binding dispute settlement procedure that could give the proposed code real legal force and, thirdly, the EU had direct negotiating rights on behalf of its members before that organisation. Notwithstanding EU preferences for the WTO, and the discussion among OECD ministers in 1996 of a possible link between the OECD negotiations and the WTO at some unspecified future time, the MAI negotiations remained centred on the OECD. This may be explained by the fact that there would have been only limited backing for similar negotiations in the WTO. Indeed when the issue was mooted at the 1996 WTO Singapore Ministerial Meeting it was opposed by a group of developing countries led by Egypt, India, Malaysia and Uganda.[29] To counter the inevitable criticism that the OECD based negotiations were unrepresentative, the MAI was envisaged as a free-standing international treaty open to all OECD Members and the European Communities and to accession by non OECD Member countries.[30] Members would have to persuade developing countries to accept the new disciplines and to sign up to the MAI. Thus from the outset the negotiating environment was lacking in a comprehensive and representative body of states. This was somewhat strange

10–015

---

[26] Elisabeth Smythe, "Your place or mine? States, international organizations and the negotiation of investment rules" 7 *Transnational Corporations* pp.85 at p. 101–102 (1998).
[27] EC Commission, "A Level Playing Field for Direct Investment World-Wide" COM(95) 42 final, March 1, 1995.
[28] See "Brittan wants WTO rules for investment" *Financial Times* January 19, 1995, p.4. and Sir Leon Brittan "Investment liberalisation: the next great boost to the world economy" 4 *Transnational Corporations* p. 1. (1995).
[29] See David Henderson, *The MAI Affair: A Story and its Lessons* (London, RIIA, 1999) p. 16.
[30] OECD *op.cit.* n. 23 at p. 11.

given that the main reason for adopting a MAI was to improve market access and investor protection in developing countries, the very group that was not represented by the OECD membership.

10–016   Thus, it may be said that the WTO, as a truly multilateral institution, with members from all geographical and political regions of the world, may be an unruly horse to control. It will not always offer a forum before which support for progressive liberalisation and sovereignty reduction can be guaranteed. This concern lay behind the American preference for the OECD. However, as things turned out, even that organisation, with its overwhelmingly developed market economy membership, could not bring about an investor and investment protection oriented multilateral agreement, given the degree to which national sovereignty would have to be limited to achieve the American objective of "state-of-the-art" protection. To this question we now turn.

4. National sovereignty and international regulation

4.1 The content of the MAI

10–017   The draft MAI consisted of 12 major sections: the general provisions and preamble; scope and application, treatment of investors and investments, investment protection, dispute settlement, exceptions and safeguards, financial services, taxation, country-specific exceptions, relationship with other international agreements, implementation and operation and final provisions.[31] It is not possible to give a detailed analysis of all the outstanding negotiating questions in this paper. Instead, the emphasis will be on the key controversies which remained unresolved during the negotiations, and which may be said to have contributed to their failure. These are: the scope of the definition of "investor" and "investment"; the extension of investor protection to the pre-entry stage and exceptions to this; the nature and content of the non-discrimination standard which lay at the heart of the draft MAI and was expressed through the national treatment and most favoured nation standards; the scope of the prohibition on performance requirements; the applicable rules on expropriation; and the proposed dispute settlement provisions which would have given MNEs direct rights to bring claims against signatory states.

4.1.1 The definition of "investor" and "investment"

10–018   It is usual for an IIA to begin with a scope and definition clause. In this the draft MAI was no different. However, the proposed formulation of the above

---

[31] OECD *Multilateral Agreement on Investment*: Consolidated Text (Final Version, April 24, 1998) DAFFE/MAI/NM (98) rev.1.http://www.oecd.org/daf/cmic/mai/negtext.htm.; OECD *Commentary to the Negotiating Text* (Final Version, April 24, 1998). For analysis of the principal provisions see: A.Fatouros "Towards an international agreement on foreign direct investment? 10 ICSID–FILJ 181 (1995); F. Engering "The Multilateral Investment Agreement" 5 *Transnational Corporations* 147 (1996); Sol Picciotto "A Critical Assessment of the MAI" in Picciotto and Mayne (eds) *op.cit.* n. 7 at p. 82, *ibid.* "Linkages in international investment regulation: the antinomies of the draft Multilateral Agreement on Investment" 19 U.Pa.J.Int'l.Econ.L. 731 (1998); UNCTAD *Lessons From the MAI* UNCTAD Series on issues in international investment agreements (New York and Geneva, United Nations, 1999); S. Canner "The Multilateral Agreement on Investment" 31 Cornell.ILJ. 657 (1998).

terms was extremely wide. Thus "investor" included not only nationals but permanent residents, as well as legal persons or other entities constituted or organised under the applicable law of a Contracting Party. "Investment" was defined in terms of, "every kind of asset owned or controlled, directly or indirectly, by an investor . . ." followed by an illustrative, though not exclusive, list that covered both equity based and contractual assets. These included *inter alia* construction contracts, loans, claims to money or performance, intellectual property rights, concessions and licences and property related contractual rights such as leases or mortgages.[32]

Although there was broad support for an asset based definition, certain **10–019** delegations argued for the exclusion of portfolio investment and others found it difficult to accept an open definition.[33] There was also concern over the extent of coverage given to investments indirectly owned or controlled by investors of a party. Indirect ownership of investments located outside a MAI country by investors from a MAI country would be covered as would investments located in a MAI country owned and controlled by an investor located in a non-MAI country. This approach would permit MNEs to manage their capital flows in a flexible manner utilising their transnational network of affiliates as they saw fit. On the other hand, some delegations favoured a denial of benefits clause which would exclude investors who lacked a substantial business presence in a MAI country from the protection of the Agreement.[34] In the event many issues remained unresolved and text refers to further work being needed in the areas of indirect investment, intellectual property, concessions, public debt and real estate.

4.1.2 Extension to pre-entry protection

The draft MAI would require the progressive liberalisation of rights of entry **10 020** and establishment. This was in line with the policy of the OECD Codes on Liberalisation and followed the precedent set by NAFTA and in bilateral investment treaties (BITs) negotiated by the United States and, more recently, Canada.[35] Historically, states have reacted differently to such proposals. While advocating greater liberalisation for outward investment, many states may prefer to restrict the flow of inward investment for protectionist purposes. Economic unions, such as the EU, may want the right to liberalise faster for internal investors than for investors from outside the economic union.[36] Federal states may encounter internal political objections from

---

[32] MAI Consolidated Text *ibid.* at p. 11.
[33] UNCTAD *Lessons From the MAI, op.cit.* n. 31 at p. 11.
[34] Commentary to the MAI Negotiating Text *op.cit.* n. 30 at pp. 6–7.
[35] See UNCTAD *Admission and Establishment, op.cit.* n. 9 at pp. 23–28. Other regional investment agreements have followed this approach albeit with variations such as transitional periods (see MERCOSUR Decision 11/93 in UNCTAD *Compendium Vol.II.op.cit.* n. 15 at p.513, ASEAN Framework Agreement on the ASEAN Investment Area 1998 see UNCTAD *Compendium Vol.IV.* (New York and Geneva, United Nations, 2000, forthcoming) p. 227) or side agreements (see Energy Charter Treaty Article 10(2)–(4) in UNCTAD *Compendium Vol.II. op.cit.* n. 15 at p. 555).
[36] See further text at n. 66–68 *infra*.

federal sub-divisions to the effect that a MAI could curtail their local competence and discretion in formulating inward investment policy.[37] A similar problem could confront local authority initiatives.[38] Developing countries in particular may prefer to exercise caution in relation to inward investment and thus to retain screening powers on entry, so as to protect indigenous infant industries from excessive competition on the part of powerful MNEs. Indeed most BITs, with the exception of the abovementioned U.S. and Canadian models, follow an investment control approach, based on the right of the receiving state to regulate the entry of foreign investors in accordance with national laws and regulations, and do not contain entry and establishment rights.[39]

10–021   Clearly, rights of entry and establishment would not be accepted without significant exceptions. Many restrictions on the rights of foreign investors may be regarded as entirely legitimate, the most obvious examples being restrictions based on public health, order or morals or on strategic and defence grounds. Indeed the draft MAI contained provisions embodying such general exceptions. In addition, it gave to contracting states the right to enter country-specific exceptions.[40] In the event numerous country-specific exceptions were put forward by states, resulting in what some have called a "swiss cheese" agreement, with more "holes" than the negotiators originally expected. This has been explained on the ground that many exceptions taken by states were mere bargaining counters to be discarded on the gaining of concessions.[41] However, the large number of exceptions may in fact be an effect of the "top-down" approach taken in the MAI.

10–022   The extension of rights of entry and establishment can be achieved in an IIA in one of two basic ways: by stating the right and allowing exceptions thereto—the "top-down" approach favoured in the MAI draft—or by giving states the discretion to open up specific sectors as and when they feel ready to do so—the "bottom-up" approach. This is the approach taken in the GATS in that contracting states are not bound to offer entry and establishment rights to investors from other contracting states.[42] Rather, by Articles XVI and XVII of that Agreement, they are given the discretion to specify which sectors will be subject to market access rights, and the extent to which full national treatment will apply. This approach may be more attractive to states that are hesitant to enter into broad commitments regarding entry and establishment. The "top-down" approach of the MAI, by contrast, places liberalisation of entry conditions at the heart of the agreement, leaving less choice to contracting states. In the event the only sure course of action may

---

[37] Such concerns led one delegation to propose an additional clause ensuring that where a subfederal entity offers more favourable treatment to its investors and investments as compared to that offered by other sub-federal entities the more favourable treatment should be extended to foreign investors and investments under the national treatment standard: see MAI Consolidated Text *op.cit.* n. 31 at p. 129.

[38] See R. Nurick *The MAI: Potential Impacts on Local Economic Development and Poverty Issues in the UK* (Oxfam, March 1998); World Development Movement "The impact of the multilateral agreement on investment on local government in the UK" (1998).

[39] See UNCTAD *Admission and Establishment op.cit.* n. 9 at p. 18.

[40] See MAI *Consolidated Text op.cit.* n. 31 at pp. 77–80 and 90.

[41] See UNCTAD *Lessons From the MAI op.cit.* n. 31 p. 12.

[42] General Agreement on Trade in Services 1994, 33 ILM 44 (1994).

be to lodge extensive general and country-specific exceptions so as to pre-serve existing national regulations, and hence host country discretion, over entry and establishment. The result is often an unwieldy agreement in which the exceptions serve to complicate its scope and interpretation. NAFTA is a case in point.[43] Furthermore, once country-specific exceptions have been made, in the absence of a transitional period within which such exceptions must be removed, the effect of the agreement may be to entrench them, thereby defeating the aim of progressive liberalisation. Even if a transitional period exists, it is quite likely that, in practice, it will be extended where the contracting states do not feel ready to espouse full liberalisation. Indeed, this issue continued to be a matter of discussion with no final agreement being reached on how the MAI would achieve its avowed aim of "rollback" on non-conforming country-specific measures.[44]

In this respect IIAs may be different from international trade agreements. A **10–023** general commitment to market access for goods and services traded across bor-ders offers less of an inroad into national sovereignty than a positive commit-ment to give rights of entry and establishment to foreign investors. The latter involves agreement to a right that permits the entry of aliens onto the territory of the receiving state, not merely goods or services of foreign origin. This has far greater political and social consequences for the receiving country. The latter is therefore likely to seek a preservation of its discretion to control the entry of aliens in the public interest. It is for this reason that the "top-down" approach of the MAI may be harder to sell on a political level than the "bottom-up" approach of the GATS, especially to developing countries, where sensitivity to foreign domination of the economy may be especially great.

4.1.3 Non-discrimination

The non-discrimination provision in the draft MAI concerned both national **10–024** treatment and most-favoured-nation treatment (MFN), which, respectively, would have ensured treatment for foreign investors "no less favourable" than that received by national investors or investors from other countries, whichever was the more favourable to the investor. The most controversial issue was the extension of the non-discrimination standard to rights of entry and establishment. As noted above, this led to considerable time and energy being devoted to the issue of exceptions. Other problems that were not resolved concerned the scope of the non-discrimination standard itself. At the outset it is worth noting that the two aspects of non-discrimination were discussed as a combined standard. This may have led to an overemphasis on national treatment issues, which are inherently more sensitive than issues relating to the MFN standard. In particular, as noted by a recent UNCTAD study on MFN treatment, "exceptions to national treatment are more fre-quent than exceptions to MFN. This reflects the fact that countries find it

---

[43] See M.Gestrin and A.Rugman "The North American Free Trade Agreement and foreign direct investment" 3 *Transnational Corporations* 77 (1994); *ibid.* "The NAFTA investment provi-sions: prototype for multilateral investment rules?" in OECD *Market Access After the Uruguay Round* (Paris, OECD, 1996) p. 63.
[44] See *Commentary on the MAI Negotiating Text* (as of April 24, 1998) p. 60.

more difficult to treat foreign and domestic investors equally than to provide for equal treatment among investors from different home countries. Furthermore, there may be special situations in which a privileged treatment of domestic enterprises can be justified."[45] It may have been better to discuss each standard in a separate provision, so as to ensure that MFN would not be overwhelmed by national treatment issues. Indeed this is the approach of the GATS where MFN is a general obligation under Article II, while national treatment is an optional obligation under Article XVII.

10–025   As regards the content of the non-discrimination standard, two closely related questions had to be answered: first, what were the factual situations in which the standard applied and, secondly, what technique of comparison should be adopted in order to determine when foreign investors or their investments were being discriminated against. As to the first issue, the draft MAI referred to, "establishment, acquisition, expansion, maintenance, use, enjoyment and sale or other disposition of investments"[46] This formulation was considered by several delegations to be a comprehensive one whose terms were designed to cover all activities of investors and their investments for both the pre- and post-establishment phases. Other delegations favoured a closed list of investment activities covered by the non-discrimination standard. Others objected to this approach on the grounds that, while such a list has the advantage of certainty, it could omit elements that were of importance to the investor.[47] A related issue concerned whether or not to include a qualifying phrase "in like circumstances". No agreement was reached on its inclusion. Some delegations thought that national treatment and MFN implicitly provided the comparative context for determining whether a measure unduly treated foreign investors and their investments differently and that the inclusion of the words was unnecessary and open to abuse. Other delegations thought that the comparative context should be indicated, following the practice of the OECD National Treatment Instrument, some BITs and NAFTA.[48] As to the second question, the formulation adopted in the MAI Negotiating Text included the phrase "no less favourable treatment".[49] This opens the possibility for treatment that may be in practice more favourable for foreign, as compared to national, investors and investments, as where, for example, the treatment of national investors falls below international minimum standards.[50] In this light there was discussion as to whether the "same" or "comparable" treatment approach should be used. However, the majority of delegates considered that this would unacceptably weaken the standard of treatment from the investor's viewpoint.[51]

---

[45] UNCTAD *Most-Favoured-Nation Treatment* UNCTAD Series on issues in international investment agreements (New York and Geneva, United Nations, 1999) at p. 31.
[46] MAI Consolidated Text *op.cit*. n. 31 at p. 13.
[47] Commentary to the MAI Negotiating Text *op.cit*. note 44 at p. 11.
[48] *ibid*.
[49] MAI Consolidated Text *op.cit*. n. 31 at p. 13.
[50] See UNCTAD *National Treatment* UNCTAD Series on issues in international investment agreements (New York and Geneva, United Nations, 1999) at p. 37.
[51] Commentary on the MAI Negotiating Text *op.cit*. n. 44 at p. 10.

4.1.4 Performance requirements

The MAI would have made the imposition of performance requirements as **10–026**
a condition of entry and establishment subject to extensive prohibitions. In
particular, it would have prohibited: trade-related requirements dealing with
the ratio of export sales to total sales, domestic content and local purchasing
rules and ratio of local sales to exports; transfer of technology requirements,
except where imposed under competition laws; location of headquarters
requirements; requirements to supply goods or services to a specific region or
the world market exclusively from the host country; local research and development targets; mandatory employment of nationals; establishment of a
joint venture with domestic participation; and minimum and maximum levels of foreign equity participation. Trade related performance requirements
would have been absolutely prohibited, while the other categories could be
allowed where they were linked to advantages granted in connection with an
investment in the territory of the host contracting party. All of these policies
entail a discretion in economic planning that might be used to favour
national investors. Indeed performance requirements can be justified as a
means of ensuring fair competition between MNEs and local firms in the
domestic market, particularly in developing countries.[52] This was one of the
issues picked up by NGOs who feared that the MAI could weaken such regulatory discretions to the disadvantage of the host state. Furthermore, delegations treated the matter with caution given the absolute nature of the
obligations and the complexity of the matters at issue.[53] The controversial
nature of these matters is further emphasised by the fact that the related issue
of incentives was postponed for discussion after the adoption of the MAI.
Had this been included on the agenda, the very right of a sub-national
authority with constitutional powers over investment matters to offer incentives would have been put into question.[54] This would have been politically
impossible to justify especially in countries with powerful sub-national entities such as the United States and Canada.

4.1.5 Provisions on expropriation

The MAI provision on expropriation sought to include the international **10–027**
minimum standards that had become commonplace in BITs. However, its
scope was to prove controversial in that it covered not only direct but indirect takings.[55] This approach could cause significant problems for countries
with strong regulatory regimes as any act of regulation which limits the
capacity of an investment to make profits could be seen as an indirect taking

---

[52] See Picciotto "Linkages in International Investment Regulation" *op.cit.* n. 31 at p. 751.
[53] UNCTAD *Lessons From the MAI op.cit.* n. 31 at p. 16.
[54] *ibid.* p. 17.
[55] According to the Consolidated Text, "A Contracting Party shall not expropriate or nationalise
directly or indirectly an investment in its territory of an investor of another Contracting Party
or take any measure or measures having equivalent effect . . . except for a purpose which is in the
public interest on a non-discriminatory basis . . . in accordance with due process of law . . .
accompanied by payment of prompt, adequate and effective compensation . . . " *op.cit.* n. 31 at
p. 57.

of property. This caused much discussion leading to the proposal that an interpretative note be added to the text explaining that the expropriation provision does not, "establish a new requirement that Parties pay compensation for losses which an investor or investment might incur through regulation, revenue raising and other normal activity in the public interest undertaken by governments."[56]

10–028   On the other hand, the provisions on taxation make clear that the provisions on expropriation will apply to taxation measures that amount to outright or "creeping" expropriation but not if the measure is, "generally within the bounds of internationally recognised tax policies and practices."[57]

4.1.6 Dispute settlement provisions

10–029   These were among the most controversial aspects of the MAI. The draft contained a chapter on dispute settlement covering both state-to-state and investor-state disputes.[58] The latter in particular gave rise to difficulties. It would have granted to foreign investors special rights to challenge national decisions concerning the observance of the substantive provisions of the MAI. This approach to dispute settlement is not new. It has become a standard feature in IIAs. For example, most BITs contain an investor-state dispute settlement provision that usually encourages amicable settlement, with third party settlement, such as arbitration before an international arbitral body, as a last resort. Similar provisions can be found in NAFTA, MERCOSUR and the Energy Charter Treaty.[59] However, the NGOs saw this provision—and similar formulations in other IIAs—as giving foreign investors special privileges enabling them to neutralise legitimate national laws and regulations by claiming before an international tribunal that they violated the protective standards of the IIA. Much was made of the recent case brought by the Ethyl Corporation against Canada under the dispute settlement provisions of NAFTA, where Ethyl claimed that a Canadian law banning the importation into Canada of the gasoline additive MMT, violated its rights as an investor under that agreement. This case was eventually settled in July 1998 with Canada lifting the import ban and paying $13 million to Ethyl.[60] The NGOs saw this case as an example of how the provisions of NAFTA could be used to invalidate a measure based on environmental concerns.[61] Similar objections were made by one delegation, while others voiced

---

[56] See MAI Consolidated Text *op.cit.* n. 31 at p. 144. Significantly this formulation is to be found in the Annex containing the package of proposals for text on environment and labour.

[57] *ibid.* at p. 87.

[58] See MAI Consolidated Text at pp. 63–76.

[59] See UNCTAD *Lessons From the MAI op.cit.* n. 31 at p.19. On investor state dispute settlement generally see P.T. Muchlinski *Multinational Enterprises and the Law op.cit.* n. 10 Chap. 15.

[60] The case is reported in relation to the jurisdictional issues under NAFTA: see 38 ILM 700 (1999).

[61] Another case that has received similar attention concerns the US Metalclad Corporation's claim under NAFTA against Mexico see M. Nolan and D. Lippoldt "Obscure NAFTA Clause Empowers Private Parties" *The National Law Journal* April 6, 1998 p.B8. On the other hand in the NAFTA case of *Robert Azanian and others v. United Mexican States*, ICSID Case No.ARB (AF/97/2) award of November 1, 1999 14 ICSID Review-FILJ 538 (1999), it was held that the NAFTA dispute settlement mechanism must operate within the limits of international law, and

opposition to the extension of the dispute settlement procedure to the pre-establishment phase.[62] Numerous unresolved questions remained after the negotiations had finished including the question of the role of local remedies, the scope of reservations and of the principle of unconditional prior consent to the MAI system.[63] A number of delegations were left feeling that much work was still needed on dispute settlement.

4.2 Other "deal breakers"

The preceding discussion has centred on the main areas of disagreement within topics that could be regarded as part of the conventional content of IIAs. In this section a number of further issues are considered. They all share the common features of going beyond this conventional content and of being highly controversial, but yet incapable of being excluded from the agenda due to the insistence of one or more delegations that had a special interest in the matter. By contrast other issues that could have raised serious controversies, namely, taxation, intellectual property and incentives, were either left out after initial debates or reserved for future discussion.[64]   **10–030**

Four such "deal-breakers" were introduced onto the agenda: in the light of the controversy over the Helms Burton Act, the issue of the extraterritorial application of investment related national laws and of the establishment of international disciplines to deal with the use of confiscated foreign owned property; the regional economic integration organisation (REIO) exception to the non-discrimination standard; the "cultural industries" exception; and labour and environmental standards.   **10–031**

4.2.1 New disciplines on the treatment of illegally confiscated property

In the course of MAI negotiations the U.S. tried to introduce new disciplines concerning the rights of owners of illegally expropriated property to pursue claims against its current owners. This emerged out of the controversy generated by the Helms-Burton Act[65] which sought to recover claims concerning property owned in Cuba by U.S. nationals, taken at the time of the Cuban revolution, and which was now owned by firms from other countries, mainly   **10–032**

---

so a mere breach of contract by the host state could not of itself give rise to a violation of NAFTA in the absence of a further violation of international law. This should prevent the NAFTA mechanism from being used by investors in any but the most serious cases of alleged violations of their rights.

[62] See UNCTAD *Lessons From the MAI op.cit.* n. 31 at p. 19.

[63] See Commentary to the MAI Negotiating Text *op.cit.* n. 44 at pp. 38–9.

[64] Taxation was carved out of the MAI, except in relation to expropriation and transparency commitments, so as to avoid clashes with double taxation agreements; intellectual property discussions were left at the stage that a separate provision excluding the application of the non-discrimination standard beyond the scope of existing commitments in intellectual property conventions would be inserted into the MAI, and incentives would have been discussed after the adoption of the MAI. See MAI Consolidated Text *op.cit.* n. 31 at pp. 87–9, 50–2 and 46–8.

[65] The Cuban Liberty and Democratic Solidarity Act 1996 U.S. Public Law 104–114, March 12, 1996, 35 ILM 357 (1996). Also of significance in generating this debate was the Iran Libya Sanctions Act 1996 U.S. Public Law 104–172, August 5, 1996, 35 ILM 1273 (1996).

Europe, Canada and Mexico. In May 1998 an understanding was reached on these issues between the U.S. and EU leaders, though with significant restrictions as to its scope. In the end two alternative country-specific proposals for new drafts existed, one on conflicting requirements and one on secondary investment boycotts. The first would prevent a Contracting Party from prohibiting outside its territory an investor from another Contracting Party from acting in accordance with that other Contracting Party's laws, regulations or express policies unless these were contrary to international law. The second would prohibit the Contracting Parties from taking measures that impose liability on investors or investments of investors from another Contracting Party, or to prohibit, or impose sanctions for, dealing with investors of another Contracting Party, because of investments an investor of another Contracting Party makes, owns or controls, directly or indirectly, in a third country in accordance with the regulations of such third country.[66]

4.2.2 The REIO Exception

10–032   The non-discrimination provision of the MAI had the potential to create a "free rider" problem. By relying on that provision, MAI contracting states could enjoy the benefits of a regional economic integration organisation (REIO), whose membership consisted of parties to the MAI, without being members of that organization. To deal with this problem, it was proposed by the EU that a REIO exception be included in the MAI.[66] There remained considerable disagreement as to the scope of such a clause at the time negotiations were suspended. Some delegations thought that this proposal struck at the very objectives of the MAI, which included the gaining of market access to REIOs on a par with access by investors from the member countries of such organisations. On the other hand, as the EU had argued, membership of such organisations carried with it additional obligations which non-members did not carry, such as, for example, the acceptance of majority voting, and extended to areas not covered by the MAI, for example recognition of diplomas. To extend the benefits of membership to non-members in such circumstances would be very difficult.[68]

4.2.3 The cultural industries exception

10–033   This exception would preserve the right of a Contracting Party to take any measure to regulate investment of foreign companies, and the conditions of activity of these companies, in the framework of policies designed to preserve and promote cultural and linguistic diversity.[69] This exception was championed by France and Canada, in particular, who feared an "Americanisation" of global media industries. It was strongly opposed by U.S.

---

[66] MAI Consolidated Text *op.cit.* n. 31 at pp. 122–7.
[67] See MAI Consolidated Text op.cit. n. 31 at pp 118–9. See further J.Karl "Multilateral investment agreements and regional economic integration" 5 *Transnational Corporations* p. 19 (1996).
[68] See UNCTAD *Lessons From the MAI op.cit.* n. 31 at pp. 14–15.
[69] See MAI Consolidated Text *op.cit.* n. 31 at p. 128.

media interests. The issues remained unresolved at the time the MAI negotiations were suspended.

4.2.4 Labour and environmental standards

Initially, the MAI was not to have included these matters. However, in response to extensive lobbying by NGOs and trade unions,[70] some general provisions were included in the preamble and an additional labour and environment clause was proposed by the Chairman of the Negotiating Conference in Annex 2 to the Draft Agreement.[71] This concentrated on the need for a balanced relationship between the MAI disciplines and other areas of public policy and on the avoidance of unintended consequences of normal regulatory practices. In particular, it was noted that the inclusion of the "in like circumstances" formulation in the non-discrimination provision would address the problem of *"de facto"* discrimination where a measure, not specifically aimed at foreign investors or investments, would have the practical effect of treating them less favourably as compared to domestic and/or other foreign investors or investments. The principal aim was to ensure that the MAI did not inhibit normal non-discriminatory governmental regulatory activity in these areas. Another aspect of this issue was the proposed inclusion of a "no lowering of standards" clause which would have ensured that countries could not use a lowering of labour environment or health standards as incentives for inward investment.[72] However, the precise content of that clause was never agreed upon and it remained subject to many drafting alternatives.

10–034

5. Analysis: lessons for the future

The problems described above proved fatal to the aim of concluding the MAI. On October 14, 1998 the French Prime Minister, Lionel Jospin, stated that France would take no further part in the negotiations, on the ground that the MAI, as currently formulated, represented an unacceptable threat to national sovereignty.[73] A week later, on October 22, the senior representatives of the OECD Members and the European Commission convened in the Executive Committee of the Special Session of the OECD in Paris. They announced that they would now proceed with further consultations on the controversies that the negotiating process had raised, thereby effectively ending the negotiations on the MAI.[74]

10–035

---

[70] On which see further Henderson *op.cit*. n. 29 at pp. 22, 27–8; Nick Maybey "Defending the Legacy of Rio: The Civil Society Campaign against the MAI" in Picciotto and Mayne (eds) *op.cit*. n. 7 p. 60.
[71] See MAI Consolidated Text *op.cit*. n. 31 at pp. 140–145.
[72] *ibid*. at p. 54.
[73] "France quits investment accord talks" *Financial Times* October 15, 1998 p.5; Henderson *op.cit*. n. 29 at pp. 30–1. For the full debate see Assemblee Nationale, Session Ordinaire de 1998–99, 8eme jour de séance, 18eme séance, 1ere séance du Mardi Octobre 13, 1998, http://www.assemblee–nationale.fr/2/cra/2aa.htm.
[74] OECD News Release Paris, October 23, 1998 "Chairman's Statement Under Secretary of State Stuart Eizenstat (USA) Executive Committee in Special Session". The negotiations were formally ended in a further informal OECD Meeting in December 1998: Henderson *op.cit*. n. 29 p. 32.

10–036   There is much debate on the actual causes of this failure. The political opposition to the Agreement generated by the NGO community undoubtedly made
a significant contribution. However, the principal reason lies in the conception
of the agreement as a pure investor and investment protection instrument. This
made it an anachronism from the start. The MAI was based on fundamental
misconceptions as to the nature of transnational economic interactions in an
era of increased privatisation and de-regulation at the national level. Thus it
started from the false premise that governmental power to control business had
to be curtailed. It lived in a world dominated by old political agendas signified
by the "right/left" axis of Cold War politics, in which the principal concerns of
foreign direct investors were to preserve existing investments in recently
decolonised and/or increasingly politically assertive host countries.

10–037   The new political environment no longer places "right/left" issues of ownership and control at centre stage. Rather there has been a transformation in
political discourse which challenges not the legitimacy and value of free private enterprise as such, but its legitimacy as a polluter, an abuser of market
power, a corruptor of state officials, an exploiter of workers and a potential
accomplice to violations of fundamental human rights. Thus, the correct
starting point should have been an acknowledgement that, in this new investment environment, new regulatory issues, of the kinds listed above, emerge.[75]
It was the complete failure to address these new questions that undermined
the MAI, based as it was on models of IIAs that were, in effect, a response
to increased state intervention and control over the national economy
through nationalisations and highly interventionist national economic plans.
In the light of the foregoing, a number of conclusions can be drawn.

10–038   As to the negotiating process, any future multilateral initiative must be made
more representative in terms of the participating countries. The active involvement of developing countries and countries in transition is essential. The developing countries in particular must come fully armed to the negotiating table.
The UNCTAD programme on issues in IIAs seeks to achieve this purpose. It
involves regional seminars for developing country officials, the publication of
specialised issues papers as guides to negotiators and ongoing analysis of the
development implications of IIAs, focused on the concept of "flexibility for
development".[76] Furthermore, to counter the perceived lack of a civic input
into the original negotiations, provision should be made for representatives of
civil society to be officially involved in the negotiations as advisers and not
merely as observers. However, the ultimate responsibility for concluding binding rules must rest with governments as the only legitimate and accountable representatives of their populations.[77] As to venue, the WTO continues to be

---

[75] On which see further the interesting paper by A.A.Fatouros "International Investment
Agreements and Development – Problems and Prospects at the Turn of the Century" in G. Hafner,
G. Loibl, A. Rest, L. Sucharipa-Berman and K. Zemanek (Eds) *Liber Amicorum Professor Seidl-
Hohenveldern – in Honour of his 80ᵗʰ Birthday* (The Hague, Kluwer Law International, 1998) p. 115.
[76] See *UNCTAD UNCTAD's Work Programme on International Investment Agreements: From
UNCTAD IX, Midrand (1996), to UNCTAD X, Bangkok (2000)* (New York and Geneva,
United Nations, 2000); UNCTAD *International Investment Agreements: Flexibility for
Development* UNCTAD Series on issues in international investment agreements (New York and
Geneva, United Nations, 2000).
[77] See Henderson *op.cit.* n. 29 at pp. 57–60.

mentioned as a possibility, given its wide membership. However, some groups have expressed caution given its commitment to free trade. They would welcome a more pluralistic venue, possibly within the UN. Another alternative might be to establish a specialist negotiating forum, composed of inputs from the WTO, UNCTAD and other relevant intergovernmental organisations.

As to content, the draft MAI was criticised as displaying an imbalance **10–039** between investor rights and responsibilities and prompted NGOs, unions, consumer groups and others to campaign for the introduction of tougher responsibilities for investors in the MAI. This may entail a binding section on investor responsibilities which, while covering many of the same issues, would go beyond the mere appending of the OECD Guidelines for Multinational Enterprises in a non-binding Annex. Numerous NGO proposals for a code based on such an approach have been formulated, and may be useful as a guide to negotiators.[78]

Secondly, with further awareness of the need for "flexibility for develop- **10–040** ment", the very structure, objectives, substantive rules and modes of implementation and monitoring of future multilateral investment rules should ensure that there is a balance between the protection of investors with the interests of countries, especially developing countries. Such future rules must avoid falling into the pitfall of the MAI, which recognised only the "legal symmetry" of the contracting parties, thereby assuming that all countries were formally equal under the law of the Agreement. However, with the active participation of developing countries, such "legal symmetry" cannot co-exist with the reality of "economic asymmetry" without resulting in the exposure of developing countries to the risk of damaging competition from often stronger foreign investors, including MNEs. Thus, the very structure, content and organisation of the agreement should aim at a minimisation of "economic asymmetry" through provisions that ensure respect for the legitimate development needs of countries. This may require the introduction of transitional provisions, commitments to co-operation and technical assistance provisions.[79]

Thirdly, the failure of the MAI shows that even the developed countries **10–041** cannot agree on a "fast-track" liberalisation agreement. The major lesson is that negotiation of a MAI-type agreement is not a zero-sum game with either full liberalisation or full protectionism as the possible outcomes. Perhaps the inevitable result will be an agreement with some liberalisation and some protectionism, much like the current example of NAFTA. One way around this, as noted above, could be to abandon the MAI's commitment to liberalisation coupled with "negative lists" of exceptions and to adopt the more cautious approach of selective liberalisation whereby a country "opts-in" to liberalisation by specifying the sectors in which it is willing to accept such disciplines while leaving non-specified sectors outside the agreement.

Fourthly, linkages with other issues such as labour standards, human **10–042** rights, environmental protection, competition, taxation and intellectual property will have to be tackled to ensure that future multilateral investment

---

[78] See examples in UNCTAD *International Investment Agreements: A Compendium Vol.V*. (New York and Geneva, United Nations, 2000); and Amnesty International UK Business Group *Human Rights Guidelines for Companies* (London, Amnesty International, 1998).
[79] For a detailed discussion and illustrative examples see UNCTAD *Flexibility op.cit*. n. 76.

rules do not interfere in a way that undermines existing international obligations of states in these areas.[80] In this regard, a new debate has arisen among NGOs. On September 15, 1999 a new group of academics and NGOs from developing countries issued a "statement Against Linkage".[81] This calls for the de-linking of environmental and labour questions from any future multilateral rules on investment, and their remaining within specialised bodies such as the ILO, on the principal ground that these constitute no more than hidden protectionism by developed countries against developing countries that may have lower standards in these areas. This position has been vigorously opposed by, among others the International Confederation of Free Trade Unions.[82] However, given the existence of a Trade and Environment Working Group in the WTO, and the growing concern over corporate responsibilities generated by Western NGOs, it is likely that this wider agenda will remain within that organisation.

10–043   Finally, certain wider implications of the lessons from the failure of the MAI should be highlighted. First, the lessons of the MAI go further than the WTO. Numerous bilateral investment agreements continue to be negotiated as do new regional investment agreements, a notable recent example being the ASEAN Framework Agreement on an ASEAN Investment Area of 1998.[83] The scope and development of such IIAs needs to reflect the experience gained under the MAI and to create a new generation of agreement types, which are more development oriented, and more sensitive to environmental and social issues. Secondly, as regards the United Kingdom's policy in this area, the Government itself asks the question whether there is a high priority for action on investor protection rules based on non-discrimination given the existing network of bilateral investment agreements.[84] On the other hand the Government believes that there is scope for action to create a single, transparent non-discrimination framework that preserves the right of governments to pursue their social, environmental and economic objectives.[85] Should the Government pursue such an objective it is crucial that it carries a truly representative voice into negotiations. To this end it may be necessary to establish improved systems of policy development, which build upon the informal networks already in existence, and which take account not only the views of civil society but also, in particular, of local and regional interests.

---

[80] See further Picciotto "Linkages in International Investment Regulation.." *op.cit*. n. 31.
[81] Third World Intellectuals and NGOs Statement Against Linkage (TWIN-SAL) September 15, 1999. This can be accessed through the Consumer Unity and Trust Society of India website: http://www.cutsjpr@jp1.dot.net.in.. This initiative has been strongly influenced by the thinking of one of the Statement's signatories, Jagdish Bhagwati, on which see further "Free trade, 'fairness' and the new protectionism: some reflections on an agenda for the WTO" (London, Institute of Economic Affairs Occasional Paper 96, April 1995).
[82] ICFTU "Enough Exploitation is Enough: a Response to the Third World Intellectuals and NGOs Statement Against Linkage" (February 2000).
[83] See n. 35.
[84] See DTI *International Investment: The Next Steps* July 21, 1999 para. 12.
[85] *ibid*. para. 45.

CHAPTER 11

MULTILATERAL AND BILATERAL APPROACHES TO THE INTERNATIONALISATION OF COMPETITION LAW: AN EU PERSPECTIVE

PROFESSOR MARISE CREMONA[1]

---

[1] Professor of European Commercial Law, Centre for Commercial Law Studies, Queen Mary, University of London.

1. Introduction

"In today's liberalised world the Community cannot be without an external dimension to its competition policy."[2]

"The WTO should begin negotiations on a basic framework of core principles and rules on domestic competition law and policy and its enforcement."[3]

1.1 The EU and multilateral trade

11–001   The European Union, in discussing EC trade policy, regularly emphasises the complementarity of its multilateral, regional and bilateral dimensions. In July 2000, in presenting its trade policy statement to the WTO's Trade Policy Review Body, the EC Commission claimed that "in terms of trade, the EU has a global vocation", a vocation which was to be realised both by using the full potential of the multilateral system and by strengthening links with individual trading partners. Its Introductory Statement on behalf of the EU the Commission emphasised three elements of EU policy, based on this "global vocation": support for the multilateral trading system, strengthened bilateral and regional relations, and the need for the WTO to respond to the challenges posed by globalisation and the concerns of civil society.

"Firstly, there is no substitute for a strong multilateral trading system. It is only in the respect of its rules that the multifaceted commercial relations between countries can truly prosper. Secondly, in terms of trade, the EU has a global vocation. It is therefore natural for it to use the full potential offered by the MTS and to deepen its trading links with a number of partners around the world. Thirdly, the WTO must take on the challenges of today or it will be disregarded and become irrelevant. Taking into account these challenges there is no other choice for us but to embark on a new round of multilateral trade negotiations."[4]

11–002   The Commission contrasts the "threat of unilateralism" and its "destructive potential for international trade" with the deepening of bilateral relations and "trade enhancing" bilateral agreements which "underpin and are mutually supportive" of the multilateral trading system.[5]

11–003   In the preparation of the EU's negotiating position prior to the Third WTO Ministerial Conference in Seattle and in its public contributions to the post-Seattle debate, the EU has also recently needed to address the future development of the multilateral trading system, represented in particular by the WTO, the part to be played by the EU in this process, its own bilateral

---

[2] Commission Communication of June 17, 1996, "Towards an International Framework of Competition Rules', COM (96) 284, at section I(b). See also Jacquemin, "The International Dimension of European Competition Policy" (1993) 31 JCMS 91; Bourgeois, "Competition Policy and Commercial Policy" in Maresceau (ed.) The EC's Commercial Policy after 1992: The Legal Dimension (Kluwer 1993); Devuyst, "The International Dimension of the EC's Antitrust Policy: Extending the Level Playing Field" (1998)3 EFA Rev 459.
[3] Conclusions of the General Affairs Council (GAC) in preparation for the WTO Ministerial Conference in Seattle, October 26, 1999.
[4] Trade Policy Review Mechanism, EU Policy Statement, European Commission Brussels, July 19, 2000, D (2000) at p. 16.
[5] *ibid.* at pp.6, 8 and 17.

preferential relations, and the relationship between them. Here the emphasis has been on the importance of the multilateral trading system, and on the priorities and role of the EU in the development of that system. In its conclusions on the preparation of its position for Seattle (which represent the Council mandate for negotiations), the Council "reaffirmed the importance it attaches to the primacy of the multilateral trading system and of its basic principles as guarantees against protectionism and unilateralism."[6] The EU stance, as a regional trade bloc committed to many regional agreements, is one of support for the multilateral trading system and for trade liberalisation whether achieved globally or regionally.

This general policy orientation has since Seattle focused on the need for a comprehensive new round of negotiations.[7] In the EU's view, a new round is needed not just in order to achieve a greater degree of trade liberalization. It is also necessary to "update the rule-book" as Commissioner Lamy put it recently in Tokyo:

    11–004

> "Trade liberalisation is generally a very good thing, and not just for business. Within that, multilateral liberalisation, and the MFN principle, is generally recognised to be the most efficient mechanism for this. But it is not, in and of itself, sufficient in this era. So we need a Round which does more than just tackle market access. We need a Round which updates the WTO rule-book."[8]

The Commissioner includes in this updating process, the need to develop a framework of rules governing foreign direct investment and competition and to re-examine the interface between trade rules and multilateral environment agreements. The trade and environment interface and the attempt to negotiate a multilateral agreement on investment are considered in chapters 9 and 10 of this volume. This chapter will take the third area mentioned by Lamy, the international dimension of competition policy; we will examine this vast subject from the particular perspective of the EU, and the distinctive combination of multilateral and bilateral initiatives in the development by the EU of a policy that reaches beyond the borders of the Community itself. It is in fact a field where a concerted attempt has been made to combine bilateral with multilateral initiatives, and even to multilateralise existing bilateral models. In this, EU policy not only demonstrates a wide variety of approaches and techniques, but can be seen as an example of the interaction between multilateral and bilateral strategies for achieving the twin objectives of underpinning increased market access with an agreed minimum level of regulatory control, and the reduction in costs represented by regulatory convergence.

    11–005

---

[6] Conclusions of GAC, October 26, 1999; these were of course adopted prior to Seattle but were subsequently confirmed by the Informal Trade Council in March 2000.

[7] The four key elements of a New Round sought by the EU are market access, new rules (covering *inter alia* competition and investment), sustainable development and a response to the concerns of civil society (notably environment and consumer issues).

[8] "Strengthening the Multilateral System", speech by Pascal Lamy to the Foreign Correspondents" Club, Tokyo, July 18, 2000; http://europa.eu.int/comm/trade/speeches_articles/spla29_en.htm.

1.2 The international dimension of competition policy

11–006   At the multilateral level, the EU has been an active participant in the debate over the need for, and possible shape of, an international framework of competition rules which would complement the TRIPS agreement on intellectual property rights within the WTO framework. In its bilateral relations, moreover, provisions on competition policy are now an inevitable accompaniment to trade commitments. These contractual provisions range from those with candidate States, such as the central and eastern European States and Turkey, to agreements with trading partners much further afield, such as Mexico or South Africa. They range from competition provisions within wider free trade or customs union agreements to specific sectoral agreements on co-operation in the enforcement and application of competition rules; and from agreements with developing countries, such as the Cotonou Convention with the ACP (African, Caribbean and Pacific) States, to agreements with industrialised States such as the USA or Canada. The remarkable spread of this external dimension to the EU's competition policy acts as a counterpoint to its rhetoric at the multilateral level, and the EU's experience bilaterally and regionally has influenced the position it takes in multilateral fora.

11–007   There is an additional element to this multidimensional approach to international competition issues. The multilateral and bilateral dimensions to EU policy should also be seen in relation to its unilateral dimension. The latter includes the application of what we may call "domestic" EU competition law to undertakings operating from outside the EU itself,[9] as well as the adoption of autonomous trade protection measures directed at anti-competitive activity under the anti-dumping or trade barriers Regulations. It is not possible in this chapter to enter into a discussion or assessment of the extra-territorial scope of domestic EU competition law; we will just note that while speaking in general terms, and avoiding specific reference to competition policy, EU statements have stressed the synergy between multilateral and bilateral approaches, in contrast to the threat to the multilateral trading system posed by unilateralism.[10] Trade protection measures such as anti-dumping legislation are of course covered by existing WTO rules, and the relationship between such measures and an effective and non-discriminatory competition policy has been one of the issues exercising the WTO Working Group on Trade and Competition Policy, established in 1996. More broadly, the development of a multilateral framework for competition raises questions as to the extent to which it could—or should—be used as a method of constraining the use of autonomous measures of both competition and trade policy.

---

[9] See Robertson and Demetriou, "But that was in another country . . ." [1994] ICLQ 41; Torremans, "Extraterritorial Application of EC and U.S. Competition Law" (1996) 21 ELRev. 280. This aspect of EU policy will not be discussed further in this chapter.

[10] On unilateralism in the context of international trade more generally, see the Symposium "Unilateralism in International Trade: What Place Can it Have in Light of the Emerging Multilateral Regime?" in 11 EJIL (2000) 249, and especially Bernhard Jansen, "The Limits of Unilateralism from a European Perspective" 11 EJIL (2000) 309.

1.3 External Community competence in matters of competition policy

Before going on to examine the multilateral and bilateral aspects of EU pol-   **11–008**
icy, we should briefly address the preliminary issue of competence. External
competence (for example, to conclude agreements) in matters of competition
policy is not expressly granted in the EC Treaty. Competence derives from
two sources.

First, where competition clauses form part of an agreement for which   **11–009**
express powers have been granted in the Treaty, that treaty provision may provide a sufficient basis for the competition dimension of the agreement. For
example, where the competition clause is ancillary to trade provisions, concerned with the effect of anti-competitive distortions on trade between the
parties, then express common commercial policy competence under Article
133 EC will provide an adequate basis for the agreement; the free-trade
agreements with the EFTA States of the 1970s are an example of this. It is
also possible to envisage competition forming part of an agreement concluded under Article 181 EC on development co-operation. The Court has
held, in relation to the scope of this provision:

> "In order to qualify as a development co-operation agreement for the purposes of [Arti-
> cle 181] of the Treaty, an agreement must pursue the objectives referred to in [Article
> 177]. . . . those are broad objectives in the sense that it must be possible for the measures
> required for their pursuit to concern a variety of specific matters. . . . the fact that a devel-
> opment co-operation agreement contains clauses concerning various specific matters
> cannot alter the characterisation of the agreement, which must be determined having
> regard to its essential object and not in terms of individual clauses, provided that those
> clauses do not impose such extensive obligations concerning the specific matters referred
> to that those obligations in fact constitute objectives distinct from those of development
> co-operation."[11]

Secondly, competence may be implied from internal powers, either directly   **11–011**
from the Treaty itself or via secondary legislation.[12] In its second Opinion on
the draft EEA, the Court of Justice said:

> "It follows from the Court's case law . . . that the Community's authority to enter into
> international agreements arises not only from an express attribution by the Treaty, but
> also from other provisions of the Treaty and measures taken pursuant to those provisions
> by the Community institutions. Consequently, the Community is empowered, under the
> competition rules in the EEC Treaty and measures implementing those rules, to conclude
> international agreements in this field."[13]

The Court also expressly confirmed that this power includes the possibility   **11–012**
of competence-sharing jurisdictional rules, providing these do not "change
the nature of the powers of the Community".[14] The competition provisions
EEA are in fact a case of indirect implied powers; the EEA was concluded

---

[11] Case C-268/94 *Portugal v. Council* [1996] E.C.R. I-6177, at paras 37-39. The Treaty Article
numbers have been changed to reflect the renumbering introduced by the Treaty of Amsterdam.
[12] The doctrine of implied external competence has been developed by the Court of Justice, in
case 22/70 *Commission v. Council* (AETR) [1971]E.C.R. 263;[1971] C.M.L.R. 335, and subsequent cases including *Opinion 2/91 (re ILO Convention)* [1993] E.C.R I-1061.
[13] *Opinion 1/92 (draft Treaty on EEA, No.2)* [1992] E.C.R I-2821 at paras 39-40.
[14] *ibid.* at para 41; see further text at n. 87.

on the basis of Article 310 EC, as an association agreement. Association agreements may include "commitments towards non-member countries in all the fields covered by the Treaty",[15] including competition policy.

11–013   External competence could be implied from the competition provisions of the Treaty and thus form part of an association agreement. The Court's statement in this case on implied external competence in the competition field is also illustrated by the Agreement between the EC and USA on competition.[16] It was ultimately concluded on the basis of Articles 83 and 308 EC; Article 83 grants a legislative competence to the Council of Ministers in the field of competition in order to give effect to the principles set out in Articles 81 and 82, but without explicit mention of external agreements. Article 308 EC was necessary, according to the Preamble of the concluding Decision, because the agreement included matters covered by the Merger Regulation (Regulation 4064/89) which is itself based on Article 308 EC. So here powers were implied from a Treaty Article directly and from secondary legislation (the Regulation). This Agreement is also of interest because it was originally concluded by the Commission; the Commission argued that it had competence to do so under Article 85 EC (then Article 89) which gives the Commission the task of ensuring the application of Articles 81 and 82 EC. However, in an action brought by France challenging the legality of the Commission Decision concluding the Agreement, the Court of Justice held that the doctrine of implied powers could not be used to justify Commission competence in this case.[17] *Community* external competence could be derived by implication from the Treaty provisions on competition but this does not imply specific institutional allocation of power. This must be derived from the specific Treaty Article dealing with the procedure for negotiating and concluding international agreements, Article 300 EC, which establishes that agreements must be concluded by the Council of Ministers. A new Decision concluding the Agreement had to be adopted by the Council of Ministers on the basis of Articles 83 and 308 together with Article 300 EC. The Court's judgment highlights the fact that (whatever the internal Treaty-based rules about institutional competence) it is the European Community itself which has legal personality (Article 281 EC) and which therefore enters into international obligations with the possibility of incurring liability at an international level.[18] The binding nature of the Agreement in international law was thus not put in question by the annulment of the Commission Decision concluding the Agreement for the Community.

11–014   Having established Community competence, we need to consider whether this is exclusive or not, whether it precludes the possibility of Member State action in the field. Where the competition clause of an agreement is simply ancillary within a trade agreement based on Article 133 EC, then competence will be exclusive.[19] Competence under the development co-operation

---

[15] Case 12/86 *Meryem Demirel v. Stadt Schwäbisch Gmünd.* [1987]ECR 3719; [1989] I.C.M.LR, 421, at para. 9.
[16] EC - USA Agreement on competition 1991 [1995] O.J. L 95/45.
[17] Case C-327/91 *France v. Commission* [1994] E.C.R I-3641; [1994] 5 C.M.L.R. 517.
[18] *ibid.* at paras 24–25.
[19] See, for example, *Opinion 1/78 (Agreement on Natural Rubber)* [1979] E.C.R 2871.

provisions of the treaty, in contrast, is shared (although this does not mean that every agreement concluded under Article 181 EC must be mixed[20]). Where, competence is based on implied powers then competence is shared, as it is internally.[21] In discussing the possibility of a multilateral competition agreement the Commission makes the point:

> "As competition is not an exclusive Community competence, international cases might involve either the Community (if trade between Member States were affected) or a single Member State (if it alone were affected). A framework of rules would have to take account of both cases, while preserving the unity of Community action in the trade field."[22]

The Member States are under a duty, in exercising their competence in this field, not to prejudice the application of Community competition rules;[23] and were an agreement to be concluded on a mixed basis (jointly by the Community and Member States) the duty of co-operation would apply: **11–015**

> "... where it is apparent that the subject-matter of an agreement or convention falls in part within the competence of the Community and in part within that of the Member States, it is essential to ensure close co-operation between the Member States and the Community institutions, both in the process of negotiation and conclusion and in the fulfillment of the commitments entered into. That obligation to co-operate flows from the requirement of unity in the international representation of the Community." [24]

A practical application of this principle can be seen in the joint submissions made by "the EC and its Member States" to the WTO Working Group on Trade and Competition Policy.   **11–016**

2. The multilateral dimension to EU policy: trade and competition

The WTO is by no means the only multilateral forum in which the development of international competition policy has been debated; the OECD and UNCTAD have engaged in their own initiatives, as well as the varied regional approaches of NAFTA, the FTAA and of course the EU itself.[25] Nevertheless the wide—and wide-ranging—membership of the WTO, and the increased attention paid in the last decade to the relationship between trade policy and regulatory policy, has meant that the work of its Working Group on Trade and Competition Policy has provided a focus for policy debate bringing together both industrialised and developing countries.   **11–017**

---

[20] Case C-268/94 *Portugal v. Council* [1996] E.C.R I-6177. A mixed agreement is concluded jointly by the Community and the Member States.

[21] Case 14/68 *Wilhelm v. Bundeskartellamt* [1969] E.C.R 1; [1969] C.M.L.R. 100.

[22] Commission Communication of 17 June 1996, "Towards an International Framework of Competition Rules', COM (96) 284.

[23] Article 10 EC and case 14/68 *Wilhelm v. Bundeskartellamt* [1969] E.C.R 1, at para 4.

[24] *Opinion 1/94 (re WTO Agreement)* [1994] E.C.R I-5267, para. 108.

[25] Initiatives outside the WTO framework include for example the draft UN Convention on Restrictive Business Practices in 1953, the 1967 OECD Recommendations on Co-operation on Anti-competitive Practices Affecting International Trade, last revised in 1995, the 1998 OECD Recommendation on Hard Core Cartels, and the work of UNCTAD and its Intergovernmental Group of Experts, in particular the (non-binding) Set of Multilaterally Agreed Equitable Principles and Rules for the Control of Restrictive Business Practices, adopted by the UN General Assembly in December 1980 (UN Doc. A/35/48 (1980)).

11–018   Although the role of competition policy in international trade does not as such form part of the "built-in agenda" for a New Round of trade negotiations,[26] it has in practice been on the agenda for some time. Indeed the abortive Havana Charter of 1947 contained a separate chapter on restrictive business practices and the issue of a possible international anti-trust agreement has been considered within GATT structures more than once since. Aspects of existing GATT law are designed to support fair competitive conditions on both import markets (Article III for example) and export markets (Article VI for example), although focused on public rather than private conduct. As WTO attention has shifted from border controls to beyond-the-border trade restrictions, and in particular the regulatory environment in which imported products are marketed and out-of-state businesses must operate, competition policy implications arise from a number of provisions in the Uruguay Round package of Agreements (such as GATS[27] and TRIPS[28]), as well as subsequent agreements (such as the Agreement on Telecommunications Services). An institutional framework for further discussion was provided when the Singapore Ministerial Conference in December 1996, the first after the coming into force of the Uruguay Round Agreements, established a Working Group "to study issues raised by members relating to the interaction between trade and competition policy, including anti-competitive practices, in order to identify any areas that may merit further consideration in the WTO framework."[29]

2.1 The rationale for an international approach to competition policy

11–019   In October 1999 the EU's Council of Ministers adopted a set of Conclusions on the planned Millennium Round negotiations, a position statement which established a negotiating mandate for the Commission. This wide-ranging and ambitious agenda was based on four "broad objectives":

> "strengthening the WTO rules-based system, promoting the further liberalisation of trade, improving the integration of developing countries into the multilateral trading system, addressing the interface between trade and related issues and policies."[30]

11–020   For the EU, the trade and competition issue relates to all four of these objectives. The Council puts its support behind a new agreement on competition:

> "The WTO should begin negotiations on a basic framework of binding core principles and rules on domestic competition law and policy and its enforcement. The WTO

---

[26] The "built-in" agenda includes those items for which further negotiations are provided within the Uruguay Round Agreements themselves, for example agriculture under Art.20 of the Agreement on Agriculture. Art.9 of the TRIMS Agreement (one of the Annex 1A Agreements on Trade in Goods) provides for a review of that Agreement within five years of its entry into force by the Council for Trade in Goods, including consideration of "whether the Agreement should be complemented with provisions on investment policy and competition policy."

[27] See Arts VIII and IX of GATS.

[28] See Arts 8, 39 and 40 of TRIPS. Smith, "A Long and Winding Road: TRIPS and the Evolution of an International Competition Framework" (1999) JIEL 435.

[29] Singapore Ministerial Declaration, WT/MIN(96)/DEC/W, December 13, 1996, para. 30.

[30] Conclusions of General Affairs Council on the preparation for the Third WTO Ministerial Conference, October 26, 1999, at para. 3.

principles of transparency and non-discrimination would provide key foundations for the development of such core principles and rules. The WTO should also aim at developing common approaches on anti-competitive practices with a significant impact on international trade and investment as well as on the promotion of international co-operation. The development dimension should also be at the centre of the considerations of such a multilateral framework by combining possible transitional periods together with technical assistance and flexibility in the rules."[31]

The link between international trade and competition based on liberalization and market access is well known to those familiar with the EC Treaty's approach to public and private barriers to cross-border trade. The market access argument is essentially that in spite of different perspectives[32] both international trade law and competition policy serve the same objective of open markets, and that the fundamental WTO principle of non-discrimination is intended to ensure equality of competitive opportunity as between products (and companies) of different national origin.[33] Competition policy is necessary to prevent prohibited public barriers to trade being replaced by anti-competitive private business practices. This argument has been sharpened by the fact that the growing membership of the WTO includes state trading (or non-market economy) countries, such as China, bringing the interface between trade liberalisation, state trading activities and competition into relief. However, there is a broader pragmatic rationale for an internationalised approach to competition policy: anti-competitive practices such as international cartels or international mergers which affect more than one State lead to simultaneous investigation and enforcement activity by more than one national competition authority, and jurisdictional and enforcement conflicts between authorities.

11–021

These essentially institutional problems are increasing with the growth of both national competition laws and the globalisation of business.[34] Combined with differences between national policies, they also increase compliance costs for companies involved in cross-border business.[35] Pitofsky, Chairman of the

11–022

---

[31] Conclusions of General Affairs Council on the preparation for the Third WTO Ministerial Conference, October 26, 1999, at para. 11(d).

[32] Tarullo points out that trade and competition authorities often have very different perspectives, which although sometimes complementary may conflict; in particular trade negotiators tend to pursue the interests of their own national businesses: Tarullo, "Competition Policy for Global Markets" (1999) JIEL 445 at 446. This issue is also discussed in the 1998 Report of the WTO Working Group on the Interaction Between Trade and Competition Policy to the General Council, December 8, 1998, WT/WGTCP/2, section C.1.(a).

[33] See the submission from the EC and its Member States to the WTO Working Group on Trade and Competition Policy, on "The relevance of fundamental WTO principles of national treatment, transparency and most favoured nation treatment to competition policy and vice versa", April 12, 1999, WT/WGTCP/W/115, section I.

[34] 82 countries have some kind of competition law and 24 are in the process of drafting or enacting such a law: Pitofsky, "Competition Policy in a Global Economy" (1999) JIEL 403, at 403.

[35] Melamed identifies three types of problem: competition problems with similar effects in several countries, such as international cartels; problems where the effects are felt in one country but much of the evidence is located in another (for example, export cartels), and cases where the effects are different for different countries, including the market access cases. Melamed, "International Co-operation in Competition Law and Policy: What can be Achieved at the bilateral, Regional and Multilateral Levels" (1999) JIEL 423 at 424. The Report of the Group of Experts, "Competition Policy in the New Trade Order: Strengthening International Co-operation and Rules", Brussels, July 1995, identifies similar problems, although they (writing from an EU perspective) also include the problem of some competition authorities' extension of jurisdiction and lack of attention to

U.S. Federal Trade Commission, emphasises the burden of divergent regulatory norms in words which reflect the confidence of a dominant model:

> "[I]nconsistent anti-trust enforcement and divergence of anti-trust rules from country to country, at least where they are unfair, unwise or enforced in a discriminatory manner, create an unlevel playing field on which firms must operate in international competition, and these are a burden on international commerce."[36]

11–023 This analysis would seem to suggest support for an international approach to competition policy from both national authorities and international business interests. It is not so simple. The need for a separate "horizontal" agreement on competition in addition to specific sectoral measures is still strongly contested, as well as its putative content. In particular, is an international competition code required, or rather a basic framework for procedural co-operation between national authorities? If a code, should this be compulsory or voluntary, how detailed should its fundamental principles be, and how should it be enforced? The three reports so far produced by the WTO Working Group on Trade and Competition Policy reflect this contention, and in particular whether the Working Group should examine all aspects of competition policy as they may affect trade, or focus primarily on aspects of the trade and competition relationship traditionally within the scope of the WTO, such as anti-competitive conduct of government or state origin, and the importance of the basic WTO disciplines of transparency, MFN and national treatment for the application of competition policy.[37]

11–024 The arguments in favour of some form of new horizontal competition agreement are, predictably but justifiably, based not only on the need for international business to be able to enter open competitive markets, but also on the need for developing and emerging economies to protect themselves against the abuse of monopoly power, whether domestic or imported.

> "The more economies are integrated into the global system the more they need competition rules to control the power of global businesses in their markets. It is argued that the absence or inappropriate enforcement of competition rules can create barriers to trade. That is certainly true. A commitment by WTO members to a common set of competition law principles would be a helpful way of addressing both issues. Countries also need to have measures to control restrictive business practices in order to reap the full benefits of trade liberalisation."[38]

11–025 The 1998 Report of the WTO Working Group on Trade and Competition Policy also reflects the complementarity of competition policy and economic development. Competition law may be adopted as part of a package with trade liberalisation, foreign investment regimes and other economic reforms

---

their partner's interests. See also Tarullo, "Competition Policy for Global Markets" (1999) JIEL 445 at 447-450; while not denying their significance, especially in the medium-longer term, Tarullo argues that these problems are still "of limited scope and urgency".

[36] Pitofsky, "Competition Policy in a Global Economy" (1999) JIEL 403, at 404.

[37] The Working Group has to date produced three reports to the General Council: November 28, 1997, WT/WGTCP/1; December 8, 1998, WT/WGTCP/2; October 11, 1999, WT/WGTCP/3.

[38] Lord McIntosh of Haringey, HL Deb, April 19, 2000, col 787; cited in House of Lords Select Committee on the European Communities, Tenth Report, June 13, 2000 "The World Trade Organisation: The EU Mandate after Seattle" at para. 184; see http://www.parliament.the-stationery-office.co.uk/pa/ld199900/ldselect/ldeucom/76/7601.htm.

such as privatisation and deregulation; in such cases "competition policy would act as a catalyst for economic reform and development based on market-oriented principles."[39] As the EU's Group of Experts Report points out, the absence of a functioning competition policy may result not only in less efficient market development but also the risk of being subjected to the extraterritorial application of third countries' competition laws by agencies which will not share the same policy interests.[40]

The EU Commissioner for Trade, Pascal Lamy, has linked the economic development arguments with the need to address the concerns of civil society over the legitimacy, transparency and responsiveness of the WTO system: **11–026**

> "Essentially, we want to fix some basic rules in the WTO so that all countries around the world start to think competition, start to put in place a basic infrastructure of competition law and policy, agreed principles, and mechanisms for co-operation between competition authorities. It's a development issue as much as a trade issue."[41]

> ". . . Surely, if we are to counter accusations that the WTO is the lap-dog of the multinationals, what better way than by starting to work on ensuring fair competition and a level playing field for all, large and small?"[42]

This objective of ensuring fair play through competition rules forms part of a rule-based approach to trade liberalisation: **11–027**

> "Indeed, a Round has to update the WTO rules across the board: not to bring us towards some utopian dream of global government, but to start to impact on global governance, in other words predictability, stability, transparency in the rules, and rule-making capacity, of the global institutions"[43]

In the discussion over possible multilateral approaches to trade and competition policy, four options[44] have emerged: **11–028**

- a multilateral agreement containing mandatory (minimum) standards for competition legislation, including enforcement;

- a sectoral approach: including specific competition provisions in sectoral agreements such as the Telecommunications Agreement;

---

[39] Report of the Working Group on the Interaction Between Trade and Competition Policy to the General Council (1998), December 8, 1998, WT/WGTCP/2, sect.C.1.(a).

[40] Report of the Group of Experts, "Competition Policy in the New Trade Order: Strengthening International Co-operation and Rules", Brussels, July 1995.

[41] Commissioner Pascal Lamy, Speech to United States Council for International Business, New York, June 8, 2000.

[42] Commissioner Pascal Lamy, Speech to Confederation of Indian Industries, March 6, 2000, cited in House of Lords Select Committee on the European Communities, Tenth Report, *op.cit.* at n. 37 at para 184.

[43] "Strengthening the Multilateral System", speech by Pascal Lamy to the Foreign Correspondents" Club, Tokyo, July 18, 2000; http://europa.eu.int/comm/trade/speeches_articles/spla29_en.htm.

[44] One might add the theoretical option of the establishment of an international competition authority with direct enforcement powers (a European Commission writ large), but even the Commission, in its 1996 Communication, does not see this as a "feasible option for the medium term": Commission Communication of June 17, 1996, "Towards an International Framework of Competition Rules', COM(96) 284, at section III.

- a multilateral framework that does not specify or require individual members to introduce any comprehensive competition law, but merely prescribes principles to be followed if a member wishes to introduce competition law.

- a plurilateral framework, such as the existing Agreement on Government Procurement, which contains mandatory rules but which does not form a compulsory part of any New Round package of commitments.

11–029   In addition, there are those who take the view that formal agreements on competition are only really feasible at a bilateral level between countries with similar approaches, expectations and levels of enforcement infrastructure. On this view, multilateral fora such as the WTO Working Group on Trade and Competition Policy are best suited to exchanges of views and experiences with the aim of gradually building convergence but without the immediate objective of an international "competition code" in any sense.

2.2 The EU position

11–030   Since the conclusion of the Uruguay Round, the European Union position, in contrast to that of the USA, has been moving towards support for a comprehensive agreement on competition, which would include "core principles and rules" as well as provisions on co-operation. In fact the rationale for the EU's position can be traced back considerably further; it derives from a sense that the EU's open approach to the external dimension of the internal market demands a degree of reciprocity from its partners. In 1988 the Commission, in seeking to categorise the 1992 single market programme as the creation of "partner Europe" rather than "Fortress Europe", stated that the Community's aim would be "to strengthen the multilateral system in accordance with the two principles of balance of mutual advantage and reciprocity".[45] A strengthening of competition policy was included as one element of this strategy although the focus was here on the international dimension of domestic EC policy rather than on developing new international rules.

11–031   In July 1995 the consultative Report of a Group of Experts commissioned by the European Commission was published.[46] In his introduction to the report, the then Competition Commissioner Karel van Miert reflects this view: open markets require effective competition policies, and the EU will look for reciprocity not only in the opening of markets but also in the development of competition principles and rules. The Report itself was not intended to represent EU policy in any formal sense, but has undoubtedly influenced its direction, particularly in its recommendation that that policy should move forward on both the bilateral and multilateral fronts in parallel:

---

[45] Commission paper, "Europe a world partner: the external dimension of the single market", Bull.EC 10-1988 p.10.
[46] "Competition Policy in the New Trade Order: Strengthening International Co-operation and Rules", Report of the Group of Experts, Brussels, July 1995. The Group of Experts included Commission officials (participating "on a personal basis") and external experts including Fréderic Jenny, now Chair of the WTO Working Group on Trade and Competition Policy.

deepening existing forms of co-operation through bilateral agreements, and at the same time developing a multilateral framework which would adopt many of the ingredients already included in bilateral agreements. In its follow-up Communication to the Council in June 1996, the Commission examines the case for the adoption of international competition rules from both a competition and a trade perspective. From both perspectives, the element of reciprocity is important, linked to equal conditions of competition and equality of market access:

> "The Community interest is to seek the same commitment to competition enforcement from our partners in their markets as we apply to operators, irrespective of their origin, on ours."[47]

The Commission agreed with the Group of Experts that bilateral and multilateral policies would be "complementary and mutually supportive", while stressing that in its judgement, bilateral co-operation agreements alone will not be sufficient; such agreements

11–032

> "remain limited in scope and in effect. In scope, because although increasing, only the EU and a limited number of countries which are very actively involved in enforcing competition policies, have entered such agreements; and, in effect, because these agreements do not contain substantive rules or principles."[48]

These 1996 proposals, although then described by the Commission as "modest" and incremental, now seem ambitious. It stresses the need for binding commitments, covering the adoption of domestic competition structures and common rules, co-operation between competition authorities and dispute settlement procedures. The Commission shares the view of the Group of Experts that the greatest scope for progress lies in a plurilateral agreement; a plurilateral framework, initially based on groups of countries where strong regional co-operation already exists[49] would allow for evolution in terms of geographical and substantive coverage and enforcement.[50] In more immediate terms, the Commission recommended that the Council's conclusions in preparation for the Singapore WTO Ministerial Meeting in December 1996 should support the creation of a WTO Working Group with a remit to explore the development of an international framework of competition rules. Following this Communication, an informal meeting of trade ministers in Dublin in September 1996 included as one of the Community's "key priorities" the need for the WTO "to broaden at Singapore its work-programme to adapt itself to new realities of the world economy in particular on investment

11–033

---

[47] Commission Communication of June 17, 1996, "Towards an International Framework of Competition Rules', COM(96) 284, at section I(b).
[48] *ibid.*, at section I(e).
[49] For example, NAFTA, EU (and the countries of central and eastern Europe) and Australia-New Zealand; however a viable plurilateral agreement should also include at least Japan and other Asian industrialized states. Apart from the EU and its Member States only 10 states are signatory to the plurilateral Government Procurement Agreement, although this does include the USA, Canada and Japan.
[50] COM(96) 284 at section IV(a). Report of the Group of Experts (see n. 31) at para. IV.1. In their view, a network of bilateral agreements will not in themselves produce a level playing field, but would make conclusion and operation of a plurilateral agreement easier: *ibid.* at para. IV.3.

and competition"[51] and the decision to approve the final text of the Ministerial Declaration was taken at a special session of the General Affairs Council in Singapore. The Ministerial Declaration established the Working Group on Trade and Competition Policy, although (unsurprisingly) with a generalised remit to "identify any areas that may merit further consideration", rather than a specific mandate to explore the possibility of a common framework of rules such as the Commission had envisaged.

11–034　　As we have seen, discussion within the Working Group reflects the very different perspectives of the WTO members as to both the desirability and feasibility of such a framework. Although the 1996 Communication still forms the basis of Community policy, the Community position has also become more nuanced since 1996, in the course of a number of internal Commission policy papers and Communications to the Working Group from the Community and Member States, in which the Community builds the case for a multilateral framework of rules.[52] The Council's negotiating mandate for the Seattle Ministerial Conference in Seattle reaffirmed the EU's support for the inclusion of competition in the agenda for a new round of negotiations, with the three-part aim of agreeing a "basic framework of core principles and rules", developing "common approaches" on certain key anti-competitive practices, and the promotion of international co-operation.[53] As a Commission discussion paper in March 1999 admitted,[54] a strategy for building support for this agenda was needed, and part of this strategy has been to emphasise the "development-friendly" aspects of these objectives, not only the benefits of an effective competition policy for development but also flexibility, transitional periods and technical assistance in the implementation of internationally agreed rules.

11–035　　Although the EU would still like to see an agreement on competition,[55] it is not looking for agreement on detailed and specific substantive rules, which would amount to a form of minimum harmonisation on the EU model, still less the creation of some form of international agency with investigative or enforcement powers. Rather, it stresses the flexibility of "core principles" and "common approaches":

---

[51] Presidency Conclusions reflecting the outcome of the informal meeting of trade ministers in Dublin on September 19, 1996, para. 3; included in Annex to Conclusions of the General Affairs Council meeting of October 1, 1996.

[52] See for example, Commission Discussion Paper of March 19, 1999 on Trade and Competition, prepared in the run-up to the Seattle Ministerial Conference in December 1999; Communication from the European Community and its Member States to the Working Group on Trade and Competition Policy, "Impact of Anti-competitive Practices on Trade", February 23, 1998; Communication from the European Community and its Member States to the Working Group on Trade and Competition Policy, "The contribution of competition policy to achieving the objectives of the WTO, including the promotion of international trade", July 12, 1999, WT/WGTCP/W/130. We cannot analyse each one of these dozen Communications in this chapter; for texts, see: http://europa.eu.int/comm/trade/miti/compet/contrib.htm

[53] Conclusions of GAC in preparation for the WTO Ministerial Conference in Seattle, 26 October 1999. See text at n. 30 *supra*.

[54] Commission Discussion Paper on Trade and Competition, March 19, 1999.

[55] See in particular, the submission from the EC and its Member States to the WTO Working Group on "A Multilateral Framework Agreement on Competition Policy", September 25, 2000, WT/WGTCP/W/152.

"The EU approach has aimed at dispelling the myth that there is no middle way between the development of a hard and fast rule and the total absence of multilateral disciplines. ... rather than seek to establish "minimum common standards" we have advocated a flexible approach based on the need to develop common approaches in relation to anti-competitive practices with a significant impact on international trade and investment."[56]

The flexibility of common approaches, using agreed assessment criteria, would allow scope for development, so that as convergence increases, consensus on rules can evolve. These will be underpinned by core principles relating to the formulation of a domestic system of competition law and its enforcement which, the Commission has argued, can be drawn from existing WTO principles, including transparency, non-discrimination and procedural fairness.[57] The third strand of this strategy is international co-operation, seeking to build on existing bilateral co-operation (whether informal or formalised in bilateral agreements), to resolve jurisdictional conflicts and to provide an institutional structure to share information, experience and good practice and provide technical assistance and advice.[58]   **11–036**

Finally, the difficult question of dispute settlement would need to be resolved. The existence of a credible dispute settlement procedure is one reason the Commission puts forward for preferring the WTO to (for example) the OECD as a forum for the development of a competition agreement.[59] Nevertheless, the Commission also resists any idea that international dispute settlement should be open to private parties; the criteria for an effective domestic competition policy should include scope for private party challenge to a competition authority's decision, but dispute settlement under any new agreement should (in the Commission's view) remain intergovernmental.[60] The Community envisages an agreement that would impose obligations on the State parties, requiring enactment of domestic legislation, but which would not directly create rights or obligations for private parties.[61] Others are sceptical as to the suitability of the WTO as a forum for resolving the problems of competition policy.[62] Even if WTO-based dispute settlement   **11–037**

---

[56] Commission Discussion Paper on Trade and Competition, March 19, 1999.
[57] See further the submission from the EC and its Member States to the WTO Working Group on "The relevance of fundamental WTO principles of national treatment, transparency and most favoured nation treatment to competition policy and vice versa", April 12, 1999, WT/WGTCP/W/115.
[58] This would encompass negative and possibly also positive comity; negative comity involves taking the interests of other states into account, positive comity involves one authority agreeing to investigate on request from another: see discussion at n. 74 below.
[59] Commission Communication of June 17, 1996, "Towards an International Framework of Competition Rules', COM (96) 284.
[60] This approach reflects the current position in relation to anti-dumping measures.
[61] Submission from the EC and its Member States to the WTO Working Group on "The relevance of fundamental WTO principles of national treatment, transparency and most favoured nation treatment to competition policy and vice versa", April 12, 1999, WT/WGTCP/W/115. The unstated implication is that private parties, as well as being denied recourse to the WTO dispute settlement procedure, would not be able to enforce the envisaged agreement in national courts. This would have to be read in the light of the so-called "*Nakajima* principle": see case C-69/89 *Nakajima* [1991] E.C.R. I-2069, and most recently, case C-149/96 *Portugal v. Council* [1999]E.C.R I-8395.
[62] See Tarullo, "Competition Policy for Global Markets" (1999) JIEL 445 at p.450-452 for a clear analysis of the difficulties inherent in using WTO mechanisms for enforcing even a limited code.

were limited to ensuring that members' domestic competition laws complied with the agreed framework of "core principles and common approaches", difficult issues would arise where a dispute ultimately challenged the legitimacy of approach or a decision of a national authority in a specific case.[63]

11–038   After Seattle, the Community's position was confirmed by the Informal Trade Council in March 2000 and in position papers since then the Community has reaffirmed its support for a multilateral agreement on competition based on core principles applying to domestic competition law and policy, international co-operation and support for the reinforcement of competition institutions in developing countries.[64] A core principles approach "does not imply harmonisation", providing instead a basis for convergence.[65] The five core principles identified by the Community in September 2000 as a basis for discussion are:

- the existence of a competition authority possessing sufficient enforcement powers;

- domestic competition law to be based on the principle of non-discrimination on grounds of the nationality of firms;

- transparency as regards the legislative framework, including any sectoral exclusions;

- guarantees of due process; and

- agreement that "hard-core" cartels should be treated as a serious breach of competition law.[66]

11–039   The Community does not see this multilateral initiative, even if successful, as replacing its bilateral and regional commitments; it predicts complementarity and synergy between the different levels and modes of co-operation. It is certainly true that we can trace a two-way process here: on the one hand, the Community has been influenced in the development of its multilateral strategy and proposals by its experience of bilateral and regional agreements; on the other, the establishment of a common approach and core principles at a multilateral level will feed into bilateral agreements, providing a basis for further and perhaps more detailed commitments. Given that provisions on competition policy are now an almost indispensable feature of the Community's bilateral agreements this synergy is important. In the next sec-

---

[63] The Commission is clear that there should be no review of individual decisions but suggests exploration of the possibility of a panel review in cases of an alleged "pattern of failure" to enforce competition laws in cases affecting the interests of other Members: Commission Discussion Paper on Trade and Competition, March 19, 1999.

[64] Submission from the EC and its Member States to the WTO Working Group on "A Multilateral Framework Agreement on Competition Policy", September 25, 2000, WT/WGTCP/W/152.

[65] *ibid.* at p.5.

[66] "Hard-core" cartels are "generally understood to be agreements among actual or potential competitors involving price fixing, bid rigging, output restrictions or customer allocation and market divisions." *ibid.* at p.8.

tion, we will turn to examine the Community's bilateral approaches to competition policy before, in the final section, drawing some conclusions as to the way in which the multilateral and bilateral interact.

3. The bilateral dimension to EU policy: from co-operation to harmonisation

There is no single model for a competition clause in a Community **11–040** agreement. As a general initial classification we can identify three basic types.

First, provision for co-operation between national (or Community) com- **11–041** petition authorities, including provision for negative and positive comity; such measures may appear as a free-standing agreement on competition co-operation or within a wider trade or association agreement.

Second, provisions which are concerned with competition in the context of **11–042** trade between the contracting parties; such clauses will be included in agreements designed to liberalize trade between the parties and are designed to prevent private actors distorting competitive conditions in a liberalized market.

Third, measures essentially concerned with substantive and/or procedural **11–043** standard-setting, or even harmonisation, within domestic legal systems; these clauses will form part of a wider agreement designed to establish closer relations with the Community and will often have a development dimension; as such they are accompanied by provision for technical assistance in developing regulatory capacity. It will be noticed that these different types of clause (which are of course not mutually exclusive) address the three different types of international competition problem identified both by the Commission and by the WTO Working Group.[67]

3.1 Bilateral co-operation agreements

Bilateral co-operation agreements have been concluded by the EC with both **11–044** the USA[68] and Canada.[69] These are agreements specifically dealing with competition policy, and are the most fully worked-out examples of co-operation agreement, but there are also co-operation provisions in other agreements, notably the European Economic Area Agreement, the Europe Agreements and the customs union Decision of the EU–Turkey Association Council. In the case of the Europe Agreements and Turkey, provisions for the implementation of co-operation on competition policy between the EC and the

---

[67] See text at n. 35 *et seq.* As summarised by the Commission, these are first, anticompetitive practices which impact on more than one market and which may therefore give rise to jurisdictional problems and the need for co-operation between national authorities; secondly, anticompetitive practices which hinder market access, whether or not the result of inadequate competition law or enforcement; and thirdly, anticompetitive practices the effects of which are felt on a third country market; see Commission Discussion Paper on Trade and Competition, March 19, 1999.
[68] EC – USA Agreement on competition 1995 O.J. L95/45; EC - USA Agreement on the application of positive comity principles in the enforcement of competition laws 1998 O.J. L173/26.
[69] Agreement between EC and Canada regarding the application of their competition laws 1999 O.J. L175/50.

respective associated states were to be adopted by Decision of the relevant Association Council. There is no bilateral agreement between the EU and Japan, but regular bilateral meetings are held to discuss competition issues and the possibility of an agreement has been discussed. Co-operation with other industrialised states such as Australia and New Zealand takes place within the framework not of a formal agreement, but of the OECD recommendation of 1986 which is limited to notification and exchanges of information.[70]

11–045   Two basic objectives underlie bilateral co-operation agreements such as that between the EC and the USA: co-operation in the implementation of the law (for example, co-operation in merger control to ensure that incompatible conditions are not imposed by the different authorities) and co-operation in the avoidance or management of disputes (including jurisdictional conflicts and positive comity provisions).[71] In principle, these agreements may establish a framework for an evolutionary process, developing from the simple exchange of non-confidential information, to more intensive co-operation including positive comity and even exchanges of confidential information. The EC – USA relationship is an example of evolution, with the 1998 agreement on positive comity building on the positive comity provision in the 1991 agreement.

3.1.1 The EC – USA Co-operation Agreements

11–046   The 1991 agreement covers notification and exchanges of information[72] co-operation in enforcement including the possibility of co-ordination,[73] and negative and positive comity.

11–047   Negative comity, essentially a self-restraint provision in relation to the extra-territorial application of competition law, seeks to avoid conflict by requiring each party to take account of the "important interests" of the other and an "appropriate accommodation" of competing interests.[74]

Under the provision on positive comity in the 1991 agreement, each party may request the other party to initiate investigative and enforcement action where it believes that its interests are adversely affected by anti-competitive practices in the other party's territory.[75] The provision does not impose any obligation, either on the requested agency to act, or on the requesting agency to refrain from acting itself.

11–048   The 1998 agreement elaborates on the application of these positive comity principles; in particular it is agreed that the requesting agency will normally suspend or defer its own enforcement activity during the continuation of enforcement procedures by the requested agency, while recognising that

---

[70] See n. 25.

[71] The agreement between the EC and Canada (see *supra* n. 69) mirrors the EC – USA Agreement of 1991. The Report for 1999 of the WTO Working Group on the Interaction between Trade and Competition Policy contains a useful discussion of the different aims and types of co-operation; Report of October 11, 1999, WT/WGTCP/3.

[72] EC – USA Agreement on competition 1995 O.J. L95/45, Arts II and III.

[73] *ibid.* Art. IV.

[74] EC – USA Agreement on competition 1995 O.J. L95/45, Art VI.

[75] *ibid.* Art. V.

sometimes action by both parties may be appropriate.[76] These clauses have two connected aims: to ensure that anticompetitive conduct with a cross-border dimension does not thereby escape the enforcement agencies, and to achieve the most effective and efficient allocation of resources between the parties.[77] In its annual Report on the operation of the EC – USA agreement covering 1998, the Commission says that the agreement on positive comity is "an important development, since it represents a commitment on the part of the European Union and the United States to co-operate with respect to antitrust enforcement in certain situations, rather than to seek to apply their antitrust laws extraterritorially."[78] Provisions of this type (as opposed to simpler information exchange provisions) clearly require a high degree of trust between the parties, which may need building up over a period of dialogue and co-operation. The Commission Report for 1998 describes this relationship:

> "In all cases of mutual interest it has become the norm to establish contacts at the outset in order to exchange views and, when appropriate, to co-ordinate enforcement activities. The two sides, where appropriate, seek to co-ordinate their respective approaches on the definition of relevant markets, on possible remedies in order to ensure that they do not conflict, as well as on points of foreign law relevant to the interpretation of an agreement or to the effectiveness of a remedy. Co-operation under this heading has involved the synchronisation of investigations and searches."[79]

As the quotation illustrates, the Commission is generally positive as to the effectiveness of the co-operation agreement. One of the major constraints has proved to be confidentiality of information. Neither the 1991 nor the 1998 agreements alter the existing laws of either party as far as confidential information is concerned. The Commission is under a duty of confidentiality under Regulation 17/62 and the agreement makes it clear that neither party may be required to disclose information where disclosure would be prohibited by the law of that party.[80] On the conclusion of the 1998 agreement the Commission made a Statement on Confidentiality of Information, in which it points out:

11–050

> "Article VII of this Agreement states that existing laws remain unchanged and that the Agreement must be interpreted consistently with those existing laws. This Agreement therefore cannot permit either of the Parties" competition authorities to do any act they do not already have the power to do. One consequence of this is that the Commission may only provide information to the U.S. authorities where it is consistent with Community law to do so."[81]

---

[76] EC – USA Agreement on the application of positive comity principles in the enforcement of competition laws 1998 O.J. L173/26, Arts III and IV.
[77] *ibid.* Art. I(2).
[78] Commission Report to the Council and European Parliament on the operation of the EC – USA competition agreement, April 2, 1999. See also Reports on 1995-96, COM (96) 479 final; on 1996, COM (97) 346 final and 1997, COM (98) 510 final.
[79] Commission Report to the Council and European Parliament on the operation of the EC – USA competition agreement, April 2, 1999 at p.2.
[80] Regulation 17 O.J. English special edition Series-I (59–62) p. 87, Art 20 (for consolidated version, see http://europa.eu.int/eur-lex/en/consleg/pdf/1962/en_1962R0017_do_001.pdf); EC – USA Agreement on competition 1995 O.J. 95/45, Art. VIII, together with an exchange of interpretative letters, and EC – USA Agreement on the application of positive comity principles in the enforcement of competition laws 1998 O.J. L173/26, Art. V.
[81] The Statement on Confidentiality of Information is quoted in the Commission's Report for 1998, April 2, 1999, p.6.

11–051   In practice this means that the consent of the undertaking concerned is needed. This may well be forthcoming as it is in the undertaking's own interest that the investigation proceeds efficiently on both sides of the Atlantic; in its Report for 1998 the Commission refers to the Microsoft case, where Microsoft agreed to the exchange of confidential information between the Commission and the Department of Justice. However, in the nature of things, such consent is less likely to be forthcoming in cartel cases. The Report of the Group of Experts in 1995 recommended increasing the level of bilateral co-operation, both in extent—the conclusion of similar agreements with more countries, including Japan[82]—and depth—with greater use of positive comity and provision for the exchange of confidential information.[83] Certainly the exchange of confidential information is much more likely to be agreed in the context of a bilateral agreement between domestic authorities that know and trust each other: the Commission has said that it would be premature to include exchange of confidential information in the co-operation provisions of a putative multilateral agreement. This example illustrates that while it will be possible to multilateralise the principle of co-operation, some of the more intensive forms of co-operation are difficult to translate from the bilateral to multilateral level.

3.1.2 Co-operation in the European Economic Area Agreement

11–052   Co-operation also forms one aspect of the extensive competition provisions in the EEA. These provisions are based on two initial decisions: first, that in spite of the overall objective of homogeneity there would be a two-pillar approach to competition enforcement within the EEA, encompassing the EC Commission and the (newly-created) EFTA Surveillance Authority;[84] and second that each individual case would be subject to investigation by one only of these two authorities. This meant that in addition to provisions for practical co-operation designed to underpin homogeneity, there was a need for clear jurisdictional rules. The EEA contains both. Article 58 provides that the Commission and the EFTA Surveillance Authority will co-operate in accordance with Protocols 23 and 24, with a view to "uniform surveillance" throughout the EEA, and the promotion of homogeneous implementation, application and interpretation of the agreement. Protocol 23 (co-operation in cases falling under Article 53 and 54 EEA, that is the equivalents of Articles 81 and 82) and Protocol 24 (co-operation in relation to control of concentrations under Article 57 EEA) cover exchanges of notification, documents and other information, mutual assistance, consultation and rights of representation at hearings. Significantly, both Protocols allow for the exchange of confidential information. In addition, Article 110 EEA provides for the mutual enforcement of decisions of the Commission, the European Court of Justice and the EFTA Surveillance Authority and EFTA Court.

---

[82] The Joint Conclusions on the Economic and Trade Partnership at the EU–Japan Summit held in Tokyo on July 19, 2000 look forward to a future bilateral agreement on competition policy.

[83] See n. 46.

[84] See Protocol 21 on the Implementation of Competition Rules Applicable to Undertakings, and Agreement between EFTA States on establishing EFTA Surveillance Authority and EFTA Court [1994] O.J. L344/1.

The jurisdictional rules in the EEA agreement are designed so as not to give rise to "any transfer of powers to the EFTA Surveillance Authority and the EFTA Court" from the Community institutions.[85] The overall effect of Articles 56 EEA is that all "mixed" cases (these are cases where both Article 81 EC and Article 53 EEA may apply) will fall within the jurisdiction of the EC Commission unless there is no appreciable effect on trade within EC. In addition, the EC Commission has jurisdiction in cases where there is no affect on trade between the EU Member States (so Articles 81 will not apply) but trade is affected between one Member State and one or more EFTA States, subject to a turnover threshold.[86] Similarly in cases of abuse of a dominant position, Article 56(2) EEA provides that cases are to be decided by the authority in whose territory a dominant position is found to exist; if the dominant position is present in both, the jurisdictional rules applicable to Article 53 apply, so that in cases where there is an appreciable effect on trade between the EU Member States, the EC Commission will have jurisdiction. In *Opinion 1/92*, the Court of Justice accepted that these provisions do not encroach on the Community's existing powers, and more importantly, that the Community had competence to enter into competence allocation agreements of this type:

11–053

> ". . . the Community may accept rules made by virtue of an agreement as to the sharing of the respective competences of the Contracting Parties in the field of competition, provided that those rules do not change the nature of the powers of the Community and of its institutions as conceived in the Treaty."[87]

The EEA therefore goes considerably further than the co-operation agreements with the USA or Canada, in its provisions on rights of representation, confidential information, and jurisdiction. They reflect the aim of the EEA to produce a "homogeneous European Economic Area"[88] with two competition authorities developing in parallel policy based on substantially identical rules in the context of a highly integrated market.

11–054

3.1.3 Co-operation in other agreements

It might have been expected that similar jurisdictional rules would be incorporated into the implementing rules on competition policy adopted by the Association Councils within the framework of the Europe Agreements.[89] However, these implementing rules instead adopt a comity-based approach,

11–055

---

[85] Summary of the Commission's request for an opinion, *Opinion 1/92* [1992] E.C.R. I-2821.

[86] Where the turnover of the undertakings concerned within the EFTA States represents more than 33% of the combined EEA turnover, then the EFTA Surveillance Authority will have jurisdiction unless trade between EU Member States is affected: Art. 56(1)(b) and (c). The concepts of "undertaking" and "turnover" are dealt with in Protocol 22. The Commission claims this jurisdiction as an "entirely new power": summary of the Commission's request for an opinion, *Opinion 1/92* [1992] E.C.R. I-2821.

[87] *Opinion 1/92* [1992] E.C.R. I-2821, at para. 41.

[88] Art.1(1) EEA.

[89] Europe Agreements have been concluded with ten Central and Eastern European States (Hungary, Poland, Romania, Bulgaria, Slovakia, Czech Republic, Estonia, Latvia, Lithuania and Slovenia). These implementing rules were to be adopted by the Association Council within three years of the entry into force of the Agreements; see, for example, the Europe Agreement

recognising that there will be overlapping jurisdiction between the EC Commission and national authorities in the Associated States. To take the Polish rules as an example:

> "The competencies of the Commission and the AMO [Polish Antimonopoly Office] to deal with these cases shall flow from the existing rules of the respective legislation of the Community and Poland, including where these rules are applied to undertakings located outside the respective territory. Both authorities shall settle the cases in accordance with their own substantive rules."[90]

11-056   Cases under the Agreements which may affect both the Community and the market of the Associated State and which may fall under the competence of both competition authorities shall be dealt by both the Commission and the relevant competition authority in accordance with the co-operation and co-ordination provisions.[91] Notification, consultation and comity (positive and negative) and the provision of information (subject to confidentiality in the same way as within the agreements with the USA and Canada) are all covered. In cases where the such procedures do not lead to a "mutually acceptable" solution, the Association Council may act as a forum for an exchange of views and may make recommendations, but these will be "without prejudice to any action under the respective competition laws in force in the territory of the Parties."[92] Again, therefore, the Commission does not cede any competence.

11-057   Other agreements, including those with less-developed economies, also contain provision for co-operation and comity. The Euro-Mediterranean Association Agreements that have been concluded with (so far) Tunisia, Morocco, Israel, Jordan and Egypt contain provisions on competition policy very similar to the Europe Agreements and it is likely that the implementing rules will follow the same pattern. The so-called "Global Agreement" with Mexico signed in 1997 provided that:

> "The Joint Council shall establish mechanisms of co-operation and co-ordination among their authorities with responsibility for the implementation of competition rules. Co-operation shall include mutual legal assistance, notification, consultation and exchange of information in order to ensure transparency relating to the enforcement of competition laws and policies."[93]

11-058   In March 2000, the EC-Mexico Joint Council adopted a Decision (which came into force on July 1, 2000) for the implementation of trade aspects of the Global Agreement which included provision for co-operation in competition.[94]

---

with Poland 1993 O.J L348/2, Art.63(3) and Decision 1/96 of the Association Council adopting the implementing rules 1996 O.J. L208/24. For an effective critique of the implementing rules, see Van den Bossche, "The International Dimension of EC Competition Law: The Case of the Europe Agreements" (1997) 18 E.C.L.R. 24

[90] Decision 1/96 of the EU – Poland Association Council adopting the implementing rules 1996 O.J. L208/24, Arts.1

[91] *ibid.*, Art.2.

[92] *ibid.*, Art.9.

[93] Economic Partnership, Political Co-ordination and Co-operation Agreement between the EC, its Member States and the United Mexican States 1997 O.J. C350/6, COM (97) 527, Art 11.

[94] The Global Agreement itself is not yet in force; however, the Interim Agreement on Trade came into force in July 1998, and Decision 2/2000 of the Joint Council of the Interim Agreement

Under Article 39 of this Decision, a "mechanism of co-operation" between the authorities of the Parties with responsibility for implementation of competition rules is established, and the details of this mechanism are set out in an Annex which covers the usual co-operation issues such as notification, exchanges of information (subject to confidentiality), co-ordination of enforcement and comity.[95] One aim of this co-operation, apart from underpinning the free-trade objectives of the Decision, is to promote mutual understanding of the parties" competition laws and to "clarify differences", and to that end mutual technical assistance will include training, seminars and joint studies.[96] Technical assistance is also included in the Trade, Development and Co-operation Agreement with South Africa, signed in 1999, along with provision for exchange of information and positive and negative comity.[97]

It is noticeable that each of these agreements or Decisions, containing provisions for co-operation and comity, post-date the specific Agreement of 1991 with the USA. Although there are still very few specific bilateral agreements on competition policy, therefore, there is a real sense in which this Agreement has provided a model for structuring co-operation in the context of a wider trade or association agreement.   **11-059**

3.2 Competition in trade agreements

3.2.1 Competition and free trade

However, the agreements that have been mentioned in the previous section have, as well as co-operation clauses, additional elements which reflect their purpose as trade agreements. Behind the EU's championing within the WTO and its Working Party of core principles and common approaches to competition policy lies a key development in its own bilateral trade policy: the recognition that an increased emphasis on reciprocal free trade leads to the need for a regulatory dimension to its external policy.[98] And for the reasons already discussed, competition policy is regarded as a centrally important dimension to the regulatory framework needed to support trade liberalisation. Both the market access and developmental aspects of this issue are relevant here: an adequate competition policy helps to create a fully competitive open market, helps to prevent the often fragile markets of emerging economies from being subverted by anticompetitive practices from private   **11–060**

---

on Trade and Trade-Related Matters brought into effect the free-trade provisions of the agreement, including competition policy, and came into force on July 1, 2000. See also Communication from the Commission to the Council and the European Parliament accompanying the Final Text of the Draft Decisions by the EC – Mexico Joint Council, January 18, 2000, COM (2000)9.

[95] Annex XV to Decision 2/2000 of the Joint Council of the Interim Agreement on Trade and Trade-Related Matters.

[96] Annex XV, Art. 9.

[97] Trade, Development and Co-operation Agreement between the EC, its Member States and South Africa 1999 O.J. L311/3, Arts. 38, 39 and 40.

[98] For a discussion of the increased emphasis on reciprocal free trade, see Cremona, "Flexible Models: External Policy and the European Economic Constitution" in de Búrca and Scott (eds.) Constitutional Change in the EU: From Uniformity to Flexibility? (Hart Publishing 2000).

undertakings (domestic or foreign) and provides a secure and friendly regulatory environment for prospective inward investors. This, at least, is the theory and helps to explain both why the EU has been keen to include competition among the "trade-related" provisions of new agreements, and why the other parties to such agreements have accepted their inclusion.

11-061   The condemnation of anticompetitive conduct where it affects the trade between the parties to a preferential trading agreement is not new. The free trade agreements with the EFTA States, now largely superseded by the EEA (or by accession to the EU) contain provisions on competition. The still extant 1972 free trade agreement with Switzerland, for example, which is typical of these early trade agreements, links together in its stated aims the promotion of bilateral trade between the Community and Switzerland, the provision of fair conditions of competition for trade between the Contracting Parties, and its contribution to the harmonious development and expansion of world trade.[99] It then declares certain anticompetitive activities "incompatible with the functioning of the Agreement in so far as they may affect trade between the Community and Switzerland".[1] Three types of conduct are specified, corresponding to Articles 81, 82 and 87 of the EC Treaty: restrictive agreements and concerted practices, abuse of a dominant position, and state aids. A very similar provision is found in the Europe Agreements and Euro-Mediterranean Association Agreements.[2] There is, however, one interesting development. The Swiss Agreement uses language which echoes the relevant EC Treaty articles; a Declaration made by the EC at the time of its conclusion states that in the context of "the autonomous implementation of Article 23(1) of the Agreement" the EC will "assess any practices contrary to that Article on the basis of criteria arising from the application of the rules of Articles 85, 86, 90 and 92 of the Treaty establishing the European Economic Community" (now Articles 81, 82, 86 and 87 EC). This explicit reference to the EC Treaty is not incorporated into the Agreement itself, however, and applies only to the Community. The later Europe and Euro-Mediterranean Agreements refer explicitly to "assessment on the basis of criteria arising from the application of the rules" of the specific EC Treaty provisions. This change, as we shall see in the next section, reflects the degree to which the Associated States are prepared to adopt a framework of competition rules aligned to those of the Community. The EEA and the Decision establishing a customs union with Turkey go even further: they both include more elaborate provisions which substantively copy the competition rules of the EC Treaty. In the former case, this is an aspect of the intended homogeneity of the EEA; in the case of Turkey the provisions reflect the high degree of integration represented by a customs union.

11-062   The substantive equivalence between the EC Treaty rules and those in the EEA and the Turkey customs union Decision has another important dimension. Anticompetitive activities are not only declared to be "incompatible"

---

[99] Free Trade Agreement with Switzerland, OJ English special edition Series-I 72 (31.12) L300 p.190, Art 1.
[1] *ibid.*, Art 23.
[2] See for example, Europe Agreement with Poland, Art.63(1) and Euro-Mediterranean Agreement with Tunisia, Art 36(1).

with the proper functioning of the agreement, they are *prohibited*; and in both cases restrictive agreements are "automatically void".[3] This of course has important implications for the enforcement of the rules. Enforcement under the bilateral free-trade agreements of the 1970's with the EFTA States (which provide for incompatibility but no prohibition) was effectively limited to intergovernmental enforcement through the Joint Committee procedure set up by the agreements; direct enforcement by private parties was not envisaged, and enforcement by respective domestic agencies depended on both the status of the Agreement within each national system and its jurisdictional rules as far as competition was concerned.

In practice, for the Community, the extra-territorial application of its own **11–063** competition law was more effective than the procedures in the free-trade agreements. One of the most significant aspects of the EEA for the Community, therefore, was the inclusion of directly enforceable competition rules, together with a regional enforcement agency (the EFTA Surveillance Authority) and Court. The Turkey customs union Decision, like the EEA, contains a firm commitment on the part of Turkey to establish an enforcement agency capable of directly enforcing the prohibition in the Decision.[4] On this point, the Europe Agreements adopt essentially the same approach as the early free-trade agreements: a declaration of the incompatibility of anticompetitive conduct, together with implementing rules under which, as we have seen, enforcement is the responsibility of the competition authority of each Party, exercising its jurisdiction on the basis of "the existing rules of the respective legislation of the Community and [the Associated State], including where these rules are applied to undertakings located outside the respective territory."[5] The requirement to adopt implementing rules pre-supposes the existence of a functioning competition authority but there is no specific obligation to create such a body.

Other trade agreements contain competition clauses, which may be more **11–064** generalised statements of principle. The free-trade Decision of the EU – Mexico Joint Council simply states that the parties "undertake to apply their respective competition laws so as to avoid that the benefits of this Decision may be diminished or cancelled out by anticompetitive activities."[6] Similarly, the Partnership and Co-operation Agreement with Russia provides that the parties "agree to work to remedy or remove through the application of their competition laws or otherwise, restrictions on competition by enterprises or caused by State intervention insofar as they may affect trade between the Community and Russia."[7] The Trade, Development and Co-operation Agreement with South Africa uses a declaration of incompatibility similar to that found in the Free Trade Agreement with Switzerland, covering

---

[3] EEA, Art. 53(2); Decision 1/95 of the Association Council on implementing the final phase of the customs union with Turkey, Art. 32(2).
[4] Decision 1/95 of the Association Council on implementing the final phase of the customs union with Turkey, Art. 39(2)(b).
[5] See n. 90.
[6] Annex XV to Decision 2/2000 of the Joint Council of the Interim Agreement on Trade and Trade-Related Matters, Art. 1(1).
[7] Partnership and Co-operation Agreement with Russia 1997 O.J. L327/1, Art. 53(1).

restrictive agreements and abuse of market power.[8] In an Annex, it is agreed that the Community will use criteria arising from the application of Articles 81 and 82 EC, including secondary legislation, and South Africa will use criteria arising from the application of the rules of South African competition law.[9] Enforcement will be by the respective competition authority, with the possibility of consultation within the Co-operation Council; each Party is under an obligation to introduce, if necessary, laws for the implementation of the competition clause.[10]

3.2.2 Competition policy and anti-dumping

11-065   One further aspect of the link between trade and competition policy made in these agreements should be mentioned: the relationship between competition policy and anti-dumping measures. While anti-dumping is essentially a trade measure, it is (at least in theory) a response to anticompetitive conduct on the part of the exporting undertaking. It is one way, enshrined in the GATT 1994, in which States are able to deal with one of the trade and competition problems: that of conduct in one State which has anticompetitive effects in another. This being the case, it is possible to argue that where there is an effective inter-State (and intra-State) competition policy there is no need for anti-dumping measures. Most of the agreements we have examined so far do not make this connection; the most they do is to provide for prior consultation before unilateral anti-dumping action is taken.[11] However there are three interesting exceptions.

11-066   The first is the EEA. As a direct result of the broader acceptance by the EFTA parties of the *acquis communautaire* and in particular of the competition policy of the European Community, anti-dumping measures will generally not be applicable in trade between EC states and EFTA states, any more than they are possible within the EC itself.[12] Anti-competitive practices, such as predatory or discriminatory pricing or illegal state aid should be dealt with by the EC Commission and EFTA Surveillance Authority within their respective jurisdictions, thus rendering retaliatory measures unnecessary. The link with the *acquis communautaire* is made clear in Protocol 13, applicable to this provision. Under the first paragraph of the Protocol, the application of Article 26 is limited to areas in which the *acquis communautaire* is fully integrated into the Agreement. The Community's common commercial policy towards third countries is, however, one area which is *not* integrated into the EEA. Consequently, problems may arise where third country origin products that are subject to (for example) EC anti-dumping measures, are imported indirectly into the EC via an EFTA party. In such a case, anti-dumping measures may be imposed as an anti-

---

[8] Trade, Development and Co-operation Agreement between the EC, its Member States and South Africa 1999 O.J. L311/3, Art. 35.
[9] *ibid.*, Annex VIII.
[10] *ibid.*, Arts. 36 and 37.
[11] See, for example, Euro-Mediterranean Agreement with Tunisia, Arts 24 and 27; Free Trade Agreement with Switzerland, Arts 25 and 27.
[12] Art. 26 EEA.

circumvention measure at the border between the EC Member State and EFTA state.[13]

The second example is the Turkey customs union Decision. In spite of its extensive competition provisions, and in spite of the fact that the Community's anti-dumping Regulation is one of the measures to be implemented by Turkey as part of its alignment to the Community's external commercial policy, the Turkey customs union Decision does not go as far as the EEA in abandoning anti-dumping in trade between the Community and Turkey. The Additional Protocol of 1970, which sets out the details for the transitional stage for the establishment of the customs union, contains procedures for the implementation of anti-dumping measures and these are preserved by the customs union Decision of 1995.[14] However, the Decision does give the Association Council the power to review the application of trade defence instruments at the request of either party, during which

11–067

> "the Association Council may decide to suspend the application of these instruments provided that Turkey has implemented competition, State aid control, and other relevant parts of the acquis communautaire which are related to the internal market and ensured their effective enforcement, so providing a guarantee against unfair competition comparable to that existing inside the internal market."[15]

Two points are notable here; first, the staged nature of the customs union implementation; unlike the EEA, this was to be achieved over a period of time allowing for the adjustment of Turkish legislation and policy.[16] Secondly, the need for anti-dumping and other trade defence measures is linked not only to competition policy but also to other elements of the internal market *acquis communautaire*. This suggests that although competition policy provides support for market liberalization, market-opening measures which provide the foundation for the internal market are themselves, in an international context, supportive of an effective competition structure.

11–068

Thirdly, we turn again to the Europe Agreements. These association Agreements have less ambitious aims as far as immediate economic integration is concerned, and preserve anti-dumping mechanisms subject to consultation procedures. However, the Commission has stated that in the case of full and effective application of competition rules by and within Associated State, it may be possible to regard anti-dumping measures as no longer necessary. This statement, made in July 1994 in a Communication that was designed to prepare the way for the major decisions on accession strategy taken by the European Council at Essen in December 1994, was also a response to criticism from the central and eastern European States over the

11–069

---

[13] Protocol 13, para. 2. Complex anti-circumvention rules mean that even products manufactured in an EFTA state may be covered, if the components or parts have been imported from a third country in order to circumvent the anti-dumping origin rules applicable to the finished product.

[14] Additional Protocol to the Association Agreement, of November 23, 1970, Art. 47; Decision 1/95 of the Association Council on implementing the final phase of the customs union with Turkey, Art. 44(2).

[15] Decision 1/95 of the Association Council on implementing the final phase of the customs union with Turkey, Art. 44(1).

[16] See Arts. 8-10 of Decision 1/95 on technical barriers to trade for another example of this staged approach.

continued use of anti-dumping measures by the EU against their exports. Emphasising the priority to be given to competition policy and State aids control in the prospective programme of harmonisation, the Commission's language is very close to that incorporated into the Turkish customs union Decision the following year:

> "Once satisfactory implementation of competition policy and state aids control, together with the application of those parts of Community law linked to the wider market, has been achieved, the Union could decide to progressively reduce the use of commercial defence instruments for industrial products for the countries concerned, since it would have a level of guarantee against unfair competition comparable to that existing inside the Internal Market."[17]

11–071   As a unilateral statement, this does not of course have the status of Article 44 of Decision 1/95; it nevertheless shows that in Community thinking at the time the link between competition and anti-dumping was well established, as well as illustrating the Community strategy towards the central and eastern European States based on incentives targeted at those countries managing to achieve goals set by the Community institutions.

In 1995 the Group of Experts also addressed the link between competition and anti-dumping in the context of strengthened bilateral co-operation, concluding that

> "Co-operation between competition authorities will not in the foreseeable future make it possible to relinquish trade protection instruments. However, as the effectiveness of co-operation increases, instances of conflict likely to lead to the use of these instruments will decrease."[18]

11–072   In its 1996 Communication, the Commission expressed the view that from an economic perspective anti-dumping measures are less efficient than the development of domestic law in dealing with the problem of inadequate regulation of competition on export markets, because they tackle the effect of the anti-competitive behaviour but not its root cause in the export country.[19] We are here moving towards the attempt to build the core principles of domestic competition policy into bilateral agreements, alongside provisions which focus on inter-party trade.

3.3 Standard-setting and harmonisation

11–073   Devuyst has pointed out that the EC has been "very active in extending its own competition policy model to countries that do not yet have a tradition in the enforcement of antitrust rules. The instrument used to achieve this goal has been linkage with preferential and non-preferential trade agreements."[20]

---

[17] Commission Communication, "Follow up to 'The Europe Agreements and Beyond: A Strategy to Prepare the Countries of Central and Eastern Europe for Accession', July 27, 1994, COM(94) 361 final, section B(ii) p.7.
[18] "Competition Policy in the New Trade Order: Strengthening International Co-operation and Rules", Report of the Group of Experts, Brussels, July 1995, at para. IV.2.1.
[19] Commission Communication of June 17, 1996, "Towards an International Framework of Competition Rules", COM (96) 284 at section 1(c).
[20] Devuyst, "The International Dimension of the EC's Antitrust Policy: Extending the Level Playing Field" (1998)3 EFA Rev. 459 at 469.

The rationale for this policy is in many ways similar to the arguments used by the EU in support of an international competition agreement, centred on the role of competition policy in developing and emerging economies.

3.3.1 The development of domestic competition law

This rationale does not, of course, in itself require use of the EU's own model of competition policy. The agreements in which approximation to the EU model is found are those which envisage a high degree of economic integration with the EU and in particular agreements with the Community's own near neighbours: the EEA, the Europe Agreements with the countries of central and eastern Europe, the Decision on the customs union with Turkey, the Euro-Mediterranean Agreements, and the Partnership and Co-operation Agreements (PCAs) with the countries of the former Soviet Union. Other agreements will commit the parties to an effective domestic competition policy but without reference to the EU standard: the free trade Agreement with Mexico, the new Partnership Agreement between the African, Caribbean and Pacific States and the EU (the Cotonou Convention), the Trade, Development and Co-operation Agreement with South Africa.   **11–074**

The Cotonou Convention exemplifies this latter approach. The provision on competition policy starts with a statement of principle; the Parties: **11–075**

> "agree that the introduction and implementation of effective and sound competition policies and rules are of crucial importance in order to improve and secure an investment friendly climate, a sustainable industrialisation process and transparency in the access to markets."[21]

Then follow two commitments; a commitment to implement national and regional rules and policies regulating anticompetitive agreements and abuse of a dominant position (the terminology reflects Articles 81 and 82 EC but without an explicit reference); and a commitment to support and assistance including "assistance in the drafting of an appropriate legal framework and its administrative enforcement with particular reference to the special situation of the least developed countries."[22] This Convention is essentially a framework convention and is designed to be followed by regional agreements moving towards WTO-compliant reciprocal free trade; it is likely that the new agreements will contain more detailed provisions on competition. As we have seen, the Trade, Development and Co-operation Agreement with South Africa contains a declaration of the incompatibility with the Agreement of certain anticompetitive activities; this is supported by a commitment to adopt the "necessary laws and regulations" within three years.[23]   **11–076**

The EEA regime is very different. Here the need was not to establish national competition authorities in the individual EFTA states, but to set up an EFTA Surveillance Authority that would fulfil the competition policy functions of the EC Commission for the EFTA States as a   **11–077**

---

[21] Cotonou Convention, Art. 45(1).
[22] *ibid.* Art 45(3).
[23] Trade, Development and Co-operation Agreement with South Africa, Art. 36; for the incompatibility clause see n. 8.

group.[24] The "two-pillar" system was designed so that as far as possible it would mirror the EC system:

> "It was decided that the same competition rules and policies had to apply throughout the EEA. It was felt that this situation even called for identical and largely parallel enforcement structures and procedures in the Community and in the EFTA countries."[25]

11–078   As with the EU Member States, there is no obligation in the EEA requiring the implementation of any specific model of *national* competition law; rather, the EEA competition rules apply in the EFTA States, enforced by the EFTA Surveillance Authority and EFTA Court. The key to the system are thus the jurisdictional and co-operation rules applicable to the EC Commission and EFTA Surveillance Authority.[26]

3.3.2 Approximation of laws

11–079   In other Association and Partnership Agreements with emerging economies —those closer to the EU—we begin to see provision for the approximation of laws with reference to Community standards, and competition is normally among the areas of law included.[27] The competition provisions in the non-preferential PCAs do not use the terminology of Articles 81, 82 or 87 in their reference to anticompetitive practices, but the approximation of laws provision makes reference to Community law. The PCAs with the "non-European" states such as Kazakhstan contain a provision on legislative co-operation, including competition, under which the partner state is to "endeavour to ensure that its legislation will be gradually made compatible with that of the Community". The Parties also agree "to examine ways to apply their respective competition laws on a concerted basis in such cases where trade between them is affected."[28] In the PCA with Russia, the parties "shall ensure that they have and enforce laws addressing restrictions on competition by enterprises within their jurisdiction"[29] and "rules on competition" are among the areas covered by the approximation of laws provision: "Russia shall endeavour to ensure that its legislation will be gradually made compatible with that of the Community".[30]

11–080   The Europe Agreements also include competition among the areas of law which are to be approximated to Community norms.[31] Here, approximation is expressly linked to integration; the Agreement with Poland, for example, states:

---

[24] See Stragier, "The Competition Rules of the EEA Agreement and their Implementation" [1993] 1 ECLRev 30; Diem, "EEA Competition Law" [1994] 5 ECL Rev. 263.

[25] European Commission, 22nd Report on Competition Policy (1992).

[26] See text at n. 84 *et seq.*

[27] The Euro-Mediterranean Agreements have only a general approximation clause, specifying that co-operation will aim at helping the Associated State to bring its legislation closer to that of the Community in the areas covered by the Agreement: see, for example, Euro-Mediterranean Agreement with Tunisia 1998 O.J. L97/2, Art. 52.

[28] PCA with Kazakhstan 1999 O.J. L196/1, Art. 43.

[29] PCA with Russia 1997 O.J. L 327/1, Art. 53.

[30] PCA with Russia, Art 55.

[31] Europe Agreement with Poland, Art. 69.

"The Contracting Parties recognize that the major precondition for Poland's economic integration into the Community is the approximation of that country's existing and future legislation to that of the Community. Poland shall use its best endeavours to ensure that future legislation is compatible with Community legislation."[32]

We have already seen that competition has been prioritised as an area of implementation by the Commission,[33] and that the rules implementing the inter-State trade competition provisions of the Europe Agreements pre-suppose a functioning domestic competition authority in the Associated States.[34] Indeed, the implementing rules appear in some respects to pre-empt the approximation process by applying aspects of EC competition law, even though the underlying principle of the rules is that each competition authority is to apply its own legislation. In the Polish rules, for example, "the competition authorities shall ensure that the principles contained in the block exemption Regulations in force in the Community are applied in full" in applying the competition provisions of the Agreement.[35] Difficulties on the Polish side caused by the Community rules are to be resolved through consultation within the Association Council, "having regard to the approximation of legislation as provided for in the Europe Agreement".

11–081

In practice, the approximation provisions in the Europe Agreements themselves are now part of the larger pre-accession process. The Commission's White Paper of 1995 on the Preparation of the Associated Countries of Central and Eastern Europe for Integration into the Internal Market has a section on competition policy which gives an analysis of EU competition policy, including state aids, merger control, restrictive agreements and abuse of a dominant position, and the rules relating to state monopolies and public undertakings. The White Paper indicates the infrastructure conditions which are a necessary precondition for the operation of competition law, and sets out recommendation for the first stage of implementation.[36] Competition (both substantive law and administrative ability to apply to *acquis*) is included in the Commission's regular reports on progress in compliance with the accession criteria, which includes the ability to assume the obligations of membership. To take just one example, the report on Poland in October 1999 concluded:

11–082

"Poland has achieved a reasonable level of alignment in the field of *antitrust* and *mergers*. Amendments to the Law on Counteracting Monopolistic Practices have entered into force in January 1999 and have improved the situation. Further alignment in particular regarding block exemptions remains to be completed. . . . Poland should establish a legal and regulatory framework for the control of state aids to ensure full compliance with the *acquis* in order to prepare for the competitiveness of the internal market. The need for an effective public aid control and enforcement system remains an urgent priority for Poland."[37]

---

[32] *ibid.*, Art. 68.
[33] See text at n. 17.
[34] See text at n. 89.
[35] Decision No 1/96 of the EU - Poland Association Council 1996. O.J. L208/24, Art.6.
[36] Commission White Paper on the Preparation of the Associated Countries of Central and Eastern Europe for Integration into the Internal Market of the Union", May 3, 1995, COM (95) 163 final, chap. 3.
[37] Regular Report from the Commission on Progress towards Accession: Poland, October 13, 1999, section B.3.1.

11–083   Similar regular reports are now produced by the Commission with respect to Turkey, now accepted as a candidate State.[38] This process takes place within the context of the customs union Decision of the EC-Turkey Association Council which, as we have already seen, contains extensive provisions on competition policy as it affects trade between the parties. However, competition also features as part of the programme of approximation of laws, "with a view to achieving the economic integration sought by the Customs Union;" Turkey was to pass a competition law modelled on that of the EC (including block exemption regulations and "the case law developed by the EC authorities") and establish a competition authority before the entry into force of the customs union, and adapt its State aids to Community rules and guidelines.[39] The provisions for state aid control are of interest; they have to accommodate the fact that while not a Member State, Turkey's position within the customs union requires a degree of State aid control which could not be provided by a national agency. The solution has been to provide for notification by Turkey to the EC Commission of proposed State aid in the same way as an individual EU Member State. The Commission may then "raise objections" against an aid which it would have deemed unlawful if granted by a Member State; if Turkey cannot accept the Commission's view, the case may be referred to arbitration. On the other side, Turkey may raise objections within the Association Council to aids granted by EU Member States, in which case the matter, if not resolved within the Association Council, may be referred by the Council to the Court of Justice. The system thus avoids the Commission issuing individual decisions binding on Turkey, while giving it a role together with international forms of dispute settlement. It is too early to tell whether this system will work in practice. In October 1999, the Commission's regular report on Turkey's progress in meeting the accession criteria concluded:

> "As far as the implementation of *anti-trust* rules is concerned, the situation remains satisfactory. However, progress still remains to be made in order to finalise the approximation on the *acquis* as foreseen in the customs union Decision. Regarding *state aid*, information on Turkey's state aid schemes have already been submitted to the Commission. Their conformity with EC rules still needs to be discussed between the Commission and the Turkish authorities."[40]

11–084   In the case of the candidate States, approximation has a clear goal, and the regular reports by the Commission (although not part of the regime instituted by the agreements themselves) provide an effective practical incentive towards implementation. Substantive commitments made by other States are much less easy to enforce and may not have much more practical effect than aspirational statements of intent. It is perhaps ironic, if understandable, that whereas a certain political dimension has become a prerequisite for economic

---

[38] See Conclusions of the European Council, Helsinki, December 1999.

[39] Decision 1/95 on the Customs Union between the EU and Turkey, Art 39. Turkish legislation on competition has been adopted, see Law No. 4054 on Protection of Competition Official Gazette 22140, December 13, 1994; Law No. 97/9090 on Appointment of the Competition Board Official Gazette 22918, February 27, 1997. See WTO Secretariat Report and government policy statement for WTO Trade Policy Review Body in October 1998, available at http://www.wto.org/wto/reviews/turkey.htm.

[40] Regular Report from the Commission on Progress towards Accession: Turkey, October 13, 1999, section B.3.1.

integration agreements, the economic and institutional infrastructure necessary to support economic liberalisation does not yet form part of the "essential elements" of most agreements.[41]

4. Conclusion

In the previous section we have examined three different types of competition clause in the Community's bilateral agreements: co-operation clauses, dealing with procedural and jurisdictional issues; substantive clauses which focus on supporting the inter-State trade liberalisation envisaged by the agreement; and approximation clauses, with or without reference to the Community standard, which seek to ensure the existence of functioning competition law at the domestic level. To what extent are any of these models likely to prove helpful in the debate over a putative multilateral agreement on competition?

11–085

The rationale for adoption of the Community model of competition policy in the agreements with candidate states is linked to their need to adopt the *acquis communautaire* as part of the pre-accession process (even where the negotiation of the Agreement pre-dates the formal membership application). The rationale is clear, although the suitability of the Community model (especially its detailed rules beyond the "hard core cartel", such as those on vertical restraints) for emerging economies some distance from accession may be questioned. It is necessarily even more questionable for countries outside the accession process, such as the Euro-Mediterranean Partnership States of the Maghreb and Mashreq, or the States of the former Soviet Union with Partnership and Co-operation Agreements.

11–086

As the Commission now recognises, any commitment to substantive standards of competition law at a multilateral level would have to be based on more generally applicable (and more generalised) principles. It is also the case that Community competition rules have been developed within the context of the treaty's market integration objectives and the development of purely domestic policy will not necessarily require the same balance of objectives:

11–087

> "Community competition policy therefore, unlike competition policy of Member States or our trading partners, has not only had to take account of the need for a system of undistorted competition but also the market integration objective."[42]

This history and context does however make Community experience valuable in identifying priorities for a competition policy designed to underpin a trade liberalisation agreement. If the adoption of a multilateral agreement containing even core principles to be applied in a domestic context is a distant and possibly unrealistic prospect, it may be more possible to achieve consensus on competition principles as they affect inter-state trade. The

11–088

---

[41] The new Cotonou Convention includes the principles of a market economy among those contributing to the agreement's objectives, without giving them "essential element" status: "The Parties recognise that the principles of the market economy, supported by transparent competition rules and sound economic and social policies, contribute to achieving the objectives of the partnership." Cotonou Convention, Art. 10(2).

[42] Commission Green Paper on Vertical Restraints in EC Competition Policy COM(96) 721 at p. 1.

"incompatibility clauses" of the Community's trade and association Agreements provide a precedent which could in principle be translated into a multilateral context. However the inclusion of norms affecting the conduct of private parties in an essentially inter-State Agreement is still problematic. The ineffectuality of these clauses in the Community's free-trade Agreements of the 1970s, as well as the contentious operation of GATT-based anti-dumping, bear witness to the difficulty of enforcing this type of trade rule. We have earlier touched on the difficulties of WTO dispute settlement in this context.[43] It will in practice be essential to combine even this level of agreement on substantive principles with some form of agreement on co-operation, and it is this aspect of Community bilateral policy which appears to offer most prospect of success at the multilateral level.

11–089   It is clear that the EU is committed to maintaining, and developing, its bilateral co-operation policies. Nevertheless, the Commission is emphatic that a bilaterally-based policy is insufficient to deal with international competition issues and the needs of the developing and emerging economies. The conclusion of bilateral agreements between each of the over eighty (and rising) countries with competition authorities is inconceivable and would be unworkable:

> "The costs of administering such a complex network would be prohibitive for all competition authorities. Therefore, if co-operation is to develop exclusively at the bilateral level, the interests of competition authorities in developing countries or in small economies are likely to be neglected."[44]

11–090   In contrast, the Commission argues, multilateral commitments play a useful role in reinforcing the position of domestic agencies and "contribute to the spread of a 'competition culture'".[45] Support for a multilateral agreement is, however, by no means universal, either within the WTO Working Group or among commentators. In 1998 the Working Group reported on discussion on the levels at which co-operation could take place:

> "It was suggested, further, that it was desirable to discuss institutional linkages between trade and competition policy, and the feasibility and desirability of expanded co-operation in competition law enforcement, at three levels. First, within individual countries, much would be gained through closer institutional linkages and dialogue between institutions responsible for trade policy and competition law enforcement. Second, at the regional level, a significant strengthening of co-operative approaches to competition law enforcement, coupled with selective substitution of competition law for existing trade instruments, could be envisioned. At the multilateral level, a more cautious and gradual approach was warranted. Consideration could be given to two elements: (i) the fostering of shared understanding and voluntary convergence through the sharing of national experiences, legislation and jurisprudence; and (ii) deliberations on possible basic standards to be incorporated in Members" competition legislation."[46]

---

[43] See text at n. 63.
[44] Submission from the EC and its Member States to the WTO Working Group on "A Multilateral Framework Agreement on Competition Policy", September 25, 2000, WT/WGTCP/W/152, at p. 3.
[45] *ibid.*
[46] 1998 Report of the WTO Working Group on the Interaction Between Trade and Competition Policy to the General Council, December 8, 1998, WT/WGTCP/2, section C.1.(a).

It is noticeable that the possibilities of multilateral action set out by the **11–091**
Working Group do not explicitly include a binding agreement, although
"deliberations on possible basic standards" may ultimately lead to such an
agreement. This is consistent with the Working Group's role; as the
Commission points out:

> "the decision on whether to launch negotiations on competition is essentially political in
> nature, and as such, does not correspond to this Working Group, whose mandate is
> exploratory and analytical; the elements of a possible future WTO agreement on com-
> petition could only be determined as a result of multilateral negotiations and, on the
> basis of input from all WTO members."[47]

A "cautious and gradual approach" is also favoured by commentators. The **11–092**
suggestion is that an evolutionary approach, whereby the practice of co-
ordination and co-operation may lead to "slow but steady convergence of
review and mutual respect"[48] and the "evolution of common views",[49] is
likely to be more successful than an immediate attempt to reach agreement
on common principles. This informal convergence has the advantage of flexibility compared with an international code.[50] "We should . . . resist the temptation to codify principles that may well be either too vague to be useful or,
if precise, unsuited to the disparate interests involved and unlikely to pass the
test of time and experience."[51]

We have already seen how the bilateral agreement on co-operation between **11–093**
the USA and the EU has served as a model for co-operation clauses in other
Community bilateral agreements. Could a bilateral agreement such as this
serve as a model for a multilateral agreement? Not all aspects of such an
agreement are equally easy to multilateralise. Co-operation ranges from
exchanges of ideas and policy, through technical assistance, to case-specific
enforcement assistance. Case-specific enforcement assistance is likely to
remain bilateral for the present; it requires trust, and relatively similar legal
systems and economic experience.[52] Co-operation at the level of exchanges of
information (excluding confidential and maybe even case-specific information) and technical assistance is likely to be more feasible at a multilateral
level, but would not by themselves go far to address the problems of international competition that have been identified. However, it may serve to
build up confidence, and more importantly capacity, so as to provide a basis
for more ambitious initiatives.

Apart from the negotiating weight of the Community, no doubt one rea- **11–094**
son for the widespread direct or indirect reference to EC competition rules

---

[47] Submission from the EC and its Member States to the WTO Working Group on "A Multilateral
Framework Agreement on Competition Policy", September 25, 2000, WT/WGTCP/W/152, at p. 1.
[48] Pitkofsky, "Competition Policy in a Global Economy" (1999) JIEL 403, at p. 407, referring to
the effect of the co-operation agreement between the USA and EU However, Pitkofsky also
cautions, "procedural co-operation does not lead ineluctably to common attitudes or approaches." *ibid.* at 406.
[49] Melamed, "International Co-operation in Competition Law and Policy: What can be
Achieved at the bilateral, Regional and Multilateral Levels" (1999) JIEL 423 at 425. See also
Tarullo, "Competition Policy for Global Markets" (1999) JIEL 445 at 446.
[50] Pikofsky, *ibid.* n. 48 at p. 411.
[51] Melamed, *ibid.* n. 49 at p. 433.
[52] Frédérik Jenny, cited by Melamed, *ibid.* n. 49 at p. 432.

in the Community's bilateral agreements, reflected in the language chosen to describe anticompetitive conduct, lies in the absence of any internationally agreed set of norms. In this, competition policy differs, for example, from Intellectual Property protection, where it is common to define bilateral obligations by reference to lists of multilateral Conventions, including the TRIPS Agreement.[53] From the Community perspective, then, an international agreement on competition containing not only co-operation provisions but also core principles would offer the advantage of a model which could be used in negotiation, especially with countries with no long-term reason to adopt the Community's own model. We have here the potential for a two-way interaction, as multilateral regulatory standards influenced by the EU's own laws themselves provide a model for the development of EU policy commitments in a bilateral context. For this purpose, the international agreement would not need to be all-encompassing or contain mandatory standards. The EU position within the WTO Working Group now puts stress not on an attempt at mandatory harmonisation but on agreement on core principles with the emphasis on those principles which are already accepted within the WTO, such as non-discrimination and transparency.

11–095   A plurilateral agreement, or even one which sets out an agreed but optional framework for a national competition policy, would provide a reference point for bilateral interlocutors. At the same time, the Community has a clear interest in influencing the content and approach of the (plurilateral or multilateral) core principles. Such influence is not only the direct result of the Commission's position papers and participation in the WTO Working Group; it is also assisted by the growing number of non-Member States having already agreed, at a bilateral level, to principles of competition policy which reflect the EU approach. In this way, bilateral commitments help to build multilateral consensus.

---

[53] For example, see the Agreement with South Africa on Trade, Development and Co-operation, Art. 46.

PART THREE

MODERN TRENDS IN CONFLICT OF LAWS

CHAPTER 12

PLEADING ACTIONS AND DEFENCES UNDER FOREIGN LAW

Oskar Hartwieg[1]

§ 27. Independent of the almost insurmountable difficulties, in which the continental jurists admit themselves to be involved, in the attempt to settle the true character of these mixed cases of international jurisprudence, and about which they have been engaged in endless controversies with each other, ... admonish us, that it is far easier to give simplicity to systems, than to reconcile them with the true duties and interests of all nations in all cases.

(Joseph Story, *Commentaries on the Conflict of Laws*, Edinburgh MDCCCXXXV, p. 28).

[1] My first and enduring thanks to Alfons Bürge, Tobias Eckardt, Dagmar Feig, Alejandro M. Garro, Akira Ishikawa, Stephan Knottnerus-Meyer, Klaus-Jürgen and Christiane Lehmann, Stephan Meder, Loukas A. Mistelis, Lydia A. Reimer, Dieter Stauder for helpful criticism, comments and encouragement, for fruitful discussions. Errors of fact, judgement and taste are of course mine.

1. Electronic commerce and the legal patchwork

1.1 The challenge: contracts, torts, property rights in e-commerce

12–001   The World Wide Web,[2] electronic data interchange (EDI)[3] and e-commerce[4] have often made irrelevant the use of the traditional legal patchwork for settling disputes arising from international trade, *i.e.* an accumulation of rulings from different countries under choice of law provisions.[5] New challenges call for reconsidering the analytic status of private international law, a matter which has remained indistinct for decades.[6] The most urgent needs of e-commerce arise in the areas of contracts, torts and property rights.

12–002   Meanwhile, new chapters of a law merchant emerged from the traditional fields of private law, directly relevant and applicable to e-commerce.[7] International conventions, model laws, legal guides and collections of other legal

---

[2] Gigante, Blackhole in Cyberspace: The Legal Void in the Internet, in XV *The John Marshall Journal of Computer & Information Law* (1997) pp. 413–436.
[3] Terminology: the U.S. Uniform Electronic Transactions Act (1999) (UETA), section 2 Definitions; available at http://www.law.upenn.edu/bll/ulc/fnacl99/1990s/ueta99.htm; the U.S. Uniform Computer Information—Transactions Act (UCITA), section 102 Definitions, with Official Comment, available at http://www.ucitaonline.com/ucita.html, *i.e.* the former draft of UCC, Art. 2B; the United Nations, *UNCITRAL Model Law on Electronic Commerce with Guide to Enactment* 1996, available at http://www.uncitral.org. For co-operation of the U.S. and UNCITRAL: Boss *Electronic Commerce and the Symbiotic Relationship Between International and Domestic Law Reform*, in 72 *Tulane L. Rev.* 1931–84 (1998).
[4] See Geller From Patchwork to Network, in 31 *Vanderbilt Journal of Transnational Law,* 553–574 (1998), sub I., II. pp. 554–559.
[5] Surveys: Allen and Widdison Can Computers Make Contracts? in 9 *Harv. J. Law & Tec* 25–52 (1996); Anil, Heralding a New Jurisprudence in Cyberspace, in *Copyright Policy* (1999) 1 no 3; Hayakawa, Private Law in the Era of Internet, in Basedow and Kôno (ed.), Legal Aspects of Globalisation, The Hague, *et al.* 2000, 27–33; Johnson and Post, *Law and Borders—The Rise of Law in Cyberspace*, in 48 *Stanford Law Rev.* 1367–1402 (1995–96); Kaufman Winn, Clash of the Titans: Regulating the Competition Between Established and Emerging Electronic Payment Systems, in 14 *Berkeley Technology Law Journal* 675–709 (1999); Louis-Jacques and Alvarez *Legal Research on International Law Issues Using the Internet*, at http://www.lib.uchicago.edu/~llou/ forintlaw.html; Mankowski, Das Internet im Internationalen Vertrags- und Deliktsrecht, in *RabelsZ* (1999) 63 pp. 203–294; Mankowski, Das Internet und besondere Aspekte des Internationalen Vertragsrechts (I), in *Computer-Recht* (1999) pp. 512–522; Taupitz and Kritter, Electronic Commerce—Probleme bei Rechtsgeschäften im Internet, in *JuS* 1999 pp. 839–846 (pp. 843–844); Nimmer, *Principles of Contract Law in Electronic Commerce, infra,* chap 24; Slutsky, Jurisdiction Over Commerce On The Internet, in *The Data Law Report* (1996), at http://www.kslaw.com/menu/jurisdic.html; Uchida, *E-Commerce and Civil Law*, in Shôjihô Kenkyûkai (ed), *Saikenhô Kaisei no Kadai to Hôkô—Minpô Hyakushûnen o Keiki to Shite -*, "New Business Law", Special Edition, Tôkyô (1998) No 51, pp. 269–326; Witzleb, Martiny, Thoelke and Frericrks, Comparative Law and the Internet, (1999) Vol. 3.2 E.J.C.L. = http://law.kub.nl/ejcl/32/at32-1.html.
[6] Gully, Need for Consumer Protection Guidelines, in *Newsletter of the International Law Office*, 28.04.00 http://www.internationallawoffice.com/Ld.cfm?Newsletters_Ref=1681, reports about 700 New Zealand-based internet shopping sites, from which 90% failed to advise customers what laws applied to their transactions, 78% failed to explain how to lodge a complaint, 75% and no privacy policy, 62% provided no refund or exchange policies, 50% failed to outline their payment security mechanisms, 25% showed no physical address.
[7] For the "law merchant" (= *lex mercatoria*) as legal authority in the U.S. see: Gabor Stepchild of the New Lex Mercatoria: Private International Law from the United States Perspective, in 8 *Northwestern J. Int'l L. & Bus.s* 538–560 (1988), also at http://www.cisg.law.pace.edu/cisg/biblio/gabor.htm; Reese, *Commentary on Professor Gabor's, Stepchild of the New Lex Mercatoria*, at http://www.cisg.law.pace.edu/cisg/biblio/reese.htm; UK: Lord Mustill, The New Lex Mercatoria: The First Twenty-five Years, in *Liber Amicorum for Lord Wilberforce,* Oxford 1987, 149–83; Germany: Sonnenberger, *Der Ruf unserer Zeit nach einer europäischen Ordnung des Zivilrechts*, in JZ (1998) 53 pp. 982–991; a more realistic approach has taken: Nygh, *Autonomy in International Contracts*, Oxford 1999 pp. 172–198.

principles, etc., have been drafted by the World Trade Organisation (WTO),[8] the World Custom Organisation (WCO),[9] OECD,[10] United Nations Commission on International Trade Law (UNCITRAL), the United Nations Economic Commission for Europe (UN/ECE), the EC, the Asean-Pacific Economic Co-operation[11] and by half-official organisations like the UNIDROIT,[12] the ICC,[13] the Gibed,[14] a Commission on European Contract Law, [15] and, last but not least, the EU and the U.S.

Pendant needs for reliability of electronic data transfers have led to domestic legislation in many countries,[16] in order to establish contractual fidelity for negotiations, for choice of law rulings applicable in contract law and to secure performance of contractual obligations via EDI.[17] But domestic legislation, even in the EC, has only limited effects in international business.[18]   **12–003**

The most urgent needs for suitable connecting factors may come from contracts agreed upon in and performed by means of cyberspace.   **12–004**

1.2 The way out: to open up an ("early") perspective for choice of law

Academic writers tend to approach problems about ascertaining the law applicable under a traditional *ex post* perspective.[19] This view is moulded by   **12–005**

---

[8] General Agreement on Trade in Services, Art. II, at http://www.wto.org.
[9] WCO, in http://www.wcoomd.org.; Kyoto Convention, in http://www.wco-omd.org/ky-01e0.htm.
[10] OECD, in http://www.oecd.org/dsti/sti/index.htm.
[11] About co-operation between the U.S. government and the EC to establish standards for privacy protection in international data transfers see Kuner, European Standardisation and Electronic Commerce, in *Business Law International* 2000 pp. 102–108, *cf.* the "Draft International Safe Harbor Privacy Principles" of the U.S. Department of Commerce (November 15, 1999), at http://www.ita.doc.gov/ecom/menu.htm. *cf.* APEC & Electronic Commerce at http://www.dfat.gov.au/apec/ecom/POHAYE.html.
[12] UNIDROIT, *Principles of International Commercial Contracts*, Rome 1994; Lando / Beale (ed.), *The Principles of European Contract Law, Part I and II combined and revised*, The Hague, London, Boston, 2000.
[13] *cf.* ICC / Alliance for Global Business for Electronic Commerce, in Business and Industry Advisory Committee to the OECD (BIAC) etc., *A Global Action Plan for Electronic Commerce Prepared by Business with Recommendations for Governments*, 2nd ed., Paris, 1999, at http://www.iccwbo.org/home/electronic_commerce/word_documents/SJAPFIN.doc. This document is the result of ICC initiatives supported by the business community.International Chamber of Commerce, *UNCID—Uniform Rules of Conduct for Interchange of Trade Data by Teletransmission*, ICC Publication No 452, Paris, 1987.
[14] *Global Business Dialogue on Electronic Commerce*, Paris published "*The Paris Recommendations*", September 13, 1999, in http://www.gbde.org/conference/recommendations.html.
[15] Lando and Beale, *supra* at n. 12.
[16] United States: *supra* at n. 3.; Germany: *Gesetz zur digitalen Signatur,* Art. 3, June 13, 1997, http://www.netlaw.de.; Japan: see Uchida, *supra* at n. 5.; Europe: Directive 99/93 [2000] O.J. L13/12. on Community framework for electronic signatures.
[17] *cf.* UETA, *supra* at n. 3; UNCITRAL Legal Guide on Electronic Funds Transfers (1986); UNCITRAL Model Law on International Credit Transfers (1992); UNCITRAL *supra* at n. 3; access to UN at: http://www.un.org.
[18] The same applies to the conventions, statutory instruments and directions of the European Union, *e.g.* Directive 99/93 *supra* at n. 16; *cf.* Directive on E-Commerce of May 4, 2000, yet unpublished.
[19] UK: Dutson, The Internet, the Conflict of Laws, International Litigation and Intellectual Property: the Implications of the International Scope of the Internet on Intellectual Property Infringements, in JBL (*Journal of Business Law*) (1997) pp. 495–513. Australia, New Zealand and other common law countries: Gully, The Treatment of Electronic Records (February 8, 2000), in http://www.bellgully.co.nz. USA: Fram / Purcell, *Choice of Law in Internet-Based*

existing codes, statutes, precedents and conventions.[20] Accordingly, legislation and case law are contemplated under the final view of judges reasoning
to a decision already found.[21] A new global market ("death of distance")
needs new flexibility to decide new types of disputes. Guidelines for pleading
choice of law matters during the "early stages" of litigation might assist such
flexibility, since they have remained in an obscure analytical status and seldom have attracted academic writings.[22]

12–006   This article attempts to contribute genuine demands of e-commerce by
comparing pleading and practice before American, English (common law)
and German (civil law) courts. To begin with analytic affiliations on substantive law-, choice of law- and procedural rules on pleading and practice
(see section 2, 2.1 and 2.2), this essay deals with party autonomy and the
most real connection as connecting factors in contract law (see sections 2,
2.2, 2.2.1 and 2.2.2). Section three reflects shortly the pleading of remedies
under historical aspects (3.). The conclusion rests on Roman Law and reflects
advantages of an inherent flexibility in adversarial modes of procedure for
surmounting pending uncertainties of global e-commerce.

2. The analytic view on pleading and conflicts

2.1 Procedure

12–007   The analytic status of rules of pleading and rules of choice of law likewise
appears as somewhat vague.[23]

12–008   While matters of procedure (jurisdiction, practice, pleading and evidence)
are governed by the domestic law of the country in question,[24] choice of law

---

Controversies, White Paper, January 1998, in http//:www.ljx.com/internet/irjuris.html; Germany:
Junker, Internationales Vertragsrecht im Internet, in RIW 1999 pp. 809–818 (809, 814);
Mankowski, *supra* at n. 5.*Cf.* Dogauchi, Law Applicable to Torts and Copyright Infringement
through Internet, in Basedow and Kono, *supra* at n. 5 pp. 49–65 (57–63).

[20] The traditional view *ex post* appears as *implied,* for the U.K. see Collins, *Dicey and Morris on
the Conflict of Laws,* 13th ed., 2000 Vol. 1, § 1–014—1–059 (7–26); for the USA: Scoles and Hay,
Conflict of Laws (Hornbook) 2nd ed., 1992 (West Publishing), §§ 2.1–2.17 pp. 4–44; for
Germany: Kegel and Schurig, *Internationales Privatrecht,* 8th ed., München 2000, § 1 II. – VII
pp. 4–36; Kropholler, *Internationales Privatrecht,* 3rd ed. Tübingen 1997, § 3 pp. 16–24; § 59 pp.
538–542; von Bar, *Internationales Privatrecht,* Vol. 1, München 1987, § 1 pp. 9–10.
[21] In civil law countries "the courts reasoning" appear as laconic; in consequence pleadings, facts
and the procedural development of a case at hand are rarely reported in detail, while the courts
take much attention to their (often highly abstract) legal arguments. *cf.* Hartwieg, *Auslandsurteile
im Wirkungsvergleich,* in Hof / Schulte (ed.), *Wirkungsforschung zum Recht—Folgen von
Gerichtsentscheidungen,* Baden-Baden 2000 (in print).
[22] To quote Fentiman, *Foreign Law in English Courts, Pleading, Proof and Choice of Law,* Oxford
1998 p. 21: "It is commonly supposed, for example, that all choice of law rules are optional, in
the sense that the application of foreign law can always be prevented if neither party pleads it."
[23] Restatement 2nd, § 133 Burden of Proof: "The forum will apply its own local law in determining which party has the burden of persuading the trier of fact on a particular issue unless the primary purpose of the relevant rule of the state of the otherwise applicable law is to affect decision
of the issue rather than to regulate the conduct of the trial. In that event, the rule of the state of
the otherwise applicable law will be applied." The comment b. offers as an confession: "On which
side of the line a given rule belongs may present a difficult problem for decision."
[24] UK: Collins, *supra* at n. 20, § 7R–001—7–051 (substance and procedure). USA: ALI,
Restatement Second, Conflict of Laws, § 122 Issues Relating to Judicial Administration "A court
usually applies its own local law rules prescribing how litigation shall be conducted even when it

matters are more closely connected with substantive law.[25] The connecting factors to international contracts include two rather different aspects: first, (both) counsels' preliminary deliberations as to whether or not to plead facts related to foreign law, and secondly, the judges' task to decide about the law applicable, which may arise either during preliminary steps (pleading, discovery, etc.), or after public hearing.

The adversarial system, taken as a guideline, leaves it entirely up to the lit-   **12–009** igants and their counsels' discretion whether and in how far they will rely on foreign law in their pleadings. Coincidentally, foreign substantive law is regarded or treated as a fact.[26] Statements of claims and defences may either include elements pointing to the choice of law questions (pleading foreign elements, fact or law) or may circumvent such difficulties.[27]

Comparable principles of procedure before civil law countries' law courts   **12–010** have been under dispute for decades. The German code of civil procedure (1879/1898) shared much of an adversarial liberal concept expressed by the *Dispositionsmaxime* and the *Verhandlungsmaxime*.[28] More stringent attitudes

---

applies the local law rules of another state to resolve other issues in the case." About the dichotomy of substance and procedure see comment b. *ibid.*; Scoles / Hay, *supra* at n. 20, §§ 5.1 – 5.8 pp. 215–223, §§ 12.1—12.19 pp. 395–429; Friedenthal, Kane and Miller, *Civil Procedure*, 2nd ed., 1993 (West Publishing), §§ 5.1—5.28 pp. 237–312.

[25] UK: Collins, *supra* at n. 20, §§ 1–004, 1–017, §§ 1–032—1–059 (choice of law); USA: Scoles and Hay, *supra* at n. 20, § 3.1—3.12 pp. 48–67; Friedenthal, Kane and Miller, *supra* at n. 24, §§ 1.1 – 1.2 pp. 1–3, §§ 2.15—2.17 pp. 37–44.

[26] Collins, *supra* at n. 20, §§ 9–001—9–012 pp. 221–225; Sir Jack I. H. Jacob and Goldrein, *Bullen & Leake & Jacob's Precedents of Pleadings*, Vol. 1, 2, 13th ed. 1990 pp. 1169–1170 (Section 41: Foreign Law); Scoles and Hay, *supra* at n. 20, §§ 12.15—12.19 pp. 418–429; Friedenthal, Kane and Miller, *supra* at n. 24, §§ 5.14–5.16 (pp. 271–278); *Federal Civil Judicial Procedure and Rules*, 1996 (West Publishing Co), rule 8 (a)(2), on behalf of a claim: "a short and plain statement of the claim showing that the pleader is entitled to relief", rule 8 (c), on behalf of an affirmative defence: "in pleading to a preceding pleading, a party shall set forth affirmatively . . . and any other matter constituting an avoidance of affirmative defense", rule 8 (e)(1): "Each averment of a pleading shall be simple, concise, and direct". Since 1966 rule 44.1 provides for pleading foreign law pleading: "A party who intends to raise an issue concerning the law of a foreign country shall give notice by pleadings or other reasonable written notice." *cf.* Moore, *Moore's Federal Practice*, Vol. 2A, 2nd ed., 1996 (Matthew & Bender), 8.17[10.–1—10.–2]. For the future see the Hazard, Jr. / Taruffo, TRCP, draft 1996 of Transnational Rules of Civil Procedure, in 30 Cornell Int'l L. J. 493–539 (1997) (Rules 10, 11 about statements of claim and statements of defense, containing no provision about foreign law [p. 499], while the comment [no. 10.1 p. 516] explains: "This rule calls for more particularity, such as that traditionally required in U.S. "code pleading" and which is required in most other legal systems. In addition, the plaintiff must refer to the legal rules on which he relies to support his claim." Despite that there is no comment on affirmative defenses (*exceptio iuris*), the same principle may be recognised from the direct wording in rule 11 (a): "The defendant shall . . . and may assert affirmative defenses." [p. 499]).

[27] UK: Collins, *supra* at n. 20, §§ 9–001—9–025 pp. 221–232; US: (Federal Rules) see *supra* at n. 26.

[28] Stein and Jonas, *Kommentar zur Zivilprozeßordnung*, 21st ed., Tübingen 1994, § 138 ZPO, Rn 7; *cf.* Lücke and Walchshöfer, *Münchner Kommentar zur Zivilprozeßordnung*, München 1992, § 138 (1) ZPO, Rn 23 (per Peters); Bruns, *Zivilprozeßrecht*, 2nd ed., München, 1979, §§ 82—83 pp. 98—100. Both maxims are mirrored by provisions of the Code of Civil Procedure as follows, translation taken from Goren, *The Code of Civil Procedure Rules of the Federal Republic of Germany*, 1990 (Fred B. Rothman & Co): *Dispositionsmaxime*: § 308 (1) [1] ZPO *"The court is not empowered to award by judgement a party anything which has not been demanded."* *Verhandlungsmaxime*: § 138 (2) ZPO *"Each party shall answer facts asserted by the opponent."* (3) *"Facts which are not expressly denied shall be deemed as admitted, unless"* . . .

about the litigants' duties to plead "the whole truth" have gained influence since 1933.[29] Furthermore, it is up to the court itself to ascertain the connecting factors and the content of foreign law relevant in the case *ex officio*, which no longer is regarded as a fact.[30] Consequently, the burden of proof is less attributed as an element of adjective law.[31]

12–011   As an intermediary result, we may note that rules on pleading belong to the sphere of procedure in all three countries mentioned, and, consequently, courts will always follow their own rules.

12–012   Coincidentally, in common law litigation the parties are free whether or not to plead foreign law as a fact, while in civil law courts the judges are obliged to ascertain all relevant aspects *ex officio* and the litigants are only "allowed" to contribute to the court's own efforts on foreign law; there is less room for predisposition by way of pleading.[32]

2.2 Pleading choice of law

12–013   Comparatists have rarely troubled to analyse interrelations between modern[33] rules of pleading and choice of law.[34] Recently, Mistelis in his study on characterisation has established that in different stages during litigation the lawyers' efforts on characterisation face different subject matters.[35]

---

(4) "*A declaration of lack of knowledge concerning facts is permissible only concerning facts which were not personally dealt with by the party or subject of his concern.*" *Cf.* the equivalents to § 138 (3) ZPO in England (RSC O.18 r. 13 [1], CPR 16.5 [3]) and in the US Federal Rules, *supra* at n. 25, Rule 8 (d).

[29] § 138 (1) ZPO as amended in 1933: "*The declarations given by the parties concerning factual circumstances shall be complete and truthful.*" The German Supreme Court often keeps a traditional distant view on § 138 (1) ZPO (BGH, June 11, 1990, in MDR 1991 pp. 226–227), *cf.* Stein and Jonas, *supra* at n. 28, § 138 (1) ZPO, Rn 1–23 (Rn 23a about pleading foreign law); Bruns, *supra* at n 28, § 85 pp. 101–106; some commentators cultivate a more stringent view *cf.* Lücke / Walchshöfer, *supra* at n 28, § 138 (1) ZPO, Rn 1–17 (per Peters); Baumbach and Lauterbach, *Zivilprozeßordnung*, 58. ed., München 2000, § 138 (1) ZPO, Rn 1–26 (per Hartmann); for the historical aspects see: Olzen, *Die Wahrheitspflicht der Parteien im Zivilprozeß*, in ZZP 98 (1985) pp. 403–426, pp. 415–426.

[30] § 293 ZPO provides: "Laws of another state, customary law and by-laws require proof only to such extent as they are unknown to the court." . . . . *cf.* BGH, September 29, 1995 (VII ZR 248/94), held that: "*The courts are to take regard and to apply the German rules on choice of law officially*". *cf.* the commentators Stein and Jonas, *supra* at n. 28, § 293 ZPO Rn 26–51; Lüke and Walchshöfer, *supra* at n. 28, Rn 1–32. Aspects as indicated by e-commerce mentiones Junker, Neuere Entwicklungen im Internationalen Privatrecht, in RIW (1998) 44 pp. 741–750 (742, references *ibid.* n. 22).

[31] The German Civil Code and the Code of Civil Procedure do not contain any explicit general rulings about the burden of proof; in contrast to the Swiss Civil Code (1907), Art. 8: "*Subject to other rulings in the Code, everybody who pleads relief has to meet the burden of proof of those facts which he is relying upon.*"

[32] *cf. supra* at n. 29.

[33] See van Caenegem, History of European Civil Procedure, in *International Encyclopaedia of Comparative Law*, Tübingen *et al.* 1971, Vol. XVI, pp. 2–2—2–79.

[34] Exceptional: Weintraub, Critique of the Hazard-Taruffo Transnational Rules of Civil Procedure, in 33 *Texas Int'l L.J.* 413–423, 418–420 (1998): "Section 139 of the Restatement (Second) of Conflict of Laws places testimonial privileges in a limbo between substance and procedure".

[35] Mistelis, *Charakterisierungen und Qualifikation im internationalen Privatrecht*, Tübingen 1999 pp. 224–250. *cf.* Hartwieg, Classifications of Security Interests on the Highways of International Commerce, in Norton and Andenas, *Emerging Financial Markets and Secured Transactions*, London, The Hague, Boston, 1998 pp. 49–81.

During early phases litigants and their counsels realistically will contemplate how to frame their cases by way of mutual pleading with necessity. The assignment of relevant facts either to the claimant or to the defendant predisposes the burden of pleading and proof, and may well influence the decision after public hearing, as the case may be.[36] In particular, there is little theoretical demand to analyse the "inner connection" between causes of actions and defences. Both (adversarial) positions are substantially interrelated. The role of foreign adjective law and the adherent question about the law applicable under choice of law rules calls for further consideration.[37]

The interplay of strategies (on pleading options)[38] is of significance for e-commerce. New choice of law rules on concluding contracts[39] in the USA, U.K., Germany call for consideration, especially under European aspects of the Rome Convention on the Law Applicable to Contracts (1980).[40]   **12–014**

2.2.1 The party autonomy

Due to a common principle in substantive- and choice of law rules, all three countries and the EC allow the contracting parties to choose the   **12–015**

---

[36] The interrelationship of conflict of laws and pleading has attracted academic writings only rarely: *cf.* Sir Jack I. H. Jacob, *The Fabric of English Civil Justice*, London 1987 pp. 82 86 ("*cause of action*"), pp. 87–92 ("*pleadings*"); Sir Jack I. H. Jacob and Goldrein, *supra* at n. 26, pp. 1169–1170 (section 41, foreign law); for evidence of foreign law (as a fact) see Civil Evidence Act 1972, section 4 (2), *cf.* Buzzard / May / Howard, *Phipson on Evidence*, 12th ed., London 1976 pp. 2230–2231; CPR, Part 33 Miscellaneous Rules about Evidence, Rule 33.7; there are no statutory rules expressly dealing with pleading foreign law, *cf.* The Supreme Court Practice 1997, Vol. 1, London 1996, Order 39/2–3/2; the Civil Procedure Rules 1999, Part 16 (16.2–16.4 for contents of the claim form [see 16.2 (1) b. "specify the remedy which the claimant seeks"] and 16.5–16.6 contents of defence), *cf.* Lord Woolf, *Access to Justice (The Woolf Report)*, London 1998, chap. 20 pp. 152–163 (section 21 on claims: "the basic requirements for claims are that they should contain the following . . . the remedy claimed" and section 23 on defences: "A defence should state the following: . . . specific defences (voluntary assumption of risk, failure to mitigate loss, etc.) and any grounds for denying the claim arising out of the facts stated by the defendant" . . .), Lord Woolf, Access to Justice (Final Report), London 1998, chap. 12, section 1–19, pp. 115–119. Hartley, Pleading and Proof of Foreign Law: The Major European Systems Compared, in 45 Int. & Comp. L.Q. 271–292 (1996).
[37] *cf.* Sir Jack Jacob and Goldrein, *supra* at n. 26, Vol. 1 pp. 65 (pleading points of law), pp. 71–109 (statement of claim), pp. 111–137 (defence). In other countries no equivalents to the collection of standard formulas for claims and the "adherent" defences as collected in the Bullen & Leake and Jacob's Precedents of Pleadings are available; (Jacob and Goldrein, *supra*).
[38] U.K.: Collins, *supra* at n. 20, Vol. 1, § 7R–001—7–051 explaining the general rule "17– All matters of procedure are governed by the domestic law of the country to which the court wherein any legal proceedings are taken belongs (lex fori)." USA: for the "procedural approach" see Restatement Second *supra* at n. 24, § 122, comment a., § 124, comment a., § 127, comment a. no 2, 3, 4, 5, § 128, comment a.-c., § 133, comment b.; Friedenthal, Kane and Miller, *supra* at n. 24, § 1.1 pp. 1–4, §§ 4.1–4.8 pp. 191–236, in particular § 4.5 pp. 212–217; for the "conflict of law approach" in contracts see: Restatement Second, *supra* at n 24, §§ 186–187 (law of the state chosen by the parties), § 188 (law governing in absence of effective choice by the parties); Scoles / Hay, *supra* at n 20, §§ 12.1–12.19 pp. 395–429. *Germany* (civil law): Kegel / Schurig, *supra* at n. 20, § 22 IV pp. 904–905; Kropholler, *supra* at n. 20, § 56 V pp. 503–505, § 59 I pp. 538–542.
[39] UNCITRAL, *supra* at n. 3, Art. 11–15; UETA *supra* at n. 3, s. 7; UCITA *supra* at n. 3, ss. 107–108, 112–114, 201–215, cf. Nimmer, *supra* at n. 5.
[40] The U.K. and Germany, acting as members of the EC have ratified and incorporated the "Rome Convention" on the Law Applicable to Contractual Obligations (1980), by Contracts (Applicable Law) Act (1990) and the German Introductory Law of the Civil Code (1991). US: Scoles and Hay, *supra* at n. 20, § 2.18 pp. 45–47.

law applicable to their contract.[41] The American doctrine was discussed with regard to limitations of the parties' autonomy, about a substantial relationship as necessary, mandatory provisions, consumers' protection, etc.[42]

12–016   Under procedural aspects, the course of development in civil law- and common law-countries went into different directions. While the German legislator in 1974 restricted the litigants' former freedom to select a certain civil court as competent to decide their controversy,[43] the Rome Convention (1980) established a link between provisions of substantive and procedural provenance.[44] Consequently, the German rules of civil procedure leave little freedom for the litigants to prescribe the law applicable to a case by pleading (foreign) choice of law matters.[45]

12–017   Common law countries mainly follow a much wider concept at this point.[46] Judges sitting in common law courts or arbitration tribunals will accept any

---

[41] U.S.: *cf.* Fram and Purcell, *supra* at n. 19, on Restatement 1st, sub I.A.1.b. and on Restatement 2nd, sub I. A. 2., § 187 Law of the State Chosen by the Parties "(1) The law of the state chosen by the parties to govern their contractual rights and duties will be applied if the particular issue is one which the parties could have resolved by an explicit provision in their agreement directed to that issue". . . .; *cf.* Scoles and Hay, *supra* at n. 20, §§ 18.1–18.2 pp. 656–662; more recently: UCITA, *supra* at n. 3, s. 108 (a): "section 109. Choice of Law. (a) The parties in their agreement may choose the applicable law. However, the choice is not enforceable in a consumer contract to the extent it would vary a rule that may not be varied by agreement under the law of the jurisdiction whose law would apply under subsections (b) and (c) in the absence of the agreement." *cf.* Official Comment, *supra* at n. 3; Nimmer, *supra* at n. 5. UK: Collins, *supra* at n. 20, §§ 32R–001—32–029 pp. 1195—1207. Germany: Kegel / Schurig, *supra* at n. 20, § 18 I. pp. 561–612. EC: Rome Convention (1986), in Chia-Jui Cheng, *Basic Documents on International Trade*, 2nd ed., Dordrecht, Boston and London, 1990 pp. 666–676, Art. 27 (1)[1] "A contract shall be governed by the law chosen by the parties."

[42] For U.S. see: Scoles / Hay, *supra* at n. 19, §§ 18.3–18.21 pp. 662–697; *cf.* the flexible approach in Restatement 2nd, "§ 6 Choice-of-law-principles (1) A court, subject to constitutional restrictions, will follow a statutory directive of its own state on choice of law. (2) When there is no such directive, the factors relevant to the choice of the applicable rule of law include (a) the needs of the interstate and international systems, (b) the relevant policies of the forum, (c) the relevant policies of other interested states and the relative interests of those states in the determination of the particular issue, (d) the protection of justified expectations, (e) the basic policies underlying the particular field of law, (f) certainty, predictability and uniformity of result, and (g) ease in the determination and application of the law to be applied." Comments in Scoles and Hay, *supra* at n. 20, § 2.13 p. 35, § 2.15 pp. 37–39, §§ 18.28–18.41 pp. 721–728; recently UCITA, *supra* at n. 41. UK: Collins, *supra* at n. 20, §§ 32R–030—32–101 pp. 1207–1232. *Germany*: Kegel / Schurig, *supra* at n. 20, § 18 I. pp. 570–575, 583–600.

[43] The German Code of Civil Procedure, *supra* at n. 28, § 38 ZPO: "*A court of first instance, which in itself has no jurisdiction, becomes competent by express or implied agreement of the parties.*" In 1974 amended by the following restriction: "parties, if the parties to the agreement are merchants who do not belong to the traders designated in" . . .

[44] *cf.* Rome Convention (1980), Art. 14 (1) "The law governing the contract under this Convention applies to the extent that it contains, in the law of contract, rules which raise presumptions of law or determine the burden of proof. (2) A contract or an act intended to have legal effect may be proved by any mode of proof recognised by the law of the forum or by any of the laws referred to in Article 9 under which that contract or act is formally valid, provided that such mode of proof can be administered by the forum."

[45] *cf.* Code of Civil Procedure, §§ 138, 293, as cited above (n. 28–30). The civil law courts tend to accept easily only the litigants consent on German substantive law as applicable to their international contract. The Code of Civil Procedure favours by § 138 (3) ZPO, *supra* at n. 28, and by § 288 ZPO: "*Facts alleged by a party need no proof to the extent that they were admitted in the course of litigation by the opponent in an oral hearing or on the record before a commissioned or requested judge. Acceptance is not required for the effectiveness of an admission in the court.*" For equivalent procedural rulings to in English and American procedure *supra* at n. 27).

[46] *cf. supra* at section 2.1.

litigants' agreement on the substantive law applicable, unless there is an strong indication to mandatory rules, etc., as the case may be.[47]

The needs of e-commerce call for global common practice which makes **12–018** the law courts everywhere to follow the contracting parties' (the later litigants') agreements upon a certain law as governing their contract. Other solutions regarding mandatory terms, consumers' protection, etc., should be allowed only as exceptions.

2.2.2 The most real connection

Governmental interests in ascertaining the law applicable in absence of an **12–019** enforceable agreement on choice of law influenced the comprehension of rules on private international law in the U.S. and world-wide. The practical needs of e-commerce are going to replace the old common law dilemma by express rulings in UCITA.[48]

Nevertheless, the dilemma between procedural and adjective law remains **12–020** neglected in both law families and calls for analytic inquiries about the traditional dichotomy of actions and defences.

The keywords are *actio* and *exceptio* (a defence *in iure*) (terminology of **12–021** classical Roman law), cause of action and affirmative defense (American terminology), cause of action and special defence (traditional English) and *Anspruch* and *Einwand* (German).[49]

As an additional difficulty appears, that big international transactions like **12–022** sales, construction, service contracts, etc., are often composed of a variety of single transactions (contracts): a central agreement on a sale, on a construction project, on licences on intellectual property rights, on associated guarantee on payments, on receivables financing, on letters of credit, on

---

[47] References for the U.K. *supra* at n. 27, 27; Fentiman, *supra* at n. 22, pp. 60–64 (exceptions by mandatory rules). For the U.S. see Federal Rules, *supra* at n. 25, Rule 8 (a)(2), (c), (e)(1), 44.1. *cf.* Moore, *supra* at n. 26. For the future see the Hazard, Jr. / Taruffo, *supra* at n. 26. *cf.* Bishop, *International Arbitration of Petroleum Disputes*, in *Yearbook of Commercial Arbitration*, Vol. (1998) XXIII pp. 1131–1210 (1143–1152).
[48] UCITA, *supra* at n. 2, s. 109 (b)–(d):
"(1) An access contract or a contract providing for electronic delivery of a copy is governed by the law of the jurisdiction in which the licensor was located when the agreement was entered into. (2) A consumer contract that requires delivery of a copy on a tangible medium is governed by the law of the jurisdiction in which the copy is or should have been delivered to the consumer. (3) In all other cases, the contract is governed by the law of the jurisdiction having the most significant relationship to the transaction.
(c) In cases governed by subsection (b), if the jurisdiction whose law governs is outside the United States, the law of that jurisdiction governs only if it provides substantially similar protections and rights to a party not located in that jurisdiction as are provided under this [Act]. Otherwise, the law of the State that has the most significant relationship to the transaction governs.
(d) For purposes of this section, a party is located at its place of business if it has one place of business, at its chief executive office if it has more than one place of business, or at its place of incorporation or primary registration if it does not have a physical place of business. Otherwise, a party is located at its primary residence." *cf.* Official Comment, *supra* at n. 2, section 109 No. 3.
[49] For terminology in the U.S. see Federal Rules, *supra* at n. 25, (Rule 8 (a) (c) [notice pleading on causes of actions and on affirmative defenses]). U.K.: The Supreme Court Practice 1997, *supra* at n. 35, O. 15/1/3 (causes of actions) O. 18 r. 8 without defining the special defence, but see comments in 18/8/1–18/8/2; *cf.* CPR (1999), *supra* at n. 36. *Germany*: *German Civil Code* (1900), translated by Goren, Littleton, 1994, § 194 (1): "The right to demand an act or an omission from another (a claim) is" . . .; no comparable definition is available for a defence *in iure*.

guarantees for advance payments, on performance bonds, counter guarantees and the like. Under choice of law aspects these complementary instruments disclose that the whole project appears as a genuine field for dépeçage, or, in the English terminology, for splitting the contract.[51]

2.2.2.1 United States: dépeçage

12–023   The Restatement Second and, later, the UCITA favours a flexible approach.[52] If the contracting parties have not agreed validly on the substantive law applicable to their contract, the most significant relationship appears on the stage of conflict rules.[53]

12–024   The issue oriented[54] approach conveniently matches the early view on pleading conflicts and is confirmed, at least indirectly, by § 124 Restatement Second. This rule requires the forum to determine the form of action,[55] while questions involving the rights and liabilities of the parties should be determined by the otherwise applicable law.[56] Nevertheless, there is scarcely a clear consent about either the substantial or reasonable relationship.[57]

12–025   The legal systems discussed here, tend to associate the burden of proof closely to the substantive law in general and, thus, establish a close connection to pleading and to the burden of proof.[58]

12–026   The adversarial view leaves it to the claimant's and his counsel's discretion whether to rely on foreign law in their claim.[59] The opponent's contributions in defining the issue are threefold: he may either rely on the factual strategy by denying the plaintiff's averments[60] or he may raise affirmative defences (*exceptiones in iure*),[61] or he may do both and, perhaps, alternatively. The

---

[51] English examples: *Muduroglu Ltd v. TC Ziraat Bankasi*, [1986] 1 Q.B. 1225; [1986] 2 W.L.R. 606; [1986] 3 All E.R. 682–715; *Channel Tunnel Group Ltd and another v. Balfour Beatty Construction Ltd and others*, [1993] A.C. 334; [1993] 2 W.L.R. 662; [1992] 2 All E.R. 609–627, *ibid.* [1993] 1 All E.R. 664–691. For the recent draft of an *uniform law on assignment in receivables financing*, UNCITRAL, March 23, 2000, see UNITED NATIONS, General Assembly, A/CN.9/470.

[52] *Supra* at n. 42, § 6. *cf.* Fram / Purcell, *supra* at n. 19, sub I.A.2.–6., II.A, III.A-D. On Restatement 2nd, § 222 as establishing the "flexible approach" in § 6 Restatement 2nd with regard to property in general: "The interests of the parties in a thing are determined, depending upon the circumstances, either by the "law" or by the "local law" of the state which, with respect to the particular issue, has the most significant relationship to the thing and the parties under the principles stated in § 6." *cf.* UCITA, *supra* at n. 3, s. 109, Official Comment No 3–5.

[53] Restatement 2nd, § 188: "(1) The rights and duties of the parties with respect to an issue in contract are determined by the local law of the state which, with respect to that issue, has the most significant relationship to the transaction and the parties under the principles stated in § 6."

[54] *cf.* Restatement 2nd, § 6 (2)(a)-(g), *supra* at n. 42; UCITA, *supra* at n. 3, s. 109, Official Comment No 4.

[55] Restatement 2nd, *supra* at n. 24, § 124 Form of Action: "*The local law of the forum determines the form in which a proceeding may be instituted on a claim involving foreign elements.*"

[56] Restatement 2nd, *supra* at n. 42, comment a. *cf.* Restatement 2nd, § 127 Form of Action: "*The local law of the forum governs rules of pleading and the conduct of proceedings in the court.*" About the inherent dilemma regarding the burden of proof, *cf.* Restatement 2nd, § 133 Burden of Proof, *supra* at n. 23. Friedenthal, Kane and Miller, *supra* at n. 24, § 5.15 p. 276.

[57] Scoles and Hay, *supra* at n. 19, §§ 18.22–18.39 pp. 697–725; *cf.* Reese, Dépeçage: A Common Phenomenon in Choice of Law, in 73 *Columbia L. Rev.* 58–75, 65–68 (1973).

[58] Friedenthal, Kane and Miller, *supra* at n. 54).

[59] *cf.* Federal Rules, *supra* at n. 26, Rule 8 (a).

[60] Federal Rules, *supra* at n. 26, Rule 8 (b)(1): "Defences; Form of Denials. A Party shall . . . admit or deny the averments upon which the adverse party relies."

[61] Federal Rules, *supra* at n. 26, Rule 8 (c).

most persuasive concept is, and will be in all adversarial systems, mixed composites of time, cost and success.[62]

Accordingly, in international contracts agreed upon and managed by means of e-commerce, a legal dispute between the contracting parties (located in different countries) leaves choice of law, pleading-matters and alternative strategies before U.S. civil courts:

12–027

• The claimant is free to select and to plead the facts of his claim for relief by ascertaining the law applicable to the dispute.

• The defendant is free either to admit or to deny the claimant's averments, the factual elements necessary to settle the law applicable included.

• In addition, the defendant may (alternatively) raise an affirmative defense, from wherever the legal basis of this special defense may be situated as derived from the claimant's country's contract law, his own country's legal system[63] or elsewhere.[64]

Accordingly, dépeçage from the intricate field of e-commerce appears as a new issue for the Restatement Second, § 6(2).[65] While Rabel held the civil law-*synallagma* in "mutual contracts" for an obstacle against any attempt to split an contract due to several places of performances,[66] this aspect has lost much of its weight, since the CISG has replaced the German *synallagma* by means of creating a new remedy, i.e. the avoidance of a contract in case of a fundamental breach.[67]

12–028

---

[62] A strategic concept of civil litigation may appear as a cornerstone of adversial modes of procedure. *cf.* Federal Rules, *supra* at n. 26, Rule 8 (e)(2): "A party may set forth two or more statements of a claim or defense alternately or hypothetically, either in one count or defense or in seperate counts or defenses. Then two or more statements are made in the alternative and one of them if made independently would be sufficient, the pleading is not made insufficient by the insufficiency of one or more of the alternative statements. A party may also state as many separate claims or defences as the party has regardless of consistency and whether based on legal, equitable, or maritime grounds." Nevertheless, a debate about pleading in the US is still under way: Bone, Mapping the Boundaries of a Dispute, Conceptions of Ideal Lawsuit Structure from the Field Code to the Federal Rules, in 89 *Columbia L. Rev.*1–118 (1989); Cleary, Presuming and Pleading: An Essay on Juristic Immaturity, in 12 *Stanford L. Rev.* 5–28, 8–16, 21–27 (1959); Imwinkelried, The Development of Professional Judgement in Law School Litigation Courses: The Concepts of Trial Theory and Theme, in 39 *Vand L.R.* 59–81, 66 (1986); Marcus, The Revival of Fact Pleading under the Federal Rules of Civil Procedure, in 86 *Columbia L. Rev.* 433–494 (1986); cf. Hartwieg, Rechtsvergleichendes zum Gegenstand der Anwaltshaftung, in *Anwaltsblatt* (1995) 45 pp. 209–216. For the present principles as mentioned above see: Friedenthal, Kane and Miller, *supra* at n. 24, §§ 5.14 – 5.21 pp. 271–295.
[63] About the limitations under the American rules on conflict of laws see Scoles and Hay, *supra* at n. 20, §§ 18.1 – 18.7 pp. 656 – 673.
[64] The American scepticism about limits in contractual choice of law may be restricted to only few alternatives, *cf.* Scoles and Hay, *supra* at n. 20, §§ 18.1–18.7 pp. 656–673; for aspects of litigation see Friedenthal, Kane and Miller, *supra* at n. 24, § 5.20 pp. 290–293; Moore, *supra* at n. 25, ¶ 8.19. [1], ¶ 8.27. [1]–[4].
[65] *Supra* at n. 42; for the modern attitude in dépeçage see Scoles and Hay, *supra* at n. 20, § 2.14 p. 35, § 2.15 p. 38, § 3.16 p. 74, § 18.40 p. 725.
[66] Rabel, *The Conflict of Laws: A Comparative Study*, 2nd ed. Ann Arbor 1960 pp. 469–472, on the German Civil Code, §§ 323–326.
[67] CISG, Arts. 45, 49, 25.

12–029   It is to mention that the choice of law rules in UCITA relate only to access contracts, consumer contracts and submit all other cases to the jurisdiction with the most significant relationship to the transaction.[68] The present issue approach in American conflict of laws, combined with liberal principles of pleading during the early phases of litigation are likely to favour the search for new and adequate solutions for future challenges in international business transactions.

2.2.2.2 United Kingdom: splitting the contract

12–030   As far as I am aware of the English choice of law discussion, there are two approaches to meet the temptation of splitting contracts: international torts[69] and international employment contracts.[70]

12–031   As a matter of substantive and procedural law it appears that both contracting parties are free to frame their (mutual) pleadings under prospects of success.[71] North has analysed the inherent relevance of both major problems to choice of law: renvoi and characterisation. In his conclusion he says: "it may convincingly be argued that it is high time English law abandoned the double-barrelled tort rule of *Phillips v. Eyre.*[72] Meanwhile, the tort rule is abolished by the Private International Law (Miscellaneous) Act 1995,[73] and the uniform rules on the law applicable to contracts under EC Rome Convention (1980) have been ratified".[74]

---

[68] *cf. supra* at n. 48.

[69] *cf.* the"double actionability" rule; in *Phillips v. Eyre* Q.B. [1869] IV pp. 225–244 (per Cockburn, C.J.), Court of Appeal Q.B. [1870] VI pp.1–31 (per Willes J.) the defendant relied in his pleading on an Act of Indemnity which as an Act has been passed in Jamaica, the place of the wrong; and in *Chaplin v. Boys*, A.C. [1971] pp. 356–406 the double actionability rule was used as a defence on the respondent's [Chaplin's] side). Now the rule is said to be abolished by Part III of the Private International Law (Miscellaneous Provisions) Act (1995), s. 9 (3), 10, 13, 14 (2), *cf.* Collins, *supra* at n. 19, §§ 35–003 – 35–013, §§ 35–120 – 35–149 (defamation claims).

[70] The Contractual Obligations (Applicable Law) Act (1991), (ratification of the Rome Convention on the Law Applicable to Contractual Obligations (1980)), in Title II (Uniform Rules) Article 6 (Individual employment contracts), subs. 1 claims, that, "notwithstanding the provisions of Articles 3 a contract of employment" . . . "shall not have the result of depriving the employee of the protection afforded to him by the mandatory rules of the law which would be applicable under paragraph 2 in absence of choice". Art. 4 (a) (b) appoints the law of the country in which the employee habitually carries out his work of performance or the place of business through which he was engaged, "unless it appears form the circumstances as a whole that the contract is more closely connected with another country, in which case the contract shall be governed by the law of that country." *cf.* Collins, *supra* at n. 20, §§ 33R–001—33–084.

[71] *cf.* Collins, Exemption Clauses, Employment Contracts and the Conflict of Laws, in 21 ICLQ 320 (1972) regarding *Chaplin v. Boys*, *supra* at n. 67, reprint in Collins, *Essays in International Litigation and the Conflict of Laws*, 1994 p. 405 (sub (1)); North, Contract as a Tort Defence in the Conflict of Laws, in 26 ICLQ 914–931 (1977), reprint in North, *Essays in Private International Law*, 1993 pp. 89–108 (89); both relying on *Matthew v. Kuwait Bechtel Corp.* [1959] 2 Q.B. 57; [1959] 2 All E.R. 345–351, 345 E–F, 346 D–G, 348 B–D, 351 D–F dealing with service abroad and jurisdiction under RSC Order 11 r 1 (e); North, having regard to pleading choice of law either in *Coupland v. Arabian Gulf Oil Co*, [1983] 1 W.L.R. 1136; [1983] 3 All E.R. 226–229 (226 g–i, 228 k-j): "The plaintiff can advance his claim, as he wishes, either in contract or in tort and no doubt he will, acting on advice, advance the claim on the basis which is most advantageous to him." (per *Goff LJ.*), and in *Johnson v. Coventry Churchill International Ltd*, [1992] 3 All E.R. 14–26 (16j)(per *JW Kay QC*); here, the claim was pleaded as a tort committed in Germany, while, after trial, *JW Kay QC*, held that the claim fell within the scope of the exception to the dual-actionability rule and, under English law, awarded £75,000 for the plaintiff.

[72] *cf. supra* at n. 67; North, *supra* at n. 71, pp.102–104, 108.

[73] Private International Law (Miscellaneous Provisions) Act 1995, s. 10.

[74] Contractual Obligations (Applicable Law) Act 1991, Title II, Art. 4.

Nevertheless, the doctrine about law applicable to torts and contracts in **12–032**
Dicey & Morris is still based on *Sayers v. International Drilling Co.*[75] In consequence, if there is a special defence under contract law available, the law applicable to the contract is to define the validity of the defence in question.[76]In his
recent analysis on mandatory pleading in contract and tort Fentiman concluded that pleading foreign law depends on the relevant choice of law rules
and whether they forbid or permit the non-introduction of foreign law.[77]
Reviewing the unsure status of principles, policy and reform of pleading,
proof and reform, he concludes that legal reform by way of legislation might
reflect six guidelines,[78] proposals which have scarcely influenced the CPR.[79] In
particular, Nygh in his comparative study did not focus on pleading choice of
law and foreign law. Thus, it remains open in how far the present rulings can
serve as suitable devices for "early approaches" or for new challenges.

2.2.2.3 Germany: the characteristic performance

Judicature, lacking express statutorial rulings on international contracts until **12–033**
1986, had developed the *hypothetical implied intention* of the contracting parties as a unique connecting factor.[80] The Rome Convention (1980), Article 4
(2)–(4) was reason enough to switch over to the "characteristic performance"
as connecting factor.[81] The fact that the Rome Convention (1980), Article 4
(1), (5) offers as a second approach "the country with which it (the contract)
is most closely connected" has been inserted into the German statute but did
not receive much theorctical attention.[82] The *genesis* of this "double
approach" has not yet been analysed in historic detail;[83] the report of
Giuliano and Lagarde scarcely discloses much about the preparatory concept
of the Convention.[84]

---

[75] [1971] 1 W.L.R. 1176; *cf.* Collins, *supra* at n. 20, §§ 35–014—35–077 (§ 35–047, § 35–060).
[76] *cf.* Fentiman, *supra* at n. 22, defines it under varying aspects on pp. 70–77 as a matter of procedure or conflict of laws if a party in his pleading relies on foreign law, on pp. 80–97 as a matter of choice of law in contract, on pp. 97–106 as a matter of choice of law in torts.
[77] Fentiman, *supra* at n. 22 pp. 3–6, pp. 286–315, mentions four principles under English law as
relevant: 1. foreign law as a question of fact, 2. proof by expert evidence, 3. pleading of foreign
law as voluntary, 4. the presumption of the same content as English law pp. 286–287.
[78] Fentiman, *supra* at n 22, pp. 312–314, reflects 1. English law as applicable, 2. mandatory
choice of law rules, 3. particulars of the law in question and about evidence at trial, 4. the
application of foreign law as a matter of private international law and not as a voluntary matter of procedure, 5. establishing foreign law by evidence of experts or by reference to relevant
materials, 6. the operation of the foregoing principles without prejudice to terms of existing
enactment.
[79] *cf.* CPR, Part 33 Miscellaneous Rules about Evidence, Rule 33.7.
[80] Kegel and Schurig, *supra* at n. 20, § 18 I. 1. d) p. 575; Reithmann and Martiny, *Internationales
Vertragsrecht*, 5th ed. Köln, 1996, § 101 pp. 114–115.
[81] Rome Convention (1980), *supra* at n. 41, Art. 4 (2).
[82] Rome Convention (1980), Art. 4 (1) (5), *supra* at n. 41; *cf.* Kegel and Schurig, *supra* at n. 20, §
18 I. 1. d) pp. 575–582; Kropholler, *supra* at n. 20, § 4 II. pp. 25–28, § 52 II. 4.–5. pp. 419–420;
Reithmann / Martiny, supra at n 80, §§ 101–108 pp. 114–123, §§ 146–151 pp. 152 156:
"*Ausweichklausel*".
[83] For the general principles in interpreting and applying international rules of law see: *Fothergill
v. Monarch Airlines Ltd* [1981] A.C. 251; [1980] 2 All E.R. 696–721; cf. Gardiner, *Treaty
Interpretation in the English Courts Since Fothergill v. Monarch Airlines* [1980], in 44 ICLQ
620–628 (1995).
[84] The Report of Giuliano and Lagarde, German version, in BT-Drucksache 10/503 (1983) pp.
33–79 (51–55) mentions that splitting a contract should be expressed in the Convention, and that
the expert group agreed the expression "*by way of exception*" in Art. 4 (1).

12–034   Germany, as a civil law country has cultivated a strict separation between substantive law (choice of law included) and procedural rulings. Accordingly, analytic studies on conflicts do not pay any attention to pleading matters. Any distinction between the "early stages of pleading" or the "late task of ascertaining the law applicable for decision" are practically unknown.[85] In particular, there is no adequate approach as to how to ascertain the law applicable to contracts concluded by EDI.[86]

2.2.2.4 The EC: The double approach

12–035   Except for the final Giuliano and Lagarde report,[87] there are only a few preparatory papers published and open for comparative studies.[88] It is my impression that two phases and approaches (civil- and common law) are distinct in the preparatory work on European harmonisation of private international law.[88] At least three salient questions may demonstrate the course of the European negotiations.

12–036   First, discussions about Article 4 on the proper law of contract as connected with the characteristic performance and with Article 7 on application of mandatory rules[89] illustrate, in how far flexibility had become a salient topic of compromise. Secondly, as a fundamental difficulty appears in how far the burden of proof (Article 14) is a matter of procedural or adjective law, since the former position would render all relevant questions to the *forum.* The third "early aspect" about pleading choice of law alternatives, as contemplated in this study, never appeared during preparatory work on the Rome Convention.

12–037   During a first period (1967–73) the civil law members remained among themselves and succeeded in drafting a comprehensive set of rules.[90] The first subject (Article 4) then was strongly based on the "characteristic performance", which was understood as a material reflection of the "proper law of contract" and thus, was not intended to leave much room for judicial discretion.[91] Article 7 appeared as restricted to mandatory rulings in states, the law of which might claim application even if not relevant under choice of law rules at hand. Here, an application was allowed as a last resort only with hesitation.[92] In summary, the draft of both rules did not expressly concede any dépeçage or splitting of a contract.[93]

---

[85] For the impact and different attitudes to classification see Mistelis, *supra* at n. 35.
[86] See Junker, *supra* at n. 19; Mankowski, *supra* at n. 5.
[87] *Supra* at n. 84.
[87] Collins, supra at n 20, §§ 32–008—32–019.
[88] The European Commission refused to disclose preparatory documents, Knottnerus-Meyer provided me with some of the papers of the late Karl Arndt who had served as a German reporter during preparation of the Rome Convention (the "*Arndt Papers*").
[89] Citations on Articles follow the present figures of the Rome Convention (1980), *supra* at n. 40.
[90] *Preliminary Draft of a Convention on the Law Applicable on Contracts and Quasi Contracts*, Paper XIV/399/72 D, explained and annotated by Giuliano, Lagarde, Van Sasse and Van Ysselt, in European Commission, SEK (72) 4430 of December 6th, 1972 = XIV/408/72 D pp. 1–97.
[91] Giuliano, Lagarde, Van Sasse and Van Ysselt, *supra* at n. 20, pp. 36–38 (no 3).
[92] *Preliminary Draft*, *supra* at n. 89; Giuliano, Lagarde, Van Sasse and Van Ysselt, *supra* at n. 91, pp. 44–45 No 1.
[93] Giuliano, Lagarde, Van Sasse and Van Ysselt, *supra* at n. 91, p.40 No 5.

The commissioners' work on Article 14 was involved with the burden of **12–038** proof as a difficulty at the borderline between substantive and procedural law and as going along with different questions about evidence in contractual matters (deeds, etc).[94] Finally, a clear position was agreed upon in Article 14, section 1, by claiming for a strong relationship with substantive law.[95]

The second period (1973–80) hallmarks by a much broader perspective **12–039** introduced by the British delegates.[96]

The characteristic performance, the proper law of the contract (Article 4), **12–040** the application of mandatory rules (Article 7) and dépeçage now caused laborious discussions.[97] Finally, in March, 1976, the British side favoured the proper law of contract as a general principle containing flexibility for further developments.[98] The commissioners of civil law countries insisted on more definite provisions and preferred that the characteristic performance as leading legislative authority for ascertaining the law applicable to contracts by reliance to Article 4, sections 2–4, while Article 4, sections 1 and 5 should be regarded as exceptional.[99] Art. 7 was restricted by way a reservation clause in Germany and in the U.K., even though the reasons may have been quite adverse in substance.[1]

The coincident vaguenesses of the burden of proof (substantive versus **12–041** procedural) were agreed upon much easier,[2] perhaps due to the ambivalent remnants of the *Praetors'* formulas in classical Roman Law.[3]

---

[94] Preliminary Draft, *supra* at n. 90, Art. 19 p. 37; *cf*. Giuliano, Lagarde, Van Sasse and Van Ysselt, *supra* at n. 90, pp. 82–88 (no 1–5).

[95] Art. 19 (1) [1]: "*Vorhandensein und Stärke gesetzlicher Vermutungen werden ebenso wie die Beweislast nach dem Recht beurteilt, das für das Rechtsverhältnis maßgeblich ist.*" *supra* at n. 90, p. 37.

[96] The first British contribution in the "*Arndt Papers*" contains a report of Trevor C. Hartley, *Some Aspects of the Draft Convention from the Point of View of British Law* (1972/1973) (= XIV/426/72–D), translated into German containing 147 pages; Memoranda 1–20 followed from November 1975 to October 1978.

[97] *Arndt Papers*, *supra* at n. 88, XIV/79/73/-D pp. 10–12; The Law Commission and The Scottish Law Commission, *Private International Law, E.E.C. Preliminary Draft convention on the Law Applicable to Contractual and Non-Contractual Obligations*, Consultative Document, August 1974, pp. 17–33, 37–43, *Arndt Papers*, *supra* at n. 88, XIV/70/75-D pp. 13–17; XI/727/75-D pp. 2–8; XI/745/75-D pp. 1–17, 19–27; XI/79/76-F pp. 10–17; XI/104/76-D pp. 9–14; XI/127/76-D pp. 2–8, 10–22; XI/514/76-D pp. 8–12; III/749/77-D pp. 5–8; III/148/78 pp. 1–10 (British proposal to limit the scope of the Convention to contractual obligations); III/581/79-D p. 5 (British proposal to strike out Article 7 with regard to difficulties in practice).

[98] The Law Commission, *supra* at n. 97, pp. 26–33; later, *cf. Arndt Papers*, XI/127/76-D p. 2, the English commissioners redrafted Article 4: "(1) To the extent that the law applicable to the contract has not been validly chosen under Article 2 [or 3] the contract shall be governed by the law of the country with which it is most closely connected: provided that a particular aspect of the contract may, if it has a special connection with another country, be governed by the law of that other country;" "(3) The preceding paragraph shall not apply if the characteristic performance cannot be determined or it appears from the circumstances as a whole that the contract is more closely connected with another country."

[99] *Arndt Papers*, *supra* at n. 88, XI/127/76-D pp. 3–4: a "majority'of the working group voted against any dépeçage and followed Art. 4 (1) redrafted (Appendix XI/127/76 D p. 26); the expression "*by way of exception*" was inserted and, thus (for the English point of view), turned the hierarchy of rule and exception upside down.

[1] The final Version of Art. 4 (1) and (5) is identical to the English Contractual Obligations (Applicable Law) Act 1991. For a comparative review see Hartley, *supra* at n. 96, pp. 271–292 (292).

[2] The Law Commission, *supra* at n. 97, pp. 77–81 (then Art. 19(1)); III/1610/77-E (Memorandum no 15 by the UK Experts) pp. 1–3; III/1627/77-FR (then Art. 19 (2) p.15; III/77/76 E p. 7; III/77/79-D p. 8.

[3] Details *post* 3. (1); The Law Commission, *supra* at n. 96, expressly referred to legal history.

12–042   Finally, in 1978 the British commissioners succeeded in restricting additional work to the law applicable on contractual obligations.[4]

12–043   As an interim result, we may summarise that both groups (civil law- versus common law-countries) owing to their divergent attitudes about interrelations between legislation and precedents, scarcely attained a reliable consent about flexibility as essential for handling future challenges in choice of law. Present difficulties of international business transactions can hardly find any easy answer from rulings based only on a "European consent" which 20 years ago in Rome was reached only as a poor compromise.

2.2.3 Summary: the global fall-back to *Audiatur et Altera Pars*

12–044   Gradually a first generation of cases about e-commerce appears in law reports. Discrepancies, as mentioned above, become detectable by comparison and, certainly, more will follow.[5] The present challenges render (among other alternatives) to look back to the roots as promising. The following section focuses on the affirmative or special defences as the salient remedy and relief in legal history.

3. Three highlights in history

12–045   Meticulous studies have disclosed historical influences world-wide,[6] but the legal concept of rights and remedies, or (speaking more exactly) the procedural dichotomy of causes of actions versus exceptions have remained under a veil of analytical uncertainty. Three historic highlights echoing the Praetors' formulas, by Savigny and Story and, finally, from recent German legislation on conflict of laws disclose that dépeçage and legally split contracts appeared early in international business and that flexibility has continuously remained of influence, even if hidden behind requirements for simple structured certainty on the surface.

3.1 Flexible structures in formulas of classical Roman law

12–046   Comprehensive legislation soon overshadowed the traditional attention to the historical school in Germany after 1900. Coincidentally, Roman law lost relevance in legal practice and education. Later, new and exclusive research began to disclose the whereabouts behind Justinian's great code. Kaser in his

---

[4] *Arndt Papers, supra* at n. 88, Memorandum no 19 of February, 1978 = III/148/78 no 1 pp. 1–10.
[5] Coincident distinction on burden of pleading versus burden of proof in civil- and in common law countries are distinguishable from the German BTX-Case Landgericht Aachen and Oberlandesgericht Köln, both in CR 1997 pp. 153–155, CR 1998 pp. 244–248 and *Evolution Online Systems, Inc. v. Koninklijke Nederland N. V.* 41 F.Supp. 2d 447. Nevertheless the German Courts misjudged the conclusion of a contract under German law with regard to an *invitatio ad offerendum* and consequently, but likewise wrongfully, displaced the burden of pleading and proof. Contrasting: *Rakoff J.* (District Court of New York) strictly followed and completely argued about the relevant rules on contracting, jurisdiction (long arm jurisdiction and *forum non convenience*) and pleading.
[6] Dawson, *The Oracles of the Law*, Ann Arbor, 1968; Watson, Aspects of Reception of Law, in 44 *Am. J. Comp. L.* 335–351 (1996); Stein, *The Character and Influence of the Roman Civil law*, 1988 pp. 151–165; Kaser, *Das Römische Privatrecht, Erster Abschnitt, Das Altrömische, Das Vorklassische und Klassische Recht*, 2nd ed. München 1971.

two voluminous studies on civil law and the law of civil procedure opened new perspectives about the *formulas*.[7] Their later influence to civil law systems[8] likewise became evident as *formulas* had coined the early common law and have remained as of relevance in modern practice, world-wide.[9]

The origin of the Praetors' *exceptio* illustrates its multifold and likewise flexible function. Initially the Praetors might have granted *exceptions* as adherent parts of the *action*, introduced by *si . . . non*. Later, for unmistakable guidance in procedure before a private judge, the *exceptio* was clearly separated and granted to a defendant who was going to prove his opposite legal position by giving evidence, if necessary.[10] The Praetors' tradition to grant an *exceptio* only if a future defendant applied for it, underlined the procedural nature for defences—much in contrast to the easy definitions of rights and remedies (*actio*) which were not easily at hand. Traditions and receptions at this point appear as difficult.   12–047

Simple examples demonstrate the chameleon-like character of such defences. A buyer of goods which have been delivered in defective condition may claim repayment of the price only if he has paid already for the goods. Whether he likewise might have a right or remedy in case that no payment was made, will appear as a defence only, if the seller would claim for payment of the price.   12–048

Such varying structure in (real or affirmative) defence has substantially survived, untouched by many receptions. In consequence, under aspects of litigation there is freedom for a defendant to choose his own course of pleading defences in common law[11] and likewise *cum grano salis* in civil law.[12] The winding ways of receptions in history and the legal structure of real or special defences are yet to be analysed.   12–049

3.2 Story and Savigny: places of performance

Rights and remedies rarely hallmark academic writings on conflict of laws, and perhaps even less under early views of pleading defences.   12–050

---

[7] Kaser, *ibid*, and Kaser and Hackl, *Das Römische Zivilprozeßrecht*, 2nd ed. München 1969.

[8] As prototypes for later rulings served among others the classical *actio venditi*: in German BGB, § 433 (1), French Code Civile, Artt. 1602–1604, Italian Codice Civile, Art. 1476 [1], [2]) and (*vice versa*) the *actio empti* BGB, § 433 (2), Code Civil, Art. 1650, Codice Civile, Art. 1498 [1]). *cf.* Kaser, *supra* at n., § 130 V. 1., 2. pp 550 551; the same applies to the *formulas* in tort, the later claim for compensation of damages caused by animals in form of an *actio de pauperie* (BGB, § 833 (1), Code Civil, Art. 1385, Codice Civile, Art. 2052) Kaser, *supra* at n. 104, § 42 II. p 165, 147 II. p 633.

[9] *cf.* Friedenthal, Kane and Miller, *supra* at n. 24, §§ 5.1–5.3, pp. 237–243; Sir William Holdsworth, *A History of English Law*, Vol. 2, 1982, pp. 244–290; Sir Frederick Pollock / Maitland, *The History of English Law*, 2nd ed. 1984, Vol. 2, § 1 (form of action, pp. 558–572), § 4 (Pleading and Proof pp. 598–619); Kaufmann, *Zur Geschichte des aktionenrechtlichen Denkens*, in JZ 1964 pp. 482–489; Schmitthoff, *Der Zivilprozeß als Schlüssel zum englischen Rechtsdenken*, in JZ 1972 pp. 38–43; Peter, *Actio und Writ: eine vergleichende Darstellung römischer und englischer Rechtsbehelfe*; Tübingen, 1957.

[10] Kaser, *supra* at n. 6 (para. 12–046), § 55, pp. 223–227, (aspects of substantive law); Kaser and Hackl, *supra* at n. 7 (para. 12–047), § 35 pp. 256–266 (procedural aspects); for the intricate traditions up to the present day see Kaser, *supra* at n., § 47 pp. 188–194; Peter, *supra* at n. 9 (para. 12–046).

[11] See *supra* at sections 2.2.2.1 and 2.2.2.2

[12] See *supra* at section 2.2.2.3

Story[13] and von Savigny[14] may likewise serve as famous examples, though antagonistic reasons in choice of law on contracts may lead to resembling results only at a first glance.[15] Both men, after discussing the validity of a contract, claimed the place of performance as the suitable connecting factor, which evidently may lead to different results in contracts imposing reciprocal obligations. Story strongly included views of pleading insofar and mentioned many examples which nowadays might be characterised as dépeçage,[16] while von Savigny, under correspondent ideas about the place of performance, expressly excluded elements of procedure.[17]

12–051   In consequence, the place of performance mirrors the parties' autonomy under substantive- and procedural aspects, while the same approach in the conflict rulings of civil law are strictly isolated from rules of procedure. The "closest connection" (*Sitz des Rechtsverhältnisses*) under German conflict of laws has rarely been characterised as genuine autonomy of the contracting parties, the (later) litigants.

3.3 The German legislation (1874–1900): the elaborated dispense

12–052   Travaux préparatoires on German legislation during the last quarter of the nineteenth century have ever since been clearly evident publicly, except for private international law.[18] Only in the 1970s did it become discernible that Gebhard, in drafting the General Part of the later Civil Code, included private international law and carefully relied on comparative studies, especially on Wharton.[19] Nevertheless, the "First Commission" in 1888 rejected both of Gebhard's proposals about international contracts in favour of the

---

[13] Story, *Commentaries on the Conflict of Laws, Foreign and Domestic*, Edinburgh, London, Dublin 1835. Modern analysis of Story's writings in conflict presents Lipstein, *Principles of the Conflict of Laws National and International*, The Hague, Boston, London, 1981 pp. 17–28.

[14] Von Savigny, *System des heutigen römischen Rechts*, Aalen 1974 (reprint of 1849); *cf.* Lipstein, *ibid.*

[15] Obviously Reimann took no notice of the fact, that Savigny expressly refrained from any aspect of practice and procedure (see Savigny, *supra* at n. 112, Vol. 1 § 1 p. 3), *cf.* Reimann, *Historische Schule und Common Law*, Berlin, 1993; The Historical School Against Codification: Savigny, Carter, and the Defeat of the New York Civil Code, in *The American Journal of Comparative Law* (1989) 37 pp. 95–119; Savigny's Triumph? Choice of Law in Contracts Cases at the Close of the Twentieth Century, in *Virginia Journal of Intern'l Law Association* (1999) 39 pp. 571–605.

[16] Story, *supra* at n. 13 (para. 12–050), §§ 231–373 pp. 193–307, §§ 231–262 pp. 193–219 (validity of a contract), §§ 263–373 pp. 219–307, § 280 p. 233 (place of performance). Story himself mentioned examples of performances as a defence under procedural aspects. His book on pleadings, published much earlier (Story, *Selection of Pleadings in Civil Actions, subsequent to the Declaration*, Salem 1805) demonstrates already reflections on private international law, by giving examples of dépeçage, *cf.* §§ 263, 264, 267, 269, 287, 289, 297, etc.

[17] Von Savigny, *supra* at n. 13 (para. 12–050), Vol. 8, §§ 369–370 pp. 200–233 (place of performance); *cf. supra* at n. 12 (para. 12–050).

[18] "Secret documents" have been published late: Hartwieg and Korkisch, *Die Geheimen Materialien zur Kodifikation des Internationalen Privatrechts*, Tübingen 1973.

[19] Niemeyer, *Zur Vorgeschichte des Internationalen Privatrechts im Bürgerlichen Gesetzbuch*, München, Leipzig, 1915, on contracts: § 11 pp. 133–155 (140–151); Wharton, *A Treatise on Conflict of Laws*, Vol. I., 3rd ed. Rochester, 1905, §§ 393–397 pp. 858–860 (complexity of obligations involves complexity of jurisdictions), §§ 398–404 pp. 862–867 (place of agreement and performances, Gebhard in 1881 used an older edition).

"contracting place."[20] Finally, the German Hansa-Towns succeeded in eliminating all choice of law rules on contracts as being inflexible and completely useless.[21]

4. Conclusion

International Business via the internet and EDI challenges conflict lawyers. **12–053** It appears as uncertain, in how far the old (and fragile) concepts may serve modern and future demands. The usual method just to continue with old connecting factors might hardly appear as promising, since neither simple concepts, or clearly convincing results are available. In addition, the laconic mode of civil law judges' reasoning scarcely discloses the full set of facts relevant for their legal arguments, much in contrast to common law practice.

Choice of law questions arising from cyberspace need broad views and **12–054** detailed explanations. Issues of pleading and the burden of proof are always to be kept in mind. In particular, there is no *natural* preponderance on the claimant's or the defendant's side, or on any of their mutual remedies (causes of actions or special defences). As an international principle of practice and procedure it can be noted that only two different constellations may appear:

- If the contracting parties have ascertained the law applicable to their contract, there is not much need for new devices, except consumers' protection and perhaps convincing interference by mandatory rules.

- If the parties disagree on a single legal system as applicable, courts may be well advised to wait and to trust on the ancient and flexible model of *act* and *except*, which leaves the risk with the litigants. Their mutual roles as plaintiffs and defendants coincides the burden of pleading and proof automatically with their allocation of risks to succeed with the remedy in question.

The claimant, by pleading his claim as based upon a certain country's **12–055** law, has to face the risk that the defendant might question both, fact and law.

Vice versa, the defendant may make use of his natural right (*audiatur et* **12–056** *altera pars*) by contesting all three elements, the plaintiff's facts, "his" (foreign) law and its applicability, thus, he may drive his opponent to evidence.

Furthermore, the defendant can plead and adduce affirmative or special **12–057** defences by relying on his own version of facts. In doing so, he likewise has to face the risk going along with his strategy of pleading a remedy (defence). He is well advised to expect that the plaintiff not necessarily

---

[20] Gebhard, in § 11 of both of his drafts (1881/1887) favoured the domicile of the debtor, the First Commission in § 5 proposed the place where the contract was agreed upon. *cf.* Hartwieg / Korkisch, *supra* at n. 18 (12–052), pp. 63, 69, 90–95, 179.
[21] For details see Hartwieg/Korkisch, *supra* at n. 18 (12–052), pp. 12–22, 42–55, 297–324 (300–304), 326, 336–338, 358.

might retreat. If his right (and remedy) is based on the law of another country, it will likewise be his, the defendant's, risk to persuade the court that his defence is resting adequately on a contract, insofar governed by that foreign law. As far as the claimant denies the content of the foreign law, he is obliged to give evidence.

12–058   This procedural principle of pleading rights and remedies which still is a vivid part of litigation world-wide may serve as an intermediate instrument to answer new challenges of international business transactions until balanced and effective criteria for ascertaining the law applicable to contracts in e-commerce are available.

CHAPTER 13

RENVOI: A NECESSARY EVIL
OR IS IT POSSIBLE TO ABOLISH IT BY STATUTE?

PROFESSOR KURT SIEHR[1]

---

[1] Professor of Law, University of Zurich, Faculty of Law (Switzerland).

1. Renvoi discovered

13–001   Discoveries may be dangerous. The discoverer may have found new territories, unknown plants or strange animals but he does not manage to get out of these new territories, cannot protect himself against poisonous plants and is not able to tame wild animals. This also happened when renvoi was "discovered" more than a hundred years ago. The discoverers did not even realise that renvoi is a wild animal and up to now there are very few proposals how to master this creature. The title of my paper is an almost correct expression of this still prevailing perplexity.

1.1 Early cases[2]

13–003   It is interesting to note that it was law courts which *applied* a renvoi first and answered questions without even realizing that they dealt with serious problems. These problems arose especially in succession cases in which persons died domiciled abroad in a foreign country. In the English case *Collier v. Rivaz*, decided in 1841,[3] a British subject died domiciled in Belgium and left codicils which were formally invalid under Belgian domestic law but valid under English law. The English court, seized of the case, referred to the Belgian *lex domicilii* and accepted a Belgian renvoi to the English *lex patriae* because according to Belgian private international law the formalities of codicils of English deceased persons were governed by the deceased's *lex patriae*. Twenty years later the predecessor court of the German Reichsgericht, the *Oberappellationsgericht* in Lübeck, had to decide a conflict between local laws of two different German regions, between the Gemeines Recht (common law) governing in the Imperial town of Frankfurt on Main and the French law valid in the Rhineland. The court admitted a renvoi of the *lex ultimi domicilii* (Mainz in

---

[2] The early French, Belgian, German, Italian, Swiss, English, American, Canadian cases and cases from some other jurisdictions (*e.g.* Netherlands and Greece) are discussed by Emile Potu, *La question du renvoi en droit international privé* (Paris 1913) 16–144; early Italian cases are treated by Maximilien Philonenko, *La théorie du renvoi en droit comparé* (Paris 1935); and Rodolfo De Nova, *Historical and Comparative Introduction to Conflict of Laws: Recueil des Cours* 118 (1966–II) 435–621 (484–538).

[3] *Collier v. Rivaz*, (1841) 2 Curteis 855; 163 E.R. 608. This case has been qualified so far as renvoi is concerned, as "the *fons et origo mali* in English conflict of laws". *cf.* John Delatre Falconbridge, *Characterization in the Conflict of Laws: 53 Law Quarterly Review* 235–258, 537–567 (552) (1937). To this case and other English renvoi–cases *cf.* Albrecht Mendelssohn–Bartholdy, Renvoi in Modern English Law (Oxford 1937) 58, *et seq.*

the Rhineland) to the *lex patriae* of the deceased (Frankfurt) if such a reference back were proven.[4] It was not until 1882 that the French *Cour de cassation* handed down the well known *Forgo case*[5] and thereby started the discussion about the renvoi problem which made *François-Xavier Forgo* one of the best known figures of the choice of law-stage. The Bavarian subject Forgo died domiciled in France. Under French choice of law-rules his Bavarian *lex patriae* governed succession and this law was held to refer back to French substantive law and, hence, French law governed the distribution of Mr. Forgo's estate. Since then, many succession cases turn out to be a person's ultimate adventure into the unknown.

The English, German and French courts were not aware of these adventures. They did not discover, discuss and evaluate the very problem of any renvoi, the vicious circle of a reference back and forth. The French court did not ask whether Bavarian law to which reference has been made, would do the same and, if Bavarian courts were seized of the case, apply Bavarian law. This eternal problem of any renvoi was revealed very soon[6] and much ink has been spilt discussing it.

13–004

1.2 Problem discovered

Hardly any problem of private international law has been discussed so often and so intensively as the problem of renvoi. *"Le renvoi a fait littéralement tache d'huile"*.[7] The reason is very simple. If a choice of law rule refers to foreign law, it has to be decided whether this reference is a reference to foreign internal law (*Sachnorm-Verweisung*) or whether foreign private international law has also to be taken into consideration (*IPR-Verweisung*). I do not want to summarise this discussion in detail. I rather should like to draw the attention to two experiences. First, it is obvious that renvoi refers to a real problem and it is not just a scientifically interesting but hardly important toy of

13–005

---

[4] Oberappellationsgericht Lübeck March 21, 1861 (*Krebs w. Rosalino*), 14 Seuffert's Archiv der Entscheidungen der obersten Gerichte der deutschen Staaten 164 (1861).
[5] Cour de cassation (Ch.req.) February 22, 1882, Recueil Sirey 1882. 1.393 (*Forgo c. Administration des Domaines*), with note by J.–E. Labbé, and Bertrand Ancel/Yves Lequette (eds.), Grands arrêts de la jurisprudence française de droit international privé (3d ed. Paris 1998) No. 8 (p. 54). As to this case *cf. Maximilien Philonenko*, L'Affaire Forgo (1874–1822). Contribution à l'étude des sources du droit international privé français: 59 Clunet 281–322 (1932).
[6] J.–E. Labbé, Du conflit entre la loi nationale du juge saisi et une loi étrangère relativement à la détermination de la loi applicable à la cause: 12 Clunet 5–16 (1885); Reichsgericht May 31, 1889, 24 Entscheidungen des Reichsgerichts in Zivilsachen 326, 331 *et seq.*; Albert Venn Dicey, *A Digest of the Law of England with Reference to the Conflict of Laws* (2nd ed. London 1908) 716, *et seq.* (Appendix: Meaning of "Law of a Country", and the Doctrine of the renvoi). The first edition of Dicey of 1896 does not discuss the case *Collier v. Rivaz, supra* n. 2, and does not mention the word "renvoi". John Westlake, *A Treatise on Private International Law or the Conflict of Laws* (London 1858) 36 *et seq.*, mentions this case when discussing the acquisition of domicile; the same does John Alderson Foote, *A Concise Treatise on Private International Law* (2nd ed. London 1890) p. 25, 27, 30 and 40.
[7] Antoine Pillet/Jean–Paulin Niboyet, *Manuel de droit international privé* (Paris 1924) 385. *cf.* the bibliographies given by J. Georges Sauveplannes, Renvoi, in: *3 International Encyclopedia of Comparative Law*, chap. 6. (Tübingen/Dordrecht 1990) 36; Gerhard Kegel/Klaus Schurig, *Internationales Privatrecht* (8th ed. Munich 2000) 334 *et seq.*, and the books of Phocion Francescakis, *La théorie du renvoi et les conflits de systèmes en droit international privé* (Paris 1958); *Philonenko, supra* n. 2; *Potu, supra* n. 2; and Peter A. Reichart, *Der Renvoi im schweizerischen IPR* (Zürich 1996).

crazy law professors. The question raised (do we have to care for foreign private international law?) has to be answered. You may ignore the problem and thereby answer it tacitly but an answer has to be given. A court decision or a statutory provision declining to accept a renvoi is such an answer to a real problem. Still open is whether such an answer is correct, proper and practical.

13–006   The other experience is more complex. A superficial reading of papers, discussions and lectures on renvoi seems to convey a rather simple line of reasoning: If everybody accepts a renvoi of foreign choice of law-rules, there may be an endless reference forth and back. This should be avoided and, in addition, the ascertainment and application for foreign private international law is burdensome and courts should be relieved of this burden. A closer look at the renvoi discussions, however, reveals interesting attitudes and theories about private international law and its purpose, functions and qualities, and these attitudes also influence the problem of renvoi. Some different attitudes shall be mentioned briefly.

1.2.1 Fundamentals of private international law

1.2.1.1 Historical Background
13–007   The nineteenth century can be called the formative years of modern private international law with *Friedrich Carl von Savigny* (1779–1861), *Joseph Story* (1779–1845), *Andrés Bello* (1781–1865) and *Pasquale Stanislao Mancini* (1817–88) as the "grand old men"[8]. It was only *Mancini*, the youngest of them, who experienced the early discussion of renvoi and who started the belief in the law-of-nations doctrine in the conflict of laws. This was a commonly supported opinion of the founders (*e.g. T.M.C. Asser, Carl Ludwig von Bar, Johann Caspar Bluntschli, Gustave Rolin-Jaequemyns, John Westlake*) of the Institute of International Law (founded in Ghent in 1873), of the International Law Association (founded in Brussels in 1873 as Association for the Reform and Codification of the Law of Nations) and of the Hague Conference on Private International Law (held for the first time in 1893). It is the time of international conferences where many multilateral conventions of a non-political nature were drafted and recommended for ratification by states. Optimistically it was held that private international law is part of public international law in general and that it might be possible to find common rules of choice of law in customary international law or, if this is impossible, to create common rules of universal application within the newly founded organisations of the Institute of International Law (Institut de Droit international), the International Law Association and the Hague Conference on Private International Law. It is this background of public international law which is shaping the early discussion of the renvoi problem. Some of these opinions shall be summarised in order to demonstrate that serious questions were raised and fundamental problems were discussed which still wait for definite answers.

---

[8] Max Gutzwiller, Internationalprivatrecht: Die drei Großen des 19. Jahrhunderts, in: Festschrift Frank Vischer (Zürich 1983) 131–140; Jürgen Samtleben, La relacion entre derecho internacional publico y privado en Andrés Bello: 34 Revista española de derecho internacional 399–408 (1982).

1.2.1.2 Applicable law vesting rights

Is it really possible and even allowed to divorce private international law from internal substantive law? Is it not true that choice of law-rules determine the sphere of application of substantive law and vest private rights to be recognised everywhere?[9] True theory of vested rights, once supported also by Justice *Oliver Wendell Holmes* (1841–1935),[10] should not be held as an approach in favour of renvoi. *Joseph H. Beale* (1861–1943), the reporter of the first Restatement of the Law of Conflict of Laws (1934) and a partisan of the vested rights theory, declined to accept a renvoi.[11] He incorrectly held that by a renvoi foreign law imposes the application of a certain law on the forum state.[12] It is, however, up to the forum state whether to accept such a renvoi or not. Foreign choice of law–rules are not binding the domestic forum.

13–008

1.2.1.3 Competent jurisdiction

A reference to foreign law can be qualified as declining to assume jurisdiction and to designate a foreign competent jurisdiction to deal with the subject matter.[13] If foreign law declines to accept this designation it does not conflict with the forum state and hence there is no danger of any *circulus inextricabilis*. The forum state may accept this attitude and designate another jurisdiction or apply the *lex fori*.

13–009

If the *lex fori* is applied this may be explained by a renvoi[14] but not necessarily. There may be also a subsidiary choice of law-rule of the forum state taking the renvoi of foreign law as a condition for a rule referring subsidiarily to the *lex fori*.[15] Also a conditional reference to foreign law has been proposed very early. This was done in the Zurich Civil Code of 1853/55 prepared by *Johann Caspar Bluntschli* (1808–81)[16] and by the Swiss Choice of Law-Statute of 1891.[17] Such a conditional reference is very similar or almost

13–010

---

[9] John Westlake in: 18 Annuaire de l'Institut de Droit international 35–40 (1900); *id., A Treatise on Private International Law* (3rd ed. London 1890) 4 *et seq.*

[10] *cf.* Justice Oliver Holmes in *Slater v. Mexican National R. Co*, 194 U.S. 120 (1904). Similar Judge Maugham in *Re Askew*, [1930] 2 Ch. 259, 267: ". . . and the phrase [applying foreign law] is really a short way of referring to rights acquired under the lex domicilii."

[11] Joseph H. Beale, *A Treatise of the Conflict of Laws*, Vol. 1, (New York 1935) 62 *et seq.*

[12] Beale, Treatise (last note) pp. 55–57; *Restatement of the Law of Conflict of Laws* (St. Paul/Minn. 1934) § 7.

[13] Carl Ludwig von Bar, Theorie und Praxis des internationalen Privatrechts vol. 1 (2nd ed. Hannover 1889, reprint Aalen 1966) 108 *et seq.; id., The Theory and Practice of Private International Law* (2nd ed. Edinburgh 1892) 79 *et seq.; id.,* Die Rückverweisung im internationalen Privatrecht: 8 Niemeyers Zeitschrift für internationales Recht 177, 178 *et seq.* (1898).

[14] Paolo Picone, Ordinamento competente e diritto internazionale privato (Padova 1986) 165 *et seq.; id.,* La méthode de la référence à l'ordre juridique compétent en droit international privé: Recueil des Cours 197 (1986–II) 229–419 (321 *et seq.*); *id.,* Les méthodes de coordination entre ordres juridiques en droit international privé: Recueil des Cours 276 (1999–II) 9–296 (119 *et seq.*)

[15] Rolando Quadri, Critica del c.d. problema del rinvio: 10 Giurisprudenza comparata di diritto internazionale privato 153 (1944), reproduced in: *id., Studi critici di diritto internazionale,* Vol. 1, (Milano 1958) 355 *et seq.*

[16] According to § 2 (2) sent 2 of the Zurich Civil Code (Privatrechtliches Gesetzbuch) foreigners are governed by their *lex patriae* "if this is provided by the law of the State of which they are subjects." Text in: *Friedrich Meili,* Die Kodifikation des internationalen Civil- und Handelsrechts. Eine Materialiensammlung (Leipzig 1891) 52 *et seq.*

[17] Art. 28 no. 2 of the Swiss Federal Statute on the Private Law Relations of the Domiciliaries and Residents of 1891 reads: "If, according to the foreign legislation, those Swiss citizens [living

identical with the application of *"Näherrecht"*, the law primarily competent to govern the case because of its proximity to the case and which has to be asked first before designating a secondarily applicable law.[18]

1.2.1.4 Reference to internal substantive law

13–011   Already at the Neuchâtel session in 1900 the Institut de Droit international voted 31:6 against any reference of domestic choice of law rules to foreign private international law and thereby rejected a renvoi.[19] The majority of scholars declined to accept a reference forth and back or a "lawn tennis" as it was called by *Giulio Cesare Buzzati* (1862–1920) one of the drafters of the proposal to disregard any renvoi.[20]

13–012   The main rationale for the attitude was based on principles of doctrine and practical considerations. The major reason was the last one mentioned: if every state would refer to foreign choice of law-rules, many cases would be stuck up a blind alley. In order to avoid such a courteous "after you"[21] a renvoi should be rejected and foreign law also be applied even if it does not want to govern the case.

1.2.2 International harmony of laws and homeward trend

13–013

A renvoi has been supported in order to achieve uniform results on an international level.[22] Limping relations should be reduced or avoided altogether and an incentive for forum shopping be eliminated. Of course, these noble objectives can only be achieved if the potentially conflicting jurisdictions do not do the same and apply their own law by accepting a renvoi of the same kind. If one jurisdiction accepts a renvoi and applies its own law, the jurisdiction referring back should apply the altruistic foreign court theory and accept

---

abroad] are not governed by the foreign law, it is the law of the canton of origin which is applied to them, and it is likewise that canton which exercises jurisdiction." Translation taken from: John Delatre Falconbridge, *Renvoi in New York and Elsewhere: 6 Vanderbilt Law Review* pp. 708–742 (728) 1953 = id., Essays on the Conflict of Laws (2nd ed. Toronto 1954) pp. 233–263 (241). French version of Article 28 in: Asser Instituut (ed.), *Statutory Private International Law* (Oslo 1971) 107, 114.

[18] Such an idea of "Näherrecht" is provided in Art. 86 (2) Swiss Private International Law Statute and in Art. 3 (3) of the German EGBGB (Introductory Statute to the Civil Code). English translations of the Swiss Statute in: 37 American Journal of Comparative Law 193, 216 (1989) and of the German one by Gerhard Wegen in: *27 International Legal Materials 1*, 6 *et seq.* (1988).

[19] 18 Annuaire de l'Institut de Droit international 176 *et seq.* (1900) concerning the proposal submitted to the members on p. 34.

[20] Buzzati in: *18 Annuaire de l'Institut de Droit international 146* (1900).

[21] A more subtle description of military history is chosen by Justice Maughan: "The English judges and the foreign judges do not bow to each other like the officers at Fontenoy". *cf.* In re Askew, *supra* n. 9, 267. – During the Austrian Succession War (1740–48) at the battle of Fontenoy (Belgium) on May 11, 1745 the officers of the Allies (England, Austria, Hanover, Netherlands) on the one side and the officers of the French army on the other side after reciprocal cheers are said to have asked each other to fire first.

[22] Martin Wolff, *Internationales Privatrecht* (1st ed. Berlin 1933) 50, mentions the term "Entscheidungseinklang" which has been accepted as one argument supporting renvoi; *id.*, *Private International Law* (2nd ed. Oxford 1950) 17 (harmony of laws). *cf.* also Paul Heinrich Neuhaus, *Die Grundbegriffe des Internationalen Privatrechts* (1st ed. Berlin/Tübingen 1962). 38 *et seq.*; Max Pagenstecher, Der Grundsatz des Entscheidungseinklangs im internationalen Privatrecht. Ein Beitrag zur Lehre vom Renvoi (Wiesbaden 1951).

that foreign law applies. Such a recipe works between various jurisdictions in some circumstances but it cannot be prescribed by a single jurisdiction.

The theory of international harmony is rather narrowly defined. It wanted **13–014** to achieve an *"Entscheidungsharmonie"* without taking into account that different results can be avoided and uniformity also be achieved by recognition of foreign decisions or acts. Such a uniformity of results (*Ergebnisharmonie*) is very likely today because the application of the "correct law" is hardly any obstacle to non-recognition any more.[23]

Authors supporting the "Entscheidungsharmonie" tend to argue very **13–015** pragmatically. They are aware of the pitfalls of renvoi and yet they accept a renvoi where a sensible solution can be achieved by doing the same as the designated law is doing.[24]

Apart from this supranational objective of international harmony, renvoi **13–016** has been welcomed because it facilitates procedure insofar as the well known domestic law may easily be applied instead of unknown foreign law. It is one device to support a certain "homeward trend" (*Heimwärtsstreben*).[25]

1.3 Interim summary

As soon as the renvoi problem had been discovered, the discussion started **13–017** and the question was raised whether to accept it or not. The answer was not a simple affirmative or declining one. Several different objectives of private international law in general favoured a renvoi or declined to accept it.

2. Renvoi codified

As soon as renvoi had been discovered as a problem, every legislator of pri- **13–018** vate international law had to make up his mind whether to accept a renvoi, decline it or make some compromises. I do not want to repeat a survey on national and international legislation already prepared recently.[26] I rather like to look at legislation under a specific historical angle.

2.1 National legislation

2.1.1 Early codification

Some of the earliest comprehensive modern codifications of private interna- **13–019** tional law are the Privatrechtliches Gesetzbuch (PGB; Civil Code) of the

---

[23] An exception to this general rule is laid down in Art. 27 No. 4 of the Brussels/Lugano Convention of 1968/1988 on Jurisdiction and the Enforcement of Judgments in Civil and Commercial Matters [1972], O.J.E.C. L299/32 and [1988] O.J.319/9.

[24] Members of this group of pragmatic scholars are well known authors and law professors such as Martin Wolff, *supra* n. 22, and Leo Raape. *cf.* Staudinger (-Raape), Kommentar zum Bürgerlichen Gesetzbuch mit dem Einführungsgesetz, vol. VI/2 (9th ed. Munich/Berlin/Leipzig 1931) Einleitung E VI 2 (p. 22 *et seq.*).

[25] The term "Heimwärtsstreben" has been coined by Arthur Nussbaum, *Deutsches internationales Privatrecht* (Tübingen 1932) 43.

[26] *Kurt Lipstein*, La prise en considération du droit international privé étranger. The Taking into account of foreign private international law: 68 I Annuaire de l'Institut de Droit international 13–53 (1999).

Swiss Canton of Zurich(1853/55),[27] the Codigo Civil of Chile of 1855[28] and the Italian Codice Civile of 1865.[29] All of these codifications ignore the renvoi problem not yet discovered but not all of them ignore foreign private international law. The Zurich Civil Code of 1853/33 takes into consideration the foreign *lex patriae* of foreigners domiciled in Zurich (§ 3 Civil Code). In matters of family law these foreigners are governed by their *lex patriae* insofar as that law provides so. That means that the *lex domicilii* governs if the *lex patriae* does not want to be applied in family matters.[30] The first codifications dealing with the renvoi problem were the Swiss statute of 1891 on Private Law Relations of the Domiciliaries and Residents (NAG),[31] the Introductory Law to the German Civil Code of 1896 (EGBGB)[32] and Japanese Horei of 1898.[33] For the first time special rules accepting a renvoi were formulated. Interesting are three details. In Germany the drafter of the bill of the EGBGB was not in favour of a renvoi,[34] yet it was provided in the new statute. The same happened 90 years later when the German Council on private international law proposed to accept the foreign court-theory[35] and parliament chose the present traditional version of Article 4 EGBGB.[36] Apparently renvoi is more attractive to practitioners than to scholars.

13–020   The second interesting observation is that the renvoi was limited to a reference back to German law. Court and scholars did not take this decision very seriously and extended the renvoi principle to references on to a third jurisdiction.[37]

13–021   The last peculiarity is the restriction of renvoi to matters of personal status, family matters and succession. This limitation is due to inherent limits of the EGBGB and other similar statutes. But also in this respect courts and scholars extended the renvoi principles to almost all matters.[38]

---

[27] See *supra* n. 16.

[28] The conflict of law-provision of this Code are reproduced in: *Meili, supra* n. 16, 46 *et seq.*

[29] *cf.* also Meili, *supra* n. 16, 29 *et seq.*

[30] See *supra* n. 16.

[31] See *supra* n. 17.

[32] Reproduced in: Alexander N. Makarov, Quellen des internationalen Privatrechts. Nationale Kodifikationen (3rd ed. Tübingen 1978) 82 *et seq.*

[33] Reproduced in: Makarov, *supra* n. 32 148 *et seq.*

[34] *cf.* Theodor Niemeyer, Zur Vorgeschichte des Internationalen Privatrechts im Deutschen Bürgerlichen Gesetzbuch ("Die Gebhardschen Materialien") (Munich and Leipzig 1915) 39 and comments to § 31 of the drafts on p. 252 and 366; and Oskar Hartwieg, *Der Renvoi im deutschen Internationalen Vertragsrecht* (Frankfurt/Berlin 1967) 85 *et seq.*; critical to this draft *cf.* Franz Kahn, *Der Grundsatz der Rückverweisung im deutschen Bürgerlichen Gesetzbuch und auf dem Haager Kongreß für internationales Privatrecht*: 36 Jherings Jahrbücher für die Dogmatik des heutigen römischen und deutschen Privatrechts 306–408 (1896) = *id.,* Abhandlungen zum internationalen Privatrecht Vol. 1 (Munich/Leipzig 1928) pp. 124–160.

[35] "Renvoi" "If the law of another state is applicable, it has to be decided as the foreign judge would decide." *cf.* Günther Beitzke (ed.), Vorschläge und Gutachten zur Reform des deutschen internationalen Personen-, Familien- und Erbrechts (Tübingen 1981) 15 (text) and 70 (explanation).

[36] Art. 4 (1) EGBGB reads: "If reference is made to the law of another state, its private international law shall also be applied so far as it does not contradict the meaning of the renvoi. If the law of the other state refers back to German law, German substantive provisions shall apply." Translation by Gerhard Wegen, *supra* n. 18, 7.

[37] Reichsgericht November 8, 1917, 91 Entscheidungen des Reichsgerichts in Zivilsachen 139 (Belgian lex patriae of deceased referred to Russian lex rei sitae).

[38] Oberlandesgericht Hamburg March 22, 1933, 1933 Die deutsche Rechtsprechung auf dem Gebiete des internationalen Privatrechts No. 28 (renvoi of English law with respect to a maritime lien on a ship).

2.1.2 Legislation up to 1945

Some states revising their private international law during the first half of **13–022**
last century rejected any reference back or on. This was done in Greece
(1940/46),[39] Italy (1942)[40] and Brazil (1942).[41] This policy seems to be inspired
by influences from scholars like *Roberto Ago* (1907–95)[42] and *Georgios
Maridakis* (1890–1979).[43] They wanted to codify conflicts rules which can be
limited and applied universally. But a renvoi does not deserve universal
recognition. It only works if states apply different rules and do not prefer the
same form of renvoi.

2.1.3 Post-war legislation

There have never been promulgated so many statutes on private international **13–023**
law as after the Second World War. Most of the Central and East European
countries revised their old statutes or enacted new ones. Almost all of them
accepted a renvoi back.[44]

Also in Western Europe, Austria, Germany, Italy, Liechtenstein, Portugal, **13–024**
Spain, Switzerland and Turkey enacted new statutes on private international
law. None of these statutes ignore the renvoi problem.[45] These provisions
range from very detailed rules in the Portuguese Civil Code[46] to less

---

[39] Art. 32 of the Greek Astikos Kodix of 1946 reads: "The choice of law – rules of foreign law governing according to Greek private international Law has not to be applied." *cf.* Wolfgang Riering, IPR-Gesetze in Europa (Bern, Munich 1997) 18 and 26 (Greek and German).

[40] Art. 30 of the Disposizioni sulla legge in generale of 1942 (Introductory Provisions to the Italian Civil Code of 1942) reads: "If according to the preceeding articles foreign law governs, the [substantive] provisions of exactly this foreign law apply without paying regard whether this foreign law refers to another law." Riering (*supra* n. 39). 28 and 34 (Italian and German).

[41] Article 16 of the Brazilian Código civil of 1942 reads: "If according to the proceeding articles foreign law governs, the provision of this law applies without paying regard to any reference which this law makes to another law." *cf.* Jan Kropholler/Hilmar Krüger/Wolfgang Riering/Jürgen Samtleben/Kurt Siehr (eds.), Aussereuropäische IPR–Gesetze (Hamburg/Würzburg 1999) 108 and 118 (Portughese and German).

[42] *Roberto Ago,* Teoria del diritto internazionale privato (Padova 1934) 221, 259 *et seq.*; *id.,* Règles générales des conflits de lois: 58 Recueil des Cours 243–469 (380, 409 *et seq.*) (1936–IV).

[43] *cf.* Georgios Maridakis, Le renvoi. Rapport provisoire: 47 I Annuaire de l'Institut de Droit international 17–53 (1957); *id.,* Le renvoi en Droit international privé: 50 I Annuaire de l'Institut de Droit international 497–509 (1963).

[44] *cf.* the following states with the pertinent articles in parenthesis: Albania (25), Czech Republic (35), Estonia (126), Hungary (4), Lithuania (607), Poland (4), Rumania (4) and Yugoslavia (6).

[45] *cf.* the following states with the pertinent articles in parenthesis: Austria (5), Germany (4), Italy (13), Liechtenstein (5), Portugal (18, 19), Spain [12 (1)], Switzerland (14) and Turkey [2 (3)].

[46] *cf.* Art. 16–18 of the Portuguese Código Civil of 1966 reads:
"Art. 16. The reference of a choice of law-provision to any foreign law fixes, unless provided differently, the application of international law of this foreign law.
Art. 17. (1) If the choice of law-rules of the law designated by the Portuguese choice of law-rules refer on to another [third] law and this law provides the competence to decide the case, the internal law of this [third] state governs
(2) The preceding paragraph does not apply if the law designated by a Portuguese choice of law-rule is the law of the personal status and the relevant person is habitually resident in Portuguese territory or in a state the choice of law-rules of which refer to the internal law of the state of the person's nationality.
(3) Paragraph 1 applies to cases of guardianship, curatorship, patrimonial relations between spouses, parental responsibility, the relation between adopting and adopted persons and succession

complicated articles in Austria and Germany.[47] Even Italy gave up its declining attitude towards any renvoi, refused any superstition and enacted Article 13 of the new statutes on private international law.[48]

2.2 International activities

2.2.1 Institute of international law

13–025   The Institute of International Law, without drafting a bill, discussed the problem of renvoi three times: during the years of 1896–1900,[49] again between 1957 and 1965,[50] and it ultimately at its Berlin session passed a resolution in 1999 under the title "Taking Foreign Private International Law into Account".[51] This is the problem correctly stated for the first time and I shall return to the 1999-resolution later.

---

if the lex patriae designated by the choice of law-rule refers on to the lex rei sitae of immovables and this law itself provides its competence.
Article 18. (1) If the choice of law-rule of the law designated by [Portuguese] choice of law-rules refers back to the internal Portuguese law, this law is applicable.
(2) In cases of personal status, however, Portuguese law only applies if the relevant person is habitually resident in Portuguese territory or if the law of the state in which he is habitually resident, also designates Portuguese internal law as applicable."

[47] § 5 (1) and (2) of the Austrian Private International Law Statute of 1978 reads:
(1) Reference to a foreign legal order includes also its conflicts rules.
(2) If the foreign legal order refers back, Austrian internal rules (rules excepting conflicts rules) shall be applied; if reference is made to a third jurisdiction, further references shall be considered, but the internal rules of the legal order which itself does not refer to any other law or to which another law refers back for the first time shall be determinative.
 Translation by Edith Palmer in: *28 American Journal of Comparative Law* 197, 222, 223 (1980).
Art. 4 (1) of the German Introductory Code to the EGBGB (*supra* n. 36).

[48] Article 13 of the Italian Private International Law Statute of 1995 reads:
1. Whenever reference is made to a foreign law in the following articles, account shall be taken of the renvoi made by foreign private international law to the law in force in another State if:
(a) renvoi is accepted under the law of that State.
(b) renvoi is made to Italian law.
2. Paragraph 1 shall not apply.
(a) to those cases in which the provisions of this law make the foreign law applicable according to the choice of law made by the parties concerned;
(b) with respect to the statutory form of acts;
(c) as related to the provisions of Chapter XI [non-contractual obligations] of this Title.
3. In the cases referred to in Articles 33 [filiation], 34 [legitimation] and 35 [recognition of an illegitimate child], account shall be taken of the renvoi only if the latter refers to a law allowing filiation to be established.
4. Where this law makes an international convention applicable in any event, the solution adopted in the convention in matters of renvoi shall always apply.
Translation by the Italian Ministry of Justice as revised by A.B. Zampetti and M.B. Deli in: 35 International Legal Materials 760, 765, 767 *et seq.* (1996).
[49] *cf.* Annuaire de l'Institut de Droit international 15 (1896) 366 (Venice); 16 (1897) 47, 181, 184 (Copenhagen); 17 (1898) 14, 36, 212, 230 (The Hague); 18 (1900) 34 *et seq.* (Neuchâtel).
[50] *cf.* Annuaire de l'Institut de Droit international 47 (1957–II) 176, 47 (1957–I) 16, 54, 104 (Amsterdam); 49 (1961–II) 272 *et seq.* (Salzburg); 51 (1965–II) 145 *et seq.*, 258 (Warsaw).
[51] *cf.* 68 I Annuaire de l'Institut de Droit international 54–46 (1999); 13–56 (Report by *Kurt Lipstein*): *supra* n. 26.

2.2.2 Hague Conference on private international law

The early Hague conventions paid regard to foreign certain choice of law   **13–026**
rules in family matters[52] but did not provide a reference to foreign choice of
law rules because a renvoi does not make sense for uniform conflicts rules in
contracting states.

In 1955 the Hague Conference prepared the Convention of June 15, 1955   **13–027**
to regulate the conflict between the national law and that of the domicile, the
so–called renvoi convention.[53] This convention never entered into force. The
main reason for this failure may be that the convention could not solve
the clash between the principles of nationality and domicile in cases in which
the person's *lex patriae* applies the principle of nationality and the law of the
person's domicile the principle of domicile, thereby leaving open one of
the main problems.

2.2.3 Other organisations

The Geneva Conventions on cheques and bills of exchange provide a renvoi   **13–028**
for the capacity to draw a cheque or a bill of exchange.[54]

2.3 Interim Summary

The survey of national legislation reveals that a renvoi has a different impor-   **13–029**
tance for states with different connecting factors. It seems that a renvoi is
more important for states with the principle of nationality than for those
with the principle of domicile. A second observation refers to the restriction
of renvoi if a renvoi would conflict with the spirit of a specific reference to
foreign law.[55] On the international level the principle of renvoi lost any importance. Uniform conflicts rules should not be weakened by a renvoi.

3 Renvoi discussed

The principle of renvoi has been discussed during the last century. Many   **13–030**
scholars of private international law contributed to the list of special
terms of this strange weapon of our conflicts arsenal. Instead of reviewing

---

[52] *cf.* Art. 7 of the Hague Convention of July 17, 1905 on the Law Governing the Effects of
Marriage; Art. 12 of the Hague Convention of July 17, 1905 on the Incapacitation and Similar
Measures of Protection. In these Articles exceptions are made with respect to immovables which
are subject to special rules under the lex rei sitae.
[53] Convention of June 15, 1955 to Regulate Conflicts between the Law of Nationality and the
Law of Domicile, Hague Conference on Private International Law (ed.), Recueil des
Conventions, Collection of Conventions (1951–96) (Den Haag 1997) No. VI. As to this
Convention Cf. First Report of the Private International Law Committee (Cmd. 9069) (London
1954) 11.
[54] Geneva Convention of June 7, 1930 for the Settlement of Certain Conflicts of Laws in
Connection with Bills of Exchange and Promissory Notes Article 2 (1) sentence 2; Geneva
Convention of March 19, 1931 on the Settlement of Certain Conflicts of Laws in Connection
with Cheques Article 2 (1) sentence 2, in: Konrad Zweigert/Jan Kropholler (eds.), *Sources of
International Uniform Law*, Vol. 1 (Leiden 1971) Nos. E 181 and 184.
[55] *cf.* especially Art. 4 (1) EGBGB, *supra* n. 36, and Art. 13 (1) of the Italian P.I.L. Statute of
1995, *supra* n. 48.

once more the renvoi discussion I should like to mention some of the attributes given to a renvoi without any guarantee that a "copyright" of the original inventor of a term will not be violated. Renvoi has been described as:

- carosello giuridico[56]

- circulus inextricabilis, vicious circle, cercle vicieux[57]

- Trojan Horse[58]

- expédient[59]

- lawn-tennis[60]

- moto perpetuo[61]

- endless oscillation backwards and forwards form one law to the other[62]

- ping-pong game[63]

- chasse-croisé[64]

- logisches Spiegelkabinett (logical cabinet of mirrors, cabinet de miroirs)[65]

- eindeloze terugkaatsing[66]

- Schicksalsfrage (fateful question)[67]

13–031   The problem of renvoi, however, cannot be solved by catchwords. A closer look at the discussion reveals interesting details, especially with respect to special bilateral problems and to certain general questions.

---

[56] Giuseppe Sperduti, *Saggi di teoria generale del diritto internazionale privato* (Milan 1967) 131.
[57] John Westlake, *A Treatise on Private International Law* (5th ed. London 1912) 31; Roberto Ago, *Teoria del diritto internazionale privato* (Padova 1934) 249; *id.,* Règles générales des conflits de lois: 58 Recueil des Cours 243–469 (402) (1936–IV); Francescakis, *supra* n. 7, 96 (vicious cercle); J. Kosters, *Het internationaal burgerlijk recht in Nederland* (Haarlem 1917) 140 (circulus vitiosus); Armand Laine, *De l'application des lois étrangères en France et en Belgique: 23 Clunet 241, 257* (1886) (cercle vicieux).
[58] Arthur Taylor von Mehren/Donald Theodore Trautman, *The Law of Multistate Problems* (Boston, Toronto 1965) 513.
[59] Renault in: 18 Annuaire de l'Institut de Droit international 174 (1900); John Delatre Falconbridge, The Problem of the Renvoi, in: *id.,* Essays, *supra* n. 16, pp. 139–169 (141).
[60] Buzzati, *supra* n. 20, 146.
[61] Sperduti, *supra* n. 56.
[62] Luxmore, J. in: *In re Ross,* [1930] 2 Ch. 377, 389.
[63] Falconbridge, Essays, *supra* n. 17, 187; Leo Raape, Internationales Privatrecht (5th ed. Berlin/Frankfurt a.M. 1961) 81.
[64] Paul Lerebours-Pigeonnière, Observations sur la question du renvoi: 51 Clunet 877–903 (901) (1924).
[65] Franz Kahn, Gesetzeskollisionen: 30 Iherings Jahrbücher für die Dogmatik des heutigen römischen und deutschen Privatrechts 1–143 (23) (1891) = *id.,* Abhandlungen, *supra* n. 34, 1–123 (20); Raape, *supra* n. 73, 81.
[66] J. Kosters/C.W. Dubbink, Algemeen deel van het nederlandse internationaal privaatrecht (Haarlem 1962) 284.
[67] Max Gutzwiller, Internationalprivatrecht, in: Rudolf Stammler (ed.), Das gesamte Deutsche Recht, Vol. 1 (Berlin 1931) 1515–1661 (1581).

3.1 Bilateral problems

Everybody recalls English court practice with respect to English subjects who **13–032** die domiciled abroad. By accepting a double or total renvoi English courts applied the same law which French or Italian courts apply to the estates of foreigners dying in France or Italy.[68] Similar bilateral problems have been solved also in other countries. If, *e.g.*, an American or English citizen domiciled abroad leaves immovable property in Germany or Switzerland, these countries will apply the German or Swiss *lex rei sitae* by accepting partial renvoi.[69] Even if a German citizen dies domiciled in England, German authorities will recognise any probate decree based on English law although according to German choice of law-rules the German *lex patriae* governs probate.[70] The principles on recognition of foreign decisions supersede German choice of law-rules as to the law applicable.

This court practice in England and on the continent could be expressed by **13–033** the following guidelines:

- If a person dies domiciled in the forum state, the authorities in this state are free to apply their own *lex domicilii* directly (England; Switzerland) or indirectly by simple or partial renvoi (Germany with respect to English, American or Swiss citizens) or apply their own *lex patriae* to their citizens (Austria and Germany).

- Every other state seized of the same case (person dies—from their perspective—domiciled abroad) should apply the same law as applied in the *forum domicilii* or recognise the probate decree.

- As far as the *lex domicilii* does not apply in the *forum domicilii* (*e.g.* with respect to immovable property located abroad) or as far as the probate decree does not cover certain aspects, the foreign court is free to decide on own its principles.

My point is that in certain areas and between certain countries the renvoi has **13–034** worked quite well for several decades, even if applied differently in the respective states. If a renvoi were not accepted, the problem of co-ordination has to be solved differently, *e.g.* by rules on recognition of foreign decisions or by creating a rule of subsidiary jurisdiction for immovable property. In most of these solutions foreign conflicts rules have to be taken into consideration. If any co-ordination is desired, foreign rules of private international law have to be considered. To this extent also we cannot escape the question of renvoi in a comprehensive sense.

---

[68] *cf.* the English cases In *re Annesley*, [1926] Ch. 692 (French law applied because France accepted a renvoi of the English lex patriae to the French lex domicilii); In *re O'Keefe*, [1940] Ch. 124 (Irish law applied because Italian law of domicile referred to substantive law of the Irish lex patriae).

[69] *cf.*, *e.g.*, Bundesgerichtshof June 5, 1957, 24 Entscheidungen des Bundesgerichtshofs in Zivilsachen 352; Obergericht Zürich February 1, 1990, 89 Blätter für Zürcherische Rechtsprechung no. 4 (1990).

[70] *cf.* § 16a of the Gesetz über die Angelegenheiten der freiwilligen Gerichtsbarkeit (Statute on Matters of Non-Contentious Jurisdiction).

3.2 General attitude

13–035   A hundred years after the discovery of renvoi the problems surrounding this phenomenon have not been solved and are still debated. Legislators provided for the acceptance of a renvoi, scholars have different views and the Institute of International Law again discussed renvoi.[71] Therefore the question arose: is renvoi really necessary?

4 Renvoi reconsidered

4.1 Problem restated

13–036   Sometimes a problem could not be solved because it had not been identified properly. The same may have happened to renvoi. If renvoi is still an open question, it may be that renvoi proper is not the problem at all but only one of possibly several responses to the true problem. The true problem is the fact that there are still competing national legal systems with different rules of substantive law and different choice of law-rules. This problem is a genuine one and renvoi is only one possible solution of this problem.

4.2 Solutions evaluated

4.2.1 Renvoi accepted

13–037   Accepting a renvoi is only one solution of the problem of different choice of law-rules in different jurisdictions. There are, however, two main types of accepting a renvoi: an egoistic renvoi and an altruistic one.

4.2.1.1 Egoistic Renvoi (Partial Renvoi)
13–038   According to an egoistic renvoi any reference back to the *lex fori* (renvoi of first degree) is treated as a reference back to substantive law.[72] Such a renvoi is provided in Austria and Germany. The pertinent sections provide in substance: "Any renvoi back to Austrian/German law is treated as a reference to Austrian/German substantive law." The problem of such a solution, openly admitting a "*Heimwärtsstreben*" (homeward trend), is that it gives up the idea of international harmony because this goal can only be achieved if the jurisdiction referring back accepts this egoistic attitude of Austrian or German private international law.

4.2.1.2 Altruistic Renvoi (total Renvoi)
13–039   A renvoi can be also handled differently in an altruistic manner. This was done first by English courts. They tried to do the same as what the foreign courts of the *lex causae* would do in fact if seized of the case: either applying their own internal substantive law (as, *e.g.* in the English case *Re Annesley*

---

[71] See *supra* n. 51.
[72] Art. 4 (1) sentence 2 German Introductory Einführungsgesetz zum BGB, *supra* n. 36; § 5 (2) first part Austrian Private International Law Statute, *supra* n. 47.

with respect to French succession law applicable in French courts)[73] or the foreign internal substantive law governing in the foreign forum (as, *e.g.* in the English case *Collier v. Rivaz* with respect to English law applicable in Belgian courts).[74] The considerable advantage of this attitude is the fact that international harmony can be achieved. The only problem is created if the foreign courts adhere to the foreign court—theory as well and are altruistically minded.

4.2.2 Renvoi rejected

If any renvoi is rejected as, *e.g.* in Greece,[75] this does not mean that foreign **13–040** choice of law–rules are never taken into consideration. In many instances of general rules of choice of law this has to be done. Vested rights have to be recognized (see *infra* section 4.2.5.2) and incidental questions have to be answered by foreign choice of law-rules (see *infra* section 4.2.5.3).

4.2.3 Conditional application of the *lex fori*

4.2.3.1 *Expressly provided conditions*
A very early method of taking foreign choice of law-rules into considerations **13–041** has been applied in Switzerland. Swiss law referred to Swiss law unless a designated foreign law wanted to be applied. This was done by the Zurich Civil Code of 1853/55[76] and by the Swiss Conflicts Statute of 1891.[77] Also *Brainerd Currie's* (1912–65) governmental interest-theory may be mentioned here. The *lex fori* of an enlightened forum applies if foreign law does not create a true conflict or has no stronger interest overriding the forum's own interest.[78]

4.2.3.2 *Escape clauses*
There are very few general escape clauses of the type of Article 15 (1) of the **13–042** Swiss Private International Law Act of 1987.[79] This provision reads: "As an exception, any law referred to in this Act is not applicable if, considering all the circumstances, it is apparent that the case has only a very loose

---

[73] In *re Annesley*, *supra* n. 68: English subject passed away domiciled in France. French law governs because French court would refer to the English *lex patriae* and accept an English renvoi to the French *lex domicilii*.

[74] See *supra* n. 3, where J. Jenner expressly said:" ... and the Court, sitting here to determine it, must consider itself sitting in Belgium under the particular circumstances of the case": (1841) 2 Curteis 859; 163 E.R. 609. In *re Ross*, *supra* n. 62, the English *lex patriae* was applied because Italian law did not accept an English renvoi to the *lex domicilii.*

[75] See *supra* n. 39.

[76] See *supra* at n. 16 and 30.

[77] See *supra* n. 17.

[78] Brainerd Currie, The Disinterested Third State: 28 Law and Contemporary Problems 754–794 (1963).

[79] The only other general escape clause is Art. 3082 of the Quebéc Civil Code: "Exceptionally, the law designated by this Book is not applicable if, in the light of all attendant circumstances, it is clear that the situation is only remotely connected with that law and is much more closely connected with the law of another country. This provision does not apply where the law is designated in a juridical act." A special escape clause is provided by Art. 4 (5) sentence 2 of the Rome Convention of 1980 on Law Applicable to Contractual Obligations (*infra* n. 83).

connection with such law and that the case has a much closer connection with another law."[80] When applying this escape clause foreign choice of law-rules may be taken into consideration. If the foreign law governing according to a black letter choice of law-rule of Swiss conflict law does not want to be applied, this indicates a lack of interest and eventually another law may be applied as the law of "much closer connection".[81] This kind of "false conflict" avoids the application of a "hidden renvoi"[82] and has a certain similarity with a subsidiary application choice of law-rule (see *infra* section 4.2.4).

4.2.3.3 Foreign mandatory rules

13–043 The reverse situation may happen and a foreign law not being designated as governing wants to be applied. This is the problem of foreign mandatory rules or foreign "lois d'application immédiate" or foreign law which wants to be applied extraterritorially. This type of situation is envisaged by Article 7 (1) of the Rome Convention of 1980 or the Law Applicable to Contractual Relations[83] or by Article 19 of the Swiss Private International Law Act.[84] In all of these instances foreign choice of law-rules, openly codified or hidden in provisions of substantive law, have to be recognised and applied.

4.2.4 Subsidiary choice of law-rules

13–044 A solution similar to expressly provided conditions (see *supra* section 4.2.3.1) was proposed by *Rolando Quadri* (1907–76). If foreign law does not want to be applied, a subsidiarily provided choice of law-rule of the forum state has to try anew to designate the law governing.[85] The same is done in case of a "hidden" renvoi when a designated foreign law only regulates unilaterally the application of its own internal substantive law to be applied by the competent domestic forum and does not refer to foreign law. This should be treated as a decline to be applied and an incentive to formulate subsidiarily applicable choice of law-rules of the forum state.[86]

---

[80] Translation taken from *Andreas Bucher/Pierre-Yves Tschanz* (eds.), Private International Law and Arbitration. Basic Documents (Basle/Frankfurt .M. 1996) 4.

[81] *cf.* Swiss Federal Court. January 27, 1992, 118 II Entscheidungen des Schweizerischen Bundesgerichts 79.

[82] *cf. Lipstein, supra* n. 26, 46 *et seq.*

[83] Rome Convention of June 19, 1980 on the Law Applicable to Contractual Obligations: Official Gazette of the European Communities 1980 No. L 266/1.

[84] Art. 19 of the Swiss Private International Law Act on "Taking into consideration mandatory provisions of foreign law" reads:
" (1) When interests that are legitimate and clearly preponderant according to the Swiss conception of law so require, a mandatory provision of another law than the one referred to in this Act may be taken into consideration, provided that the situation dealt with has a close connection with such other law.
(2) In deciding whether such a Provision is to be taken into consideration, one shall consider its aim and the consequences of its application, in order to reach a decision that is appropriate having regard to the Swiss conception of law."
Translation taken from Bucher/Tschanz (*supra* n. 80).

[85] Quadri, *supra* n. 15.

[86] Günther Beitzke, Zuständigkeitsrückverweisung und versteckte Rückverweisung in Adoptionssachen: 37 Rabels Zeitschrift für ausländisches und internationales Privatrecht 380, 390–393 (1973).

4.2.5 Recognition of facts, rights and relations

4.2.5.1 Recognition of relations established abroad

Famous is an example discussed by my teacher of private international law   **13–045**
Leo Raape (1878–1964).[87] Swiss nationals (uncle and niece) domiciled in
Russia, married in Russia and the validity of this marriage had to be determined by German authorities. According to German private international
law the *lex patriae* of the parties governed the substantive validity of a marriage. Under Swiss civil law a marriage between uncle and niece had to be
declared *ex officio* null and void. According to Swiss choice of law, however,
the validity of a marriage celebrated abroad was governed, also as to substance, by the Russian *lex loci celebrationis*. Hence, the marriage was valid in
Russia and in Switzerland. In order to achieve the same result for Germany,
Raape advocated for a renvoi of a second degree to Russian law. Such a
necessity has been put into question.[88] Germany could, as Switzerland did
and still does,[89] recognise a family relation created abroad. Such a rule is all
the more preferable as a marriage is solemnised by public or ecclesiastical
authorities according to statutory rules.

4.2.5.2 Recognition of rights vested abroad

The creation, transfer and loss of property rights are governed in many juris-   **13–046**
dictions by the *lex rei sitae*. This implies that property rights acquired under
a foreign *lex rei sitae* will be recognised as vested rights unless such a recognition violates public policy of the state in which recognition is requested. In
order to find out whether a right has been vested under the respective *lex rei
sitae*, foreign private international law has to be taken into account. If the
actual *lex rei sitae* does not want to be applied because, *e.g.* objects to be
exported are governed by the *lex loci destinationis*,[90] no right is vested under
the actual *lex rei sitae* and has to be recognised abroad.

4.2.5.3 Answering preliminary questions

Preliminary or incidental questions arose in substantive law as well as in pri-   **13–047**
vate international law. You cannot escape them. They have to be answered,
expressly or tacitly. Even if not recognised as a problem, the preliminary
question is answered without being aware of it. When answering these questions arising under the law governing, foreign choice of law-rules have to be
taken into consideration. This has already been discussed for vested rights or
relations established abroad (see *supra* section 4.2.5).

In the English case In *re Askew*[91] German law governed the main question.   **13–048**
Whether a child legitimated under German law by subsequent marriage of
the deceased, was to be answered as an incidental question under German

---

[87] Raape, in: *Staudinger (-Raape)* (*supra* n. 24) Einleitung E VI 2b (p. 24); *id.,* Les rapports
juridiques entre parents et enfants: 50 Recueil des Cours 401–544 (413) (1934–IV); *id.,*
Internationales Privatrecht (*supra* n. 63) 69 *et seq.*
[88] Alfred E. von Overbeck, Les questions générales du droit international privé à la lumière des
codifications et projets récents: 176 Recueil des Cours 9–258 (171) (1982–III).
[89] Article 45 Swiss Private International Law Statute, *supra* n. 18.
[90] *cf., e.g.*, Art. 103 Swiss Private International Law Statute, *supra* n. 18.
[91] In *re Askew, supra* n. 10.

law governing the main problem. The English court correctly took German conflicts law into consideration and answered the incidental question in the affirmative according to German conflicts rules. Similar decisions have been handed down in other jurisdictions.[92]

4.2.6 *Lex fori*

13–049   The application of the *lex fori* may be the acceptance of a renvoi (see *supra* section 4.2.1) or a conditional or subsidiary application of domestic law (see *supra* sections 4.2.2 and 4.2.3). It is not a solution on its own.

4.3 **Special exclusions**

13–050   A special rule may be mentioned here because I contributed to its creation and because it has been subscribed by the Institut de Droit international[93]and by commentaries in other countries.[94] The German codification of Private International Law (EGBGB) favours a renvoi extensively. There is, however, one exception which has not been discussed very much. This exception of Article 4 (1) sentence 1 EGBGB reads: "If reference is made to the law of another state, foreign private international law of this state has to be applied unless this is incompatible with the spirit of this reference."[95] This restriction originates in the Hamburg Max-Planck-Institut and was conceived especially for alternative choice of law-rules favouring certain solutions.[96] A renvoi should be declined if it reduces the number of alternatively applicable substantive rules of different countries. It may be also applied if reference is made to foreign conflicts rules violating fundamental rights (*e.g.* equality of husband and wife) or if reference is made to the law of country with which the case is most closely connected.[97] If this has been determined a renvoi of the designated law should declined to be accepted.

5 Renvoi summarised

13–051   1.   Renvoi is one of several potential solutions of a worldwide problem of differing national choice of law-rules and differing national substantive law.

---

[92] Reichsgericht November 30, 1906, 64 Entscheidungen des Reichsgericht in Zivilsachen 389.
[93] *cf.* section 4b of the Berlin Resolution, *supra* n. 51.
[94] *cf.* Kurt Siehr, in: Anton Heini/Max Keller/Kurt Siehr/Frank Vischer/Paul Volken, IPRG Kommentar (Zurich 1993) Art. 72 marginal n. 12.
[95] Art. 4 (1) German Introductory Law to the BGB, *supra* n. 18.
[96] These 3 (2) of the "Thesen zur Reform des Internationalen Privat- und Verfahrensrechts": "References by choice of law or by alternative choice of law-rules normally do not comprise the choice of law-rules of the designated jurisdiction." *cf.* 44 Rabels Zeitschrift für ausländisches und internationales Privatrecht 344–366 (355) (1980) and in: *Peter Dopffel/Ulrich Drobnig/Kurt Siehr* (eds.), Reform des deutschen internationalen Privatrechts (Tübingen 1980) 145, 146 and 75–77 (Explanation by Jürgen Samtleben und Diskussion); hierzu kritisch *Konrad Schmidt*, Die Sinnklausel der Rück- und Weiterverweisung im Internationalen Privatrecht nach Artikel 4 Absatz 1, Satz 1 EGBGB (Frankfurt a.M. u.a. 1998) 141–143.
[97] There is a general rule according to which a reference by very individual connecting factors is less renvoi-minded.

2. As long as such national rules create conflicts or at least differ, the question has to be answered by every forum whether it has to take foreign choice of law-rules into consideration.

3. This problem of conflicting national law may also be solved by:

(a) rejecting a renvoi;

(b) conditional application of the *lex fori*;

(c) subsidiary choice of law-rules;

(d) recognition of facts, rights and relations;

(e) application of the *lex fori*.

4. These solutions are guided by different policies, basic attitudes towards private international law in general and pragmatic considerations.

5. The solution by accepting a renvoi, be it an egoistic or altruistic one, has been applied by law courts and is not a mysterious invention by learned but eccentric law professors.

6. There are two principal reasons for accepting a renvoi:

(a) promoting international harmony (*internationaler Entscheidungseinklang*);

(b) easy administration of justice by applying the *lex fori* ("*Heimwärtsstreben*").

7. International harmony can only be achieved if the forum state and the foreign state of the *lex causae* avoid a *circulus vitiosus* of a reference forth and back and do not apply the same solution of the problem of conflicting legal systems.

8. Therefore renvoi cannot be recommended as a universal solution. Solutions have to be different.

9. There are renvoi-minded connecting factors and others are less renvoiphile.

10. The more formal a connecting factor (*e.g.* nationality) is or the more comprehensive (*e.g.* covering movable and immovable) it is, the more a renvoi should be accepted. The more flexible or open-ended a reference (*e.g.* law of the closest connection) is or the more specific (*e.g.* different types of tangibles) it is, the more a renvoi should be rejected and the foreign court theory be applied.

11. In international conventions all references should be directed exclusively to internal substantive law eliminating any renvoi.

12. If rights vested abroad are recognised in the forum state, foreign conflicts law has to be taken into account by logic in order to find out whether there is a vested right.

13. Evaluating some general problem of private international law foreign conflicts law has to be taken into account. This is true especially for:

(a) preliminary questions answered by foreign law governing the principal question;

(b) qualifications of foreign phenomena and their treatment in foreign conflicts law;

(c) the application of evasion clauses and the attitude of the foreign law of closer relation towards the problem to be decided.

14.   My answer to the question of my paper is:

(a) The question is incorrectly formulated. Renvoi is only one solution of the major problem of conflicting national legal systems.

(b) Foreign conflicts law has to be taken into consideration in several instances.

(c) Which instances those are, depends to a large extent on the connecting factors used by national conflicts law.

(d) Some general problems of private international law cannot be solved properly without taking foreign conflicts law into account.

CHAPTER 14

PROPERTY RIGHTS IN THE SECURITIES MARKETS, COMPUTERISATION AND CONFLICT OF LAWS[1]

DR JOANNA BENJAMIN
CENTRE FOR COMMERCIAL LAW STUDIES,
QUEEN MARY AND WESTFIELD COLLEGE

"Assuredly this is true of our real property law, it has been secreted in the interstices of the forms of action."[2]

---

[1] This discussion is based on chapters entitled "Property Rights in Interests in Securities" and "The Conflict of Laws and Securities Collateral" in J. Benjamin, *Interests in Securities*, Oxford University Press, Oxford, 2000.
[2] (F.W. Maitland, *The Forms of Action at Common Law*, Ed., A. H. Chaytor & W.J. Whittaker, 1997, Cambridge University Press (first published 1909), p. 1, paraphrasing Maine.)

1. Overview

14–001 This discussion will consider the asset of a client for whom an intermediary holds investment securities on an unallocated basis, commingled with the interests of other clients. This asset will be called "interests in securities". As against the intermediary, it will be argued, the rights of the client are proprietary under English domestic law.

14–002 This argument is not uncontroversial, particularly for civil lawyers. Some commentators reject the possibility of property rights subsisting in relation to intangible assets, especially where such rights are asserted through intermediaries and in the absence of allocation. However, this paper will seek to show that, although the assertion of property rights in such circumstances is relatively recent, it accords with the traditional principles of classical and English property law. This paper will go on to consider why such property rights have been developed only relatively recently, and seek to explain why there is some conceptual resistance to their development, particularly among civil lawyers.

14–003 To support this discussion, this paper will briefly consider the historical development of the law of property in the writings of a small number of key authors in the classical and common law traditions, particularly Justinian, Bracton, Blackstone, Maitland and Hohfeld.

14–004 Further, it will be argued that, under English private international law, questions concerning such proprietary rights should be determined by *lex situs*. Again, this argument is not uncontroversial, as interests in securities comprise intangible assets, having no physical location. However, it will be argued that the attribution of a notional location to interests in securities is appropriate and helpful.

2. Property rights in relation to intangible assets

14–005 This section will argue that the assertion of property rights in relation to intangible assets accords with the traditional principles of the law of property. In order to do this, it is necessary to return to the real actions from which property rights have historically been extrapolated in ancient[3] and common law.[4]

2.1 Real and personal actions

14–006 Justinian distinguishes real actions from personal actions as follows:

> "A plaintiff may sue a defendant who is under an obligation to him, from contract or from wrongdoing. The personal actions lie for these claims. . . .Or else he may sue a

---

[3] "So great is the ascendancy of the Law of Actions in the infancy of Courts of Justice, that substantive law has at first the look of being gradually secreted in the interstices of procedure." Maine, Early Law and Custom p. 398, quoted in Maitland, *The Forms of Action at Common Law*, 1909, Cambridge University Press, p. 1.
However, by the time Blackstone was writing, the original real actions had fallen into disuse. See *Commentaries*, volume 3, pp. 266, 267.

[4] ". . .[T]he forms of action are given, the causes of action must be deduced therefrom." Maitland, *The Forms of Action*, p. 5, commenting on Bracton.

defendant *who is not under any kind of obligation to him* but is someone with whom he is in dispute about a thing. Here the real actions lie." [author's italics][5]

The term "real actions" is a translation of *"actiones in rem"*. *"Rem"* is the accusative form of the word *"res"* or "thing"

2.2 Things include intangibles

Crucially, in Justinian, things include *intangible* things such as obligations: **14–007**

> "Some things are corporeal, some incorporeal. . . . Incorporeal things cannot be touched. They consist of legal rights—inheritance, usufruct, obligations however contracted."[6]

This reification of obligations is continued in *Bracton on the Laws and* **14–008** *Customs of England*[7] and in *Blackstone's Commentaries on the Laws of England*, in which discussion of things includes choses in action.[8] If an intangible is a thing or *res*, linguistically and therefore conceptually it is a candidate to be the subject of a *real* action.

2.3 All actions concern things

As obligations are things to Justinian and the Western legal tradition which **14–009** follows him, a personal action (which relates to the obligation of the defendant to the plaintiff) involves a thing as much as a real action. The difference between the two types of action is not the presence or absence of a thing (for things are present in both). Rather it is the presence or absence of an obligation of the defendant to the plaintiff (which is present in a personal action and absent in a real action).[9]

3. Intermediated property rights in intangible assets

It follows that an intangible asset may be the subject of a real action, but **14–010** only as against a third party.[10] For example, as against the debtor, the creditor can only assert personal rights in relation to the debt. However, if the debt is held through an intermediary, the creditor can assert real rights in relation to the debt, as against the intermediary.[11] On this basis,

---

[5] J.4.6.2, Justinian's *Institutes*, Birks and McLeod Transl. Duckworth, London, 1987, p. 129.
[6] J.2.2.pr- 2. The reification of obligations by Gaius before Justinian is described by Birks and McLeod as "a brilliant leap" (p.15).
[7] "Incorporeal things are such as are intangible, which exist in contemplation of law, as inheritance, usufruct, advowsons of churches, obligations, actions and the like." Volume II, p. 48. Bracton is described as ". . .that great cathedral of the thirteenth century. . ." Introduction to *Justinian's Institutes, op. cit.*, p. 26.
[8] See Chapter XXV. Of course, the legal French term "chose" means "thing", and is a fair translation of the Latin "res".
[9] This point has been somewhat obscured by the terms "actions in personam" and "actions in rem". More helpful terminology might have been "actions in personam" and "other actions".
[10] *i.e.* someone other than the obligor.
[11] Professor Schroeder has clearly shown that the proprietary nature of a chose in action arises only in the hands of third parties. See, for example, *Chix Nix Bundle-O-Stix*, 93 Mich. L. Rev. 239 (1994).

intermediation is not merely compatible with property rights in relation to intangibles; it is their precondition.

14–011   The question arises how a client may enjoy property rights in relation to assets held by an intermediary. In English law, while property rights in *tangible* assets may be intermediated under a bailment, property rights in *intangible* assets may only be intermediated under a trust. Thus, the law of property rights in relation to intangibles is the law of trusts.[12]

14–012   Incidentally, the author would suggest that the old vexed question of whether the rights of the beneficiary under a trust are personal or proprietary,[13] may be readily answered by applying Justinian's test of real and personal actions. *As against the trustee*, the rights of the beneficiary are personal: the courts of equity are the courts of conscience, and the law of trusts is built on the personal obligations of the trustee to the beneficiary.[14] This accords with the Justinian definition of a personal action as one where the defendant owes a personal obligation to the plaintiff. However, if the trustee becomes insolvent, the beneficiary may be obliged to protect the trust assets from the trustee's general creditors. The general creditors owe no personal obligation to the beneficiary, so that *as against them*, the rights of the beneficiary are proprietary. Thus, the trust assets are not available to creditors of the insolvent trustee. The same reasoning protects the trust assets against judgment creditors of the trustee, and persons to whom the trustee transfers the trust assets in breach of duty (other than the bona fide purchaser for value without notice of the legal estate).[15]

---

[12] Hence perhaps their strangeness to civil lawyers.

   Another historic reason for the greater readiness of common lawyers then civil lawyers to see the rights of clients in (heavily) intermediated interests in securities as proprietary, may be that common law (unlike civil law) has developed uninterrupted from the middle ages. The English law of property originated with indirect rights of land tenure. "Almost all the real property of this kingdom is by the policy of our laws supposed to be granted by, dependent upon, and *holden* of some superior or lord. . .The thing holden is therefore stiled a *tenement*, the possessors thereof *tenants*, and the manner of their possession a *tenure*." Blackstone, Book 2, p. 59. The author has been struck by the likeness of interests in securities, held through chains of financial intermediaries, with feudal land tenures, held through chains of landlords. Both are intangible: see Jeremy Waldron, "Property Law", in *A Companion to Philosophy of Law and Legal Theory*, Dennis Patterson Ed., Blackwell, London 1996, p.4; see also Blackstone, *Commentaries on the Law of England*, Vol. 1, p. 18 and Vol. 2 pp. 59–60.

[13] See, for example, the opening passages of Hohfeld, *Fundamental Legal Conceptions* Yale University Press, New Haven 1919; Maitland, "Trust and Corporation" in *Selected Essays*, Cambridge University Press, 1936, pp. 144–147; and, more recently, Kam Fan Sin, *The Legal Nature of the Unit Trust*, 1997, Clarendon Press, Oxford, p. 265 and the materials referred to there.

[14] Hence the maxim, "Equity acts in personam". "The Courts of Equity in England are, and always have been, Courts of conscience, operating in personam and not in rem. . ." *Ewing v. Orr Ewing* (1883) 9 App Cas 34, per Lord Selborne at 40.

[15] Admittedly, in theory, the historic development of the class of third parties against whom the beneficiary could assert its rights has been based on the proposition that the conscience of those persons is affected: see Maitland, "Trust and Corporation", in Selected Essays, 1936, Cambridge University Press, pp. 165, 166, 169. See also Blackstone, *Commentaries on the Laws of England*, Vol. 2, p. 328.However, ". . . it is to be remembered that the making of grant theories is not and never has been our strong point. The theory that lies upon the surface is sometimes a borrowed theory which has never penetrated far, while the really vital principles must be sought for in out-of-the-way places." Maitland, "Trust and Corporation", *op. cit.*, pp. 218, 219.

4. Property rights in unallocated intangible assets

This section will argue that interests in securities confer on clients property **14–013** rights in relation to the client assets held by intermediaries, even though there is no allocation of particular interests in securities to particular client assets.

The further question arises how property rights can arise in relation to an **14–014** unallocated part of a pool of client assets (the allocation question). There are two possible answers. The first answer is that the interest of each client relates to the whole of the pool, which she co-owns with each other client. This approach serves to allocate the client's interest,[16] but at the cost of reducing it to a co-ownership interest.

Where the pool of assets held by the intermediary for clients comprises **14–015** intangible assets such as (interests in) shares, the second possible answer to the allocation question is as follows: the client owns part of the pool outright, without allocation. This is on the basis that there is no requirement for property interests in intangible assets to be allocated. This argument accords with the judgments in *Hunter v. Moss*[16a] and *CA Pacific*[16b]. In the author's view, these were bold judgments, which went beyond the settled scope of English law. However, it will be argued below that they can be reconciled with the traditional principles of the law of property, and may therefore indicate the way in which English law should develop in the future.

To support this argument, the requirement for allocation will be consid- **14–016** ered in relation to tangible assets and intangible assets in turn.

4.1 Allocation required for property rights in tangible assets

As discussed below, property rights originated in real actions, and the origi- **14–017** nal real action was vindication. Vindication enabled the plaintiff to recover a specific asset *in specie* from the defendant.[17] As a practical matter, a plaintiff cannot succeed in *recovering* a specific asset without first *identifying* that asset, and therefore allocation is a precondition of vindication.

The historic link between property and vindication may explain the con- **14–018** ceptual difficulty lawyers often experience in considering unallocated property rights.[18] However, vindication is no longer relevant to property rights in the securities markets. As a technical matter, vindication cannot take place in relation to fungible assets such as interests in securities.[19]

---

[16] The interest is allocated by exhaustion.
[16a] [1993] 1 WLR 934; [1994] 1 WLR 452.
[16b] [2000] BCLC 494.
[17] And not merely an asset equivalent to it, or its monetary value. See, for example, Bracton, II. 292: "Actions in rem are those given against a possessor...as where one claims a specific thing, an estate or a piece of land, from another and asserts that he is its owner, and seeks the thing itself, not its price or its value or an equivalent of the same kind. . ."
[18] One way around the difficulty, indicated by Hohfeld as discussed below, is to understand property rights, not as relationships between persons and things, but as relationships between persons in respect of things. This approach accords with the author's suggestion below that the functional purpose of asserting property rights in interests in securities is not to recover particular assets, but rather to achieve "super priority" in the insolvency of an intermediary.
[19] This is because the individual identity of the client's assets is lost on commingling within the pool held by the intermediary.

14–019   However, even in the absence of vindication, it might be argued that there remains a conceptual requirement for allocation where property rights are asserted in *tangible* assets. This is because tangible assets exist physically, whereas legal rights are notional. In order to show that (notional) property rights relate to (physical) assets, some step is required to link the two. Such a link is required, because the notional and physical worlds are discontinuous.[20]

4.2 Whether allocation required for property rights in intangible assets

14–020   By the same token, it might be argued, no link is required between property rights and intangible assets, because both are notional. Obligations are deemed by the law to be things, and therefore the establishment of an obligation automatically causes a notional thing to arise.[21] Because the law reifies obligations, an obligation automatically attaches to the thing which is its notional reification. No act of allocation is required, because both the right and the thing come into being together.

14–021   However, this reasoning, although compatible with old authority, is (as far as the author knows) novel. In contrast, a number of cases have held that, in order to assert property rights in a third party obligation, the plaintiff must link that obligation with a particular *asset* in the defendant's hands, which can serve as the thing to which her claim relates. Thus, in order for a trust of a debt to arise, the trust asset must be segregated in an empirically observable manner, for example by the opening of a separate bank account; a purported trust over part of a bank balance cannot take effect.[22] The same reasoning lies behind the rule that a proprietary claim can only be traced into a continuing trust fund,[23] so in general that it is not possible to trace through an overdrawn account. [24] While it was argued in *Space Investments*[25] that a beneficial interest could take effect without allocation, as a general charge over the assets of the defendant, this approach was rejected in *Bishopsgate Investment Management Ltd v. Homan.*[26]

---

[20] "... .for it is not enough to say 'I claim a thing,' unless it is said 'I claim such a thing.'" *Bracton on the Laws and Customs of England*, Thorn Transl., Harvard University Press, Cambridge Mass, 1968, pp. 342, 343.

[21] See Blackstone's discussion of the original form of the action for debt (detinue), which involved the creditor claiming the debt *as a thing* in the hands of the debtor. "The form of the writ of *debt* is sometimes in the *debet* and *detinet*, sometimes in the *detinet* only: that is, the writ states, either that the defendant *owes* and unjustly *detains* the debt or thing in question, or only that he unjustly *detains* it." Commentaries on the Laws of England, Book III, Chap. 9, p. 155.

This approach also accords with the language of a recent House of Lords judgment, which described a creditor as *owning* a debt which was owed to it: "The relationship of the bank with the solicitors was essentially that of debtor [574] and creditor, . . . It must follow. . .that the solicitors *as owners of the chose in action constituted by the indebtedness of the bank to them* in respect of the sums paid into the client account, could trace their property in that chose in action into its direct product, the money drawn from the account by Cass." [author's italics] *Lipkin Gorman v. Karpnale Ltd* [1991] 2 A.C. 548, per Lord Goff at 573, 574.

[22] See for example *Mac-Jordam Construction Ltd v. Brookmount Erostin Ltd (in receivership)* [1992] BCLC 350.

[23] See *Re Diplock* [1948] Ch. 465 per Lord Greene at 521.

[24] See, for example, *Westdeutsche Landesbank Girozentrale v. Islington LBC* [1996] A.C. 669, *per* Lord Browne-Wilkinson at 706.

[25] *Space Investments Ltd v. Canadian Imperial Bank of Commerce Trust Co (Bahamas) Ltd* [1986] 1 W.L.R. 1072, *per* Lord Templeman at 1074.

[26] [1995] Ch. 211 *per* Dillon LJ at 271 and Leggatt LJ at 221.

These cases have attracted criticism, and arguably wrought hardship on the unsuccessful plaintiffs.[27] It might be argued that these decisions are not well founded, and conflate notional things (to which property rights automatically attach) with physical things (to which property rights require to be allocated). It is therefore hoped that the ideas which are implicit in *Hunter v. Moss* will be judicially developed in the years ahead.[28] In the meantime, clients of unallocated custody and settlement arrangements may rely on the classical law of co-ownership when asserting property rights against intermediaries.[29]

14–022

5. Late development of property rights in obligations

This paper has argued that it is possible to assert property rights in relation to intangible assets such as interests in securities, and further that such proprietary rights accord with the traditional principles of the law of property. It might be objected that if such property rights did accord with such traditional principles, they would have a long history, and it must be conceded that they are relatively novel. To answer this possible objection, this section will seek to explain this late development of property rights in obligations.

14–023

English common law has always allowed real actions in relation to incorporeal hereditaments (*i.e.* servitudes).[30] These are intangible rights associated with land, such as rights of way.[31]

14–024

However, neither Roman nor English law developed real actions in relation to other types of intangibles such as obligations. Thus, although Justinian created, and the traditional common law authors sustained, the conceptual possibility of property rights in relation to third party obligations, they did not write of them. The reasons for this are both practical and procedural.

14–025

5.2 *Practical reasons*

In order to understand the practical reasons for the relatively late development of property rights in relation to obligations, it is helpful to consider the purposes that have been served by the assertion of property rights at different periods in legal history.

14–026

As indicated above, the original real action was vindication. Of course, an obligation cannot be vindicated, because the enforcement of an obligation discharges it.[32] This is an obvious practical reason that early lawyers did not assert property rights in relation to obligations.

14–027

---

[27] It is hard to see how justice is served by penalising a plaintiff for the defendant's inadequate banking arrangements.
[28] This development may involve resurrecting the concept of a "general charge" in the judgment in *Space Investments Limited.*
[29] See the discussion of co-ownership in Justinian (J2.125–29, Transl. Birks and McLeod (pp. 57–9)); Bracton (discussion of acquiring dominion by confusion, vol. 2, p. 47); and Blackstone (vol. 2, pp. 180, 191, 192).
[30] "Incorporeal herediaments are principally of ten sorts: advowsons, tithes, commons, ways, offices, dignities, franchises, corodies or pensions, annuities, and rends." Blackstone, *Commentaries on the Laws of England*, Vol. 2, p. 21.
[31] "It is called an action *in rem* because you are claiming your incorporeal *res*, that is, the right of going over his land. . ." Bracton, Book 2, p. 294.
[32] See Justinian, 3.29.pr., Transl. Birks and McLeod p. 119.

14–028   During the late medieval and early modern periods, a benefit of property rights was transferability.[33] In order to render bearer debt securities transferable, they were re-categorised as chattels.[34] It was not possible to assert property rights in debt securities as obligations, for policy reasons.[35]

14–029   The enduring usefulness of property rights in the securities markets lies in their ability to bind third parties. If a client places assets with an intermediary, she faces the risk that the intermediary will have a judgment debt enforced against it or become insolvent. She will only be able to protect her assets against these risks if she can assert property rights in the assets, which will bind third party creditors.[36] Thus, property rights are needed in the contemporary securities markets in order to address intermediary credit risk, in effect by giving the client "super priority" in the insolvency of the intermediary, so that the client ranks ahead of all creditors.

14–030   Since ancient times, domestic and international trade has been conducted through agents, and commercial people have been obliged to entrust their goods, bearer instruments and other tangible assets to intermediaries. Traditionally, tangible assets have been protected in the hands of intermediaries by the law of bailment, under which the client retains title to the assets as bailor.

14–031   However, in relation to intangible assets, the project of reserving property rights so as to protect the assets in the hands of intermediaries, is more recent. The two most commercially important categories of intangible asset are intellectual property rights and financial assets. Intellectual property rights are not regularly intermediated. Among financial assets, cash at bank is not protected from the bank's creditors,[37] and securities have only recently been dematerialised.

14–032   With the computerisation of the securities markets, the asset of the investor has become both intangible (with the elimination of paper instruments) and intermediated (as the investor is unable to participate directly in computerised settlement systems). With the advent of interests in securities,

---

[33] The late medieval period to the early modern period, property rights were transferable, but a policy against maintenance, or the trafficking in claims, prohibited the transfer of obligations. Therefore an important consequence of establishing proprietary status for an asset was to render that asset transferable. With the rise of commerce, it became economically necessary to deliver debt obligations person to person.

See the interesting discussion in J. E. Penner, *The Idea of Property in Law*, Clarendon Press, Oxford, 1997, p 112, in which the test of "contingency" is preferred to the test of "transferability".

[34] This was achieved by a legal fiction which conflated a debt obligation with the negotiable instrument issued in respect of it; a piece of paper was transferred, with the debt locked up inside it.

Other techniques were developed over time to by-pass the common law restrictions, including equitable assignment. With the Judicature Act of 873, the assignment of choses in action was generally permitted at common law, subject to certain formalities. With these developments, the old rule against the transfer of personal rights was overcome, and the second historical purpose of asserting property rights became otiose.

[35] It was necessary to resort to the fiction, which had the effect of notionally converting intangibles into tangible assets, because any attempt to assert proprietary (and therefore transferable) status on intangible debt obligations would have been defeated by the policy against maintenance.

[36] Where the intermediary is an individual, assets held for clients are excluded from the intermediary's bankruptcy by section 283(3)(a) of the Insolvency Act 1986. Where the intermediary is a company, the same result is achieved by the general principle that only assets beneficially owned by the company are available to its creditors, as reflected in case law. See, for example, *Barclays Bank Ltd v. Quistclose Investors Ltd* [1963] 3 All E.R. 651 and *Re Kayford Ltd* [1975] 1 All E.R. 604.

[37] *Foley v. Hill* [1848] 2 H.L Cas 28.

very significant values of intangible assets are entrusted to intermediaries, in circumstances where clients seek to avoid the intermediaries" credit risk.[38] Therefore the urgency of asserting property rights in intangible assets is associated with the rise of interests in securities, and thus with a period of time starting with the last quarter of the twentieth century. In terms of legal history, it is a recent problem.

5.2 Procedural reasons

There are also procedural reasons why real actions did not develop in rela- 14–033
tion to obligations. The class of assets for which real actions were traditionally available comprised land, tenements and hereditaments. As indicated
above, this class included certain intangibles (incorporeal hereditaments). It
also excluded certain tangible assets.[39] The criterion for the inclusion of an
asset in that class was not its tangibility, but rather its association with land.[40]

The land-based values of feudal society receded in favour of commercialism 14–034
in the early modern period. However, prior to the procedural reforms of the
nineteenth century, the class of assets for which real actions were available
was closed.

With the abolition of the fixed forms of action,[41] no obstacle remained to 14–035
bringing real actions in relation to obligations, should the need arise. As indicated above, this need arose with the computerisation of the securities markets.

6. Physical Model

It was argued above that the development of property rights in intangible 14–036
assets such as interests in securities was long delayed for practical and procedural reasons. In addition, there is a mistaken but widespread conception of
property rights which must be overcome in order to assert property rights in
relation to intangible assets, particularly where such rights arise indirectly
and without allocation. This mistaken view will be called the Physical Model.

The Physical Model (mistakenly) conceives of property rights as a legal 14–037
relationship between a person and a physical asset, as distinct from personal
rights (which are legal relationships between persons).

---

[38] The culture of the financial markets, including the policies of the credit rating agencies and regulatory, taxation and accounting authorities, requires that investors and collateral takers are protected from the intermediaries" credit risk.
[39] Real actions were not available for chattels until the nineteenth Century (when section 78 of the Common Law Procedure Act of 1854 enabled Court to order restitution of a chattel to a plaintiff, and removed the defendant's traditional option of paying its value. See Maitland, *The Forms of Action at Common Law, op. cit.*, p. 58.
[40] See *e.g.* Blackstone, Book 2 p. 384: "Under the name of things *personal* are included all sorts of things *moveable*, which. . .are not esteemed of so high a nature, nor paid so much regard to by the law, as things that are in their nature more permanent and *immoveable*, as lands, and houses, and the profits issuing thereout. These being constantly within the reach, and under the protec-tion of the law, were the principal favourites of our first legislators: who took all imaginable care in ascertaining the rights, and directing the disposition, of such property as they imagined to be lasting, and which would answer to posterity the troubles and pains that their ancestors employed about them; but at the same time entertained a very low and contemptuous opinion of all personal estate, which they regarded only as a transient commodity."
[41] The Common Law Procedure Act 1852 and the Judicature Acts 1873–75.

6.1 Possessory basis

14–038   "It should be remembered that there has always been a very close association between ownership and possession in English law."[42] It seems clear that the origin of the Physical Model is the historic legal association between property and possession.[43] This association continues to be very strong.[44] "The law of *England* has always been, that personal property passes by delivery of possession; and it is possession which determines the apparent ownership."[45] Property confers the right to possession; possession raises the presumption of ownership,[46] and long-standing possession confers it.[47]

14–039   Property rights were originally developed in English law in relation to the possession of land, and applied other assets including intangibles by analogy.[48] The factual relationship of control between a person and the physical assets in her possession was used as a metaphor for the notional relationship between a person and the intangibles in which she has a property interest.[49]

14–040   It can take tremendous intellectual energy always to remember that a metaphorical statement is not a literal statement, and hence the understandable tendency to conflate intangibles with the tangible assets to which they are metaphorically linked in legal writing.

14–041   Another aspect of the basis of the Physical Model in possession is vindication. As indicated above, property rights originated historically and conceptually in legal remedies, and the original legal remedy was vindication. Because vindication was not available for chattels until the Common Law Procedure Act of 1853, chattels were long considered not to be subject to *in rem* rights, and are still excluded from the definition of real property. The

---

[42] N. Palmer and A. Hudson, "Pledge", in *Interests in Goods*, Ed. Palmer and McKendric, 2nd Ed., LLP, London, 1998, p. 633

[43] Possession involves the physical control of a tangible asset. The association between property and possession is discussed in Pollock & Wright, *An Essay on Possession in the Common Law*, 1888, Clarendon Press, Oxford.

[44] "The common law has recognised the taking of possession as essential to the [85] transfer of title in various ways, in the delivery of chattels, for example, or in the ancient common law ritual of 'livery of seisin', in which the transferor of land picked up a piece of the earth and placed it in the hand of the transferee before witnesses." J. E. Penner, *The Idea of Property in Law*, Clarendon Press, Oxford, 1997, pp. 84, 85. See Blackstone, *Commentaries on the Laws of England*, Vol. 2, pp. 312, 313 and Vol. 3 p. 201.

[45] *Dearle v. Hall* (1828) 38 E.R., 475, *per* Sir Thomas Plumer MR at 483.

[46] In Chap. 3 of *Interests in Goods* (Ed. Palmer and McKendrick, 2nd Edition, LLP, London, 1998) N. Palmer offers a fascinating discussion of possessory title. Following a careful analysis of case law, he concludes that ". . .in some respects at least, the immediate right to possession partakes of the nature of property." (p. 89). See the discussion of the doctrine of false wealth in Philip Wood, *The Principles of International Insolvency*, London, Sweet & Maxwell, 1995 at pp. 36, 37.

[47] See the law of prescription. "To prevent uncertainty over title, the old state law laid down that, where someone dealt with a non-owner in the belief that he was dealing with an owner, and obtained something in good faith by purchase or gift or on some other legally sufficient basis, he should become owner by usucaption, *i.e.* possession over time." J.2.6.pr, Transl. Birks and McLeod, p. 63.

[48] See for example, Bracton Vol. II p. 121: ". . .incorporeal things cannot be possessed. . .They therefore are said to be quasi-possessed [and] can be transferred or quasi-transferred by acquiescence and use."

[49] ". . .you must give notice to the legal holder of the fund; in the case of a debt, for instance, notice to the debtor is, for many purposes, tantamount to possession." *Dearle v. Hall*, *supra*, n. 45 *per* Sir Thomas Plumer MR at 848.

connection between property and vindication is so ancient that for many it still remains counterintuitive to assert property rights in fungible assets such as interests in securities, where vindication is not sought and indeed not possible. Whereas vindication is the ancient purpose for asserting property rights, the current purpose in the securities markets (avoiding the credit risk of intermediaries) is fairly recent: corporate insolvency only dates from 1844.[50]

6.2 Rationalist Basis

Another factor contributing to the persistence of the Physical Model is its conceptual attraction to rationalist thinkers. This factor also explains why English common lawyers, who belong to an empirical intellectual traditional, have been better able to resist the Physical Model than continental civil lawyers.[51]   **14–042**

In order to develop these comments, it is necessary to return to the real and personal actions from which property rights and obligations have historically been derived.   **14–043**

6.2.1 Actions

Early Roman law ". . . can be very fully expounded as nothing but a law of actions",[52] and the early textbooks of English law are collections of writs.[53] In both classical and common law, the forms of action precede substantive law, both historically and conceptually.[54]   **14–044**

6.2.2 Persons, things, actions[55]

The induction of substantive law from the forms of action begins with the classical trinity around which Justinian's Institutes is organised: **14–045**

---

[50] With the Joint Stock Companies Act of 1844.

[51] Whereas the judges who wrote English commercial law in the eighteenth and nineteenth centuries read John Locke, and though empirically, the civilians who wrote the civil continental civil codes read Descartes, and thought a priori.

Another factor in assisting English judges in resisting rationalist thought is the role of Equity: "Equity thus depending, essentially, upon the particular circumstances of each individual case, there can be no established rules and fixed precepts of equity laid down, without destroying its very essence. . ." Blackstone, *Commentaries on the Laws of England*, Vol. 21 p. 61.

(In contrast, it might have been supposed that empirical thought, with its emphasis on the world available to the senses, would have been more drawn to the Physical Model, but English judges seem to have resisted this danger.)

[52] Introduction to Justinian's *Institutes*, p. 17.

[53] *The Treatise on the Laws and Customs of the Realm of England commonly called Glanvill*, ("Glanvill") probably written around 1198 "is the first textbook of the common law." (*Glanvill*, Ed. Hall, Clarendon, Oxford, 1965, Introduction, p. xi.) "Writs, and the procedure connected with them, bulk so large is this treatise that it is tempting. . .to regard the work as a commentary on writs." ibid, p. xxxvii). The reader will search in vain for substantive law. Moreover, "Bracton, with the Institutes scheme before him, gives about 100 folios to Persons and Things and about 350 to the law of Actions." *ibid*, p. 8.

[54] With Bracton ". . . [T]he forms of action are given, the causes of action must be deduced therefrom." Maitland, The Forms of Action, p. 5.

[55] In the introduction to their translation of Justinian's *Institutes*, Peter Birks and Grant McLeod discuss two points concerning the Roman conceptual trichotomy of persons, things and actions. "One is the strength of its grip of the law of modern Europe. The other is the proper credit for it. Unless he too had predecessors whom we do not know, it was Gaius, not Justinian,

"All our law is about persons, things, or actions."[56]

In the thirteenth century this trinity is picked up in Bracton:

". . . the whole of the law with which we propose to deal relates either to persons or to things or to actions . . .".[57]

14–046 In the early modern era, the same conceptual framework is fundamental to the structure of Blackstone's *Commentaries*.[58]

14–047 In Blackstone and Bracton, as in Justinian before them, the difference between persons and things is not an a priori distinction, but a technique for categorising actions.[59]

6.2.3 Induction

14–048 Justinian did not induce property rights from real actions. In English law, the induction of substantive law from legal procedure has been a very slow process. Indeed, it has never been completed.[60] From their emergence in the twelveth century until their abolition in the nineteenth, the forms of action provided the conceptual framework of English law, and "they still rule us from their graves."[61] Arguably, the process of abstraction only became plainly visible with Blackstone,[62] and did not develop very far. Common law has never been a rationalist science.[63]

"I think that the courts should be very slow to declare[64] a practice of the commercial community to be conceptually impossible. Rules of law must obviously be consistent and

---

who invented it. . . .the truth is that the inventor of the institutional scheme was a genius and deserves to be remembered as a Darwin among lawyers." (*op. cit.*, p. 13, 18.)

[56] J.1.2.12. Justinian's *Institutes*, Birks and McLeod Transl. *op. cit.*, p. 39.

[57] *Bracton on the Laws and Customs of England*, Thorne Transl., Harvard University Press, Cambridge Mass., 1968, p. 29.

[58] "The one great institutional writer of the common law still derived his structure ultimately from Justinian." Introduction to Justinian's *Institutes*, *op. cit.*, p. 24. Vol. 1 is entitled "Of Rights of Persons", Vol. 2 "On Rights of Things", and Vol. 3 is devoted to legal procedure under the title "Of Private Wrongs". Book four discusses criminal law, under the title "Of Public Wrongs". The four books reflect the division of Justinian's *Institutes* into four books, the first dealing with persons, the second and third dealing with things, and the fourth dealing with actions as well as criminal law.

[59] In the history of Roman law, the distinction between persons and things did not predate and inform the forms of action, but was induced from them. In their Introduction, Birks and McLeod discuss the fundamental importance of forms of action in Gaius. "Gaius's book 4 is crucial . . .it gives a unique account of the classical and pre-classical forms of action. Gaius. . .was genuinely interested in legal history and rightly believed it essential to a proper understanding of law . . . the law can be very fully expounded as nothing but a law of actions." (p. 17). See also Bracton: "The first classification of actions . . .is this, that some are *in rem*, some *in personam* and some are mixed.", Vol 2, p. 290.

[60] "This dependence of right upon remedy. . .has given English law that close texture to which it owes its continuous existence despite the temptations of Romanism." Maitland, *The Forms of Action at Common Law*, p. 63.

[61] Maitland, *The Forms of Action at Common Law*, p. 1.

[62] However, Blackstone followed a scheme devised by Sir Matthew Hale in the seventeenth century.

[63] "Also it is to be remembered that the making of grand theories is not and never has been our strong point." Maitland, *Selected Essays*, Cambridge University Press, 1936, *Trust and Corporation*, pp. 218, 219. See also P. Birks and G. McLeod, *Justinian's Institutes, op. cit.*, Introduction, p. 24: ". . .Halsbury, the practitioner's work of reference in many volumes, sticks to the alphabet, much the commonest system of classification throughout the history of English law."

[64] In *re BCCI (No 8)* [1998] A.C. 214, *per* Lord Hoffmann at 228.

not self-contradictory . . . But the law is fashioned to suit the practicalities of life and legal concepts like "proprietary interest" and "charge" are no more than labels given to clusters of related and self-consistent rules of law. Such concepts do not have a life of their own from which the rules of law are inexorably derived."

(The author would argue that the empirical, "bottom up" approach of English law is its strength, [65] for it enabled English lawyers better to resist the Physical Model than their continental colleagues, for the reasons given below). **14–049**

In contrast, continental civil lawyers extrapolated rights from Roman actions in the medieval period.[66] When continental civil law was codified in the early modern era, the forms of action were forgotten. In Grotius" *Introduction to the Jurisprudence of Holland*,[67] in the Napoleonic Code and in continental civil law generally, one reads only of persons and things, and not of actions. The distinction between persons and things ceases to be a technique for categorising actions, and becomes an a priori distinction. **14–050**

6.2.4 Relative nature property rights in relation to obligations

As discussed above, obligations can only be subject to property rights as against someone other than the obligor.[68] Personal or proprietary status is not unchangeably inherent in the asset, but depends upon whom one is suing. In other words, property is a function of particular actions, and not of particular assets. **14–051**

However, in modern civil law, the relative, action-based nature of property is lost, and the distinction between the personal and the proprietary becomes an a priori distinction. The cost of such abstract thought is clear. If one starts with the distinction between the personal and the proprietary, and then categorises assets in the light of it, property status is taken to be an invariable quality of certain assets. If obligations are personal for some purposes, they are considered to be personal for all purposes. Thus civil lawyers may be drawn to the Physical Model, and consider the assertion of property rights in relation to intangible assets to be misconceived. **14–052**

6.2.5 Critique of the Physical Model

A distinguished line of Anglo-American legal writers including, notably, Hohfeld, have developed a critique of the Physical Model.[69] There are two key themes in this critique. **14–053**

---

[65] For a famous defence of this approach, see *The Common Law Tradition*, Karl N. Llewellyn, Little, Brown and Company, Boston 1960.

[66] "The terms *'jus in rem'* and *'jus in personam'* were devised by the Civilians of the Middle Ages, or arose in times still more recent. . ." Austin, *Lectures on Jurisprudence or The Philosophy of Positive Law*, (5th Ed, 1885) Vol I., p. 369, quoted in Hohfeld, Fundamental Legal Conceptions, p. 82.

[67] Published 1631.

[68] For example, if I invest in debt securities, as against the issuer my rights are personal, so that my investment is at risk in the insolvency of the issuer. However, if I hold my debt securities through a custodian, as against the custodian my rights are proprietary, so that my investment is not at risk in the insolvency of the custodian.

[69] See in particular Hohfeld, *Fundamental Legal Conceptions* and Schroeder, *The Myth that the UCC Killed "Property"*, (1996) 69 Temple Law Review 1282–1341.

14–054   First, it is shown that rights of property are not rights *against things*, but rather rights against persons in respect of things.[70] As Hohfeld famously pointed out in *Fundamental Legal Conceptions*, legal rights are enforced by action,[71] and all legal actions, whether personal or real, are brought against the person of the defendant. By remembering the action-based nature of legal rights, their interpersonal nature becomes clear: "All proceedings, *like all rights*, are *really against persons*.[72] Thus:

> "A right *in rem* is not a right "against a thing". . . . all rights *in rem* are against persons . . ."[73]

14–055   Although a real action *relates to* a thing in the hands of a person, it necessarily *lies against* a person, for only a person can be a defendant in a legal action.[74]

14–056   The inter-personal nature of property rights is particularly clear in the English law of property, because of its derivation from the rules of medieval land tenure.[75] Moreover, the continuing close association in English law between rights and actions assists English lawyers in remembering that property rights lie against persons. However, civilian lawyers who approach law *a priori*, and seek to understand the law of property without reference to the practicalities of real actions, may face the danger of mistaking property rights for rights *against assets* and, on the basis of this false premise, as rights against *physical* assets only.[76]

14–057   The second element in the common law critique of the Physical Model is as follows. It is argued that, by equating property with physical things, the Physical Model conflates rights of property with the assets in relation to which they are asserted. This is a danger against which Justinian[77]

---

[70] "The law of property is about *things*, and our relations with one another in respect of the use and control of things." Jeremy Waldron, "Property Law", in *A Companion to Philosophy of Law and Legal Theory*, Ed. Dennis Patterson, Blackwell, London 1996, p. 4. See also *Property in Thin Air*, Kevin Grey, (1991) 51 Cambridge Law Journal 252

[71] (with the exception of limited "self help" remedies; see Blackstone Vol. 3 p. 22)

[72] Chief Justice Holmes in *Tyler v. Court of Registration* (1900) 175 mass., 71, 76, quoted by Hohfeld, *op. cit.*, p. 75.

[73] pp. 74, 76.

[74] Thus, the nature of personal and real rights can only be understood by reference to the potential actions whereby they might be enforced, and (Hohfeld argues) the difference between such rights is the identity of the potential defendants to such actions. (Intriguingly, Hohfeld refuses to understand rights in terms of actions; see p. 69, 102 *et seq.* The emphasis on actions is the author's)

[75] Under the rules of feudal land tenure, a freeholder does not own land, but rather an interest in land. The nature of that interest is defined by the mutual rights and duties arising between the freeholder and his feudal lord. This is a reciprocal personal relationship, as symbolised by the ceremony of fealty. See Blackstone, *Commentaries on the Laws of England*, Vol. 1, p. 57.

[76] This error is forgivable because of the traditional terminology, which has been a false friend. If one uses Justinian's terminology for categorising actions (without carefully reading his definitions), one is tempted to take actions (and therefore rights) *in personam* as lying against persons, and actions (and therefore rights) *in rem* as lying against things. An opposition between rights against persons and rights against things suggests (falsely) that a personal obligation (which clearly confers a right against the obligor) cannot be a thing. If an obligation were not a thing or *res*, it could not be the subject of an *in rem* right. The attraction of this false conclusion is linguistic as much as logical.

[77] See, for example, Bracton: "It is irrelevant that an inheritance may include corporeal things. What a usufructuary takes from the land will also be corporeal. And what is owed to us by virtue of an obligation is usually corporeal, such as land, a slave, or money. The point is that the actual

warned us, and the warning has been repeated by common lawyers ever since. [78]

Hohfeld points out that property is intangible, because property comprises **14–058** legal rights, which are notional and not physical things, even if they happen to relate to tangible assets.[79]

Historically, much of our commercial law was developed in the pre- **14–059** electronic era, in relation to the sale and delivery of tangible assets. The conflation of intangible rights of property with tangible things presented no conceptual problem in the pre-electronic era.[80] However, in the electronic era, the Physical Model is burdensome, because it cuts across the assertion of property rights in intangible assets. In relation to interests in securities, therefore, it is important to reject the Physical Model.

This paper has argued that the traditional principles of the law of property **14–060** are quite equal to the challenge of computerisation. The impression that they are not, and that the law of property is the law of tangible things, involves conflating legal rights of property with the things to which they relate, and further conflating things with tangible things.

6.2.6 Cultural context of the Physical Model

The Physical Model conflates the intangible with the physical. The same **14–061** materialism is a characteristic of modern Western culture, with the decline of popular religion and the rise of empirical science. It may therefore be unsurprising that the Physical Model belongs to the modern period, and coincides historically with these cultural developments.

This links financial law to the wider culture in which it has been developed. **14–062** The role of the Physical Model, and the history of Western lawyers in alternately resisting and succumbing to it, has a direct parallel, for example, in the history of Western theology. The historic debate among financial lawyers on the status of the bearer bond (whether it constitutes, or merely represents, the debt) recalls the debate between transubstantiation and consubstantiation, and may express the same underlying concerns. This may explain the beautiful and haunting quality of problems that recur in this area of law, and the great cultural status of the leading judgments.

It is all too human to mistake the physical for the intangible. But just as **14–063** Moses taught us not to worship the golden calf, and just as Lacan advised us that tangible possessions will never make us happy,[81] so the computerisation

---

right of inheritance is an incorporeal, as is the actual right to the use and fruits of a thing, and the right inherent in an obligation." J.2.2.2, p. 61.

[78] See, for example, Bracton: "Incorporeal things are such as are intangible, which exist in contemplation of law, as inheritance, usufruct, advowsons of churches, obligation, actions and the like. It is no objection to this that corporeal things are comprised in inheritance, usufruct and such, for what is due us under an obligation is in most cases corporeal, as land, a slave, money and the like, but the right of succession itself, that is the right of inheritance, is incorporeal." Vol. II, p. 48. See also Blackstone, Book II, pp. 20, 21.

[79] Even a microscopic physical examination of a shipment of grain will not reveal its ownership.

[80] Although incorrect, the Physical Model is not burdensome in a physical commercial environment. This is because, in relation to tangible assets, the legal results of Physical Model coincide with the legal results of the correct model of property rights as intangible and interpersonal legal rights.

[81] See also *Pirke Avot*, Chap. 2, verse 8.

of the international financial markets reminds us to return to Justinian, and the knowledge that the law has never belonged to the physical world.

7. Lex Situs

14–064 This section will argue that, in cross border disputes before the English courts concerning clients" property rights in interests in securities, the correct connecting factor is *lex situs*, or the law of the place where the asset is located.

14–065 The *lex situs* rule provides that property rights in an asset are determined by the law of the place where the asset is located, or *lex situs*. "If personal property is disposed of in a manner binding according to the law of the country where it is, that disposition is binding everywhere".[82] Thus, for example, the English courts will apply Norwegian law to a question concerning property rights in a cargo of goods located in Norway.[83]

14–066 In the relevant case law, the chief policy reason which is given for the *lex situs* rule is commercial convenience. "I do not think that anybody can doubt that with regard to the transfer of goods, the law applicable must be the law of the country where the movable is situate. Business could not be carried on if that were not so."[84] A number of cases stress the importance of the rule in enabling the purchaser of goods to establish title with certainty.[85] In this way, the *lex situs* rule also serves to protect the courts from unnecessary litigation: "A little imagination will show that any different rule might produce a multiplicity of claims and confusing and unnecessary question of competing priorities."[86] Some cases justify the rule on the basis of the comity of nations; it would be incompatible with the United Kingdom's recognition of a foreign state as sovereign for the English courts to seek to interfere with property rights in assets located in that foreign state.[87]

---

[82] *Cammell v. Sewell* (1858) 3 H & N 617, *per* Pollock C.B. at 624.

[83] *Cammell v. Sewell* (*supra*).

[84] In *re Ansiani* [1930] 1 Ch 407, *per* Maugham J. at 420.

[85] See for example, *Cammell v. Sewell* (1860) 5 H & N 728, *per* Crompton J. at 1374 (if the rule did not apply, "A purchaser would have no secure title, and consequently a fair price would not be obtained."), and 1378; *Winkworth v. Christie* [1980] 1 Ch 496, *per* Slade J. at 512,3 (Commercial convenience may be said imperatively to demand that proprietary rights to movables shall generally be determined by the *lex situs* under the rules of private international law. Were the position otherwise, it would not suffice for the protection of a purchaser of any valuable movables to ascertain that he was acquiring title to them under the law of the country where the goods were situated at the time of the purchase. . ."). See also *Embraces v. Anglo-Austrian Bank* [1904] 1 K.B. 677, *per* Vaughan Williams L.J. at 684, in which the *lex situs* rule is compared with the market overt rule.)

[86] *Schemer v. Property Resources Ltd and others* [1974] Ch D 451, *per* Gelding J. at 458.

[87] Any other approach is "is contrary to all the rules of the comity of nations. . ." *Norton v. Florence Land and Public Works Company* (1877) 7 Ch D 332, *per* Jesse M.R. at 337. See also *Cammel v. Sewell* (1858) 3 H & N 617, *per* Pollock C.B. at 627; *Castrique v. Imrie* (1870) L.R.4 H.L. 414, *per* Blackburn J. at 437; *In re Maudslay* [1900] 1 Ch 602, *per* Cozens-Hardy J. at 609; and *Winkworth v. Christie* [1980] 1 Ch 496, *per* Slade J. at 513
Many of the relevant cases concern the nationalisation of private property by the Soviet government following the Russian revolution. See *Askionairenoye Obsechestvo A.M.Luther v. James Sagor & Co* [1921] 3 KB532, *per* Scrutton L.J. at 556: "But it is impossible to recognise a government and yet claim to exercise jurisdiction over its person or property against its will." "It is no business of mine to criticise the decrees or to express any view as to their propriety..." *Re Bank des Marchands de Moscou* [1952] 1 All E.R. 1269, *per* Vaisey J. at 1275. (See also *Re Helbert Wagg*

In cross border situations, third parties are most likely to assess the availability of assets under the law of the place where the assets are located, and hence the *lex situs* rule. **14–067**

The rule may in part be attributable to the pragmatic desire of judges to avoid making futile orders. Because an order relating to, for example, French land can only be enforced in France with the co-operation of the French judiciary, such an order which is at odds with the mandatory provisions of French law will be unenforceable in practice. **14–068**

In matters before the English courts, the identification of the situs of an asset will be determined by English law as the law of the forum.[88] **14–069**

7.1 Applicability of the rule

There is an active debate in the legal community concerning application of the lex situs rule to interests in securities. This debate concerns two questions. The first is whether the rule applies to intangibles such as interests in securities. The second question (which becomes relevant if the answer to the first question is positive) concerns the identification of the situs of interests in securities. The second question is beyond the scope of this discussion,[89] which will consider the first question. **14–070**

7.2 Extension of the lex situs rule to intangible assets

The *lex situs* rule has long been applied to tangible assets such as land and chattels.[90] More recently, the Court of Appeal decision in the case of *Macmillan v. Bishopsgate*[91] has confirmed that the rule applies to tangible and intangible assets alike.[92] Case law provides authority that the *lex situs* rule applies to intangibles. In re *Maudslay*[93] the question of whether a debt owed by a French firm was subject to a debenture was determined by lex **14–071**

[1956] Ch 323, *per* Upjohn J. at 346.) The *lex situs* rule also defines when such nationalisation order will not be effective: see *Sedgwick Collins v. Rossia Insurance Co of Petrograd* [1925] 1 KB 1, *per* Sargant L.J. at 15. (See also *The El Condado* (1939) 63 Lloyds Rep 83 and 330, *per* Lord Jamieson at 87, *per* Lord Mackay at 338.)

Any other approach is "is contrary to all the rules of the comity of nations..." *Norton v. Florence Land and Public Works Company* (1877) 7 Ch D 332, *per* Jessell M.R. at 337. See also *In re Maudslay* [1900] 1 Ch 602, *per* Cozens-Hardy J. at 609; and *Winkworth v. Christie* [1980] 1 Ch 496, *per* Slade J. at 513

[88] *Rossano v. Manufacturers' Life Insurance Co* [1963] 2 Q.B. 352, at 379–380. See *Dicey and Morris*, 13th Edition, 1999, 1–076.

[89] See the discussion in chap 7 of *Interests in Securities, op. cit.*

[90] See, for example, *Inglis v. Usherwood* (1801) 1 East 525 (chattels) and *Norris v. Chambers* 29 Beav 246 (1860)(land).

[91] *Macmillan v. Bishopsgate (No. 3)* [1996] 1 W.L.R. 387, 404, 405 (*per* Staughton L.J.), 410, 411, 412 (per Auld LJ) and 423, 424 (per Aldous LJ). This complex judgment indicates overall that *lex situs* is relevant, rather than *lex loci actus*, which was favoured by Millett J. in the first instance decision [1995] 1 W.L.R. 978. (It would be interesting if the issue came before Lord Millett again in the House of Lords.)

[92]

[93] [1900] 1 Ch 602

[94] "It seems to me that I must treat the debt due from Delaunay & Cie. As being situate in France, and subject to French law, and I cannot therefore prevent the claimants, at the suit of the debenture-holders, from taking any proceedings the law of France allows from recovering their debt out of this French asset." Per Cozens-Hardy J. at 609.

situs;[94] in *New York Life Insurance Company v Public Trustee*[95] *lex situs* was applied to the question of whether insurance policies were subject to a charge; and in *Jabbour v. the Custodian*[96] *lex situs* was applied to determine whether an insurance policy was subject to an expropriation order.[97]

7.3 Relevance for Collateral

14-072   This issue has clear relevance where interests in securities are used as collateral. If property rights in intangibles are determined by *lex situs*, it follows that security interests require to be perfected under *lex situs*.[98] Arguably it also follows that, where interests in securities are delivered under outright transfer arrangements, recharacterisation risk must be considered under *lex situs* (as well as under the governing law of the collateral contract and the law of the insolvency jurisdiction of the counterparty).

14-073   Of course, in cross border collateral arrangements, the English law position is not the end of the matter, as the courts of other countries may assume jurisdiction in relation to the collateral arrangements. However, for the London financial markets, English law is a very important part of the picture. In particular, clarity on this issue will offer a significant advantage to lawyers in drafting the English legal opinions routinely sought by clients.

7.4 The governing law argument

14-074   Some commentators have argued that the Court of Appeal decision in *Macmillan* was mistaken. This is on the basis that the *lex situs* rule properly applies to tangible things (which have physical locations) and not to claims (which do not). It is unhelpful (they argue) to reify claims by artificially attributing locations to them.

14-075   Rather, such commentators argue, questions concerning assets that arise under contract are properly answered by the law of contract. The Rome Convention[99] applies "to contractual obligations in any situation involving a choice of the laws of different countries".[1] Article 12(2) relates to assignments of contractual rights, and indicates (broadly) that the position of the assignee is governed by the governing law of the assigned right (and not by

---

[95] [1924] 2 Ch 101

[96] [1954] 1 All E.R. 145

[97] *per* Pearson J. at 151: "It is established by the decided cases that not only debts, but also other choses in action, are for legal purposes localised and are situated where they are properly recoverable and are properly recoverable where the debtor resides."

[98] A long line of cases applies *lex situs* to determine the validity or perfection of security interests. See, for example, (lien on land) *Norris v. Chambers* (1860) 29 Beav, 246 at 253; on appeal 3 De. G. F. & J. 583, *per* the Lord Chancellor at 548; (pledge of goods) *City Bank v. Barrow* (1880) 5 App Cas 664, *per* Lord Blackburn at 677; (pledge of share certificates) *Williams v. Colonial Bank* (1888) 38 Ch D 388(CA), *per* Lindley L.J. at 403; (pledge of documents of title to goods) *Inglis v Robertson* [1898] AC 616, *per* Earl of Halsbury LC at 625; (charge on real property under a debenture) *Mount Albert Borough Council v. Australasian Temperance and General Mutual Life Assurance society Ltd* [1937] 4 All E.R. 206, *per* Lord Wright at 213, 217.

[99] The Convention on the Law Applicable to Contractual Obligations, implemented in the UK by the Contracts (Applicable Law) Act 1990.

[1] Art. 1

the law of its notional situs).[2] It follows analogously from this (it is argued), that the perfection of a security interest over interests in securities should be governed by the governing law of that asset. This argument will be called "the governing law argument".

There is persuasive authority that the Rome Convention does not apply to property rights.[3] However, this does not hinder the governing law argument, because that argument rests on the premise that contractual claims are not subject to property rights; it is argued that personal rights bind persons, and this distinguishes them from property rights, which relate to things. On this basis (it is argued) contractual claims (which bind persons) cannot be subject to property rights. Therefore (it is argued) the *lex situs* rule (which relates to property rights) cannot apply to intangibles such as contractual claims, and the Court of Appeal decision in *Macmillan* was wrong.[4]

14–076

7.5 The counter argument

The author's counter argument to the governing law argument is as follows. Briefly, contractual and other claims have been treated as things in Western law since Justinian. They may be subject to property claims (and therefore property rights) in the hands of third parties (*i.e.* persons other than the obligor). The client holding interests in securities through an intermediary is able to recover its asset in the insolvency of that intermediary because *as against the intermediary* its interests are proprietary. If the client grants a security interest to a collateral taker over its interests in securities, the collateral taker is able to enforce its security interest in the insolvency of the client because *as against the client* its interest is proprietary. Therefore there is clear (to the author at least) that interests in securities are legal things, and may be subject to property rights.

14–077

In this connection the author has long argued in favour of the approach now endorsed by the thirteenth edition of Dicey & Morris. In its discussion of dealings in immobilised securities, the new edition rejects the governing law argument.[5]

14–078

---

[2] Art. 12. "Voluntary Assignments. . . .2. The law governing the right to which the assignment relates shall determine its assignability, the relationship between the assignee and the debtor, the conditions under which the assignment can be invoked against the debtor and any questions whether the debtor's obligations have been discharged."

[3] ". . .since the Convention is concerned only with the law applicable to contractual obligations, property rights. . .are not covered by these provisions." See *Council Report on the Convention on the Law Applicable to Contractual Obligations*, M. Guiliano and P. Lagarde, [1980] O.J. L266, comments on Art. 2 of the Convention.

However, the contrary view has been expressed. For discussion of the relevant issues, see *The Proprietary Aspects of International Assignment of Debts and the Rome convention, Art. 12*, Strucken [1998] LMCLQ 345.

[4] See the discussion in *Dicey & Morris*, paras 24–048, 24–059.

[5] "If the investor seeks to enter into a transaction such as a loan, and purports to transfer title to, or pledge or charge, his interest in the securities as security for the loan, a question arises to determine which law governs . . .the purported assignment of such interest as he may have. In analysing the proprietary aspect of such facts, it . . .seems improbable that Art. 12 of the Rome Convention was designed to be applied." 24–64.

A further argument for not applying Art. 12 to deliveries of interests in securities as collateral, is that book entry transfers of interests in securities to not take effect by assignment, but rather by novation; see chap. 4.

14-079   The question remains whether it is helpful artificially to attribute locations to claims by legal fiction. The author would argue that it is. Legal fictions have a long and successful history in English law. More fundamentally, Western law has always dealt with intangible things by analogy with tangibles. The use of analogy has long served as a powerful technique for extending settled rules to new circumstances. This has contributed to the flexibility of the common law, which has enabled it to remain alive for a millennium. Law is a system of ideas, and provided the attribution of a situs to a claim is helpful, it matters not that it is notional.[6]

14-080   Whether or not it is helpful to confer a situs on a claim, must be assessed at a practical level. The conflict of laws is abstract in its theory, but in practice often turns on pragmatic considerations of enforcement. The rules for attributing a situs to an intangible are based on enforcement; broadly speaking, a claim is located where it may in the ordinary course be enforced.[7] Herein lies the usefulness of applying the *lex situs* rule to intangibles. The English courts apply French law to the perfection of a security interest in a debt owed by a French-resident person, because France is the situs of the debt. In practice the chargee sees the sense of obtaining the opinion of a French lawyer in relation to the charge, because it knows that in practice it is likely it will need the co-operation of the French courts to enforce its interest. In this way the application of the lex situs rule to intangibles permits theory and practice to coincide.

---

[6] (Because the subject matter of financial law largely comprises notional things such as corporations and debts, financial law is a metaphysical subject. The tendency to mistake it for an empirical subject has always been a source of confusion.)

[7] "Choses in action generally are situated in the country where they are properly recoverable or can be enforced." *Dicey and Morris* 22R–023, rule 112(1).

CHAPTER 15

THE HAGUE GLOBAL JURISDICTION AND JUDGMENTS PRELIMINARY DRAFT CONVENTION

CATHERINE KESSEDJIAN
PROFESSOR, UNIVERSITY OF PARIS II PANTHÉON, ASSAS
FORMER DEPUTY SECRETARY GENERAL, HAGUE CONFERENCE ON
PRIVATE INTERNATIONAL LAW

When the work started in 1992 on a possible Hague Convention on Jurisdiction and Judgments, there was a common understanding, among all countries who participated then,[1] that the future Convention should remain as close as possible to the successful Brussels and Lugano Conventions.[2] Thus, it was with that understanding in mind that preliminary work was begun.[3] However, it soon appeared that what was possible with a small group of countries[4] was not desirable in a worldwide convention. Hence, the necessity to depart from some well established European rules, and to take into consideration other cultures and ways to approach international litigation, became evident. As a result, the draft Hague Convention presents certain specific features which allow it to be potentially well accepted by a wide variety of countries.   **15–001**

First, it is a text which offers some clear and fixed rules of jurisdiction hence providing certainty and foreseeability to parties to a dispute. One may argue, although it is now contested by some,[5] that these are the two main goals of the work undertaken at The Hague. Whoever has been involved actively in international litigation knows it is not possible at present to evaluate the judicial risk unless one is prudent enough to include an arbitration   **15–002**

---

[1] A working group was convened in 1992 to study the proposal of the United States that the Hague Conference undertake work in this area. Not all participating countries were European as the list shows: Argentina, China, Egypt, Finland, France, Hungary, U.K, USA and Venezuela.

[2] The Brussels Convention was adopted on September 27, 1968 and entered into force in 1973. It is to be applied within the European Union States. The Lugano Convention, adopted on September 16, 1988, is parallel to the Brussels text and is to be applied to relations between the EU Member States and EFTA countries. It is also extended to third countries who are to become EU Members in the future. Documents distributed by the United States to the delegates at the working group showed clearly the concept of a "mixed convention" (see below) and were drafted fairly closely modeled on the Brussels and Lugano Conventions.

[3] For a complete background on the initial work see C. Kessedjian, International Jurisdiction and Foreign judgments in civil and commercial matters, Prel do. No.7 of April 1997 accessible on http://www.hcch.net. It is not suprising that the work started with a strong inspiration by the European conventions as many well renowned scholars around the world, and particularly in the United States, had followed closely the evolution of European endeavors in this respect and recognised the important innovations built into it.

[4] It should be noted that the Brussels Convention was negotiated by six countries only, all of which were civil law countries. No major changes occurred in the text when common law countries acceded to it.

[5] At the IBA meeting in Amsterdam in September 2000, a participant from the United States said certainty and foreseeability were not the main goals of the draft Hague Convention.

clause in the contract.[6] Even if one looks at contractual matters only, and supposing the contract contains a choice of court clause, no certainty exists. Indeed the criteria for appraising the validity of the clause vary from country to country and some courts apply the *forum non conveniens* theory even in presence of such a clause.[7] For reasons unclear to this writer, two Conventions on choice of court have had no success. The Hague Convention on the jurisdiction of the selected forum in the case of international sales of goods of April 15 1958[8] was signed by four States only[9] and ratified by none. Likewise, the Convention on the Choice of Court of November 25 1965 was signed only by Israel. Hence neither of the two texts are in force. If only the new draft Convention could bring clarity and certainty in this area, it would certainly have advanced and eased the life of international business operators.

15–003   While providing foreseeability, the text allows, at the same time, some flexibility for a better adequation between the jurisdictional rules chosen and real life disputes as they crystallise before a judge. Thus, within the future Hague Convention, the role of the judge is greater than what he/she would enjoy under traditional civil law systems, but somewhat narrower than the one granted by common law systems. Articles 21 on *lis pendens* and 22 on declining jurisdiction embody this principle. The respect for certainty is shown by the fact that a court may not decline jurisdiction when it is seised under an exclusive choice of court agreement or by virtue of some other exclusive jurisdiction (Article 12) or when the matters in dispute pertain to sensitive areas such as consumer or labour contracts (Articles 7 and 8). The necessity for flexibility is embodied in paragraphs 6 and 7 of Article 21 providing, in summary, for cases in which the automatic *lis pendens* rule, giving priority to the court first seised, must give way. As we know, the rigid automaticity of the *lis pendens* rule in the Brussels and Lugano Conventions has given rise to abuses.[10] These abuses would be impossible with the Hague provisions.

15–004   Secondly, it is a Convention that is not exhaustive, *i.e.* which allows national law on jurisdiction to apply to certain cases, notwithstanding a provision in the Convention. Thus, the system proposed by the Convention is not a closed one and leaves some freedom for national laws on jurisdiction and foreign judgments to co-exist with the Convention system. This feature (the so–called "mixed" model) is very useful at least in two respects:

---

[6] This is good for contractual relations among businesses but, obviously, does not work for tort or consumer contracts to name only two of the areas in which arbitration is either not allowed or problematic.

[7] See, for example, G. Born, *International Arbitration and Forum Selection Agreements*, Kluwer Law International, 1999, pp. 33 and 34; W.W. Park, *International Forum Selection*, Kluwer Law International, 1995, pp. 25–32.

[8] This Convention was drafted in French only and no English translation is available see www.hcch.net/e/conventions/text05e.html.

[9] Austria, Belgium, Germany and Greece.

[10] This is particularly true in the intellectual property area. See for example, forthcoming proceedings of the Fordham Conference held in New York in April 2000.

1) it allows national rules to adapt to new developments in international litigation;

2) the Convention does not upset national systems.

If, in addition, as is proposed by the Permanent Bureau, the Convention would include a provision defining an easy and flexible mechanism to revise the text, after it has been applied for a certain period and once practice has evolved, the Convention can become the best tool for the management of international litigation.[11] **15–005**

The draft Convention is also very useful at least in two respects:

1) for choice of court clauses and

2) in respect of provisional and protective remedies.

As far as choice of court clauses are concerned, the present situation is unsatisfactory as explained above. Depending on the court seised of the matter, the clause can be held valid or invalid. Thus, parties can never be entirely assured that their will, as expressed in their contract, will be respected by some courts. The future Convention, by providing clear criteria for the validity of those clauses, eases greatly the management of international disputes and gives the parties to such disputes the means to define precisely and quantify their risks. In that aspect alone, the Convention is invaluable. Its Article 4 provides for a clear criterion of validity of a choice of court agreement in line with the most recent practice in the field, particularly in the numeric world.[12] **15–006**

But the draft text offers another very helpful feature when providing rules of jurisdiction on provisional and protective measures together with rules on their recognition and enforcement. Because international litigation is becoming increasingly complex, it is not seldom that a dispute be initiated by one party with a request before one or more courts for the granting of some protective measures. The present lack of uniformity on jurisdiction and the effects of such measures, renders often very difficult and costly the granting of effective transnational measures. The Convention would thus provide a system through which parties may be assured to obtain such measures in an efficient manner. It is true that the Convention does not unify the measures themselves,[13] but it already offers great assistance to potential litigants. **15–007**

From the point of view of the effects of judgments, the Convention is the very tool needed by countries whose legal system prohibits recognition or **15–008**

---

[11] Inspiration may be taken from Conventions in the field of environment protection. See for example: Ch. Chinkin and C. Kessedjian, "A new international regime governing the taking of security in high–value mobile assets", *Uniform Law Review* Vol. IV 1999 pp. 323, where different methods are explored.

[12] Although the Special Commission had no time to fully consider all the consequences of electronic commerce, it incorporated into Art. 4 the necessary adjustments.

[13] This is very difficult considering the wide variety of measures existing in the national systems, see C. Kessedjian, Note on Provisional and Protective Measures in Private International Law and Comparative Law, Prel.Doc.No.10 of October 1998 available at http://www.hcch.net. Such unification may perhaps be done under the auspices of Unidroit which is presently working on civil procedure rules for transnational disputes (see the American Law Institute project entitled "Transnational Rules of Civil Procedure", Preliminary draft No.2 March 17, 2000).

enforcement of foreign judgments without a treaty. Hence, it would favour a better circulation of judgments among trading partners and would, once again, facilitate the management of international disputes. Having said that, however, the Convention provides for a strict set of safeguards so that only judgments which conform with minimal standards of justice and reasonableness can benefit from the conventional system. It is striking to note that on this matter, concepts, principles and their concrete implementation in draft rules have not changed much in 30 years. Indeed, if one looks at the *Hague Convention of 1 February 1971 on the Recognition and Enforcement of Foreign Judgments in Civil and Commercial Matters*[14] and compares its provisions with that of the current preliminary draft, the similarity is quite evident.

15–009   Finally, it must be mentioned that, if the negotiating partners agree to include in the Convention a provision on uniform interpretation along the lines proposed in Article 40 of the draft, the Convention would be one of the most modern texts in the recent history of unification of private law. It is to be hoped that all of the efforts, work and resources put into this project since 1992, the momentum maintained since then and the expectations created for the practitioners will contribute to a successful Diplomatic Conference.

---

[14] This Convention is in force among the following States: Cyprus, the Netherlands and Portugal.

CHAPTER 16

MODERN PERSPECTIVES OF INTERNATIONAL
JURISDICTION

Konstantinos D. Kerameus
Professor of Civil Procedure, Athens University,
President of the International Academy of Comparative Law

1. Introduction

Having the benefit of presenting the last paper in this section, I take a look **16–001** at its title which also refers to departure from localisation and territoriality with a question mark. Under this question mark I was asked to present some observations on modern perspectives of international jurisdiction. The combination of the function assigned to me with the larger framework of the session within which it is included leads to the assumption that what is expected is probably a reflection about the present status and the future fate of international jurisdiction in an era which apparently tries to restrain local connections in favour of global rules. In other, more technical, terms the question is whether it is advisable and feasible to substitute (wholly or partly) uniform rules for the present multitude of national rules governing international jurisdiction. Thus jurisdiction, being conceptually the point where law meets geography and complies with territorial divisions, would be in a certain sense de-territorialised, at least as far as the source of its delineation is concerned. Under this aspect I will try to make three points. They consecutively address, first, the reasons for the success of the Brussels Convention, secondly, the lessons to be drawn from the Brussels-connected experience, finally, some considerations on the comparison between jurisdiction and substance in the contemporary endeavours towards legal approximation.

2. Autonomous procedural unification: Brussels Convention and New York Convention

16–002   All existing texts on uniform jurisdictional rules, be it the Brussels,[1] the Lugano[2] or the Hague Convention (both the existing and the draft one), belong to the so-called autonomous procedural unification, *i.e* they do not rely upon any uniform body of substantive law with respect to which to accomplish an implementing and auxiliary function.[3] Like most international conventions on procedural matters, conventions on international jurisdiction as well do not refer to any set of common substantive norms. Since no particular substantive law is addressed, procedure is freed from its generally auxiliary character and is called upon to occupy a place of its own. This uncoupling of procedure from substance in the international field implies both a degree of upgrading of procedure, and a need to search for new values. In most cases, these values will display a specific procedural colour and, in the case of international jurisdiction, they will pertain to the proper allocation of adjudicatory power among the contracting states. Therefore, the autonomous character of international procedural unification includes not only the negative aspect of severing substance and procedure[4] but also the positive aspect of inserting independent values. If procedural change may pursue social reform,[5] procedural unification is apt to result in a specific elaboration of values and principles proper to adjudication.[6]

16–003   Since the substratum of a uniform substantive law is here missing, there must exist other conditions which make procedural unification both desirable and feasible. Such conditions may be related to either the legal or the factual level. In the first instance, they may include an already existing degree of uniformity among the various legal systems which come under consideration to be mutually approximated. Always on the legal level, such

---

[1] Brussels (EC) Convention on International Jurisdiction and Recognition and Enforcement of Judgments in Civil and Commercial Matters 1968, as amended. The Convention is currently under revision. Current text or the proposed regulation for the reform of the Brussels Convention, COM (2000) 689, at http://www.europa.eu.int/eur–lex/en/com/greffe_index.html.

[2] Lugano Convention on International Jurisdiction and Recognition and Enforcement of Judgments in Civil and Commercial Matters 1988.

[3] For a more extensive discussion on the distinction between autonomous and derivative procedural unification see Kerameus, "Procedural unification: The need and the limitations", I. R. Scott (ed.), *International Perspectives on Civil Justice. Essays in honour of Sir Jack I. H. Jacob Q. C.* (London, 1990) 47, at 53–55 = Kerameus, *Studia iuridica III* (Sakkoulas/Kluwer, 1995) 21, at 29–32.

[4] Separating procedure and substance is a tricky matter. See R. M. Cover and O. M. Fiss, *The Structure of Procedure* (1979) 47–104; D. W. Louisell and G. C. Hazard, Jr., *Cases and Materials on Pleading and Procedure, State and Federal* (4th ed., 1979) 433–436; M. D. Green, *Basic Civil Procedure* (2nd ed., 1979) 5–9, at 8 ("Any procedural point could, conceivably, affect substantive rights"), 9 ("the age–old struggle to distinguish between substance and procedure"); J. G. Collier, *Conflict of Laws* (1987) 319–328; W. Henckel, *Prozessrecht und materielles Recht* (1970).

[5] *cf*. H. Smit, La procédure comme instrument de réforme sociale, Rev. int. dr.Comp. 28 (1976) 449–460.

[6] Additional values in other areas of procedural unification include making available all appropriate means of defence in transnational adjudication, providing for a reasonable and efficient taking of evidence across national borders, or permitting the unencumbered flow of judgments and arbitral awards within the international community.

conditions may also call for a legal structure under which procedural unification is facilitated, welcome, or even required; similar legal structures may exist in a federal state, if one thinks about procedural unification among the various federate entities, or in other forms of regional political or economic integration. Of course not every federal state displays procedural diversity. The Federal Republic of Germany, for instance, not only is a federal state but allocates most of the courts to the various *Länder* as well. Only the highest courts in each jurisdictional branch belong to the Federal Republic itself and are specifically mentioned in the Constitution.[7] However, all civil courts, irrespective of whether they are organs of the Federal Republic or of the *Länder*, are called upon to apply the same code of civil procedure; state law on procedural matters has an extremely limited function.[8] Nevertheless, in many federal structures federal law governs procedure only in the federal courts,[9] and the constituent states are permitted to enact their own procedural rules for their courts. The United States and Switzerland belong to this group.[10] In both countries there is a substantial degree of convergence among the procedural systems of the constituent states or cantons; however, occasional differences may grow to considerable dimensions.

Still no major endeavour to remove these differences and to bring about formal uniformity appears to be forthcoming in the near future.[11] The reason for this could well be that it is believed that a sufficient degree of unification is achieved through the inherent unifying force of the constitutional superstructure rather than any insensibility to practical needs or indolence of mind. Indeed, the federal constitutions of both the United States and Switzerland indicate or even impose the same solution upon many procedural issues in all constituent states or cantons. The relevance of the constitution becomes more obvious with the increasing degree by which procedural questions rise to constitutional eminence. Thus, the most striking difference between internal and international procedural unification is the interference of considerations immediately drawn from norms of higher ranking in the former but not in the latter case; public international law cannot with regard to international procedural unification assume a function even remotely similar to the one attributed to the constitution within a federal setting.[12]

16–004

---

[7] Fundamental Law of May 23, 1949, Arts 92, 94, 95, 96, 96a.
[8] Rosenberg, Schwab and Gottwald, *Zivilprozessrecht* (15th ed., 1993) § 5 III 2 p. 27.
[9] See C. A. Wright, *The Law of Federal Courts* (4th ed., 1983); M. H. Redish, *Federal Jurisdiction: Tensions in the Allocation of Judicial Power* (1980); J. W. Howard, *Courts of Appeals in the Federal Judicial System* (1981).
[10] In the United States the expression "bifurcated justice" has been coined: Louisell and Hazard (see *supra*, n. 4) at 363. For a modern treatment of the interaction between federal and canton law of civil procedure in Switzerland see H. U. Walder–Bohner, *Zivilprozessrecht nach den Gesetzen des Bundes und des Kantons Zürich unter Berücksichtigung anderer Zivilprozessordnungen* (3rd ed., 1983) § 3 pp. 23–38. In that country federal procedural rules cover a wider scope than in the United States to the extent that they also include the law of enforcement with respect to money judgments, orders and other enforceable instruments.
[11] In Switzerland a Committee was recently established in order to envisage the feasibility of a procedural unification among the 26 cantonal codes, but no results have been so far reported.
[12] *cf.* generally G. Maridakis, *The Enforcement of Foreign Judgments Under the Law Applicable in Greece* (3rd ed., 1970; in Greek) 2–6.

16–005   Turning now to the two most successful pieces of international procedural unification, *i.e.* the New York Convention on recognition and enforcement of foreign arbitral awards and the Brussels Convention on jurisdiction
and the enforcement of judgments in civil and commercial matters, we may
discern several of the aforementioned conditions in both instances. The
New York Convention built upon an advanced level of convergence
throughout the world with regard to the concept as well as the attributes of
arbitration, such as the form of the arbitration agreement, the obligation of
the court to refer the parties to arbitration, the otherwise expected assistance by the court to the arbitral tribunal, the appointment of arbitrators,
the authority of the arbitral tribunal to rule on its jurisdiction, the equal
treatment of the parties, the form and contents of the award, the limited
grounds for setting aside an award, or the conditions for its recognition or
enforcement.[13]

16–006   On the factual level, the New York Convention addressed a particular
and highly uniform group of persons and legal entities, that is, the international business community. Not only did the cohesion of this group grow
and intensify with the development of international business relations and
the gradual elimination of national frontiers but, furthermore, the usage
and customs preferred by members of the group have in recent times
aspired to collective recognition under the name of *lex mercatoria*.[14] No
matter how vague and ambiguous the notion may be, it is characteristic as
the legal (or para-legal) instrument of businessmen conscious of their own
identity and eager to disregard national law limitations. Such a closed and
conforming community constitutes the proper recipient for internationally
uniform rules. Of course, the New York Convention lacks otherwise a larger
legal structure since neither the United Nations Charter as such nor general
international law may be understood as issuing mandates with respect to
commercial arbitration.

16–007   Compared to the New York Convention, the Brussels Convention presents
both similarities and dissimilarities. Its constituency is made up of all people,
regardless of their nationality, domiciled in (which, as a practical matter,
means living in) any of the Member States. This constituency, although less
uniform than the international business community, is more integration-
minded. The deeper and faster the integration process, in particular against
the background of the Economic and Monetary Union, the more homogeneous will the group of the addressees become. In sum, the Brussels Convention also has a cohesive factual infrastructure, whereby global integration

---

[13] See generally R. David, *L'arbitrage dans le commerce international* (Paris, 1982), chap. V,
183–230.
[14] See in the volume *Le droit des relations économiques internationales: Études offertes à Berthold
Goldman* (1982), in particular the studies by J.–D. Bredin, La loi du juge, at pp. 15–27; Ph. Kahn,
Droit international économique, droit du développement, lex mercatoria: concept unique ou pluralisme des ordres juridiques?, at pp. 97–107; P. Lagarde, Approche critique de la lex mercatoria,
at pp. 125–150; A.T. von Mehren, To what extent is international commercial arbitration
autonomous?, at pp. 217–227; M. Virally, Un tiers droit? Réflexions théoriques, at pp. 373–385.
Also G. Delaume, "Comparative analysis as a bar of law in state contracts. The myth of the lex
mercatoria", Tulane L. Rev. 63 (1989) 575–611; K. Highet, "The enigma of the lex mercatoria",
ibid., at 613–628.

rather than common business aspirations constitutes the main connecting factor.

Similarly, the Brussels Convention, in spite of its highly innovative character with regard to certain crucial points, organised the partial unification of several legal systems which did not have any spectacular pre-existing divergences among them. Of course, exorbitant bases of jurisdiction, which are eliminated within the scope of the Convention,[15] are admitted to a different extent and with varying content by the various national systems. But the important aspects of the law of jurisdiction and enforcement provided for by the Convention have more or less been familiar to most of the national systems within the European Community. Thus, this Convention focused on areas of procedural law that were ripe for unification.   **16–008**

Besides the common features shared with the New York Convention which aided acceptance of procedural unification, the Brussels Convention considerably benefited from two additional circumstances. First, the Brussels Convention is not a usual arrangement in that is does not derive its force solely from the will of the concluding parties. The Convention, without belonging to primary or secondary Community law properly speaking, is not independent of the entire legal structure starting from, and culminating in, the Treaties of Rome, Maastricht and Amsterdam. Methods of interpretation with regard to the Convention are similar to the ones used with regard to Community law in general, and the objectives pursued by the Founding Treaties are often relied upon when dealing with questions arising under the Convention.[16] This means that procedural unification, as brought about by the Brussels Convention, is linked to a pre-existing legal scheme that is dominated by the Founding Treaties as a set of quasi-constitutional norms. One is reminded here of the situation in the United States, where the inherently unifying force of constitutional superstructure may well have made formal procedural unification among the various states superfluous.[17]   **16–009**

The second circumstance that greatly enhanced the unifying effect of the Brussels Convention lies in the interpretative authority granted to the Court of Justice of the European Communities and exercised by preliminary rulings upon referrals by national courts.   **16–010**

3. Experience and lessons from the Brussels Convention

Precisely this aspect leads us to the second point, to wit what lessons may be drawn from the experience obtained so far in connection with the Brussels   **16–011**

---

[15] Art. 3.

[16] *e.g. Tessili v. Dunlop,* October 6, 1976, E.C.R. [1976] 1473, paras 6–11, in particular at 9; *Somafer v. Saar-Ferngas,* November 22, 1978, E.C.R. [1978] 2183, paras 4, 7: *Duijnstee v. Goderbauer,* November 15, 1983, E.C.R. [1983] 3663, [1983] paras 11–14.

[17] For a comparison between U.S. practice and the Brussels Convention see, in particular, A.T. von Mehren, "Recognition and enforcement of sister–state judgments: Reflections on general theory and current practice in the European Economic Community and the United States," Columbia L. Rev. 81 (1981) 1044–1060; F. Juenger, "Judicial jurisdiction in the United States and in the European Community: A comparison", Michigan L. Rev. 82 (1984) 1195–1212.

Convention. In fact, the draftsmen of the Convention by entrusting its interpretation to the Court of Justice eliminated the single most important obstacle to the unification of law in general, that is the deficiency of common
interpretation.[18] Such deficiency had been, for instance, blamed for the only
partial success of the Geneva Conventions of June 7, 1930 and March 19,
1931 on negotiable instruments.[19] In contrast, the preliminary rulings handed
down by the Court of Justice with respect to the Brussels Convention are not
only binding for the purposes of the particular case; the principles contained
therein are relevant with regard to other cases also arising under the same
Convention. As the European Court of Justice puts it, the interpretation proceeds in accordance with the basic principles of the Convention itself (which
are sometimes called "Community" principles)[20] and on a broad comparative
basis. Indeed, the unification of the law of jurisdiction and enforcement
within the European Union has not been completed by concluding the
Brussels Convention. Rather, the unifying work unfolds every day through
the case law of the national courts and, in particular, the European Court of
Justice. Therefore, entrusting the authoritative interpretation of uniform
rules to a single, permanent, high-quality, multinationally-composed and
generously-equipped jurisdictional organ also constitutes a condition for
successful procedural unification.

16–012   What has just been said may also give an answer to the question how the
chances of success for the Lugano Convention are to be assessed. In fact, this
Convention comes into an ambivalent position. Formally, it is deprived of
the benefit of uniform interpretation by the European Court of Justice. Nevertheless, since the text is almost identical to the Brussels Convention, it is
reasonably expected that case law produced under the latter will have an indirect effect upon the former.[21] For the rest, the Lugano Convention will probably have, at least in Europe, a decreasing constituency since most of its
Member States are at the same time candidates for accession to the European
Union and, therefore, to the Brussels Convention as well.

16–013   Furthermore, the judicial interpretation of the Brussels Convention has
had some side-effects which go well beyond its scope of application. First, it
significantly contributed to a convergence in the method of understanding
the law on both sides of the Channel. As already indicated, the principles
enunciated in interpreting the Convention also enjoy a persuasive force in

---

[18] See R. Rodière, *Introduction au droit comparé* (Paris, 1979) nos 52–53 pp. 94–97; R. David, The
international unification of private law, Int. Enc. Comp. Law, Vol. II, chap. 5, s. 247–316, in particulars. 248–259.
[19] *cf.* H. Kötz, "Rechtsvereinheitlichung - Nutzen, Kosten, Methoden, Ziele", RabelsZ 50 (1986)
1, at 7–8.
[20] See Collier (*supra* n. 4) 114 and specifically n. 11.
[21] Protocol 2 to the Lugano Convention on the uniform interpretation of that Convention
requires the courts of each contracting state to pay due account to any relevant rulings delivered
by courts of the other contracting states, and provides for a system of exchange of information
covering "relevant judgments under the Brussels Convention" as well (Art. 2). It remains to be
seen to what extent the Brussels Convention, as interpreted and developed by the European
Court of Justice, will be in fact conceived as a kind of ratio scripta which may inspire solutions
imperio rationis, although not ratione imperii; see Kerameus, "Das EuGVÜ innerhalb einer
Vielzahl von Rechtsquellen: Griechische Erfahrungen und Perspektiven", in E. Jayme (ed.), *Ein
internationales Zivilverfahrensrecht für Gesamteuropa* (1992) 383–390, at 387.

cases other than the one referred to the European Court of Justice. The Court itself regularly follows its previous opinions. Where, exceptionally, it does not, it proceeds to a typical common-law-influenced approach of distinguishing. This is in fact what the Court did in 1990 in *Dumez*[22] when restricting potential consequences from the earlier 1976 judgment in *Bier*[23] with regard to the scope of application of the tort-connected special basis of jurisdiction. By doing so, it came as close as any court on the European Continent to a *stare decisis* practice.

The second side–effect of the jurisdictional opinions of the Court of Justice consists in making clear to lawyers throughout the Member States the relevance of judicial cases in general. In fact, an essential part of lawyers' job consists in continuously reading considerable amounts of texts, among other things statutes, private contracts and judicial opinions. It is not revealing a professional secret by saying that most lawyers, if asked about their preferred kind of materials, would probably put judicial opinions in first place. I do not think that such choice is necessarily influenced by either quality or length of the materials: there are instances where legislative drafting is better than judicial opinion writing; there are also instances in which judicial opinions do not lag in length behind even sophisticated private arrangements. If nevertheless judicial opinions remain the preferred kind of reading materials, the explanation may be that only judicial opinions are made out of both, fact considerations and a full set of reasons. By contrast, statutes, even if accompanied by an introductory statement of reasons or other recitals, never include facts. And private agreements, while primarily dealing with facts, never include reasons. Thus, at the end of the day, only judicial opinions are built upon both facts and reasons and satisfy the human inclination towards the qualities of reality and reasoning.

16–014

4. Conclusion

My concluding point will be short, and a little worried. We have been witnessing in recent years stronger attention being paid to issues of procedure than substance. This seems to be true with respect to both, attempts at legal approximation and the actual discussion on legal matters of international trade. Important books on conflicts devote a substantial part of their contents to international procedure. Significant journals on the same topic deservedly flourish in the European Union as well as elsewhere. As far as I am concerned, I will be the last one to deny the relevance of procedure. In legal history as well as in the legal present, leading legal systems, such as Roman law, the common law or, for that matter, the law of the European Convention on Human Rights, have essentially focused on procedural issues. Article 6 of the ECHR, dealing with fair trial, currently draws about as much of the attention of the European Court on Human Rights as the rest of the Convention. Nevertheless this ostensible preponderance of procedure may generate some risks, for instance to unduly suppress the merits of a case or

16–015

---

[22] *Dumez v. Hessische Landesbank,* January 11, 1990, E.C.R. [1990] I–49, paras 10–20.
[23] *Bier v. Mines de potasse d'Alsace*, November 30, 1976, E.C.R. [1976] 1735 paras 13–25.

to artificially exaggerate the importance of distinguishing procedure from substance, which is already a tricky matter[24] and certainly does not need to be further encouraged. This situation, if correctly detected, might be improved by still stronger intensifying attempts also at comparison and approximation in the field of substantive law. My final suggestion would then be towards re-establishing a functional equilibrium rather than reducing the relevance of international civil procedure.

---

[24] See *supra* n. 4.

PART FOUR

CURRENT ISSUES IN INTERNATIONAL
COMMERCIAL ARBITRATION

CHAPTER 17

ARBITRATORS' CONTROL OF TACTICAL AND PROCEDURAL ISSUES IN THE 21ST CENTURY

DR JULIAN D. M. LEW

PARTNER, HERBERT SMITH, LONDON; HEAD OF THE SCHOOL OF INTERNATIONAL ARBITRATION, VISITING PROFESSOR, CENTRE FOR COMMERCIAL LAW STUDIES, QUEEN MARY, UNIVERSITY OF LONDON

1. Introduction

In his day Professor Clive Schmitthoff was a revolutionary exponent of the **17–001** *lex mercatoria*.[1] He believed there were in existence a set of international norms and rules which could, and which in some circumstances did, regulate international commercial agreements between parties from different countries. Professor Schmitthoff believed that for a more harmonious and effective international trade regime the development of the *lex mercatoria* was essential and inevitable.

Professor Schmitthoff was concerned about the substantive rules which **17–002** could be applied to international agreements as neutral, non-national or even transitional norms. They were intended to apply to the substance of an arrangement rather than the procedure in an arbitration.

---

[1] See, for example, Clive M. Schmitthoff, "The Law of International Trade", in *Commercial Law in A Changing Economic Climate*, 2nd ed, London 1981, pp. 18–33.

17–003   Over the last 25 years and in particular in the past decade, there has been a harmonisation of arbitration rules and procedures applied in international commercial arbitration. These procedures have been developed by practical compromises reflecting the essentials of national laws and the absolute of due process. The UNCITRAL Model Law,[2] the UNCITRAL Arbitration Rules,[3] and the New York Convention[4] have all directly influenced the way arbitrations are conducted. Institutional rules are increasingly close in their fundamental procedures and requirements.[5]

17–004   Professor Schmitthoff was a purist. He was concerned with the practical daily application of legal principles to determine the substantive issues in dispute. He was not concerned or involved with the tactical issues which parties adopt and which are fundamental to the way they present their cases in arbitration. In every arbitration, the parties' main interest is to win. They wish to achieve a result which vindicates the positions they have taken in pre-arbitration discussions. The parties' positions are often polarised. The reasons for the positions of the parties have taken may be pragmatic or tactical. The object of the parties' intention varies. Justice and the enforcement of rights in many cases become confused with the parties' ulterior motives and wider interests.

2. Fundamental tactical issues in international commercial arbitration

17–005   We will look at a selection of tactical issues which are fundamental in international commercial arbitration proceedings:

- Presentation of the arbitral issues (see section 2.1)

- Tactical issues for parties and arbitrators (see section 2.2)

- Duty of parties to comply with and perform the arbitration agreement (see section 2.3)

- The selection of suitable arbitrators is a key element (see section 2.4).

1. Presentation of the arbitral issues

17–006   In the preparation of every case, parties develop factual scenarios which form the basis for their contentions. The claim or defence, and the remedies

---

[2] UNICTRAL Model Law on International Commercial Arbitration, 1985. Currently adopted by more than 35 jurisdictions. Updates as to the status of the Model Law can be found on the UNCITRAL Web site at http://www.un.or.at/uncitral.
[3] United Nations Commission on International Trade Law Arbitration Rules (Resolution 31/98 adopted by the General Assembly on December 15, 1976).
[4] United Nations Convention on Recognition and Enforcement of Foreign Arbitral Awards Done at New York, June 10, 1958, United Nations Treaty Series, Vol. 330, p. 38 no. 4739 (1959). Updates as to the status of the New York Convention can be found on the UNCITRAL Web site at http://www.un.or.at/uncitral.
[5] See, for example, the emerging convergence of the Rules of the International Chamber of Commerce, of the London Court of International Arbitration, the American Arbitration Association, the Singapore International Arbitration Centre and the Stockholm Chamber of Commerce.

sought are dependant on the existence of certain facts. If these facts vary, the result may not be the same. The establishment of these facts is therefore crucial to the success of a party in any arbitration. Much depends on how the evidence is adduced and presented.

Often, arbitrators are told that the facts are not in real dispute. However, the story changes as the two parties present their arguments and contentions from their different perspectives: sometimes, it is like ships passing in the night, rather than colliding head on. This should not really be surprising because the facts are the real basis to the dispute and each party identifies them subjectively. The law and the money involved follow quickly behind.   **17–007**

In determining facts, one is reminded of the often-quoted example of the invitation to different people to look out of a window and to describe what they see. Without reference to one another and without some specific direction, invariably the individuals will see and describe something different. The analysis and identification of facts in an arbitration scenario does not differ greatly.   **17–008**

The facts on which a party chooses to base its case are often tactically determined. Time is spent deciding on what evidence to base the case. What documents should be presented? What information should be withheld unless asked for? Should experts be relied upon? Which witnesses should be presented? What questions should be posed and in what terms? Even issues of the applicable legal rules and the remedies sought are often carefully selected to comply with the facts as claimed. These are all tactical issues which are carefully considered.   **17–009**

2.2 Tactical issues for parties and arbitrators

How can arbitrators control the presentation of facts and tactical decisions taken by parties? Should arbitrators seek to control the arbitration process or should they remain passive and rely on the parties? Does international arbitration provide the basis for arbitrators to control the procedure within the confines of the respective claims of the parties?   **17–010**

Parties may take other tactical decisions to control, delay or expedite a hearing. Frequently this can involve seeking to place burdens and unbalance or disadvantage the other party.   **17–011**

A most obvious example is with the selection of arbitrators. There are many issues which are taken into account when parties nominate an arbitrator: expertise, reputation, availability and nationality. There are other factors which are less objective: will the arbitrator support or be sympathetic to the case to be presented? Has the arbitrator written and expressed opinions on relevant subjects?   **17–012**

Other tactics include seeking interim measures, security for costs, document discovery, etc. which impose a burden of time concerns on the other party. Even if such applications are unsuccessful, they put down a marker for the tribunal and place additional pressure on the other party. This may be particularly significant when there is a disparity in size of the parties, the law firms representing them and the international approaches and experience of those involved.   **17–013**

Sometimes parties will tactically try anything which they consider will provide them with an edge. This can mean something as simple as filing   **17–014** submissions late, failing to deliver all the documents relied on and perhaps untranslated, challenging or ignoring orders of the tribunal, and bombarding the other side with abusive correspondence.

17–015   None of these tactics are illegal, illegitimate or unfair. Their objective is to obtain the best result for the party using them. However, few people believe that the genuine right result will come from objective presentations alone. Whilst this might succeed in a national court, the composition of international tribunals are often considered by the parties to require "educating" in the needs of the specific case.

17–016   There may be little the arbitrators can do about it at the time. On the other hand, it can bode ill if the tribunal develop a poor view of the party concerned. This will not undermine a good case, but it may make the burden harder.

2.3 Duty of parties to comply with and perform the arbitration agreement

17–017   One should never forget that by agreeing to submit to arbitration certain disputes, parties have agreed to attend and participate in the arbitration process. This means co-operating in the appointment of the arbitrators, filing its case, following the tribunal's directions and then performing the ultimate award.

17–018   This obligation was given effect to in section 40 of the English Arbitration Act 1996 (hereafter all references to section are references to the Act). This provides:

(1)   The parties shall do all things necessary for the proper and expeditious conduct of the arbitral proceedings.

(2)   This includes–

(a)   complying without delay with any determination of the tribunal as to procedural or evidential matters, or with any order or directions of the tribunal, and

(b)   where appropriate, taking without delay any necessary steps to obtain a decision of the court on a preliminary question of jurisdiction or law (see sections 32 and 45).

17–019   Section 33 sets out the duties of arbitrators simply, concisely and uncontroversially. They must "act fairly and impartially as between the parties giving each party a reasonable opportunity of putting his case and dealing with his opponent".[6]

---

[6] This is a universally accepted principle. See, *e.g.*, Article IX (1)(b) of the European Convention on International Commercial Arbitration 1961, Art. V (1)(b) of the New York Convention on the Recognition and Enforcement of Foreign Arbitral Awards 1958, Art. 1460 of the French Code of Civil Procedure 1981, sections 1036 and 1042 of the German Code of Civil Procedure 1998, Sections 8 and 24 of the Swedish Arbitration Act 1999, Art. 12 and 18 of the UNCITRAL Model Law on International Commercial Arbitration 1985, Art. 16 of the AAA International Arbitration Rules 1997, Art. 15 of the ICC Rules of Arbitration 1998, Art. 14 of the LCIA Arbitration Rules 1998, and Art. 15 of the UNCITRAL Arbitration Rules 1976.

This breaks down to two fundamental objectives: the absence of bias and due process. This relates to the quality of the arbitrators and procedure according to which the arbitration is conducted.

17–020

2.4 The selection of suitable arbitrators is a key element

If the character, quality and ability of the arbitrators are right then the probability is that the arbitration will be properly and appropriately managed and controlled. Not only will due process be respected, but procedures can be adopted that will expedite and assist the arbitration process.

17–021

The question is whether either or both parties will be happy with this type of control, especially if their wider objectives in the arbitration are frustrated.

17–022

To ensure and assist in the due process obligations of arbitrators, the second limb of section 33(1) instructs the criteria for the procedures to be followed. Arbitrators must "adopt procedures suitable to the circumstances of the particular case, avoiding unnecessary delay or expense, so as to provide a fair means for the resolution of the matters falling to be determined".[7]

17–023

Here again there are two fundamental objectives: firstly, the procedure must reflect the circumstances of the particular case, and secondly, have the objective of minimising delay and expense.

17–024

These are welcome attributes, especially in international cases where parties come from different backgrounds, legal, cultural and political systems. Whatever their origins, the parties and their lawyers (and frankly some arbitrators as well) believe the legal system from which they come is the only real, pragmatic and fair way for a dispute to be determined.

17–025

Accordingly, for the common lawyer, lengthy hearings become an essential of justice. For the civil lawyer, the obligation to produce documents which are unhelpful to one's own case is considered to infringe a fundamental norm of the burden of proof and justice. Others from some countries do not consider there to be any objection to *ex parte* communications between the party and the arbitrator it nominated; this can work both to pass information to the party or to the tribunal.

17–026

This is not the place to analyse these attitudes or to suggest what is right or wrong. Suffice it to say here, subject to the prerequisite of partiality, none of these approaches should be rejected as wrong, or preferable to another. Each has its strengths, purposes and weaknesses. It also suffices to say here that the task for the qualified, experienced and able arbitrator is to blend all these systems and select aspects which are suitable for the characteristics and needs of each particular case.

17–027

---

[7] Although this principle is not expressly stated in any of the arbitration laws of major international arbitration centres, arbitral tribunals, no matter where their seats are, observe it. See, *e.g.*, Art. 14 of the Model Law on International Commercial Arbitration 1985, and Art. 24(1) of the ICC Rules of Arbitration 1998. See, also A. Redfern & M. Hunter, *Law and Practice of International Commercial Arbitration*, para. 5–19, 256 (3rd Ed. Sweet & Maxwell 1999), and *Fouchard, Gaillard & Goldman on International Commercial Arbitration*, para. 1194, 645 (E. Gaillard & J. Savage eds,) (Kluwer 1999).

3. Fixing an appropriate procedure for the case

17–028   Section 34 gives maximum authority to the arbitrators in fixing the procedural and evidentiary issues for the arbitration, subject to party autonomy. Accordingly, section 34(2) sets out a whole series of procedural and evidentiary matters which include:[8]

> "(c) whether any and if so what form of written statements of claim and defence are to be used, when these should be supplied and the extent to which such statements can be later amended;
> (d) whether any and if so which documents or classes of documents should be disclosed between and produced by the parties and at what stage;
> (e) whether any and if so what questions should be put to and answered by the respective parties and when and in what form this should be done;
> (g) whether and to what extent the tribunal should itself take the initiative in ascertaining the facts and the law;
> (h) whether and to what extent there should be oral or written evidence or submissions."

17–029   Sections 33, 34 and 40 separately and jointly give arbitrators the right to control the arbitration process and at least to limit the misuse in subjective terms of tactics that are adopted. They equally give parties the opportunity to persuade arbitrators to adopt procedural and evidential rules which will assist in their respective positions. The procedure adopted must be fair to both parties and should not place one party at an unfair advantage over another. In fixing the procedure the arbitral tribunal should look to the needs of the parties rather than the desires and experience of their lawyers.

17–030   In the context of conducting an effective, expeditious and reasonably priced arbitration there are various approaches which arbitrators can adopt. Each of these procedures is a blend of the approach of different legal systems. These include:

- Taking control of establishing the facts (see section 3.1);

- Proof of substantive law (see section 3.2);

- Appointment and instruction of experts (see section 3.3);

- Assistance with settlement (see section 3.4);

- Limiting time for oral argument and examination of witnesses (see section 3.5); and

- Interim awards and bifurcation of determinative issues (see section 3.6).

---

[8] See, also, on this matter generally 1996 Report on Arbitration Bill of the Departmental Advisory Committee on Arbitration Law, paras 166–176.

3.2 Taking control of establishing the facts

This is often the lengthiest and costly aspect of any arbitration. Traditionally, each party collects and presents the facts from its own files and witnesses, despite the fact that there is much overlap between them. This inevitably results in a lengthy battle over relatively minor but important facts. If elicited differently and in a less contentious way, the crucial facts may be more easily identified and more clearly referable to the dispute.   17–031

Section 34(2)(g) entitles the tribunal to decide itself whether and to what extent it should take the initiative in ascertaining the facts and the law. This is a real alternative to the partial and subjective presentation of the parties. This would suggest the arbitrators analysing the documents which the parties have presented and perhaps seeking additional documents so as to draw up a picture on facts. This could be done without each party presenting the statement of its facts within the context of its own submission.   17–032

The tendency today is with a presentation by each party of witness statements. Lawyers fluent in the language of the arbitration frequently prepare the witness statements. The half of the story is often contained in what the witness says. The other half is contained in what the witnesses do not say. The question is whether the whole story is ever shown.   17–033

If arbitrators were to take control of the collection of evidence, they themselves could directly interview witnesses and ask the questions they consider necessary. This would not preclude the parties subsequently examining the witnesses themselves: however this detailed examination would follow that of the tribunal. This could necessitate the presentation of an abstract by each party of the evidence that the witness could give, in light of his/her particular role in the conduct of the contract in the dispute in question.   17–034

3.2 Proof of substantive law

There are two main ways of determining the substantive law rules which are to be applied by the arbitral tribunal.   17–035

The first is to "argue" the law. This involves a presentation of the law, relying on the authorities, *i.e.* statute, case law and textbooks, to show and to persuade the tribunal what the law actually is. This approach follows the presumption in some civil legal systems,[9] and often considered appropriate in international commercial arbitration, that the arbitrators know the law.[10] The lawyers' role is only to assist the tribunal to understand what the relevant substantive law rules actually are.   17–036

The alternative is for the parties to state the law and to present opinions from professors and experts versed in that particular law. In this latter case, the tribunal find the law and the applicable rules as a question of fact. It is   17–037

---

[9] See, *e.g.*, Redfern & Hunter, *supra* n. 7, paras. 6–61—6–65 at 311–314; Julian Lew. "Proof of Applicable Law in International Commercial Arbitration", in *Festschrift für Otto Sandrock* 281–301 (K.-P. Berger, ed, 2000).
[10] Redfern & Hunter, *id.* at para. 6–61 at 311. See Lew & Shore, "International Commercial Arbitration: Harmonising Cultural Differences" 54–Aug *Disp. Resol. J.* 33, 36–7 [1999].

another piece in the factual jigsaw to be pieced together by the arbitrators. This is very much the common law approach.[11]

17–038   Once again here the parties' submissions suggest the answers to a question that each party wishes the arbitrator to answer. Sometimes the questions to which the parties proffer the law differ, or are at least different to the questions the arbitrators consider to be relevant. Whatever the question is the tribunal is still left with the necessity of trying to find the relevant law.

17–039   As already seen, section 34(1)(g) of the Arbitration Act 1996 gives arbitrators the power to decide whether it should itself take the initiative in determining the law to apply.[12] Unlike the national court judge who genuinely does know or should know the law which he is to apply, this is often not the case in international arbitration. Hence, to give arbitrators the power to ascertain the law would enable them to focus on the issues that they consider essential. In doing this a tribunal must follow an impartial and clear approach so that the parties understand the issues which concern the arbitrators and can have an input into the arbitrators' discussions and conclusions.

17–040   Whichever route a tribunal takes it should be clear and instruct the parties, if they are not agreed, how they wish the legal proof to be brought. A mixed system will only work if the parties are aware of how the arbitrators wish matters to be presented.

17–041   Section 37(1)(a)(i) gives the arbitrators power to appoint legal advisers to report to it and to the parties. This has a very special purpose. In no way should this detract from the right of parties to monitor and comment on the legal arguments and evidence that has been presented to the tribunal. If the tribunal identifies the legal issues which it wishes to determine, it will facilitate that the legal argument will be focused, limited and responsible to the substantive dispute.

3.3 Appointment and instruction of experts

17–042   Section 37(1)(a)(i) also gives the power for a tribunal to appoint and instruct its own technical experts. Parties rarely appoint an expert who does not support their case. Once again, frequently it is not what the expert says but what he does not say that is crucial to the case. In some circumstances, arbitrators can be faced with two diametrically opposed experts. Parties ask experts to answer the question to which an answer will support their case. This immediately places the arbitration on a direction that may be what one of the parties wants but which does not answer the arbitrators' concerns.[13]

17–043   The real issue may be more easily resolved if the technical issue is neutrally defined. Each case can be objectively described. If the experts are then asked to address these objectively defined issues, their answer would probably have been different and perhaps the issues agreed or at least narrowed.

---

[11] Redfern & Hunter, id. at paras 6–61—6–65 at 311–314. See Lew & Shore, *id.*

[12] See also, *e.g.*, Art. 1042 of the Netherlands Arbitration Act 1986, section 25 of the Swedish Arbitration Act of 1999, and Art. 27 of the UNCITRAL Model Law 1985.

[13] See in this respect *National Justice Compania Naviera S.A. v. Prudential Assurance Co. Ltd. (The "Ikarian Reefer")* [1993] 2 Lloyd's Rep. 68; [1993] FSR 563.

The advantage of appointing a tribunal expert, at the outset, rather than a party appointed expert, is to take control of the expert process. Nothing precludes the parties from having access to the expert, provided the tribunal's instructions are clearly understood. Nothing should be done which is not open to the parties. They should have the opportunity to hear all the questions put to the expert, to challenge that and to examine the expert. If there are visits to a technical facility both parties and their expert advisers should be entitled to attend at the time. Whatever the tribunal appointed expert does must be done openly, in front of both parties, and the arbitral tribunal.

17–044

3.4 Should arbitrators assist the parties with settlement?

Our contemporary western mindset is against arbitrators becoming involved in settlement discussions. The right of an arbitrator to become a mediator, in part or in whole, is generally considered inappropriate. The concerns of subsequent partiality because of views expressed and information received are overriding.

17–045

However, is it time for a change to this prejudice? Although cases are often polarised, arbitrators can frequently see, at an early stage, the real issues. If the parties were aware of the tribunal's views the dispute could be narrowed. This would enable the parties to settle. If the arbitrators were to indicate to the parties they believed that a certain issue could be resolved in a particular way and with some expedition, this might help the parties to resolve the problem and to settle their differences.

17–046

The concern of prejudice may be overstated. Experienced arbitrators (like judges and lawyers) are able to see both sides of the coin. The majority of cases have right and wrong on both sides. An indication from the tribunal, simply, at an early stage, that the tribunal does not find a particular argument convincing, will help parties to reassess their case and perhaps facilitate settlement discussions.

17–047

The desire to keep the arbitrators out of expressing an opinion on issues until the award could be rethought. Whilst not appropriate in every case, there are many disputes where parties wish to settle quickly, without excessive cost and on fair and reasonable terms. It is only where the parties succeed to settle with or without the direct help of the arbitrators, they can revert to the arbitration process.

17–048

3.5 Limiting time for written submissions and oral hearings

There is often a tendency to believe that one needs lengthy periods of time to prepare and present a case. Counsel state that they need several months to prepare written arguments and assemble evidence, and then numerous days or weeks to present a case at hearing. Sometimes this will be justified: the case may be complicated, the evidence strewn around the world and witnesses not easily contactable. However, there are equally cases where these lengthy delays are unnecessary. A debtor may be happy to delay the process, as this will add pressure to a party awaiting payment of significant moneys. There are also cases where one party has other tactical or commercial reasons to delay the proceedings for as long as possible.

17–049

17–050   The duty for arbitrators is to identify what is the genuine reason for the delays sought, and to fix the timetable in a fair and reasonable way. Provided the parties are able to present their case and answer that of the other side, lengthy periods of time are not necessary. If the tribunal takes control or at least some responsibility for collecting evidence and proving the law (as described above) it will be well able to determine appropriate times for submissions.

17–051   When it comes to fixing the time for hearings, one must presume that arbitrators will have read the papers and understand the case and what has been submitted to them. What the arbitrators do not understand, or what the arbitrators find unconvincing, they can raise directly with the parties in correspondence or at the hearing.

17–052   Lawyers sometimes ask for long periods of time for the examination of witnesses. Is this really necessary? If by the time of the arbitration hearing the issues have been narrowed and are clear there may not be that much difference between the parties. In some ways this supports the suggestion that examination of witnesses should be conducted by arbitrators, in the first instance at least. This would give the tribunal the opportunity, without prejudice to the arguments of the parties, to isolate and determine issues on those matters that they consider of particular importance.

17–053   For this reason, it will often be of great help where arbitrators are able to set down, well in advance, the time parties will have to present their arguments and their case. Experience shows that within reason even the drastic limitations of time rarely prejudice the presentation of the case of a party. It does, however, have the advantage of ensuring equality between the parties and can preclude one party hijacking an arbitration and the presentation of evidence or argument. The fact that an argument is repeated many times, or that a case is presented over a longer period of time, does not *per se* make the case stronger than a case that is simply and succinctly presented.

3.6 Bifurcation and interim awards

17–054   The proposal of an interim award is invariably branded, by the party that is opposed to it, as a delaying tactic. The request may contain a delaying factor. However, properly used, the identification of specific issues and their determination on an interim or partial basis can greatly help to expedite the proceedings. If issues can be identified which are determinative of the differences or the dispute between the parties, this will have the effect of saving time and money in the long run.

17–055   Where possible, arbitrators should identify the specific issues which are in themselves determinative of all or important parts. This too will expedite and simplify the arbitral procedure and will assist the overall dispute settlement procedure.

4. Conclusion

17–056   The motives and expectations of parties to arbitration differ. The parties may employ different tactics to achieve those motives and expectations. Whatever the form the motives and expectations take, the essential duties of parties and arbitrators do not change: parties have a duty to co-operate in the formation and functioning of the agreed method of dispute resolution. Arbitrators have a duty to act fairly and impartially, with reasonable expedition and always complying with the requirements of due process.

However, ultimately, the parties are seeking a resolution to their dispute. Arbitrators are the selected instruments to achieve this resolution. By taking control of the arbitration process and the definition of the issues in dispute, the tribunal can efficiently and expeditiously determine all or some of the issues. This will increasingly enhance arbitration as the preferred dispute resolution mechanism for the twenty first century.

CHAPTER 18

ARBITRATION'S DISCONTENTS: OF ELEPHANTS AND PORNOGRAPHY

PROFESSOR WILLIAM W. PARK

William W. (Rusty) Park is Professor of Law at Boston University, Counsel to the firm Ropes & Gray and Vice President of the London Court of International Arbitration. Currently he serves as Arbitrator on the Claims Resolution Tribunal for Dormant Accounts in Switzerland.

1. Abuse in Arbitration

1.1 Sources of unhappiness

18–001 Arbitrators often complain about frivolous motions and excessive requests for documentary discovery. Scholars worry that arbitration allows business managers to evade statutory norms that further vital public policies. Winning claimants grumble that judicial review of awards impairs neutrality and finality. Losing litigants lament that arbitrators apply the law either too strictly or not strictly enough, with insufficient court supervision. Discontent aims principally at the abuse of otherwise legitimate procedures, whether in arbitration itself or in related court actions.

18–002 Arbitrators and judges are increasingly aware of the need to discourage litigants from frustrating the basic aims of business arbitration: dispute resolution that is both relatively efficient and reasonably free from excessive judicial intervention. Although these aspirations do not lend themselves to facile analysis, they can help frame a dialogue that promotes reasonable choices about acceptable tactics, with sensitivity to the inevitable cultural predispositions existing in today's international commercial community.

1.2 "We know it when we see it"

For better or for worse, international commercial arbitration lacks any universally recognised standard-setting body. No arbitral "Miss Manners" sets worldwide procedural etiquette. Statutes and conventions contain only general principles (arbitrators must be free of bias, respect the limits of their authority and give each side an opportunity to present its case), and arbitral institutions leave arbitrators wide discretion in establishing facts and interpreting contracts. Treatises on international arbitration have only persuasive authority.[1]   **18–003**

Attempts to define "abuse" in arbitration bring to mind the line by U.S. Supreme Court Justice Potter Stewart reversing a movie theater's pornography conviction. Admitting an inability to define "hard core" pornography, Stewart added, "But I know it when I see it."[2]   **18–004**

British judges sometimes apply a similar (but less risqué) characterisation test in deciding that a floating crane was not a "ship or vessel" for purposes of insurance policy, Lord Justice Scrutton referred to the gentleman who "could not define an elephant but knew what it was when he saw one."[3]   **18–005**

Like pornography and elephants, abuse in arbitration is often easy to recognise but hard to define, leaving many fuzzy edges that frustrate rigorous discussion. A "we-know-it-when-we-see-it" approach has merit *faute de mieux*, as an analytic starting point that serves until something better appears. However, arbitrators and judges who apply such subjective tests for abuse must do so humbly, recognising their own cultural blinders and predispositions.   **18–006**

---

[1] See *e.g.*, W. Laurence Craig, William W. Park & Jan Paulsson, *International Chamber of Commerce Arbitration* (3rd ed., 2000); Alan Redfern & Martin Hunter, *Law & Practice of International Commercial Arbitration* (3rd ed., 1999); Yves Derains & Eric Schwartz, *Guide to the New ICC Rules of Arbitration* (1998); Philippe Fouchard, Emmanuel Gaillard & Berthold Goldman, *Traité de l'arbitrage commercial international* (1996); (English ed., also with John Savage, 1999).

[2] See *Jacobellis v. Ohio*, 378 U.S. 184 (1964) at 197 (concurring opinion), examining when erotic expression falls outside the limits of Constitutionally protected speech. The object of inquiry was a Louis Malle film *Les Amants* about a woman in an unhappy marriage. Justice Stewart concluded, ". . . the motion picture involved in this case is not that." See also Paul Gewirtz, On "I Know It When I See It", 105 *Yale L.J.* 1023 (1996).

[3] See *Merchants Marine Insurance Co. Ltd. v. North of England Protecting & Indemnity Association*, [1926] 26 Lloyd's Rep. 201, at 203; 32 Com. Cas. 165, at 172. In the Charente river near Rochefort, a steamship had collided with the crane. If the crane was a "ship or vessel" then the insurance company apparently paid three-fourths of the damages; otherwise the damage was paid by the North of England Protecting & Indemnity Association. See also *O'Callaghan v. Elliot* [1966] 1 QB 601 (a Denning decision that attributes the saying to Balfour); and *Cole Brothers Ltd. v. Phillips* [1981] STC 671, 55 Tax Cas 188.

1.3 Baselines

18–007   As Einstein reminded us, most things are relative. To speak of a practice as abusive requires some contemplation of alternatives: abusive compared to what? Since no consensus exists on what should be included within the malleable notion of abuse, conduct usually gets labelled "abusive" when pushed just a bit further than the observer's comfort level.

18–008   In some instances pettifoggery pure and simple (what the French call *objections de pure chicane*) results in time-wasting and costly motions.[4] More often, however, perceptions of abuse rest on cultural assumptions about the baselines and yardsticks that measure "normal" procedure.[5] Thus procedural diversity in arbitration serves both to enliven the game (allowing constant re-invention of civil procedure) and to frustrate the players (creating divergent perceptions of fairness that lead to a sense of abuse). Presuming one's own conclusion poses a constant risk.[6]

18–009   In a legally heterogeneous world, unfamiliar fact-finding techniques may leave litigants feeling short-changed or mistreated with respect to cross-examination, witness statements, experts (party-appointed and tribunal-selected) and the way law is proven.[7] It is as if one is playing both American football and British rugby at the same time, never knowing whether the ball can be thrown forward.

1.3.1 Documentary discovery

18–010   Seeking a cautionary tale about the importance of cultural baselines in arbitration, it would be hard to do better than documentary discovery, always a fertile source of irritation and conflict.[8] In many parts of the world, discovery means no more than giving the other side any documents to be relied upon during the hearings, so as to avoid undue surprise. In the United

---

[4] Arbitration, of course, has no monopoly on cheap litigation tactics. See *In Re Mailman Steam Carpet Cleaning*, 196 F.3d 1 (1st Cir. 1999), in which Judge Selya rejected a jurisdictional challenge based merely on an incorrect citation in the pleadings.

[5] On legal baselines in other contexts, see Richard Pildes & Cass Sunstein, "Reinventing the Regulatory State", 62 *U. Chicago L.Rev.* 1 (1995); Jack Beermann & Joseph Singer, "Baseline Questions in Legal Reasoning: The Example of Property in Jobs", 23 *Georgia L.Rev.* 991 (1989); Cass Sunstein, "Constitutionalism after the New Deal", 101 *Harv. L. Rev.* 421 (1987).

[6] For recent contributions to understanding cultural differences in this area, see; Yves Fortier, "The Minimum Requirements of Due Process in Taking Measures Against Dilatory Tactics: Arbitral Discretion in International Commercial Arbitration—A Few Plain Rules and a Few Strong Instincts", *ICCA Working Group III: Achieving Efficiency Without Sacrificing Due Process, Improving the Efficiency of Arbitration Agreements and Awards: 40 Years of Application of the New York Convention* (ICCA, Gen Ed. A.J. van den Berg, 1999) (quoting from W. Wordsworth's 1809 poem, "Alas! What Boots the Long Laborious Quest?"); Fali Nariman, "The Spirit of Arbitration", 16 *Arb. Int'l* 261 (2000), taking for prooftext II Corinthians 3:6 ("The letter kills but spirit gives life.")

[7] See *e.g.*, Julian Lew & Larry Shore, "Harmonizing Cultural Differences in International Commercial Arbitration", 54 *Dispute Resolution J.* 32 (August 1999); Julian Lew, "Proof of Applicable Law in International Commercial Arbitration", *Festschrift für Otto Sandrock* 581 (K.-P. Berger, ed., 2000); Michael Bühler & Carroll Dorgan, "Witness Testimony Pursuant to the IBA Rules of Evidence in International Commercial Arbitration," 17 *J. Int'l Arb.* 3 (No. 1, 2000).

[8] See generally, Peter Griffin, "Recent Trends in the Conduct of International Arbitration: Discovery Procedures and Witness Hearings", 17 *J. Int'l Arb.* 19 (No. 2, 2000).

States and England, however, lawyers must often produce documents to prove the adversary's case.[9]

For Americans, discovery sometimes serves as a vacuum cleaner to suck up all the minimally relevant pieces of paper that might possibly yield "information ... reasonably calculated to lead to the discovery of admissible evidence."[10] Analogous practices in England exist notwithstanding recent Woolf reforms abrogating the "*Peruvian Guano* rule" that gave entitlement to documents leading to a "train of inquiry" toward evidence.[11] **18–011**

Continental lawyers often complain about the abusive "fishing expeditions" and scatter-gun tactics of American lawyers. To this, American lawyers reply that in bargaining for arbitration their client did not agree to give up basic procedural rights. "How can we prove our claim or defense without your documents?" they ask.[12] **18–012**

In dealing with requests for documents, the concept of "proportionality" is often invoked. Arguably, the time and expense of producing documents should bear a reasonable relationship to the expected enlightenment. However, assumptions about what type of discovery is normal inevitably affect conclusions on this cost/benefit calculation. **18–013**

At the heart of this divergence lie fundamentally different ideas of what commercial dispute resolution should be. Is the arbitrator actively seeking to learn the whole truth? Or is the arbitrator's role simply to see whether one side can support a claim or defence using its own resources? **18–014**

1.3.2 Costs

Similar cultural differences arise with respect to allocation of costs. While in many places the loser bears the prevailing party's legal costs, this practice is the exception in the United States. Most institutional arbitration rules give the arbitrators discretion to award costs against the loser, often leading to lively discussions within the arbitral tribunal. European arbitrators sometimes dismiss American objections to the "loser pays" rule by saying, "But this is an international arbitration." Their presumption seems to be that European practices are by definition international, a premise that brings to **18–015**

---

[9] The alleged benefits of such discovery include a better perspective of the strengths and weaknesses in one's case, leading to settlement or sharper definition of issues, as well as a greater ability to identify an adversary's misleading evidence. For comparisons of national practices, see Julius Levine, *Discovery* (1982) (England and the United States); Arielle Elan Visson, *Droit à la production de pièces et discovery* (1997) (England and Switzerland).

[10] Federal Rules of Civil Procedure, Rule 26(b)(1). Sanctions for non-compliance, set forth in Rule 37, include preclusion of introduction of the evidence, striking certain pleadings and even fines for contempt of court. See generally, Thomas Mauet, *Pretrial* (4th ed. 1999); John Beckerman, "Confronting Civil Discovery's Fatal Flaws", 84 *Minn. L. Rev.* 505 (2000); Michael Silberberg, "Federal Discovery", *N.Y. Law J.*, 6 July 2000, at p. 3.

[11] See Court of Appeal decision in *Compagnie Financière et Commercial du Pacifique v. Peruvian Guano Co.*, [1882] QB 55 (documents in plaintiff's possession might have contradicted alleged oral agreement). For the current state of play on English discovery, see *1998 Civil Proceedings Rules*, Part 31.

[12] The American lawyer might go even further, arguing that to prepare the case requires depositions of the other side's witnesses.

mind the obverse North American arrogance which gives the label "World Series" to a set of entirely regional baseball games.

18–017   On occasion, the reasonableness of legal fees can also cause problems. For an American, there may be nothing inherently unreasonable about a contingency fee based on a percentage of the amount in dispute. Less certain is whether this amount should be assessed against the loser in an international arbitration, or should instead be replaced by a healthy hourly rate.

2. Neutrality and efficiency

18–018   International business managers usually agree to arbitrate as a way to enhance both neutrality and efficiency in the resolution of disputes. Focusing on these goals can help identify two types of abusive practices: (i) court actions that unduly inject intervention by natural judges; and (ii) excessive emphasis on procedural rights that adds cost and delay.

2.1 Abuse of court procedures

18–019   When contracting parties from different countries mistrust each other's legal system, arbitration can level the playing field in the event of disputes, reducing the risk of unfamiliar procedures, perhaps in foreign language before xenophobic judges.[13] Controversies can be settled under rules that give neither side an improper advantage, with a presiding arbitrator who shares neither side's nationality.

18–020   Immoderate requests for judicial intervention in arbitration thus constitute one form of abuse. Overly zealous recourse to courts sabotages the aspiration toward a more neutral form of dispute resolution. Perspectives differ widely on when judicial recourse is unreasonable. An arbitration's winner protests that it never anticipated ending up in court, while the losing side complains that it did not expect to relinquish all right to appeal on the merits of the case. A claimant argues that pre-award judicial attachment of assets enhances arbitration's potential effectiveness, while the respondent says that its agreement to arbitrate was predicated on exclusion of national courts until after the award.[14]

18–021   Sometimes recourse to courts take the form of an improper action to enjoin arbitration.[15] More commonly, however, problems lie in excessive review of awards.

---

[13] The perception of litigation bias may be as harmful to the development of cross-border commerce as its reality. One study found evidence that in federal civil actions in the United States, foreigners actually fare better than domestic parties. See Kevin Clermont & Theodore Eisenberg, "Xenophilia in American Courts", 109 *Harvard L. Rev.* 1122 (1996). An explanation for this counter-intuitive finding might lie in a fear of American courts that leads foreign litigants to settle rather than continue to final judgment, unless they have particularly strong cases.

[14] Compare *McCreary Tire & Rubber v. CEAT*, 501 F.2d 1032 (3rd Cir. 1974) (pre-award attachment denied) with *Carolina Power & Light v. Uranex*, 451 F. Supp. 1044 (N.D.Cal 1977) (pre-award attachment allowed).

[15] For a complex situation in which a Montréal court was asked to enjoin part or all of an ICC arbitration abroad, see *Lac d'Amiante du Québec v. Lac d'Amiante du Canada*, Cour d'appel, Province de Québec, December 6, 1999 (participation in Québec litigation deemed a waiver of right to bring claims in New York arbitration).

Most arbitral centres provide some judicial scrutiny of awards rendered **18–023** within their territory, at least as a default rule absent contractual exclusion of such review.[16] An efficient framework for arbitration requires balancing concern for finality against the need for some procedural safeguards. While a golden mean remains elusive, modern arbitration statutes usually seek a counterpoise between arbitral autonomy and judicial control.

The most popular model for judicial review grants a right to challenge awards **18–024** only for excess of authority and basic procedural defects such as bias or denial of due process.[17] Another paradigm supplements scrutiny of an arbitration's procedural fairness with a right to appeal an award's substantive legal merits.[18] Some countries provide options (requiring litigants either to elect[19] or to reject[20] merits appeal), while others supply hybrid grounds for vacatur, such as "manifest disregard of the law"[21] or "arbitrariness,"[22] which imply something beyond a simple mistake, but not necessarily clear excess of authority.

Even the best of judicial review procedures inevitably open the door to **18–025** potential abuse. The very existence of court supervisory powers can work mischief when high stakes tempt attorneys to adopt aggressive strategies that involve court intervention. The lawyer for a disappointed party can hardly tell a client to be gracious about a multi-million dollar loss. Inevitably, counsel will be urged to exploit the smallest opening for judicial scrutiny of the award.

One solution to abusive court proceedings might be to eliminate *all* judi- **18–026** cial review at the arbitral situs,[23] or at least to permit complete arbitral autonomy as an option.[24] While courts must scrutinize awards before granting

---

[16] See generally W. Laurence Craig, William W. Park, Jan Paulsson, *International Chamber of Commerce Arbitration,* chap. 28 (3rd ed, 2000).

[17] See, *e.g.,* Federal Arbitration Act §10; French *NCPC* Art. 1502; Swiss *LDIP* Art. 190; UNCITRAL Model Law Art. 34. While these last three statutes do not enumerate bias explicitly, some of their other bases for vacatur (such as lack of due process or violation of public policy) could serve to deal with this defect.

[18] See 1996 English Arbitration Act §§67–69. *See* William W. Park, "The Interaction of Courts and Arbitrators in England", 1 *Int'l Arb. L. Rev.* 54 (1998), reprinted in 13 *Mealey's Int'l Arb. Rep.* 21 (June 1998).

[19] Perhaps the most widely-discussed American case on opting for judicial review is *Lapine Technology v. Kyocera,* 130 F.3d 884 (9th Cir. 1997).

[20] See 1996 English Arbitration Act §69 (requiring exclusion of appeal on questions of English law).

[21] Introduced by the U.S. Supreme Court through dictum in *Wilko v. Swan,* 346 U.S. 427 (1953), "manifest disregard of the law" builds on notions of arbitrator excess of authority. See *Advest, Inc. v. McCarthy,* 914 F.2d 6, 9 (1st Cir. 1990). Court decisions have made clear that in international arbitrations, awards rendered in the United States may be vacated for "manifest disregard." See *Alghanim v. Toys "R" Us,* 126 F.3d 15 (2nd Cir. 1997). An expanded notion of "manifest disregard" has been applied in employment discrimination claims. See *Halligan v. Piper Jaffray,* 148 F.3d 197 (2nd Cir. 1998), *cert. denied,* 526 U.S. 1034 (1999).

[22] Swiss *Concordat intercantonal sur l'arbitrage,* Art. 36(f) (defining arbitrariness to include "evident violations of law or equity").

[23] At least one scholar suggests complete elimination of pre-enforcement judicial review. See Philippe Fouchard, "La Portée internationale de l'annulation de la sentence arbitrale dans son pays d'origine", 1997 *Rev. Arb.* 329, 351–352. On the problematic aspects of this proposal, see William W. Park, "Duty and Discretion in International Arbitration", 93 *Am. J. Int'l L.* 805 (1999); William W. Park, "Why Courts Review Arbitral Awards", in *Festschrift für Karl-Heinz Böckstiegel* 579 (Jens Bredow *et al.,* ed. 2001).

[24] For example, if neither party has a Swiss residence or place of business, federal arbitration law in Switzerland allows an explicit exclusion of all pre-enforcement court review (*déclaration expresse/ ausdrückliche Erklärung*). See *LDIP,* Article 192. Otherwise, federal standards provide

them *res judicata* effect, an arbitral venue chosen only for convenience or neutrality might dispense with judicial review before the enforcement stage, particularly for disputes that have no effect at the place of arbitration.

2.2 Abuse of procedural rights[25]

18–027   Business managers choose arbitration not only to promote neutrality, but also in the hope that it will make dispute resolution cheaper and quicker. Undue invocation of procedural rights derails advancement of this objective of efficiency in arbitral proceedings.

2.2.1 The tension between fairness and efficiency

18–028   Even the best of rules have unintended consequences, like ripples on a still pond after a stone is thrown across the water's surface. Thus an arbitrator often walks a tightrope, trying to balance efficiency against careful consideration of all arguments—desiderata which in practice do not always marry easily.

18–029   The inevitable tension between efficiency and fairness takes different forms depending on the stage of a business relationship. Both sides may want some ideal of efficiency when a contract is signed. However, after the dispute arises, the party with the weaker case may look for a fuller opportunity to present its case. Consequently, cheerful talk of arbitration's speed and economy is often belied by the unhappy experience of proceedings turned extremely sour, ending up as long and costly as court actions.

18–030   For example, well into the arbitration, one side may wish to make a new claim that requires the arbitrators' approval. In deciding whether to authorise the claim, arbitrators must be mindful of the need to move the proceedings along in an orderly manner, while still allowing each side to present substantially all of its case.

18–031   The contrast between fairness and efficiency appears crisply in the English Arbitration Act's first canon of construction, which calls for "fair resolution of disputes . . . without unnecessary delay or expense." The path to promoting this worthy objective will not always be self-evident, since the thoroughly fair examination of an argument sometimes makes the arbitration slower and more expensive. What appears as undue delay to a claimant expecting an easy win may be dressed as essential due process to a defendant anxious to present its case more fully. Grants of discretion to the arbitral tribunal (such

---

judicial scrutiny of awards related to matters of procedural integrity and public policy (*LDIP* Article 190). The parties may also choose the more expansive scrutiny under cantonal standards, which include vacatur for "arbitrariness." Belgium allows exclusion of recourse to courts if no party is a Belgian resident or citizen. See Art. 1717 (4), *Code judiciaire*. This right does not apply to a Belgian office of a foreign company ("*une personne morale ayant en Belgique son principal établissement ou y ayant une succursale*").

[25] Continental legal systems have a particularly strong tradition of struggling with how to deal with abuse of otherwise legitimate rights. See *e.g.*, Art. 2 of the Swiss *Code civil*. The stipulation that the law will not protect a clear abuse of a right (*abus manifeste d'un droit*) operates in tandem with a requirement of good faith. See generally, *Abuse of Procedural Rights: Comparative Standards of Procedural Fairness* (*Festschrift für Rolf A. Schütze*, Michele Taruffo, ed., 1999).

as UNCITRAL Model Law Article 19, giving arbitrators power to act in an "appropriate manner") provide some help through the procedural thicket. However, more specific principles and cases are often needed for guidance on dealing with the conflict between efficiency and due process.

2.2.2 Problematic elements of arbitral procedure

In addition to excessive documentary discovery, other candidates for the label   **18–032**
of arbitral pollutants include refusal to pay a portion of the advance on costs, spurious challenges to subpoenas and abusively high arbitrators" fees. Four in particular merit special notice: (i) too much paper, (ii) spurious attacks on arbitrators" independence, (iii) improper jurisdictional challenges, and (iv) claims, defensces and motions that are frivolous in nature. The difficulty in dealing with these offenders, of course, is that they are linked to elements of arbitral procedure which, in their right place, can serve the ends of justice.

2.2.2.1 Excessive submissions
In many proceedings, arbitrators are needlessly bombarded with documents.   **18–033**
Requests for a "core bundle" often go unheeded, with litigators unable to understand (either intentionally or innocently) that emphasis requires selectivity.

2.2.2.2 Spurious attacks on arbitrators' independence
While it is entirely appropriate for arbitrators to disclose financial links and   **18–034**
close personal connections with parties, the search for independence can sometimes become harassment. One sees unwarranted objections to the other's nominee because of experience in industry, "unconscious bias" or friendship with another arbitrator. Even if a challenge is ultimately rejected, dealing with it takes time and money.[26]

2.2.2.3 Improper jurisdictional challenges
Occasionally, challenges to arbitral jurisdiction form part of strategies to   **18–035**
derail proper consideration of a claim. Thus arbitrators must resist requests for interim jurisdictional awards that are only dilatory tactics, while still mindful that some initial jurisdictional determinations do make sense as a way to avoid the cost of hearings on matters beyond their power.

2.2.3 Objections to evidence

Arbitrators decide cases neither by flipping a coin nor by cutting a baby   **18–036**
in half, but by weighing evidence. This implicates hearing objections to

---

[26] For recent case law on arbitrator impartiality under English law, see the Court of Appeal decision in *AT&T Corp. & Lucent Technologies Inc. v. Saudi Cable Co.*, [2000] 2 Lloyds Rep. 127 (2000 W.L. 571190), first reported in *The Times*, May 23, 2000 (arbitrator's links to a competitor of one party in the arbitration), and *Laker Airways v. FLS Aerospace Ltd.*, [1999] 2 Lloyd's Rep. 45 (arbitrator and advocate were barristers in the same chambers). See also Armen H. Merijan, "Caveat Arbitor: Laker Airways and the Appointing of Barristers as Arbitrators in Cases Involving Barrister-Advocates from the Same Chambers", 17(1) *J. Int. Arb.* 31 (2000).

admission or exclusion of testimony and documents. In the absence of clear evidentiary standards for international arbitration, both the objections and the rulings thereon can appear unfair and arbitrary.

18–037   Understandably, trial lawyers often try to have evidence excluded merely because it might hurt their client. During hearings, objections are often raised in abbreviated form ("lack of foundation" or "leading question") which may or may not be familiar to counsel from another legal system. What is or is not admissible can vary significantly from one place to another. In some but not all countries corporate officers can testify for their company. Approaches to hearsay evidence can vary considerably from one jurisdiction to another.

18–038   While everyone seems to agree that the normal rules of evidence do not apply in arbitration, there is less consensus about what rules do apply. The 1999 version of the *IBA Rules on the Taking of Evidence in International Commercial Arbitration* provide five grounds for exclusion of testimony: (i) lack of relevance, (ii) privilege, (iii) commercial or technical confidentiality, (iv) political sensitivity and (v) compelling "considerations of fairness or equality".[27]

18–039   Many of the reasons underlying exclusion of evidence in court do not apply to arbitration. Since arbitration is not subject to appeal on the merits, there is less need to worry about what does or does not get into the record.[28] However, to protect an award from annulment, arbitrators are generally careful *not* to exclude evidence in a way that could arguably prejudice one side's right to present its case.

18–040   The predisposition of many arbitrators for admitting evidence does not mean that an arbitrator should allow undue surprise, misleading questions or testimony with little probative value. But it does mean that counsel should be encouraged to think carefully before making objections.

18–041   One way to reduce the prospect of abusive objections is for counsel to give arbitrators the "benefit of the doubt," in the sense of trusting them to understand the probative value of testimony. Admittedly, this may not come easily to advocates who feel compelled to adopt aggressive behavior to impress clients.

18–042   Arbitrators accept some documents and testimony *de bene esse*, avoiding any attribution of fixed weight. One frequently hears expressions such as, "We take the document for whatever it's worth" or "*Ça vaut ce que ça vaut.*" In addition to relevance and privilege (included within the IBA tests mentioned above) the following questions are often helpful: Is the testimony reliable? Has the witness misunderstood the question? Is counsel genuinely surprised by a question or a document? Is there privilege? Is there a clearly defined policy reason (for example, fishing for information to be used in another proceeding) to keep a question from being answered or a document from being produced?

---

[27] Art. 9, IBA Rules of Evidence (1999 Version). The same Art. also permits production of documents to be resisted on the ground of "unreasonable burden" and "loss or destruction".

[28] This principle may change, at least in the United States, to the extent American courts follow the approach in *Halligan v. Piper Jaffray*, 148 F.3d 197 (2nd Cir. 1998), *cert. denied*, 526 U.S. 1034 (1999), where the court exhibited great zeal in setting aside an award for "manifest disregard of the law."

Opting for arbitration may imply accepting a different calculus in the search   **18–043**
for truth, with both costs and benefits. In most commercial arbitrations the
purpose of the hearing will be to find out what the parties" shared expectations were at the time they entered into the contract. Normally, this goal will
be served by letting a witness answer the question.

3. Searching for fairness

It is sometimes said that arbitration provides an avenue to achieve greater   **18–044**
commercial equity. This search for fairness, however, carries its own potential for abuse.

A business manager who gets the rough side of the law appeals to notions   **18–045**
of "right" that go beyond statute, precedent or the letter of the contract.
However, for the counter party who is denied the result mandated by law and
the language of the agreement, the "fair" result will seem an unjust re-writing
of parties" agreement.

Requiring awards to be reasoned may affect the arbitrator's ability to   **18–046**
stretch for extra-contractual notions of fairness. In the United States, traditionally arbitrators were encouraged to give no explanation for their decisions. Such "check the box" awards were seen as reducing the hooks on which
the unhappy loser could hang a challenge for "manifest disregard of the
law."[29]

By contrast, under the international arbitration model, represented by   **18–047**
ICC and LCIA arbitration as well as the new AAA international rules, arbitrators typically explain why they decided as they did. One result is that decisions based on concepts of general commercial fairness rather than specific
contract language become difficult. Arbitrators who arrogate to themselves
unauthorised power to decide *ex aequo et bono* or in *amiable composition*
may find their awards vacated for exceeding their mandate.

4. Discouraging abuse

4.1 Arbitral proceedings

Few anti-abuse mechanisms are more effective than an experienced and capa-   **18–048**
ble arbitral tribunal.[30] Just as in real estate the three most important elements
are "location, location, location," so in private dispute resolution the golden
trilogy is "arbitrator, arbitrator, arbitrator."

In addition, the parties will want to be clear about the procedural ground   **18–049**
rules, which may involve choices about discovery and standards of evidence,
perhaps with an election of the IBA Rules. Often, of course, these matters are
not high on the priority list of contract drafters, whose focus is more on

---

[29] However, in *Halligan v. Piper Jaffrey, supra*, the court noted an absence of reasoned opinion
as one element in its decision to vacate an award for "manifest disregard of the law."
[30] Facetiously, one might suggest that a party whose arguments are fundamentally flawed might
be minded to nominate a less-gifted arbitrator not sharp enough to see through the smoke and
mirrors of specious arguments. This can backfire, however, if the opposing side nominates a
competent arbitrator with a significant influence on the tribunal's chairman.

domestically-nurtured concerns related to agreement's substantive provisions than on dispute resolution mechanisms.

18–050   In some cases, the threat of cost allocation can deter abuse. In extreme situations, frivolous motions and unfounded claims may even justify an order requiring the winner to bear the loser's legal fees. The *in terrorem* effect of allocating costs against the abusive party works best when understood early in the proceedings, and will probably have more impact on sophisticated lawyers who have seen such punishment administered.

4.2 Court-related abuse

18–051   The best way to avoiding court-related abuse is to choose the right arbitral situs. In this context, the most appropriate model of judicial review is one in which courts exercise limited control over matters of basic procedural fairness while leaving the arbitrators a relatively free rein on the merits of the controversy.

18–052   This paradigm, however, loses much of its force when arbitration implicates consumer contracts[31] or conflicts with basic public policies.[32] Ironically, the value of fair adjudication that justifies arbitration in international business will often condemn it in a domestic context. While it is entirely proper to prefer cool-headed arbitrators rather than juries swayed by unduly emotional rhetoric, it is quite another matter to impose arbitration without informed consent,[33] at a prohibitive cost[34] or with an arbitrator selected directly or indirectly by the industry drafting the contract.

---

[31] Theoretically arbitration permits consumers to benefit from lower prices reflecting reduced litigation expenses. In practice, of course, such cost savings can just as well go into the pockets of the business owners. For an economic analysis of arbitration, see Eric Posner, "Arbitration and the Harmonization of International Commercial Law", 39 *Va. J. Int. Law* 647 (1999); Keith N. Hylton, "Agreements to Waive or to Arbitrate Legal Claims: A Legal Analysis", 8 *Supreme Court Economic Review* 209 (2000).

[32] Justice Stevens' dissent in the landmark U.S. decision allowing arbitration of international antitrust disputes argued that "the elected representatives of the American people would not have us dispatch an American citizen to a foreign land in search of an uncertain remedy for the violation of a public right." *Mitsubishi v. Soler*, 473 U.S. 614, at 666 (1985). The dissenting justice, of course, took his own system as the baseline for normalcy, rather than the specter of foreign courts that may have haunted the business manager when signing the contract.

[33] See *Hill v. Gateway 2000 Inc.*, 105 F.3d 1147 (7th Cir. 1997) (arbitration clause in box containing computer ordered by mail). Compare *Badie v. Bank of America*, 67 Cal. App. 4th 779, 79 Cal. Rept. 2d 273 (1st Dist.) (1998), review denied February 24, 1999, refusing to enforce an arbitration clause included in a bank's routine statement of account. While some countries have statutory safeguards against abuse in consumer contexts (*e.g.* EU Council Directive 93/13/EEC, [1993] O.J. (L95) 29 and *French Code civil* Art. 2061), the United States have none.

[34] One recent decision struck down as "unconscionable" (under UCC § 2–302) an ICC arbitration clause in a consumer sale of computer products, due to the high costs. *Brower v. Gateway 2000*, 676 N.Y.S. 2d 569 (A.D. 1 Dept. 1998). One must note, however, that the high cost of arbitration can come from exaggerated requests for punitive damages, particularly when an advance on costs is calculated in proportion to amount in dispute.

CHAPTER 19

POWER OF ARBITRATORS TO FILL GAPS AND REVISE CONTRACTS TO MAKE SENSE

PROFESSOR DR. KLAUS PETER BERGER, LL.M.,
CENTER FOR TRANSNATIONAL LAW (CENTRAL), MÜNSTER
UNIVERSITY, GERMANY

1. Introduction

The issue of the power of arbitrators to fill gaps and revise contracts in international commercial arbitration is of extreme practical relevance. It also belongs to the most controversial issues of arbitral scholarship of the past three decades.[1]   **19–001**

---

[1] See Craig, Park and Paulsson, *International Chamber of Commerce Arbitration* (2nd ed. 1990) at p. 143.

Two of the greatest comparative lawyers of the twentieth century, *René David* and *Clive Schmitthoff*, have inspired this discussion in the late 1970s and early 1980s. *David's* contribution to the Tenth International Congress of Comparative Law in Budapest in 1978[2] and *Schmitthoff's* groundbreaking article on "Hardship and Intervener Clauses" in the Journal of Business Law of 1980[3] have set the stakes for a discussion that is still continuing today. In fact, their views of and approaches to this intricate problem are more topical than ever.[4] The following arguments are intended to shed some light on the current state and the future prospects of the search for the arbitrators' power to fill gaps and revise contracts.

2. The traditional dogma: adaptation and supplementation between contract and procedure

19–002   The main reason for the quasi perpetual search for a satisfactory solution lies in the fact that this discussion is centred around a seemingly clear-cut dogma: the procedural character of arbitration is said to be incompatible with the contractual nature of adaptation and gap-filling. This dogma has two aspects. The first is of a contractual (see section 2.1), the second of a procedural nature (see section 2.2).

2.1 The contractual perspective

19–003   The contractual perspective relates to the natural weakness of complex long-term "relational" contracts. The time factor makes these contracts vulnerable to the change of technological, political or economic circumstances or the omission of certain contractual provisions. Given the significance of long-term contracts, these problems are "a fact of life"[5] and arbitrators as the natural judges of international trade and commerce should be able to cope with them. However, their resolution requires a balancing of two antagonistic classical principles of contract law. The principle *"pacta sunt servanda"* stands for the sacrosanct character of the parties' initial agreement. The notion of *"clausula rebus sic stantibus"* reflects the idea of creating a certain flexibility of the initial party agreement over the duration of the contract in order to maintain the initial economic equilibrium. In this contractual context, a decision in favour of or against an arbitrator's power to fill gaps or revise contracts depends on how the "eternal dilemma"[6] between the ideal of sanctity of contracts and the need for commercial flexibility is resolved.

---

[2] David, "La technique de l'arbitrage comme procédé de révision des contrats" in *Reports to the Tenth International Congress of Comparative Law Budapest 1978* (Péteri and Lamm eds.) (1981) at pp. 269 *et seq.*
[3] Schmitthoff, "Hardship and Intervener Clauses" (1980) *J.B.L.* at pp. 82 *et seq.*
[4] See *infra* section 6.
[5] Bernini, in *New Trends in the Development of International Commercial Arbitration and the Role of Arbitral and other Institutions* (Sanders, ed.) (ICCA congress series no. 1,1983) at p. 193.
[6] Bruner, in (2000) *Int'l Constr.L.Rev.* at p. 47.

2.2 The Procedural Perspective

The procedural perspective relates to the traditional view of arbitration as it **19–004**
is reflected in Article 7 (1) of the UNCITRAL Model Law on International
Commercial Arbitration and provisions of other domestic arbitration laws.
These provisions are said to reflect a notion of arbitration that is limited to
traditional legal "disputes", requiring from the arbitrator a "yes or
no"—decision with respect to a party's non-performance or violation of contractual duties.[7] It is argued that this procedural notion of arbitration is
incompatible with the creative character of decisions required in cases of
adaptation and gap-filling which involve the evaluation of economic issues
and the rewriting of the parties' contract.[8] From this perspective, gap-filling
and contract adaptation are not arbitrable, unless the arbitrator is freed from
the constraints of substantive law and is authorised by the parties to act as
"*amiable compositeur*".[9]

Ultimately, the discussion on the admissibility of contract adaptation and
supplementation by arbitrators boils down to a clash of two basic philosophies: the idea of creating rights through contractual intervention is generally regarded as a matter of contract law which seems to be reserved to the
parties or to third party interveners acting on their behalf. The notion of
adjudication of pre-existing rights is considered as a matter of procedural
law. The formal character of the latter seems to be irreconcilable with the creative character of the former.[10] In his well-known study on hardship clauses
published in 1976,[11] *Fontaine* has asked the question that is still discussed
today with respect to gap-filling and contract revision by international arbitrators: "Is this still arbitration?".

3. Classification

Much has been written about possible classifications of situations where the **19–005**
filling of gaps or the adaptation of contracts is necessary. Over the past
decades two classifications have emerged, according to which we will structure the discussion.

3.1 Initial gaps—supervening gaps

A first distinction relates to the filling of "initial" and of "supervening" **19–006**
gaps.[12]

---

[7] See the statement of the German delegation during the drafting of the Model Law in UN Doc.
A/CN.9/263, para. 15: ". . .the activity of the arbitral tribunal is concentrated on the interpretation and application of contractual agreements and legal provisions".
[8] See Vagts, in *International Investment Disputes: Avoidance and Settlement* (Rubin and Nelson,
eds.) (1985) at pp. 29, 36 *et seq.*
[9] Fouchard/Gaillard/Goldman, *On International Commercial Arbitration* (1999) No. 37.
[10] See David, *supra* n. 2, at p. 271.
[11] Fontaine, "Hardship Clauses" in (1976) *DPCI* at pp. 51, 79.
[12] See Bernini/Holtzmann, in (1975) *Revue de l'Arbitrage* at pp. 18, 43 *et seq.*; Sanders, *Quo Vadis
Arbitration?* (1999) at p. 141 *et seq.*; Peter, *Arbitration and Renegotiation of International
Investment Agreements* (2nd ed. 1995) at p. 254.

Initial gaps are those deliberately left open by the parties during the drafting of the contract. In this case, the arbitrator is not regarded as competent to fill the gap.[13] Supervening gaps occur after the conclusion of the contract and are unforeseen at that moment. Here, the arbitrator may be authorised to fill the gap if the conditions of the applicable procedural and substantive law[14] are met. The justification for this distinction is drawn from a procedural and a substantive aspect.

19–007   The procedural aspect relates to the fact that in the case of initial gaps the parties have agreed from the outset to have a certain point decided by them later or, failing such agreement, settled for them by the arbitrator. It is thus the most obvious case where one may argue that there is no "dispute" as required by the arbitration laws. However, if the parties later fail to reach an agreement on the filling of the gap, there is at least a "difference" between them which suffices to establish the competence of an arbitral tribunal, *e.g.* under section 82 (1) of the English 1996 Arbitration Act.[15]

19–008   The second argument is related to the first but touches upon the substantive side of the problem. It is based on a particularity of English[16] and American[17] contract law. If the parties, instead of agreeing on all material terms, have concluded a mere "agreement to agree" or a "contract to negotiate", English and American courts refuse to enforce such agreements because the terms are too indefinite to fashion a legal remedy based on the parties' intent. The parties may perhaps avoid these problems by conveying to the arbitrators the power to fill gaps only for clearly specified matters such as the period of performance and the price and any consequential damages, as compared to a general revision clause.[18] However, the risk remains that such agreements to agree are considered unenforceable by an international arbitral tribunal acting under English or American law.[19]

---

[13] Fouchard, Gaillard and Goldman, *supra* n. 9, no. 33.

[14] See for the interaction of the *lex arbitri* and the *lex causae infra* sections 4.2 and 4.3.

[15] Section 82 (1) of the Arbitration Act 1996 reads: "In this Part..., 'dispute' includes any difference"; see Kröll, *Ergänzung und Anpassung von Verträgen durch Schiedsgerichte* (1998) at pp. 66 *et seq.*; see for adaptation Fouchard, Gaillard and Goldman, *supra* n. 9, no. 41.

[16] *May and Butcher v. R.* [1934] 2 K.B. 17; *Walford v. Miles* [1992] 2 A.C. 128 *et seq.*; McKendrick, *Force Majeure and Frustration of Contract* (2nd. ed. 1995) at p. 110: ". . .it is. . .questionable whether a clause can validly provide, in an entirely general and open-ended manner, that the parties shall use their best endeavours to agree "whatever modifications to the contract may be fair and reasonable'. It is considered that the modifications have to be confined to specified matters, such as the period for performance and the price, and any consequential changes".

[17] *Lahaina-Maui Corp. v. Tau Tet Hew,* 362 F 2d. 419; *Transamericana Equipment Leasing Corporation v. Union Bank*, 426 F 2d. 273, 275; *Joseph Martin Jr., Delicatessen v. Schumacher*, 52 NY 2d. 105; *Magna Development Co. v. Reed,* 228 Cal. App. 2d. 230, 236; *White Point Company v. Paul B. Herrington et al.*, 268 Cal. App. 2d. 458, 468: "The rule is that when something is reserved for the future agreement of both parties, the promise can give rise to no legal obligation until such future agreement. Since either party, by the very terms of the promise, may refuse to agree to anything to which the other party will agree, it is impossible for the law to affix any obligation to such a promise".

[18] McKendrick, *supra* n. 16, at p. 110; Mann, in *Further Studies in International Law* (Mann ed.) (1990) at pp. 252, 259; Maskow, in *Die Anpassung langfristiger Verträge im internationalen Wirtschaftsverkehr* (Kötz and von Marshall eds.) (1984) at pp. 81, 97; see also Hunter, Paulsson, Rawding and Redfern, *The Freshfields Guide to Arbitration and ADR* (1990) at p. 45.

[19] See *infra* 4. for the assumption of "implied terms" in these cases.

3.2 Authorisation—no authorisation

During the drafting of the UNCITRAL Model Law the question whether a **19–009** provision should be included dealing with the problem of contract revision and gap-filling was discussed. The discussions in the Working Group have revealed that there is one decisive classification that can and should be made here.[20] This distinction relates to the prior authorisation by the parties.[21] The same differentiation has been made in many arbitral proceedings such as the well-known *AMINOIL*-arbitration.[22]

3.2.1 Authorisation by the parties

There is an important reason why things look different if the parties have **19—010** authorised the arbitrators to adapt or supplement the contract. In these cases, the principle of *"pacta sunt servanda"* does not speak against but *in favour* of the arbitrators' competence to reshape the contract.[23] They are called upon to implement the agreement of the parties on gap-filling or contract adaptation. Such an authorisation may be included in the standard arbitration agreement. Thus, in the ICC arbitration no. 7544, the parties had authorised the tribunal to decide on "all disputes arising out of the contract *including a change of the contract itself*".[24] By including such a clause in the contract, the parties have made it clear beyond doubt that they consider the fair distribution of mutual profits and gains over the duration of the contract more important than legal certainty.[25]

Thus, the primacy of party autonomy in international commercial arbi- **19–011** tration[26] may have a decisive influence on the determination of an arbitrator's power to adapt contracts or fill gaps. It should be inherent in the principle of party autonomy that the parties may entrust a third party to decide on how a contract should be adapted or supplemented.[27] It would even be desirable to subject this process to the same procedural safeguards which arbitrators have to observe, thus enhancing legal certainty in international trade.[28] The German delegation in the UNCITRAL Working Group has made it clear that such a party agreement does not have to be made *expressis verbis* but may also be derived from the significance and

---

[20] See Redfern and Hunter, *Law and Practice of International Commercial Arbitration* (3rd ed. 1999) nos. 8–17 *in fine*; *cf. also* for proposals to include in the Model Law a provision dealing with the arbitrator's authority to adapt contracts and fill gaps and requiring an "express authorisation" by the parties, UN Doc. A/CN.9/WG.II/WP.41, para.11; A/CN.9/WG.II/WP.44, para. 32.
[21] Fouchard, Gaillard and Goldman, *supra* n. 9, Nos. 34 *et seq.*
[22] *Kuwait v. The American Independent Oil Company (AMINOIL)*, ILM 1982, 976, 1015: ". . .there can be no doubt that. . .a tribunal cannot substitute itself for the parties in order to make good a missing segment of their contractual relations—or to modify a contract—unless that right is conferred upon it by law, or by the express consent of the parties"; see Mann, *supra* n. 18, *ibid.*
[23] Draetta, Lake and Nanda, *Breach and Adaptation of International Contracts* (1992) at p. 202.
[24] ICC (Partial) Award No. 7544 in (1999) *Clunet* at pp. 1062, 1063 with n. Hascher, *ibid.*, at pp. 1064, 1065.
[25] Baur, in *Festschrift Steindorff* (1985) at pp. 511, 512; see also Harms, in (1983) *Der Betrieb* at pp. 322, 325.
[26] See generally Berger, in (1993) *The American Revue of International Arbitration* at pp. 1 *et seq.*
[27] See the UNCITRAL Working Group, in UN Doc. A/CN.9/233, para. 16.
[28] UN Doc. A/CN.9/WG.II/WP.44, para. 19.

purpose of the agreement.[29] Thus, the issue of whether the parties did actually confer such a power on the arbitral tribunal is one of contract interpretation.[30] At the same time, the German delegation emphasised that in the second category of cases, where the parties have not authorised the arbitrators, a stricter perspective should be taken because "if the parties do not want an arbitration of this kind, it should not be imposed on them".[31]

3.2.2 No authorisation

19–012   If no express or implied authorisation can be found in the contract the arbitrators are left with a tough task. They have to look for legal authority to intervene in the parties' contract without their consent. Such an authorisation can be found in the applicable law, *i.e.* the arbitration law or the law applicable to the substance of the dispute. As will be seen later,[32] this search for authority is made difficult mainly for two reasons. First, the absence of a provision in the contract allowing adaptation or gap-filling necessarily emphasises the principle of sanctity of contracts. Secondly, even if the arbitrators conclude that adaptation or gap-filling is just and fair in a given case, the complex interaction between procedural law and contract law often stands in the way to such a modification or supplementation of the parties' rights under the contract.[33]

3.3 Incidental decisions on contract adaptation and gap-filling

19–013   There is a third group of cases which can be excluded from the following discussion because it falls outside the problem area. It relates to traditional disputes over a legal issue in which an incidental decision is required from the arbitral tribunal with respect to the validity, meaning, scope or effect of a hardship or other adaptation clause, *e.g.* because the respondent raises a relevant defence.[34] The same applies if an arbitrator is called upon to decide whether a party has violated its duty to renegotiate the contract under a hardship or renegotiation clause and is thus liable for damages.[35] In these scenarios, no special authorisation is required to vest the arbitrators with a decision-making power. The issue forms an integral part of the parties' dispute. The arbitrator's decision forms an interim step in the process of making the

---

[29] UN Doc. A/CN.9/263, para. 15.

[30] Fouchard, Gaillard and Goldman, *supra* n. 9, No. 41; Hascher, in (1999) *Clunet* at pp. 1064, 1065.

[31] UN Doc., *supra* n. 29, para. 15 *in fine*.

[32] See *infra* sections 4.2 and 4.3.

[33] See *infra* sections 4.2 and 4.3.

[34] See Bernini, in (1998) *ICSID Review—Foreign Investment Law Journal* at pp. 411, 420; Berger, in (1993) *International Economic Arbitration* at p. 84; see also UN Doc. A/CN.9/WG.II/WP.44, paras 9, 13.

[35] Fontaine, *supra* n. 11, at p. 79; *see* for the intricate problems to determine whether a party's violation of its duty to (re-)negotiate can lead to a claim for damages Horn, in *Adaptation and Renegotiation of Contracts in International Trade and Finance* (Horn, ed.) (1985) at pp. 173, 188; Berger, in (2000) *RIW* at pp. 1, 8; *AMINOIL* Award, *supra* n. 22, at p. 1014; ICC Awards No. 6515 and 6516 in (1999) XXIV *Yearbook Commercial Arbitration* at pp. 80, 100 *et seq.*

final award. It is thus covered by the tribunal's general authority granted to it by the arbitration agreement.[36]

3.4 Borderline cases

Sometimes, however, this authority may go rather far, depending on the atti-   **19–014**
tude of the applicable substantive[37] law. In fact, in "real life", the distinction between gap-filling, contract adaptation and interpretation is not so easy.[38] Very often, the point becomes a matter of degree.[39] Thus, under German civil law, if a contractual stipulation for a specific issue has been omitted from the contract, judges and arbitrators may apply the principle of the "supplementary construction" (*ergänzende Vertragsauslegung*) of contractual terms derived from section 157 of the German Civil Code (*Bürgerliches Gesetzbuch, BGB*), thereby closing gaps in the contract if and to the extent that this is in line with the hypothetical will of the parties.[40] From the perspective of German substantive law, this part of the arbitrators' decision-making still falls under the arbitrator's general task to apply the *lex causae*. In fact, a judge or arbitrator may resort to the German rules of hardship only after remedies such as the supplementary construction of the contract have been exhausted.[41] Similarly, a tribunal acting under English law may avoid the unenforceability of "to be agreed"-clauses[42] by applying "principles of construction" and assuming an implied term in the contract in cases where the parties have commenced the performance of the contract.[43] Also, under American law, a court or arbitral tribunal may supply an omitted contract term by "implication" based on the expectations of the parties or on aspects of justice and fairness.[44] From a procedural perspective, however, these approaches come very close to gap-filling without express or implied authority by the parties.

4. The sources of the arbitrators' powers

The reference to the fact that an arbitrator's interference in a contractual   **19–015**
relationship may be regarded as permissible from the perspective of the applicable contract law and impermissible from the perspective of the law that governs the procedure reveals one of the major weaknesses of the present discussion on the arbitrator's power to fill gaps and adapt contracts.

The simple reference to the fact that "German law allows the adaptation of contracts by arbitrators" while "English law is hostile to the idea of

---

[36] Fontaine, *ibid.*; Berger, *supra* n. 34, at pp. 84 *et seq.*; Kröll, *supra* n. 15, at pp. 19 *et seq.*; Peter, *supra* n. 12, at p. 254.
[37] See for the interplay of procedural and substantive law in these cases *infra* section 4.
[38] Horn, *supra* n. 35, at p. 184.
[39] Mann, *supra* n. 18, *ibid.*
[40] See Nicklisch, in (No. 3 1988) *J.Int'l Arb.* at pp. 35, 38.
[41] *cf.* German Federal Supreme Court, BGHZ 81, 143; BGHZ 90, 74.
[42] See *supra* n. 16 and 17.
[43] *Hillas & Co. v. Acros Ltd* [1932] All ER 494; *Foley v. Classique Coaches* [1934] 2 K.B. 1; Kröll, *supra* n. 15, at pp. 96 *et seq.* and 160 *et seq.*
[44] Farnsworth, *Contracts* (3rd ed. 1999) § 7.16.

rewriting the contract for the parties" neglects the special scenario of the international arbitral process where aspects of substantive and procedural law are closely intertwined. The drafters of the Model Law, after extensive discussion, realised this problem. They ultimately refrained from inserting a provision on adaptation and supplementation of contracts. In their view "it was difficult to separate questions pertaining to procedural law and questions pertaining to substantive law and that, therefore, the Model Law, as a system of procedural rules, should not contain rules which might touch upon substantive rights of the parties".[45]

19–016   Thus, in order to determine the power of an arbitrator to adapt or supplement a contract in an individual case, one has to refer *simultaneously* to three different legal sources: the arbitration agreement, the law applicable to the arbitration (*lex arbitri*) and the law applicable to the substance of the dispute (*lex causae*). It is obvious that within this three-tier system, we are faced once again with the clash of substantive and procedural law mentioned above.[46]

4.1 The arbitration agreement

19–017   The arbitration agreement is the basic source of the arbitrator's powers. Usually, the traditional terminology that "all disputes arising out of or in connection with this contract" are referred to arbitration suffices to invest an international arbitral tribunal with a decision making power that covers all aspects of possible disputes. The situation is different with respect to the adaptation and supplementation of contracts. Here, the perceived contractual and creative nature of the arbitrator's decision is said to require a specific contract clause that contains an express authorisation by the parties *in addition* to the usual arbitration agreement.[47] This authorisation may be contained in the arbitration agreement itself.[48] It can also be derived from a hardship or other adaptation or renegotiation clause which refers to the arbitration agreement contained in the same contract if the adaptation or gap-filling mechanisms provided for in the contract have failed. In order to be workable in practice, the authorisation should indicate in a clear and precise manner the triggering events which confer the creative competence on the arbitrators and guidelines which indicate the scope and extent to which adaptation or supplementation should be effected.[49]

19–018   In view of this significance and effect of the authorisation in the arbitration agreement, the main issue is whether an arbitral tribunal may do so even *without* special authorisation by the parties.[50] The answer to this question

---

[45] UN Doc. A/CN.9/245, para. 21; see also UN Doc. A/CN.9/WG.II/WP.44, para. 10: ". . .the. . . model law would only regulate procedural aspects of adaptation of contracts; it would not regulate substantive conditions, as may be contained in a contract clause or in substantive law provisions, for the right of the party to request an adaptation of the contract".

[46] See *supra* section 2.

[47] Craig, Park and Paulsson, *supra* n. 1, at p. 144; Bernini, *supra* n. 34, at p. 421.

[48] See for a practical example *supra* n. 24.

[49] Craig, Park and Paulsson, *supra* n. 1, at p. 144; Bernini, *supra* n. 34, at p. 421; Berger, *supra* n. 35, at p. 8; see also *infra* IV.

[50] See UN Doc. A/CN.9/WG.II/WP.35, para. 21; Sanders, *supra* n. 12, at p. 141.

depends on whether the traditional wording of arbitration clauses covers the adaptation and supplementation of contracts. In 1988, an ICC tribunal presided by Lord *Wilberforce* held that the traditional ICC arbitration clause may be interpreted as covering the adaptation of contracts if the clause is contained in a long-term contract that contains "a number of provisions which may require adjustment over the period of that contract".[51] This interpretation was based on the particular circumstances of the case. The tribunal emphasised that "in other contexts [the standard ICC arbitration agreement] might be given a narrower scope".

In fact, it is by no means clear whether a traditional arbitration clause can **19–019** be interpreted in such a wide manner.[52] The case decided by the *Wilberforce* tribunal comes close to an implied authorisation by the parties that was derived from the significance and purpose of the agreement and the large number of "open" contract clauses contained therein.[53] Absent such an implied authority, international arbitral tribunals are reluctant to accept such a far reaching competence. This reluctance is based on a reasonable interpretation of the contract and the increased responsibility of business-men for their contractual relations. This responsibility is derived from the presumption of the professional competence of the parties of international business contracts which is generally regarded by international arbitrators as a principle of transnational commercial law.[54] This presumption serves an important function in this context. It is regarded by the arbitrators as a mea-surestick for the distribution of risks in the contract. Based on this presumption, international arbitrators assume that it is up to the parties to take precautions in their contract against unforeseen circumstances. If no such clauses are inserted into the contract, arbitrators are reluctant to overrule the principle of "*pacta sunt servanda*" in favour of contract adaptation and gap-filling.[55] They assume that absent a special clause in the contract, the parties

---

[51] ICC Award no. 5754 (unpublished) cited by Craig, Park and Paulsson, *supra* n. 1, at p. 112.

[52] See UN Doc. A/CN.9/WG.IIWP.41, para. 8 *in fine*: ". . . the usual arbitration clauses may be interpreted as being limited to the mandate to adjudicate legal disputes arising from breach or non–performance of contracts".

[53] See the proposal of the German delegation during the drafting of the UNCITRAL Model Law, *supra* n. 29.

[54] See ICC Award No. 1990 in (1974) *Clunet* at p. 897; no. 1512 in (1974) *Clunet* at p. 905; no. 2291 in (1976) *Clunet* at p. 989; no. 2438 in (1976) *Clunet* at p. 969 with n. *Derains, ibid.* at p. 971; no. 3130 in (1981) *Clunet* at p. 932; no. 3380 in (1981) *Clunet* at p. 927; no. 5364 in (1991) *Clunet* at p. 1059; *cf. generally* Berger, *The Creeping Codification of the Lex Mercatoria* (1999) at p. 236.

[55] See, *e.g.* ICC Award No. 1512 reprinted in *Collection of ICC Arbitral Awards* (Jarvin and Derains eds.) (1990) at pp. 3, 4: "As a general rule, one should be particularly reluctant to accept [the doctrine rebus sic stantibus] when there is no gap or lacuna in the contract and when the intent of the parties has been clearly expressed . . . Caution is especially called for, moreover, in international transactions where there is generally much less likely that the parties have been unaware of the risk of a remote contingency or unable to formulate it precisely"; *cf.* also ICC Award No. 6281 in (1990) *Yearbook Commercial Arbitration* at pp. 96, 98: ". . .otherwise [*i.e.* if the tribunal would adapt or supplement the contract] any business transaction would be exposed to uncertainty, or even rendered impossible altogether, whenever the mutual covenants are not performed at the time at which the contract is concluded"; see also n. by Derains to ICC Award no. 2291, reprinted in *Collection of ICC Arbitral Awards* (Jarvin and Derains eds.) (1990) at pp. 275, 277; no. 2291 in (1976) *Clunet* at p. 989; no. 2404 in (1976) *Clunet* at p. 995; n. *Derains* to ICC Award No. 8486 in (1998) *Clunet* at p. 1050; Carbonneau, in (1985) *Col.J.Transn'l L.* at pp. 589, 593 ("Given the parties" [presumed] professional sophistication as international merchants, ICC arbitrators interpret party silence about possible future contingencies as a conscious decision to

have indicated that the principle of sanctity of contracts shall prevail. The risk of changed circumstances or discovery of gaps beyond the requirements of hardship or similar institutions of the applicable substantive law is to be borne by the parties. The financial reward stipulated in the contract already discounts the business risk resulting from the particular transaction.[56] Since the parties do not want an arbitration of that kind, adaptation and supplementation may not be imposed on them by the arbitrators.

4.2 The arbitration law (lex arbitri)

19–020   While the arbitration agreement provides the basic authority to adapt or supplement a contract, it is the law applicable to the arbitration, the *lex arbitri*, which determines whether the arbitrators are procedurally authorized to decide on the contract adaptation or supplementation. If no such authority exists, there is no enforceable award under the New York Convention since the question whether a decision constitutes an enforceable award is decided not by the *lex fori* of the enforcement court but by the law applicable to the arbitral procedure.[57]

19–021   There is, however, a significant problem with this relationship between the arbitration agreement and the *lex arbitri*. Only very few arbitration laws contain express provisions dealing with the arbitrators' authority to adapt or supplement contracts. Among them is the 1986 Dutch Arbitration Act. It provides in Article 1020 (4) that "the parties may agree to submit . . . to arbitration . . . the filling of gaps in, or the modification of, the legal relationship between the parties . . .". Likewise, section 1 (2) of the 1999 Swedish Arbitration Act provides that "the parties may authorise the arbitrators to supplement contracts beyond the boundaries of the principles of the construction of contracts".[58] With their reference to an agreement of the parties, both the Dutch and Swedish Act confirm the two basic premises of this field of international arbitration law. First, the arbitrator needs an authorisation from the parties in order to intervene in the contractual relationship between the parties. Secondly, it is not the arbitration agreement alone, but the agreement *in its combined effect* with the *lex arbitri* which conveys the necessary authority to the arbitral tribunal. Article 1 (2) of the 1988 Bulgarian Law on International Commercial Arbitration as amended in 1993 contains a similar provision without, however, requiring an agreement of the parties.[59]

---

assume the risk of such eventualities"); Poznanski, in (no. 3 1987) *J.Int'l Arb.* at pp. 71, 80 *et seq.* ("Parties intending to contract can protect themselves [against the risk of changed circumstances] by fortuitous events clauses, and in the absence of such clauses, the contract is presumed to be speculative"); Fouchard, Gaillard and Goldman, *supra* n. 9, no. 36.

[56] Bernardini, in *New Trends in the Development of International Commercial Arbitration and the Role of Arbitral and other Institutions* (Sanders ed.) (1983) at pp. 211 *et seq.*: ". . . in today's world the contractual know–how is sufficiently developed and accessible so as to permit the parties to an international contract, experienced as they normally are and assisted by skillful legal counsels, to appreciate in advance the advantages and disadvantages of incorporating in their contract a hardship clause . . .".

[57] Van den Berg, *The New York Arbitration Convention of 1958* (1981) at p. 46.

[58] Para. 1 (2) Swedish Arbitration Act of April 1, 1999; see generally Ek, in (2000) *RIW*, at pp. 31 *et seq.*

[59] Art. 1 (2) Bulgarian Law on International Commercial Arbitration, reprinted in *International Handbook on Commercial Arbitration Vol. I* (van den Berg and Sanders eds.) at Bulgaria Annex I–1: "The [sic] international commercial arbitration resolves civil property disputes arising from

In those frequent cases where the applicable arbitration law remains silent   **19–022**
on the arbitrator's authority to fill gaps and adapt contracts, one has to refer
back to the competence of domestic courts in that particular jurisdiction.
Here, the principle of synchronised competences applies: if the courts have
the authority to adapt or supplement the contract, then the arbitral tribunal
acting under the arbitration law of that jurisdiction enjoys the same competence.[60] If the domestic procedural law does not provide a rule for national
courts, one has to go back to the substantive law of that jurisdiction which
serves as an indicator for contract adaptation and gap-filling by courts and,
accordingly, by arbitral tribunals. By way of example, German procedural
law does not provide an express authorisation for contract adaptation or gap-
filling by courts or arbitral tribunals. However, section 317 of the German
Civil Code contains a rule of substantive law which, according to a predominant view of German legal doctrine, allows contract adaptation by German
courts if both parties cannot agree on the adaptation modus.[61] Using this
rule of substantive law as a statutory basis, arbitral tribunals are also allowed
to adapt contracts.

If, however, neither the arbitration law nor the procedural law nor the sub-   **19–023**
stantive law of the seat of the arbitration provides any basis for contract
adaptation or supplementation by arbitrators, the arbitrators are acting as
third party interveners outside the procedural realm of an arbitration, irrespective of the fact that the parties wanted to have an "arbitral tribunal"
decide the case.[62] The effects of any decisions taken by the "tribunal" in that
direction can only be interpreted according to the law of obligations. Consequently, they have to be judged according to the law applicable to the contract.[63] This law also decides on the review or correction of that decision by
the ordinary courts. In this case, the tribunal is acting outside the procedural
ambit of the applicable arbitration law.[64]

4.3 The law applicable to the substance (lex causae)

The tribunal's authorisation by the parties and its procedural competence to   **19–024**
adapt contracts and fill gaps have to be distinguished from the substantive
requirements and validity of that decision. A strict distinction has to be
drawn between the formal question of whether the contractual intervention
required from the arbitrator may be called arbitration in the proper sense
and the related but distinct inquiry of whether the tribunal considers the

---

foreign trade relations as well as disputes about the filling of gaps in a contract or its adaptation
to newly arisen circumstances. . .".

[60] Sanders, in (1975) *Revue de L'Arbitrage* at pp. 83, 84; Sanders, *International Encyclopedia of
Comparative Law*, Vol. XVI, Chap. 12 at p. 70; Schlosser, *Das Recht der internationalen privaten
Schiedsgerichtsbarkeit* (2nd ed. 1989) no. 29; Schmitthoff, *supra* n. 3, at p. 88; Nicklisch, *supra* n.
40, at pp. 38 *et seq.*; Nicklisch, in (1989) *RIW* at pp. 15, 18; Peter, *supra* n. 12, at p. 257;
Bernardini, *supra* n. 56, at p. 214; Berger, *supra* n. 34, at p. 86; Kröll, *supra* n. 15, at p.19;
Holtzmann and Neuhaus, *A Guide to the UNCITRAL Model Law* (1994) at pp. 1126, 1131;
Fouchard, Gaillard and Goldman, *supra* n. 9, no. 43.
[61] See BGH LM § 157 (Ga) No. 14; Kröll, *supra* n. 15, at pp. 58 *et seq.*
[62] Peter, *supra* n. 12, at p. 256.
[63] See Zweigert and von Hoffmann, in *Festschrift M. Luther* (1976) at pp. 203, 211.
[64] Berger, *supra* n. 34, at pp. 86 *et seq.*; Peter, *supra* n. 12, at pp. 256 *et seq.*

requirements of the adaptation process to be met or not. These substantive standards are governed by the *lex causae*. It is the law applicable to the substance of the dispute which has to be consulted to decide on the validity of the adaptation clause and of the adaptation standards agreed upon by the parties, the canon of interpretation to be applied to such clauses and the methods of adaptation to be applied by the arbitrators if the contract does not contain specific instructions for the tribunal.[65] Also, the *lex contractus* has an important effect on the outcome of the contract adaptation or supplementation by the arbitrators. The contract terms established by the tribunal in adapting or supplementing the contract may not violate the mandatory rules of the law applicable to the contract.[66]

4.4 The interaction of the legal sources

19–025   This survey on the combined effect of the arbitration agreement, the applicable arbitration law and the *lex causae* reveals that provisions such as the one included in the 1986 Dutch Arbitration Act do not provide a final answer to the search for the arbitrator's power to adapt or supplement the contract. If the applicable arbitration law allows contractual interference by the arbitrator but the *lex causae* does not provide for an adequate substantive basis for this interference, the arbitrator is acting in a legal vacuum and cannot modify or adapt the contract.[67] Conversely, the provisions on contract adaptation and supplementation contained in the *lex causae* remain without effect if the applicable arbitration law does not contain a corresponding procedural authority for the arbitrator.[68]

19–026   From a practical perspective, however, it has to be borne in mind that in view of the restriction on the setting aside of awards at their seat, the significance of the *lex arbitri* in this complex interaction of different legal sources is substantially reduced. In practice, therefore, international arbitrators focus more on the law applicable to the substance of the dispute in order to determine the basis and scope of their power to adapt and supplement contracts.[69]

5. Contract adaptation "that makes sense"

19–027   From the perspective of international business practice, the practical question "does contract adaptation or supplementation by international

---

[65] Horn, in Horn, Fontaine, Maskow and Schmitthoff, *Die Anpassung langfristiger Verträge* (1984) at p. 37; Briner, in (1989) *Yearbook Commercial Arbitration* at p. 12; Berger, *supra* n. 34, at p. 87; see for an instructive example from recent arbitral practice ICC Awards nos 6515 and 6516, *supra* n. 35, at pp. 96 *et seq.* ("Amendment Clauses" in Service Agreement and Sub–Contracts).

[66] See UN doc. A/CN.9/WG.II/WP.44, para. 30.

[67] See Briner, in *Planning Efficient Arbitration Proceedings, The Law Applicable in International Arbitration* (van den Berg ed.) (1996) at pp. 362, 371; Berger, *supra* n. 34, at p. 87; Horn, in (1992) *Tel Aviv University Studies in Law* at pp. 137, 147: "As a rule, the arbitrator — like the court — must decide according to the rules of the applicable law. If German law is the *lex causae*, the arbitrator may adopt [or adapt?] the contract if circumstances result in the collapse of the foundation of the transaction (*Wegfall der Geschäftsgrundlage*)".

[68] See Berger, *supra* n. 34, at pp. 87 *et seq.*; Berger, *supra* n. 35, at p. 9; Kröll, *supra* n. 15, at pp. 9 *et seq.*; Peter, *supra* n. 12, at p. 257.

[69] Briner, *supra* n. 67, at pp. 370 *et seq.*; Kröll, *supra* n. 15, at p. 245; Berger, *supra* n. 35, at p. 9.

arbitrators lead to a result that makes sense" is almost as important as, if not more important than the dogmatic and technical issues relating to the arbitrators' legal authority.

It is certainly true that the parties to an international contract may trust **19–028** the arbitrators' ability to appraise the economic relations between the parties and, for this reason, may give them the mandate to adapt or supplement their contract.[70] There is, however, an obvious difference in the degree of competences required from an arbitrator called upon to settle a traditional dispute and one whose task is to reorganise the parties' contractual relationship in a manner "that makes sense". In the latter case, the arbitrator must be competent not only in the legal field but also in the economic, technical, financial etc.[71] He is faced not with "commercial" but with "economic" arbitration. Relying solely on the arbitrator's commercial experience and his sensitivity to the economic expectations and commercial interests of the parties is no guarantee for a result "that makes sense". Therefore, the parties are always well advised to provide the tribunal with concrete criteria which may guide them in their decision making. Frequently, however, the contract merely refers to **19–029** such "soft" criteria as "fair and equitable", "reasonable" or the arbitrators' duty to "restore or maintain the economic equilibrium of the contract" or to modify the contract "along the lines and the philosophy of the present agreement".[72] There are two reasons for this stealth of workable criteria for contract adaptation and gap-filling. First, the circumstances which surround the need to refashion the contract cannot be foreseen by the parties at the moment of the conclusion of the contract. Secondly, refashioning the contract requires sufficient flexibility and leeway. A tight framework of prefabricated rules and principles would not do justice to this multi-dimensional character of the arbitrators' decision making. This creative quality of the arbitrators' task finds its counterpart in the parties' duty to renegotiate. The prevailing international opinion maintains that this does not imply a duty to reach agreement but only a duty to use one's best efforts in the negotiation process.[73] The main reason for this is that there is usually a broad range of possible results of these negotiations which are equally acceptable to both sides so that it makes no sense to force the parties into an agreement.

Ultimately, the arbitrators' decision boils down to a comprehensive evalu- **19–030** ation of the wording and (non-risk taking) nature of the contract, the purpose and interests which the parties have pursued with their contract, the previous business practice between them, the usages and practices of the trade concerned and the nature and quality of the risk that has materialised.[74] This complex evaluation process and the resulting search for a solution that is

---

[70] See UN Doc. A/CN.9/WG.II/WP.41, para. 7 *in fine.*

[71] Fontaine, *supra* n. 11, at p. 79.

[72] See ICC Awards Nos. 6515 and 6516, *supra* no. 35, at p. 96; see also Horn, in *Adaptation and Renegotiation of Contracts in International Trade and Finance* (Horn, ed.) (1985) at pp. 15, 28: "We cannot expect very clear rules"; see also Fontaine, *supra* n. 11, at pp. 77 *et seq.*

[73] Schmitthoff, *supra* n. 3, at p. 87; Fontaine, *supra* n. 11, at p. 75; Peter, *supra* n. 12, at p. 247; Nassar, *Sanctity of Contracts Revisited: A Study in the Theory and Practice of Long–Term International Transactions* (1995) at pp. 180 *et seq.*; Berger, *supra* n. 35, at p. 7; *AMINOIL* Award, *supra* n. 22, at p. 1004 ("An obligation to negotiate is not an obligation to agree").

[74] Horn, *supra* n. 72, *ibid.*; Berger, *supra* n. 35, at p. 7; Draetta, Lake and Nandra, *supra* n. 23, at p. 204.

"fair" in the given situation should be guided by the "no profit-no loss rule", meaning that, absent contrary indications in the contract, neither party should be allowed to profit or should be forced to suffer a loss as a result of the restructuring.[75]

19–031   Apart from an extensive practical know-how, the arbitrator has to have a sufficient degree of sensitivity to the spirit and atmosphere that exists between the parties. As *Norbert Horn* has stated: "no court or arbitrator in the world, at least in international business transactions, can render an award that could serve as the legal basis for a complex future co-operation against the will of one of the parties".[76] With this particular feature of the adaptation or supplementation process, the procedure comes close to a mediation or conciliation which can only be successful if both parties are willing to accept the proposal of the mediator. The famous *IBM/Fujitsu* arbitration provides a perfect example for this aspect. There, the arbitrators entered into a restructuring of a complex copyright relationship between the parties only after the parties had empowered them to act as mediators.[77] The complexity of the revision or gap-filling process makes international arbitrators, outside the realm of mere price determinations, reluctant to restructure the contractual relationship between the parties. Finally, there may be even cases where the parties want a decision by the arbitrator but do not want to be bound by it.[78] They trust each other and merely want to use the arbitrators' recommendation as a basis for their own negotiations. In these cases, the technical issue of whether the arbitrators were procedurally authorised to render this decision and whether it constitutes an award is overruled by commercial pragmatism and reasonableness. In these cases, the parties themselves decide whether the arbitrators' adaptation or gap-filling really "makes sense" for them.

6. Overcoming the dogma: towards the "oneness of arbitration"?

19–032   Are there ways to escape the dogma in which the discussion on the arbitrators' power to adapt and supplement contracts has been trapped so far? Is it possible to reconcile procedure with contract?

19–033   Back in the late 1970s and early 1980s, *René David* and *Clive Schmitthoff* have both shown possible ways to escape the dilemma which are still valid today.

6.1 René David's concept of the "oneness of arbitration"

19–034   In his Report to the Tenth International Congress of Comparative Law as well as in his magnus opus on "Arbitration in International Trade", *René*

---

[75] Horn, *supra* n. 72, *ibid.*; see also ICC Award no. 2291 reprinted in *Collection of ICC Arbitral Awards* (Jarvin and Derains eds.) (1990) at p. 274: "...toute transaction commerciale est fondée sur l'equilibre des préstations réciproques et...nier ce principe reviendrait à faire du contrat commercial un contrat aléatoire, fondé sur la spéculation ou le hasard"; see also Lörcher, in (1996) *Der Betrieb* at pp. 1269, 1271; Steindorff, in (1983) *Betriebs-Berater* at pp. 1127, 1129.
[76] Horn, *supra* n. 35, at p. 182.
[77] See generally Büring-Uhle, in (1991) *Am. Rev. Int'l Arb.* at pp. 113 *et seq.*
[78] Horn, *supra* n. 35, at p. 178.

David has pursued the idea of a uniform concept of arbitration comprising traditional dispute settlement as well as contract adaptation and gap-filling. In his view, the strict distinction between the two kinds of decision making should be given up as a relic from the nineteenth century:

> "The arbitrators may be given by the parties the task of solving a legal dispute or of intervening in the regulation of the contractual relationship. In both cases the situation is, in essence, the same. . .It is artificial and in many respects deplorable that a distinction should be drawn between the two varieties of arbitration: the one aiming at the settlement of a legal dispute, the other at the regulation of a contractual relationship. In both cases the same technique is resorted to, the same result is aimed at, and the application of the same rules is desirable."[79]

According to *David*, this approach should be taken in particular in the field **19–035** of international commerce, where the trend towards the transnationalisation of substantive law does no longer require the strict adherence to traditional legal concepts of domestic law but requires pragmatic solutions.[80] Given the recent renaissance of transnational law,[81] this argument is more valid than ever. Thus, Article 6.2.3 (4) of the UNIDROIT Principles of International Commercial Contracts provides that in case of hardship, the court may, if reasonable, adapt the contract with a view to restoring its equilibrium. Pursuant to Article 1.10 of the Principles, the term "court" includes an "arbitral tribunal". Ultimately, this notion of the *"unité de l'arbitrage"* was also recognised during the deliberations of the Model Law when the Working Group, in deciding to include in the Model Law a provision on contract adaptation and gap-filling was called upon to "take account of the trend towards a broader concept of arbitration".[82] This view was confirmed in the recent ICC arbitration no. 7544. The respondent had claimed that the task of fixing the contract price was of a purely contractual nature as provided for by Article 1592 of the French Code Civil. The tribunal, however, assumed its competence to fill the gap in the contract stating that "the filling of gaps by arbitrators is considered an important element in long-term commercial relations".[83] Thus, more than 20 years after it had been introduced, *David's* notion of a uniform concept of arbitration comprising both contractual and procedural decision-making powers, seems to have been accepted as the model for future discussions on this subject.[84]

---

[79] David, *Arbitration in International Trade* (1985) No. 452; see also David, *supra* n. 2, at *p.* 285; Sanders, *supra* n. 12, at p. 142.

[80] David, *supra* n. 2, at p. 285.

[81] See, *e.g.* Berger, *supra* n. 54, at pp. 32 *et seq.*; see also the contributions of Bonell, Lando and Berger, in *Transnational Law in Commercial Legal Practice* (ed. CENTRAL) (1999).

[82] UN doc. A/CN.9/WG.II/WP.44, para. 22.

[83] ICC Award no. 7544 in (1999) *Clunet* at pp. 1062, 1063 with Note Hastier, *ibid.*, at pp. 1064, 1066; the arbitration clause contained a specific authorization for the arbitrators to adapt the contract, see *supra* n. 24.

[84] See Fouchard, Gaillard and Goldman, *supra* n. 9, no. 40 *in fine*: ". . .any distinction between so-called contractual arbitration and judicial arbitration is extremely tenuous. It is therefore preferable, both for theoretical and practical reasons, to define arbitration relatively broadly, at least as far as the adaptation of contracts is concerned"; Bernini, *supra* n. 34, at p. 422: "The evolution is certainly in the direction of considering that the arbitrator's role. . .embraces more and more functions which do not strictly partake of a purely jurisdictional nature but aim at regulating a contractual element with a view to securing the stability of the contract. . .[This] should permit the conclusion that the activity of the arbitrator, whatever the role and power assigned to the

6.2 Clive Schmitthoff's vision of the progressive effect of the English Arbitration Act

19–036 In his article on Hardship and Intervener Clauses in the 1978 Journal of Business Law, *Clive Schmitthoff* has hinted at the important role which the 1979 English Arbitration Act played in the shaping of the English legal system as a modern system of commercial law that allows gap-filling and revision of contracts.[85] As we all know, the 1979 Arbitration Act has not lived up to these expectations. Due to its arbitration-friendly character, the new English Arbitration Act 1996, however, is generally praised as a milestone in modern arbitral legislation.[86] *Clive Schmitthoff's* vision of the English Arbitration Act as a forerunner for a broad understanding of the arbitrators' competences under English law is therefore more up to date than ever. As *Stefan Kröll* has stated in his study on gap-filling and contract adaptation by Arbitrators: ". . .last doubts of a legal or procedural nature — concerning the arbitrators' authority [to fill gaps and adapt a contract under English law] should have been dissipated with the new Arbitration Act".[87] Again, the drafters of the Model Law foresaw this trend towards the dissociation of court and arbitral competences by stating that it is by no means clear that "the mere fact that arbitration is to the exclusion of court competence does necessarily mean that the competence of the arbitral tribunal cannot be wider than the (excluded) competence of the court".[88]

6.3 The changing paradigm of international contract law

19–037 Finally, it is the changing paradigm of international contract law which speaks in favour of a broad competence of international arbitrators to adapt contracts and fill gaps.[89]

19–038   Today, good faith and fair dealing have become the central yardstick for the "social control" of business behaviour and of the substantive fairness of any business agreement under the UNIDROIT Principles.[90] This has serious repercussions on the quality of transnational contracts.

19–039   The emphasis on good faith and fair dealing signals the transition to a new form of contractual morality in international business. The "all or nothing rule" of the sanctity of contract principles is being replaced by a more flexible, pragmatic approach. This approach seeks to produce results that are perceived to be just and fair and in consonance with commercial common sense. Modern commercial contract doctrine is developing away from the discrete

---

arbitrator by the parties, *should receive a unitary consideration* so that its decision may take the form of an award with all the resulting attributes, including enforceability" (emphasis added); *see also* Oppetit, *Théorie de l'arbitrage* (1998) at p. 77.

[85] Schmitthoff, *supra* n. 3, at p. 91.
[86] *cf.* Merkin, *Arbitration Act 1996* (1996) at pp. 1 *et seq.*
[87] Kröll, *supra* n. 15, at p. 305 (translation by the author).
[88] UN Doc. A/CN.9/WG.II/WP.44, Para. 17.
[89] See Berger, *supra* n. 35, at pp. 9 *et seq.*
[90] See Farnsworth, in (1994) *Tulane J.Int'l & Comp.L.* at pp. 47 *et seq.*; Bonell, in (1994) *Tulane J.Int'l & Comp.L.* at pp. 73, 75 *et seq.*; Hartkamp, in (1994) *Tulane J.Int'l & Comp.L.* at pp. 65 *et seq.*

model of the one-time exchange of goods and money to the co-operative and complex long-term transactions where the parties are depending to a substantial extent on the compliance of their counterparts with good faith and fair dealing as conduct-related legal standards over a long period of time. Also, this shift in emphasis reflects the fact that in the commercial context, various extra–contractual devices such as cooperation, flexibility, and the intrinsic willingness of the parties to adjust terms operate to reduce the rigid use of contract law and may often involve the "entangling strings of friendship, reputation, interdependence, morality and altruistic desires".[91] Thus, "the sacred principle of *pacta sunt servanda* should not be betrayed by means of a blind, and sometimes hypocritical, compliance".[92]

7. Conclusion

This study has shown that there is good hope that doctrine, courts and arbitral tribunals alike will finally accept the international arbitrators' power to fill gaps and revise contracts. Various developments of the past three decades, both in the field of arbitration and contract law, reveal that pragmatism has finally won over dogmatism. We should thus start with a broad modern understanding of the arbitral process into the twenty-first century comprising both settlement of traditional disputes and contract adaptation *viz* gap-filling. If arbitrators refuse to fill gaps or revise the contract, they should not do it because they do not feel authorised to act but because the distribution of risks in the contract prevents them from doing so.   **19–040**

In this context, the strength of terminology should not be underestimated. The concept of the "oneness of arbitration" should lead to a oneness of terminology symbolising the synthesis of contract and procedure. In his 1998 Freshfields Lecture, *Gerold Herrmann* has hinted at the tendency in modern doctrine to draw artificial distinctions in what is one and the same natural process.[93] He has added to this statement a whole array of fascinating names and abbreviations such as "Cruisation", "Intermediation", "Aloha" and "Orbitration", for which he claims a copyright. Let me add one more for which the present author claims the copyright: "It is not arbitration, it is not adaptation, it is *"adaptration"*.   **19–041**

---

[91] Sharma, in (1999) *N.Y.L.Sch.J.Int'l & Comp.L.* at pp. 95, 120 (citing Macneil, in (1974) *Va.L.Rev.* at pp. 589, 595).
[92] Bernini, *supra* n. 5, at p. 197.
[93] See Herrmann, "The 1998 Freshfields Lecture" in (1999) *Arbitration International* at pp. 211, 227 *et seq.*

PART FIVE

INTERNATIONAL CONTRACTS — HARMONISATION OF
SALES CONTRACTS AND COMMERCE

CHAPTER 20

UNIFORMITY IN THE CISG IN THE FIRST DECADE OF ITS APPLICATION

CAMILLA BAASCH ANDERSEN
UNIVERSITY OF COPENHAGEN LAW SCHOOL

1. Introduction: the CISG map of the world

I am honoured to take this opportunity to express some of my thoughts on my **20–001** favourite subject, namely the uniformity of the CISG. As most of you will know, the CISG is the 1980 United Nations Convention on Contracts for the International Sale of Goods, the uniform international sales law. There was a reference to it as an unusual Convention, and that it is; if for no other reason than for its astounding popularity. As of April 30, 2000, the UN Treaty section reports that the CISG has been ratified by 57 countries[1] throughout the world, effectively representing international transactions equivalent to two-thirds of global trade. Although the CISG has yet to be ratified in the British Isles and also has yet to be ratified in Japan, it is certainly safe to say that most industrial countries are represented by the CISG in foreign trade.[2]

---

[1] Argentina, Australia, Austria, Belarus, Belgium, Bosnia & Herzegovina, Bulgaria, Burundi, Canada, Chile, PR China, Croatia, Cuba, Czech Republic, Denmark, Ecuador, Egypt, Estonia, Finland, France, Georgia, Germany, Greece, Guinea, Hungary, Iraq, Italy, Kyrgystan, Latvia, Lesotho, Lithuania, Luxembourg, Mauritania, Mexico, Moldova, Mongolia, Netherlands, New Zealand, Norway, Peru, Poland, Romania, Russian Federation, Singapore, Slovakia, Slovenia, Spain, Sweden, Switzerland, Syrian Arab Republic, Uganda, Ukraine, USA, Uruguay, Uzbekistan, Yugoslavia and Zambia.

[2] But there is reliable information from the British Department of Trade and Industry that the proposal for a British ratification is again underway, albeit on a slow low-priority back-burner, on request from the new labour government, so perhaps there is hope; at least I am sure that British ratification will not positively *require* public demonstrations through the streets of London demanding that it be done, as Professor Kronke suggested yesterday.

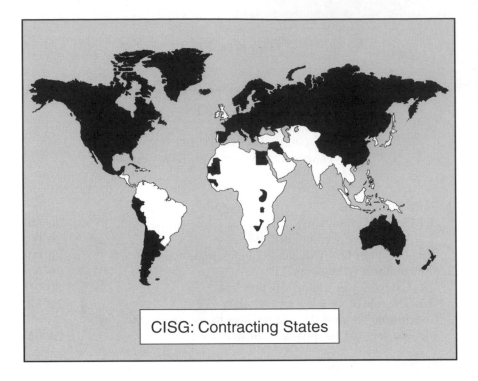

CISG: Contracting States

I should like to draw your attention to the CISG map of the world which illustrates this.[3]

20–002   This map will be used as a tool to get a point across, one might say it is a cheap trick. There is much talk of the global village, the removal of boundaries and how the world is everyone's back yard. And although it cannot be disputed that the world seems smaller due to travel, communication, media and other means of insight and co-operation, I want to use this map to stress an important point. What you see when you look at this map is not a village nor a backyard, but a very large world spanning many continents, and covering a multitude of very different languages, cultures, legal systems and peoples. It is a complicated and very varied world out there, and we must keep this in mind when we refer to harmonisation, global equalisation and uniformity. The CISG is an example of how these differences can surface: it applies throughout most corners of the world, and given the differences which abound in many aspects of the different Member States, it is not surprising that problems of uniformity surface.

1.1 Defining Uniformity

20–003   But what exactly is "uniformity"? Logically, it is impossible to isolate problems of uniformity without at least attempting to define what uniformity is,

---

[3] Taken from the Pace University Institute of International Commercial Law CISG database, available at .http://www.cisg.law.pace.edu/cisg/cisgintro.html.

and what standards it sets. As mentioned, the CISG is a *uniform* international sales law, as gleaned from Article 7 and the Preamble to the Convention. Linguistically, the term "uniform" sounds as if the application and use of the Convention is required to be absolutely the same, with no variations. Uniform, *but*, such absolute complete uniformity is unarguably a utopian concept even within the boundaries of a small legal community—in the end all law is applied by human beings who are influenced by their own concepts of justice and legal ethics, and variation will occur. Even in a regional context, uniformity may often be undermined by the party autonomy. This is all the more so where a global convention is concerned, since the people applying the convention stem from completely different cultures and legal backgrounds, and their interpretations of the Convention (at least potentially) can vary immensely.

So how *do* we define uniform law? What does uniformity mean? Is it the same as harmonisation? Are the two terms mixed up and applied at random? Perhaps. My research, however, would seem to indicate that uniformity is just a little bit more legal equality than harmonisation, which does not (on the surface of things) set out to equalise legal regulations. But then, since total uniformity is unrealistic, can we speak of different levels of uniformity? Do we determine this from what we take to be the intention of the drafters, despite the uncertain status of *travaux preparatoires?* I may be splitting hairs, and indeed I do not portend to suggest answers to these questions. And I doubt that anyone ever will be able to define uniformity precisely, although I should welcome a debate with anyone who finds this interesting.   **20–004**

1.2. Why do we need uniformity?

Global harmonisation, uniformity, equalisation and, legal equilibrium are all very much buzz-words when it comes to international law—especially where international sales law is concerned—and justifiably so. The reason for the popularity of these concepts is the need to promote similar or equal rules and regulations which will enable a certain predictability in contracts. As the world grows ever smaller in terms of trade, travel and communication, people from different countries and continents become ever more likely to enter into contractual relationships, and this leads to a need to know the legal basis of the contracts in question; a need for predictability. In short, a need for international similar rules is created by the need to foresee the basis of different contractual situations, for contracting parties to be able to meet on "common ground".   **20–005**

1.3. The quest for predictability in international contracts

What would be the situation without uniform international rules? Even if the utopian aim of private international law to ensure that jurisdiction and choice of law rules always led to the same application of rules were realised, the need for predictability would not be satisfied as the rules referred to would still be the domestic rules of one party, and the other party will in all likelihood not be able to fully comprehend these rules, or even be able to become familiar with them. It would be difficult to foresee the basis of the   **20–006** contract, and more importantly, it would be difficult to foresee what gap-filling rules would apply if a problem with a contract were to surface. Some might then inject that this problem might be solved by choice-of-law clauses, but this would necessitate that the parties reach agreement on a set of domestic rules, which might be difficult, for at least one of the contracting parties, to gain insight into. Private international law does not, and cannot, hold the key to the problem of predictability in contracts.

20–007   The only viable solution is to seek to make international rules which are similar. Thus, harmonisation and uniform rules are most certainly justifiable, and it is no wonder that in the area of international trade law, modern work on uniform international regulation has been underway since before the Second World War, with roots of harmonisation dating back to Roman law.

2. How uniform is "uniform"?

20–008   However, having determined that the harmonisation and uniformity is the proper path to tread, with respect to creating predictability in contracts, many problems and questions arise. Especially concerning uniformity. One of the first problems which emerges is: How is uniformity to be achieved? And, perhaps even trickier than that, is the question: to which extent must the rules be equal? To what degree must the certainty of rigid predictability outweigh the reasonableness of flexibility? In other words: to what degree is uniformity required?

20–009   The standard answer to the latter question is, that rules which are uniform must be interpreted in a uniform manner (equally) before all courts, globally. Apparently, this sort of perfect uniformity is a utopian idea; even within the boundaries of a smaller community there will always be an element of individual subjectivity and influence when a judge decides a case, and unless one man makes all decisions, based on the same norms, influencing factors and thought- process, interpretations will never be perfectly uniform. This is all the more true for uniform laws which apply across boundaries of very different cultural, historical and legal backgrounds. Further, judges or arbitrators would only consider rules which are deemed applicable. Interpretation is normally subject to methods which are used for domestic law; arguable, there are no uniform methods for the interpretation of international (uniform) law.[4]

20–010   The Convention is not uniform just because it claims to be—at least not everywhere. In the eternal words of George Orwell: "Everyone is created equal, but some are more equal than others". With some poetic license, this may apply to the legal interpretations of alleged "uniform" legal text as well as it may apply to the questions of personal freedom to which it was meant. The level of uniformity which is intended for different uniform laws differs greatly according to their setting, their drafting and their general aim. A set

---

[4] The House of Lords, for example, in *Fothergill v. Monarch Airlines Ltd* [1980] 2 All E.R. 696–721, has expressed the view that the interpretation of international conventions should be performed cautiously, at least under historical aspects. *c.f.* Richard Gardiner, "Treaty Interpretation in the English Courts Since *Fothergill v. Monarch Airlines* (1980)", 44 ICLQ 620–628 (1995). The principles of Fothergill were reiterated in *Antwerp United Diamonds and Air Europe* [1995] 3 All E.R. 424–432. For the possibilities for dynamic interpretation see recently Michael Van Alstine, "Dynamic Treaty Interpretation", 146 *University of Pennsylvania Law Review* 687–793 (1998).

level of uniformity will be difficult to establish for all uniform laws, and the present paper thus focuses on the uniformity of the CISG without supposing to establish guidelines for the uniformity of any other uniform laws. The uniformity, or alleged uniformity, of the CISG is unique.

Another somewhat unique position of the CISG which should be mentioned when discussing the uniformity of the CISG—especially in connection with concerns for the impact it will have on existing trade upon its ratification (such as the British anxieties to preserving the status quo of the sale of commodities)—is its hierarchy and the fact that the CISG is not the beast of uniformity that some may think. The CISG merely fills gaps in the contract between parties—there is a firm hierarchy in the Convention of (i) Contract, (ii) Customs in trade and (iii) Convention provisions, which is gleaned from Articles 6 and 9. Thus, any trade contract can merely agree to ignore the CISG, or agree on other terms which will overwrite it (by way of Article 6), and existing trade with established trade customs will automatically overrule any gap-filling rules of the Convention (by way of Article 9). **20–011**

This openness to diversity by means of party autonomy (including opting out) and trade usages may seem like an obstacle to uniformity since it hinders predictability, but this is not the case. Where contract terms have been agreed upon or where trade usage has been established, the parties are certainly aware of the contents of the agreement, and the predictability of the contract for third parties is not an issue with which the CISG is concerned. **20–012**

So how uniform is "uniform"? If it is so elusive to define positively, then perhaps we should look at what constitutes a problem of uniformity and define it negatively. It appears that one of the best definitions, to date, of what constitutes a problem of uniformity was offered by Professor Sundberg on the subject of a different uniform convention (Warsaw Air Charter) a decade before the CISG was even drawn up.[5] He stated that a margin of imperfection is not a defect with regards to uniformity as long as it does not encourage forum shopping. Leaving aside the advantages or pitfalls of forum shopping,[6] which in certain circumstances is desirable in international transactions we will concentrate on the other aspects of the definition. Although this definition is perhaps a tad vague—since one might hope that uniformity should be more than that—it is still a valid guideline for determining that which is a problem of uniformity, and for lack of a better definition I will use it in the following to set the "minimum standard" of uniformity. **20–013**

I was very fond of Professor Herrmann's metaphor of the nail-cutting vending machine which inadvertently harmonises finger-lengths by cutting nails of standard-length fingers, because it so clearly illustrates two of my fine "pet-points" concerning uniformity: **20–014**

---

[5] "Air Charter" from 1963, quoted in O.C. GILES "Uniform Commercial Law—An essay on international conventions in national courts" at pp.23–24.
[6] See the debate between Professors Friedrich Juenger and Brian Opeskin. Friedrich Juenger, "What's Wrong with Forum Shopping?", *16 Sydney L. Rev.* 5–13 (1994); Brian R. Opeskin, "The Price of Forum Shopping: A Reply To Professor Juenger", 16 *Sydney L. Rev.* 14–27 (1994); Friedrich Juenger, "Forum Shopping: A Rejoinder", *16 Sydney L. Rev.* 28–31 (1994). See also X, "Forum Shopping Reconsidered", *103 Harvard L. Rev.* 1677–1696 (1990).

(a)   Anyone who feels a knife rush towards his fingers will surely move his hands when his digits are in danger. Similarly, practitioners will move away from the use of any uniform law which inhibits their sense of law or justice, rending the instrument useless. And,

(b)   Is it truly an acceptable side-effect of a nail-cutter that it mercilessly chops off fingertips of a non-standardised length? In the same way we can ask ourselves if it is proportional to disregard any aspects of uncommon legal systems in the drawing up and in the application of uniform law. In these times of standardisation, we sometimes seem keen to equalise the law at any price. The quest for uniform law may seem ruthless to some . . .

So, where are the problems of uniformity in the CISG? Which provisions vary in their application so as to possibly encourage forum shopping?

2.1. Categories of uniformity problems

20–015   Most of the problems of uniformity fall into some "categories" of different problems, and although I realise the danger of rigidly pigeonholing caselaw into categories, it is nonetheless an efficient way of lending an overview, so I will briefly try to illustrate some of them and give you examples of provisions which present problems.

20–016   (i) First of all, the *sphere of application of the Convention*, a problem which spills over into the other categories, but nonetheless deserves its own, for how can we begin to speak of uniformity if the CISG does not even apply to the same cases in the different member states? One of the examples of this is one of interpretation of terms, found in Article 2: Is software "goods"? If it is, then the convention will apply to software transactions, lending itself to the security of both buyer and seller in the absence of any other contract, and giving predictability to such transaction *providing*, of course that it is predictable whether or not it applies, *i.e.* whether or not software is "goods". Now, any legal counsel representing a party who has breached an agreement in some way would be well advised to encourage his client to hurriedly forum-shop to a venue where software is not considered goods, to avoid the provisions of the pro-contractual CISG for breach.

20–017   (ii) Another example is that of *Fauxs Amis*, i.e. the "false friend" in a term which seems familiar to a practitioner but which in fact is defined differently in the uniform law than it is in the system where the practitioner is used to it. This is found in Article 47, which was—rather unfortunately—referred to as a *"Nachfrist"* rule by the Secretariat's commentary, prompting some German courts to equate it to their own Nachfrist rule in the BGB, and causing them to apply it to cases of delay in delivery and not just in cases of non-conformity of goods as was intended. The forum shopping advantages here are clear; a buyer who has not given a seller Nachfrist in a case of late delivery, should flee from all German courts as it is only here that such a Nachfrist would be required under Article 47.

20–018   (iii) *domestic influence on uniform law* is felt throughout many of the problems of uniformity, including the instances of vague terms and the interpretation of the more flexible provisions. One of the best examples of this is found in Article 39(1) concerning the timeliness of a notice of non-conformity from a buyer to a seller in cases where the buyer wishes to exercise any rights under the convention. Such a notice must be given within *"reasonable time"*, and what is that? In available case law this time-period has varied from several days to over a month, and there is evidence that there is a tendency for the buyer-friendly French courts to allow longer time-frames, whereas German courts, which I think I can safely call seller-friendly, lean towards much briefer timeframes. There is a rising trend for standardising the way the timeframe is measured by using a "grosszügige Monat" as a vantage point to which accepted criteria for setting the time frame are applied, but to date this has only been applied in three member States.[7]

(iv) The last example of a problem category regarding uniformity that I **20–019** share with you today is that of *Gap-filling and Article 7*. According to Article 7, gaps in CISG provisions which are within the sphere of the convention are to be resolved either via otherwise applicable law or general principles. On top of these options, some courts have referred to standard gap-fillers (such as the UNIDROIT principles)[8] in lieu of CISG solutions. An example of a provision with such a gap is the question of rate of interest in Article 78. Some courts apply the principle of full compensation found throughout the convention as a principle to award compensatory interest at the cost of not having the money, others apply the otherwise applicable law (using private international law) in determining the rate, and then there is a worrying trend to apply UNIDROIT principle 7.4.9 as a standard gap-filler to the question, regardless of whether the parties have agreed to apply them in part or in whole or otherwise have referred to general principles of international law. This question of interest rate, which is relevant for almost every CISG case lodged, is a central issue which must in my mind find some standardised solution in the interest of predictability; it is difficult to point to any nationalised trends which may promote forum shopping, but there are fundamental differences, and the issue is certainly a problem of uniformity.

2.2. The role of case law[9] and scholars[10]

This brings me to the first of some of the practical problems in the applica- **20–020** tion of the convention which influence its uniformity, namely the role of international case law. For the question of interest rate is most certainly one

---

[7] With a comment in his paper, Professor Bonell gave me an opportunity to elaborate that the flexibility of terms which represents the compromise which is the CISG is a good solution, but one which requires guidelines or yardsticks for interpretation, lest they stand completely alone and allow predictability to disappear through too diverse interpretations of the same provision. See chap. 21 by Professor Bonell in this book.

[8] See Bonell, *infra* chap. 21.

[9] For case law on CISG see the Pace University Web Site at http://www.cisg.law.pace.edu with links to the autonomous CISG network, the UNCITRAL Case Law on Uniform Texts (CLOUT) at http://www.un.or.at/uncitral/ the dedicated CD-ROM and database UNILEX.

[10] There is a substantial number of excellent commentaries on the CISG. See, for example, Cesare Massimo Bianca and Michael Joachim Bonell, Commentary on the International Sales Law—The 1980 Vienna Sales Convention, Giuffrè: Milan (1987); Fritz Enderlein and Dietrich Maskow, International Sales Law—United Nations Convention on Contracts for the International Sale of Goods—Convention on the Limitation Period in the International Sale of

which has offered up much international case law which may be of aid in determining the best way to settle the issue, yet there are no references to be found in any CISG cases concerning this question to other solutions to the problem from courts or tribunals from other countries. In fact I can present you with an unfortunate statistic: of the almost 500 cases I have read for my thesis concerning a wide variety of CISG issues, only two !,[11] have referred to international case law in compliance with the duty in Article 7 which scholars agree is there. This is a problem caused by many factors: accessibility of case-law, language barriers, legal traditions for including cases from other countries, etc., and with the arrival of extensive internet databases the situation can hopefully be remedied slightly—I will return to this in a moment. There is, however, an Italian case which makes references to 47 foreign judgments.[12]

20–021   Another, perhaps even more serious problem, is the question of the CISG being overlooked. There is an alarming scarcity of case law from many CISG Member States, and my own country, Denmark, is certainly no angel in that department. There is a grand total of two reported CISG cases from Denmark, a figure which does not accurately represent the number of cases concerning international sales. Practicing lawyers from my own generation tell me of instances where the CISG is pleaded by them but consciously pushed aside by judges of an older generation who prefer the domestic sales law they know. This is a deplorable problem which will hopefully be amended with time, as judges who have been trained in the international sales law emerge to the benches.

20–022   All this is aggravated by the fact that there is no monitoring or official legal watch-dog who guards the CISG, there is no court before which questions of interpretation can be lodged or complaint of cases can be brought. It is all up to scholars. And so my plea to you all; an active participation in the monitoring of cases concerning international sales amongst scholars and practitioners, and a publishing of criticism can help bring about less flippant negligence of the CISG and encourage more careful uniform approaches in case law. It is up to us to spy, spot, cry out and publish. A major effort to col-

---

Goods, New York, London and Rome (1992); John O. Honnold, Uniform Law for International Sales under the 1980 United Nations Convention, 3rd ed., The Hague (1999); John O. Honnold, Uniform Law for International Sales under the 1980 United Nations Convention, 2nd ed., Deventer and Boston (1991); Albert H. Kritzer, Guide to Practical Applications of the UN Convention on Contracts for the International Sale of Goods, Deventer / Boston (1989); Peter Schlechtriem, Commentary on the UN Convention on the International Sale of Goods (CISG), 2nd ed., Oxford (1998); UNCITRAL SECRETARIAT Commentary, Official Records.

[11] The first, from Italy from January 31, 1996 Tribunale Civile di Cuneo *(Sport D'Hiver di Genevieve Culet v. Ets. Louys et Fils)* (available at http://cisgw3.law.pace.edu/cases/960131i3. html), the next from the U.S. from May 17, 1999 U.S. Dist. Ct. *(Medical Marketing International, Inc. v. Internazionale Medico Scientifica, S.r.l.)* (available at: http://cisgw3.law.pace.edu/ cases/990517u1.html). The latter case is very interesting as the Defendant sought to have an arbitral ruling overturned on the grounds that "the arbitrators misapplied the United Nations Convention on Contracts for the International Sales of Goods . . . and that they refused to follow a German Supreme Court Case [BGH 8 March 1995] interpreting the CISG." Although the Court was unwilling to accept this argument, they double checked that the tribunal had in fact referred to international case law, and thus acknowledged the duty to do so.

[12] See Tribunale di Vigevano in composizione monocratica Giudice: dott. Alessandro Rizzieri Sentenza 12 luglio 2000, n. 405, available at http://cisgw3.law.pace.edu/cases/000712i3.html.

lect, translate in English and publish all cases (almost 800) relating to CISG is currently underway in a co-operation between the Institute of International Commercial Law at Pace University Law School and the Centre for Commercial Law Studies, at Queen Mary, University of London. In this effort co-operation with other institutions and scholars is needed and required.[13]

3. Conclusion: so what else can be done to constructively alleviate some of the problems of uniformity?

Some scholars have suggested that the general principles of the convention can help to ensure that all interpretations of the convention are carried out uniformly, but I do not agree with that. The general principles are diffuse and difficult to glean, and it is certainly unclear whether practitioners from different countries would spot the same general principles from which to interpret provision. **20–023**

A more passable road would seem to be a compliance of the recognised duty for practitioners to look to international case law. The databases available on CD-ROM and those on the Internet have done a lot to alleviate the problems of accessibility and language barriers, and an international respect for other tribunals and courts would seem to be the easiest and most realistic way of obtaining a more similar way of interpreting CISG provisions and stepping closer to the elusive goal of uniformity. **20–024**

I leave you with my hope for the future, namely the evolution of a "watchdog" to monitor the CISG. I understood from Professor Herrmann's chapter[14] that—maybe—my hope that CLOUT will grow to become a more encompassing monitor of CISG practice and perhaps even a venue for posing CISG judicial questions and/or having blatantly wrong cases reversed is not so utopian after all. I shall cross my fingers and hope to see it in my lifetime.[15] **20–025**

---

[13] For further information, contact L.Mistelis@qmw.ac.uk and/or Akritzer@law.pace.education.

[14] See *supra* chap. 2.

[15] Another very recent development is that the Centre for Commercial Law Studies, Queen Mary, University of London, and Pace University, Institute of International Commercial Law, are co-ordinating a CISG-Interpretative Council which will have its formative meetings in April 2001.

CHAPTER 21

THE UNIDROIT PRINCIPLES OF INTERNATIONAL
COMMERCIAL CONTRACTS AND THE HARMONISATION
OF INTERNATIONAL SALES LAW

MICHAEL JOACHIM BONELL
PROFESSOR OF LAW, UNIVERSITY OF ROME I "LA SAPIENZA"
CONSULTANT, UNIDROIT

1. Introduction

"We are beginning to rediscover the international character of commercial law [. . .] The
general trend of commercial law everywhere is to move away from the restrictions of
national law to a universal, international conception of the law of international trade".

21–001   It was Clive M. Schmitthoff, in whose honour our seminar is being held, who
made this statement almost 50 years ago in a lecture he gave at the University of Helsinki.[1] What then may have appeared rather visionary, is today
very close to reality. The last decades have seen the proliferation initiatives to
unify or harmonise the law governing cross-border economic relationships.
Such efforts were sometimes confined to particular regions and sometimes
had a universal dimension. The techniques used likewise varied considerably,
ranging from the adoption of binding instruments, such as conventions and
uniform laws, to the preparation of non-binding sets of rules in the form of
model contracts or model clauses, codes of conduct and legal guides. As a
result we are experiencing what has been described as an "emerging global
legal culture, largely shaped by the dominance of global economic markets".[2]

---

[1] C.M. Schmitthoff, *Modern Trends in English Commercial Law*, in Tidskrift utgiven av Juridiska
Foreningen i Finland, 1957, p. 349 *et seq.* (at p. 354).
[2] A. Rosett, United States (Part I), in M.J. Bonell (Ed.) *A New Approach to International
Commercial Contracts*, 1999, p. 388 *et seq.* (at p. 390).

The unification process has proved to be particularly successful with respect **21–002** to contract law in general and sales law in particular, and in both fields Clive M. Schmitthoff has played a major role. In the late 1960s he was one of the founders of UNCITRAL which eventually produced the 1980 UN Convention on Contracts for the International Sale of Goods (CISG); likewise in the early 1970s he was one of the three "wise men" entrusted by UNIDROIT with the task of laying down the foundation of a project that led, two decades later, to the adoption of the UNIDROIT Principles of International Commercial Contracts.[3]

Both CISG and the UNIDROIT Principles represent landmarks in the **21–003** process of international unification of law. CISG, unanimously adopted in 1980 by a diplomatic Conference with the participation of representatives from 62 States and eight international organisations, has been ratified by 57 countries from the five continents, including almost all the major trading nations.[4] The UNIDROIT Principles, published in 1994, are likewise a worldwide success: translated into over two dozen languages, they are not only the subject of a substantial body of legal writings, but are more and more frequently being used in international contract practice and dispute resolution.[5]

The present paper will focus on the relationship between CISG and the **21–004** UNIDROIT Principles in the context of international sales contracts. After a brief description of the nature and content of the two instruments (See Section 2), I shall demonstrate that, far from being competitors, they may indeed complement one another (See Section 3). This is true not only in cases where CISG is not applicable (See Section 3.1), but also with respect to sales contracts governed by CISG (See Section 3.2): in this latter case the UNIDROIT Principles may be used to interpret and supplement CISG either because expressly referred to by the parties or even in the absence of any such reference. In discussing the various items, particular attention will be given to the growing body of case law.

2. CISG and the UNIDROIT Principles: international uniform sales law v. "restatement" of general contract law

When back in 1929 Ernst Rabel launched the idea of preparing uniform rules **21–005** on international sales contracts, it was taken for granted that the envisaged rules were to be prepared in the form of a binding instrument. Even after the poor reception of the two 1964 Hague Sales Conventions, when in 1968

---

[3] The other two members of the Steering Committee were René David and Tudor Popescu.
[4] For the list of the Contracting States, as well as some 350 cases and an exhaustive bibliography on CISG, see. M.J. Bonell *et al* (eds.), *UNILEX—International Case Law & Bibliography on the UN Convention on Contracts for the International Sale of Goods*, Transnational Publishers Inc., Ardseley, NY, (ed. February 28, 2000).
[5] For an exhaustive bibliography on the UNIDROIT Principles as well as some 50 cases in which the UNIDROIT Principles are referred to, see M.J. Bonell *et al* (eds.), *UNILEX— International Case Law & Bibliography on the UNIDROIT Principles* , Transnational Publishers Inc., Ardseley, NY (to be published in December 2000); see also the UNIDROIT Principles Internet web site [http://www.unidroit.org/english/principles/pr-main.htm].

UNCITRAL decided to make a fresh start, the legislative option was the only conceivable one.[6]

21–006　　Yet the option in favour of uniform legislation inevitably restricted the drafters" room for manoeuvre. Due to the differences in legal tradition and at times, even more significantly, in the social and economic structure prevalent in the States participating in the negotiations, some issues had to be excluded at the outset from the scope of CISG, while with respect to a number of other items the conflicting views could only be overcome by compromise solutions leaving matters more or less undecided.

21–007　　Thus, some categories of sale—among which are also transactions of considerable importance in international trade practice, such as sales of shares and other securities, of negotiable instruments and money, of ships and aircraft—are expressly excluded from its scope.[7] But also in regard to ordinary sales contracts a number of important issues have not been taken into consideration. CISG itself expressly mentions the validity of the contract, the effect of the contract on the property in the goods[8] and the liability of the seller for death or personal injury caused by the goods to the buyer or any other person.[9] In addition, one may recall, for instance, the conclusion of the contract through an agent, the problems arising from the use by one or both of the parties of standard terms, or the impact which the different kinds of State control over the import and/or export of certain goods or the exchange of currency may have on the contract of sale as such or on the performance of any of its obligations.

21–008　　Of the provisions laying down not too convincing compromise solutions between conflicting views some openly refer the definite answer to the applicable domestic law.[10] Others use the technique of a main rule immediately followed by an equally broad exception thereby leaving the question open as to which of the two alternatives will ultimately prevail in each single case.[11] Others still hide the lack of any real consensus by an extremely vague and ambiguous language.[12]

21–009　　The UNIDROIT Principles represent a totally new approach to international trade law. First of all, on account of their scope which, contrary to that of all existing international conventions including CISG, is not restricted to a particular kind of transaction but covers the general part of contract law.[13]

---

[6] For a discussion of some of the reasons for this preference, see M.J. Bonell, *An International Restatement of Contract Law*, (Transnational Publishers Inc.) (2nd ed. 1997, pp. 62–63).

[7] Art. 2, CISG.

[8] Art. 4, CISG.

[9] Art. 5, CISG.

[10] *cf. e.g.*, Arts. 12 and 96, CISG with respect to the formal requirements of the contract; Art. 28, CISG concerning the possibility of obtaining a judgment for specific performance; Art. 55, CISG with respect to the possibility of a sales contract being validly concluded without an express or implied determination of the price.

[11] *cf. e.g.* Art. 16, CISG dealing with the revocability of the offer; Arts. 39(1), 43(1) and 44 CISG as to the notice requirement in case of delivery of non-conforming goods or goods which are not free from third parties" rights; Art. 68, CISG concerning the transfer of risk where the goods are sold in transit.

[12] *cf. e.g.* the reference to good faith in Art. 7(1), CISG; the definition of "fundamental breach of contract" in Art. 25, CISG; Art. 78, CISG concerning the right to interest on sums in arrears.

[13] On the possibility of the UNIDROIT Principles playing the role of general contract law otherwise allotted to a national law, see M. Bridge, *The International Sale of Goods: Law and Practice*, (Oxford University Press) 1999, pp. 54 *et seq.*

Moreover, and more importantly, the UNIDROIT Principles —prepared by a private group of experts which, though acting under the auspices of a prestigious Institute such as UNIDROIT, lacked any legislative power—do not aim to unify domestic law by means of special legislation, but merely to "re-state" existing international contract law. Finally, the decisive criterion in their preparation was not just which rule had been adopted by the majority of countries ("common core approach"), but also which of the rules under consideration had the most persuasive value and/or appeared to be particularly well suited for cross-border transactions ("better rule approach").

Yet precisely because the UNIDROIT Principles were not conceived as a binding instrument they could address a number of matters that had either been completely excluded or insufficiently regulated by CISG.   **21–010**

Thus, in the chapter on formation, new provisions were included on the manner in which a contract may be concluded, on writings in confirmation, on the case where the parties make the conclusion of their contract dependent upon reaching an agreement on specific matters or in a specific form, on contracts with terms deliberately left open, on negotiations in bad faith, on the duty of confidentiality, on merger clauses, on contracting on the basis of standard terms, on surprising provisions in standard terms, on the conflict between standard terms and individually negotiated terms and on the battle of forms.[14]   **21–011**

Further, a whole chapter on validity was added which moreover is not restricted to the classical cases of invalidity, *i.e.* the three defects of consent such as mistake, fraud and threat, but also addresses the much more controversial issue of "gross disparity".[15]   **21–012**

Equally new are, among others, the *contra proferentem* rule, the provision on linguistic discrepancies and that on supplying an omitted term in the chapter on interpretation,[16] the provision on implied obligations in the chapter on content;[17] those on payment by cheque or other instruments, on payment by funds transfer, on currency of payment, on the determination of the currency of payment where it is not indicated in the contract, on the costs of performance, on the imputation of payments, on public permission requirements and on hardship in the chapter on performance;[18] the provisions on the right to performance, on exemption clauses, on the case where the aggrieved party contributes to the harm, on interest rates and on agreed payment for non-performance in the chapter on non-performance.[19]   **21–013**

---

[14] *cf.* UNIDROIT Principles, Arts. 2.1, 2.12, 2.13, 2.14, 2.15, 2.16, 2.17, 2.19, 2.20, 2.21 and 2.22, respectively.
[15] *cf.* UNIDROIT Principles, Arts. 3.4–3.9 and 3.10, respectively.
[16] *cf.* UNIDROIT Principles, Arts. 4.6, 4.7 and 4.8, respectively.
[17] UNIDROIT Principles, Art. 5.2.
[18] *cf.* UNIDROIT Principles, Arts. 6.1.7–6.1.9, 6.1.10, 6.1.11, 6.1.12, 6.1.14–6.1.17 and 6.2.1–6.2.3, respectively.
[19] *cf.* UNIDROIT Principles, Arts. 7.2.1–7.2.5, 7.1.6, 7.4.7, 7.4.9 and 7.4.13, respectively.

3. CISG and the UNIDROIT Principles: two complimentary instruments

3.1 International sales contracts not governed by CISG

21–014   Notwithstanding the world-wide acceptance of CISG there might still be sales contracts not governed by CISG. According to Art. 1 CISG this is the case whenever at least one of the parties is not situated in a Contracting State or the rules of private international law of the forum lead to the application of the law of a non-Contracting State. It is also the case when the parties decide to opt out, *i.e.* to exclude in part *or* in whole the application of the CISG pursuant Art. 6. In all such cases the UNIDROIT Principles may be applied as an alternative set of internationally uniform rules, either because of an express choice to this effect by the parties themselves or because the contract is governed by "general Principles of law", "*lex mercatoria*" or the like, and the UNIDROIT Principles are considered to be a particularly authoritative expression thereof.

21–015   In actual practice, more and more cases are being reported in which the UNIDROIT Principles have been applied as *lex contractus* of international sales contracts which do not fall within the scope of CISG.

21–016   In one case the parties themselves had expressly chosen the UNIDROIT Principles as the law governing their contract.[20] The case concerned a sales contract entered into between a Hong Kong export company and a Russian trade organisation. The contract did not contain any choice of law clause, but when the dispute arose, the parties agreed that the Arbitral Tribunal should apply the UNIDROIT Principles to resolve any questions not expressly regulated in the contract.

21–017   In two other cases the UNIDROIT Principles were applied even without any express reference to them by the parties.

21–018   One is the ICC Award No. 8502[21] concerning a contract for the supply of rice entered into between a Vietnamese exporter and French and Dutch buyers. The contract did not contain any choice of law clause. The Arbitral Tribunal decided to base its award on "trade usages and generally accepted Principles of international trade" and to refer "in particular to the 1980 Vienna Convention on Contracts for the International Sale of Goods (Vienna Sales Convention) or to the Principles of International Commercial Contracts enacted by UNIDROIT, *as evidencing admitted practices under international trade law*" (emphasis added). The individual provisions it then referred to were Arts. 76, CISG and 7.4.6 (*Proof of harm by current price*) of the UNIDROIT Principles.

21–019   Yet another example is the award rendered by an *ad hoc* Arbitral Tribunal in Buenos Aires in 1997.[22] The case concerned a contract for the sale of shares between shareholders of an Argentine company and a Chilean company. The

---

[20] See Award No. 116 of January 20, 1997 rendered by the International Arbitration Court of the Chamber of Commerce and Industry of the Russian Federation (for an abstract see M.J. Bonell, *supra* n. 4, pp. 252–253).
[21] ICC Award No. 8502 of 1996, in *ICC International Court of Arbitration Bulletin, op. cit.*, pp. 72–74.
[22] Award of December 10, 1997: *c.f. Uniform Law Review*, 1998, 178.

contract did not contain a choice of law clause and the parties authorised the Arbitral Tribunal to act as *amiables compositeurs*. Notwithstanding the fact that both parties had based their claims on specific provisions of Argentine law, the Tribunal decided to apply the UNIDROIT Principles. The Tribunal held that the UNIDROIT Principles constituted *"usages of international trade reflecting the solutions of different legal systems and of international contract practice"* (emphasis added), and that as such, according to Art. 28(4) of the UNCITRAL Model Law on International Commercial Arbitration, they should prevail over any domestic law.[23] The individual provisions of the UNIDROIT Principles applied to the merits of the case were Arts. 3.12 (*Confirmation*), 3.14 (*Notice of avoidance*) and 4.6 (*Contra proferentem* rule).

Yet it is particularly in the context of so-called "state contracts" that the UNIDROIT Principles are frequently applied even in the absence of an express reference by the parties. **21–020**

A first example is provided by the ICC Partial Awards in Case No. 7110.[24] The dispute concerned contracts for the supply of equipment concluded between an English company and a Middle Eastern governmental agency. While most of the contracts were silent as to the applicable law, some did refer to settlement according to "rules of natural justice". In a first partial award dealing with the applicable law, the Arbitral Tribunal, by majority, held that the parties had intended to exclude the application of any specific domestic law and to have their contracts governed by general Principles and rules which enjoy wide international consensus. According to the Arbitral Tribunal such *"general rules and Principles [. . .] are primarily reflected by the UNIDROIT Principles"* (emphasis added), and in the other partial awards dealing with substantive issues it referred to Arts 1.7 (*Good faith and fair dealing*), 2.4 (*Revocation of offer*), 2.14 (*Contracts with terms deliberately left open*), 2.18 (*Written modification clause*), 7.1.3 (*Withholding performance*) and 7.4.8 (*Mitigation of harm*) of the UNIDROIT Principles, considering them all to be expressions of generally accepted Principles of law. **21–021**

Other examples are ICC Awards No. 7375 and No. 8261 relating to contracts for the supply of goods between a United States company and a Middle Eastern governmental agency,[25] and between an Italian company and another Middle Eastern governmental agency,[26] respectively. In both cases the contracts were silent as to the applicable law. The Arbitral Tribunal, assuming that neither party was prepared to accept the other's domestic law, decided in the first case to apply *"those general Principles and rules of law applicable to international contractual obligations [. . .], including [. . .] the UNIDROIT Principles, as far as they can be considered to reflect generally accepted Principles and rules"* (emphasis added), while in the second it declared that it would base its decision on the "terms of the contract, **21–022**

---

[23] Art. 28(4) provides that "[i]n all cases the arbitral tribunal shall decide in accordance with the terms of the contract and shall take into account the usages of the trade applicable to the transaction."

[24] For abstracts of the three partial awards rendered in 1995, 1998 and 1999 respectively, see *ICC International Court of Arbitration Bulletin*, Vol. 10, no. 2 (1999), pp. 39–57.

[25] ICC Award No. 7375 of June 5, 1996: *c.f.* 11 *Mealey's International Arbitration Report* 1996, A-1 *et seq.*; *Uniform Law Review* 1997, p. 598.

[26] ICC Award No. 8261 of September 27, 1996, in *Uniform Law Review* 1999, 171.

supplemented by general Principles of trade as embodied in the *lex mercatoria"* and eventually applied some individual provisions of the UNIDROIT Principles with no further explanation.

21–023 Finally mention may be made of ICC Award No. 7365.[27] The case concerned contracts for the delivery of sophisticated military equipment, entered into in 1977 between a U.S. corporation and the Iranian Air Force. The contracts contained a choice-of-law clause in favour of the law of the Government of Iran in effect at the date of the contracts, but when the dispute arose the parties eventually agreed to the supplementary application of "general Principles of international law and trade usages". The Arbitral Tribunal declared that as to the contents of such general Principles and rules it would be guided by the UNIDROIT Principles and indeed, when deciding the merits of the case, on a number of occasions based its solutions, exclusively or in conjunction with similar rules to be found in Iranian law, on individual provisions of the UNIDROIT Principles such as Arts 5.1–5.2 on express and implied obligations, 6.2.3(4) (*Effects of hardship*), 7.3.6 (*Restitution*) and 7.4.9 (*Interest for failure to pay money*).

21–024 It is worth noting that the award was challenged by the U.S. corporation before the District Court, S.D. California precisely on the ground, among others, that the Arbitral Tribunal, by resorting to the UNIDROIT Principles, whereas the parties had only referred to "general Principles of international law" as the rules applicable to the substance of the dispute, had exceeded the scope of the submission to arbitration thereby violating Article V(1)(c) of the 1958 New York Convention on the Recognition and Enforcement of Foreign Arbitral Awards. However the Court expressly rejected this argument, thereby confirming the Arbitral Tribunal's implicit assumption that the UNIDROIT Principles represent a source of "general Principles of international law and usages" to which arbitrators may resort even in the absence of an express authorisation by the parties.[28]

3.2 International sales contracts governed by CISG

21–025 On account of its binding nature, CISG will normally take precedence over the UNIDROIT Principles whenever the requirements for its application are met.

21–026 It is true that according to Art. 6 CISG parties may exclude the Convention wholly or in part. While there may be cases where parties choose to replace individual articles of CISG by the corresponding provisions of the UNIDROIT Principles which they consider to be more appropriate, an exclusion of CISG in its entirety in favour of the UNIDROIT Principles is, at least for the time being, rather unlikely. As a matter of fact, parties do quite often exclude CISG, but this is generally because they are afraid of the

---

[27] ICC Award No. 7365 of May 5, 1997. For a summary of the award see *Uniform Law Review*, 1999, p. 796 *et seq.*

[28] *cf. The Ministry of Defence and Support for the Armed Forces of the Islamic Republic of Iran v. Cubic Defense Systems, Inc.*, 29 F.Supp. 2d 1168: for a comment see M.J. Bonell, A Significant Recognition of the UNIDROIT Principles by an United States Court, in Uniform Law Review 1999, pp. 651–663.

uncertainties surrounding the application of any novel instrument. In such cases, they will prefer the safety of domestic law rather than venture into the application of something as novel as the UNIDROIT Principles, whatever their intrinsic merits.

It remains to be seen, however, what will happen if the parties, either **21–027** because they are not aware of the existence of CISG, or because they do not know that their contract falls within the scope of application of CISG, refer to the UNIDROIT Principles as the applicable law, without expressly excluding CISG. The view has been expressed that such reference is tantamount to a tacit exclusion of CISG as a whole, just as occurs, for example, if the parties choose the law of a non-Contracting State or refer to Principles and rules typical of the non-unified domestic law of any State, whether or not a party to CISG.[29] This argument, however, is difficult to accept. There is not the same degree of incompatibility between the UNIDROIT Principles and CISG as exists between CISG and the domestic law of whichever State: on the contrary, they are both instruments of international origin which, apart from their different scope, at most differ in specific provisions. It follows that reference to the UNIDROIT Principles as the law governing the contract cannot be construed as indicating the parties" intention to exclude CISG in its entirety; the sole consequence of such reference is that, within the limits of party autonomy according to Article 6, CISG, the UNIDROIT Principles will prevail over any conflicting provision of CISG. CISG, however, will continue to govern the individual contract as the applicable law; hence all issues peculiar to sales contracts and as such neglected by the UNIDROIT Principles, such as for instance the seller's liability for defective goods, and the specific remedies granted to the buyer, will be governed by CISG, not by the otherwise applicable domestic law, as would be the case if CISG were to be completely excluded by the parties.

3.2.1 The UNIDROIT Principles as a means of interpreting and supplementing CISG

Yet even in cases where the international sales contract is governed by CISG, **21–028** the UNIDROIT Principles may serve an important purpose.

According to Article 7(1), CISG, "[i]n the interpretation of this Conven- **21–029** tion regard is to be had to its international character and to the need to promote uniformity in its application [. . .]", while Article 7(2) states that "[q]uestions concerning matters governed by this Convention which are not expressly settled in it are to be settled in conformity with the general Principles on which it is based [. . .]".[30]

In the past the Principles and criteria for the proper interpretation of **21–030** CISG have had to be found by the judges and arbitrators on an *ad hoc* basis. After publication of the UNIDROIT Principles the question arises whether,

---

[29] K. Boele-Woelki, *The Principles and Private International Law*. The UNIDROIT Principles of International Commercial Contracts and the Principles of European Contract Law: How to Apply Them to International Contracts, in *Uniform Law Review* 1996, p. 652 *et seq.* (p. 670).
[30] Only in the absence of such general Principles does the same article permit as a last resort reference to the domestic law applicable by virtue of the rules of private international law.

and if so, to what extent they can be used as a means of interpreting and supplementing CISG.

21–031 Opinions among legal scholars are divided. On the one hand there are those who categorically deny that CISG can be interpreted on the basis of the UNIDROIT Principles, invoking the rather formalistic and not necessarily convincing argument that as the latter were adopted later in time than the former they cannot be of any relevance.[31] On the other hand there are those who, perhaps too enthusiastically, justify the use of the UNIDROIT Principles as a means of interpreting or supplementing CISG on the mere ground that they are "general Principles of international commercial contracts".[32] The correct solution would appear to lie between these two extreme positions. In other words, there can be little doubt that in general the UNIDROIT Principles may well be used to interpret or supplement even pre-existing international instruments such as CISG; on the other hand in order for individual provisions to be used to fill gaps in CISG, they must be the expression of general Principles underlying also CISG.[33]

21–032 Among the provisions of the UNIDROIT Principles which might serve to clarify rather ambiguous provisions of CISG, reference has been made to Art. 7.1.4(2), which states that the right to cure is not precluded by notice of termination, in connection with Article 48 CISG; Article 7.1.7(4), which expressly indicates the remedies not affected by the occurrence of an impediment preventing a party from performance, in connection with Article 79 (5) CISG; and Article 7.3.1(2), which specifies the factors to be taken into account for the determination of whether or not there has been a fundamental breach of contract, in connection with Article 25 CISG.[34]

21–033 As to the provision of the UNIDROIT Principles to be used to fill veritable gaps in CISG, reference has been made to Articless 2.15 and 2.16 on negotiation in bad faith and breach of a duty of confidentiality, respectively; Article 6.1.6(1)(a) stating the general principle according to which a monetary obligation is to be performed at the obligee's place of business; Articles. 6.1.7, 6.1.8 and 6.1.9 which provide an answer to the questions, likewise not expressly settled in CISG, of whether, and if so under what conditions, the seller is entitled to pay by cheque or by other similar instruments, or by a funds transfer, and in which currency payment is to be made; Article 7.4.9(1) and (2) on the time from which the right to interest accrues and the rate of interest to be applied; and Article 7.4.12 on the currency in which to assess damages.[35]

---

[31] See F. Sabourin, Quebec, in M.J. Bonell (Ed.), *A New Approach*, p. 245.

[32] See J. Basedow, Germany, in M.J. Bonell (Ed.), *A New Approach, supra* n. 29, pp. 149–150. For a similar view see K.-P. Berger, *The Creeping Codification of the Lex Mercatoria*, 1999 (Kluwer Law International), p. 182.

[33] See, also for further references, M.J. Bonell, *An International Restatement, supra* n. 4, pp.75–82. More recently, F. Ferrari in P. Schlechtriem (Ed.), *Kommentar zum Einheitlichen UN-Kaufrecht—CISG*, (3rd ed. 2000), p. 138 (No. 64); C. W. Canaris, Die Stellung der "UNIDROIT Principles" und der "Principles of European Contract Law" im System der Rechtsquellen, in J. BASEDOW (Ed.), *Europäische Vertragsrechtsvereinheitlichung und deutsches Recht*, Tübingen (Mohr Siebeck), 2000, p. 5 *et seq.*, at p. 28

[34] See, also for further references, M.J. Bonell, *An International Restatement, supra* n. 4, pp. 76–77.

[35] See, also for further references, M.J. Bonell, *An International Restatement, supra* n. 4, pp.77–82.

Turning to actual practice, it is worth noting that courts and arbitral **21–034** tribunals have so far generally taken an extremely favourable attitude to the UNIDROIT Principles as a means of interpreting and supplementing CISG.

Significantly only in a few cases has recourse to the UNIDROIT Principles **21–035** been justified on the ground that the individual provisions invoked as gap-fillers could be considered an expression of general Principles underlying also CISG.

Thus, in two awards of the International Court of Arbitration of the **21–036** Federal Chamber of Commerce of Vienna[36] the sole arbitrator applied Article 7.4.9(2) of the UNIDROIT Principles, according to which the applicable rate of interest is the average bank short-term lending rate to prime borrowers prevailing at the place for payment for the currency of payment, in order to fill the gap in Article 78, CISG on the ground that it could be considered an expression of the general principle of full compensation underlying both the UNIDROIT Principles and CISG. Likewise the Court of Appeal of Grenoble,[37] in referring to Article 6.1.6 of the UNIDROIT Principles to determine under CISG the place of performance of the seller's obligation to return the price unduly paid by the buyer, stated that this provision expressed in general terms the principle underlying also Article 57(1) CISG, *i.e.* that monetary obligations have to be performed at the obligee's place of business.

On two other occasions Article 7.4.9(2) of the UNIDROIT Principles on **21–037** the applicable rate of interest was applied with no further justification at all,[38] or because it was considered *"one of the general Principles according to Article 7(2) CISG"* (emphasis added).[39]

Finally, in other cases the arbitral tribunal went even further by stating in **21–038** general terms that it would apply "the provisions of [CISG] *and its general Principles, now contained in the UNIDROIT Principles* [. . .]"[40] or that in applying CISG it was "informative to refer to [the UNIDROIT Principles] *because they are said to reflect a world-wide consensus in most of the basic matters of contract law"* (emphasis added).[41] The individual provisions of the

---

[36] *cf.* Schiedsspruche SCH 4318 and SCH 4366 of June 15, 1994: see them published in the original German version in Recht der internationalen Wirtschaft 1995, p. 590 *et seq.*, with note by P. SCHLECHTRIEM (p. 592 *et seq.*); for an English translation see M.J. Bonell (ed.), UNILEX. International Case Law & Bibliography on the UN Convention on Contracts for the International Sale of Goods, (Transnational Publishers, Inc.) Ardsely, NY, December 1998 release, E.1994-13 and E.1994-14.

[37] *cf.* Cour d'Appel de Grenoble, October 23, 1996, in *Uniform Law Review* 1997, p. 182.

[38] *cf.* ICC Award No. 8769 of December 1996 in ICC *International Court of Arbitration Bulletin*, p. 75.

For a similar approach see also ICC Award No. 8908 of 1998, ICC *International Court of Arbitration Bulletin*, pp. 83–87 (at p.87): after having pointed out that "Art. 78 [CISG] [. . .] does not lay down the criteria for calculating the interest" and that "[i]nternational case law presents a wide range of possibilities in this respect, the Arbitral Tribunal, though without expressly mentioning Art. 7.4.9(2) of the UNIDROIT Principles, concluded that "amongst the criteria adopted in various judgments, the more appropriate appears to be that of the rates generally applied in international trade for the contractual currency . . . in concrete terms, since the contractual currency is the dollar the the parties European, the applicable rate is the 3-month LIBOR on the dollar, increased by one percentage point, with effect from the due date not respected up until full payment has been made."

[39] *cf.* ICC Award No. 8128 of 1995, in *Journal de droit international* 1996, p. 1024, with note by D. Hascher, *ibid.*, p. 1028; *Uniform Law Review* 1997, p. 810.

[40] *cf.* ICC Award No. 8817 of December 1997, in *ICC International Court of Arbitration Bulletin*, p. 75–78.

[41] *cf.* ICC Award No. 9117 of March 1998 in *ICC International Court of Arbitration Bulletin*, pp. 96–101.

UNIDROIT Principles applied in these two cases were Articles 1.8 on usages and 7.4.8 on mitigation of harm, and Articles 2.17 on merger clauses, 2.18 on written modification clauses and 4.3 on the relevant circumstances in contract interpretation, respectively.

3.2.2 UNIDROIT Principles and CISG side by side

21–039 In view of the more comprehensive nature of the UNIDROIT Principles, parties may well wish to apply them in addition to CISG for matters not covered therein. To this effect, they may include a clause in the contract which might read as follows:

> "This contract shall be governed by CISG, and with respect to matters not covered by this Convention, by the *UNIDROIT* Principles of International Commercial Contracts".

21–040 A similar provision has been included in the International Trade Centre UNCTAD/WTO *Model Contract for the International Commercial Sale of Perishable Goods* (1999), Article 14 (*"Applicable Rules of Law"*) of which states:

> "In so far as any matters are not covered by the foregoing provisions, this Contract is governed by the following, in descending order of precedence: The United Nations Convention on Contracts for the International sale of Goods; the UNIDROIT Principles of International Commercial Contracts, and for matters not dealt with in the above-mentioned texts, the law applicable at [. . .] or, in the absence of a choice of law, the law applicable at the Seller's place of business through which this Contract is to be performed."

21–041 The difference between the role attributed to the UNIDROIT Principles under such a clause and the role which, as has been shown, they may play under Article 7(2) CISG is, at least in theory, clear. Under Article 7(2), the UNIDROIT Principles merely serve to fill in any lacunae to be found in CISG, *i.e.* to provide a solution for "[q]uestions concerning matters governed by [CISG] which are not expressly settled in it [. . .]" and with respect to which recourse to domestic law is permitted only as a last resort. By contrast, by virtue of a parties" reference to the UNIDROIT Principles of the kind described above, the latter are intended to apply to matters actually outside the scope of CISG and which otherwise would fall directly within the sphere of the applicable domestic law.

21–042 Given the non-binding nature of the UNIDROIT Principles the impact of such a reference is likely to vary according to whether a domestic court or an arbitral tribunal is seized of the case.

21–043 Domestic courts will tend to consider the parties" reference to the UNIDROIT Principles as a mere agreement to incorporate them into the contract and to determine the law governing that contract on the basis of their own conflict-of-law rules.[42] As a result, they will apply the UNIDROIT Principles only to the extent that the latter do not affect the provisions of the

---

[42] For more on this point, *cf.* M.J. Bonell, *An International Restatement of Contract Law*, *supra* n. 4, p. 180 *et seq.*

proper law from which the parties may not derogate. This may be the case, for instance, with the rules on contracting on the basis of standard terms (*cf.* Articles 2.19, 2.22) or on public permission requirements (*cf.* Articles 6.1.14, 6.1.17). On the other hand, the rules relating to validity (*cf.* Chapter 3) or to the court's intervention in cases of hardship (*cf.* Article 6.2.3) will only be applied to the extent that they do not run counter to the corresponding provisions of the applicable domestic law.

The situation is different if the parties agree to submit their disputes aris- **21–044**
ing from the contract to arbitration. Arbitrators are not necessarily bound to base their decision on a particular domestic law.[43] Hence they may well apply the UNIDROIT Principles not merely as terms incorporated in the contract, but as "rules of law" governing the contract together with CISG irrespective of whether or not they are consistent with the particular domestic law otherwise applicable. The only mandatory rules arbitrators may take into account, also in view of their task of rendering to the largest possible extent an effective decision capable of enforcement, are those which claim to be applicable irrespective of the law otherwise governing the contract ("*loi d'application nécessaire*"). Yet the application, along with the UNIDROIT Principles, of the mandatory rules in question will as a rule not give rise to any true conflict, given their different subject-matter.[44]

4. Conclusion

The foregoing remarks amply demonstrate that even in the context of **21–045**
international sales contracts CISG and the UNIDROIT Principles are not alternatives but complementary instruments.

This is only too evident with respect to international sales contracts lying **21–046**
outside the scope of application of CISG. In such cases the UNIDROIT Principles represent a set of internationally uniform rules which the parties may—and actually increasingly do—choose as the *lex contractus*, or which arbitral tribunals may—and actually increasingly do—apply as an expression of "general Principles of law", the *lex mercatoria* or the like.

Yet even with respect to international sales contracts governed by CISG, **21–047**
the UNIDROIT Principles may play an important role. In the absence of an express reference by the parties, they may be—and actually increasingly are bcing—uscd, though not indiscriminatcly, as a mcans of intcrprcting or supplementing CISG. In the presence of an express reference by the parties, the UNIDROIT Principles may moreover apply to matters outside the scope of CISG and which otherwise would fall within the sphere of the applicable domestic law.

In conclusion it may well be said that both CISG and the UNIDROIT **21–048**
Principles are the right instruments at the right time: each one has its own *raison d'être*.

---

[43] See M.J. Bonell, *An International Restatement of Contract Law*, *supra* n. 4, p. 183 *et seq.*
[44] One of the few potential examples of such conflict may be where arbitrators have to decide between the law of the place of payment imposing the payment in local currency and the different solution provided for in the UNIDROIT Principles that otherwise governs the contract.

CHAPTER 22

RULE-SETTING BY PRIVATE ORGANISATIONS, STANDARDISATION OF CONTRACTS AND THE HARMONISATION OF INTERNATIONAL SALES LAW

ALEJANDRO M. GARRO[1]

1. Introduction

22–001 More than 40 years ago, at a time when the international codification of the law of sales was still in doubt, Professor Schmitthoff examined the role of the standardisation of contracts in the harmonisation of international commercial law.[2] Standard or model contract forms, general conditions of business, and rules adopted by professional organisations are included among a broad range of rule-making activities adopted by the international business community and they claim, as such, some role in the progressive harmonisation of international commercial law.

22–002 Regardless of the mode or shape taken by these rules, they may be loosely regarded as quasi-formal sources of a constantly evolving *lex mercatoria*. While praising the involvement of the business community in

---

[1] Adjunct Professor of Law, Columbia University; Senior Research Scholar, Parker School of Foreign and Comparative Law, Columbia Law School, 435 W. 116th St., New York, NY 10027, e-mail: garro@law.columbia.edu.

[2] See Clive M. Schmitthoff, The Unification or Harmonisation of Law By Means of Standard Contracts and General Conditions, 17 Int. & Comp. L. Q. 551 (1968). See also, Clive M. Schmitthoff, *Schmitthoff's Export Trade. The Law and Practice of International Trade* 63–80 (9th ed. 1990), 669–690 (10th ed. 2000).

what he perceived as an increasing trend towards self-regulation, Professor Schmitthoff noted that the active participation of all sectors of the business community, exporters as well as importers, was a key factor in developing useful, reliable and fair set of rules capable of complementing incipient codification efforts at an international level. It is particularly fitting to recall Schmitthoff's critical view on the self-regulation of international sales in connection with the current expansion of private rule-formulating agencies and parallel efforts of codification undertaken by international agencies such as UNCITRAL and UNIDROIT.

This re-examination of the role of standard terms calls for some concep-   **22–003**
tual distinctions. First, it is necessary to distinguish between the treatment standard or model contracts and general conditions that are relevant to international trade, from the adhesion contracts that are so common to domestic consumer transactions. Next, once identified the type of model contracts and clauses that are most relevant to the harmonisation of international sales, it is necessary to explore the extent to which the standardisation of contracts may be regarded by a given legal system as a more or less formal source of international trade (business or commercial) law. This calls in turn for some discussion of the complex interaction between standard contracts and other types of self-regulatory rules issued by those engaged in a particular branch of trade (or the professional organisations that represent the interest of those traders) and the more formally recognised sources of law such as national laws, international conventions and instruments, and customary international law or more informal practices or usages of trade.

Also relevant to this is to explore possible parallelisms between the contribu-   **22–004**
tion of standard contracts and general conditions to the cause of harmonisation with the contribution provided by more formal international instruments. Which are the non-governmental organisations that have assumed the responsibility of self-regulation, what have they accomplished so far, and which methods they followed in this rule-setting business. Who decides to use model contracts or general conditions and what gets decided in terms of the content of a particular standard contract or term are separate but related issues. The "political economy" of self-rulemaking processes is admittedly complex, but even a modest glance to the interests pursued by a particular private industry may explain much of the type of rules that get produced. Finally, and as a sort of afterthought on this trend towards self-regulation, one should ponder how to ensure that the validity of standard terms is uniformly upheld and are subject to consistent, if not uniform interpretation. Also on this subject Professor Clive Schmitthoff reflected with great insight 30 years ago.

2. Standard contracts and general conditions: total and partial standardisation

2.1 Standard contracts and adhesion contracts

Standard or model contracts, as well as standard or model clauses or terms,   **22–005**
are always written, always prepared in advance, invariably submitted by one party to another who generally accepts the terms without much discussion or negotiation. Yet, it is arguably possible to draw a distinction between the policy approach toward standard contracts and model clauses commonly used

in international business transactions between parties of relatively equal bargaining power, as opposed to standard contracts prevailing in domestic consumer transactions, typically confronting a powerful commercial firm with a much weaker party, who is likely to acquire property or contracts services for his or her personal use.

22–006   Accordingly, standard contracts or terms used in international business transactions may be properly identified with boilerplate formulae to which international practitioners will turn for guidance in drafting an international contract, and which are susceptible of alteration or adaptation by the parties during the course of their negotiations in order to meet their needs. In contrast, an adhesion contract may be identified with the type of specimen submitted by the stipulator to the adherent in a typical "quick-hand" transaction, on a "take-it-or-leave-it" basis, generally intended to be inalterable and whose terms are unlikely to be negotiated.[3]

22–007   The noted difference between standard terms used in international business transactions and adhesion contracts typically envisioned by domestic consumer legislation does not deny the existence of some kind of connection between the two. International contracts are not always concluded between parties of equal bargaining power, and even though the possibility of changing the standard terms offered by one party is always there, it often happens that the party who is in a weaker bargaining position ends up accepting the standard contract or term in the form in which it is made. However, unlike the typical consumer transaction, in the typical international business transaction a stringent standard term may have been accepted by the other party for a *quid pro quo* or a good business reason, or at least this is what in most cases it may be fairly presumed to have happened. If that was not the case, a court or arbitral tribunal will be required to police the terms of the contract in the same way as if it would be an adhesion contract in a domestic setting.

2.2 Total and partial standardisation of contracts

22–008   Further distinctions may be drawn from business practices between a total or comprehensive standardisation of contracts, represented by a complete model contract form in which the parties merely fill in the blank spaces (*e.g.*, names, price terms, specifity of the goods), as opposed to a partial standardisation of terms through the inclusion of a typical or recurrent catalogue of clauses or terms that may serve as aide-memoir to the person drafting a contract (*e.g.*, price escalation, reservation of title, exemption of liability, choice of law and forum). Samples of model contracts are those prepared by the International Chamber of Commerce[4] on the sale of manufactured goods

---

[3] For further conceptual clarification on this issue, the reader is referred to a seminal contribution by Professor Ole Lando on the so-called "General Conditions" (G.C.) issued by rule-setting organisations. See Ole Lando, *Standard Contracts. A Proposal and A Perspective*, in 10 *Scandinavian Studies in Law* 127 (1966).

[4] In its latest brochure on *ICC and Rule-Setting* distributed in 2000 (hereinafter "ICC and Rule-Setting"), the ICC defines ICC model contract forms as those "giving the parties a neutral framework for their contractual relationships: their provisions have been drafted to ensure consistency with the parties" legal systems without expressing a bias for any one particular legal system. They are flexible and user-friendly contractual tools, and are used in countless daily transactions."

intended for resale,[5] commercial agency,[6] distributorship agreements,[7] model conract for privacy protection in telecommunications,[8] and many others currently in preparation.[9] Many international commodity transactions are almost exclusively concluded with the use of these forms. On the other hand, partial standardisation through the adoption of terms covering only a segment of the contract is represented by standard terms such as the *ICC Force Majeure Clause* recommended for all major international contracts (sales, distribution, engineering, building, etc.) as well as domestic sales. Even more well known are the *Incoterms* issued by the ICC, first published in 1936 and periodically revised until 2000 to take into account the latest developments in international trade such as containerisation, development of multimodal transport, and the use of electronic data interchange.

3. The binding force of standard contracts depends on the applicable law

How do standard contracts and general conditions acquire binding force and won what hierarchy do those standard terms occupy *vis-à-vis* other sources of law? The answer to this question rests on the recognition given by the applicable law to the parties' freedom to choose the law applicable to their contract. Eventually, other types of self-regulation may acquire the force of customary law or trade usages, in which case the binding force of the standard terms may derive from a constructive or fictional consent that the applicable law attaches to the parties as a matter of law.   **22–009**

Assuming that most Western legal systems will recognise the autonomy of the parties to adopt their own rules, it must be borne in mind that the binding force of those rules, hence the validity of the standard contracts or terms, cannot be determined with absolute independence from the law that is applicable to the contract. In other words, standard contracts do not and cannot stand alone; they must be interpreted and understood against a legal background provided by law applicable to the transaction in question.   **22–010**

Standard contracts and terms operate within the limits of public policy, as reflected in the mandatory rules of the applicable law. And public policy is likely to be concerned, for example, with the genuineness of the parties' freedom to consent to the application of the standard terms. Thus, in order to compensate for the imbalance of economic bargaining power between,   **22–011**

---

[5] *ICC Model Sale Contract (Manufactured goods intended for resale)* (1997), which has been used as a model by the International Trade Centre (a joint UNCTAD/WTO organisation) for the elaboration of the 1999 model contract and user's guides for the international commercial sale of perishable goods.

[6] *ICC Model Commercial Agency Contract* (1991).

[7] *ICC Model Distributorship Contract* (1993)

[8] *Model Contract for Privacy Protection in Transborder Data Flows* (1992). This model contract, which the ICC suggested for incorporation into contracts requiring the cross-border transmission of personal data, has been jointly endorsed by ICC, the Council of Europe and the European Commission.

[9] According to the International Chamber of Commerce, there are a series of model contract forms currently under elaboration, including the ICC Model International Franchising Contract, ICC Model Mergers & Acquisition Contract, ICC Model Agency Contract (short form), ICC Model Distributorship Contract (short form), and ICC Model Turnkey Contract. See ICC and Rule-Setting at 2–3.

say, shippers and carriers, the applicable law or international convention (*e.g.*, Brussels Convention or Hague Rules) may prohibit the parties from contracting out the carrier's liability or may force the parties to contract in certain provisions. In this regard, it has been noted that standard contracts or terms, though a useful tool of conflict avoidance, they do not provide for a full-proof conflict-avoidance device. There is a limit as to the extent to which standard contracts or terms may "evade" the application of municipal law. Confronting this reality calls for a consideration of the interrelationship between standard contracts and trade usages.

4. Standardisation of contracts and international trade usages

22–012   No standard contract or term may bind a party who has not accepted to be governed by it. Yet repeated patterns of behaviour may give rise to a practice, usage, or custom, which in turn may give rise to a series of expectations to which a given legal system may attach binding force, equivalent to a contractual clause expressly consented by the parties or to formally sanctioned norm. Thus, if merchants engaged in a certain area of trade resort very often to certain model contracts or standard terms, they may be imputed with knowledge of those forms to the point of being considered to have implicitly adopted those standard terms into their contract.

22–013   Mere standardisation of a certain term or clause does not suffice to conclude that such a term has turned into a custom or usage, and domestic legal systems differ as to how immemorial or universal a given habit must be to attain the category of "usage" or "custom" in any given branch of trade.[10] Be this as it may, the answer to the question when does the standardisation of a certain term actually become a genuine usage or custom is likely to be inconclusive in most municipal systems, for any given practice is likely to go through a period of evolution before it becomes crystallised. Thus, it is not uncommon for a certain rule to start as a business procedure followed by a few leading enterprises, then turn into a practice generally observed in a particular area of trade, eventually growing into a trade usage at a national level in a particular industry and later expanding to an international usage.

22–014   It is the degree of acceptance enjoyed by the alleged practice or usage what determines its legitimacy as a source of law. Since the use of standard terms is bound to be always *in fieri*, it is not easy to ascertain the point in time when commercial practices and usages have become so widely used that business people would expect their contracting parties to conform their behaviour to those practices. One of the elements influential in this determination is the promulgation of a given set of standard contracts or terms by an international agency of recognised prestige in the business community. This is a subject to which Professor Clive Schmitthoff considered of relevance to ascertain whether a given usage enjoyed acceptance to a considerable degree,[11] and this is the theme to which our attention now turns.

---

[10] For a thorough and insightful treatment on this matter, see Filip De Ly, *International Business Law and Lex Mercatoria* 134–182 (T.M.C. Asser Institut, The Hague, 1992).
[11] Clive M. Schmitthoff, *The Law of International Trade, Its Growth, Operation and Formulation*, in *The Sources of the Law of International Trade* 16 (Schmitthoff, ed. London, 1964).

5. Standard contracts and terms adopted by recognised "professional organisations"

The rule-making activity of professional organisations has been acknowledged **22–015** for a long time, and so is the fact that the degree of acceptance of a given usage may be influenced by its adoption in the form of a model contract or term by a reputable professional organisation. By way of an example, we may refer to the contributions made several decades ago to the harmonisation of international sales law made by organisations as different as the Economic Commission for Europe of the United Nations ("UN/ECE") and the International Chamber of Commerce ("ICC"). Other international trade associations in traditional export commodities have been largely responsible for achieving a *de facto* harmonisation of commercial terms.[12] A glimpse to the kind of rule-making activity in which these organisations have been engaged may provide some clue as to the role they occupy in the harmonisation process.

The UN/ECE elaborated the General Conditions of Sale and Standard **22–016** Form Contracts, incorporating model contract forms developed by international trade associations in the trade of commodities.[13] The model forms varied from country to country and from trade to trade, including various forms for the sale of plant and machinery, durable consumer goods, cereals, timber and miscellaneous goods (*e.g.*, citrus fruit, solid fuels). The ICC provides yet another model of rule-making activity which has managed to contribute significantly to the cause of harmonisation of the law of sales. Perhaps the most well-known contribution has been the codification of trade terms under the name of Incoterms.

Unlike the standard model contracts prepared by the UN/ECE, the **22–017** Incoterms do not represent a total standardisation device, but rather a partial standardisation of certain price-delivery terms and the allocation of risks and costs between the parties to the contract of sale. It started in 1923 with a survey on the interpretation of six trade terms in 13 countries, leading to the publication of the first edition in 1936. By 1953 the Incoterms expanded its coverage to provide a uniform interpretation of 10 trade terms in 18 countries. Subsequent editions in 1967, 1976, 1980, 1990 and 2000 sought to confirm and expand on the greatest "common measure of practice" (the *"fond commun"* or common core) around those trade terms. Six months after launching the Incoterms 2000, they are the already the most widely used version of Incoterms ever. As reported by the ICC, they are constantly used in countries as the United States and China, where the use of the previous version, Incoterms 1990, was not systematic.[14]

In addition to the codification of standardised trade terms, the rule-setting **22–018** activity of the ICC has expanded to the fashioning of rules adopted by

---

[12] Among the more traditional international trade associations should be included the London Corn Trade Association (1877), the Grain and Feed Trade Association (GAFTA), the Federation of Oil Seeds & Fats Association, the Association of Corn Merchants of Hamburg (1968), the Bremen Cotton Exchange (1872), the Silk Association of America (1873), etc.
[13] See P. Benjamin, *The ECE General Conditions of Sale and Standard Forms of Contracts*, [1961] JBL 113.
[14] ICC and rule-setting at 3.

members of the organisations that adhere to those rules. Under the heading of "voluntary codes", the ICC has elaborated other rules in areas as diverse as arbitration,[15] banking and finance,[16] marketing and advertising,[17] insurance,[18] customs,[19] telecommunications and information technologies,[20] transport,[21] environment,[22] and exortion and bribery.[23] Regardless of the form these "uniform rules" may take (codes of conduct, guides, customs and practices, etc.) they have been adopted by the ICC with the aspiration to influence national legislation, the development of what may represent increasingly accepted trade usages, or at least offer a set of rules that may be adopted by companies, professional associations and self-regulatory bodies.[24]

22–019   Despite the absence of legislative authority, many of those rules developed by the ICC have become widely respected and by industry and business circles worldwide. It was Professor Schmitthoff who attributed much of the practical success of the Incoterms to the wisdom of adopting only a partial standardisation of business terms, limiting the harmonisation effort to a few trade practices and only after a serious effort to ascertain a common measure of globally accepted standards.

22–020   This prudent approach allow us to realise that there are many areas of the law that are not yet ripe for the formulation of standard contracts or rules, at a time when the issuance of mere "guidelines" may be more appropriate

---

[15] The International Court of Arbitration has been in business since 1923 and has played a prominent role in securing the worldwide acceptance of international commercial arbitration.

[16] Among the many international banking instruments elaborated by the ICC are included the *Uniform Customs and Practice for Documentary Credits* (UCP 500, Revised 1993). More than 100 countries have signed up to the UCP adherence list on the ICC website (http://www.iccwbo.org). Other banking instruments include the *Uniform Rules for Demand Guarantees* (URDG 458, 1992) and the *Uniform Rules for Collection* (URC 522). The newest banking instrument is represented by the *International Standby Practices* (ISP 98, adopted 1999). The ICC estimates that 15% to 20% of standby letters of credit use ISP 98, but it is difficult as yet to judge their impact as genuine trade usages. See ICC and rule-setting at 1.

[17] See, *e.g.*, the *ICC International Code of Adverstising Practice* , the *ICC International Copde of Direct Selling* (1999), *ICC Guidelines on Advertising and Marketing on the Internet* (1998), and the *ICC/ESOMAR International Code of Marketing and Social Research Practice*.

[18] See *ICC Rules for Contract Bonds* (URCB, 1994), regulating the increasing use of performance bonds in different countries of the world.

[19] In this field the World Customs Organisations joined the ICC to elaborate a set of business principles on customs administrations embodied in the *ICC International Customs Guidelines*. See ICC and rule-setting at 2.

[20] See, *e.g.*, *ICC Uniform Rules of Conduct for Interchange of Trade Data by Tele-transmission* (1988), which has provided significant support to the growth in the use of Electronic Data Interchange (EDI) in all business sectors; *ICC General Usage in Digitally Ensured Commerce* (GUIDEC, 1997), attempting to set worldwide standards for e-signature practices.

[21] In 1992 were issued the UNCTAD/ICC Rules for multimodal transport documents.

[22] *ICC Business Charter for Sustainable Development—Principles for Environmental Management*; *Environmental Management System Resource Training Kit*; and the *ICC Code on Environmental Advertising* (1991).

[23] Part of the struggle to combat extortion and bribery in international trade included a 1997 ICC Report on Extortion and Bribery in business transactions, which later evolved into the *ICC Rules of Conduct to Combat Extortion and Bribery in International Business Transactions*, which were subsequently accompanied with the publication of the *ICC Corporate Practices Manual: Fighting Bribery* (1999).

[24] ICC and rule-setting at 1 ("ICC codes are often applied as a reference point for solving national or cross-border disputes. They can be effective in three ways: through enactment in national legislation; they can be applied directly by companies, professional associations and self-regulatory bodies; or they can be adapted to local or specific professional requirements.")

than the standardisation of terms that are subject to rapidly changing practices. Other commercial practices may enjoy some consensus in certain commercial circles, in which case one may assert their binding force among participants in that branch of the trade. For example, there is no question that a great number of banking associations have endorsed the *ICC Uniform Customs and Practice for Documentary Credits* ("UCP"), whose binding force to interbank relationships can hardly be contested, at least among those banks who belong to those banking associations. However, the binding force of the UCP to relationships between the bank, account party, the beneficiary of the credit or its assignees may call for further evidence that they actually accepted to be bound by those rules.

Certain "practices" may be surrounded by a degree of controversy   **22–021** suggesting that it may be premature to standardise terms that are far from attending the category of genuine "trade usages." Thus, the controversy surrounding the carriers' adoption of superimposed clauses in a bill of lading, qualifying the representation that the shipped goods are in good order and condition, should not claim the status of "trade usages" unless and until one can really ascertain an acceptable compromise between shippers and carriers. In fact, the success of many harmonisation efforts rests on the possibility of achieving reasonable compromises among competing interests, a point which is not always easy to reach and to which our attention now turns.

6. The representation of competing interests in the formulation of standard terms and contracts

Older model contracts sponsored by powerful and traditional business   **22–022** organisations showed a tendency to favour members of the association, grossly shifting the balance to the advantage of the economically stronger. Yet, while weighing the legitimacy of the movement towards the standardis-ation of contracts and its potential contribution to the harmonisation of commercial practice, it is important to consider the extent to which this trend towards self-regulation actually incorporates a component of fairness, with-out which standard contracts cannot aspire to achieve widespread voluntary acceptance.

Much of the acceptance of standard terms formulated by private organi-   **22–023** sations depends on the chance given to parties holding competing interests to have a voice in the formulation of those terms. Not much attention has been paid to this point by the existing literature, even though model contracts and standard terms should be aimed at reaching an agreed balance of fairness between the economically stronger and weaker contracting parties. Thus, model contracts and clauses, as well as the uniform rules and voluntary codes prepared by the ICC are said to be issued only "after extensive consultations with business worldwide" in order to provide a "neutral framework"[25] to contractual relationships.

It is submitted that if genuinely wide representation is sought, then the   **22–024** participation of the business community in the elaboration of standard

---

[25] ICC and rule-setting at 1.

terms and contracts requires an additional effort towards reaching out those countries and organisations that are not commonly heard in business circles. I am referring to state agencies in developing countries as well as other participants in international commerce who have traditionally been mistrustful of the "spontaneous" trade usages elaborated by transnational enterprises with a main office of operations in industrialised nations. It is common for the working groups and parties leading the discussion and adoption of these "voluntary codes" to be staffed with representatives of leading multinational corporations engaged in a particular trade, many of whom are able to rely on the assistance of able and well prepared counsel. In contrast, many developing countries, if present at all, tend to be represented by civil servants from government ministries, whose participation tends to lack continuity and many of whom are not always prepared or even interested on the topic of discussion. This reality calls for new approaches aimed at recruiting more meaningful participation of representatives from developing countries, a task that may require the financial assistance of international organisations.

7. Validity and interpretation of standard contracts

22–025   Concern against the easy application of self-regulatory schemes of trade organisations in which the interest of some sectors of the business community are not represented are reflected in Article 9.2 of the Vienna Convention on Contracts for the International Sale of Goods ("CISG") calling for the application of trade usages only if widely known and regularly observed, or those which the parties ought to have known. This approach is narrower than the one adopted by CISG's predecessors, providing that "terms, forms, clauses usually used in the trade should be interpreted according to the meaning that is common in that trade."[26]

22–026   On the one hand, terms forced into the contract cannot acquire a binding force under the guise of standard terms turned into "usages", because Article 9.2 establishes a veritable link between the application of a particular usage and the parties' constructive consent. On the other hand, the requirement that the usages must be not only regularly observed but also widely known within a particular trade to which the parties belong (*e.g.*, wheat trade, industrial machinery trade, etc.) appears to ensure that usages followed by dominant trade associations within a particular country or region are not necessarily applicable to international transactions with a company from a country or region where such usage was not widely followed or known.

8. Harmonisation of international commercial law and standard texts

22–027   It may be easier for active participants in international trade to agree on the use of model contracts and standard terms than for legal scholars and government officials to reach a consensus as to the type of uniform law that should be adopted for recurring international transactions. At least that was the prevailing sentiment several decades ago was one of scepticism as to the

---

[26] See ULF Art. 13.2 and ULIS Art. 9.3.

possibility of adopting an international convention on the law of sales. According to some, the efforts towards the harmonisation and unification of international commercial law through the adoption of common terminology and rules in model contract forms could prove more fruitful than the adoption of international conventions.[27]

According to Professor Clive Schmitthoff, whose memory we evoke at this colloquium, the harmonisation efforts by agreeing on standard contracts and terms was not conceived as an alternative, but rather as a complement, to the harmonisation efforts sought to be achieved by international conventions.[28] After all, the rule-making activity of international agencies who are in the business of formulating standard texts seek to ascertain the existence of prevailing practices in a given area of trade, rather than the adoption of a more desirable and doctrinally improved set of rules pursued by the drafters of international conventions.[29] It is sober and stimulating to realise, now that more than 60 trading nations have adopted a uniform sales law, and the codification of international commercial law advances at a pace hardly imaginable at the time Professor Schmitthoff wrote his seminal contributions, that standard texts in the shape of model contracts, standard forms, and guidelines continue to play a significant role in the harmonisation of the law.

22–028

---

[27] See Kopelmanas, International Conventions and Standard Contracts as Means of Escaping from the Application of Municipal Law, in *The Sources of the Law of International Trade* 118 (Schmitthoff, ed., London, 1964) ("In the long run, the harmonisation of international trade law by means of model contracts may prove more fruitful than by means of international conventions."); Ole Lando, Standard Contracts. A Proposal And A Perspective, 10 *Scandinavian Studies in Law* 129, 140 (1966) ("International cooperation should, perhaps, not aim at making uniform rules on Standard Contracts but at making Standard Contracts.").

[28] Schmitthoff, The Unification or Harmonisation of Law by Means of Standard Contracts and General Conditions, 17 *Int. & Comp. L.Q.* 661, 569 (1968) ("The gradual establishment of a codified world trade law, essentially identical in all national jurisdictions, can only be achieved by a series of international conventions. This lofty ideal presupposes an international understanding to establish such a law, and at the present stage, on a realistic appreciation of the position, it would be premature to contend that such understanding already exists among the nations of the world. In the meantime, however, much practical preparatory work in the field of unification can be done by the ascertainment of standard contract texts.").

[29] Schmitthoff, *ibidem*, at pp.568–69. In these passages, Professor Schmitthoff contrasts what he calls the "consolidating method" followed to ascertain the content of standard texts, with the "codifying method" followed in the drafting of international conventions. Both are conceived as practical and useful exercises in applied comparative law, to which Professor Schmitthoff dedicated much of his teaching and scholarship.

CHAPTER 23

REVISITING THE AUTONOMOUS CONTRACT[1]—TRANSNATIONAL CONTRACT "LAW", TRENDS AND SUPPORTIVE STRUCTURES

RALPH AMISSAH

---

[1] This contribution is based on a previous work by the author: The Autonomous Contract: Reflecting the borderless electronic-commercial environment in contracting was published in Elektronisk handel—rettslige aspekter, Nordisk †rsbok i rettsinformatikk 1997 (Electronic Commerce—Legal Aspects. The Nordic Yearbook for Legal Informatics 1997) Edited by Randi Punsvik, or at http://www.jus.uio.no/the.autonomous.contract.07.10.1997.amissah/doc.html

1. Reinforcing trends: borderless technologies, global economy, transnational legal solutions?

Globalisation is to be observed as a trend intrinsic to the world economy.[2]   **23–001**
Rudimentary economics explains this runaway process, as being driven by competition within the business community to achieve efficient production, and to reach and extend available markets.[3] Technological advancement particularly in transport and communications has historically played a fundamental role in the furtherance of international commerce, with the Net, technology's latest spatio-temporally transforming offering, linchpin of the "new-economy", extending exponentially the global reach of the business community. The Net covers much of the essence of international commerce providing an instantaneous, low cost, convergent, global and borderless: information centre, marketplace and channel for communications, payments and the delivery of services and intellectual property. The sale of goods, however, involves the separate and distinct element of their physical delivery. The Net has raised a plethora of legal and other questions and has frequently offered solutions. The increased transparency of borders arising from the Net's ubiquitous nature results in an increased demand for the transparency of operation. As economic activities become increasingly global, to reduce transaction costs, there is a strong incentive for the "law" that provides for them, to do so in a similar dimension. The appeal of transnational legal solutions lies in the potential reduction in complexity, more widely dispersed expertise, and resulting increased transaction efficiency. The Net reflexively offers possibilities for the development of transnational legal solutions, having in a similar vein transformed the possibilities for the promulgation of texts, the sharing of ideas and collaborative ventures. There are however, likely to be tensions within the legal community protecting entrenched practices against that which is new, (both in law and technology) and the business community's goal to reduce transaction costs.

Within commercial law an analysis of law and economics may assist in   **23–002**
developing a better understanding of the relationship between commercial law and the commercial sector it serves.[4] ". . . [T]he importance of the interrelations between law and economics can be seen in the twin facts that legal change is often a function of economic ideas and conditions, which necessitate and/or generate demands for legal change, and that economic change is

---

[2] As Maria Cattaui Livanos suggests in *The global economy—an opportunity to be seized* in Business World the Electronic magazine of the International Chamber of Commerce (Paris, July 1997) at http://www.iccwbo.org/html/globalec.htm "Globalisation is unstoppable. Even though it may be only in its early stages, it is already intrinsic to the world economy. We have to live with it, recognise its advantages and learn to manage it. That imperative applies to governments, who would be unwise to attempt to stem the tide for reasons of political expediency. It also goes for companies of all sizes, who must now compete in global markets and learn to adjust their strategies accordingly, seizing the opportunities that globalisation offers."

[3] To remain successful, being in competition, the business community is compelled to take advantage of the opportunities provided by globalisation.

[4] Realists would contend that law is contextual and best understood by exploring the interrelationships between law and the other social sciences, such as sociology, psychology, political science and economics.

often governed by legal change."[5] In doing so, however, it is important to be aware that there are several competing schools of law and economics, with different perspectives, levels of abstraction, and analytical consequences of and for the world that they model.[6]

23–003   Where there is rapid interrelated structural change with resulting new features, rather than concentrate on traditionally established tectonic plates of a discipline, it is necessary to understand that underlying currents and concepts at their intersections, (rather than expositions of history)[7], is the key to commencing meaningful discussions and developing solutions for the resulting issues.[8] Interrelated developments are more meaningfully understood through interdisciplinary study, as this instance suggests, of the law, commerce/economics, and technology nexus. In advocating this approach, we should also pay heed to the realisation in the sciences, of the limits of reductionism in the study of complex systems, as such systems feature emergent properties that are not evident if broken down into their constituent parts. System complexity exceeds sub-system complexity; consequently, the relevant unit for understanding the systems function is the system, not its parts.[9] Simplistic dogma should be abandoned for a contextual approach.

2. Common property—advocating a common commercial highway

23–004   Certain infrastructural underpinnings beneficial to the working of the market economy are not best provided by the business community, but by other actors including governments. In this paper mention is made for example of the United Nations Convention on the Recognition and Enforcement of Foreign Arbitral Awards (New York, June 10, 1958), which the business community regularly relies upon as the back-stop for their international agreements. Common property can have an enabling value, the Net, basis for the "new" econ-

---

[5] Part of a section cited in Nicholas Mercuro and Steven G. Medema, *Economics and the Law: from Posner to Post-Modernism* (Princeton, 1997) p. 11, with reference to Karl N. Llewellyn *The Effect of Legal Institutions upon Economics*, American Economic Review 15 (December 1925) pp. 655-683, Mark M. Litchman *Economics, the Basis of Law*, American Law Review 61 (May–June 1927) pp. 357–387, and W. S. Holdsworth *A Neglected Aspect of the Relations between Economic and Legal History*, Economic History Review 1 (January 1927-28) pp. 114–123.

[6] For a good introduction see Nicholas Mercuro and Steven G. Medema, *Economics and the Law: from Posner to Post-Modernism* (Princeton, 1997). These include: Chicago law and economics (New law and economics); New Haven School of law and economics; Public Choice Theory; Institutional law and economics; Neo-institutional law and economics; Critical Legal Studies.

[7] Case overstated, but this is an essential point. It is not helpful to be overly tied to the past. It is necessary to be able to look ahead and explore new solutions, and be aware of the implications of "complexity" (as to the relevance of past circumstances to the present). History merely provides unique (circumstance bound) events, which theory (assuming such exists) may be tested against.

[8] The majority of which are beyond the scope of this paper. Examples include: encryption and privacy for commercial purposes; digital signatures; symbolic ownership; electronic intellectual property rights.

[9] Complexity theory is a branch of mathematics and physics that examines non-linear systems in which simple sets of deterministic rules can lead to highly complicated results, which cannot be predicted accurately. A study of the subject is provided by Nicholas Rescher, *Complexity: A Philosophical Overview* (New Brunswick, 1998). See also Jack Cohen and Ian Stewart, *The Collapse of Chaos: Discovering Simplicity in a Complex World* (1994).

omy, would not be what it is today without much that has been shared on this basis, having permitted "Metcalf's law"[10] to take hold. Metcalf's law suggests that the value of a shared technology is exponential to its user base. In all likelihood it applies as much to transnational contract law, as to technological networks and standards. The more people who use a network or standard, the more "valuable" it becomes, and the more users it will attract. Key infrastructure should be identified and common property solutions where appropriate nurtured, keeping transaction costs to a minimum.

The following general perspective is submitted as worthy of consideration (and support) by the legal, business and academic communities, and governments.   **23–005**

(a)   Abstract goals valuable to a transnational legal infrastructure include, certainty and predictability, flexibility, simplicity where possible, and neutrality, in the sense of being without perceived "unfairness" in the global context of their application. This covers the content of the "laws" themselves and the methods used for their interpretation.

(b)   Of law with regard to technology, "rules should be technology-neutral (*i.e.*, the rules should neither require nor assume a particular technology) and forward looking (*i.e.*, the rules should not hinder the use or development of technologies in the future)."[11]

(c)   Desirable abstract goals in developing technological standards and critical technological infrastructure, include, choice, and that they should be shared and public or "open" as in "open source", and platform and/or program neutral, that is, interoperable. (On security, to forestall suggestions to the contrary, popular open source software tends to be as secure or more so than proprietary software).

(d)   Encryption is an essential part of the mature "new" economy but remains the subject of some governments' restriction.[12] The availability of (and possibility to develop common transnational standards for) strong encryption is essential for commercial security and trust with regard to all manner of Net communications and electronic commerce transactions, *vis-à-vis* their confidentiality, integrity, authentication, and non-repudiation. That is, encryption is the basis for essential commerce related technologies, including amongst many others, electronic signatures, electronic payment systems and the development of electronic symbols of ownership (such as electronic bills of lading).

(e)   As regards the dissemination of primary materials concerning "uniform standards" in both the legal and technology domains, the Net should be used to make them globally available, free. Technology

---

[10] Robert Metcalf, founder of 3Com.
[11] *US Framework for Global Electronic Commerce* (1997), at http://www.whitehouse.gov/WH/New/Commerce.
[12] The EU and US have recently lifted such restrictions. For an overview of considerations surrounding public access to cryptography in the digital age from a US perspective, see Steven Levy, *Crypto* (2001).

should be similarly used where possible to promote the goals outlined under point (a). Naturally, as a tempered supporter of the market economy,[13] proprietary secondary materials and technologies do not merit these reservations. Similarly, actors of the market economy would take advantage of the common property base of the commercial highway.

3. Modelling the private international commercial law infrastructure

23–006　Apart from the study of "laws" or the existing legal infrastructure, there are a multitude of players involved in their creation whose efforts may be regarded as being in the nature of systems modelling. Of interest to this paper is the subset of activity of a few organisations that provide the under-pinnings for the foundation of a successful transnational contract/sales law. These are not amongst the more controversial legal infrastructure modelling activities, and represent a small but significant part in simplifying international commerce and trade.[14]

23–007　Briefly viewing the wider picture, several institutions are involved as independent actors in systems modelling of the transnational legal infrastructure. Their roles and mandates and the issues they address are conceptually different. These include certain United Nations organs and affiliates such as the United Nations Commission on International Trade Law (UNCITRAL),[15] the World Intellectual Property Organisation (WIPO)[16] and recently the World Trade Organisation (WTO),[17] along with other institutions such as the International Institute for the Unification of Private Law (UNIDROIT),[18] the International Chamber of Commerce (ICC),[19] and the Hague Conference on Private International Law.[20] They identify areas that would benefit from an international or transnational regime and use various tools at their disposal, (including: treaties; model laws; conventions; rules and/or principles; standard contracts), to develop legislative "solutions" that they hope will be subscribed to.

23–008　A host of other institutions are involved in providing regional solutions.[21] Specialised areas are also addressed by appropriately specialised institutions.[22]

---

[13] Caveats extending beyond the purview of this paper. It is necessary to be aware that there are other overriding interests, global and domestic, that the market economy is ill suited to providing for, such as the environment, and possibly key public utilities that require long term planning and high investment. It is also necessary to continue to be vigilant against that which even if arising as a natural consequence of the market economy, has the potential to disturb or destroy its function, such as monopolies.

[14] Look for instance at national customs procedures, and consumer protection.

[15] See http://www.uncitral.org.

[16] See http://www.wipo.org.

[17] See http://www.wto.org.

[18] See http://www.unidroit.org.

[19] See http://www.iccwbo.org.

[20] See http://www.hcch.net.

[21] See, for example, ASEAN http://www.aseansec.org, the European Union (EU) http://europa.eu.int/, MERCOSUR http://embassy.org/uruguay/econ/mercosur/, and North American Free Trade Agreement (NAFTA) http://www.nafta-sec-alena.org/english/nafta.

[22] *e.g.* large international banks; or in the legal community, the Business Section of the International Bar Association (IBA) with its membership of lawyers in over 180 countries. http://www.ibanet.org.

A result of globalisation is increased competition (also) amongst States, which are active players in the process, identifying and addressing the needs of their business communities over a wide range of areas and managing the suitability to the global economy of their domestic legal, economic, techno-logical and educational[23] infrastructures. The role of States remains to iden-tify what domestic structural support they must provide to be integrated and competitive in the global economy.

In addition to "traditional" contributors, the technology/commerce/law   **23–009** confluence provides new challenges *and opportunities, allowing, the emergence* of important new players within the commercial field, such as Bolero,[24] which, with the backing of international banks and ship-owners, offers elec-tronic replacements for traditional paper transactions, acting as transaction agents for the electronic substitute on behalf of the trading parties. The acceptance of the possibility of applying an institutionally offered lex has opened the door further for other actors including add hoc groupings of the business community and/or universities to find ways to be engaged and actively participate in providing services for themselves and/or others in this domain.

4. The foundation for transnational private contract law, arbitration

The market economy drive perpetuating economic globalisation is also active   **23–010** in the development and choice of transnational legal solutions. The potential reward: international sets of contract rules and principles, that can be counted on to be consistent and as providing a uniform layer of insulation (with minimal reference back to State law) when applied across the landscape of a multitude of different municipal legal systems. The business community is free to utilise them if available, and if not, to develop them, or seek to have them developed.

The kernel for the development of a transnational legal infrastructure gov-   **23–011** erning the rights and obligations of private contracting individuals was put in place as far back as 1958 by the *UN Convention on the Recognition and Enforce-ment of Foreign Arbitral Awards ("NY Convention")*,[25] now in force in over 122 States. Together with freedom of contract, the *"NY Convention"* made it possi-ble for commercial parties to develop and be governed by their own lex in their contractual affairs, should they wish to do so, and guaranteed that provided their agreement was based on international commercial arbitration, (and is not against relevant mandatory law) it would be enforced in all contracting States. This has been given further support by various more recent arbitration laws and the *UNCITRAL Model Law on International Commercial Arbitration 1985*,[26]

---

[23] For a somewhat frightening peek and illuminating discussion of the role of education in the global economy as implemented by a number of successful States see Joel Spring, *Education and the Rise of the Global Economy* (Mahwah, NJ, 1998).
[24] See http://www.bolero.org/ also http://www.boleroassociation.org.
[25] See http://www.jus.uio.no/lm/un.arbitration.recognition.and.enfor-cement.convention.new.york.1958.
[26] See http://www.jus.uio.no/lm/un.arbitration.model.law.1985.

which now explicitly state that rule based solutions independent of national law can be applied in international commercial arbitration.[27]

23–012   International commercial arbitration is recognised as the most prevalent means of dispute resolution in international commerce. Unlike litigation, arbitration survives on its merits as a commercial service to provide for the needs of the business community.[28] It has consequently been more dynamic than national judiciaries in adjusting to the changing requirements of businessmen. Its institutions are quicker to adapt and innovate, including the ability to cater for transnational contracts. Arbitration, in taking its mandate from and giving effect to the will of the parties, provides them with greater flexibility and frees them from many of the limitations of municipal law.[29]

23–013   In sum, a transnational/non-national regulatory order governing the contractual rights and obligations of private individuals is made possible by:

(a)   States' acceptance of freedom of contract (public policy excepted);

(b)   Sanctity of contract embodied in the principle *pacta sunt servanda;*

(c)   Written contractual selection of dispute resolution by international commercial arbitration, whether ad hoc or institutional, usually under internationally accepted arbitration rules;

(d)   Guaranteed enforcement, arbitration where necessary, borrowing the State apparatus for law enforcement through the *"NY Convention"*, which has secured for arbitration a recognition and enforcement regime unparalleled by municipal courts in well over a hundred contracting States;

(e)   Transnational effect or non-nationality being achievable through arbitration accepting the parties' ability to select the basis upon which the dispute would be resolved outside municipal law, such as through the selection of general principles of law or *lex mercatoria*, or calling upon the arbitrators to act as *amiable compositeur* or making decisions *ex aequo et bono*.

23–014   This framework provided by and at arbitration opened the door for the modelling of effective transnational law default rules and principles for contracts independent of State participation (in their development, application, or choice of law foundation). Today we have an increased amount of certainty

---

[27] Lando, Each Contracting Party Must Act In Accordance with Good Faith and Fair Dealing in Festskrift til Jan Ramberg (Stockholm, 1997) p. 575. See also UNIDROIT Principles, Preamble 4a. Also Arthur Hartkamp, *The Use of UNIDROIT Principles of International Commercial Contracts by National and Supranational Courts* (1995) in *UNIDROIT Principles: A New Lex Mercatoria?*, pp. 253-260 on p. 255. But see Goode, *A New International Lex Mercatoria?* in Juridisk Tidskrift (1999-2000 nr 2) pp. 256 and 259.

[28] Arbitration being shaped by market forces and competition adheres more closely to the rules of the market economy, responding to its needs and catering for them more adequately. See also Yves Dezalay and Bryant G. Garth, *Dealing in Virtue—International Commercial Arbitration and the Construction of a Transnational Legal Order* (University of Chicago Press 1996).

[29] As examples of this, it seeks to give effect to the parties" agreement upon: the *lex mercatoria* as the law of the contract; the number of, and persons to be "adjudicators"; the language of proceedings; the procedural rules to be used, and; as to the finality of the decision.

of content and better control over the desired degree of transnational effect or non-nationality with the availability of comprehensive insulating rules and principles such as the *UNIDROIT Principles of International Commercial Contracts ("PICC")* or the *Principles of European Contract Law ("European Principles"* or *"PECL")* that may be chosen, either together with, or to the exclusion of a choice of municipal law as governing the contract. For electronic commerce a similar path is hypothetically possible.

5. "State contracted international law" and/or "institutionally offered lex"? CISG and PICC as examples

An institutionally offered lex ("IoL", uniform rules and principles) appears to have a number of advantages over "state contracted international law" ("SiIL", model laws, treaties and conventions for enactment). The development and formulation of both "ScIL" and "IoL" law takes time, the *CISG* representing a half century of efforts.[30] The *CISG* may be regarded as the culmination of an effort in the field dating back to Ernst Rabel,[31] followed by the Cornell Project, (Cornell Project on Formation of Contracts 1968[32] and connected most directly to the *UNIDROIT inspired Uniform Law for International Sales[33]*), the main preparatory works behind the *CISG* (*Uniform Law on the Formation of Contracts for the International Sale of Goods* (ULF) and the *Convention relating to a Uniform Law on the International Sale of Goods* (*ULIS*) The Hague, 1964).

23–015

The first edition of the *PICC*[34] were finalised in 1994, 23 years after their first conception, and 14 years after work started on them in earnest. The *CISG* by UNCITRAL represents the greatest success for the unification of an area of substantive commercial contract law to date, being currently applied by 57 States,[35] estimated as representing close to 70 per cent of world trade and including every major trading nation of the world apart from England and Japan. To labour the point, the USA, most of the EU (along with Canada, Australia, Russia) and China, ahead of its entry to the WTO, already share the same law in relation to the international sale of goods. "ScIL" however has additional hurdles to overcome:

23–016

(a)   In order to enter into force and become applicable, it must go through the lengthy process of ratification and accession by States.

(b)   Implementation is frequently with various reservations.

---

[30] *UNCITRAL Convention on Contracts for the International Sale of Goods 1980* see at http://www.jus.uio.no/lm/un.contracts.international.sale.of.goods.convention.1980.
[31] Das Recht des Warenkaufs, Bd. I&II (Berlin, 1936-1958). Two volume study on sales law.
[32] Rudolf Schlesinger, *Formation of Contracts. A study of the Common Core of Legal Systems*, 2 vols. (New York, London 1968)
[33] See *ULIS* at http://www.jus.uio.no/lm/unidroit.ulis.convention.1964/ at and *ULF* at http://www.jus.uio.no/lm/unidroit.ulf.convention.1964/.
[34] *UNIDROIT Principles of International Commercial Contracts* commonly referred to as the *UNIDROIT Principles* and within this paper as *PICC* see at http://www.jus.uio.no/lm/ unidroit.contract.principles.1994 and http://www.jus.uio.no/lm/unidroit.international.commercial. contracts.principles.1994.commented.
[35] As of February 2000.

(c)   Even where widely used, there are usually as many or more States that are exceptions. Success, that is by no means guaranteed, takes time and for every uniform law that is a success, there are several failures.

23–017   Institutionally offered lex ("IoL") comprehensive general contract principles or contract law restatements that create an entire "legal" environment for contracting, has the advantage of being instantly available, becoming effective by choice of the contracting parties at the stroke of a pen. "IoL" is also more easily developed subsequently, in light of experience and need. Amongst the reasons for their use is the reduction of transaction cost in their provision of a set of default rules, applicable transnationally, that satisfy risk management criteria, being (or becoming) known, tried and tested, and of predictable effect.[36] The most resoundingly successful "IoL" example to date has been the ICC's *Uniform Customs and Practices for Documentary Credits*, which is subscribed to as the default rules for the letters of credit offered by the vast majority of banks in the vast majority of countries of the world. Furthermore uniform principles allow unification on matters that at the present stage of national and regional pluralism could not be achieved at a treaty level. There are, however, things that only "ScIL" can "engineer", (for example that which relates to priorities and third party obligations).

23–018   PICC: The arrival of PICC in 1994 was particularly timely. Coinciding as it did with the successful attempt at reducing trade barriers represented by the World Trade Agreement,[37] and the start of general Internet use,[38] it allowed for the exponential growth of electronic commerce, and further underscored the transnational tendency of commerce. The arrival of *PICC* was all the more opportune bearing in mind the years it takes to prepare such an instrument. Whilst there have been some objections, the *PICC* (and *PECL*) as contract law restatements cater to the needs of the business community that seeks a non-national or transnational law as the basis of its contracts, and provide a focal point for future development in this direction. Where in the past they would have been forced to rely on the ethereal and nebulous *lex mercatoria*, now the business community is provided with the opportunity to make use of such a "law" that is readily accessible, and has a clear and reasonably well defined content, that will become familiar and can be further developed as required. As such the *PICC* allow for more universal and uniform solutions. Their future success will depend on such factors as:

(a)   Suitability of their contract terms to the needs of the business community.

(b)   Their becoming widely known and understood.

---

[36] "[P]arties often want to close contracts quickly, rather than hold up the transaction to negotiate solutions for every problem that might arise." Honnold (1992) on p. 13.

[37] See http://www.jus.uio.no/lm/wta.1994.

[38] See Amissah, *On the Net and the Liberation of Information that wants to be Free* in ed. Jens Edvin A. Skoghøy Fra institutt til fakultet, Jubileumsskrift i anledning av at IRV ved Universitetet i Tromse feirer 10 †r og er blitt til Det juridiske fakultet (Tromse, 1996) pp. 59–76 or the same at http://www.jus.uio.no/lm/on.the.net.and.information.22.02.1997.amissah/.

(c)   Their predictability evidenced by a reasonable degree of consistency in the results of their application.

(d)   Recognition of their potential to reduce transaction costs.

(e)   Recognition of their being neutral as between different nations' interests (East, West; North, South).

In the international sale of goods the *PICC* can be used in conjunction with more specific rules and regulations, including (on parties election[39]) in sales the *CISG* to fill gaps in its provisions.[40] Provisions of the *CISG* would be given precedence over the *PICC* under the accepted principle of *specialia generalibus derogant*,[41] the mandatory content of the *PICC* excepted. The *CISG* has many situations that are not provided for at all, or which are provided for in less detail than the *PICC*.

Work on *PICC* and *PECL* under the chairmanship of Professors Bonell and Ole Lando respectively, was wisely cross-pollinated (conceptually and through cross-membership of preparatory committees), as common foundations strengthen both sets of principles. A couple of points should be noted. First, despite the maintained desirability of a transnational solution, this does not exclude the desirability of regional solutions, especially if there is choice, and the regional solutions are more comprehensive and easier to keep of uniform application. Secondly, the European Union has powers and influence (within the EU) unparalleled by UNIDROIT that can be utilised in the future with regard to the *PECL* if the desirability of a common European contract solution is recognised and agreed upon by EU Member States. As a further observation, there is, hypothetically at least, nothing to prevent there being developed an alternative extensive (competing) transnational contract lex solution, though the weighty effort already in place as represented by *PICC* and the high investment in time and independent skilled legal minds, necessary to achieve this in a widely acceptable manner, makes such a development not very likely. It may, however, be the case that for electronic commerce, some other particularly suitable rules and principles will in time be developed in a similar vein, along the lines of an "IoL".

23–019

6. Contract Lex design. Questions of commonwealth

The virtues of freedom of contract are acknowledged in this paper in that they allow the international business community to structure their business relationships to suit their requirements, and as such reflect the needs and working of the market economy. However, it is instructive also to explore the limits of the principles: freedom of contract, *pacta sunt servanda* and *caveat*

23–020

---

[39] Also consider present and future possibilities for such use of *PICC* under *CISG* Arts. 8 and 9.
[40] Drobnig comments that the *CISG* precludes recourse to general principles of contract law in Article 7. This does not refer to the situation where parties determine that the *PICC* should do so, see *CISG* Art. 6. Or that in future the *PICC* will not be of importance under *CISG* Arts. 8 and 9. Ulrich Drobnig, The use of the UNIDROIT Principles by national and Supranational Courts, in UNIDROIT Principles: A New Lex Mercatoria? (1995), pp. 223–229 on p. 228.
[41] "Special principles have precedence over general ones." See Huet, *Synthesis* (1995) p. 277.

subscriptor. These principles are based on free market arguments that parties best understand their interests, and that the contract they arrive at will be an optimum compromise between their competing interests. It not being for an outsider to regulate or evaluate what a party of their own free will and volition has gained from electing to contract on those terms. This approach to contract is adversarial, based on the conflicting wills of the parties, achieving a meeting of minds. It imposes no duty of good faith and fair dealing or of loyalty (including the disclosure of material facts) upon the contracting parties to one another, who are to protect their own interests. However, in international commerce, this demand can be more costly, and may have a negative and restrictive effect. Also, although claimed to be neutral in making no judgment as to the contents of a contract, this claim can be misleading.

6.1 The neutrality of contract law and information cost

23–021   The information problem is a general one that needs to be recognised in its various forms where it arises and addressed where possible.

23–022   Adherents to the *caveat subscriptor* model point to the fact that parties have conflicting interests, and should look out for their own interests. However, information presents particular problems which are exacerbated in international commerce.[42] As Michael Trebilcock put it: "Even the most committed proponents of free markets and freedom of contract recognise that certain information preconditions must be met for a given exchange to possess Pareto superior qualities."[43] Compared with domestic transactions, the contracting parties are less likely to possess information about each other or of what material facts there may be within the other party's knowledge, and will find it more difficult and costly to acquire. With resource inequalities, some parties will be in a much better position to determine and access what they need to know, the more so as the more information one already has, the less it costs to identify and to obtain any additional information that is required.[44] The converse lot of the financially weaker party, makes their problem of high information costs (both actual and relative), near insurmountable. Ignorance may even become a rational choice, as the marginal cost of information remains higher than its marginal benefit. "This, in fact is the economic rationale for the failure to fully specify all contingencies in a contract."[45] The argument is tied to transaction cost and further elucidates a general role played by underlying default rules and principles. It also extends further to the value of immutable principles that may help mitigate the problem in some circumstances. More general arguments are presented below.

---

[42] The more straightforward cases of various types of misrepresentation apart.
[43] Trebilcock, (1993) p. 102, followed by a quotation of Milton Friedman, from *Capitalism and Freedom* (1962) p. 13.
[44] Trebilcock, (1993) p. 102, note quoted passage of Kim Lane Scheppele, *Legal Secrets: Equality and Efficiency in the Common Law* (1988) p. 25.
[45] See, for example, Nicholas Mercuro and Steven G. Medema, *supra* n. p. 58.

6.2 Justifying mandatory loyalty principles

Given the ability to create alternative solutions and even an independent lex   **23–023**
a question that arises is what limits if any should be imposed upon freedom
of contract? What protective principles are required? In what circumstances?
Should protective principles be default rules that can be excluded? Should
they be mandatory? Should mandatory law only exist at the level of municipal law?

A kernel of mandatory protective principles with regard to loyalty may be   **23–024**
justified, as beneficial, and even necessary for "IoL" to be acceptable in international commerce, in that they (on the balance) reflect the collective needs of
the international business community. The present author is of the opinion
that the duties of good faith and fair dealing and loyalty (or an acceptable
equivalent) should be a necessary part of any attempt at the self-legislation or
institutional legislation of any contract regime that is based on "rules and
principles" (rather than a national legal order). If absent a requirement for
them should be imposed by mandatory international law. Such protective
provisions are to be found within the *PICC* and *PECL*.[46] As regards *PICC*:

(a)   The loyalty (and other protective) principles help bring about confi-
        dence and foster relations between parties. They provide an assurance
        in the international arena where parties are less likely to know each
        other and may have more difficulty in finding out about each other.

(b)   They better reflect the focus of the international business community
        on a business relationship from which both sides seek to gain.

(c)   They result in wider acceptability of the principles within both gov-
        ernments and the business community in the pluralistic international
        community. These protective principles may be regarded as enabling
        the *PICC* to better represent the needs of the commonweal.

(d)   Good faith and fair dealing[47] are fundamental underlying principles
        of international commercial relations.

(e)   Reliance only on the varied mandatory law protections of various
        States does not engender uniformity, which is also desirable with
        regard to that which can be counted upon as immutable. (Not that it
        is avoidable, given that mandatory State law remains overriding.)

More generally, freedom of contract benefits from these protective principles
that need immutable protection from contractual freedom to effectively serve
their function. In seeking a transnational or non-national regime to govern
contractual relations, one might suggest this to be the minimum price of

---

[46] Examples include the deliberately excluded validity (Art. 4); the provision on interest (Art. 78);
impediment (Art. 79); and what many believe to be the inadequate coverage of battle of forms
(Art. 19).
[47] The commented PECL explain "Good faith" means honesty and fairness in mind, which are
subjective concepts . . . 'fair dealing' means observance of fairness in fact, which is an objective
test".

freedom of contract that should be insisted upon by mandatory international law, as the limitation which hinders the misuse by one party of unlimited contractual freedom. They appear to be an essential basis for acceptability of the autonomous contract (non-national contract, based on agreed rules and principles/ "IoL"). As immutable principles they (hopefully and this is to be encouraged) become the default standard for the conduct of international business and as such may be looked upon as "common property." Unless immutable they suffer a fate somewhat analogous to that of "the tragedy of the commons."[48] It should be recognised that argument over the loyalty principles should be of degree (which will vary *inter alia* with regard to the nature of the transaction and relationships involved, *e.g.* from discrete commodity transactions to long term relational contracts), as the concept must not be compromised, and needs to be protected (even if they come at the price of a degree of uncertainty), especially against particularly strong parties who are most likely to argue against their necessity.

7. Problems beyond uniform texts

7.1 In support of four objectives

23–025　　In the formulation of many international legal texts a pragmatic approach was taken. Formulating legislators from different States developed solutions based on suitable responses to factual example circumstances. This was done, successfully, with a view to avoiding arguments over alternative legal semantics and methodologies. However, having arrived at a common text, what then? Several issues are raised by asking the question, given that differences of interpretation can arise and become entrenched, by what means is it possible to foster a sustainable drive towards the uniform application of shared texts? Four principles appear to be desirable and should insofar as it is possible be pursued together: (i) the promotion of certainty and predictability; (ii) the promotion of uniformity of application; (iii) the protection of democratic ideals and ensuring of jurisprudential deliberation, and (iv) the retention of efficiency.

7.2 Improving the predictability, certainty and uniform application of international and transnational law

23–026　　The key to the (efficient) achievement of greater certainty and predictability in an international and/or transnational commercial law regime is through the uniform application of shared texts that make up this regime.

23–027　　Obviously a distinction is to be made between transnational predictability in application, that is "uniform application", and predictability at a domestic level. Where the "uniform law" is applied by a municipal court of State "A" that looks first to its domestic writings, there may be a clear and predictable manner of application, even if not in the spirit of the "Convention".

---

[48] Special problem regarding common/shared resources discussed by Garrett Hardin in Science (1968) 162 pp. 1243–1248. For short discussion and summary see Trebilcock, (1993) p. 13–15.

State "B" may apply the uniform law in a different way that is equally predictable, being perfectly consistent internally. This however defeats much of the purpose of the uniform law.

A first step is for municipal courts to accept the *UN Convention on the Law*   **23–028**
of Treaties 1969 (in force 1980) as a codification of existing public international law with regard to the interpretation of treaties.[49] The relevant articles on interpretation are Articles 31 and 32. A potentially fundamental step towards the achievement of uniform application is through the conscientious following of the admonitions of the interpretation clauses of modern conventions, rules and principles[50] to take into account their international character and the need to promote uniformity in their application,[51] together with all this implies.[52] However, the problems of uniform application, being embedded in differences of legal methodology, go beyond the agreement of a common text, and superficial glances at the works of other legal municipalities. These include questions related to sources of authority and technique applied in developing valid legal argument. Problems with sources include differences in authority and weight given to:

(a)   legislative history;

(b)   rulings domestic and international;

(c)   official and other commentaries;

(d)   scholarly writings.

There should be an ongoing discussion of legal methodology to determine the methods best suited to addressing the problem of achieving greater certainty, predictability and uniformity in the application of shared international legal texts. With regard to information sharing, again the technology associated with the Net offers potential solutions.

7.3 The Net and information sharing through transnational databases

The Net has been a godsend permitting the collection and dissemination of   **23–029**
information on international law. With the best intentions to live up to admonitions to "to take into account their international character and the need to promote uniformity in their application" of "ScIL" and "IoL", a

---

[49] This is the position in English law, see Lord Diplock in *Fothergill v. Monarch Airlines* [1981], AC 251, 282 or see http://www.jus.uio.no/lm/england.fothergill.v.monarch.airlines.hl. 1980/2_diplock.html also FA Mann (London, 1983) at p. 379.

[50] Examples: The *CISG*, Art. 7; The *PICC*, Art. 1.6; *PECL*, Art. 1.106; *UN Convention on the Carriage of Goods by Sea* (The *Hamburg Rules*) 1978, Art. 3; *UN Convention on the Limitation Period in the International Sale of Goods* 1974 and 1978, Art. 7; *UN Model Law on Electronic Commerce 1996*, Art. 3; *UNIDROIT Convention on International Factoring 1988*, Art. 4; *UNIDROIT Convention on International Financial Leasing 1988*, Art. 6; also *EC Convention on the Law Applicable to Contractual Obligations 1980*, Art. 18.

[51] Such as the *CISG* provision on interpretation—Art. 7.

[52] For an online collection of articles see the Pace *CISG* Database http://www.cisg.law.pace. edu/cisg/text/e-text-07.html and amongst the many other articles note Michael Van Alstine *Dynamic Treaty Interpretation* 146 University of Pennsylvania Law Review (1998) 687–793.

difficulty has been in knowing what has been written and decided elsewhere. In discussing solutions, Professor Honnold in "*Uniform Words and Uniform Application*"[53] suggests the following: "General Access to Case-Law and Bibliographic Material: The development of a homogenous body of law under the Convention depends on channels for the collection and sharing of judicial decisions and bibliographic material so that experience in each country can be evaluated and followed or rejected in other jurisdictions." Honnold then goes on to discuss "the need for an international clearing-house to collect and disseminate experience on the Convention" the need for which, he writes there is general agreement. He also discusses information-gathering methods through the use of national reporters. He poses the question "Will these channels be adequate? . . ."

23–030   The Net, offering inexpensive ways to build databases and to provide global access to information, provides an opportunity to address these problems that was not previously available. The Net extends the reach of the admonitions of the interpretation clauses, providing the medium whereby if a decision or scholarly writing exists on a particular article or provision of a Convention, anywhere in the world, it will be readily available. Whether or not a national court or arbitration tribunal chooses to follow their example, they should be aware of it. Whatever a national court decides will also become internationally known, and will add to the body of experience on the Convention.[54]

23–031   Such a library would be of interest to the institution promulgating the text, governments, practitioners and researchers alike. It could place at your fingertips:

(a)   Convention texts.

(b)   Implementation details of contracting States.

(c)   The legislative history.

(d)   Decisions generated by the convention around the world (court and arbitral where possible).

(e)   The official and other commentaries.

(f)   Scholarly writings on the Convention.

(g)   Bibliographies of scholarly writings.

(h)   Monographs and textbooks.

---

[53] Based on the CISG, and inputs from several professors from different legal jurisdictions, on the problems of achieving the uniform application of the text across different legal municipalities. J. Honnold, *Uniform words and uniform applications. Uniform Words and Uniform Application: The 1980 Sales Convention and International Juridical Practice.* Einheitliches Kaufrecht und nationales Obligationenrecht. Referate Diskussionen der Fachtagung. am 16/17–2–1987. Hrsg. von P. Schlechtriem. Baden-Baden, Nomos, 1987. p. 115–147, at p. 127–128.

[54] Nor is it particularly difficult to set into motion the placement of such information on the Net. With each interested participant publishing for their own interest, the Net could provide the key resources to be utilised in the harmonisation and reaching of common understandings of solutions and uniform application of legal texts. Works from all countries would be available.

(i)   Student study material collections.

(j)   Information on promotional activities: lectures, moots, etc.

(k)   Discussion groups/ mailing groups and other more interactive features.

With respect to the *CISG* such databases are already being maintained.[55]

The database by ensuring the availability of international materials, used in conjunction with legal practice, helps to support the forenamed four principles. That of efficiency is enhanced especially if there is a single source that can be searched for the information required.   **23–032**

The major obstacle that remains to being confident of this as the great open and free panacea that it should be is the cost of translation of texts.[56]   **23–033**

7.4 Judicial minimalism promotes democratic jurisprudential deliberation

How to protect liberal democratic ideals and ensure international jurisprudential deliberation? Looking at judicial method, where court decisions are looked to for guidance, liberal democratic ideals and international jurisprudential deliberation are fostered by a judicial minimalist approach.   **23–034**

For those of us with a common law background, and others who pay special attention to cases as you are invited to by interpretation clauses, there is scope for discussion as to the most appropriate approach to be taken with regard to judicial decisions. U.S. Judge Cass Sunstein's suggestion of judicial minimalism[57] which despite its being developed in a different context[58] is attractive in that it is suited to a liberal democracy in ensuring democratic jurisprudential deliberation. It maintains discussion, debate, and allows for adjustment as appropriate and the gradual development of a common understanding of issues. Much as one may admire farsighted and far-reaching decisions and expositions, there is less chance with the minimalist approach of the (dogmatic) imposition of particular values. Whilst information sharing of decisions and judicial reasoning offers the possibility of the percolation[59] of   **23–035**

---

[55] Primary amongst them Pace University, Institute of International Commercial Law, *CISG* Database http://www.cisg.law.pace.edu/ which provides secondary support for the CISG, including providing a free on-line database of the legislative history, academic writings, and case law on the *CISG* and additional material with regard to *PICC* and *PECL* insofar as they may supplement the *CISG*. Furthermore, the Pace CISG Project, networks with the several other existing Net based "autonomous" *CISG* projects. *UNCITRAL* under Secretary Gerold Herrmann, has its own database through which it distributes its case law materials collected from national reporters (*CLOUT*).

[56] In that respect Pace University (Professor Albert Kritzer) and the Centre for Commercial Law Studies at Queen Mary, University of London (Dr Loukas Mistelis) have formed an alliance with the aim of improving the translation service of cases relating to CISG, PECL and PICC. For further information contact L.Mistelis@qmw.ac.uk and/or Akritzer@law.pace.edu.

[57] Cass R. Sunstein, *One Case at a Time—Judicial Minimalism on the Supreme Court* (1999).

[58] His analysis is developed based largely on "hard" constitutional cases of the U.S.

[59] D. Stauffer, *Introduction to Percolation Theory* (London, 1985). Percolation represents the sudden dramatic expansion of a common idea or ideas thought he reaching of a critical level/mass in the rapid recognition of their power and the making of further interconnections. An epidemic like infection of ideas. Not quite the way we are used to the progression of ideas within a conservative tradition.

good ideas and convergent legal reasoning. Much as we admire the integrity of Dworkin's Hercules,[60] that he can consistently deliver single solutions suitable across such disparate socio-economic cultures is questionable. In examining the situation his own "integrity" would likely give him pause and prevent him from dictating that he can.[61]

23–036   This position is maintained as a general principle across international commercial law, despite private (as opposed to public) international commercial law not being an area of particularly "hard" cases of principle, and, despite private international commercial law being an area in which over a long history it has been demonstrated that lawyers are able to talk a common language to make themselves and their concepts (which are not dissimilar) understood by each other.

23–037   In 1966, a time when there were greater differences in the legal systems of States comprising the world economy Clive Schmitthoff was able to comment that:

> "22. The similarity of the law of international trade transcends the division of the world between countries of free enterprise and countries of centrally planned economy, and between the legal families of the civil law of Roman inspiration and the common law of English tradition. As a Polish scholar observed, "the law of external trade of the countries of planned economy does not differ in its fundamental principles from the law of external trade of other countries, such as *e.g.*, Austria or Switzerland. Consequently, international trade law specialists of all countries have found without difficulty that they speak a "common language'
> 23. The reason for this universal similarity of the law of international trade is that this branch of law is based on three fundamental propositions: first, that the parties are free, subject to limitations imposed by the national laws, to contract on whatever terms they are able to agree (principle of the autonomy of the parties" will); secondly, that once the parties have entered into a contract, that contract must be faithfully fulfilled (*pacta sunt servanda*) and only in very exceptional circumstances does the law excuse a party from performing his obligations, *viz.*, if force majeure or frustration can be established; and, thirdly that arbitration is widely used in international trade for the settlement of disputes, and the awards of arbitration tribunals command far-reaching international recognition and are often capable of enforcement abroad."[62]

7.5 Non-binding interpretative councils and their co-ordinating guides can provide a focal point for the convergence of ideas—certainty predictability, and efficiency

23–038   A respected central guiding body can provide a guiding influence with respect to:

(a)   the uniform application of texts;

(b)   information management control;

(c)   dissemination of information.

Given the growing mass of writing on common legal texts (academic and by way of decisions), we are faced with an information management problem.[63]

---

[60] Ronald Dworkin, *Laws Empire* (Harvard, 1986); *Hard Cases* in Harvard Law Review (1988).
[61] Hercules was created for U.S. Federal Cases and the community represented by the U.S.
[62] *Report of the Secretary-General of the United Nations, Progressive Development of the Law of International Trade* (1966). Report prepared for the UN by C. Schmitthoff.
[63] Future if not current.

Supra-national interpretative councils have been called for previously[64] **23–039**
and have for various reasons been regarded impracticable to implement
because of problems associated with getting States to formally agree upon
such a body with binding authority.

However, it is not necessary to go this route. In relation to "IoL" in such **23–040**
forms as the *PICC* and *PECL* it is possible for the promulgators themselves[65]
to update and clarify the accompanying commentary of the rules and principles, and to extend their work, through having councils with the necessary
delegated powers. In relation to the *CISG* it is possible to do something
similar, of a non-binding nature, through the production of an updated
commentary by an interpretative council[66] (that could try to play the role of
Hercules).[67]

With respect, despite some expressed reservations, it is not true that it would **23–041**
have no more authority than a single author writing on the subject. A suitable
non-binding interpretative council would provide a focal point for the convergence of ideas. Given the principle of ensuring democratic jurisprudential
deliberation, that such a council would be advisory only (except perhaps on
the contracting parties election) would be one of its more attractive features,
as it would ensure continued debate and development.

7.6 Capacity building

> ". . . one should create awareness about the fact that an international contract or trans-   **23–042**
> action is not naturally rooted in one particular domestic law, and that its international
> specifics are best catered for in a uniform law."[68]

Capacity building—raising awareness, providing education, creating a new **23–043**
generation of lawyers versed in a relatively new paradigm. Capacity building in
international and transnational law, is something relevant institutions including arbitration institutions; the business community, and far-sighted States,
should be interested in promoting. Finding means to transcend national
boundaries is also to continue in the tradition of seeking the means to break
down barriers to legal communication and understanding. However, while the
business community seeks and requires greater uniformity in their business

---

[64] UNCITRAL Secretariat (1992) p. 253. Proposed by David (France) at the second UNCI-
TRAL Congress and on a later occasion by Farnsworth (USA). To date the political will backed
by the financing for such an organ has not been forthcoming. In 1992 the UNCITRAL
Secretariat concluded that "probably the time has not yet come". Suggested also by Louis Sono
in Uniform laws require uniform interpretation: proposals for an international tribunal to
interpret uniform legal texts (1992) 25th UNCITRAL Congress, pp. 50–54. Drobnig,
Observations in Uniform Law in Practice at p. 306.
[65] UNIDROIT and the EU
[66] Ideally constituted primarily of respected academics from around the globe.
[67] For references on interpretation of the *CISG* by a supranational committee of experts or
council of "wise men" see Bonell, *Proposal for the Establishment of a Permanent Editorial Board
for the Vienna Sales Convention in International Uniform Law in Practice/ Le droit uniforme
international dans la practique* [Acts and Proceedings of the 3rd Congress on Private Law held by
the International Institute for the Unification of Private Law (Rome, 1987)], (New York, 1988)
pp. 241–244.
[68] UNCITRAL Secretariat (1992) p. 255.

relations, there has been paradoxically, at a national level, a trend towards a nationalisation of contract law, and a regionalisation of business practice.[69]

23–044   As an example, Pace University, Institute of International Commercial Law, plays a prominent role with regard to capacity building in relation to the *CISG* and *PICC*. Apart from the previously mentioned *CISG* Database, Pace University organises a large annual moot on the *CISG*[70] in 2000 involving students of 79 universities from 28 countries, and respected arbitrators from the world over. Within the moot the finding of solutions based on *PICC* where the *CISG* is silent, is encouraged. Pace University also organises an essay competition[71-72] on the *CISG* and/or the *PICC*, which next year is to be expanded to include the *PECL* as a further option.

8. Marketing of transnational solutions

23–045   Certain aspects of the Net may already be taken for granted, but was the Net recognised for what it was, or might become, when it arrived?

23–046   As uniform law and transnational solutions are in competition with municipal approaches, to be successful a certain amount of marketing is necessary and may be effective. The approach should involve ensuring the concept of what they seek to achieve is firmly implanted in the business, legal and academic communities, and through engaging the business community and arbitration institutions, in capacity building and developing a new generation of lawyers. Feedback from the business community, and arbitrators will also prove invaluable. Whilst it is likely that the business community will immediately be able to recognise their potential advantages, it is less certain that they will find the support of the legal community. The normal reasons would be similar to those usually cited as being the primary constraints on its development "conservatism, routine, prejudice and inertia" (René David). These are problems associated with gaining the initial foothold of acceptability, also associated with the lower part of an exponential growth curve. In addition the legal community may face tensions arising for various reasons including the possibility of an increase in world-wide competition.

23–047   There are old well-developed legal traditions with developed infrastructures and roots well established in several countries, that are dependable and known. The question arises why experiment with alternative non-extensively tested regimes? The required sophistication is developed in the centres providing legal services, and it may be argued that there is not a pressing need for unification or for transnational solutions, as the traditional way of contracting provides satisfactorily for the requirements of global commerce. The services required will continue to be easily and readily available from existing centres of skill. English law, to take an example, is for various reasons (including perhaps language, familiarity of use, reputation and widespread

---

[69] Erich Schanze, New Directions in Business Research in Bʳrge Dahl & Ruth Nielsen (ed.), *New Directions in Contract Research* (Copenhagen, 1996) p. 62.
[70] See http://www.cisg.law.pace.edu/vis.html.
[71-72] See http://www.cisg.law.pace.edu/cisg/text/essay.html.

Commonwealth[73] relations) the premier choice for the law governing international commercial transactions, and is likely to be for the foreseeable future. Utilising the Commonwealth as an example, what the "transnational" law (*e.g. CISG*) experience illustrates however, is that for States there may be greater advantage to be gained from participation in a horizontally shared area of commercial law, than from retaining a traditional vertically integrated commercial law system, based largely for example on the English legal system.

Borrowing a term from the information technology sector, it is essential to guard against FUD (fear, uncertainty and doubt) with regard to the viability of new and/or competing transnational solutions, that may be spread by their detractors, and promptly, in the manner required by the free market, address any real problems that are discerned.   **23–048**

9. Tools in future development

An attempt should be made by the legal profession to be more contemporary and to keep up to date with developments in technology and the sciences, and to adopt effective tools where suitable to achieve their goals. Technology one way or another is likely to encroach further upon law and the way we design it.   **23–049**

Science works across cultures and is aspired to by most nations as being responsible for the phenomenal success of technology (both are similarly associated with globalisation). Science is extending its scope to (more confidently) tackle complex systems. It would not hurt to be more familiar with relevant scientific concepts and terminology. Lawyers might benefit in their conceptual reasoning from an early dose of the philosophy of science,[74] what better than Karl Popper on scientific discovery and the role of "falsification" and value of predictive probity.[75] And Thomas Kuhn on scientific advancement and "paradigm shifts"[76] has its place. Having mentioned Karl Popper, it would be unwise not to go further (outside the realms of philosophy of science) to study his defence of democracy in both volumes of *Open Society and Its Enemies*.[77] Howard Bloom's "*Global Brain: The Evolution of Mass Mind from the Big Bang to the 21st Century*" (2000) is a remarkable theoretical work that provides insight into the working of organic complex adaptive systems including those of a socio-political/economic/legal nature.   **23–050**

Less ambitiously there are several tools not traditionally in the lawyers set, that may assist in transnational infrastructure modelling. These include further exploration and development of the potential of flow charts, fuzzy thinking, "intelligent" electronic agents and Net collaborations.   **23–051**

In the early 1990s I was introduced to a quantity surveyor and engineer who had reduced the *FIDIC Red Book*[78] to over a hundred pages of intricate   **23–052**

---

[73] See http://www.thecommonwealth.org.
[74] An excellent, approachable introduction is provided by A.F. Chalmers *What is this thing called Science?* (1978, 3rd ed., 1999).
[75] Karl R. Popper *The Logic of Scientific Discovery* (1968).
[76] Thomas S. Kuhn *The Structure of Scientific Revolutions* (1962, 3rd ed., 1976).
[77] Karl R. Popper *The Open Society and Its Enemies: Volume 1, Plato* (1966) and *The Open Society and Its Enemies: Volume 2, Hegel & Marx.* (1966)

flow charts (decision trees), printed horizontally on roughly A4 sized sheets. He was employed by a Norwegian construction firm, who insisted that based on past experience, they knew that he could, using his charts, consistently arrive at answers to their questions in a day, whereas law firms took weeks to produce. Flow charts can be used to show interrelationships and dependencies, in order to navigate the implications of a set of rules more quickly. They may also be used more proactively (and *ex ante* rather than *ex post*) in formulating texts, to avoid unnecessary complexity and to arrive at more practical, efficient and elegant solutions.

23–053   Explore such concepts as "fuzzy thinking"[79] including fuzzy logic, fuzzy set theory, and fuzzy systems modelling, of which classical logic and set theory are subsets. Both by way of analogy and as a tool fuzzy concepts are better at coping with complexity and map more closely to judicial thinking and argument in the application of principles and rules. Fuzzy theory provides a method for analysing and modelling principle and rule based systems, even where conflicting principles may apply, permitting *inter alia* working with competing principles and the contextual assignment of precision to terms such as "reasonableness". Fuzzy concepts should be explored in expert systems, and in future law. Problems of scaling associated with multiple decision trees do not prevent useful applications, and structured solutions. The analysis assists in discerning what lawyers are involved with.

23–054   "Intelligent" electronic agents can be expected both to gather information on behalf of the business community and lawyers. In future electronic agents are likely to be employed to identify and bring to the attention of their principals "invitations to treat" or offers worthy of further investigation. In some cases they will be developed and relied upon as electronic legal agents, operating under a programmed mandate and vested with the authority to enter certain contracts on behalf of their principals. Such mandate would include choice of law upon which to contract, and the scenario could be assisted by transnational contract solutions (and catered for in the design of "future law").

23–055   Another area of technology helping solve legal problems relates to various types of global register and transaction centres, amongst them property registers being an obvious example, including patents and moveable property. Bolero providing an example of how electronic documents can be centrally brokered on behalf of trading parties.

---

[78] FIDIC is the International Federation of Consulting Engineers http://www.fidic.com.
[79] Concept originally developed by Lotfi Zadeh, *Fuzzy Sets Information Control* 8 (1965) pp. 338–353. For introductions see Daniel McNeill and Paul Freiberger, *Fuzzy Logic: The Revolutionary Computer Technology that is Changing our World* (1993); Bart Kosko, *Fuzzy Thinking* (1993); Earl Cox, *The Fuzzy Systems Handbook* (New York, 2nd ed. 1999). Perhaps to the uninitiated an unfortunate choice of name, as fuzzy logic and fuzzy set theory is more precise than classical logic and set theory, which comprise a subset of that which is fuzzy (representing those instances where membership is 0 per cent or 100 per cent). The statement is not entirely without controversy, in suggesting the possibility that classical thinking may be subsumed within the realms of an unfamiliar conceptual paradigm, that is to take hold of the future thinking. In the engineering field much pioneer work on fuzzy rule based systems was done at Queen Mary College by Ebrahim Mamdani in the early and mid-1970s. Time will tell.

Primary international commercial law (as open technology protocols) **23–056** should be available on the Net free, and this applies also to "IoL" and the static material required for their interpretation. This should be the policy adopted by all institutions involved in contributing to the transnational legal infrastructure. Where possible larger databases also should be developed and shared. The Net has reduced the cost of dissemination of material, to a level infinitesimally lower than before. Universities now can and should play a more active role. Suitable funding arrangements should be explored that do not result in proprietary systems or the forwarding of specific lobby interests. In hard-copy to promote uniform standards, institutions should also strive to have their materials available at a reasonable price. Many appear to be unacceptably expensive given the need for their promotion and capacity building, amongst students, and across diverse States.

Follow the open standards and community standards debate in relation to **23–057** the development of technology standards and technology infrastructure tools, including operating systems,[80] to discover what if anything it might suggest for the future development of law standards.

10. As an aside, a word of caution

I end with an arguably gratuitous observation, by way of a reminder and **23–058** general warning. Gratuitous in the context of this paper because the areas focused upon[81] were somewhat deliberately selected to fall outside the more contentious and "politically" problematic areas related to globalisation, economics, technology, law and politics.[82] Gratuitous also because there will be no attempt to concretise or exemplify the possibility suggested.

Fortunately, we are not (necessarily) talking about a zero sum game, how- **23–059** ever, it is necessary to be able to distinguish and recognise that which may harm. International commerce/trade is competitive, and by its nature not benign, even if it results in an overall improvement in the economic lot of the peoples of our planet. "Neutral tests" such as Kaldor-Hicks efficiency, do not require that your interests are benefited one iota, just that whilst those of others are improved, yours are not made worse. If the measure adopted is overall benefit, it is even more possible that an overall gain may result where your interests are adversely affected. The more so if you have little, and those that gain, gain much. Furthermore such "tests" are based on assumptions and/or axioms, which at best are approximations of reality (*e.g.* that of zero transaction costs, where in fact not only are they not, but they are frequently proportionately higher for the economically weak). At worst they may be manipulated *ex ante* with knowledge of their implications (*e.g.* engineering to

---

[80] See for example *Open Sources : Voices from the Open Source Revolution—The Open Source Story* http://www.oreilly.com/catalog/opensources/book/toc.html also Peter Wayner, *Free for All: How Linux and the Free Software Movement Undercut the High-Tech Titans* (2000).
[81] Sale of goods (*CISG*), contract rules and principles (*PICC*), related Arbitration, and the promotion of certain egalitarian ideals.
[82] It is not as evident in the area of private international commercial contract law the chosen focus for this paper, but appears repeatedly in relation to other areas and issues arising out of the economics, technology, law nexus.

ensure actual or relative[83] asymmetrical transaction cost). It is important to be careful in a wide range of circumstances related to various aspects of the modelling of the infrastructure for international commerce that have an impact on the allocation of rights and obligations, and especially the allocation of resources, including various types of intellectual property rights. Ask what is the objective and justification for the protection? How well is the objective met? Are there other consequential effects? Are there other objectives that are worthy of protection? Could the stated objective(s) be achieved in a better way?

---

[83] Low fixed costs have a "regressive" effect.

CHAPTER 24

PRINCIPLES OF CONTRACT LAW IN ELECTRONIC COMMERCE

RAYMOND T. NIMMER
UNIVERSITY OF HOUSTON LAW CENTER

1. Introduction

This paper overviews contract law pertaining to e-commerce. The paper **24–001**
focuses on United States law, but will also touch on several international
laws. Within the United States, this paper will focus primarily on general
statements of contract law, contained in the following:

- Article 2 of the Uniform Commercial Code ("Article 2") (dealing with
  sales of goods)

- Uniform Computer Information Transactions Act ("UCITA") (formerly entitled "Article 2B" approved by the National Conference of
  Commissioners on Uniform State Laws; dealing with the formation
  and terms of transactions in digital information)

- Restatement (Second) of Contracts (approved in 1971 and widely, but
  not uniformly followed as "common law" in the states)

- Uniform Electronic Transactions Act ("UETA") (approved by the National Conference of Commissioners on Uniform State Laws; setting out general principles for electronic messages and transactions)

24–002   The basic inquiry here is to set out a framework that identifies issues that arise in applying general contract law to transactions conducted electronically. The core policy principle, common to all who have discussed this question, is that electronic trade (on the Internet and otherwise) is rapidly becoming the distribution system of choice in many areas of commerce and an important distribution system in all areas. As in "traditional" commerce, a basis for this economic activity lies in contract law. The relevant questions of private law here relate to determining whether, or to what extent, the change in methods of interaction among parties engender changes in the nature of the private contract law regime that applies to Internet transactions. The basic approach in the United States has been that there is a need for tailoring some principles to the Internet, but that this tailoring derives from, rather than radically altering core concepts of contract law.

2. Formation of a contract

24–003   A contract is formed by an offer and an acceptance, but more broadly by any conduct of the parties showing agreement.[1] The basic principle in United States law is that the offer *and* the acceptance may be expressed in any manner appropriate to the circumstances as may conduct adequate to show agreement.[2] This principle was most recently stated in section 202(a) of UCITA:

---

[1] Discussions of electronic commerce often devote substantial time to whether electronic messages or computer files satisfy formalities requirements found in some laws, especially in the U.S., such as the rule that an executory contract is not enforceable unless expressed in a signed writing. Although billions of dollars of commerce have been conducted over the Internet, there are no reported cases raising this question. At present count, at least 21 states recognise the equivalence between electronic "records" and writings. Both UETA and UCITA adopt a convention initiated in Art. 8 of the UCC in using the term "record", rather than "writing", a "record" being defined as "information that is inscribed on a tangible medium or that is stored in an electronic or other medium and is retrievable in perceivable form." UCITA Section 102(58). UCITA recognises the equivalence of electronic processing and "traditional" signatures; this has been followed in UCC Art. 9 (dealing with secured transactions). UETA has the same concept. The model law proposed by UNICTRAL likewise provides similar rules of equivalence. All in all, while the formalities debate continues, its commercial relevance is greatly reduced and need not detain us as a matter of general private law. The issue remains important, however, in the continued existence of regulatory rules in some states and in federal law that require writings as a matter of regulation, and have not been fully updated to fit electronic commerce.

[2] In mass markets especially, there is often an ambiguity about which act of which party is the offer and which is the acceptance. For example, on an Internet site, is the making available of information or other commodities for a stated fee the "offer" which is "accepted" by the customer's assenting to the terms, or is the site an advertisement or a solicitation for offers, the customer's conduct being the "offer" to purchase on the vendor's terms, which is "accepted" when the vendor acts in response? Deciding this question is often not important, but it can relate to questions about when and where a contract is formed and about what regulatory regime applies. There are no United States cases dealing with this issue in Internet contexts.

A contract may be formed in any manner sufficient to show agreement, including offer and acceptance or conduct of both parties or operations of electronic agents which recognize the existence of a contract.[3]

Notice that this formulation contains an express reference to agreements being shown by the operations of "electronic agents" which recognise the existence of a contract.[4] This rule establishes the validity of purely automated contracting, a practice that has already developed in several information industries and has variants in other areas of commerce in the United States. This formulation from UCITA, including the electronic agent concept, is followed in the approved draft of UETA and also in the current draft of proposed revisions of Article 2, although the status of that revision has been called into doubt by recent political events.

24–004

The idea that agreement can be shown by conduct is a common law premise in the United States that was carried forward into Article 2, the Restatement (Second) of Contracts and UCITA. The term used in the Restatement for assent by conduct is that a party "manifests assent" to the contract or to the terms of a particular writing ("record").[5] As expressed in UCITA, the concept of manifesting assent reads as follows:

24–005

> A person manifests assent to a record or term if the person, acting with knowledge of, or after having an opportunity to review the record or term or a copy of it . . . intentionally engages in conduct or makes statements with reason to know that the other party or its electronic agent may infer from the conduct or statement that the person assents to the record or term.[6]

The conduct must be voluntary or intentional in the sense that a decision to act (or not to act) occurs. The U.S. case law establishes that inaction can constitute a manifestation of assent. A recent case illustrating that principle was *Gateway 2000, Inc. v. Hill*,[7] in which the purchaser of a computer system was bound by the terms of a contract contained within the computer system box when the customer failed to return the computer within thirty days after its receipt and the contract provided that this failure would constitute assent to the terms of the contract.

24–006

The rules here do not focus on determining whether there was a *subjective* intent to be bound, but on whether the objective manifestations indicate such an intent.[8] A key term in both the *Restatement* and UCITA is that the

24–007

---

[3] Accord Uniform Commercial Code [UCC] § 2–202(a).
[4] UCITA section 102(28) defines "electronic agent" as "a computer program, or electronic or other automated means used independently to initiate an action or respond to electronic messages or performances without review or action by an individual at the time of the action, response or performance."
[5] See *Restatement (Second) of Contracts* § 19.
[6] UCITA § 112(a). Accord *Restatement (Second) of Contracts* § 19.
[7] *Gateway 2000, Inc. v. Hill*, – F.3d – (7th Cir. 1997). See also *Brower v. Gateway 2000, Inc.*, 676 NYS.2d 569 (N.Y.A.D. 1998) (contract formed, but particular term relating to arbitration was unconscionable and, at least in part, unenforceable).
[8] In U.S. law, one measures intent by objective manifestations of intent, rather than subjective intention. This means that the person responding is held to intend "what appeared from his expression to be his intention." *Restatement (Second) of Contracts* § 18, 19. Calamari & Perillo, *The Law of Contracts* 2–13 (1987). The UNIDROIT rules are consistent. *UNIDROIT Principles* Art. 2.2, comment 2 ("Since such an intention will rarely be declared expressly, it often has to be inferred from the circumstances of each individual case.").

conduct or inaction must occur with "reason to know" that it will yield an inference of assent on the part of the other party. The idea of "reason to know" is fluid and captures a wide range of circumstances that occur in cases, many of which circumstances will fall far short of actual knowledge. As discussed in both the Restatement and UCITA, a person has reason to know a fact if the person has information from which a reasonable person of ordinary intelligence would infer that the fact does or will exist based on all the circumstances, including the overall context and ordinary expectations in that context.[9] The party is charged with commercial knowledge of any factors in a particular transaction which in common understanding or ordinary practice are to be expected, including reasonable expectations from usage of trade and course of dealing. If a person has specialised knowledge or superior intelligence, reason to know is determined in light of whether a reasonable person with that knowledge or intelligence would draw the inference that the fact does or will exist.

24–008   "Reason to know" is distinguished from knowledge. Knowledge means conscious belief in the truth of a fact. Reason to know need not entail a conscious belief in the existence of the fact or its probable existence in the future. Of course, a person that has knowledge of a fact also has reason to know of its existence. Reason to know is also to be distinguished from "should know." "Should know" imports a duty to others to ascertain facts; the term "reason to know" is used both where the actor has a duty to another and where the person would not be acting adequately in protecting its own interests if it did not act in light of the facts of which it had reason to know.

24–009   UCITA goes beyond the *Restatement* in expressly requiring that the conduct manifesting assent must occur after the party has an *opportunity to review* the terms of the contract.[10] A person has an *opportunity to review* a record only if the record "is made available in a manner that ought to call it to the attention of a reasonable person and permit review." This standard tailors the general concept of manifesting assent in a manner that gives potentially important protection against inconspicuous or hidden records. It does not require that the assenting party actually read the record before agreeing to it. This is consistent with general U.S. contract law, including the rules outlined in the *Restatement*, and with ordinary practice; under U.S. law, a party does not avoid being bound by the terms of a record fairly presented for review simply because the party fails to seize the opportunity to review the terms before assenting to the contract. On the other hand, as implemented in UCITA and, arguably, in general contract law, one party cannot obtain assent to a record that it has not at least fairly made available for the other party's review.

2.1 Assent online by individuals

24–010   These general concepts set the basic framework for consideration of the mechanics of contractual assent in Internet transactions under U.S. law.

---

[9] *Restatement (Second) of Contracts § 19, Comment b*; UCITA section 102 (56), *Reporter's Notes* (July, 1999 proposed draft).
[10] UCITA 112(a) (July 1999, approved draft).

I will defer, for the moment, the question of "given general assent to a contract, is the assenting party bound by all of the terms?" This section deals with the question of assent itself.

A fair reading of U.S. case law and general contract law sources leave **24–011** little doubt that, as a general principle, assent expressed in the form of a click or other expression of assent in a context clearly indicating (giving "reason to know") that the click on the screen will create an inference of assent is adequate to bind the party to the contract. While there are relatively few U.S. decisions on point, there seems to be little doubt that a party by reacting to a choice, clearly presented, to either assent to a contract or decline assent and leave a particular transactional context, manifests assent if it chooses the option that it has reason to know will yield that result.[11]

There is little reason to believe that the electronic acts indicating assent do **24–012** not do so. Behaviour and non-verbal assent have long been treated in most countries as adequate to form a contract and adopt terms relating to that contract.[12] Although there are few cases, all reported cases in the U.S. hold that an indication of assent online by clicking "I agree" forms a contract.[13] A Canadian court in *Rudder v. Microsoft Corp.*[14] reached the same result, holding that a choice of forum clause in an online agreement controlled the forum (jurisdiction) issue. The court rejected the premise that presentation of the clause electronically was deficient because of the "click, I agree" formats. While not all terms of the agreement were displayed at the same time, the court held that this did not change the fact that assent was effectively given. There was no basis to selectively invalidate any particular term. The court commented:

> [Plaintiffs] seek to avoid the consequences of specific terms of their agreement while at the same time seeking to have others enforced. Neither the form of this contract nor its manner of presentation to potential members are so aberrant as to lead to such an anomalous result. To give effect to the plaintiff's argument would, rather than advancing the goal of commercial certainty [and] move this type of electronic transaction into the realm of commercial absurdity. It would lead to chaos in the marketplace, render ineffectual electronic commerce and undermine the integrity of any agreement entered into through this medium. On the present facts, the Membership Agreement must be afforded the sanctity [given] to any agreement in writing.

However, there are a number of assumptions made about the context, the **24–013** failure of which assumptions might yield the result that there was no contract formed. For example, if a party has no alternative but to proceed in a particular manner (*e.g.*, it cannot withdraw from the site), proceeding in that particular manner does not indicate assent because there was no choice

---

[11] See, *e.g.*, *Caspi v. The Microsoft Network*, L.L.C. *et. al.*, – N.E.2d – (NJ Super. Ct. 7/2/99) (choice of forum clause in online contract which consumer could review entire contract and click "I Agree" or "I disagree" enforceable); *Storm Impact, Inc. v. Software of the Month Club*, 44 U.S.P.Q.2d 1441 (N.D. Ill. 1997) (online agreement preventing commercial use); *Hotmail Corp. v. Van$ Money Pie, Inc.*, 47 U.S.P.Q.2d 1020 (N.D. Cal. 1998).
[12] Restatement (Second) of Contracts § 19.
[13] See, *e.g.*, *Caspi v. Microsoft Network*, LLC, 323 NJ Super. 118, 732 A2d 528 (NJ Super. AD 1999); *Storm Impact, Inc. v. Software of the Month Club*, 13 F.Supp.2d 782 (N.D. Ill. 1998).
[14] *Rudder v. Microsoft Corp., Ontario Superior Court* (Canada, Oct. 8, 1999).

involved.[15] Similarly, at least under the UCITA formulation, there might be no assent if the terms of the contract are not available for review before the alleged assent or if the reference to them was inconspicuously buried in a screen in a manner that would not come to the attention of an ordinary person. Terms not made available until after the conduct that allegedly constitutes assent are not assented to *by that conduct*, although subsequent conduct may be sufficient.

24–014   This type of contextual analysis, shaped by standards, rather than specific mandatory rules, is a common approach in U.S. contract law. From the perspective of a party transacting on the Internet, these standards set out guidelines which, if followed, provide fair notice to the other party in addition to establishing assurance that the terms will be binding. The provider must create a setting in which:

- the terms of the contract are fairly presented for review in a manner that ought to call their availability to the attention of a reasonable person; and

- the user's choice to take a particular action is clearly indicated as yielding assent to the contract.

24–015   For example, a prominent hyperlink to the contract terms followed by a clearly delineated option to accept the terms or refuse them would clearly satisfy this standard. Of course, this system of contract law does not allow the other party to demand the information or other commodity that is being marketed on *its own terms*, but that is the nature of the marketplace and, in U.S. law, cases of potential abuse of market are dealt with under law other than those associated with contract formation.

24–016   This being said, in the U.S., as in other countries, some have expressed doubt about whether a single manifestation of assent to an alternative made explicit on the screen of a computer should be sufficient to constitute assent for purposes of contract formation. The bases for this position have never been fully articulated and the concept of "enhanced assent" that it postulates has not been adopted in any U.S. case or general contract law statute formulation applicable to Internet contracting.[16] Under U.S. common law and under UCITA, the issue is simply whether the conduct occurred in a context where there was reason to know that it would indicate assent. To this writer, the principle concern appears to be grounded in the risk that a mistake might bind an individual to an unwanted contract and the proposition that the risk of such mistakes is more pronounced in Internet transactions than elsewhere. As an empirical matter, the latter point is unsubstantiated: indeed, in

---

[15] This, of course, does not mean that the party must be given an alternative of making the purchase without assenting to the terms. The idea of choice here resides at the transactional level: the party must have the capability of refusing the terms and declining the transaction. There is no principle embedded in U.S. law which dictates that a vendor cannot generally insist on the terms under which it chooses to distribute (or not distribute) its product.

[16] Some indications of enhanced assent requirements can be found in consumer protection regulatory laws regarding disclosure rules, however, but a review of these is beyond our scope here.

a properly constructed Internet site, the idea that mistaken assent is more likely than elsewhere is counterintuitive and factually incorrect.

UCITA contains provisions specially dealing with the risk of mistake in **24–017** Internet and UETA adopts a similar concept in modified form. I discuss these later. In addition, however, UCITA establishes a statutory incentive for providers to employ a so-called "double-click" technology to reduce the risk of mistake. UCITA section 112(d) provides:

> Conduct or operations manifesting assent may be shown in any manner, including a showing that a person or an electronic agent obtained or used the information or informational rights and that a procedure existed by which a person or an electronic agent must have engaged in the conduct or operations in order to do so. *Proof of compliance with [the required conduct occurring with reason to know] is sufficient if there is conduct that assents and subsequent conduct that electronically reaffirms assent.* [emphasis added]

In discussing contract formation issues with respect to Internet contracting, **24–018** two general policy points should be kept in mind.

The first involves the reality that, while enhanced assent requirements *may* provide protection to some purchasers on Internet, that protection comes at a *cost* measured by (i) the cost of compliance with the enhanced require-ment; (ii) the uncertainty for the vendor created if the adequacy of compli-ance cannot be judged at the outset; and (iii) the consequences of non-compliance with enhanced assent concepts. This is an especially cogent formulation when one considers requirements grounded in, and associated with, the world of goods in traditional commerce in the form of paper-based disclosures and the like, where the requirements themselves sometimes dis-able the very benefits of electronic commerce itself. It is also especially cogent when one acknowledges that, like all other venues of commerce, electronic commerce is not merely a consumer marketplace, but increasingly a com-mercial market involving transactions among and between businesses.

The second point focuses on the consequences of concluding that no con- **24–019** tract is formed and on the question of, as a matter of policy, under what cir-cumstances the cost or risk of those consequences *should be* imposed on either of the transacting parties. If we assume that no performance has occurred by either party, the consequences of concluding that there was no enforceable contract may be, as we discuss below, simply a matter of allow-ing the customer to avoid the alleged deal. For consumer transactions, this may be trivial, but it may not be trivial in a business-to-business transaction where supply-chain structures cause early reliance on the contract. If we assume that the value has been provided to the customer, but in law no con-tract was formed, the consequences vary depending on the subject matter of the transaction.

- In the world of goods, the consequence may be that the vendor has delivered goods without the benefit of a contract or, alternatively, with-out the benefit of the terms of contract under which it has decided to market the goods. Assume that there were no egregious terms in the contract. In either case, the result in either case is that the vendor is in the marketplace under terms it did not desire, with unknown economic consequences. For the buyer, either it is in possession of goods it did not purchase and must return them, or it has purchased goods under terms that were not those offered. Clearly, for the buyer, the latter is the optimal result, but when is it appropriate? Of course, in all countries, various principles of law may exist to equitably adjust these circumstances, but these are often costly and uncertain and, in an Internet context, may be applicable to millions of purchases, rather than one or two.

- In the world of information, the consequences are equally difficult, but involve somewhat different considerations. Let's look at two cases. In the first, Client obtained access to and read a copy of the latest court decision pursuant to a contract requiring payment of two dollars for the access time, but the contract is unenforceable. Having read the case, the knowledge cannot be returned. However, equitable remedies against each of the one hundred thousand clients who used the same access under the same invalid contract is impossible. In the second case, Client obtains by downloading a copy of copyrighted software under a license that allows use for commercial purposes by up to ten simultaneous users or with up to ten copies, but the license is not enforceable. The licensee may be in possession of an infringing copy, if downloading was contingent on the licensee. Even if not, it cannot make additional copies without infringing, because the copyright owner did not effectively transferred the right to do so.[17]

2.2 Assent and contracting by computers

24–020 A number of years ago, at a conference in the United States, I asked over 100 lawyers in the audience whether they thought that a computer could enter into a contract with another computer. After allowing several moments for the subdued chuckles to die down, I followed my question with the following statement: "The answer to that question *must* be yes in order to realize the potential of electronic commerce because, as the technology evolves, that will be exactly the way in which contracts are increasingly formed and, in the arena of information commerce, performed." Subsequent years have merely underscored the accuracy of that observation. The use of "electronic agents" (or "bots") has developed rapidly in Internet. Indeed, their development and the predictable use *by consumers* of such agents to "shop" an international marketplace is a distinguishing characteristic of electronic commerce that contrasts to commerce at the storefront, in the shopping mall, or from the factory.[18]

24–021 An "electronic agent" is "a computer program, or electronic or other automated means used independently to initiate an action or respond to electronic messages or performances without review or action by an individual at

---

[17] See, *e.g., Micro Star v. Formgen Inc.*, 154 F.3d 1107 (9th Cir. 1998) (enforceability of license in downloaded software not material to infringement claim; if license was enforceable, actions exceeded the license, but if license was not enforceable, there was no right to make any copies of the software).

[18] See Lorin Brennan, "The real technological revolution," *Nevada Lawyer* 16 (June 2000).

the time of the action, response or performance."[19] There are few reported cases in the U.S. on fully automated contract formation,[20] but, as described above, UCITA and UETA expressly recognise that electronic agent operations can form an enforceable contract, and proposed revisions of Article 2 have the analogous concept. The key issue will be under what circumstances do the operations of the agents recognise the existence of a contract.

The idea that contracts can be formed between two computer programs **24–022** represents either a mere expansion of concepts of assent under U.S. contract law or a fundamental philosophical shift that has great significance in electronic commerce. It is a fundamental change in concept if one looks solely to the interaction of programs as the basis for judging adequate assent to a contract. Computer programs increasingly have capabilities associated with "intelligence", such as the basic capability to rapidly make "choices" among options, including not only particular products, but the price and contract terms associated with those products. Yet, this type of choice and the operations that it causes are not equivalent to the human choice that characterises the assent associated with contracting. They might be treated as such for purposes of legal effect, but they are not the same. Equally important, of course, it is not the computer program itself that is bound to a contract, but the person on whose behalf the program ("electronic agent") operates.

This suggests casting backward for a finding of assent, focusing on the **24–023** decision to use the electronic agent. Under both the UCITA and the UETA formulations, an electronic agent is a program *used* to engage in independent actions associated with the creation or performance of contracts. The "user" here is akin to the principal in a principal-agent relationship, although neither UCITA nor UETA rely on that fiction to support the contract-related consequences of use of the electronic device. The basic principle on which responsibility for electronic operations lies, instead, in the initial choice and the imposition of resulting obligations. "Use" of an electronic agent implies a conscious decision to rely on that agent's independent operations. That decision corresponds to a resulting acceptance of the obligations that ensue from that use.

UCITA section 107 specifies that a "person that uses its own electronic **24–024** agent for authentication, performance, or agreement, including manifestation of assent, is bound by the operations of the electronic agent, even if no individual was aware of or reviewed the agent's operations or the results of the operations." This is the basic attribution rule. However, there is also a need to provide a buffer against fraud and gross mistake in the fully automated contracting arena. To this end, UCITA section 206(a) indicates that, if the interaction of electronic agents "results in the electronic agents engaging in operations that the circumstances indicate acceptance, a contract is formed but a court may grant appropriate relief if the operations resulted from fraud, electronic mistake, or the like." On this latter point, the Reporter's Notes to an earlier draft of UCITA state:

---

[19] UCITA section 102(28) (1999 Approved Draft).
[20] See *Corinthian Pharmaceutical v. Lederle Laboratories*, 724 F. Supp. 605 (SD Ind. 1989) ("When Corinthian placed its order, it merely received a tracking number from the computer. Such an automated, ministerial act cannot constitute an acceptance.").

Assent from the operations of the two electronic agents does not arise if the operations are induced by mistake, fraud or the like. Formation of a contract does not occur if a party or its electronic agent manipulates the programming or response of the other electronic agent in a manner akin to fraud. Such acts, in essence, vitiate the inference of assent which would occur through the normal operations of the agent. Similarly, the inference is vitiated if because of aberrant programming or through an unexpected inter-action of the two agents, operations indicating the existence of a contract occur in circumstances that are not within the reasonable contemplation of the person using either electronic agent. In such cases, the circumstances are analogous to mutual mis-take. In some cases, especially if the electronic agent is supplied by one party to the purported agreement, it would be appropriate for a court to avoid results that are clearly outside the reasonable expectations of the other party. The concept here is more akin to the law of unilateral mistakes except that it places the risk on the party that supplied the agent for and required its use in a particular transaction.[21]

3. Terms of a contract on the Internet

24–025   U.S. contract law follows a concept of contractual freedom associated with the open-market economy. Under this policy, the agreement controls and contract law provides, at most, background or default rules that govern in the event that the parties' agreement fails to address the particular issue.[22] This policy permeates the Uniform Commercial Code and UCITA, and was explained in comments to Article 2A on leases of goods: "This article was greatly influenced by the fundamental tenet of the common law as it has developed with respect to leases of goods: freedom of the parties to con-tract . . . These principles include the ability of the parties to vary the effect of the provisions of Article 2A, subject to certain limitations including those that relate to the obligations of good faith, diligence, reasonableness and care."[23]

24–026   This legal structure creates an interaction between the two sources of con-tractual provisions (underlying law and over-riding agreement). While some contract law rules are expressly invariable, most can be altered by the agree-ment. As a consequence, in defining the terms of a contract, one looks first to the agreement and, in particular, to any record of the agreement, and only thereafter to the underlying default rules.

24–027   Most Internet contracts are standard forms to which the other party assents. In Internet, the assenting party may be either the vendor or the pur-chaser, depending on the nature of the transaction. General U.S. law holds that a party is bound by the terms of a standard form if it manifests assent to that form.[24] This includes all the terms of the contract whether or not the party has read or actually understood them. This principle, which flows from a general concept of blanket assent to a record containing terms of a con-tract, is not without exceptions, however.

---

[21] UCITA Section 206, Reporter's Notes (July 1999 Proposed Draft).
[22] "Agreement" is a defined term in the UCC and in UCITA, referring the entire bargain of the parties in fact, not just the written (or recorded) contract. See UCC § 1-201.
[23] UCC 2A-101, Comment. See also Randy E. Barnett, "The Sound of Silence: Default Rules and Contractual Consent", 78 *Va. L. Rev.* 821 (1992); Ian Ayres & Robert Gertner, "Strategic Contractual Inefficiency and the Optimal Choice of Legal Rules", 101 *Yale L.J. 729*, 734 (1992).
[24] *Restatement (Second) of Contracts* § 211. See also UCITA Section 209(a)(c) (1999 Approved Draft).

3.1 Rules invalidating some terms.

The most broadly applicable rule in U.S. contract law that allows a court to invalidate some terms of the contract comes from the doctrine of "unconscionability." This doctrine was created in the 1950s in Article 2 of the UCC.[25] It was subsequently adopted in Article 2A (leases of goods) and embodied in the Restatement (Second) of Contracts. It has been carried forward into the field of computer information transactions in UCITA.   **24–028**

The doctrine of unconscionability gives the court power to invalidate aspects of contracts that produce untoward results. As stated in Article 2, the doctrine provides: **24–029**

> If a court as a matter of law finds the contract or any term thereof to have been unconscionable at the time it was made, the court may refuse to enforce the contract, or it may enforce the remainder of the contract without the unconscionable term, or it may so limit the application of any unconscionable term as to avoid any unconscionable result.[26]

Unconscionability as a theory lacks substantive focus. As initially promulgated, it centred on creating an important organising principle that established the right of courts to "police" against abusive contract terms.[27] The theory thus sets out a limited right of a court to rewrite contracts. As unconscionability doctrine evolved, it came to focus excluding contractual clauses that reflect a combination of procedural unconscionability (adhesion contracts) and substantive unconscionability (oppressive terms).[28] As the comments to the Article 2 section that created the concept indicate, the "basic test is whether, in light of the general commercial background . . . the clauses involved are so one-sided as to be unconscionable at the time and place of the making of the contract."[29] The concept bears some resemblance to the ideas expressed in the European Union Directive on Unfair Contract Terms in consumer contracts, although it lacks anything resembling the lengthy list of terms contained in that Directive as illustrative of unfair and, thus, avoidable terms.[30]   **24–030**

One could spend hours discussing the scope of unconscionability without placing firm limits on that scope. It is, in fact, a general overview standard within which courts can police contracting practice to avoid extreme abuses. Within that overall standard, the case law pattern that has developed invalidates a term of a contract only if based on a conjunction of procedural problems and substantive abuses. The earliest litigation centred on consumer cases and this continues to be its major focus. However, it also applies to commercial contracts.[31]   **24–031**

---

[25] UCC § 2-302. Interestingly, this doctrine is not expressly applicable to secured transactions (UCC Art. 9) or to transactions involving securities (UCC Art.8).

[26] UCC § 2-302(a).

[27] U.C.C. § 2-302, Comment 1.

[28] Arthur Leff, "Unconscionability and the Code–The Emperor's New Clause," 115 *U. Pa. L. Rev.* 485 (1967) (describing procedural and substantive unconscionability);

[29] U.C.C. 2-302, Comment 1 (1962 Approved Draft).

[30] EU Directive 93/13 on Unfair Terms in Consumer Contracts. [1993] O.J. L95/29.

[31] See, *e.g., Brower v. Gateway 2000, Inc.*, 676 NYS.2d 569 (N.Y.A.D. 1998) (arbitration clause in standard form contract that was otherwise enforceable is unconscionable because it effectively deprived buyer of computer of the ability to pursue a claim); *Intergraph Corp. v. Intel Corp.*, – F. Supp. –, 1998 WL 180606 (ND Ala. 1998) (termination provision in technology contract used in an anti-competitive manner had an unconscionable effect).

24-032 Unconscionability doctrine was controversial when first introduced and engendered extensive litigation. More recently, however, the parameters of the doctrine, although ultimately flexible, have stabilised. A less-well-accepted invalidation rule is suggested in section 211 of the *Restatement*. Although promulgated in 1971, this rule has been adopted in less than 10 states.[32] Section 211 proposes that a person who manifests assent to a standard form is bound by the terms of that form, except terms that the party proposing the form has reason to believe would cause the other party to reject the writing if it knew that the egregious term were present.[33] In form, this creates a "refusal term" concept that extends beyond unconscionability and creates an *additional* basis for avoiding some contract terms even if the term itself is not unconscionable.

24-033 While the black letter of the *Restatement* refers to "refusal terms", however, some courts in the few states that adopt the theory go further and allow a court to avoid any term that the judge believes is outside the "reasonable expectations" of the other party, whether or not that other party is a consumer or a business.[34] The *Restatement* comments mention this phrase, but focus on other issues. They state in relevant part:

> Although customers typically adhere to standardised agreements and are bound by them without even appearing to know the standard terms in detail, they are not bound to *unknown* terms which are beyond the range of reasonable expectations. ... Reason to believe may be inferred from the fact that the term is bizarre or oppressive, from the fact that is eviscerates the non-standard terms explicitly agreed to, or from the fact that it eliminates the dominant purpose of the transaction.[35]

24-034 The interest protected here is associated with the bargaining process itself. The *Restatement* recognizes, as any contract law must, that parties agree to and are bound by standard forms every day. This is central to modern commerce, especially in the Internet. The *Restatement* section goes beyond the idea of unconscionability, however, to deal with concerns about unfair surprise. Basically, the goal seems to be to give a party an opportunity to convince a court that the term was not known to it and that the other party should have known that the adhering party would refuse the contract had the term been disclosed.

24-035 Variations of the *Restatement* standard were presented and debated in both the process leading to the promulgation of UCITA and the process of revising Article 2. The concept was rejected in UCITA, being replaced with enhanced procedural protections and a reliance on general theories of unconscionability. A general adoption of the concept was also rejected in the Article 2 revision process. The most recent draft of revisions for Article 2 provided a variation of the expectations test limited to consumer contracts, but that proposal has been controversial and its status is uncertain in light of a recasting of the Article 2 revision process in the face of the controversy.

---

[32] See James J. White, "Form Contracts Under Revised Article 2" 75 *Wash. U. L. Q.* 315 (1997).
[33] *Restatement (Second) of Contracts* § 211(3).
[34] James J. White, "Form Contracts Under Revised Article 2", 75 *Wash. U. L. Q.* 315 (1997).
[35] *Restatement (Second) of Contracts* 211, Comment f.

Both unconscionability and the *Restatement* test share a concern about **24–036** unknown or undisclosed terms. From the perspective of the party seeking enforcement of contract terms, they indicate a need to affirmatively disclose important terms if this is possible. However, because of the substantive aspect of unconscionability doctrine, mere disclosure may not be adequate to overcome a challenge under that doctrine.

A third source of *term* invalidation under U.S. law is present throughout **24–037** U.S. contract law, but has been codified only in UCITA and the *Restatement*. This principle recognises that some contract terms are invalid because they conflict with the fundamental public policy of a state and that public policy overrides the interest in the enforcement of contracts. As described in UCITA, the test is:

> If a term of a contract violates a fundamental public policy, the court may refuse to enforce the contract, may enforce the remainder of the contract without the impermissible term, or so limit the application of the impermissible term as to avoid any result contrary to public policy, in each case, to the extent that the interest in enforcement is clearly outweighed by a public policy against enforcement of the term.[36]

Not surprisingly, this "public policy" invalidation seldom arises in ordinary **24–038** commercial practice. Comments to the *Restatement* suggest that: "In doubtful cases . . . a decision as to enforceability is reached only after a careful balancing, in light of the circumstances, of the interests in the enforcement of the particular promise against the policy against the enforcement of such terms. . . . Enforcement will be denied only if the factors that argue against enforcement clearly outweigh the law's traditional interest in protecting the expectations of the parties, its abhorrence of any unjust enrichment, and any public interest in enforcement of the particular term."[37]

In a recent illustration of this concept, a California court invalidated a con- **24–039** tractual choice of law provision.[38] The basis for this was that the choice of law (the state of Maryland) if enforced, would circumvent fundamental public policy of California which denies enforcement, except in exceptional cases, to contract terms precluding an employee from competing with the employee's former employer. By denying enforcement to the contract choice of law, the court applied California law to the dispute and declared the no-competition clause invalid (in effect, a dual application of the public policy invalidation theme). As here, in most cases, the concept when applied stems ether from a specific state statute or from well-established principles of common law.

In principle, there is nothing unique in Internet transactions that would affect the applicability or non-applicability of the public policy concept.

3.2 Required procedures for presenting terms

In addition to the foregoing invalidation rules, U.S. law contains a number of **24–040** specific rules which require particular disclosures associated with a contract or

---

[36] UCITA § 105(b). See also *Restatement (Second) of Contracts* § 178.
[37] *Restatement (Second) of Contracts* § 178, Comment b.
[38] *Application Group, Inc. v. Hunter Group, Inc.*, 61 Cal. App4th 881, 72 Cal. Rptr2d 73 (Cal. App. 1998).

which specify format or form for particular types of contractual clauses. Many of these are embedded in particular state or federal regulations, most often associated with consumer protection issues. In some cases, failure to comply with the particular disclosure rule invalidates a contract or term, while in others it exposes the non-complying vendor to an administrative sanction.

24–041   In general, these consumer rules were developed for a paper-based economy and reflect methods of disclosure and discourse associated with that economy such as in the form of requirements that disclosures occur *in writing* or that *terms* be presented in a specified manner associated with size and location deriving from an expectation that the contract be handed over in print form. Many of these regulations have not been updated to reflect the Internet commerce environment. In some states, however, electronic commerce legislation broadly preempts aspects of the regulations that require either a writing or a traditional signature, in each case permitting electronic surrogates of these traditional commerce concepts. UCITA contains similar preemptive language.[39]

24–042   In the U.S., many consumer protection themes are contained in federal regulations. U.S. Federal agencies appear ready to recognise conceptually the equivalence between electronic records and writings, but seem to be pursuing disconnected policy approaches to adjusting regulatory disclosure and similar rules to Internet. For example, the Federal Reserve Board, which administers various consumer regulatory systems (including truth in lending and electronic funds transfer rules) has a adopted an open-ended, flexible approach to the Internet variations, allowing systems that fairly comply with underlying disclosure policies,[40] while the Federal Trade Commission (which administers a variety of other consumer rules) has proposed a more limited approach which will restrict commercial development in Internet contexts.[41] Neither view is consistent with the approach apparently being developed within the European Union.

24–043   Beyond regulatory requirements, general contract law in the U.S. in some situations imposes format requirements in order to obtain enforceability of particular types of contract terms, despite assent to the overall contract. The most common is a requirement that certain terms be "conspicuous." This concept exists in current Articles 2 and 2A dealing with sales and leases of goods. These statutes require that, if a disclaimer of an implied warranty is contained in a "writing", the disclaimer must be "conspicuous" in order to be enforceable.[42] UCITA adopts this same standard with respect to disclaimers in a record in transactions involving computer information.[43] UCITA also requires that, in a mass market transaction, a restriction on transfer of the license must be conspicuous to be enforceable.[44]

---

[39] UCITA § 105(d).
[40] See, *e.g.*, Federal Reserve System, 63 Fed. Reg. 14548-01 (March 25, 1998); Federal Reserve System, Interim Rule Regarding Reg. E, 63 FR 14528-01 (March 25, 1998).
[41] Federal Trade Commission, Proposed Statement Regarding E-Commerce, 63 Fed. Reg. 24996-01 (1998).
[42] UCC § 2-316.
[43] UCITA § 406(b)(5) (1999 approved draft).
[44] UCITA § 503(4) (1999 approved draft). UCITA also allows the parties to agree that it applies to aspects of transactions otherwise outside its scope, or does not apply to aspects otherwise within its scope. In a mass market transaction, such a choice must also be conspicuous. UCITA § 103(e)(3).

The functions of a conspicuousness requirement are to provide fair notice   **24–044**
of the term to the other party and, as a related matter, to give contract
drafters guidance on how to present terms that will make them enforceable
under general contract law. In the UCC, a term is "conspicuous" if presented
in a manner that ought to call it to the attention of a reasonable person.[45]
The statute specifies several methods of making a term conspicuous, such as
by presenting it in all caps distinct from surrounding text. UCITA follows
this approach of giving guidance on how to make a term conspicuous,
expanding the guidance to fit Internet contexts. It provides in relevant part
that a term is conspicuous if it is:

- a heading in capitals in a size equal to or greater than, or in contrasting
  type, font, or colour to, the surrounding text;

- language in the body of a record or display in larger or other contrasting
  type, font, or colour or set off from the surrounding text by symbols or
  other marks that call attention to the language;

- a term prominently referenced in an electronic record or display which
  is readily accessible and reviewable from the record or display; or

- a term or reference to a term that is so placed in a record or display that
  the person or electronic agent can not proceed without taking some
  action with respect to the term or reference.[46]

This same language is replicated in the most recent draft of revisions of
Article 2.

In contrast to these approaches to the requirement of a term being "con-   **24–045**
spicuous", one can compare a draft policy by the Federal Trade Commission
which it placed out for comment. The proposal received significant negative
comment. The draft sought to provide interpretation of standards administered by the Commission requiring "clear and conspicuous" disclosures in
advertising. The Commission noted that generally its current standards of
administering there rules would continue to apply, but that electronic media
with scrolling and other functions create special difficulties. In assessing these
settings, it suggested that the following factors be considered:[47]

> **a. Unavoidability.** "The Commission believes that, to ensure effective-
> ness, disclosures ordinarily should be unavoidable by consumers acting
> reasonably. On the Internet or other electronic media, this means that
> consumers viewing an advertisement should necessarily be exposed to
> the disclosure in the course of a communication without having to take
> affirmative action, such as scrolling down a page, clicking on a link to
> other pages, activating a "pop up," or entering a search term to view the
> disclosure."

---

[45] UCC § 1-201.
[46] UCITA § 102 (15) (1999 approved draft).
[47] Federal Trade Commission, Proposed Statement Regarding E-Commerce, 63 Fed. Reg.
24996-01 (1998).

b. Access to disclosures. "The Commission believes that in order to be effectively communicated, disclosures should remain accessible by consumers at all times during the communication. Therefore, after initially viewing a Web page that contains disclosures, a consumer who hyperlinks to another page should not be prevented from returning to the page containing the disclosures."

c. Proximity and placement. "Internet and other electronic media advertisements often include many pages and the length of each individual page can far exceed that of a traditional off-line page. Consumers may choose not to scroll completely through each page and not to link to each available page on the Web site, thus possibly missing important disclosures. Based on its experience in evaluating disclosures in traditional media, the Commission believes that the effectiveness of disclosures is ordinarily enhanced by their proximity to the representation they qualify."

d. Prominence. "Disclosures that are large in size and/or emphasised through a sharply contrasting colour, and remain visible or audible for a sufficiently long duration, are likely to be more effective than those lacking such prominence."

e. Non-distracting factors. "Even if a disclosure is large in size and long in duration, other elements of an advertisement may distract consumers so that they fail to notice, read, or listen to the disclosure. For example, Web pages may contain large flashing images, background sounds, or other items that are separate from the disclosure and may reduce the prominence of the disclosure."

24-046 In contrast, in discussing adaptation of its rules to electronic commerce, the Federal Reserve Board commented: "The act and Regulation Z require creditors to present required information 'clearly and conspicuously.'" Under the proposed rule, the "clear and conspicuous" requirement applies to electronic communication. *The Board does not intend to discourage or encourage specific types of technologies.* Regardless of technology, however, the disclosures provided by electronic communication must meet the "clear and conspicuous" standard. While a creditor is generally not required to ensure that the consumer has the equipment to read the disclosures, in some circumstances a creditor would have the responsibility of making sure the proper equipment is in place." (emphasis added)[48]

24-047 Standards evolved in general law for general applicability should be more open-ended than standards developed pursuant to specific regulatory regimes of limited and focused applicability. Additionally, of course, the contract law standard that some terms be "conspicuous" is on its face potentially different from a standard that a disclosure be "clear and conspicuous." Besides the language differences, the terms come from a different legislative and policy background.

---

[48] Federal Reserve System, 63 Fed. Reg. 14548-01 (March 25, 1998).

4. Under what circumstances can a contract be rescinded

U.S. Contract law contains no general right of rescission applicable to Internet **24–048** transaction analogous to that provided for in the EU Distance Contracts Directive.[49] Disclosure rules are created under federal law for certain forms of telemarketing, but these are not as broadly applicable as under the Directive.[50] While limited rights of rescission are created in U.S. law for particular types of transactions, these are associated with intrusive or otherwise sensitive sales environments and have not bee extended into Internet contexts.[51]

In general contract law, however, a variety of doctrines permit the avoidance **24–049** of an otherwise apparently enforceable contractual obligation and these doctrines apply to Internet transactions.[52] In U.S. law, these doctrines generally deal with circumstances which vitiate the conclusion that there was actual assent to the contract. For example, a contract may be rescinded for fraud. More relevant to the Internet situations are doctrines which allow avoidance of a contractual obligation based on "mistake." The reported decisions are far more likely to support the defense in cases of "mutual mistake", than in cases of "unilateral mistake", but even then the availability of the defense is limited.

A leading U.S. statement of the law of mutual mistake is in the *Restate-* **24–050** *ment (Second) of Contracts*. Section 152(1) in relevant part provides:

> Where a mistake of both parties at the time a contract was made as to a basic assumption on which the contract was has a material effect on the agreed exchange of performances, the contract is voidable by the adversely affected party unless he bears the risk of the mistake . . . [53]

---

[49] EU Distance Sales Directive. Council Directive on the Protection of Consumers in Respect of Distance Contracts 97/7, [1997] O.J. L144/19. Importantly, while the Directive contains a mandatory rescission right, that right does not apply to contracts for the supply of video recordings, records or computer software, where the risk of customer fraud is high.

[50] FTC regulates long distance contracting through a focus on "telemarketing." 16 CFR Part 310 (Aug. 23, 1995). The telemarketing rules prohibit various deceptive acts and require disclosure *prior to when the customer pays* of the following items: total cost and quantity of goods or services involved, all material restrictions on the purchase, receipt, or use, existence of any policy of not making refunds, cancellations or the like, in a prize promotion, elements of the promotion. Telemarketing is a defined term which includes a campaign to induce the purchase of goods or services "by use of one or more telephones". 16 C.F.R. 310.2(u). While electronic medium used in electronic contracts might entail use of telephones under this rule, a number of exemptions will ordinarily exclude online contracting and focus the rule on cases of telephone solicitation, rather than on all cases involving telephones used in a marketing or contracting environment.

[51] Door-to-door sales are subject to a mandatory right of withdrawal (rescission). FTC rules define a door-to-door sale as one involving consumer goods or services in which "the seller . . . personally solicits the sale . . . and the buyer's agreement . . . to purchase is made at a place other than the place of business of the seller." 16 C.F.R. 429.1, note 1(a). FTC rules exempt transactions conducted and consummated entirely by mail or telephone without "any other contact" between the parties prior to performance of the contract. The focus of the rules and resulting withdrawal period are to protect against deception and high pressure techniques possible in in-home environments. The better view is that electronic contracting typically does not entail "personal solicitation."

[52] In addition to the theories noted in the text, it could be said the U.S. statute of frauds, when applicable, allows avoidance of a contract in that, in theory, it prevents a party from enforcing the contract unless it is represented in a sufficient, signed writing. Under both Art. 2 and UCITA, however, the statute of frauds prevents assertion only of entirely executory contracts. See UCITA § 201; UCC § 2-201. Performance offered and accepted precludes assertion of the defense as to that performance.

[53] *Restatement (Second) of Contracts* 152 (1981).

24-051 The rule is not available where one party assumed the risk, either expressly in the contract or by virtue of its knowledge about the circumstances.[54]

24-052 In U.S. law, the idea of avoiding a contract because of mutual mistake is a relatively limited doctrine, reflecting the fact that it runs contrary to the basic tenant of contract law that the parties *by their agreement* allocate risks and undertake opportunities. The *Restatement* comments:

> Before making a contract, a party ordinarily evaluates the proposed exchange of performances on the basis of a variety of assumptions with respect to existing facts. Many of these assumptions are shared by the other party, in the sense that the other party is aware that they are made. The mere fact that both parties are mistaken with respect to *such an assumption* does not, of itself, afford a reason for avoidance of the contract by the adversely affected party.[55]

24-053 This implies simply and correctly that mistake principles are not used to set aside bargains simply because the bargained for exchange proved to be disadvantageous for one party.

24-054 Avoidance of a contractual relationship because of mutual mistake is an unusual remedy, not casually undertaken. It is generally not appropriate in situations where the complained of mistake is simply that the one party's expectations of gain under the transaction are not achieved.[56] Similarly, relief is not appropriate where the transaction was undertaken amid acknowledged uncertainty and as events materialised the uncertainties worked to the detriment of one party. Allocation of risk in such cases should be in the contract, not in the fact review of a court.

24-055 The *Restatement* states: "A mistake is a belief that is not in accord with the facts."[57] The comments to this section of the *Restatement* further point out that the idea of "mistake" as used in this area of law does not "refer to an improvident act, including the making of a contract, that is the result of such an erroneous belief." Thus, to establish a basis for relief under this standard of mutual mistake, it is not sufficient to show that entering the contract proved to have been improvident.

24-056 The *Restatement* provides that relief for mutual mistake is not to be granted where the adversely affected party bears the risk of the mistake.[58] It goes on to provide: "A party bears the risk of a mistake when . . . the risk is allocated to him by agreement of the parties, or . . . the risk is allocated to him by the court on the ground that it is reasonable in the circumstances to do so."[59]

24-057 While the *Restatement* suggests a broader applicability, case law in most U.S. jurisdictions looks even less favourably on claims to rescind a contract based on claims of "unilateral mistake." As a general principle, unilateral mistakes do not absolve compliance with a contract. Each party should protect its own position in reference to the handling of errors and the like. This

---

[54] In *re Schenk Court, Inc.*, 69 B.R. 906 (Bankr. E.D. N.Y. 1987).
[55] *Restatement (Second) of Contracts* 152, Comment a (1981).
[56] See *Leasco Corp. v. Taussig*, 473 F.2d 777 (2d Cir. 1972).
[57] *Restatement (Second) of Contracts* 151.
[58] *Restatement (Second) of Contracts* 152(1) (1981).
[59] *Restatement (Second) of Contracts* 154 (1981).

common law principle has been somewhat readjusted in modern case law to hold that the unilateral mistake allows an avoidance of the contract if enforcement against the party making the mistake would be oppressive and rescission of the contract would impose no substantial hardship on the other party.[60] In practice, few such claims of rescission are granted in U.S. courts, with the dominant policy being that the other party (the one who did not labour under the supposed mistake) is entitled to the benefit of the contractual arrangement that it established.

In Internet, especially with respect to open-context transactions, the law of mistake may have a particularly significant role.[61] Consider the case of a customer who claims to have mistakenly entered an identification code for a $1,000 software package, having intended to enter the code for a $20 video game. The message offering to purchase the software is received by the vendor's computer system, a cash debit is entered on the customer's debit card, and the software is automatically shipped. When the software package is received, what are the customer's rights? Obviously, at least where the software is in an unopened package (as compared to having been downloaded online or contained in a package that was opened), most reputable vendors will entertain the customer's claim of error if coupled with prompt return of the package. This is a matter of good business practice, however, rather than of legal mandate.

24-058

Suppose that the vendor doubts that there was an error. What is the customer's ability to rescind the contract? The answer may lie in how the law of mistake applies in this case where one party claims mistake and the other party is represented by an automated system (an electronic agent) that accurately responds to the information it receives. There is no U.S. case law on point, but the matter may turn on whether the events are treated as mutual or unilateral mistake. Arguably, the electronic agent did not act on a mistaken impression, but on the fact of the order as received. Mistaken intent often is not sufficient to vitiate a contract, especially in the case of a unilateral error.[62]

24-059

UCITA provides a right of rescission that does not depend on mistake doctrine; a similar right is provided for in UETA.[63] The UCITA provision

24-060

---

[60] 3 *Corbin on Contracts* 608. See Calamari & Perillo, *The Law of Contracts* pp.9-27.
[61] We are here discussing the case where one party (or both) makes a mistake. Another source of error might come in the transmission itself. In the U.S., as between buyer and seller, in cases involving errors by telegraph companies, the majority approach is that the sender of the message is liable for errors created by the intermediary it chose to communicate the message unless the other party should have known that the message was mistaken. See Calamari & Perillo, *The Law of Contracts* 2-24. See also 1 *Williston on Contracts* 94. A minority position exists which holds that no contract exists in such a situation because the sender is not responsible for the actions of an independent contractor. *Restatement (Second) of Contracts* 64, Comment b. This rule applies even if the intermediary service provider was not an agent of the sender. The *UNIDROIT* Principles of International Commercial Law state: "An error occurring in the expression or transmission of a declaration is considered to be a mistake of the person from whom the declaration emanated. *UNIDROIT* Principles Art. 3.6.
[62] There is, of course, a practical solution for the conceptual problem. The use of a system which requires reconfirmation of the order, such as by displaying the name and price of the ordered software, and requesting a second indication of intent to order it, would go a long way toward vitiating any claim by the customer that a mistake actually occurred.
[63] See UCITA § 216 (1999 approved draft).

gives a consumer the right to rescind the results of its mistake occurring in an automated transaction of the type described above. For this right to apply, several things must be established:

- the electronic system of the vendor must not have provided a reasonable method to detect or avoid the error

- the consumer promptly notifies the other party of the error

- causes delivery to the other party of all copies of the information or, pursuant to reasonable instructions received from the other party, delivers to another person or destroys all copies; and

- has not used or received any benefit from the information or caused the information or benefit to be made available to a third party.

24-061   This rescission right is limited in UCITA to cases involving consumer because in business-to-business transactions, the equities entailed in particular contexts are not predictable. The provider might, for example, be linked into a just in time inventory system and have made numerous, irrevocable commitments based on the message before being notified of the mistake. If the statutory right does not apply, the general law of mistake governs the right to rescind the transaction.

5. Choice of law

There is a basic issue of what law applies.

24-062   Traditional methods of deciding this within the U.S. and internationally often rely on location: location of a transaction, location of performance, the location of an effect, etc., to reach a conclusion about which laws control.[64] Alternatively, they rely on a court determining which state or

---

[64] See especially *Restatement (First) of Conflicts of Law* (1934). See Perry Dane, "Vested Rights, "Vestedness" and Choice of Law", 96 *Yale LJ* 1191 (1987). Choice of law under the *Restatement (First)* generally followed a "vested rights" approach. For contracts dealing with personal property or services it breaks down essentially to three parallel rules. The first, applicable to questions of validity, such as consideration and capacity, requires application of the law of the location where the contract was made. *Restatement (First) of Conflict of Law* § 332. As a result, the *Restatement* devotes substantial attention to defining when and where a contract is created. The basic principle describes the place of making as the location at which "the principle event necessary to make a contract" occurs. *Restatement (First) of Conflict of Laws* § 311, Comment d. That event, according to the Restatement differs depending on the type of contract involved and on whether the contracting occurred in a person to person context or over a distance through the use of mail, telephone and the like. The following primary rules apply: (i) formal contract: place of delivery, *Restatement (First of Conflict of Laws* § 312; (ii) unilateral contract: place of offeree performance, *Restatement (First) of Conflict of Laws* § 323; (iii) bilateral contract: place of offeree promise, *Restatement (First) of Conflict of Laws* § 325. In defining the place of a promise for purposes of contracting at a distance, the *Restatement* uses a mailbox rule, making the promise effective when sent and then goes on to specify illustrations of this rule applicable to mail, telegraph and telephonic contracting. *Restatement (First)* § 326. See Ian MacNeil, "Time of Acceptance: Too Many Problems for a Single Rule", 112 *U. Pa. L. Rev.* 947 (1964).

country has the most significant interest in the transaction.[65] These indicia for choice of law are attenuated and often made irrelevant by the fact that physical location in electronic information commerce has little or no importance. Trade in information occurs without regard to distance or borders. Guessing what law governs a given electronic contract or a group of electronic commerce events is just that, a guess. It is a guess that occurs in a context where the consequences of being wrong can be quite significant.

From a transactional perspective, the resulting uncertainty and risk entails **24–063** significant cost and, in some cases, an impossibility of compliance (*e.g.*, country A requires a step that Country B prohibits). The desire to reduce cost and avoid conflict that the need to stabilise what law applies, either in terms of what state's law governs or in terms of what are the substantive provisions of that law. The alternative is that parties are subject to inconsistent and often indeterminate rules.[66] The question is how to stabilise the law applicable to the global transactional context of electronic commerce.

There are various approaches, all of which will ultimately contribute to an **24–064** international solution of the problem of complexity in law and regulation in global electronic commerce.

One approach argues for international harmonisation of law to supplant **24–065** conflicting rule with internationally harmonised rules and fill important gaps where no law exits at all. Greater uniformity in contract law is clearly important as the information economy emphasises global commerce in a way that was not possible and did not exist before. UCITA, as well as directives in Europe and initiatives in the United Nations, address this. We need more of that effort. We especially need more of it for commerce in services and information where the modern economy predominantly resides. But full harmonisation is an impossible dream. It may be socially undesirable since the richness of global society consists in part in its diversity. In any event, the issues in harmonization and the differences in cultural approach are too complex and too diverse to resolve.[67]

---

[65] See generally *William Richman & William Reynolds, Understanding Conflict of Laws* 241 (2d ed. 1992); Patrick J. Borchers, "The Choice of Law Revolution: An Empirical Study", 49 *Wash. & Lee L. Rev.* 357, 372 (1992) (more than 20 years after the promulgation of the *Restatement (Second)* with its radically different approach to choice of law, approximately thirty percent of U.S. states continued to use the old doctrine and the new doctrines as adopted in other states were not uniform). Modern choice of law theories refer to governmental interests, while others refer broadly to the idea of "contacts", some of which entail ideas of location. The *Restatement (Second) of Conflicts of Law* (1971) uses a similar test, describing a test that requires consideration of various factors including the: (i) place of contracting, (ii) place of negotiation, (iii) place of performance, (iv) location of the subject matter of the contract, (v) domicile, residence, nationality, place of incorporation and place of business of one or both parties, (vi) needs of the interstate and international systems, (vii) relative interests of the forum and other interested states in the determination of the particular issue, (viii) protection of justified expectations of the parties, and (ix) promotion of certainty, predictability and uniformity of result.

[66] Based in part on this risk, UCITA proposes that absent fundamental public policy or specific, mandatory consumer rules, the parties can by agreement establish what law governs their transaction. In the absence of such contractual choice, an online transaction in computer information is governed by the law of the licensor's location. UCITA § 109 (1999 Official Text). See also EU Proposed Council Directive on Electronic Commerce (1999).

[67] For example, a Convention on the International Sales of Goods dealing with basic contract law issues was developed based on United Nations sponsorship and approved by a number of countries. However, even though it deals with the much more stable and settled law relating to goods, the Convention is often not used by parties and, in any event, by its own terms applies only to true *international* transactions between entities *located* in two different countries.

While waiting for harmonisation, trillions of dollars of commerce transpire in electronic commerce subject to costs associated with national laws built on a reference to an older forms of international trade.[68]

24–066   There is a way out. Harmonisation efforts assume that a common ground can be established and that a controlling force should be formal legal rules. An alternative view is that, rather than a controlling force, law should support the marketplace and contract choices, subject to restrictions that prevent abuse and choices that contradict fundamental public policy. The market entails choices, expressed in contracts. This argues that the choices should generally be supported. Most states in the United States enforce contractual choices of law;[69] that rule is restated in UCITA.[70] It is generally followed in the *Restatement*. The rationale, even extrapolated to global commerce, is simple. Commerce consists of markets and markets are shaped by choices. These choices are best able generally to establish rules of the road for commercial transactions. If a party makes information or services available on terms that provide that the law of a designated state governs contract issues and the other party does not refuse to accept that term, that agreed designation should be enforced in order to allow the parties to shape their own deal and identify their own level of risk. In UCITA, as in some other law, the contractual choice is reined in by the requirement that it not violate fundamental public policy of the otherwise applicable state law.[71] In addition, UCITA provides that the contractual choice of law cannot alter the effect of a mandatory consumer protection rule which cannot otherwise be altered by agreement under the law of the state whose law would otherwise have applied to the transaction.

24–067   Law in other countries is not always as fully accepting of contract choices, especially in consumer transactions. European rules, for example, allow contract choices to govern in commercial (business–business) transactions, but invalidate some choices in consumer contracts. These rules generally invalidate contract choices that deny the consumer coverage under *either* the law of the country where the consumer resides or the law of the country where the transaction occurred.

24–068   Why do states adopt this rule? The reason is surprising. The overt explanation is that the rule is a "consumer protection" rule. But that is not a reasonable answer. In some cases, law other than the law of the consumer's domicile better protects the consumer, while in other cases the law of the consumer's residence will be better. For example, the law of Texas gives

---

[68] How can that be, a lawyer might ask. This reflects a myopic view of business that is uniquely lawyerly in character. It can be because for business, legal risk is simply one of many forms of risk that any area of commerce entails. It is a risk (read cost) that should be minimised, but not one the existence of which is necessarily disabling, especially when one realises that thousand of transactions occur without legal problems or disputes for every one that has any semblance of a legal dispute raised with respect to it.

[69] See *Restatement (Second) of Conflicts of Law* § 187.

[70] UCITA § 109 (1999 Official Text).

[71] UCITA § 105(b) (1999 Official Text). *Application Group, Inc. v. Hunter Group*, Inc., 61 Cal. App.4th 881, 72 Cal. Rptr.2d 73 (Cal. App. 1998). *Compare Lowry Computer Products, Inc. v. Head*, 984 F. Supp. 1111 (E.D. Mich. 1997).

consumer far greater rights than the law of many other states. If consumers resident in those other states cannot be governed by Texas law, they lose.

There is no consumer-protection basis for an absolute, mandatory rule. **24–069** Instead, the reason lies less in protecting consumers than in protecting sovereign prerogatives. The basic policy, although often not explicit, is that contracts should not alter the rules of a given country or state as to its own consumers because those states have a right to control the rights of their own residents, wherever they may be. Not surprisingly, until recent ferment caused by Internet commerce, few states sought to extend the scope of their consumer protection law to transactions in other locations, but after that advent of global commerce, assertions of state sovereignty are common.

If applied generally to electronic commerce, this approach to choice of law **24–070** in consumer contracts in electronic commerce guaranties huge legal compliance costs and legal compliance risk in electronic transactions. In effect, the rule means that even the smallest e-commerce vendor could not function on the Internet unless it either (i) restricted its commerce to designated countries (or states) in which it knows and can comply with the law, or (ii) learns and complies with the law of all countries and all states. The first option creates an undesirable and artificial legal restraint on the capabilities for global information commerce, while the second option states an impossible task even for the world's largest companies.

In the absence of a contract term that chooses the law applicable to the **24–071** transaction, what law governs? More particularly, what rules should determine the answer to this question in a practical, transactional context?

To answer this, we need to recognise the difference between rules that **24–072** determine choice of law as (i) a body of law that provides a means of resolving litigated disputes, and (ii) law that gives guidance to commercial relationships. For litigation, it may be acceptable (especially in tort cases) to say that a judicial or other tribunal should have broad flexibility to choose a law that reflects what it believes to be a fair, acceptable result for *that* litigation. Indeed, in the United States, since many choice of law doctrines evolve in judicial decisions made in the course of litigation or in academic literature focused on litigation, that flexibility is a hallmark of most modern doctrine. At their core, such doctrines consist of allowing a court to apply a variety of factors that are differently weighed under different doctrines and by different courts. The result in terms of predictability from a perspective centered on planning transactions before any dispute arises is, in a word, chaotic.[72] The benefits in fair litigation contrast with the detriments of uncertainty when persons engage in planning multistate, multinational and global transactions.

If choice of law doctrine is addressed from a planning perspective, how- **24–073** ever, the goal is to give parties guidance about what contract (or other) law states the basis on which they should structure their transaction to achieve its intended effects. This perspective facilitates commercial relationships and reduces costs for commercial and consumer commerce. It has been adopted

---

[72] William Richman & William Reynolds, *Understanding Conflict of Laws* 241 (2nd ed. 1992) ("[C]hoice-of-law theory today is in considerable disarray . . . [It] is marked by eclecticism and even eccentricity.").

as a primary rule in several revisions of the Uniform Commercial Code.[73] The predictability approach achieves cost savings among the many transacting parties achieved against unknown losses or gains grounded loss of the flexibility for courts to choose *after-the-fact* based on often uncertain factors.

24-074   In online commerce in information assets, there is only one rule that implements the goals of certainty and cost savings associated with a planning perspective. UCITA provides that rule. It states that, in the absence of contrary contract terms, the default of law rule is that the applicable law is the law of the place where the licensor is located.[74] In effect, an information and service provider should be governed by the law of the origin of the service. UCITA, in adopting a "place of origin" rule for applicable law in online information commerce, further provides that:

> For purposes of this section, a party is located at its place of business if it has one place of business, at its chief executive office if it has more than one place of business, or at its place of incorporation or primary registration if it does not have a physical place of business. Otherwise, a party is located at its primary residence.[75]

24-075   The point is to establish a predictable and discernible basis for what law applies in electronic commerce as a means of reducing uncertainty and resulting cost, which both are artifacts of law unless tailored to true and persuasive policy interests.

24-076   The most recent draft of the European Union directive on Electronic Commerce[76] uses a similar approach, at least in part, for business–business transactions. The draft directive states:

> Information Society services should be supervised at the source of the activity, in order to ensure an effective protection of public interest objectives; to that end . . . it is essential to state clearly this responsibility on the part of the Member State where the services originate; moreover, in order to effectively guarantee freedom to provide services and legal certainty for suppliers and recipients of services, such Information Society services should in principle be subject to the law of the Member State in which the service provider is established . . .[77]

24-077   The idea of where a company is "established" does not focus on where the computer or data reside, but on where there is an ongoing business presence. This rule focuses on regulatory scope and right to control. The draft does not deal with consumer law on this point, and declines any intent to establish additional rules on private international law on conflicts of law or the jurisdiction of courts.

24-078   To understand why the licensor's location is the appropriate rule for online information commerce, imagine the information service as at the centre (or hub) of a wheel consisting of numerous spokes, each one of which leads to a

---

[73] UCC § 4A-507(a)(3). Section 507(b) expressly rejects any "reasonable relation" test with respect to the enforceabililty of agreed choice of law. UCC § 5-116(b) (choice of law is issuer's location regarding any issue of its liability).

[74] UCITA § 109(b)(1) (1999 Official Text).

[75] UCITA § 109(d) (1999 Official Text).

[76] Directive 2000 EC of the European Parliament and of the Council, on certain legal aspects of Information Society services, in particular electronic commerce, in the Internal Market ("Electronic Commerce Directive"), Interinstitutional File 98-325(COD) (February 28, 2000).

[77] Electronic Commerce Directive (21).

client (licensee) in a different location. The economies of the Internet involving information and related services transactions lie in part in the fact that the provider can service clients around the world in a frictionless, often automated manner from a single location. Where the subject matter is computer information, this can be done without even the need for costly and cumbersome delivery systems. Electronic communication through the same medium through which the contract was formed are an increasingly viable alternative that most information providers expect to be the dominant delivery system of the very near future.

In this framework, we might imagine three possible choice of law rules. **24–079**

One could *first* identify the applicable law by referring to some general, flexible concept, such as choosing the law of the state with the greatest interest in resolving the issue or the law of the state with the most significant relationship to the transaction. Under that approach, what law would govern, for example, a transaction in which a licensee company based in Michigan, places an order for information to be delivered electronically to Texas from a provider located in Maryland? The answer is not immediately clear. Should the answer change if the order were placed by the licensee's agent while she attended a meeting in New Jersey? Uncertainty such as this is a cost. It is difficult to see the commensurate transactional benefit for any party.

A *second* choice of law principle would have the law of the licensee's state **24–080** govern the transaction. There are obvious problems of locating a licensee in the virtual world of Internet when or if the licensee is a multistate or multinational entity, or determining what is the relevant location where the licensee is mobile. Let's put those problems aside. The more fundamental problem is that this rule would in all cases choose as applicable law the outer ends of each spoke in our hypothetical wheel. For a licensor, sitting at the hub of this wheel, this result has a very specific and costly effect. A rule that presumes that the transferee's location governs would require (i) that the information provider learn and comply with the law of countries and all states, (ii) that it arrange its contracting and distribution system to forego transactions with persons in jurisdictions whose law it does not know or to which it does not wish to conform (if such restrictions are technologically feasible), or (iii) that it simply ignore the law of most states on the assumption that no bad results will occur from what will be non-compliance with at least some of those laws.

- Even for the largest companies, learning all state's laws within the United States and the laws of all countries is a daunting and expensive task. For ordinary sized companies or for individuals, it is impossible.

- Even if technologically feasible, an approach that restricts online transactions to states whose law the provider has learned and will comply with truncates a valuable efficiency of Internet information commerce.

- Ignoring the laws of most states, while a likely result, is hardly an effect of a choice of law regime about which a law-maker should be proud.

24–081 A *third* choice of law approach would select the law of the state in which the provider of the information is located. There are definition problems about where a multifaceted entity is located and mobility issues. This rule has several important effects in that it gives guidance for transactions and reduces costs of legal analysis of foreign laws and resulting legal risks. The rule eliminates reliance on the fictions that dominate modern choice of law doctrine, such as determining which state has the dominant interest, or in determining where a contract was created or performed in the Internet. Also, it creates a stable and identifiable base for planning and implementing trans-actions. Rather than a dispersed set of legal compliance requirements, the point of origin rule focuses all transactions for a provider on the law of a single state or country.[78]

Should this rule apply to consumer transactions?

24–082 Some assert that it should not and these have had an impact on the recent European Union draft. The apparent reasoning is that a consumer should have the *benefit* or the fall-back choice of being governed by the consumer's own national or local law. In online electronic commerce in information, however, that rule would create the costs and risks described above for any transaction involving a consumer. If we are to create those costs it would seem that we should demand an off-setting benefit, or else the policy choice to create the costs is not appropriate. An answer to what benefit is obtained is that this rule is a consumer protection rule, since consumers are better off being treated under their own local law. That is misleading. In one-half of all cases, the *other* law will be equal or better for the consumer. Consider, for example, a country that provides no consumer protections at all, but whose citizens routinely do business with information providers in the state of Maryland, which has a well-developed consumer protection regime. Is the consumer benefited by having its own national law govern (with no consumer protections at all), or would the consumer benefit by having Maryland law apply?

24–083 The consumer issue ultimately is not a question of consumer protection, but one of a state's assertion or retention of sovereign rights and control in a virtual world where the relevance of distance and physical location are diminished. Electronic commerce in information highlights this as a major issue. If assertions of sovereignty in this form are pursued, they will sub-stantially impede realisation of the advantages of electronic commerce in information and, ultimately, harm the states that insist on the sovereignty claim. On the other hand, of course, it is naïve to think that sovereign

---

[78] No approach to this issue is perfect. This rule, for example, creates a risk that vendors will "race to the bottom", by relocating to jurisdictions where the law is most beneficial to them. There are many reasons to believe that electronic commerce will not experience that. Empirically, for example, corporate governance issues in the U.S. are heavily dominated by states such as Delaware that encourage information in that state. Yet, while Delaware has a sophisticated cor-porate law regime, it is not one that benefits corporate insiders at the cost of others. Also, the risk in electronic commerce would be offset by the frictionless ability of other entities to compete by offering customers and trading parties more desirable legal regimes. Additionally, however, UCITA contains a provision which alters the choice of law rule if the effect of applying it would be to select a law that is fundamentally less protective of the consumer than law that would oth-erwise apply. UCITA § 109(c) (1999 Official Text).

claims or positions will not be staked out in the virtual world of the Internet and electronic commerce. How this will occur is a major unanswered issue in modern commerce. The hope is that sovereignty here will be buffered by the fact that the virtual commerce systems enable a fluid, international commerce that will move away from states that impose serious tariffs on it.

Arguably, the default choice of law rule (at least for consumers) could be different for transactions in goods conducted in the Internet. If the subject matter of a transaction is goods or other tangibles, the transaction requires physical delivery to the transferee. Because of this, there is a greater opportunity for a vendor to make decisions about where to ship or not ship based on a particular destination. Yet, even here, the questions must be: "what social benefits are obtained at the cost of a rule that requires vendors to forego the international commerce benefits of electronic systems by excluding some states or some countries from their commerce?" **24-084**

6. Technology adequacy

Many discussions of contract law suggest that the most important issues for electronic commerce deal with the *technology* of electronic commerce and whether contract law *permits* use of that technology. Yet, adequacy is the simplest issue of all, and will become even less difficult as familiarity with and use of the technology continues to grow. The rule should be: except in extreme and limited cases, there is no reason to not allow electronic records and signatures to fulfill former written requirements. Indeed, I suspect that most courts and regulatory entities, faced with a statutory requirement of a writing or a signature, would readily conclude that digital equivalents suffice under the same standards as would written equivalents.[79] As it has played out, however, the *adequacy* issue has not remained that simple; uneasiness and fear of new technologies has led to potentially harmful proposals that have been adopted in at least a few states. **24-085**

6.1 The general principle

Issues about electronic adequacy in law involve whether electronic (digital) files, digital entries, or other digital acts satisfy requirements of a *writing* or a *signature* in cases where such requirements are imposed by law.[80] While this might seem to be a core issue, billions of dollars of commerce have been conducted electronically for over a decade without serious judicial challenge **24-086**

---

[79] Of course, this does not mean that anything electronic will always suffice for a written or traditional equivalent. For example, the traditional definition of signature, carried forward into UCC Art. 9 and UCITA in the concept of authentication, is that the symbol or act must be taken with an intent to authenticate a record. UCITA § 102; UCC § 1-201 (1998 Official Text).
[80] There are many situations where a writing or a signature may be used, but is *not* required by law. For example, under UCC § 2-201, a signed writing is required to enforce a contract only if the goods to which the contract refers have not already been delivered. When they have been delivered, that conduct satisfies the rudimentary documentation purposes of the Art. 2 statute of frauds.

to the premise that electronics suffice.[81] Why is this true? One answer is that the commercial world long ago accepted that electronics suffice in order to enable commerce of a type in which many companies and consumers now participates. Courts, thus, are seldom presented with the adequacy issue because the parties assume that digital surrogates suffice for simple contract law ideas. When presented with the issue, courts are unlikely to get it wrong. The world has moved past when the general rule that digital records supplant paper can be seriously questioned.

24–087   Thus, at one level, there is no principled argument that electronic records and electronic signatures should not suffice under general law requirements of a "writing" or "signature." In many countries, for example, a signed writing that contains the contract terms is never required; there is in these countries no statute of frauds rule. That rule is generally followed in the United Nations Convention on the International Sales of Goods, although that convention allows countries to derogate from this permissive rule. Clearly, where no legal mandate of a writing exists, "technology adequacy" is not an issue.

24–088   In other contexts, general contract law requires a "signed writing" for enforceability under a statute of frauds.[82] But in commercial practice, that requirement is no more than a small impediment to commerce, seldom invoked. Indeed, if one asked business transaction lawyers how often they had any concern about whether a transaction conformed to the statute of frauds, none would say that they ever considered that issue. In that environment, allowing electronic records and electronic signatures to suffice for written records and written signatures is not a major policy change.

24–089   At present, at least 25 states in the United States and five countries expressly recognise as a matter of law the equivalence between electronic "records" and writings in at least some contexts.[83] Both UCITA[84] and the draft EU Directive on Electronic Commerce adopt the concept of electronic equivalence. The Uniform Electronic Transactions Act (UETA) similarly adopts this principle, but limits when it applies.[85] The draft EU Directive

---

[81] Among the very few judicial expressions of concern about this issue is found in *Zemco Mfg., Inc. v. Navistar Intern. Transp. Corp.*, 186 F.3d 815 (7th Cir. 1999). There, the court held that genuine issues of fact existed about whether computer printouts allegedly representing extensions of a contract for sale of machined parts met the signature requirement under the applicable statute of frauds under Art. 2 of the UCC. The question is whether the symbol was executed or adopted by the party with present intention to authenticate the writing. "This court, applying Illinois" version of the UCC, has previously held that typed initials or a letterhead could suffice as a signature. We cannot say, on this record, that all of the computer printouts in this case are not adequately signed. The name Navistar is stamped or typed on some of these documents. There is an issue of fact regarding whether these markings were executed with the intention of authenticating the documents." Notice, of course, that the issue was not adequacy of electronics, but whether the particular symbols were done with the requisite intent.

[82] See, *e.g.*, UCC § 2-201 (1998 Official Text).

[83] For a collection of state and international law on this issue, see http://www.MBC.com.

[84] UCITA § 107 (1999 Official Text).

[85] UETA § 5(b) (1999 Official Text). The existence or non-existence of an agreement is to be determined from the context, including the conduct of the parties. As enacted in non-uniform form in California, the requirement of agreement is much more demanding. The California rule provides that: "Except for a separate and optional agreement the primary purpose of which is to authorise a transaction to be conducted by electronic means, an agreement to conduct a transaction by electronic means may not be contained in a standard form contract that is not an

provides that "Member States shall ensure that their legal system allows contracts to be concluded by electronic means. Member States shall in particular ensure that the legal requirements applicable to the contractual process neither create obstacles for the use of electronic contracts nor result in such contracts being deprived of legal effectiveness and validity on account of their having been made by electronic means."[86] UCITA provides: "A record or authentication may not be denied legal effect or enforceability solely because it is in electronic form."[87]

Both UCITA and UETA adopt a convention initiated in Article 8 of the UCC in using the term "record", rather than "writing", a "record" being defined as "information that is inscribed on a tangible medium or that is stored in an electronic or other medium and is retrievable in perceivable form." UCITA recognises the equivalence of electronic processing and "traditional" signatures; this is implemented in UCITA through a new term, "authentication" which encompasses both electronic and traditional signatures. That convention has been followed in UCC Article 9 (dealing with secured transactions). UETA has the same concept. The model law proposed by UNICTRAL likewise provides a rule of equivalence. All in all, while the formalities debate continues, its commercial relevance is reduced and need not detain us as a matter of *general* private law. The issue remains important, however, in the myriad regulatory rules that in some jurisdictions require writings and have not been updated to electronic commerce. **24–090**

6.2 The special cases: commercial.

"Solving" the technology adequacy issue has been a consistent theme in law revisions on electronic commerce *contract* law. As this focus has extended over time, however, the premise that electronic records and signatures should be adequate for paper equivalents has been affected by other issues and has shifted in some surprising ways. The discussion of equivalence has taken on a new theme of conflict, grounded in consumer protection issues centred on perceived uncertainty regarding electronic systems. **24–091**

The new theme often belies the issue to which contract law reform of this type was originally addressed. That issue is that billions of commerce occur electronically even though many laws require a writing or a written signature which, under one view, cannot be created in the electronic world. Internet and other electronic interchanges are accepted as fundamental technology by their users. The new debate, however, often seems to ignore that and asks, instead, whether there may not be many cases where electronics should not suffice to meet are requirement of a writing and, thus, that there should be some places where electronic commerce cannot function. Debates on technological **24–092**

---

electronic record. An agreement in such a standard form contract may not be conditioned upon an agreement to conduct transactions by electronic means. An agreement to conduct a transaction by electronic means may not be inferred solely from the fact that a party has used electronic means to pay an account or register a purchase or warranty. This subdivision may not be varied by agreement." Cal. Civil Code § 1633.5(b) (1999).

[86] Electronic Commerce Directive Art. 9.
[87] UCITA § 107(a).

adequacy thus have taken on issues associated with a fundamental uneasiness among some about the modern economy and the digital environment itself. The changes in methods of communicating and contracting challenge the settled order and create uncertainty for those wedded to it.

24–093   Are some *commercial* cases so different that the required "writing" or written "signature" should not be changed by a general law allowing electronic commerce?

24–094   If one asks this question seriously, there may indeed be some cases where commercial law truly incorporates a policy that can be met only by a *signed paper* rather than an *authenticated electronic record*. To decide when or if this is true would require that the person asking the question focus on why a writing requirement made sense as part of the particular rule and ask whether that policy in fact precludes a rule that electronic records suffice for the same purpose. For example, should it be sufficient to make disclosures about proposed private investments or securities electronically? Can accounting records be retained solely in electronic form for an audit? Are electronic records of a contract adequate evidence of a contract or a notice in litigation?

24–095   Asked in this way, in most cases, the answer will be that digital records are sufficient if the proponent or user of the record can establish the authenticity and receipt of the record. These same issues, of course, are important for paper records and signatures.

24–096   Yet, in any ordinary jurisdiction, there may be literally thousands of existing rules in which a statute or a regulation requires a written record or signature. The practical question becomes: "should the electronic commerce reform approach be that such requirements are met by digital equivalents unless the contrary is proven to be important, or should the approach be that advocates of electronic adequacy must prove their case for each situation in which an existing rule requires a writing?"

24–097   The proper answer is that electronic computer systems ordinarily suffice and that a decision that this is not so in reference to a particular rule should be based the particular policy underlying that *specific* rule. It should be up to the proponents of the exception to make the case that a paper record is actually required. Digital commerce methods entail low friction and high speed with resulting cost savings and market options that do not exist in old commerce. This benefits both the person acquiring information and the person providing it. Multiple and often conflicting requirements that might be created among numerous jurisdictions would encumber an otherwise transparent and largely frictionless transactional system. This produces a net loss.

24–098   Each decision that a writing requirement is not satisfied by a digital record imposes a cost. That cost reduces the benefits that the digital systems enable. If the exceptions expand among different states and jurisdictions in different ways and with respect to different rules, the cost multiples and may eventually seriously impede commerce. A decision to deny digital adequacy for particular requirements should be reached only if the clear benefits of that choice exceed the harm it causes. What should happen is that we should ask why policy-makers in a paper world chose to require a writing and how should the actual policies influencing that decision be exported to the modern electronic environment.

The reality does not always approach this. Most electronic commerce **24–099** statutes validate electronic records and electronic signatures, at least in providing that they should not be denied legal effect because they are electronic. As we have seen, many modern bodies of law reflect this rule. But, often, the adequacy principle is limited in scope. In some cases, such as in UCITA, this is a product of the limited substantive focus of the law. UCITA governs contracts in computer information transactions, but not goods or personal services transactions.[88] Its statement of the adequacy principle is thus limited to those cases. The same will be true if a revised Article 2 containing electronic commerce rules is enacted. In other contexts, some statutes take a broad validating approach, but others do so only within limits. Why this is so is not clear, but works off of a concern about and uneasiness with the new technology and an inability to come to grips with why any writing requirement exists in any law. In most cases, the answer to that question is simply that there was no alternative to paper in a case where the goal was to require a contract or term to be in a recorded form.

Broad direct validation of adequacy is most clearly illustrated in the Euro- **24–100** pean Directive on Electronic Commerce.[89] This Directive requires countries in the European Union to remove barriers to enforcement of electronics as equivalent to paper records and signatures, except in narrow contexts. In the Directive as in UCITA, the approach is to validate, *as a matter of law*, the principle that electronics should not be discriminated against in any case where a writing is otherwise required. The policy judgment is that, in principle, there is nothing sufficiently different in law and legal policy between a writing (or written signature) and electronic counterparts that justifies the costs that different treatment would impose on electronic commerce. If the parties were to agree to not treat electronics as being equivalent to paper, that agreement would be enforced. But in the absence of such an agreement, the presumption should be that electronics are not per se less acceptable than are writings. This, UCITA provides that:

> A record or authentication may not be denied legal effect or enforceability solely because it is in electronic form. . . . In any transaction, a person may establish requirements regarding the type of authentication or record acceptable to it.[90]

UETA, a statute of broad applicability, takes a different approach. It **24–101** includes the same general validation rule, but the effect is different. UETA does not apply to a transaction unless the parties *agree* to use electronic systems for *that* transaction.[91] A transaction is any exchange of an electronic record. Furthermore, consent to electronics that allows application of UETA continues for future transactions only if a party does not withdraw its agreement to use electronics. These rules transform the idea of adequacy. The UETA rule is not that electronics should not be discriminated against. Rather, the rule is that if the parties agree to use electronics, law should not

---

[88] UCITA § 103(a) (1999 Official Text).
[89] Electronic Commerce Directive Art. 9.
[90] UCITA § 107(a)(c) (1999 Official Text).
[91] UETA § 5(b) (1999 Official Text).

discriminate against the agreed use in cases where the form of the law requires use of a writing or traditional signature.

24–102   What is meant by the requirement that the parties agree as a precondition to UETA applying at all? One reading would render the requirement of an agreement meaningless: it would infer "agreement" in broad terms. An "agreement" is the "bargain of the parties in fact" and that it can be inferred from all of the circumstances. Does a business card handed out during a cocktail party constitute a tacit "bargain" (agreement) to use electronic communications if that card contains a physical address and an e-mail address? One suspects that a court would say "no," but some argue that this is enough "agreement" for UETA.[92] Yet, if that interpretation works, what does one do with the UCC concept that an "agreement" is a "bargain" and that the idea of a bargain seems to be that two parties agree to something? In any event, if a broad interpretation hinging agreement on the use of a business card is followed, it renders the statutory requirement largely meaningless. If that were intended, one wonders why the requirement is present at all, except as a basis for litigation.

24–103   If the requirement of agreement was intended to have substance and bite, then where does that bite fall and why? Other laws directly declare electronics as adequate (precluding discrimination against them simply because they are electronic) except in delineated cases. The agreement requirement transforms the function of the statute: instead of an affirmative public policy statement, it becomes an acquiescence in the choice of the parties. That is indeed useful, but a person relying on it must be sure to obtain that agreement.

24–104   Under UETA, an agreement to conduct transactions electronically can be withdrawn and the party can refuse to do so for other transactions.[93] This right to withdraw cannot be varied by agreement. The term "transaction" does not refer to an overall contract or its performances, but to any specific interaction that involves electronics. Thus, apparently, an assent to accept notices electronically in an online relationship can be unilaterally withdraw after the initial agreement.

6.3 The special cases: consumer issues

24–105   Although not designated as a consumer protection, the focus on requiring on-going agreement to use electronic messages as a precondition for their adequacy under UETA relates to a concern that broad use of electronics may detrimentally affect consumers such as, for example, where the individual is entitled in law to a mailed notice and might now receive only an e-mail notice. For some, then, the adequacy issue seems more complicated and more threatening in consumer contracts.

"Why?"

24–106   The technical arguments claim that an electronic message should not suffice for a written notice because the two are different, but that argument typically leaves the *ways* in which they are different unstated, except for

---

[92] UETA § 5, Official Comments.
[93] UETA § 5(c).

general statements that electronic messages are not given as much attention as written messages. For me the difference goes the other way: I am actually *more* likely to pay attention and respond to an e-mail than a form letter. The fact is that increasingly many individuals ("consumers") actively use the Internet, computers and e-mail. Electronic commerce creates a new and more consumer-friendly market where myriad potential vendors can be contacted and prices or services compared with little effort by the consumer. It seems awkward to compromise those *consumer* benefits on the altar of a general concern that the new systems are less vivid than their paper counterparts, especially since this was not the policy reason for the rules requiring a writing or a mailing because no option then existed for electronic message systems.

Of course, I may not have an e-mail address or other electronic message or recording system that I use. Some say that this means that generally validating electronic systems is inappropriate because some consumers do not use electronic mail or equivalent systems. Of course, it will always be the case that some individuals will not use electronic mail or analogous systems. However, the principle of technological equivalence does not erase other indicia of whether a notice, record or signature is effective. A signature requires an intent to sign (whether electronic or on paper), a record requires some level of reliability in reproducing the information (whether electronic or in writing) and a notice must be sent to a location from which it can reasonably be expected to be received (whether electronic or otherwise). If I do not have an e-mail address, to what location could an e-mail notice be sent and still described in law as a reasonable notice?[94] Equating electronics to writings has no impact on this.

The truth is that, although presented as *consumer* issues, the concerns that advocates raise most often reflect *their* fundamental discomfort with the new economy and the idea of electronic commerce. That discomfort, focused on technology adequacy, is misplaced. There are important consumer issues in electronic commerce, but the *adequacy* of a digital record or electronic signature is not one of those issues.

So far, the consumer debate on technology adequacy has focused on:

- whether a consumer must indicate specific assent to the use of electronic methods such as e-mail notices and the like,

- are electronic records and signatures equivalent to writing or signature requirements in specific situations such as written notices of foreclosure or other consumer protection rules, and

- should detailed disclosure rules, such as requiring a disclosure in no less that 30 point font, be altered to suit electronic commerce?

The first state to adopt UETA was California. Unfortunately, the California statute broke *far* from the UETA which Act, in itself, contains some

24–107

24–108

24–109

---

[94] The UCC requires that notice entail sending the information in a manner reasonable calculated to be received, an element of the definition of notice that would seem to be assumed in any system or rule. UCC § 1-201 (1998 Official Text).

questionable themes as seen above. The California Act contains a number of rules that address "consumer" issues, but that are not limited to consumer cases as the statute was drafted. Rather than benefit electronic commerce, the California UETA creates new unwarranted risks and costs. One California rule limits how a party (consumer or otherwise) can effectively agree to engage in electronic transactions or to accept electronic notices in a manner under which the Act will allow electronics to supplant a required writing. Under this rule, an agreement is unenforceable if it is contained in a standard form *written* contract unless that contract deals solely with assent to electronic transactions and assent to it is optional. The rule is that:

- Except for a separate *and* optional agreement the primary purpose of which is to authorise a transaction to be conducted by electronic means, an agreement to conduct a transaction by electronic means may not be contained in a standard form contract that is not an electronic record.

- An agreement in such a standard form contract may not be conditioned upon an agreement to conduct transactions by electronic means.

- An agreement to conduct a transaction by electronic means may not be inferred solely from the fact that a party has used electronic means to pay an account or register a purchase or warranty.

- These rules may not be varied by agreement.[95]

24–110   What interest is protected by this rule? Presumably, the answer is that the Act protects against a concern about over-reaching and abuse in standard form contracts that allow a party to send notices by e-mail or the like.[96] The justification hinges on the view that consumers must be protected against unknowingly agreeing to electronic transactions, but the rule also applies to business-business transactions governed by California law.

24–111   "Unknowing agreement" when an agreement to accept e-mail notices is stated in a written "standard form" that deals with other contract issues. Of course, written agreements are often in "standard forms" and they often have terms that deal with to what location a notice should be sent and how it should be sent. Singling out assent to electronic notices or the like is inappropriate and can only be justified by a belief that some people who have electronic addresses are uncomfortable using them and should not be allowed casually to agree to do so and that the applicable law requiring a written notice could not adequately cope with cases where this is done in an abusive manner. More generally, the reason for singling out electronic messages reflects a discomfort among the advocates of "consumer" positions about the

---

[95]   Cal. Civil Code § 1633.5(b) (1999).

[96]   On important point to note is that this rule does not apply if the agreement itself is contained in an electronic record. Presumably, this is because, in such cases, the consumer or other party knows that its engaged in electronic commerce and, thus, a clause providing that further electronic transactions are permitted cannot constitute a surprise. UCITA does not address this issue, but by definition all UCITA transactions involve computer information as the transactional subject matter.

entire idea of electronic commerce. One wonders whether this discomfort is shared by the alleged constituency to an extent sufficient to impose a cost on all those who do not share the concern and who do business electronically all of the time.

In a digital economy, the idea that agreements to use digital messages require special formalities is absurd. It is even more absurd when, as in California, the special formalities are not limited to consumer transactions. For example, in a franchise or distributorship agreement, the California rule seemingly precludes the parties from agreeing in the written contract (ordinarily a standard form) that future "transactions" will be electronic (*e.g.*, electronic orders, financial reports). **24–112**

Five years from now, the idea that one must prove an agreement to use electronics in order to be legally enabled to do so will seem quaint. Five years from now, the California restrictions will have been repealed, ignored by commercial parties, or viewed as a barrier to electronic commerce in California. **24–113**

7. Responsibility for the contract (attribution rules)

While the Internet contains a huge number of transactional and other efficiencies which provide a new world of commerce for consumers and business, the fundamentals of Internet create anonymous forms of transacting business. When I receive e-mail or other messages over Internet, unless there are indicia in the message on which I can rely, I have no idea of who the sender of the message may be. When anonymity is placed in a context in which the messages of the parties are intended to have binding and legally significant effects, the context creates **24–114**

The core question is when a party can be held responsible for message purporting to have come from that party of its agent. When can the message be *attributed* to that party? For our purposes, we can approach this issue in terms of three levels or contexts in U.S. law. **24–115**

7.1 Attribution in the absence of any special arrangement

The easiest case to state conceptually, but the most difficult for the parties occurs in the situation where there are no special arrangements between the parties as to how one identifies the other and there are no specific applicable laws providing guidance on this matter. This context can be viewed as the most basic form of an open system: in effect, it assumes that I send a performance based on your e-mail and that when you receive that performance you assume that it is from me because of my e-mail to you, neither one of us having dealt with each other before. **24–116**

To a lawyer, this type of transaction appears to be the height of folly. But it occurs constantly in all commerce. It is based on the proposition, true empirically, that the vast majority of all transactions do not involve fraud or deception, but a coming together of two parties who desire to and in fact do fully perform the agreement. Of course, as the stakes grow higher, the likelihood of willing reliance on this open model becomes less, but in ordinary commerce, it is common. **24–117**

24-118   The legal framework is relatively clear-cut. The obligation or burden to establish that a message or performance should be attributed to the other party is on the person who seeks to rely on that attribution. If you wish to establish that you obtained a copy of my copyrighted software from me with authority to use it, the burden is on you to establish that the message or the software came from me or from a person authorised by me to send it. If I wish to obtain payment from you for the television that I shipped based on a message that may have come from you, it is up to me to establish that the message came from you or a person authorised by you to send it. This is the situation in most states in the U.S. regarding electronic commerce, including those states that have enacted legislation validating the use of electronic signatures and electronic records, without stating more about their effect. It is the position adopted in both UCITA and UETA applicable to this open context. The UCITA formulation reads:

> An electronic event is attributed to a person if it was the act of that person or its electronic agent, or the person is otherwise bound by it under the law of agency or other law. The party relying on attribution of an electronic event to another person has the burden of establishing attribution.[97]

24-119   How one goes about proving this in an open environment is unclear and may depend on the context in cases where attribution is disputed. For example, if I can show that I shipped the television to your address and that it is currently in your living room in use, I have gone a long way toward attributing the order to you or your son. If your son, it is likely that I can infer he was acting as your agent or that, at least, you ratified his acts by keeping and using the television. On the other hand, the case is more difficult in the trade in services or information, where tangible indicia may not exist to support my claim.

7.2 Attribution when using a procedure

24-120   The second context occurs when the parties have allegedly engaged in a transaction using a procedure established by agreement or by law for purposes of identifying themselves. UCITA describes this type of procedure as an "attribution procedure." UETA describes it as a "security procedure", a perhaps confusing use of a term also used in Article 4A of the UCC with a much different legal effect. In any event, the concept is the same: the key additional ingredient in this context is the existence and use of a procedure that better enables identification of a party.

24-121   The policy question here is what effect should be given to the use of that procedure? This issue is under heated dispute in the U.S. (and internationally), having generated conflicting schools of theory whose debate sometimes approaches a degree of bitterness out of keeping with the context itself.

While there are many nuances in the various approaches taken, there are three general models.

24-122   The *first* has been described as some as a "minimalist" approach, but might better be described as on relying on rules of evidence and the common

---

[97] UCITA § 214(a) (1999 Approved Draft).

sense of courts to resolve cases in the event of a dispute. This approach is reflected in both UCITA and UETA, each of which provides that in reaching a decision on attribution of a message or performance, a court should consider the character and effectiveness of any attribution (security) procedure used by the parties. This same concept can be inferred as the law in those U.S. jurisdictions that have not adopted any particular legislative approach to this issue. The strength of this approach is that it is open-ended and will allows standards and technological approaches to develop over time. The weakness, however, is that this open-ended approach provides little guidance for assessing risk in creating a system, conducting a transaction or, indeed, in receiving a performance. Also, it provides little incentive to develop effective systems of attribution except the obvious practical incentive that the better the system, the more defensible it will be in the case of litigation.

The *second* approach is exemplified by the Illinois electronic signature statute which generally validates the use of electronic signatures and records, but goes further to deal with so-called secure electronic signatures. This concept entails electronic identification technologies that achieve enhanced levels of reliability as gauged by standards in the Act. When these are used (as an attribution procedure) by the parties, the statute creates various *presumptions* about attribution and the absence of error in a message. The presumptions, while rebuttable, provide the relying party with some advantage in the event of litigation. The effect, arguably, is to create an incentive for use of better procedures and to provide some guidance for risk assessment and structuring attribution procedures in commerce. **24–123**

The *third* approach is commonly associated with Digital Signature statutes, but is more generally described as an approach that gives strong legal benefits associated with the use of reliable attribution systems. For example, Article 4A of the UCC, dealing with electronic funds transfers, provides that the burden of establishing attribution shifts if the parties established and used a commercially reasonable attribution (security) procedure.[98] Digital Signature statutes have been enacted in four U.S. jurisdictions. The original prototype was enacted in Utah. The statutes generally create certification systems and give enhanced legal status to electronic exchanges made using particular technologies within that certification process. **24–124**

The Utah Digital Signature Act (*Signature Act*)[99] sets out a system for certification authorities and public key encryption to encourage use of "digital signatures" involving enhanced security and authenticity attributes. The goal of the *Signature Act* is to "facilitate commerce by means of reliable electronic messages." A "digital signature" means a transformation of a message using an asymmetric crypto-system such that a person having the initial message and the signer's public key can accurately determine: (a) whether the transformation was created using the private key that corresponds to the signer's public key; and (b) whether the message has been altered since the **24–125**

---

[98] UCC § 4A-203.
[99] 46 Utah Code Ann. ch. 3, Utah Administrative Code RI 54-2-101, *et seq.*

transformation was made.[1] The *Signature Act* adds a system of licensed entities who can issue, control and certify keys for the public key encryption system. The certifying authority issues and maintains the security and accuracy of the key. Complying with the requirements gives two results. One involves the reality of security and authentication: these systems are in fact more reliable than many other systems. The second is in the legal consequences. The *Signature Act* provides that the use of a "digital signature" coupled with the use of a licensed certification authority to issue and control security of the keys, means that the resulting signature *and* text of an electronic message constitute: a signature under applicable law, a writing under applicable law, an original of the document under applicable law, and an acknowledged writing or signature under applicable law.[2]

24–126   In the *Signature Act*, for attribution of messages the key measure lies in the control of the private key issued to a user of the system. The *Act* links liability or attribution to use and control of that key. It imposes liability on the customer if the customer failed to exercise reasonable care in control of the private key and that failure resulted in a loss to another party. This choice reflects the importance of the key to the reliability of the system. The Utah Act itself suggests that other states might adopt different approaches. The alternatives suggested range from strict liability for any use of the key to a system of imposing liability on consumers for lack of reasonable care, while holding all other key holders to a standard of diligence defined in part in terms of having used reasonable security procedures as against an intruder.

24–127   The long term position of the U.S. and its states on the choice among these approaches can best be described as in flux. States laws differ on approach. A former draft of UCITA contained an approach modeled after the "commercially reasonable" standard of Article 4A. At the meeting that adopted both UCITA and UETA, this Article 4A approach was deleted in favour of an approach parallel to UETA by a narrow majority vote (63 - 60). The ultimate federal position on the issue is unclear.

7.3 The role of contract

24–128   As we have seen, one way to establish an attribution or security procedure is by agreement of the parties. However, the contract has a potentially broader role. Consider the following case:

> WestCo and Customer agree to allow Customer to access WestCo databases for a fee of $1,000 per hour of actual access time. The parties agree that Customer will use an ID code to access the databases and that this code will identify customer. Additionally, the parties agree that Customer will be responsible for the cost of any use of the databases made pursuant to its ID code.

24–129   This agreement not only establishes an attribution procedure, but specifies the effect of use of that procedure: Customer is responsible for uses made pursuant to its code.

---

[1] *Signature Act* 103(10).
[2] *Signature Act* 401–405.

Both UCITA and UETA expressly provide that the effect of their provi-   **24–130**
sions can be varied by agreement, except as otherwise indicated, and both
statutes permit modification by agreement of the effect of the use of an attribution (security) procedure. This same approach is also apparently true in
states that have not expressed a legislative position on the efficacy of attribution procedures. The policy judgment made in UCITA and UETA is that
market forces along with tradition contract law doctrines about avoiding
fraud and unconscionable terms adequately control for potential abuse in the
marketplace.

A different approach is possible, for example, the Article 4A formulation   **24–131**
of the effect of a security procedure limits the effects of a procedure created
by agreement to only those cases where the procedure is commercially reasonable. An earlier draft of UCITA, modelled after Article 4A, also provided
that the rules it established and the effect of an agreement on attribution were
limited only to cases involving commercially reasonable procedures. These
rules were deleted when the UCITA approach was modified to conform to
UETA on this point.

7.4 Liability limitations

Attribution issues are ultimately connected to the policy question of how   **24–132**
to allocate the cost and risk of fraud. In Internet transactions, especially
those involving information and services, the risk of fraud moves in both
directions.

In the U.S., loss and risk allocation for fraud in analogous situations is   **24–133**
approached in a number of different ways, depending on the nature of the
system involved. For example, in the traditional check system, the risk of loss
for forgery is generally placed on the person who took the forged check from
the thief or on the drawee bank if it did not discover the forgery of its customer's name. The loss remains there unless the customer (or other party)
was negligent and that negligence contributed to the forgery. In the telephone
system, in contrast, the loss is generally placed (in law if not in practice) on
the customer whose equipment is fraudulently used for unauthorised long
distance charges.

The most widely known loss allocation system entails liability caps placed   **24–134**
to protect the consumer in cases of fraudulent use of the consumer's credit
card. A relatively low maximum liability is permitted. This in effect precludes
the card company from collecting against the consumer. As between the card
company and merchants, the agreement typically shifts the loss to the merchant. The merchant is then faced with accepting the loss or attempting to
prove that, in fact, the use of the credit card is properly attributable to the
consumer.

The credit card rules, of course, apply to Internet transactions involving a   **24–135**
credit card. Beyond that, however, none of the existing or proposed laws
relating to Internet attribution place liability limits on consumer transactions. The reason lies in the rich diversity of Internet commerce. This is a setting in which vendors may range from huge corporations to single
individuals, while purchases occupy the same range.

8. Conclusion

24–136   As we have seen, online digital systems create a "death of distance" and a change in how parties do business and how people and organisations interact. It affects how law should be formulated. While changes of the sort we have experienced often engender desire for regulation, modern information markets are, and should be, largely defined by agreements and other manifestations of market choice, rather than by regulation. In effect, the market chooses its own direction. If we focus on the computer information industries and commerce in information and services, we can see a vivid demonstration of how that market context generates an expanding productivity and a burgeoning diversity in product, service and opportunity. No regulatory scheme could approximate this.

24–137   What from one person's vantage appears to be burgeoning diversity and vibrant economic activity, is sometimes viewed from another vantage as disruptive challenge to the existing social order and comfortable patterns of business and law. This essay shows, I think, that the challenge to law is real, but that the remedy is not to seek a retraction or retrenchment. Even were that possible, it would be undesirable. But it is not possible. A genie has left the bottle and has transformed our economy and the way we lead our lives. It blurs legal categories, eliminates or greatly reduces concepts of location and distance, diversifies the marketplace, allows small entities to compete with large entities, and fundamentally calls for new ways of understanding law and business, as well as their interaction.

24–138   I have not even scratched the surface of the issues that the information economy and the emergence of computer information as a significant commercial resource present. As we have seen, however, they are already being debated and discussed, with some patterns of tentative resolution emerging. This is an exciting time for law and lawyers; perhaps somewhat less so than for businesses and business persons, but nonetheless existing. We have begun to rework our ideas of law as we respond to the new information economy and the challenges it presents.

CHAPTER 25

THE CURIOUS DYNAMICS OF FREE TRADE IN THE WESTERN HEMISPHERE: PROSPECTS FOR THE FTAA

PROFESSOR JOSEPH J. NORTON[*]

---

[*] Sir John Lubbock Professor of Banking Law (CCLS, Queen Mary, University of London); James L. Walsh Distinguished Faculty Fellow in Financial Institutions Law, Professor of Law, and Director of the Law Institute of the Americas (SMU Law School); and Vice Chancellor's Distinguished Visiting University Professor of Law (Univ. of Hong Kong) 2000–2001. Professor Norton is Editor–in–chief of the *NAFTA Review: Law and Business in the Americas* and of *The International Lawyer,* and is co–editor and contributor to *NAFTA and Beyond: A New Framework for Doing Business in the Americas* (Kluwer 1995). This Chapter speaks as of May 2000. The author has used internal references consistent with U.S. social science citations in lieu of formal legal footnoting.

1. Introduction

25–001   Clive Schmitthoff, as a premier international trade lawyer and academic and as the first Deputy Chair of our Centre for Commercial Law Studies (CCLS), well understood that the historic, current and future driving force underpinning the range of international economic, monetary, financial business and commercial relationships was trade. In trying to systematise the legal framework for international trade, Clive was not timid about crossing over and interconnecting public-private law and domestic-regional-international subject-matter. It is with this richness of approach and vision that Clive made his lasting tribute to the foundations of the CCLS.

25–002   My International Financial Law Unit at the CCLS had the great privilege of working with Clive on the CCLS's last collaborative effort with him, a tribute volume honouring him concerning international bank supervision. Clive well appreciated that for international trade to flourish, the world needed not only responsive commercial law systems and viable judicial and non-judicial dispute resolution mechanisms, but also robust, yet "safe and sound" banking and other financial systems.

25–003   This inextricable connection between trade and finance (and, accordingly, trade law and financial law) is no more evident today than in the current WTO focus on trade in services (particularly financial services) and the importance of this essential linkage to regional economic integration efforts (*e.g.*, respecting the European Union and its internal market and economic and monetary union).

25–004   Respecting the geographic focus of this presentation (*i.e.*, the Western hemisphere), these linkages of public and private law and of trade and financial law became readily apparent with the 1994 entry into force of the North American Free Trade Agreement among Canada, Mexico and the United States and the concerted intergovernmental resolution of the 1994 Mexican peso crises. The NAFTA, in fact, contains a special section (Chapter 14) on cross-border financial services and investments.

25–005   Since 1994, the dynamics of intergovernmental economic and co-operative efforts among the nations of the Western hemisphere have expanded significantly. However, as will be discussed more fully below, the new dynamics have unfolded in a most "curious" way. On the one hand, there appears to be a linear attempt to expand the NAFTA into a Free Trade Area of the Americas by 2005 [*e.g.*, see 1994 Miami Summit of the Americas] yet the reality is a very complex and disparate pattern of bilateral, sub-regional and regional treaty arrangements.

25–006   Ironically, if FTAA occurs in 2005, as currently planned, it will most probably be a practical non-event for Western hemisphere business, as adjustments *under* the FTAA will have been and will continue to be incremental—pre and post-adoption. A similar view could have been postulated respecting the NAFTA in 1994. [Norton and Bloodworth, 1995, Chapter 1]. And, if FTAA fails to come about as planned, U.S. business activities within the Americas most probably will continue as usual, lest this failure portrays a fundamental political or economic crisis and destabilisation within the Hemisphere. [Lawrence, 1999, at p. 6].

However, this author suggests that the critical importance of FTAA for **25–007** U.S. business is as a "code word" for an ongoing environmental process that is now two decades of age. This process reflects and supports a general ongoing search within our hemisphere for nations to pursue sustainable economic development through the creation of a favourable, predictable, transparent and stable hemispheric "climate" for liberalising trade and investment, including the financial services area. Correspondingly, this process is concerned with developing and strengthening free market infrastructures, more democratic and accountable political institutions, and a more rule-based and rule of law civil society [*e.g.,* Bush, 1990]. Thus, the ongoing process, perhaps, is more significant than the end result; and the supportive climate created and sustained, perhaps, is more important than the specificity of any treaty provisions.

The remaining sections of this presentation will elaborate more fully on **25–008** these views of the author. To this end, section 2 will reflect upon the notion of FTAA as a code word for this ongoing environmental process from the respective vantage point of the developed and the developing nations of the hemisphere. Section 3 will consider the primary expectations of U.S. enterprises for doing business within the hemisphere and the extent these can be met *without* a formal FTAA though *within* the FTAA process. Section 4 will explore how the FTAA process entails a complex matrix of existing bilateral, regional and sub-regional treaty arrangements *within* and *without* the hemisphere. Section 5 will provide some concluding observations on the prospects for a specific hemispheric FTAA process.

2. A "code word" for an ongoing environmental process for economic, political and legal reform

As the NAFTA could be viewed as a code word for an ongoing environmen **25–009** tal process respecting trade and direct investment liberalisation, so also can the FTAA. Here two related, but distinct perspectives are germane: that of the developing countries of the hemisphere (*i.e.* 32 of the 34 FTAA nations, excluding Cuba) and that of the two developed countries of the hemisphere (*i.e.* the United States and Canada).

2.1 The developing countries' perspective

The underlying movement toward trade and direct investment liberalisation **25–010** in the hemisphere can be substantially attributed to a fundamental shift in the early 1980s in the domestic economic policies of Mexico, as followed subsequently by other key Latin American countries such as Argentina and Chile [Abbott and Bowman, 1994]. During the 1960s and 1970s Mexico, the other Latin American states, and (for that matter) most "Third World" countries espoused an economic development model rooted in (i) public ordering and state planning of the economy and society; (ii) reliance on state enterprises as economic actors; (iii) restriction and regulation of private enterprise; and (iv) limitation and control of the country's economic relations with the outside world [Salacuse, 1999, at p. 877]. In addition, most of these Latin American countries were characterised by authoritarian regimes under a one-party state or military regime. Economic, political and social life of these countries were largely state-oriented and state-directed [Linz & Stepan, 1978; and W.C. Smith, 1993].

2.1.1 The Mexican situation

25–011   The two "six year periods" of Presidents Escheverria and Lopez Portillo, beginning in December 1970, saw the Mexican economy go from a new exuberance that the Mexican State could funnel significantly new resources to meet the country's significant social needs while fostering new industrial growth to severe economic crises. Much of the exuberance was rooted in the country's estimation of its national control of petroleum resources in light of rocketing oil prices in the 1970s. This new-found national wealth led the government and its state-controlled enterprises to undertake significant indebtedness in world money and capital markets. The unforeseen dilemma was that such sovereign-related indebtedness was tied to "floating rate" debt instruments and that the 1970s and 1980s would witness unprecedented national and global inflation.

25–012   Also, during this period, Mexico (as with most Third World countries) held to an economic policy of import-substitution and severe restrictions on foreign direct investment. This economic policy complemented a national foreign policy based on a perceived "North-South" struggle between the industrialised nations and the developing nations.

25–013   While the Mexican economy grew at a robust pace, external debt quadrupled between 1976 and 1982 (to reach two-thirds of the country's GNP by the end of 1982). This situation, coupled with the dramatic drop in world oil prices, led to the devaluation of the peso and a government moratorium on sovereign external debt. The ensuing nationalisation of the Mexican banking system added further erosion to public confidence, leading to increased capital flight. The new government of President de la Madrid, taking over in December 1982, undertook a fundamental reordering of the Mexican economy. A tough anti-inflationary policy (*i.e.* austerity, shock plan), with a price freeze and a fixed exchange rate, was introduced. At the same time, a more favourable environment for foreign direct investment was being gradually put into place. Further, by mid 1985 Mexico had embarked upon a broad trade program, including reduction of the use of import licenses, major tariff cuts, and phasing-out of official import pricing. Even more significant, the government announced it was prepared to enter into the world trade order by opening membership negotiation with GATT. Within a year, the GATT accession negotiations were completed.

25–014   Moreover, in early 1985, President de la Madrid, trying to stave off the adverse impact of possible U.S. trade sanctions and (more generally) to better manage and promote Mexico-U.S. trade relations began bilateral discussions on a wide range of trade issues with the U.S. This led to a Mexico-U.S. Commercial Framework Agreement on Trade and Investment signed in November 1987. [On above historical aspects, see, *inter alia*, Norton *et al.*, 1990 Chs. 2 & 3].

25–015   This 1987 Framework Agreement can be seen as a landmark in Mexico-U.S. commercial relations and a direct forerunner of the NAFTA. The

Agreement touched upon such subject matter as incipient dispute resolution mechanisms; improved data exchange; an "Immediate Action Agenda" covering such sensitive matters as textiles, electronic products, agricultural products and steel; foreign investment; and an initial approach to services. This Agreement also set into play ongoing, bilateral sectoral consultations and consultation groups on matters (*e.g.* foreign investment). The focused co-operative efforts were to prove invaluable as the U.S. and Mexico moved toward the NAFTA. [U.S.-Mexico Joint Statement, 1998].

As domestic and economic reform progressed in Mexico, so did infra-structural legal reform in the business, property and commercial law areas and so did gradual political reform toward a greater democratisation of Mexican political society [Norton *et al.*, 1990]. 25–016

This was the new, but fragile, environment, President Salinas came into. How to help consolidate and to solidify these reform efforts became a major concern of Salinas. Also of continuing concern, was the fear U.S. trade policy might turn more protectionist to the detriment of Mexico's economic development. 25–017

In a real sense, NAFTA became feasible because of this decade of domes-tic reform in Mexico and these related concerns of President Salinas and his Government. As such, Salinas initiated with U.S. President Bush the concept of a Mexico-U.S. FTA, which idea quickly became translated into the trilat-eral NAFTA negotiations, including Canada. In doing so, Salinas and the Mexican Government signalled that a new model of economic development was in place; that Mexico and other Latin and Third World nations were desirous of being equal players in the new world economic order; and that the worn paradigm of North-South conflict was now one of North-South co-operation [Bello and Holmer, 1993, at p. 593]. 25–018

2.1.2 The broader Latin American situation

This fundamental reform process was not limited to the Mexico experience; but the Mexican situation served as a new model for domestic reform and transition among the other Latin American nations. Argentina and Chile, and to a lesser degree the mammoth economy of Brazil, came to forge their own new dynamic and more market-oriented economic reform processes. In addition, new regional and sub-regional arrangements (*e.g.* LAIA, Mercosur and CACM) emerged, demonstrating a greater substance, direction and commitment than the defunct integration efforts of the 1970s (*e.g.* LAFTA); and a pre-existing, protectionist arrangement such as the Andean Compact transformed itself into a more open and externally positive Community [Hufbauer and Schott]. 25–019

Moreover, as will be discussed more fully below, the Latin countries in the 1990s and currently have taken the initiative to enter into numerous bilateral trade and investment arrangements among their Latin and North American partners and external to the hemisphere [FTAA Investment Agreement Compendium, OAS, 1999]. These external relations have even included comprehensive arrangements with the European Union [Irela website; and R. Bouzas, 1998]. 25–020

The reality is that a dynamic and evolving process of economic reform has been in play in Latin America now for nearly two decades. The FTAA, for 25–021 our Latin neighbours, becomes another dimension and catalyst to this ongoing process, even within the current vacuum of U.S. leadership as to this process (as exemplified by the U.S. President's inability to bring fast track authority to the 1998 Santiago Summit respecting the Chilean accession to NAFTA and the FTAA more generally) [Otero Lathrop, 1998].

2.2 The developed countries' perspective

2.2.1 The U.S.

25–022   U.S. direct involvement in regional integration is of recent vintage. Post World War II U.S. involvement has largely been indirect, for example, in its support of European integration through the EFTA, European Community (and now the European Union), or in condoning a qualified free trade area exception under the GATT/WTO. U.S. concern for Latin American integration efforts, until this past decade, has been largely indifferent, filtering primarily through the OAS and the IDB [J.J. Norton, 1986]. In particular, Latin American integration efforts of the 1970s and early 1980s often were viewed as hostile to American economic interests [T. O'Keefe, Transnational, 1997].

25–023   U.S. attention to trade and investment issues were essentially bilateral (through FCN or BIT treaties) or multilateral through the GATT (now WTO) processes. In fact, the U.S. FTA model arose with the bilateral arrangement with Israel in the mid-1980s [Israel U.S. FTA of 1985] and a few years later with the bilateral FTA with Canada [Canadian-U.S. FTA of 1988; and J. Bello and A. Holmer, 1990]. As originally proposed, NAFTA itself started as a bilateral FTA with Mexico; but, through Canadian diplomacy, converted itself into the current trilateral NAFTA.

25–024   Perhaps, the first clear, comprehensive national statement of a U.S. hemispheric foreign policy and foreign trade approach (notwithstanding the 1960s euphoric *Alliance for Progress* of President Kennedy) came with President Bush's *Enterprise for the Americas Initiative* speech of June 27, 1990 (subsequent to President Salinas" initial initiatives for a U.S.-Mexico FTA). In his remarks, President Bush reflected upon the general movement of the Latin American and Caribbean nations toward more democratic political institutions and a more civil society and away from statistic economic policies. This belated U.S. recognition of a new political and economic environment emerging within the LAC led the U.S. President to propose a "genuine partnership" throughout the hemisphere for free market reform based on "trade and not aid" [Bush, 1990].

25–025   The three pillars of the EAI were to be trade, investment and debt restructuring. No grand umbrella arrangement was proposed as there is "no blueprint, no one-size-fits-all approach to [such] reform, with the primary responsibility for achieving economic growth [resting] with each individual country." President Bush welcomed and encouraged the various individual, bilateral, subregional and regional efforts that were underway in the LAC. [*Id*]

25–026   It was only with the NAFTA safely "put to bed" in late 1993 that U.S. policy-makers came to theorise on how hemispheric FTAs could be used as a program of continuous progressive expansion that would lock-in the hemispheric economic and political reform processes. The goal of hemispheric free trade was viewed as long-term. Ongoing usage of bilateral FTAs with appropriate countries in Latin America and the Caribbean, and possibly some Asian countries, was viewed as the way forward. Moving from fair trade to free trade was to be a progressive process through sectional ("building block") agreements. [see, *e.g.* USTR, 1994].

NAFTA accession would be carefully explored on a case-by-case basis, but **25–027** bilateral FTAs were the preferred expansion instruments. Though the concept has been since abandoned, it was thought that the building of a hemispheric free trade zone over the long-term could be achieved through a hub-and-spoke of bilateral FTAs between the U.S. and other countries by NAFTA accession, or by some combination. In fact, a separate FTA might be a predecessor to an eventual NAFTA accession [USTR, 1994].

Thus, in a manner similar to President Salinas' desire to solidify a decade **25–028** of fundamental reform in Mexico through the NAFTA, the U.S. was desirous of solidifying and further fostering hemispheric economic and political reforms, while maintaining for the U.S. maximum flexibility to enter agreements that are in our (*i.e.* U.S.) best interest. [*Id*] As will be discussed below, the post NAFTA U.S. embrace of a more coherent and comprehensive FTAA hemispheric approach, though not inconsistent with the EAI, does mark a fundamental advancement of U.S. foreign and trade policy toward the LAC area.

2.2.2 Canada

Though Canada's trade and other economic relations with Mexico and Latin **25–029** America were not entirely non-existent historically, Canada's economic relations were deeply entwined to a very significant degree with the United States and to a lesser degree with Western Europe and the Commonwealth nations. The initial incentive for Canada to seek NAFTA membership was a fear that a strong U.S.- Mexico bilateral FTA might come to undermine or to diminish Canada's position under the CUFTA. However, in many ways, Canada has proven to be a most constructive force in fostering the NAFTA and broader Western Hemispheric integration efforts and has reaped far greater economic and political benefits from NAFTA than had been originally anticipated [Swanson, April 2000].

3. Doing business without an FTAA, but within the FTAA process

The current push toward an FTAA has not been a driving consideration of **25–030** American business [*cf.* Portras 2000]. The Canadian/U.S. Free Trade Arrangement made recognisable business sense [See, *inter alia*, Abbott and Bowman]. The NAFTA, though perceived as having net benefits for U.S. businesses (at least in the Southwest U.S.), must be seen as largely a political event. To date, one can readily find numerous conflicting studies and analyses of experts arguing over the overall economic gains of NAFTA [*cf.* Weintraub, 2000]. This quandary is not unique. In fact, even after 50 years of economic integration in Western Europe, the true *raison d'etre* for this ongoing integration process remains essentially *political* [See, *inter alia*, Davey, 1993].

25–031   Certainly, putting aside whether one country's economy or a business sector gains or loses economically, it cannot be denied that a North America with an NAFTA presents a more favourable *environment* for cross-border trade and investment and new, cross-border, economic and business opportunities among the three Contracting Parties, than a North America without an NAFTA [Garten, 1995]. Equally so, a FTAA also can be viewed as being more favourable for those businesses of the 34 involved nations seeking cross-border trade and investment opportunities within the hemisphere than a hemisphere without the FTAA. General reduction of trade and investment barriers, promotion of a top-class intellectual property regime, creation of a viable dispute resolution mechanism for the Contracting Parties (and in some instances for private parties)—these all can only be estimated as "business facilitators." [See, *e.g.* Trakman, 1997].

25–032   However, NAFTA and an FTAA do not so much forge new territory as solidify and support what are generally viewed as the fundamental preconditions for effective, long-term trade and direct investment liberalisation in an overall favourable trade and investment environment. Such pre-conditions might include for a particular country:

- sound and consistent macro-economic policies,

- a stable and accountable political system,

- fair, transparent and efficient administrative system,

- a viable legal and judicial infrastructure receptive to business and commercial, activities (including modern property, contract, commercial, secured transactions, corporate and insolvency laws),

- effective and enforceable judicial and non-judicial dispute resolution mechanisms,

- sound corporate governance and accounting systems,

- developing, but stable and transparent financial markets/systems,

- a suitable public transportation, and technological infrastructure,

- a sufficient, stable and trained workforce,

- reasonable and predictable tax regime (preferably with a favourable double taxation treaty(ies)),

- minimum and contained corruption, criminality and terrorism,

- currency convertibility and free capital exchange movements,

- geographic proximately or centrality for trade/business expansion, and

- a true atmosphere of trust and confidence in engaging in local partnership or other business contractual arrangements [Norton, 1999b, sections III and IV].

When looked at in this context, all of the above factors are not directly dealt with by the FTAA or an FTA.

The reality is that while the actual reduction/elimination of barriers to　**25–033**
cross-border trade and investments are centrally important for businesses,
these other key, infrastructural elements rest largely within the domain of
domestic reform initiatives or of extra-FTAA intergovernmental co-operative
efforts. For instance, sound and consistent macroeconomic policies and political stability clearly facilitate exchange rate stability, which is itself undoubtedly a pre-condition for effective international trade within any country or
region. This is a matter for government policy and decision-makers.

Additionally, for another example, transparency and accountability in　**25–034**
commercial law regimes, particularly regarding corporate and insolvency
laws, financial regulation and dispute resolution mechanisms, are essential in
attracting foreign trade and direct investment. Many countries in this region
have made cognisable legal and regulatory reforms in these and other critical
areas of domestic law reform [*e.g.,* in financial regulation/supervision area,
see, E. Aguirre and J. Norton].

As a general position the FTAA *process* should continue to facilitate　**25–035**
implementation of these preconditions in the various LAC countries as part
of an ongoing economic law reform process into the first part of this twenty-
first century [Barshefsky, 1999].

3.1 External factors on reform

The movement toward market-oriented economic policies by Mexico and　**25–036**
other LAC countries came largely from the self-realisation of these nations
that the old economic development model simply did not work and had
become largely counter-productive. This was reinforced in many instances
through the IMF, World Bank and IDB structural adjustment and assistance
packages. The IMF and World Bank structural adjustment packages have
traditionally focused on macro-economic criteria, but increasingly have come
to incorporate both structural economic and infrastuctural legal reforms, a
trend that became quite evident in packages resulting from the recent
1994–95 Mexican Peso Crises and the more recent 1997–98 Asian Financial
Crisis. The incorporation of law reform requirements as meaningful aspects
of structural adjustment packages and particularly the continuous monitoring of implementation of such law reforms by the international financial
institutions as pre-requisites to receipt of ongoing multilateral financial
assistance in tranches over time, have become modern realities of economic
markets [Norton, 1999b].

Thus, modernisation and upgrading of domestic economic and financial　**25–037**
systems have come about through responsible domestic government and
intergovernmental reactions to crises and otherwise through co-operative
efforts within the hemisphere. Illustrative is the movement toward international approaches to financial supervisory standards. The development of
international financial supervisory standards has manifested through
global public-private fora such as the Basle Committee on Banking Supervision and the International Organisation of Securities Commissions.
These multilateral forums have, in recent times, consistently developed
supervisory standards for implementation in home country statutory and
regulatory frameworks based on input from both regulatory agencies and

financial market participants. In particular, the Basle Committee and IOSCO have developed frameworks of "core" principles or standards in recent years for banking and securities markets that should be incorporated into any financial market infrastructure. The global economic order now necessitates that member countries and regional organisations adopt, implement and enforce these principles and standards, as they will undoubtedly continue to be used by IFIs as a meaningful part of continued adjustment packages and ultimately by corporates as a "stability factor" in evaluating potential international banking, finance and trade opportunities. The LAC countries themselves have taken and are taking significant initiatives in these areas (*e.g.* Association of Latin American and Caribbean Bank Supervisors).

25–038   A meaningful but often overlooked aspect of implementing global financial, trade, and legal infrastructures is the necessity of addressing corruption, criminality and terrorism. The FTAA nations have begun to address these issues through distinct domestic, bilateral regional, international co-operative efforts, many of which also address money laundering in attempts to comply with the globally derived OECD Financial Action Task Force (FATF) Recommendations and Basle Committee "Core Principles." Joint, co-operative efforts are also being undertaken as to anti-terrorism measures [Zagaris and Olive, 1999]. All these efforts will need to continue indefinitely as these perils will continue to erode legal infrastructures, political stability, regulatory regimes and economic and financial market policies [See, Norton, 1999a].

25–039   Tax policy is another example that is essentially domestic driven, though also subject to IFI adjustment program commitments. An incidence of domestic policy being influenced by the integration process was evident with the 1993 U.S.–Mexico Double Taxation Treaty. While the public focus was on the NAFTA negotiations, the U.S. and Mexico successfully completed the most advanced bilateral income treaty. Such a treaty was seen as a concomitant to providing greater certainty in cross-border business activities and in further converging national tax laws and practices [Dell and Polma, 1995].

3.2 Ongoing domestic reform

25–040   The reform of commercial and property laws, and the quality of judicial administration all remain subject to domestic initiatives and reforms. A case in point can be seen in the secured lending area. Cross-border business depends, to a large extent, upon cross-border financing. Such financing may often be tied to the taking of security. This, in turn, is linked to the degree of "legal security" and legal certainty a cross-border lender can obtain within a particular jurisdiction. Given the division of approach between "common law" jurisdictions (*e.g.* U.S. and to a large extent Canada) and "civil law" jurisdictions (*e.g.* Mexico), building legal and practical bridges among the laws of the differing jurisdictions becomes important. This may entail a number of domestic options, including innovative and proactive reviews of one's current laws, the adoption of new laws under one's particular legal tradition, or the wholesale or partial adoption of foreign or international models [Banowsky and Guabardi, 1995].

3.3 The transparency factor

For a business to properly evaluate cross-border business opportunities, the   **25–041**
quality, predictability, security and transparency of the local economic, political, legal and social environments are largely determinative; and these factors remain essentially domestic in character. For instance, transparency is critical so all the various "players" understand and can evaluate the rules of the game and so the game can continue successfully and fairly. As such, legal, accounting, financial, economic and administrative transparency is of the utmost importance in the long-term development of a country's financial system, and trade and investment regimes. Transparency is necessary not only for international investors and business people, but for their domestic counterparts also, and also for the corresponding economic and financial markets and for the involved governmental and intergovernmental policy-makers [Norton, 1999b, at pp. 305–308].

Thus, a FTA network or an FTAA has a practical effect of consolidating   **25–042**
and fostering the desired domestic business/commercial orientation and environments of the involved countries.

4. FTAA as a matrix of treaty arrangements v. singular goal

What exists within our hemisphere is a complex and enlarging matrix of   **25–043**
diverse trade and economic treaty arrangements, notwithstanding the move toward an FTAA. In fact, the FTAA is not intended to pre-empt or to supercede these arrangements, but to supplement and to "overarch" these [*cf.*, Garcia, 1995 and 1997].

4.1 The bilateral trade treaty

Such treaty configurations include over 50 bilateral trade and/or investment   **25–044**
treaties among the intended FTAA members, most of which came on stream only during this past decade. As to some 58 hemispheric bilateral investment treaties (BITs) reviewed by the OAS Trade Unit for the FTAA Negotiating Group on Investment, 55 were concluded after 1990. The broad domestic economic reform undertaken by many LAC nations from the mid-1980s to the present has as its logical corollary the need to adopt new investment regimes. This could be accomplished by domestic law and administrative reform and through BITs. With a shift from the Latin aversion to arbitration under the "Calvo doctrine", these BITs incorporated new cross-border, private dispute mechanisms. These bilateral treaties further advanced the pervasive use of the "national treatment standard" and helped reduce or eliminate restrictions in cross-border capital flows and profits repatriation. Thus, the increasing prevalence of BITs has served as a leveler and "liberaliser" of the cross-border business "playing field" within the hemisphere [OAS Compendium, 1999].

4.2 The integration arrangements

25–045   Then, there are the integration arrangements including the customs union/ common market configuration of Mercosur, the Group of Three (Mexico, Columbia, and Venezuela), the Central American Common Market (CACM), and the Caribbean Community and Common Market (CARICOM), and the restructured and revitalised Andean Community. The most "integration intensive" of these arrangements is MERCOSUR. MERCOSUR goes beyond the level of free trade among the members to embrace a customs union (*i.e.* with a common external tariff), a common internal market to cover not only goods, but services, establishment, labour and capital, and an incipient institutional governmental structure [O'Keefe, 1994; and Haines-Ferrari, 1993].

25–046   Equally significant, MERCOSUR has actively pursued accession arrangements with Chile and Bolivia, and is endeavouring to consult and work closely with other Latin American groupings (*e.g.* with the Andean Community). In fact, we see other cross-grouping linkages coming on stream (*e.g.* G-3 with CARICOM and possibly with CACM).

25–047   All this is occurring notwithstanding active, direct and ongoing FTAA negotiations among the 34 countries. As such, the hemispheric "playing field" is in a state of constant flux. Further, the various hemispheric groupings are beginning to adopt common positions on FTAA related matters– a fact which could well change the dynamics of the FTAA negotiations process [*cf.*, Guira, 1997].

4.3 The hemispheric FTAs

25–048   Add to the above, a half-dozen or so FTAs among the FTAA members-to-be. For example, FTAs have been concluded between Mexico and Bolivia, Mexico and Costa Rica, Mexico and Nicaragua, and Mexico and Chile. In fact, Canada has entered into a FTA with Chile, even though Chilean accession to NAFTA has been forestalled. Chile itself has been active in spinning a web of trade and investment arrangements throughout the hemisphere: as mentioned above, FTAs with Canada and Mexico, associate status and now full status with MERCOSUR and separate bilaterals with Columbia, Ecuador, and Venezuela.

4.4 The externals

25–049   What makes this matrix even more intriguing and interesting are the EU arrangements with Mexico and MERCOSUR, and other external negotiations such as with the Pacific Five. The EU configuration fills part of a void created by the diminishment of U.S. leadership in the current hemispheric trade negotiation processes. The significance of the new external factor to the overall FTAA dynamics remains to be seen [see www.eurosur.org/eurosur].

25–050   As to a Pacific Five grouping involving the U.S., this most likely could be negotiated without "fast track" authority as the involved Asian Nations are developed non-low-cost labour economies [*i.e.* Australia, New Zealand and Singapore, with the U.S. and Chile being the Western hemisphere members].

4.5 Attempted evaluation of the matrix

Certainly this matrix evidences an ongoing and proactive desire among our hemispheric partners for freer trade and investment and even, in some instances, for genuine levels of economic integration. But, where do U.S. businesses fit into the maze? Can conflicting or differing rules of origin be reconciled so as not to disadvantage U.S. interests? Will new sub-regional trade blocks such as MERCOSUR prove to be overtly or laterally protectionist *vis-à-vis* the U.S.? Will the new Latin and Caribbean flirtations with the EU cut against U.S. interests? These are very real but incredibly difficult issues to decipher.

25–051

On a positive note, the matrix does appear to lend itself to enhanced transparency for doing business within and throughout the hemisphere: this can only benefit U.S. cross-border business activities. In fact, transparency may be the most significant consequence and characteristic. U.S. businesses and business lawyers have traditionally shown themselves to be quite innovative when faced with complexities. So long as they have sufficient "hard" information upon which to evaluate the systemic complexities, then, this (somewhat cynically) could even lead (on a short-term, medium-term basis) to competitive advantages through "jurisdictional and legal arbitrage."

25–052

Also, the matrix favours an increase in cross-border joint ventures; generally greater enforcement of liberal trade and investment policies; the creation of new dispute resolution mechanisms; and for upgrading of domestic commercial and business law infrastructures. Where there exist complexities, but with shared policy objectives (*i.e.* an embrace of trade and investment liberalisation), the tendency of business could be to go forward with local partners. The local partners can assist in managing better these complexities and can be more reliable co-venturers as the broad governmental objectives will probably (in most, but not all instances) be more closely aligned than divergent. Moreover, such an environment may probably also encourage the further development of alternative, cross-border, commercial dispute resolution mechanisms, and greater practical intergovernmental and inter-bureaucratic co-operation and collaboration [D. Lindsay and Blackaby].

25–053

One of the real challenges of the FTAA process is to bring into the sunlight this matrix of numerous and diverse treaty arrangement for analysis and possible better co-ordination and compatibility, benefiting all members of the impending FTAA [Garcia, 1997].

25–054

5. Concluding observations: prospects for the FTAA

Virtually all of this chapter has either avoided or skirted around any direct discussion of the seriousness and potential value for U.S. and hemispheric businesses of an FTAA. This should not be taken, however, as an indication that the FTAA will not be a major milestone in the history of hemispheric co-operation or not be a presenter of new and significant business opportunities for interested U.S. and hemispheric businesses. The drawback for business people is that currently it is hard to discern coherence and definitiveness in the process.

25–055

5.1 The negotiation process and structure

25–056   When one tracks through the Joint Declaration of the Leaders of State and Governments at the First Summit of the Americas (Miami, 1994) and at the Second Summit of the Americas (Santiago, 1998), and the series of five Trade Ministerial Declarations to date (Denver in 1995, Cartagena in 1996, Belo Horizonte in 1997, San Jose in 1998 and Toronto in 1999), one begins to glean a very comprehensive planning and negotiating process—a process that could well overshadow in significance any end result. With an overall "Plan of Action" being periodically assessed and refined; with the original 13 Working Groups streamlined down to nine Negotiating Groups; and with technical assistance and support from the OAS, the IDB and ECLAC, we confront what must be one of the most sophisticated multilateral trade negotiating process in history.

25–057   Let me highlight what I think are several significant points respecting the FTAA negotiation process:

1.   The process is largely transparent, with an extensive website and extensive, publicly disseminated reports making readily accessible the breadth, depth and current status of the negotiations underway.

2.   Each Negotiating Group has a set agenda, reviewed, refined and revised at each Trade Ministerial Meeting.

3.   Each Group is an active working party as to a large range of significant issues being put on the table for review, discussion and consideration by the 34 participating countries.

4.   This in-depth, broad and ongoing level of hemispheric co-operation is unprecedented. Even if many issues are not resolved and even if the FTAA target dates of 2003 (for completion of substantive negotiations) and 2005 (for formal enactment) are delayed or abandoned, such serious and open discussions over a prolonged period of time can only prove beneficial for a hemispheric environment conducive to free trade, investment and hemispheric business opportunities [Stephenson, 2000].

5.2 An FTAA by 2005?

25–058   Crystal ball gazing is generally not the "bread and butter" of sound business decision-making or of sound business law judgments. So, I will leave such prognostication to the politicians and policy-makers.

25–059   I suggest that this U.S. election year, (*i.e.*, Nov. 2000) the FTAA will not appear on either candidates "radar screen" for international trade issues: WTO, "globalisation", and probably even China (notwithstanding recent granting of permanent normal trade status by the U.S.), most probably, will occupy this turf. In actuality, both of the main presidential candidates are on record as being supportive of both NAFTA and the FTAA. Despite increasingly strong pressure from the Right and Left for a new protectionism, neither candidate will probably be drawn into the debate; but each will probably let the planned FTAA intergovernmental processes continue on course. A President-elect then will have a period of several years to leave his mark on the process and to re-evaluate and "even" redefine it.

This, however, will not ensure eventual passage. I agree with one leading **25–060** commentator that for the U.S. to obtain passage of the FTAA, the President will have to be given "fast-track authority" by the Congress [Weintraub, 2000]. Though, some speculate that President Clinton's failure to secure "fast-track" for Santiago had more to do with the person than the subject-matter, I suspect that any President is going to find it an "uproad" struggle against an increasingly recalcitrant and parochial Congress [See, *inter alia,* James and Lustig, 2000 on "fast track"].

Some speculate that the recent Seattle WTO debacle holds new opportu- **25–061** nities for the FTAA process, as it is now "the only game in town." The reality, however, may be that there is, at least at the moment, *no* trade game in town [Bergsten, 1999].

The same forces that forced comprehensive side agreements to the NAFTA **25–062** before it was passed are still there in the wings. The expanded *ménage* that disabled Seattle is growing with the disenchanted and disenfranchised from the relentless and disorientating globalisation processes. Add to this the emotionalism on drugs and immigration issues that will irrationally join the onslaught against FTAA. Not too pleasant a picture!

And this is a picture snapped during a period of unprecedented, prolonged **25–063** economic prosperity in the United States — when the "feel good factor" should be at its highest. What type of photo will emerge if the U.S. has an economic downturn at any time prior to 2005?

Also, it needs to be kept in mind that an FTAA with 34 divergent coun- **25–064** tries is a much more difficult proposition in and of itself than was the NAFTA negotiation.

Where does all this lead us—complexity, fragmentation, uncertainty, reac- **25–065** tionism? Yes, but all this may still lead us to a situation which, in fact, may hold out significant long-term opportunities and benefits for Western hemisphere businesses and economies. Even more importantly, a successful FTAA holds out a hemisphere of greater peace, prosperity, security, harmony and social justice for current and future generations of "Americans". However, on a current basis, the scenario is one most difficult to evaluate (politically, economically and financially).

What can be evaluated, as it continues to unfold, is the overall *process* itself **25–066** and its direct and indirect *consequences*. This will assume a continued general sharing of common intergovernmental objectives; good faith collaboration and consultations respecting the various FTAA Working Groups, Ministerials and Summits; and ongoing and enhanced transparency in the process. With these givens, the policy-makers and the business community in the Western hemisphere should recognise their common interest respecting success of the *FTAA process,* and should be able to figure out the "course," and (at minimum) to "stay the course" of more liberalised trade and investment within the Western Hemisphere.

Abbreviations and acronyms

ACN – Andean Community
ACS – Association of Caribbean States
ALADI (LAIA) (formerly LAFTA) – Latin American Integration Association
BIT – Bilateral Investment Treaty
CACM – Central American Common Market
CARICOM – Caribbean Community and Common Market
CUFTA – Canadian U.S. Free Trade Agreement
EAI – Enterprise of the Americas Initiative
ECLAC – (UN) Economic Commission for Latin America and the Caribbean
EFTA – European Free Trade Agreement
EU – European Union
FCN – Bilateral Treaty of Friendship, Commerce and Navigation
FDI – Foreign direct investment
FTA – Free Trade Agreement
FTAA – Free Trade Area of the Americas
G-3 – Group of Three (Free Trade Agreement among Mexico, Columbia
       and Venezuela)
GATS – General Agreement on Trade in Services
GATT – General Agreement on Tariffs and Trade
Hemisphere – the Western hemisphere
HFTZ – Hemispheric Free Trade Zone
ICSID Convention – International Convention on the Settlement of
       Investment Disputes
IDB – Inter-American Development Bank
IMF – International Monetary Fund
LAC – Latin American and Caribbean Region
LAFTA – Latin American Free Trade Agreement (now ALADI-LAIA)
Latin America – includes Mexico, the Central American and South American
               Nations
MERCOSUR – Common Market of the Southern Cone (Argentina, Brazil,
           Paraguay, Uruguay)
MFN – Most-favoured-nation treatment
NAFTA – North American Free Trade Agreement
NT – National treatment
NY Convention – UN Convention on the Recognition and Enforcement of
               Foreign Arbitral Awards
OAS – Organisation of American States
OECS – Organisation of Eastern Caribbean States
SELA – Economic System of Latin America
SIECA – Permanent Secretariat of the General Treaty on Central American
        Integration
SICA – Central American Integration System
Summit of the Americas – Periodic Meeting (1994-Miami, 1998- Santiago,
2001–Toronto) of Heads of State and Governments Authority for Western
Hemispheric Nations (excluding Cuba) respecting the FTAA Process
UNCTAD – United Nations Conference on Trade and Development

UNCITRAL Rules – U.N. Committee on International Trade Law Rules on
        Arbitration
World Bank – International Bank for Reconstruction and Development
WTO – World Trade Organisation

Appendix A

List of economic and trade integration arrangements in western Hemisphere,
with country membership

A-1. Trade and integration agreements

Andean Community	*CARICOM*	*Group of Three*
Bolivia	Antigua and Barbuda	Colombia
Columbia	Bahamas	Mexico
Ecuador	Barbados	Venezuela
Peru	Belize	
Venezuela	Dominica	
	Grenada	
	Guyana	
	Haiti	
	Jamaica	
	Montserrat	
	St. Kitts and Nevis	
	St. Lucia	
	St. Vincent and the Grenadines	
	Suriname	
	Trinidad and Tobago	

MERCOSUR	*NAFTA*
Argentina	Canada
Brazil	Mexico
Paraguay	United States of America
Uruguay	

A-2. Bilateral Free Trade Agreements

Bolivia – Mexico
Canada – Chile
Central America – Dominican Republic
Chile – Mexico
Costa Rica – Mexico
Mexico – Nicaragua

Appendix B

List of trade and investment treaties intra-Western hemisphere

B. Bilateral Investment Treaties

ARGENTINA

Bolivia	Convenio entre la República de Bolivia y la República Argentina para la Promoción y Protección Recíprocas de Inversiones, 17 de marzo de 1994.
Canada	Agreement between the Government of Canada and the Government of the Republic of Argentina for the Promotion and Protection of Investments, November 5, 1991.
Chile	Tratado entre la República de Argentina y la República de Chile sobre Promoción y Protección Recíproca de Inversiones, 2 de agosto de 1991.
Costa Rica	Acuerdo entre el Gobierno de Costa Rica y el Gobierno de la República de Argentina para la Promoción y Protección Recíprocas de Inversiones, 21 de mayo de 1997.
Ecuador	Convenio entre el Gobierno de la República del Ecuador y el Gobierno de la República Argentina para la Promoción y Protección Recíproca de Inversiones, 18 de febrero de 1994.
El Salvador	Acuerdo entre la República de El Salvador y la República de Argentina para la Promoción y Protección Recíproca de Inversiones, 9 de mayo de 1996.
Guatemala	Acuerdo entre la República de Argentina y la República de Guatemala para la Promoción y Protección Recíproca de Inversiones, 21 de abril de 1998.
Jamaica	Agreement between the Government of Jamaica and the Government of the Argentine Republic on the Promotion and Reciprocal Protection of Investments, February 8, 1994.
Mexico	Acuerdo entre el Gobierno de los Estados Unidos Mexicanos y el Gobierno de la República de Argentina para la Promoción y Protección Recíproca de Inversiones, 13 de noviembre de 1996.

Nicaragua	Acuerdo entre el Gobierno de la República de Nicaragua y el Gobierno de la República de Argentina para la Promoción y Protección Recíprocas de Inversiones, 10 de agosto de 1998.
Panama	Convenio entre la República de Argentina y la República de Panamá para la Promoción y Protección Recíproca de las Inversiones, 10 de mayo de 1996.
Peru	Convenio entre el Gobierno de la República de Argentina y el Gobierno de la República del Perú sobre Promoción y Protección Recíproca de Inversiones, 10 de noviembre de 1994.
United States	Agreement between the United States of America and the Argentine Republic concerning the Reciprocal Encouragement and Protection of Investment, 14 November 1991.
Venezuela	Acuerdo entre el Gobierno de la República de Venezuela y el Gobierno de la República de Argentina para la Promoción y Protección Recíprocas de Inversiones, 16 de noviembre de 1993.

BARBADOS

Canada	Agreement between the Government of Canada and the Government of Barbados for the Reciprocal Promotion and Protection of Investments, 29 May 1996.
Venezuela	Acuerdo entre el Gobierno de la República de Venezuela y el Gobierno de Barbados para la Promoción y Protección de Inversiones, 15 de julio de 1994.

BOLIVIA

Argentina	Convenio entre la República de Bolivia y la República Argentina para la Promoción y Protección Recíprocas de Inversiones, 17 de marzo de 1994.
Chile	Acuerdo entre la República de Bolivia y la República de Chile para la Promoción y Protección Recíproca de Inversiones, 22 de septiembre de 1994.
Ecuador	Convenio entre la República de Bolivia y la República de Ecuador para la Promoción y Protección Recíproca de Inversiones, 25 de mayo de 1995.

Peru   Convenio entre el Gobierno de la República del Perú y el
                  Gobierno de la República de Bolivia sobre Promoción y
                  Protección Recíproca de Inversiones, 30 de julio de 1993.

United States Treaty between the United States of America and the
                  Government of the Republic of Bolivia concerning the
                  Encouragement and Reciprocal Protection of Investment,
                  April 17, 1998.

BRAZIL

Chile   Acuerdo entre el Gobierno de la República de Chile y el
                  Gobierno de la República Federativa de Brasil para la
                  Promoción y Protección Recíproca de Inversiones, 22 de
                  marzo de 1994.

Venezuela   Acuerdo entre el Gobierno de la República de Venezuela
                  y el Gobierno de la República Federativa de Brasil para la
                  Promoción y Protección Recíproca de las Inversiones, 4 de
                  julio de 1995.

CANADA

Argentina   Agreement between the Government of Canada and the
                  Government of the Republic of Argentina for the Promo-
                  tion and Protection of Investments, November 5, 1991.

Barbados   Agreement between the Government of Canada and the
                  Government of Barbados for the Reciprocal Promotion
                  and Protection of Investments, 29 May 1996.

Costa Rica   Agreement between the Government of Canada and the
                  Government of the Republic of Costa Rica for the
                  Promotion and Protection of Investments, March 18,
                  1998.

Ecuador   Agreement between the Government of Canada and the
                  Government of the Republic of Ecuador for the Promo-
                  tion and Reciprocal Protection of Investments, April 29,
                  1996.

Panama   Treaty between the Government of Canada and the Gov-
                  ernment of the Republic of Panama for the Promotion
                  and Protection of Investments, September 12, 1996.

Trinidad &   Agreement between the Government of Canada and the
Tobago   Government of the Republic of Trinidad and Tobago for
                  the Reciprocal Promotion and Protection of Investments,
                  September 11, 1995.

Uruguay Agreement between the Government of Canada and the Government of the Eastern Republic of Uruguay for the Promotion and Protection of Investments, October 29, 1997.

Venezuela Agreement between the Government of Canada and the Government of the Republic of Venezuela for the Promotion and Protection of Investments, July 1, 1996.

CHILE

Argentina Tratado entre la República de Argentina y la República de Chile sobre Promoción y Protección Recíproca de Inversiones, 2 de agosto de 1991.

Bolivia Acuerdo entre la República de Bolivia y la República de Chile para la Promoción y Protección Recíproca de Inversiones, 22 de septiembre de 1994.

Brazil Acuerdo entre el Gobierno de la República de Chile y el Gobierno de la República Federativa de Brasil para la Promoción y Protección Recíproca de Inversiones, 22 de marzo de 1994.

Costa Rica Acuerdo entre la República de Chile y la República de Costa Rica para la Promoción y Protección Recíproca de las Inversiones, 11 de julio de 1996.

Ecuador Convenio entre el Gobierno de la República de Chile y el Gobierno de la República del Ecuador para la Promoción y Protección Recíprocas de Inversiones, 27 de octubre de 1993.

El Salvador Acuerdo entre la República de El Salvador y la República de Chile para la Promoción y Protección Recíproca de las Inversiones, 8 de noviembre de 1996.

Guatemala Acuerdo entre la República de Guatemala y la República de Chile para la Promoción y Protección Recíproca de las Inversiones, 8 de noviembre de 1996.

Honduras Acuerdo entre la República de Honduras y la República de Chile para la Promoción y Protección Recíproca de las Inversiones, 11 de noviembre de 1996.

Nicaragua Acuerdo entre la República de Chile y la República de Nicaragua para la Promoción y Protección Recíproca de las Inversiones, 8 de noviembre de 1996.

Panama   Convenio entre la República de Panamá y la República de Chile para la Promoción y Protección Recíproca de las Inversiones, 8 de noviembre de 1996.

Paraguay   Acuerdo entre la República de Chile y la República del Paraguay para la Promoción y Protección Recíproca de las Inversiones, 7 de agosto de 1995.

Uruguay   Acuerdo entre la República de Chile y la República Oriental del Uruguay para la Promoción y Protección Recíproca de las Inversiones, 26 de octubre de 1995.

Venezuela   Acuerdo entre el Gobierno de la República de Venezuela y el Gobierno de la República de Chile sobre Promoción y Protección Recíproca de Inversiones, 2 de abril de 1993.

COLOMBIA

Peru   Convenio entre la República de Colombia y el Gobierno de la República del Perú sobre Promoción y Protección Recíproca de Inversiones, 26 de abril de 1994.

COSTA RICA

Argentina   Acuerdo entre el Gobierno de Costa Rica y el Gobierno de la República de Argentina para la Promoción y Protección Recíprocas de Inversiones, 21 de mayo de 1997.

Canada   Agreement between the Government of Canada and the Government of the Republic of Costa Rica for the Promotion and Protection of Investments, March 18, 1998.

Chile   Acuerdo entre la República de Chile y la República de Costa Rica para la Promoción y Protección Recíproca de las Inversiones, 11 de julio de 1996.

Paraguay   Acuerdo entre la República de Costa Rica y el Gobierno de la República del Paraguay para la Promoción y Protección Recíproca de Inversiones, 29 de enero de 1998.

Venezuela   Acuerdo entre la República de Venezuela y la República de Costa Rica para la Promoción y Protección Recíproca de Inversiones, 17 de marzo de 1997.

DOMINICAN REPUBLIC

Ecuador   Acuerdo para la Promoción y Protección de Inversiones entre el Gobierno de la República del Ecuador y el Gobierno de la República Dominicana, 26 de junio de 1998.

ECUADOR

Argentina	Convenio entre el Gobierno de la República del Ecuador y el Gobierno de la República Argentina para la Promoción y Protección Recíproca de Inversiones, 18 de febrero de 1994.
Bolivia	Convenio entre la República de Bolivia y la República de Ecuador para la Promoción y Protección Recíproca de Inversiones, 25 de mayo de 1995.
Canada	Agreement between the Government of Canada and the Government of the Republic of Ecuador for the Promotion and Reciprocal Protection of Investments, April 29, 1996.
Chile	Convenio entre el Gobierno de la República de Chile y el Gobierno de la República del Ecuador para la Promoción y Protección Recíprocas de Inversiones, 27 de octubre de 1993.
El Salvador	Convenio entre el Gobierno de la República del Ecuador y el Gobierno de la República de El Salvador para la Promoción y Protección Recíprocas de Inversiones, 16 de mayo de 1994.
Paraguay	Convenio entre la República del Paraguay y la República del Ecuador sobre Promoción y Protección Recíproca de Inversiones, 28 de enero de 1994.
Dominican Republic	Acuerdo para la Promoción y Protección de Inversiones entre el Gobierno de la República del Ecuador y el Gobierno de la República Dominicana, 26 de junio de 1998.
United States	Treaty between the United States of America and the Republic of Ecuador Concerning the Encouragement and Reciprocal Protection of Investment, August 27, 1993.
Venezuela	Convenio entre el Gobierno de la República de Venezuela y el Gobierno de la República del Ecuador para la Promoción y Protección Recíprocas de Inversiones, 18 de noviembre de 1993.

EL SALVADOR

Argentina	Acuerdo entre la República de El Salvador y la República de Argentina para la Promoción y Protección Recíproca de Inversiones, 9 de mayo de 1996.

Chile Acuerdo entre la República de El Salvador y la República de Chile para la Promoción y Protección Recíproca de las Inversiones, 8 de noviembre de 1996.

Ecuador Convenio entre el Gobierno de la República del Ecuador y el Gobierno de la República de El Salvador para la Promoción y Protección Recíprocas de Inversiones, 16 de mayo de 1994.

Peru Acuerdo entre el Gobierno de la República de El Salvador y el Gobierno de la República de Perú para la Promoción y Protección Recíproca de Inversiones, 13 de junio de 1996.

GRENADA

United States Treaty between the United States of America and Grenada Concerning the Reciprocal Encouragement and Protection of Investment, May 2, 1986.

GUATEMALA

Argentina Acuerdo entre la República de Argentina y la República de Guatemala para la Promoción y Protección Recíproca de Inversiones, 21 de abril de 1998.

Chile Acuerdo entre la República de Guatemala y la República de Chile para la Promoción y Protección Recíproca de las Inversiones, 8 de noviembre de 1996.

HAITI

United States Treaty between the United States of America and the Republic of Haiti Concerning the Reciprocal Encouragement and Protection of Investment, December 13, 1983.

HONDURAS

Chile Acuerdo entre la República de Honduras y la República de Chile para la Promoción y Protección Recíproca de las Inversiones, 11 de noviembre de 1996.

United States Treaty between the United States of America and the Government of the Republic of Honduras Concerning the Encouragement and Reciprocal Protection of Investment, July 1, 1995.

JAMAICA

Argentina   Agreement between the Government of Jamaica and the Government of the Argentine Republic on the Promotion and Reciprocal Protection of Investments, February 8, 1994.

United States   Treaty between the United States of America and Jamaica Concerning the Reciprocal Encouragement and Protection of Investment, February 4, 1994.

MEXICO

Argentina   Acuerdo entre el Gobierno de los Estados Unidos Mexicanos y el Gobierno de la República de Argentina para la Promoción y Protección Recíproca de Inversiones, 13 de noviembre de 1996.

NICARAGUA

Argentina   Acuerdo entre el Gobierno de la República de Nicaragua y el Gobierno de la República de Argentina para la Promoción y Protección Recíprocas de Inversiones, 10 de agosto de 1998.

Chile   Acuerdo entre la República de Chile y la República de Nicaragua para la Promoción y Protección Recíproca de las Inversiones, 8 de noviembre de 1996.

United States   Treaty between the Government of the United States of America and the Government of the Republic of Nicaragua Concerning the Encouragement and Reciprocal Protection of Investment, 1 July 1995.

PANAMA

Argentina   Convenio entre la República de Argentina y la República de Panamá para la Promoción y Protección Recíproca de las Inversiones, 10 de mayo de 1996.

Canada   Treaty between the Government of Canada and the Government of the Republic of Panama for the Promotion and Protection of Investments, September 12, 1996.

Chile   Convenio entre la República de Panamá y la República de Chile para la Promoción y Protección Recíproca de las Inversiones, 8 de noviembre de 1996.

United States   Treaty between the United States of America and the Republic of Panama Concerning the Treatment and Protection of Investment, October 27, 1982.

Uruguay   Convenio entre la República de Panamá y la República Oriental del Uruguay para la Promoción y Protección Recíproca de Inversiones, 15 de setiembre de 1998.

PARAGUAY

Chile   Acuerdo entre la República de Chile y la República del Paraguay para la Promoción y Protección Recíproca de las Inversiones, 7 de agosto de 1995.

Costa Rica   Acuerdo entre la República de Costa Rica y el Gobierno de la República del Paraguay para la Promoción y Protección Recíproca de Inversiones, 29 de enero de 1998.

Ecuador   Convenio entre la República del Paraguay y la República del Ecuador sobre Promoción y Protección Recíproca de Inversiones, 28 de enero de 1994.

Peru   Convenio entre la República del Perú y la República del Paraguay sobre Promoción y Protección Recíproca de Inversiones, 31 de enero de 1994.

Venezuela   Convenio sobre Promoción y Protección Recíproca de Inversiones entre el Gobierno de la República de Venezuela y el Gobierno de la República del Paraguay, 5 setiembre de 1996.

PERU

Argentina   Convenio entre el Gobierno de la República de Argentina y el Gobierno de la República del Perú sobre Promoción y Protección Recíproca de Inversiones, 10 de noviembre de 1994.

Bolivia   Convenio entre el Gobierno de la República del Perú y el Gobierno de la República de Bolivia sobre Promoción y Protección Recíproca de Inversiones, 30 de julio de 1993.

Colombia   Convenio entre la República de Colombia y el Gobierno de la República del Perú sobre Promoción y Protección Recíproca de Inversiones, 26 de abril de 1994.

El Salvador   Acuerdo entre el Gobierno de la República de El Salvador y el Gobierno de la República de Perú para la Promoción y Protección Recíproca de Inversiones, 13 de junio de 1996.

Paraguay	Convenio entre la República del Perú y la República del Paraguay sobre Promoción y Protección Recíproca de Inversiones, 31 de enero de 1994.
Venezuela	Convenio entre el Gobierno de la República de Venezuela y cl Gobierno de la República del Perú sobre la Promoción y Protección de Inversiones, 12 de enero de 1996.

TRINIDAD and TOBAGO

Canada	Agreement between the Government of Canada and the Government of the Republic of Trinidad and Tobago for the Reciprocal Promotion and Protection of Investments, September 11, 1995.
United States	Treaty between the Government of the United States of America and the Government of the Republic of Trinidad and Tobago Concerning theEncouragement and Reciprocal Protection of Investment, September 26, 1994.

UNITED STATES

Argentina	Agreement between the United States of America and the Argentine Republic Concerning the Reciprocal Encouragement and Protection of Investment, November 14, 1991.
Bolivia	Treaty between the United States of America and the Government of the Republic of Bolivia Concerning the Encouragement and Reciprocal Protection of Investment, April 17, 1998.
Ecuador	Treaty between the United States of America and the Republic of Ecuador Concerning the Encouragement and Reciprocal Protection of Investment, August 27, 1993.
Grenada	Treaty between the United States of America and Grenada Concerning the Reciprocal Encouragement and Protection of Investment, May 2, 1986.
Haiti	Treaty between the United States of America and the Republic of Haiti Conccrning the Reciprocal Encouragement and Protection of Investment, December 13, 1983.
Honduras	Treaty between the United States of America and the Government of the Republic of Honduras Concerning the Encouragement and Reciprocal Protection of Investment, July 1, 1995.

Jamaica	Treaty between the United States of America and Jamaica Concerning the Reciprocal Encouragement and Protection of Investment, February 4, 1994.
Nicaragua	Treaty between the Government of the United States of America and the Government of the Republic of Nicaragua Concerning the Encouragement and Reciprocal Protection of Investment, July 1, 1995.
Panama	Treaty between the United States of America and the Republic of Panama Concerning the Treatment and Protection of Investment, October 27, 1982.
Trinidad & Tobago	Treaty between the Government of the United States of America and the Government of the Republic of Trinidad and Tobago Concerning the Encouragement and Reciprocal Protection of Investment, September 26, 1994.

URUGUAY

Canada	Agreement between the Government of Canada and the Government of the Eastern Republic of Uruguay for the Promotion and Protection of Investments, October 29, 1997.
Chile	Acuerdo entre la República de Chile y la República Oriental del Uruguay para la Promoción y Protección Recíproca de las Inversiones, 26 de octubre de 1995.
Panama	Convenio entre la República de Panamá y la República Oriental del Uruguay para la Promoción y Protección Recíproca de Inversiones, 15 de setiembre de 1998.

VENEZUELA

Argentina	Acuerdo entre el Gobierno de la República de Venezuela y el Gobierno de la República de Argentina para la Promoción y Protección Recíprocas de Inversiones, 16 de noviembre de 1993.
Barbados	Acuerdo entre el Gobierno de la República de Venezuela y el Gobierno de Barbados para la Promoción y Protección de Inversiones, 15 de julio de 1994.
Brazil	Acuerdo entre el Gobierno de la República de Venezuela y el Gobierno de la República Federativa de Brasil para la Promoción y Protección Recíproca de las Inversiones, 4 de julio de 1995.

Canada	Agreement between the Government of Canada and the Government of the Republic of Venezuela for the Promotion and Protection of Investments, July 1, 1996.
Chile	Acuerdo entre el Gobierno de la República de Venezuela y el Gobierno de la República de Chile sobre Promoción y Protección Recíproca de Inversiones, 2 de abril de 1993.
Costa Rica	Acuerdo entre la República de Venezuela y la República de Costa Rica para la Promoción y Protección Recíproca de Inversiones, 17 de marzo de 1997.
Ecuador	Convenio entre el Gobierno de la República de Venezuela y el Gobierno de la República del Ecuador para la Promoción y Protección Recíprocas de Inversiones, 18 de noviembre de 1993.
Paraguay	Convenio sobre Promoción y Protección Recíproca de Inversiones entre el Gobierno de la República de Venezuela y el Gobierno de la República del Paraguay, 5 setiembre de 1996.
Peru	Convenio entre el Gobierno de la República de Venezuela y el Gobierno de la República del Perú sobre la Promoción y Protección de Inversiones, 12 de enero de 1996.

Other relevant arrangements

OAS

Antigua & Barbuda
Argentina
Bahamas
Barbados
Belize
Bolivia
Brazil
Canada
Chile
Colombia
Costa Rica
Cuba (excluded from participation since 1962)
Dominica
Dominican Republic
Ecuador
El Salvador
Grenada
Guatemala
Guyana

SELA

Argentina
Bahamas
Barbados
Belize
Bolivia
Brazil
Colombia
Costa Rica
Chile
Cuba
Ecuador
Dominican Republic
El Salvador
Grenada
Guatemala
Guyana
Haiti
Honduras
Jamaica

Haiti
Honduras
Jamaica
Mexico
Nicaragua
Panama
Paraguay
Peru
St. Lucia
St. Vincent & the Grenadines
Suriname
St. Kitts & Nevis
Trinidad & Tobago
United States of America
Uruguay
Venezuela

Mexico
Nicaragua
Panama
Paraguay
Peru
Suriname
Trinidad & Tobago
Uruguay
Venezuela

ACS
Antigua & Barbuda
Bahamas
Barbados
Belize
Colombia
Costa Rica
Cuba
Dominica
Dominican Republic
El Salvador
Grenada
Guatemala
Guyana
Haiti
Honduras
Jamaica
Mexico
Nicaragua
Panama
St. Kitts & Nevis
St. Lucia
St. Vincent & the Grenadines
Suriname
Trinidad & Tobago
Venezuela
Aruba
The Netherlands Antilles
France

OECS
Antigua & Barbuda
Dominica
Grenada
Montserrat
St. Kitts & Nevis
St. Lucia
St. Vincent & the
Grenadines
Anguilla
British Virgin Islands

Selective bibliography

A. FTAA Source Documents

- Declaration of Principles, First Summit of the Americas (Heads of States and Governments of the 34 Hemispheric Nations, excluding Cuba), with Plan of Action (Miami, USA, December 6, 1994).

- Declaration, Second Summit of the Americas (Heads of States and Governments), with Plan of Action (Santiago, Chile, April 19, 1998).

- Joint Ministerial Declaration, First Western Hemisphere Trade Ministerial (Denver, USA, June 30, 1995).

- Joint Ministerial Declaration, Second Western Hemisphere Trade Ministerial (Cartagena, Columbia, March 21, 1996).

- Joint Ministerial Declaration, Third Western Hemisphere Trade Ministerial (Belo Horizonte, Brazil, May 16, 1997).

- Joint Ministerial Declaration, Fourth Western Hemisphere Trade Ministerial (San Jose, Costa Rica, March 19, 1998).

- Joint Ministerial Declaration, Fifth Western Hemisphere Trade Ministerial (Toronto, Canada, November 4, 1999).

- FTAA Negotiating Group on Competition Policy:

  - *Inventory of Domestic Laws and Regulations Relating to Competition Policy in the Western Hemisphere* (updated version 1999).

  - *Report on Developments and Enforcement of Competition Policy and Laws in the Western Hemisphere* (updated as of October 1999).

- FTAA Negotiating Group on Dispute Resolution, *Inventory of Dispute Settlement Mechanisms, Procedures and Legal Texts Established in Existing Trade and Integration Agreements; Treaties and Arrangements in the Hemisphere and in the WTO.*

- FTAA Negotiating Group on Government Procurement:

  - *National Legislation, Regulations and Procedures Regarding Government Procurement in the Americas* (prepared by IDB for Group).

  - *Government Procurement Rules in Integration Arrangements in the Americas.*

- FTAA Negotiating Group on Investment, *Investment Agreements in the Western Hemisphere: A Compendium* (updated 1999).

- FTAA Negotiating Group on Services, *Provisions on Trade in Services in Trade and Integration Agreements in the Western Hemisphere* (updated 1999).

- FTAA Negotiating Group on Standards and Technical Barriers to Trade, *National Practices in Standards, Technical Regulations and Conformity Assessment in the Western Hemisphere.*

- FTAA Negotiating Group on Subsidies, Antidumping and Countervailing Duties (updated 1999).

- *Investment Agreements in the Western Hemisphere: A Compendium* (prepared by OAS Trade Group for FTAA Negotiating Group on Investment, 1999).

B. Other related source documents

- Agreement on Andean Subregional Integration, May 26, 1969 (Treaty of Cartegena).

- Canadian-United States Free Trade Agreement, December 22, 1982–January 2, 1988, 27 I.L.M. 281 (1988).

- Common Code for the Treatment of Foreign Capital, Trademarks, Patents, Licenses and Royalties. *Decision 291* of the Andean Commission.

- Convention between the United States and Mexico for the Avoidance of Double Taxation and the Prevention of Fiscal Evasion with Respect to Taxes on Income, September 18, 1993.

- Groupo de los Tres (G-3 Treaty), June 13, 1994.

- Israel–United States Free Trade Agreement.

- Mexico–U.S. Commercial Framework Agreement on Trade and Investment, November 6, 1987.

- North American Free Trade Agreement, drafted August 12, 1992, rev. September 6, 1992, US–Canada–Mexico, 32 I.L.M. Entered into force January 1, 1994.

- North American Agreement in Environmental Cooperation, September 14, 1993, 32 I.L.M. 1480.

- North American Agreement on Labor Cooperation, September 14, 1993, U.S.–Canada–Mexico, 32 I.L.M. 1499.

- North American Free Trade Agreement Implementation Act (U.S.), Pub. L. No. 103–182, 107 Stat. 2057 (1993).

- Treaty Establishing a Common Market (MERCOSUR), March 26, 1991 (Treaty of Asuncion).

- Treaty of Montevideo Establishing Latin American Integration Association, August 12, 1980.

- U.S.–Mexico Joint Statement, "Reflections about the Trade and Investment Relations Between Mexico and the United States (August 1998).

C. Key websites

Andean Community—http://www.imf.org/external/np/sec/decdo/acuerdo.
htm
ALADI (LAIA)—http://www.aladi.org.
CARICOM—http://www.caribrnm.net.
ECLAC—http://www.eclacpos.org.
FTAA—http://www.mac.doc.gov/ftaa2005/
G-3—see SELA website
IDB—http://www.iadb.org.
MERCOSUR—http:mercosurinvestment.com
NAFTA Secretariat—http:www.nafta-sec-alena.org
OAS—http://www.sice.cas.org
SELA—http://www.lonic.utexas.edu/onsela
2001/Summit of the Americas—http:www.americascanada.org/eventsummit
/menue.asp

D. Books and articles

K.W. Abbott and G.W. Bowman, "Economic Integration in the Americas: a
Work in Progress," 14 *Nw. J. Int'l L. & Bus* 493(1994).

Kym Anderson, "The WTO Agenda for the New Millennium," *Economic
Record*, no. 228, Vol. 75, at 77 (1999).

R. Aggarwal, "Technology and Globalization as Mutual Reinforcers in
Business: Reorienting Strategic Thinking for the New Millennium,"
Management International Review (July 15, 1999), at p. 83.

A. Aquirre and J. Norton (eds.) *Reform of Latin American Banking Systems:
National and International Perspectives,* (2000).

D. Arner, "The Mexican Peso Crisis of 1994–94: Implications for the
Regulation of Financial Markets," *2 NAFTA Rev.* 28, (1996).

D. Banowsky and C. Gabuardi, "Secured Credit Transactions in Mexico", *28
Int'l Law*. 263 (1994).

Charlene Barshefsky, "The Role of Legal Institutions in the Economic
Development of the Americans: Keynote Address", 30 *Law & Pol'y
Int'l Bus.*1 (1999).

J. Bello and A. Holmer, *Guide to the US/Canada Free Trade Agreement* (1990,
as updated periodically).

J. Bello and A. Holmer, "The NAFTA: Its Overarching Implications", 27
Int'l Law 589, (1993).

J. Bello, A. Holmer and J. Norton (eds.), *NAFTA, A New Frontier in Trade
and Investment in the Americas* (1994).

Fred Bergsten, "Trade Stalemate", *Washington Post*, September 29, 1999, at
29 (op-ed).

President George Bush, "Enterprise for the Americas Initiative" (June 27, 1990).

Maria Dakolias, "A Strategy for Judicial Reform: The Experience in Latin America", 36 *Va. J. Int'l Law* 167 (1995).

William J. Davey, "European Integration: Reflections on its Limits and Effects," 1 *Ind. J. Global Leg. Studies* 185 (1993).

J.D. Dell and Geoffrey R. Polma, "The New U.S.-Mexico Income Tax Treaty: Overview and Analysis", 1 *NAFTA Rev.* No. 1, 49 (1995).

R. Folsom and W.D. Folsom, *Understanding NAFTA and Its International Business Implications* (1997).

R. H. Folsom, M. W. Gordon and J. A. Spanogle, Jr., *International Business Transactions* (4th ed. 1999).

Frank J. Garcia, "NAFTA and the Creation of the FTAA: A Critique of Piecemeal Accession", 35 *Va. J. Int'l L.* 539 (1995).

Frank J. Garcia, "Americas Agreements—An Interim Stage in Building the Free Trade Area of the Americas", 35 *Colum. J. Trans. L.* 63 (1997).

Frank J. Garcia, New Frontiers in International Trade: Decision-Making and Dispute Resolution in the Free Trade Area of the Americas", 18 *Mich. J. Int'l L.* 357 (1999).

Jeffrey E. Garten, "The Changing Face of North America in the Global Economy", I *NAFTA Rev.* No. 1, 5 (1995).

Jeffrey E. Garten, "Business and Foreign Policy", 76 *Foreign Affairs* No. 3, 67 (1997).

Michael Gordon, "Dispute Resolution Under the North American Free Trade Agreement: A Framework to Avoid National Country", Chap. 7 in *J. Norton, Changing World* (1998) (see *infra*).

William C. Gruben, "Clean Dynamics, and the Economics of NAFTA", I *NAFTA Rev.* No. 1, 87 (1995).

William C. Gruben, "Latin American Monetary Policies" (SMU-Tower Center- March 2000; Summer 2000 *NAFTA Review*).

Jorge Guira, "MERCOSUR as an Instrument for Development," 3 *NAFTA Rev.* 53 (1997).

Marta Haines-Ferrari, "MERCOSUR: A New Model of Latin American Economic Integration," 25 *Case W. Rev. J. Int'l L.* 413 (1993).

J. Holbein and D. Musch (compilers), *North American Free Trade Agreements* (1993B).

G.C. Hufbauer and J.J. Scholt, *Western Hemisphere Economic Integration* (1994).

P. James and M. Lustig, "Predicting the Future of the FTAA" (SMU-Tower Center, March 2000; Summer 2000 *NAFTA Review*).

J. Steven Jarreau, "Negotiating Trade Liberalization in the Western Hemisphere: The Free Trade Areas of the Americas", 13 *Temp. Int'l & Comp. L. J.* (1999).

Richard Lawrence, "Free Trade in Americas on Slow Track," *Journal of Commerce* (September 27, 1999), at 6 (op ed.).

D. Lindsay and N. Blackaby, *Latin American Commercial Arbitration* (Kluwer, forthcoming, 2000).

J.J. Linz and A Stepan, *The Breakdown of Democratic Regimes* (John Hopkins, 1978).

Sergio Lopez Allyon, "The Impact of Trade Agreements in the Legal Systems of the American Continent," 19 *Hous. J. Int'l L.* 761 (1997).

J. Norton (ed.), *The European Economic Community: Trade and Investment* (Matthew Bender 1986).

J. Norton *et al.* (eds.), *Doing Business in Mexico* (3 vols, 1990).

Joseph J. Norton and Thomas L. Bloodworth (eds.) *NAFTA and Beyond: A New Framework for Doing Business in the Americas* (1995).

Joseph J. Norton, "The Mexican Peso Crisis and the Future of Financial Integration in the Americas", Chap. 12 in J. Norton *et al.* eds., *The Changing World of International Law in the 21ˢᵗ Century* (1998).

Joseph J. Norton, "New International Financial Architecture - Reflections on the Possible Law – Based Dimension", 33 *Int'l Law* 891 (1999a).

Joseph J. Norton, "International Co-Operative Efforts and Implications for Law Reform", Chap. 9, in R. Lastra and H. Shiffman (eds.), *Bank Insolvencies in Transition Economies* (1999b).

Paul A. O'Hop, Jr., "Hemispheric Integration and the Elimination of Legal Obstacles Under a NAFTA-Based System", 36 *Harv. Int'l L.J.* 127 (1995).

Thomas A. O'Keefe, "An Analysis of the MERCOSUR Integration Project From a Legal Perspective," 28 *Int'l Law*. 439 (1994).

Thomas O'Keefe, *Latin American Trade Agreements* (Transnational 1997a).

Thomas A. O'Keefe, "Potential Conflict Areas in Any Future Negotiations Between MERCOSUR and the NAFTA to Create a Free Trade Area of the Americas", 14 *Ariz. J. Int'l & Comp. L.* 305 (1997b).

M. Otero-Lathrop, "Mercosur and NAFTA: The Need for Convergence", IV *NAFTA Rev.* No. 3, 116 (1998).

G. Portras, "The Potential for the U.S. Economic Dominance" (SMU-Tower Center, March 2000; Summer 2000 *NAFTA Review*).

Jeswald Salacuse, "From Developing Countries to Emerging Markets: A Changing Role in the Third World", 33 *Int'l Law*. 875 (1999).

Peter H. Smith, "Whither Hemispheric Integration?," *Business Economics*, No. 3, Vol. 34, at p. 38 (1999).

W.C. Smith *et al.* (eds.), *Democracy, Markets and Structural Reform in Latin America* (1993).

Edward Snyder, "The Menem Revolution in Argentina; Progress Toward a Hemispheric Free Trade Area", 29 *Texas Int'l L.J.* 95 (1994).

Jinny St. Goar, "It's a Jungle Out There: Lending and Investment in Emerging International Financial Markets," *CFO*, No. 11, Vol. 15, at p. 93 (1999).

Sherry Stephenson, "The Current State of the FTAA Negotiations" (SMU - Tower Center, March 2000; Summer 2000 *NAFTA Review*).).

W. P. Streng & J. W. Salacuse, *International Business Planning: Law and Taxation - United States* (1983, as updated regularly).

Hon. J. Swanson, "Canada's Contributions to the NAFTA and FTAA Processes" (Annual SMU Law Institute of the Americas Lecture, Dallas Texas, April 2000).

Jon M. Tate, "Note: Sweeping Protectionism Under the Rug: Neoprotectionist Measures Among Mercosur Countries in a Time of Trade Liberalization", 27 *Ga. J. Int'l & Comp. L* 389 (1999).

Leon Trakman, *Dispute Settlement Under the NAFTA* (1997).

USTR Office, "Discussion Draft on Post-NAFTA Policy" (February, 1994).

Sidney Weintraub, "The Meaning of NAFTA and its Implications for the FTAA" (SMU - Tower Center, March 2000; Summer 2000 *NAFTA Review*).

Bernard Weinstein, *NAFTA after Four Years: Successes, Problems and Challenges*, IV *NAFTA Review* 109 (1998).

J. Whalley and C. Hamilton, "The Intellectual Underpinnings of North American Economic Integration", 4 *Minn. J. Global Trade* 43 (1995).

B. Zagaris and S.L. Ohri, "The Emergence of and International Enforcement Regime on Transnational Corruption in the Americas", 30 *Law & Pol'y Int'l Bus.* 53 (1999).

CHAPTER 26

FINANCING TRADE WITHIN A REGIONAL FRAMEWORK — LEGISLATIVE OPTIONS: CLIVE M. SCHMITTHOFF ON THE UNIFICATION OF THE LAW OF INTERNATIONAL TRADE REVISITED

ANNA MÖRNER[1]

> *"Global unification of the law of international trade — that, and nothing less, must be our aim. That aim should be asserted with force and without qualification although it is obvious that in the present state of international society regional unification in some instances may be more easy to attain, particularly amongst countries which have a common legal tradition or are linked by geographical, political, economic or social ties."*[2]

1. Introduction

The past few decades have seen an almost explosive increase in the number **26–001** of Regional Integration Arrangements (RIAs)[3] worldwide. Purportedly, the creation of an RIA serves a number of purposes: trade creation,[4] maintenance of peace and stability[5] and the creation and maintenance of stable and

---

[1] Anna Mörner was a Research and Teaching Fellow in Central and Eastern European Financial Law at the Centre for Commercial Law Studies, Queen Mary, University of London, until her sudden and tragic death in November 2000. This paper formed the basis of her presentation at the Symposium in honour of Clive M. Schmitthoff held at CCLS in June 2000, and was revised for publication by Anna before her death.
[2] Schmitthoff, C.M. "The Unification of the Law of International Trade" Handelshogskolan, Goteborg, Skrifter 1964–65. Reprinted in Cheng, C.J. (ed.) *Clive M.Schmitthoff's Select Essays on International Trade Law* (Dordrecht: Martinus Nijhoff)(1988).
[3] The expression Regional Integration Arrangement (RIA) is used in its widest sense in the context of this chapter to denote all regional efforts at liberalisation of cross–border trade in goods and services, ranging between free trade agreements, customs unions, political and economic union and federal bodies.
[4] Viner, J. *The Customs Union Issue* (Washington D.C.: Anderson Kramer Associates)(1961).
[5] Mohammed, N.A. & Treeck, D. "The Role of Regional Integration, Security and Development in Southern Africa" 8 *African Dev. Rev.* 1 (1996)

financial markets.[6] In this vein, RIAs are promoted by international organisations such as the Basle Committee, the G10 and the Bretton Woods institutions,[7] and existing successful RIAs are frequently promoted, and promote themselves, as models for less advanced integration efforts. Against the background of the desire to promote cross-border trade, in goods as well as in services, this paper aims to examine the extent to which successful integration efforts may be of use as models in other regions of the world. The focus is not primarily on substantial provisions (although some substantial provisions will be alluded to by way of example), but on the legislative process. RIAs are creatures of public international law. The creation of an RIA involves complex matters relating to treaty law, sovereignty, subsidiarity and matters of harmonisation and unification. Traditionally, however, the law of international trade involves matters of private international law; matters relating to the taking of security, guarantees, company law and issues of enforcement.

26–002   This chapter asks whether, in the search for inspiration[8] for regional integration efforts, the focus should be less on what has traditionally been termed the public international law aspects of RIAs, and more on regional efforts to promote the harmonisation of private law. In creating new RIAs, could regions do better than to import wholesale concepts, provisions and principles developed in entirely different environments? Would perhaps efforts to harmonise features of private law, such as matters relating to personal property law, serve the international trade community equally well?

26–003   The question may also be approached from a different angle: it is a phenomenon well recognised in recent academic comment that, increasingly, borders between private international law and public international law are being blurred. This may create an opportunity, in the creation of new RIAs, to focus less on rigid matters of treaty law and more on matters inspiring confidence in participants in international trade transactions, involving goods or services.

2. Regional integration arrangements and the promotion of cross-border trade

26–004   Regional integration arrangements[9] are increasingly common: in addition to high-profile and relatively successful RIAs such as the European Union,

---

[6] Fischer, S., Hernandez–Cata, E. and Khan, M. S. *Africa: Is This the Turning Point* (IMF: IMF Paper on Policy and Assessment)(1998)

[7] While the World Bank takes an active interest in and sponsors a number of RIAs, the GATT/WTO framework, in direct contrast to its most–favoured nation principle, contains provisions specifically providing for RIAs.

[8] The terms "model" and "model laws" have been the subject to much debate, not to be delved into in the current context. I have chosen, in order not to invoke any particular connotations, to employ the term "inspiration".

[9] In this paper, the term regional integration arrangement (RIA) is used in its widest sense. According to received economic wisdom economic relations between a group of countries within a region may be organised as follows: in a free trade area, goods and services circulate and are sold without the levying of tariffs or duties at national borders; in a customs union, Member States agree to maintain uniform tariffs and duties on external trade; a common market refers to the simultaneous existence of a customs union and a free trade area; an internal market permits free movement across borders of all factors of production, including workers and capital; in an economic union, Member States agree to maintain common economic and monetary policies. It should be noted that this is not necessarily a continuous process: many free trade areas never develop into common markets, nor, indeed, are they intended by their creators to do so.

NAFTA, Mercosur and Caricom, other groups of countries, too, are creating or re-creating regional integration arrangements.[10] Frequently, RIAs are seen as suitable tools for development: in theory, regional economic agreements enable a group of countries to reduce obstacles, including tariff and non-tariff barriers to trade, and to promote liberalisation of cross-border trade. In relation to efforts to create RIAs in Africa, for example, it has been claimed that, "The reduction or elimination of barriers to intra-African trade although in itself not sufficient, yet remains a necessary pre-condition for the accelerated economic development of African countries."[11] Faced with global liberalisation of markets and increased interdependence, developing countries are taking steps to make their economies more attractive to foreign investors. In this context, an important task facing the authorities in these countries is to reduce the perceived risk of policy reversals: membership of an RIA would be seen as a credible commitment to the policies embraced within the grouping and would, in theory, increase the cost of reneging on these commitments.[12] Recognising the importance of lowering trade barriers the World Bank is actively financing economic adjustment programmes to support tariff and tax reforms. In this context, intensive analytical work in a number of countries is focusing on trade expansion and the competitiveness of African countries in the global economy. This includes successful regional work such as the Cross-Border Initiative (CBI) and trade linkages in the Southern African Development Community and the Common Market for Eastern and Southern Africa (COMESA).[13]

Of course, a consequence of entering into an RIA through which a country grants more favourable conditions to its trade with other parties to that arrangement than to other WTO Members' trade, is breach of the guiding principles of non-discrimination and MFN treatment.[14] That creation of an RIA is seen as a beneficial development, however, is illustrated by the fact that WTO Member States are permitted to enter into RIAs under specific conditions set out within the WTO legal framework. Thus Art XXIV of GATT[15] provides for the formation and operation of customs unions and free trade areas and the so-called Enabling Clause[16] refers to preferential trade arrangements between developing country Members. GATS Article V,

26–005

---

[10] While it is difficult to find a reliable source for all RIAs currently in force, the number of RIAs notified by Member States of the WTO (previously GATT) is a good indicator: in the period 1948–1994, GATT contracting parties notified 118 RIAs relating to trade in goods, of which 38 in the five years ending in 1994. Since the creation of the WTO, 80 additional RIAs covering trade in goods and services have been notified. Of the total of 198 RIAs notified to the GATT/WTO, 119 are presently in force. A list of notified RIAs in force can be found on www.wto.org/wto/develop/webrtas.htm.

[11] Hazlewood, A. "Problems of Integration Among African States" Ch. 1 in Hazlewood, A. (ed.) *African Integration and Disintegration* (Oxford:OUP)(1967)

[12] Fischer, S., Hernandez–Cata, E. and Khan, M. S. *Africa: Is This the Turning Point* (IMF: IMF Paper on Policy and Assessment)(1998) p. 16.

[13] For an outline of the World Bank's activities in this field, see www.worldbank.org/afr/overview.htm

[14] GATT Art. I, GATS Art. II.

[15] See GATT Art. XXIV paras 4–10, as clarified in the Understanding on the Interpretation of Article XXIV of the GATT 1994.

[16] Decision on Differential and More Favourable Treatment, Reciprocity and Fuller Participation of Developing Countries 1979.

finally, governs the conclusion of RTAs in the area of trade in services. In addition, a Committee on Regional Trade Agreements (CRTA) has been established under the auspices of the WTO General Council.

26–006   It is clear, then, that in the area of promotion of international trade, RIAs are seen as desirable by international organisations and nation States alike. Many developing countries in particular are dependent on fiscal income generated for example by customs duties. Advocates of removal of tariff barriers, therefore, had to demonstrate that on the whole, the creation of an RIA would benefit the Member States, if not always equally. Early economic research indicated that "the benefit from a customs union to the customs union area as a whole derives from that portion of the new trade between the member countries which is wholly new trade (trade creation), whereas each particular portion of the new trade between member countries which is a substitute for trade with third countries (trade diversion). . .must be regarded as a consequence of the customs union which is injurious for the importing country, for the external world, and for the world as a whole, and is beneficial only to the supplying country."[17] While this theory has been the subject of much criticism,[18] in its modified form it still underlies much research in the area of RIAs. More recently, in relation to the potential of regional integration to promote economic growth, it has been argued that "countries with open, large and more developed neighbouring economies grow faster than those with closed, smaller and less developed neighbouring economies."[19] In other words, empirical evidence suggests that small economies should grow faster when they form regional trade agreements with large and more developed economies; however, testing for the impact of several RIAs in the 1970s and 1980s found that none led to faster growth. The main reason for this seemed to be that most of the agreements were between small, closed and developing economies.[20] On the whole, however, it remains the case that RIAs are created in the belief that this will lead to an increase in cross-border trade, a consequence of which will be growth of the GDP of Member States, in turn leading to an increase in welfare of the citizens of the Member States and, in the case of developing countries, a reduction of poverty.

3. Creating a supranational framework

26–007   From an analytical point of view, RIAs are creatures of public international law. The establishment of an RIA is by treaty; the institutional framework of the regional organisation is subject to the rules of public international law. It is clear that the formation of an organisation, by necessity encroaching on the sovereignty of prospective Member States, is a cumbersome process. Aside from negotiating economic terms such as reduction of tariffs and non-tariff barriers, a sustainable institutional framework must be created, the purpose of which is to ensure that the substantive provisions of the arrange-

---

[17] Viner, J. *The Customs Union Issue* (Washington D.C.: Anderson Kramer Associates)(1961).
[18] Notably by Lipsey, see Lipsey, R.G. *The Theory of Customs Unions: A General Equilibrium Analysis* (London: Wiedenfeld and Nicolson)(1970).
[19] Vamvakidis, A. "Regional Integration and Economic Growth" 12 *World Bank Econ. Rev.* 2 p. 251 (1998).
[20] *ibid.* p. 251.

ment are upheld. If the RIA is of the more advanced type, *i.e.* providing for a customs union or an internal market, for example, it will commonly entail the creation of institutions performing executive, administrative and judicial functions. In other words, a transnational constitution will be created.[21] The best-known example hereof is probably the European Union, with its Council, Commission, Parliament and Court of Justice.[22] RIAs are structured to provide for a trade-off: loss of sovereignty[23] is compensated by the economic benefits enjoyed by the Member States of the organisation; the RIA, however, may also be seen as a pooling of sovereignty, enabling Members jointly to address matters of common concern. Voting arrangements must satisfy all Member States and must define matters which will be subject to majority decision as well as matters where decisions require unanimity. In addition, many RIAs provide for some type of vote-weighting; this is seen as necessary in organisations the membership of which includes countries with wide differences in (for example) size of population and macroeconomic fundamentals such as GDP.[24] No doubt, drafting of provisions defining voting and vote-weighting are of great importance but they are no substitute for political will. Thus, on the two occasions within the EU when matters of the legal powers of Member States and voting requirements have been at issue, political compromises have enabled the Member States to move forward and integration to continue, despite lack of commitment by one or several Member States.[25]

Matters of a public international law character to be addressed within an **26–008** RIA further include law-making processes and the capacity of legal provisions adopted at a supranational level to bind individual nationals of the Member States. Here, issues such as direct effect and positive and negative harmonisation must be resolved.[26] Achieving a process of continuing integration is a feat often, within the EU, attributed to the "judicial activism" of the European Court of Justice. With its remarkable judgments, it is often claimed, the Court of Justice paved the way for developments relating to the capacity of supranational law to impose binding obligations on individuals as well as matters relating to the removal of tariff and non-tariff barriers to trade in goods and services.[27]

---

[21] One of the classical texts on these matters is Stein, E. "Lawyers, Judges and the Making of a Transnational Constitution" 75 *Am.J.Int'l L.* 1 (1981)

[22] There is vast academic literature commenting on different aspects of the institutional framework of the EU and the purpose of this paper is not to discuss these matters. It should be noted that, in the context of the EU, the division of functions between the different institutions is not organised according to the traditional functions of a municipal government: each of the institutions could be said to perform different aspects of these functions.

[23] On matters of sovereignty see for example Attanasio, J.B. "Rapporteur's Overview and Conclusions: Of Sovereignty, Globalization and Courts" 28:1 *N.Y.U.J. Int'l L. & Pol.* 1 (1995–96), or Grigera Naon, H.A. "sovereignty and Regionalism" 27 Law & Pol'y Int'l Bus. 1073 (1996)

[24] For vote weighting in the Council of the European Union, see Art.205 EC.

[25] The Luxembourg Accords and the Ioannina compromise, respectively.

[26] See Stein *supra.* n. 20 at p. 3. For a more recent discussion, see Cottier, T. & Nadakavukaren Schefer, K. "The Relationship Between World Trade Organization Law, National and Regional Law" 1 J. Int'l Econ. L. 83 (1998).

[27] While integration initially proceeded at a sluggish pace, legal provisions relating to a number of diverse areas of the internal market, were adopted as a result of the "New Approach" designed in the mid–1980s, providing for minimum requirements and mutual recognition in a number of areas of integration..

26–009   On the whole, the development of EU law and the creation of a supranational constitution has been a success and aspects of EU law and integration are often promoted as models for RIA efforts in other parts of the world.

4. The arrival of international business law

26–010   It is suggested that, while the creation of the EU must be regarded as a success this is largely due to factors unique to Europe and which cannot be found anywhere else. Thus, macroeconomic conditions, for example, are relatively similar in the Member States as a result of strong political commitment to integration, the process has moved forward despite occasional differences between Member States. Bearing in mind the underlying economic rationale underlying the creation of an RIA—promotion of liberalisation of cross–border trade—this section asks whether, rather than relying on the EU as a model for the public international law aspects of the arrangement, focusing on what may be termed private law aspects of the arrangement would serve the purpose of facilitating cross–border trade within a regional grouping. It is readily recognised that public international law and private international law[28] are both necessary features of a successful RIA. The suggestion, however, is to encourage prospective members of an RIA to examine the extent to which key features of what may be termed "international business law" may be harmonised. In other words, the focus should move away from the creation of a grand institutional design[29] to an examination of which features of private international law could usefully be harmonised.

26–011   In discussing the "The Meaning of International Business Law" Schmitthoff defines international economic law as the branch of public international law concerned with multilateral conventions such as the GATT, bilateral treaties between States, and the treatment of international economic organisations constituted by sovereign States such as the IMF and the World Bank. International business law deals with the legal organisation of business transacted on the level of private law. International business law has two main branches: the law of international trade, in particular the sale of goods abroad, and the law of international companies. International business law and international economic law overlap in two respects:

> "first, arrangements creating regional trade groups and double taxation agreements pertain, strictly speaking, to international economic law, but, to the considerable extent to which they affect the individual importer and exporter, they also form part of international business law. The planning of an international business transaction would be

---

[28] Of course, boundaries between the two disciplines are increasingly blurred, see Steinhardt, R.G. "The Privatization of Public International Law" 25 *Geo. Wash.J.Int'l L. & Econ.* 523 (1991) and Spanogle, Jr, J.A. "The Arrival of International Private Law" 25 *Geo. Wash.J.Int'l L. & Econ.* 477 (1991)

[29] Reasons for failures (or lack of success) of RIAs are frequently sought in the design of the institutional structure: see Kiplagat, P.K. "Jurisdictional Uncertainties and Integration Processes in Africa: The Need for Harmony" 4 *Tul.J.Int'l & Comp.L.* 43 (1995), Hazlewood, A. "The End of the East African Community: What Are the Lessons for Regional Integration Schemes?" 18 *J. Common Market Stud.* 40 (1979)

incomplete if the tariff requirements and the incidence of taxation in the country to which the transaction extends were disregarded." [30]

It seems to me, in promoting the public international branch of successful RIAs as models for other regions, the importance of international business law, as defined by Professor Schmitthoff, is sometimes overlooked.   **26–012**

In discussing the problem of the "decreasing utility of the ancient and hallowed distinction between "public international law" and "private international law", several commentators agree that the distinction is obsolete as an analytical tool and that lawyers in either field ignoring the developments in the other, do so at their peril.[31] The term "private international law" traditionally used in civil law countries to describe conflicts of law issues is not sufficient to describe the variety of substantive international treaties, model laws, uniform rules, principles, legal guides and harmonisation efforts within RIAs. To distinguish and describe these efforts, the term "international private law" has been proposed.[32] This paper suggests that the development of "international private law" should be given added emphasis in the creation of new RIAs, not least in arrangements between developing countries. Several ways to achieve international private law harmonisation may be identified.[33]   **26–013**

First, a uniform substantial law for a particular subject matter may be adopted, along the lines of the work of, for example, UNCITRAL[34] or UNIDROIT. Provisions of these laws may be designed to apply either to domestic or international transactions, or both. Secondly, States may adopt choice of law rules, assuring parties to a transaction that one national domestic law will govern regardless of the location of the forum where a dispute is heard. Examples of uniform choice of law include the work done by the Hague Conference on Private International Law,[35] such as the Convention on the Law Applicable to Trusts and on Their Recognition.[36] Thirdly, a quite different strand of international private law is what has been termed *lex mercatoria*. Proponents of the *lex mercatoria* argue that there is a body of supranational legal principles and rules that govern international contracts.[37] *Lex mercatoria* has two principal sources, the work of scholars in the field and accredited representatives of sovereign States. A fourth possible source of harmonisation in international trade transactions is the use of standard contracts and general conditions. Active traders in many areas of international business have developed standard forms, contracts and principles to   **26–014**

---

[30] Schmitthoff *op. cit.* n. 1 at p. 20.
[31] For a summary of this discussion, see Spanogle, Jr, J.A. "The Arrival of International Private Law" 25 *Geo.Wash.J.Int'l L. & Econ.* 477 (1991)
[32] *ibid.* p. 477.
[33] I have borrowed this categorisation from Spanogle, *ibid.* p. 490.
[34] See. www.uncitral.org.
[35] See http://www.hcch.net
[36] 23 ILM 1388 (1984). While this convention has only few signatories, it is of great importance in several civil law States where the concept of trust is only recognised in limited situations. The structuring of asset securitisation in Italy, for example, is facilitated by the fact that Italy is one of the signatories to the Convention.
[37] Schmitthoff, C.M "The Codification of the Law of International Trade" *J.Bus.L.* 34 (1985) Reprinted in Cheng, C-J (ed.) *Clive M.Schmitthoff's Select Essays on International Trade Law* (Dordrecht: Martinus Nijhoff)(1988).

govern transactions in that area of business. In the area of financial services, for example, traders in OTC swaps and derivatives rely extensively on the ISDA[38] model agreements, and issuers of international bonds frequently use principles and clauses developed by the IPMA.[39] Here, the interplay between traders, international regulators, supranational bodies and national legislature is interesting to note in passing.[40] Of paramount importance, of course, in the area of trade in goods is the Uniform Customs and Practice for Documentary Credits.[41]

5. Creating international private law at regional level

26–015   RIAs, too, are developing international private law provisions. Within the EU, the process is long–standing, resulting so far in substantial rules relating to *inter alia* company law, banking, investment services and insurance.

26–016   The efforts to harmonise substantial rules[42] within the EU, and to create international (regional) private international law, are particularly interesting, and potentially offer valuable lessons for other countries endeavouring to promote cross-border trade.

26–017   Members of the EU include common law as well as civil law countries and as a result, approaches to matters of personal property and equity, for example, differ fundamentally between the Member States. Moreover, efforts to develop a common contract law have long been hampered by the lack of mandate within the European Treaties for the creation of a European private law "as a whole".[43]

26–018   Harmonisation has, nevertheless, proceeded in narrow fields. One of the more interesting recent developments is the adoption of the so-called Finality Directive[44] which, in Article 9(2) provides for a clarification of the application of established conflicts of law rules when securities are taken as collateral. The provision is an eminent example of harmonisation of choice of law rules as a feature of the creation of international private law. Embodying the response of the European Community to a long-standing discussion on the issue of the applicable law,[45] in England triggered partly by the Macmillan case,[46] the provision aims to eliminate certain aspects of legal risk

---

[38] International Swaps and Derivatives Association.

[39] International Primary Markets Association.

[40] In particular the influence of soft law principles developed by the Basle Committee and adopted in an European Community directive on drafting within the framework for the ISDA Master Agreement is interesting.

[41] For an account of the implementation experience of the UCP 500 within an RIA, see Kozolchyk, B. "The "Best Practices" Approach to the Uniformity of International Commercial Law: the UCP 500 and the NAFTA Implementation Experience" in Cranston, R. (ed.) *Making Commercial Law* (Oxford: Clarendon Press, 1997).

[42] For a critical discussion on harmonisation of laws relating to personal property security, and on the concept of harmonisation, see, Boodman, M. "The Myth of Harmonization of Laws" 39 *Am.J.Comp.L.* 699 (1991)

[43] Basedow, J. "A Common Contract Law for the Common Market" 33 *Common Mkt.L.Rev.* 1169 (1996) p. 1173 (citing Martin Bangemann).

[44] Directive 98/26/EC on settlement finality in payment and securities settlement systems [1998 O.J.] L166, 1166/45.

[45] See for example Goode, R. "The Nature and Transfer of Rights in Dematerialised and Immobilised Securities" *Butterworths J.Int'l Banking & Fin.* 167 (1996).

[46] *Macmillan Inc v Bishopsgate Investment Trust plc* (No. 3) [1995] 3 All E.R. 747.

for certain collateral takers. The provision goes to the very heart of aspects of personal property law and choice of law rules and, while the opinions of Member States relating to the design of the directive were mixed, it constitutes a significant step forward.[47]

The broader agenda, the aim to create a common civil code for the common market, is also gaining momentum. Although, as noted from the outset, views on this concept are mixed, there are significant ongoing efforts in this area, covering *inter alia* tort law, securities and different aspects of contract law.   **26–019**

In the context of other regions, too, the promotion of international business law is proceeding. In relation to Latin America, for example, it has been observed that: **26–020**

> "Although trade among Latin American countries will not necessarily be promoted by unifying their laws, it is plausible that trade with Latin America will be fostered if countries of the region were to join global unification efforts in which Latin Americans are given the chance to express their views. After all, in a region actively seeking capital investments, unification forces are likely to succeed once they can demonstrate the practical need, or at least a significant convenience, of making their legal systems more coherent and comprehensible. . ."[48]

6. Conclusion

This paper argues that, while the public international law provisions establishing regional economic arrangements may be useful as inspiration for countries of other regions contemplating creation, or re-creation, of RIAs, they should not be adopted wholesale. Moreover, countries aiming to promote trade at a regional level should be encouraged to look further for inspiration, and should consider investigating the extent to which harmonisation and unification of laws relating to trade transactions, the creation of international business law, would be of use. A complementary approach, embracing efforts to harmonise laws within the RIA, as well as participation in international treaties and conventions, would be preferable.   **26–021**

It is not argued that relying on existing RIAs for inspiration and, to a limited extent, as models, is worthless; on the contrary, the experience gained within these bodies provides valuable lessons. The international business law aspect, however, should not be forgotten, and it should be remembered that, while there powerful economic arguments in favour of the creation of RIAs, economists also argue in favour of harmonisation of, for example, property laws. [49]   **26–022**

---

[47] Potok, R. "The Problem of Providing Securities as Collateral" 18 *Int'l Fin. L. Rev.* (December) 12 (1999).
[48] Garro, A.M. "Unification and Harmonization of Private Law in Latin America" 40 *Am. J. Comp. L.* 587 (1992) at 616.
[49] Ajani, G. and Mattei, U. "Codifying Property Law in the Process of Transition: Some Suggestions from Comparative Law and Economics" 19 *Hastings Int'l & Comp. L. Rev.* 117 (1995).

CHAPTER 27

CROSS-BORDER TRADE IN FINANCIAL SERVICES

DR. ROSA MARIA LASTRA[1]

1. Introduction

27–001 Trade in services, financial and others, was included for the first time in the Uruguay Round of trade negotiations in 1986. The General Agreement on Trade in Services (GATS) is the first multilateral agreement to provide legally enforceable rights to trade in all services. It has a built-in commitment to continuous liberalisation through periodic negotiations. The inclusion of services in the trade negotiations was a logical consequence of the increasing importance of the "service economy." Countries that have lost their comparative advantage in the production of some goods now believe their comparative advantage lies in trading certain services. However, the liberalisation of trade in services is not an easy task. To begin, the heterogeneity of services and their regulation is a problem. Furthermore, as David Leebron interestingly points out (in an unpublished manuscript on "Trade in Services"):

> "Trade in services is in a sense, the intersection of the three basic economic relations between states: trade, investment and the movement of persons. The formulation of a legal framework for trade in services is difficult in part because each of these areas has been the subject of fundamentally different norms and regimes. In trade, the basic norm is most-favored-nation treatment, and the regime is multilateral. In investment, the basic norm is reciprocity, and the regime is bilateral. And in immigration, the regime is unilateralism, and the only norm that can be said to exist (apart from the treatment of political refugees) is the sovereign right to exclude all foreigners. Countries that express a willingness to negotiate trade in services often do not have in mind any change in the regime applicable to these other aspects of economic relations."

---

[1] Senior Lecturer in International Financial and Monetary Law, Centre for Commercial Law Studies, Queen Mary and Westfield College, University of London. E-mail: R.Lastra@qmw.ac.uk.

The paper is divided into three sections. Section 1 deals with the history of **27–002** financial services trade negotiations since the Uruguay Round. Section 2 surveys the multilateral legal framework applicable to financial services under the GATS. Section 3 analyses whether trade liberalisation and prudential supervision are "companions or antagonists," *i.e.* whether their goals are complementary or conflicting and, in the case of potential conflict, it considers how such goals can be reconciled. The paper finishes with some concluding remarks.

2. History of financial services trade negotiations[2]

Financial services have proven to be a particularly difficult sector to negoti- **27–003** ate. Initial—and rather modest—commitments on financial services trade liberalisation were made by 82 countries at the end of the Uruguay Round in 1993, though the strength of such commitments varied substantially among countries.

Negotiations on financial services were re-initiated in 1995; however, the **27–004** U.S. withdrawal from the agreement in June 1995 left the European Union with the task of trying to rescue an accord.[3] An interim agreement—which expired at the end of 1997— was signed by more than 90 countries, which agreed to open their banking, securities and insurance markets to each other on the basis of most-favored nation (MFN) treatment. The commitments made in July 1995 by 95 WTO Members entered into force on September 1, 1996, with the agreement that they would only continue to apply if they were not modified or withdrawn by a deadline established at December 12, 1997.

In April 1997, negotiations on financial services were re-launched and were **27–005** successfully concluded by the established deadline of December 12, 1997. On December 13, 1997, all major trading members—including the USA— agreed to include financial services on a permanent and MFN (most-favoured nation) basis in the GATS. Under this agreement—referred to as the Financial Services Agreement (FSA)—70 WTO Members improved their commitments on market access and national treatment and 32 others maintained their existing schedules dating from the Uruguay Round or from the 1995 interim agreement.[4] The basic element of the legal framework of the

---

[2] See http://gats.info.eu.int (A Guide to the GATS—Service Sectors—Financial Services) and http://www.wto.org (press releases of December 12, 1997 and February 15, 1999).
[3] The U.S. withdrew from the accord because it was unwilling to allow emerging economies to become "free riders," *i.e.*, to enjoy the benefits from free trade in financial services without opening their own markets. See Sydney Key, "Financial Services in the Uruguay Round" in H. Scott and P. Wellons, *International Finance: Transactions, Policy and Regulation*, 3rd ed., University Casebook Series, The Foundation Press, 1996, pp. 178–181. See also Sydney Key, "Financial Services in the Uruguay Round and the WTO," Occasional Paper No. 54, Group of Thirty, Washington D.C., 1997.
[4] This was hailed as an important progress, not only in substance, but also as regards the total number of countries which undertook commitments in financial services: 102 in comparison to 95 under the 1995 interim agreement. Governments agreed: (1) to apply full "*most-favoured nation*" treatment to all financial services activity, preventing a government from discriminating between financial service suppliers based on their different foreign origins; (2) to grant *market access*, subject to limitations, in a negotiated range of financial services activities, preventing a government from applying quantitative restrictions on financial services or service suppliers; (a government could not, for example, set a maximum limit on the number of banks permitted to

deal reached in December 1997 is the *Fifth Protocol to the GATS*,[5] which was open for ratification and acceptance by WTO members until 29 January 1999[6] and which entered into force on March 1, 1999.

27–006   In late 1999, the Third Ministerial WTO Conference in Seattle should have covered all service sectors, including financial services. But the talks were "suspended" because of the failure of trade negotiators to reach agreement. However, trade liberalisation in financial services can still proceed through the route of the "in-built agenda"[7] provided by Article XIX of the GATS, which requires negotiations in all service sectors, including financial services, to begin again by the year 2000.[8]

3. Liberalisation of trade in financial services under the GATS

27–007   The General Agreement on Trade in Services, which is part of the Agreement establishing the World Trade Organisation, has three major components: a framework agreement, various annexes (one of them dealing with financial services) and schedules for each country of specific commitments and lists of MFN exemptions. In addition, for financial services, there is unique additional element, the "Understanding on Commitments in Financial Services," which provides for a higher level of minimum obligations than that provided for in the basic GATS provisions, and which has been used by most OECD countries.

27–008   The GATS recognizes—in its Article I—four "modes of supply" of services:

(a)   *Cross-border supply* or cross border provision of services. This is the supply of a service from the territory of one Member to a consumer/ user in the territory of another Member (regardless of whether such a financial service supplier has or has not a commercial presence in the territory of the Member in which the financial service is supplied).

---

operate in its market); (3) to grant *national treatment*, subject to limitations, in a negotiated range of financial services activities, thus preventing a government from discriminating between domestic and foreign financial services and service suppliers; (a government could not, *e.g.*, require that a certain proportion of board members be its own nationals). See *Clifford Chance Newsletter* (European Financial Markets), February 1998.

[5] The Fifth Protocol to the GATS provides for the replacement of the existing financial services sections of the Schedules of Specific Commitments and the Lists of MFN exemptions of the Members concerned by the corresponding lists annexed to the Protocol. This means that the agreement docs not constitute a separate agreement under the GATS, but simply that the new schedules and MFN exemptions lists will be an integral part of the corresponding Member's schedules once the results of the negotiations enter into force. The text of the Fifth Protocol can be downloaded from http://gats.info.eu.int (Legal texts and Commitments—The Related Instruments and Protocols).

[6] 52 WTO members accepted the Protocol by the due date. The Council for Trade in Services decided that the Protocol would be kept open for acceptance for the remaining 18 members until June 15, 1999. For those Members accepting after March 1, 1999, it was decided that the [Fifth] protocol would enter into force upon acceptance.

[7] By "in-built agenda" I refer to treaty clauses in the WTO agreement, which call for negotiations with an indicated deadline.

[8] Article XIX (1) of GATS reads as follows: "In pursuance of the objectives of this Agreement, Members shall enter into successive rounds of negotiations, beginning not later than five years from the date of entry into force of the WTO Agreement and periodically thereafter, with a view to achieving a progressively higher level of liberalisation. (. . .)." On May 22, 2000, the *Financial Times* reported that the services council of the WTO was to meet in Geneva on May 26, 2000 to take stock of negotiations to improve WTO rules governing trade in services.

(b)   *Consumption abroad*, which for financial services is often difficult to distinguish from the cross-border provision of services.

(c)   *Commercial presence*, means the establishment of a legal entity (foreign direct investment) for the supply of financial services and it includes wholly or partly-owned subsidiaries, joint ventures, partnerships, franchising operations, branches, agencies, representative offices or other organisations.

(d)   *Presence of natural persons*. With respect to financial services, this mode of supply refers to the temporary presence of natural persons including, for example, the non-local staff of a branch of a foreign bank.

With regard to the terminology adopted by the GATS in relation to "modes of supply," it is interesting to point out that in the European Union context, the EC Directives dealing with the cross border provision of financial services have focused on the establishment of branches (legally dependent entities) and subsidiaries (legally independent entities).[9] The so-called single banking licence applies to cross-border expansion through branches for EC credit institutions; subsidiaries are subject to a prior consultative procedure. Branches of non-EC credit institutions require an authorisation procedure, while subsidiaries are subject to a reciprocity clause.[10] The Basle Committee on Banking Supervision's initiatives on cross-border establishments focus on branches, subsidiaries and joint ventures.[11]   **27–009**

During the Uruguay Round, participants agreed to list the following activities as "financial services" under the GATS:[12]   **27–010**

•   Banking and other financial services, including: acceptance of deposits; lending of all types including consumer credit, mortgage credit, factoring and financing of commercial transactions; financial leasing; all payment and money transmission services; guarantees and commitments; trading in money market instruments, foreign exchange, derivatives, exchange rate and interest rate instruments such as swaps and forward rate agreements, securities, other negotiable instruments and other assets, such as gold; participation in issues of new securities; money broking; asset management such as portfolio management or pension fund management; settlement and clearing services for financial assets; provision and transfer of financial information and financial data processing; advisory and other auxiliary financial services.

---

[9] Of course, EC credit institutions can also consider other methods of cross-border expansion such as mergers and acquisitions, or the cross-border provision of services without a physical establishment.
[10] See, *e.g.*, Rosa M. Lastra (1996), *Central Banking and Banking Regulation,* Financial Markets Group, London School of Economics, pp. 225–230.
[11] *ibid.* at pp. 175–184.
[12] This itemised list of financial services is included in the Annex on Financial Services annexed to the GATS, para. 5.

- Insurance and other related life and non-life insurance services; reinsurance and retrocession; insurance intermediation, such as broking and agency services; services auxiliary to insurance.

27–011   The GATS Annex on Financial Services also provides—in its paragraph 1(b)—a list of "excluded activities," *i.e.*, of activities excluded from the coverage of the GATS:

- Activities conducted by a central bank or monetary authority of by any other public entity in pursuit of monetary and exchange rate policies;

- Activities, forming part of a statutory system of social security or public retirement plans; and

- Other activities conducted by a public entity for the account or with the guarantee or using the financial resources of the Government.

4. Trade liberalisation and prudential supervision—companions or antagonists?

27–012   Trade negotiations in financial services (under the umbrella of the General Agreement on Trade in Services, GATS) have typically focused on competitive issues, rather than on supervisory issues. Supervisory issues have been discussed internationally in fora such as the Basle Committee on Banking Supervision, the International Organisation of Securities Commissions and others. In the ensuing paragraphs, I will discuss briefly the goals of prudential supervision and of trade liberalisation, their complementary or conflicting character and, in the case of potential conflict, how to reconcile them. Where appropriate I will be referring to the experience of the European Union, as an interesting regional (supranational) case where liberalisation in financial services cohabits with harmonisation of prudential supervisory standards in the creation of an internal market in financial services. The EU example also helps illustrate the shift of emphasis from trade in goods to trade in services that has taken place over the last two decades in the developed world.

4.1 The goals of prudential supervision and the goals of trade liberalisation

27–013   Prudential supervision aims to safeguard the stability and soundness of the financial system, to protect individual depositors, investors or policyholders, to prevent fraud and to promote competitive equality among international financial institutions. The ultimate goal of prudential supervision is the protection of *confidence* in the financial system.

27–014   Trade liberalisation aims to promote free trade by reducing (or eliminating) tariffs and other barriers to trade and by eliminating discriminatory treatment in international commerce, facilitating the cross-border movement of goods and services.[13] The freedom of entry into a market, the freedom to

---

[13] The benefits of free trade rest upon the principle of the theory of comparative advantage, first formulated by David Ricardo. Under the theory of comparative advantage, unilateral liberalisation would be most advantageous for countries; *i.e.*, a country would profit most by pursuing a

compete and the freedom to exit a market, without government interference, discrimination, distortions or other barriers, are key elements of free trade. The opposite of free trade is protectionism.

4.2 Conflicting or complementary character of the goals of prudential supervision and trade liberalisation

The banking industry has typically been highly regulated and "protected" by   **27–015**
the Government. "Protectionism" in banking is much more subtle than in other industries; a number of policy justifications can often be put forward to shield the hidden protectionism of some particular regulatory outcome. Some supervisory policies and techniques as well as some financial regulations imply restrictions or limits on competition, which are justified on the basis of "safety and soundness" or on the grounds of depositor protection or other "consumer protection" considerations. This is, for instance, the rationale underlying the historical separation (in the U.S.) between commercial and investment banks and the subsequent restrictions in their permissible activities; the lending limits that restrict the freedom of banks in their risk-taking policies; deposit insurance premiums imposed onto banks, and others. Other restrictions, such as reserve requirements, cannot be justified on *prudential grounds* but rather on *monetary considerations* (though many bankers argue that reserve requirements are an implicit tax on the banking system). Furthermore, restrictions can also be justified invoking some kind of *"public good" consideration*.[14] Indeed, many banking prudential supervisory and regulatory standards can in a way be considered as "anti-competitive," and "discriminatory." Interestingly, such discrimination works some times in favour, some times against banks. It works in favour of banks in the case of bank crises, when the lender of last resort or the deposit insurance fund or the government directly or indirectly "protects" these institutions and bails them out (*i.e.* preferential treatment against institutions which do not enjoy this type of government assistance). It works against banks when the restrictions on activities place a "regulatory burden" upon banks *vis-à-vis* other institutions providing similar products or services but subject to lesser regulation and also to lesser protection.

The GATS acknowledges the possibility of conflicting goals in its "Annex   **27–016**
on Financial Services." This Annex includes the so-called *"prudential*

---

free trade policy whether its trading partners were free-traders or protectionists. (See J. Bhagwati (1989), *Protectionism,* MIT Press, Cambridge, MA, at p. 24). However, trade negotiations—including the GATT—generally approach trade on the basis of reciprocity; one side grants market access to its markets in exchange for access to other markets.

[14] In the EC, according to Art. 56 of the Treaty of Rome, restrictions on the freedom to provide services may be justified on the grounds of public policy, public security or public health. The Court of Justice ruled in Case C–76/90 *Säger v. Dennemeyer* [1991]; [1993] 3 C.M.L.R. I–4221639, that the freedom to provide services may be limited only by provisions which are justified by imperative reasons relating to the public interest and which apply to all persons or undertakings pursuing an activity in the host state. The following criteria were laid down for determining whether a measure can be relied upon against a service provider: the measure must be in the interest of the general good, be non-discriminatory, be objectively necessary; and be proportionate to the objective pursued. The restriction must also come within a field which has not yet been harmonised.

carve-out," in paragraph 2(a), whereby a country may take prudential measures to ensure the integrity and stability of the financial system or to protect depositors, investors or policy-holders regardless of any other provision of the GATS. paragraph 2(a) states:

> "Notwithstanding any other provision of the Agreement, a Member shall not be prevented from taking measures for prudential reasons, including for the protection of depositors, investors, policy holders or persons to whom a fiduciary duty is owed by a financial service supplier, or to ensure the integrity and stability of the financial system. Where such measures do not conform with the provisions of the Agreement, they shall not be used as a means of avoiding the Member's commitments or obligations under the Agreement."

27–017 This specific exception for prudential regulation and supervision was introduced at the insistence of financial regulators, which were concerned that a trade agreement (liberalising financial services) could interfere with their ability to regulate and supervise financial institutions. One significant implication of this broadly formulated "prudential carve-out" is that priority is given to the goals of financial regulation over the demands of competition and financial liberalisation.

27–018 At the EC level, the possibility of conflicts is also acknowledged. In the *Züchner case*[15] the Luxembourg Court of Justice recognised that the banking sector could be exempted from the competition rules to the extent that any anti-competitive conduct by banks was imposed by the monetary authorities.

27–019 A relatively recent example of the tensions between supervisory and competitive concerns is provided by the 1994 Directive on Deposit Guarantee Schemes,[16] which was deemed by the Commission to be an essential element of a properly functioning internal market in financial services (in the aftermath of the BCCI affair). Germany, which enjoys a generous deposit protection scheme, challenged this Directive in the Luxembourg Court of Justice arguing, *inter alia,* that the Directive contravened the freedom to provide services (Article 47.2 [ex. *Art* 57.2] of the Treaty of Rome).[17] In particular, Germany opposed the compulsory participation in the deposit guarantee schemes of all authorised credit institutions, the so-called host country "topping-up" clause (article 4.2 of the Directive)[18] and the "no export" clause (Article 4.1 of the Directive).[19] However, the Court of Justice reached a decision on May 13, 1997, rejecting the German claims on all grounds. The Court concluded that the Directive contributed to the abolition of obstacles to the free flow of services, as a condition for the

---

[15] Case 172/80 *Züchner v. Bayerische Vereinsbank* [1981]; C.M.L.R. 2021313.
[16] Directive 94/19/EC of May 30, 1994, O.J. L135, p. 5.
[17] Case C-233/94 *Germany v European Parliament and Council* [1997] ECR. I–2405.
[18] The "topping-up" clause allows branches to join the deposit protection scheme of the host state if the latter provides more generous coverage than the home state scheme.
[19] The "no-export" clause prevented the home state from providing—until December 31, 1999—more generous coverage than that provided by the host state. In a report on the operation of this clause in December 1999, the Commission indicated that it would not be proposing its extension beyond this date: Report from the Commission to the Council and the European Parliament on the application of the export prohibition clause, Art. 4(1) of the Directive on deposit-guarantee schemes (94/19/EC) COM(99)/722 final.

completion of the single market in the area. Nonetheless, the line between what should be harmonised—as an essential element of an internal market in financial services—and what should be left to the freedom of the Member States is a dynamic line; what is considered to be essential may change over time.

4.3 How to reconcile conflicting goals?

(1) Potential conflicts can be prevented through enhanced *harmonisation of prudential rules*, which set a prudential minimum common denominator for international banks, helping to create a "level playing field" and allowing for natural comparative advantage to be established. These rules should be shaped or reformed so as to facilitate trade, to promote competition and to channel rather than stifle innovation. The GATS Annex on financial services contains a clause (paragraph 3) which explicitly authorises members to recognise the prudential standards (achieved through harmonisation or otherwise) applied by other Members, thereby facilitating access to each others" markets for service suppliers originating in any of them.

27–020

In the EC the driving force for the creation of a single market in financial services has been the principle of mutual recognition on the basis of prior minimum harmonisation. Mutual recognition presupposes the equivalence of the objectives of national legislation and the existence of similar public-interest goals, although such goals can be reached by different means. Likewise, at an international level, the rules to be agreed upon by national regulators should be preceded by an agreement in regard to the goals to be pursued, which in turn will generate mutual trust.

27–021

(2) Greater *transparency* is also needed to help prevent the occurrence of conflicts. Transparency is indeed an essential pillar of a market economy, and one which is recognised as a "general obligation" for Members in Article III of the GATS. However, secrecy and confidentiality provisions in banking often hinder the pursuit of transparency. Paragraph 2(b) of the GATS "Annex on Financial Services" permits the non-disclosure of information:

27–022

> "Nothing in this Agreement shall be construed to require a member to disclose information relating to the affairs and accounts of individual customers or any confidential or proprietary information in the possession of public entities."

Thus, according to this paragraph 2(b), secrecy laws and confidentiality provisions prevail over GATS requirements.

27–023

(3) Rule harmonisation can help prevent conflicts, but *per se* cannot bring a solution to a conflict. Therefore, *dispute resolution* is also needed. The GATS Annex on Financial Services states in its paragraph 4 that:

> "Panels for disputes on prudential issues and other financial matters shall have the necessary expertise relevant to the specific financial service under dispute."

Prudential supervision and regulation need to be shaped or reformed to facilitate trade in financial services, to promote fair competition and to channel

27–024

rather than stifle innovation. Rules, however, will always be needed. Nobel laureate Ronald Coase convincingly argued that private, competitive markets depend on a comprehensive legal structure:[20]

> "All exchanges regulate in great detail the activities of those who trade in these markets (. . .) and they all provide machinery for the settlement of disputes and impose sanctions against those who infringe the rules of the exchange. It is not without significance that these exchanges often used by economists as examples of a perfect competition, are markets in which transactions are highly regulated (and this quite apart from any government regulation that there may be). It suggests, I think correctly, that for anything approaching perfect competition to exist, an intricate system of rules and regulations would be normally needed. Economists observing the regulations of the exchange often assume that they represent an attempt to exercise monopoly power and to aim to restrain competition. They ignore, or at any rate, fail to emphasise an alternative explanation for these regulations: that they exist in order to reduce transaction costs and therefore to increase the volume of trade.
>
> It is evident that, for their operation, markets such as those that exist today require more than the provision of physical facilities in which buying and selling can take place. They also require the establishment of legal rules governing the rights and duties of those carrying out transactions in those facilities. Such legal rules may be made by those who organise the markets, as is the case with most commodity exchanges. The main problem faced by the exchanges in this law making are the securing of the agreement of the members of the exchange and the enforcement of its rules . . .When the physical facilities are scattered and owned by a vast number of people with very different interests, as is the case with retailing and wholesaling, the establishment and administration of a private legal system would be very difficult. Those operating in these markets have to depend, therefore, on the legal system of the State."

27–025   Interestingly, prudential supervision is shifting from a lending-based system characterised by mandatory rules and government intervention to a trading-based system, which relies upon voluntary restrictions, fiduciary rules, disclosure requirements and other market mechanisms. This change should help reconcile the goals of liberalisation with those of prudential supervision and regulation of financial institutions.[20]

5. Concluding remarks

27–026   The inclusion of services in the trade negotiations during the Uruguay Round is a logical consequence of the increasing importance of the "service economy," particularly in developed countries. Financial services have proven to be a particularly difficult sector to negotiate. An agreement reached in 1997 has been hailed as a milestone by trade negotiators in this area. However, major challenges remain ahead. This paper has focused on the need to reconcile the demands of liberalisation and competition with those of financial supervision and regulation. Though the goals are often conflicting, as the GATS Annex on Financial Services recognises in its controversial "prudential carve-out," it is possible to envisage mechanism and techniques to reconcile such goals, in particular through rule harmonisation, greater transparency and dispute resolution. It is important that trade negotiators in financial services address supervisory and regulatory issues in a multilateral context so as to ensure that financial services users and providers fully benefit from trade liberalisation in this sector.

---

[20] See Ronald Coase (1988), *The Firm, the Market and the Law*, Chicago, University of Chicago Press, pp. 9–10.
[21] See Rosa M. Lastra, *supra* n. 4, at pp. 160–161.

CHAPTER 28

PAYMENT SYSTEMS IN THE 21ST CENTURY

ROBERT C. EFFROS[1]

Traditional analysis of the history of payment systems usually begins   **28–001**
with a narrative of how societies progress from barter of tangible goods
and services to payment with precious metals, the ensuing standardisation
of these into coins of the realm, the invention of paper currency, and
then development of paper non-cash items such as cheques and paper
based giros, through the use of payment cards and the electronic transfer
of funds and finally the introduction of electronic money. While some
might think that the 21st century is likely to be characterised by an
inevitable advance to widespread use of electronic money with a proportionate decrease in the use of the older means of payment, such a scenario does not seem to accord with the latest trends. In fact, the
established means of payment are likely to be with us for the immediately
foreseeable future and probably beyond. In what follows, we will (1)
review the traditional means of payment, (2) consider how the use of
these means varies among countries, (3) explore the newer developments
and finally (4) attempt a forecast.

1. Traditional payment systems

Cash comprises coins and currency notes. It may be viewed as the basic form   **28–002**
of payment. As such, it is commonly assured of this status by a legal tender
law. In accordance with such a law, a person may use cash to settle his tax and
other public obligations. Furthermore, in regard to private obligations, if a
debtor tenders cash to his creditor the latter is bound to accept it in discharge
of the obligation between them. The rules of transfer for cash are intended
to maximise the quality of transferability even at the expense of the true
owner. Thus, in the jurisprudence of many countries, if cash is stolen by a
thief, the owner from whom its was stolen cannot recover it from a third
party who has received it fairly and honestly in payment for value. Similarly,

---

[1] Copyright 2000 by R. Effros. Consultant on banking and financial law.

if cash is lost, the owner who has lost it may not recover it from an innocent finder after the latter has honestly paid it away. As a country's financial development proceeds, currency notes are likely to exceed in value the coins in circulation. Thus, in the United States, Federal Reserve notes account for about 95 per cent of the $564 billion of currency notes and coin in circulation.[2] While currency is intended to circulate within the jurisdiction of the issuing authority, in fact some currencies are held and may even circulate beyond the national boundaries of the issuer. Thus, confidence in the U.S. dollar and apprehension concerning certain local currencies has resulted in substantial holdings of U.S. dollars abroad. In fact, it has been estimated that approximately two-thirds of U.S. currency is held internationally. The deutsche mark has also been widely used and held abroad, particularly in some countries of eastern Europe. While the uses found for these currencies abroad have largely been informal, some countries (such as Panama) officially use foreign currencies and the practice may gain adherents.

28–003   Cash is typically used in payment of low cost items in face to face transactions. Thus, notes in denominations of one to twenty dollars account for about 85 per cent of the currency notes produced by the U.S. Bureau of Engraving and Printing. Cash has also adapted itself well to the advent of automatic vending machines. The anonymity of cash transactions and the finality associated with its use has made cash a part of every culture and a traditional choice for consumers as well as for the merchants and service providers who seek payment. The issuers (usually central banks) also derive an economic advantage in producing currency at low cost and reflecting its face value for the product so produced. The profit to the issuer upon its transfer to the public is recognised as seignorage. Among the disadvantages of cash are that it can be counterfeited and that it is unwieldy to use to settle transactions at long distance, difficult to carry (particularly in large amounts), hard to store, and is subject to loss and to theft. In addition, holdings of cash by its owner will not earn income on the balance of the funds.

28–004   In many countries, the *cheque* is one of the most familiar of the non-cash means of payment. A cheque is a type of negotiable instrument, specifically, a demand order drawn on a bank. The characteristic feature of negotiability is the facility with which it may pass ownership of the instrument (and the attendant right to payment) from one party to the next transferee. Under certain circumstances, the transferee of a negotiable instrument may be protected from defects in his chain of title or other defences of a prior party that, in the absence of negotiability, would jeopardise the ability of the transferee to obtain payment on the instrument. The law governing cheques around the world is basically divided between two schools. One school, composed of the civil law countries of Europe, has adopted the Geneva conventions that were signed in the 1930s. The second school is composed of the common law countries of the U.K. and the U.S. and countries whose laws are derived therefrom.

---

[2] See testimony of L. Roseman, Division of Reserve Bank Operations and Payment Systems, before the Subcommittee on Domestic and International Monetary Policy of the Committee on Banking and Financial Services, U.S. House of Representatives, March 28, 2000.

In a typical cheque transaction, a payor, the drawer, gives or sends his **28–005** cheque to the payee. The payee deposits the cheque in his bank account for collection. The cheque is sent through the collection process, which may involve one or more intermediary banks, and then is presented for payment at the drawee (paying) bank where the drawer maintains his account. The payee may receive immediate credit from the depositary bank, but in the absence of special arrangements is more likely to receive credit from that bank according to a timetable that allows time for the cheque to clear. Upon receipt of the cheque, the drawee bank will debit the account of its customer, the drawer of the cheque. If the cheque does not clear as a result of its dishonour by the drawee bank on the ground of insufficient funds, forgery, or some other reason, it may be sent back through the collection process until it reaches the depositary bank which will then refuse to give credit to its customer for the amount of the cheque (or if it has done so, seek to revoke the credit). Under some systems of cheque collection, the drawee bank must give notice of its dishonour to the depositary bank (*e.g.*, in the case of cheques drawn over a certain amount). The returned cheque may follow in reverse the same course of its initial forward collection or in some systems may be sent directly from the drawee bank to the depositary bank. In some systems, either by law or by practice, paid cheques are then returned to the drawer by the drawee bank. Alternatively, the drawee bank may hold them and return to the drawer a statement sufficiently detailed to allow the drawer to identify the paid cheques. The cheque has traditionally been paper-based and many of the rules that regulate it assume the existence, transfer and presentment of the physical cheque (the possibilities for truncation will be discussed in the final section of this paper).

The advantages of cheques include the long familiarity that the public of **28–006** many countries has had with their usage. Moreover, there is a well-developed legal framework that supports this usage so that the parties to a cheque are generally comfortable in the knowledge of their rights, risks and liabilities. Among the risks that the legal framework allocates among the various parties are: forgery of signatures, fraud, inadequate balances, mistakes, unauthorised alterations, insolvency of one or more of the banks that are party to the cheque. Unlike cash, payment by cheque is conditional upon acceptance by the creditor and the tender of a cheque is not supported by the provisions of a legal tender statute. Cheques may be used in face to face transactions as may cash, but unlike cash cheques are useful in payments made at a distance. While cheques are subject to the risks mentioned above (and to others such as stop payment orders and staleness), the protections that the legal framework has provided make them less subject to theft than cash with the result that in most countries drawers do not hesitate to put cheques into the mail even though they would hesitate to post cash. Neither cash nor cheques require their users to travel to special locations, dial special numbers or invest in sophisticated equipment to originate payments. While a creditor who is paid in cash has the immediate use of that cash, if he takes a cheque, unless he immediately negotiates it to another, he may have to wait for its clearance and settlement before he can use the funds. An unwieldy process of collection adds costs that must be allocated and, by virtue of the delays, a float that operates in favour of the drawer whose balance is last to be debited.

28–007　　In a number of countries, particularly in Europe, *giro* systems of payment have developed. Often these systems are operated by the post office, but in some countries banks have developed their own giro systems. In these systems a payor may direct his bank to make payment into the account of his payee either at the same bank or, if he keeps his account elsewhere, at that of the payee. The account of the payor is then debited and the account of his payee is credited. The system may allow a payor to instruct his bank to make payments of a recurring nature to a payee such as a utility or a single payment to a vendor. Although originally paper-based, the giro has evolved into an electronic means of payment in some countries. A giro system has certain advantages over a chequeing system. This is because a giro system is based on credit transfers while the cheque involves a debit transfer. In a giro system, the question of whether a payor has sufficient funds in his account can be determined before a payment is made. A payment will not be made if the balance is insufficient. This eliminates the problems that may arise in a chequeing system when a cheque that has been given to the payee for payment of a transaction bounces for lack of sufficient funds. In addition, the giro system does not require a system of complicated rules analogous to those that have evolved for cheque collection and settlement since the course of a giro payment is simpler than that of a cheque payment and is likely to involve fewer parties.

28–008　　An *automated clearinghouse* (ACH) is a computerised facility organised by banks to process high-volume, low value transactions. In the United States, there are four ACHs: one run by the Federal Reserve which handles the bulk of the transactions and three private ACHs. The networks are batch processing, store and forward systems. This means that transactions received during a day are stored and processed later in a batch instead of being sent individually. Instead of using paper, ACH transactions are transmitted electronically between financial institutions. The system is used primarily for recurring transactions of invariable amounts. Credits may be entered directly into a consumer's bank account. Examples include payroll, pension and social security payments which employers and the government may initiate. Debit transactions may include pre-authorised mortgage and loan installments and insurance premiums. In a debit transaction, a consumer may authorise his utility to debit his bank account monthly. The utility will then initiate this debit once a month from his account and from the accounts of all of its other customers who have similarly made the required arrangements with their banks to allow such debits. The ACH system is less costly to operate than the chequeing system and has been growing in use. However, it is not well adapted to handle individual transactions and the body of rules that govern commercial transactions is complex. Moreover, procedures have not been developed to enforce the applicable rules for such systems. The latter have been promulgated and administered by a banking trade association called NACHA (The National Automated Clearing House Association)[3].

---

[3] See Committee on the Federal Reserve in the Payments Mechanism of the Federal Reserve System, The Federal Reserve in the Payment Mechanism 26–39 (January 1998).

Debit cards evolved in the United States from *automated teller machines* **28–009**
(ATMs). The latter are used to dispense cash, accept deposits and loan payments and provide balance information. They are activated by the insertion
of a plastic card and the entry of a personal identification number (PIN).
ATMs were originally developed by banks to substitute for human tellers in
these functions, but subsequently were additionally located by the banks
beyond their premises in shopping malls and elsewhere. ATMs allow the consumer to minimise the cash that he carries with him. When located outside
bank premises, they are intended to facilitate sales in what are called point of
sale (POS) transactions. Typically, after the sale is rung up by a merchant, the
consumer swipes his debit card through a PIN pad and enters his PIN. After
he presses a key, a message is sent to a computer switch which then notifies
his bank to debit his chequeing account for the amount of the sale. If the
PIN is correct and the customer has sufficient funds in his account, his bank's
computer will confirm to the switch that the purchase is authorised. This
obligates the customer's bank to pay the merchant's bank. In accordance
with the agreement between the two banks, the consumer's bank may immediately pay the merchant's bank or pay sometime later. An immediate transfer of funds occurs in what is called an online transaction while a delayed
transfer of funds takes place as a separate step in what is called an offline
transaction.[4] If a merchant does not have a PIN pad on premises, he may ask
his customer for his signature and the transaction is offline. In the settlement
of offline POS transactions, the information concerning the sale is sent to the
central card network by the merchant's bank (called the acquirer) where the
network calculates a net position for each financial institution (acting in a
dual role as card issuer and as acquirer). On settlement date, which (in the
United States) is usually the business day after the purchase date, financial
institutions in a debtor position send wire transfers to the central network's
clearing institution and the latter sends funds transfers to financial institutions in a net credit position. In the settlement of online POS transactions
the purchase amount is immediately withdrawn from the cardholder's bank
account so that at the end of the day settlement by the central processor
involves calculating a total debit to each card-issuing bank for all of its customers' online transactions, and a total credit to each merchant's bank
account for all of its transactions.[5]

Debit cards appear to have developed in a different manner in Europe. In **28–010**
Germany most debit cards were based on the Eurocheque card, which began
as a European cheque guarantee card that allowed customers to cash cheques
across Europe up to a certain limit. In the German debit card system, as in
the debit card systems of some other countries in Europe, there is a deliber-
ate deferral of payment rather than an immediate transfer of funds. With a
deferred debit card, charges are deducted from a cardholder's account typically on a monthly basis. This provides built in float for consumers. In
Europe deferred debit cards are often reinforced with a revolving line of

---

[4] See D. Evans and R. Schmalensee, *Paying with Plastic* 298–301(MIT:1998)
[5] See Federal Reserve Bank of St. Louis Emerging Payments Primer: Debit Cards/Point of Sale
9–12(1996)

credit so that if the consumer exhausts the funds in his bank account, he may utilise the associated credit line which may be accessed through the further use of the card. While deferred debit cards exist in the United States, they are relatively rare.[6]

28–011 While debit cards are more popular in Europe, *credit cards* are easily the favourite payment card in the United States. In a typical credit card system there is a card-issuing bank, an umbrella organisation like MasterCard or Visa that sponsors the card and sets the system rules, a merchant's bank, the merchant and the cardholder. In such a system the merchant agrees to honour the credit card and the merchant's bank agrees to pay the merchant less a discount for purchases made with the card. In the process of accepting payment, a merchant will telephone or, in more modern systems, contact an electronic terminal. If the authorisation is given, the merchant will request the cardholder to sign the sales slip. In the earlier version of these systems, the merchant would send the original of the sales slip to his bank, retaining a copy for his records and giving a copy to the cardholder. In the earlier version, the merchant's copy would be left at the merchant's bank and electronically forwarded to the bank that issued the card to the holder. (In the newer version, the slip is left at the merchant's cash register instead of being transmitted to the card issuing bank. Instead, that bank learns of the transaction electronically).[7] The merchant's bank credits the merchant's account less the discount and transmits the information on the sales slip to the card–issuing bank. The card issuing bank pays the merchant's bank and then bills the customer who receives a statement monthly. The card-issuing bank earns its income from an annual fee and the finance charges payable by the card holder if he does not timely pay his statement.[8]

28–012 Payment cards, whether debit or credit enjoy certain advantages over cheques. While they can be counterfeited and are otherwise subject to fraud, these problems do not rise to the incidence of bad cheques that often develops in countries. It is for these reasons that merchants are often glad to accept payment cards even if they must allow a discount (estimated at about 2 per cent of transaction value) from the ultimate proceeds that they collect in order to participate in the systems. Moreover, the cards can be used by hotels and others to protect against customer defaults. Payment cards also offer consumers certain benefits. One of these is convenience. Thus it has been estimated that a typical chequebook is 14 times the weight of a payment card. Compared to a chequebook, a card is a much handier payment device to carry around. Because of the problem of bad cheques, it may be more easily accepted by a merchant who might have some apprehension about taking a cheque from a new customer.

28–013 The payment systems described above are classified as *retail systems*. In addition, each country tends to evolve a *wholesale payment system* when it reaches a certain stage of financial development. Such systems are used to

---

[6] See D. Evans and R. Schmalensee, n. 0 4 at 55.

[7] M. Mayer, The Bankers 116–117 (Truman Talley Books/Plume, 1997).

[8] See R. Effros, *Legal Issues in Payment Systems Reform*, 1 Journal of International Banking Regulation 193 at 202 (September 1999). See also Lawrence *An Introduction to Payment Systems*, 513–6 (Aspen: 1997).

apply to balances between the banks for their own account as well as for their corporate customers. The amounts of such transfers are typically very large, much larger than the average amount of a retail transfer that is made by the typical consumer. The average value of such payments (in 1993) was calculated as $4.9 million in Europe, $4.2 million for the United States and $93.1 for Japan.[9] The result is that the total amounts transferred through the wholesale systems tends to exceed the total amounts transferred through the retail systems even though the number of transactions of the latter exceeds that for the former. The value of wholesale transfers across seven developed countries (France, Germany, Italy, Switzerland, the U.K., Japan and the United States) varies from 11 times to 100 times the GDP.[10]

Wholesale payment systems invariably invite the attention of the central bank, which becomes the operator or supervisor of the systems by virtue of their importance to the financial system. For reasons of speed and economy, the systems assume an electronic form in which credit transfers are made between the participating banks. The structures may vary, but three basic types of system can be identified. These are called gross settlement without intraday credit, gross settlement with intraday credit and net settlement. It is useful to consider the distinctions.   **28–014**

In a *gross settlement system*, payment orders are expected to be honoured on a transaction by transaction basis. This requires banks that participate in the system to hold funds on deposit so that incoming payment orders can be implemented. If funds are not available to allow the payment order to be implemented, the system operator will return the order to the sending bank. Alternatively, it may hold the order in queue until enough funds accumulate in the account of the sending bank to permit the implementation. Such a system is called a *real time gross settlement system* (RTGS). This type of system has been recommended within the European Union. By virtue of its conservative principles such a system is unlikely to produce a domino effect if one of the member banks should fail and further unlikely to involve the central bank in the event of such failure.   **28–015**

One of the disadvantages of a gross settlement system is that banks may encounter gridlock situations in which they must wait for other banks to perform before they themselves will be funded sufficiently to enable the operator of the system to proceed to implement their own payment orders. This situation can be addressed if it is provided that the operator may extend credit on an intraday basis in the event that the account of the sending bank lacks adequate funds to effect its payment order. Such a system is characterised as incorporating *gross settlement with intraday credit*. In such a system, the operator (normally the central bank) will assign limits to the credit that it may extend to each of the participant banks. It will expect to be repaid before the close of the day. An example of such a system is FedWire, which is run by the Federal Reserve System.   **28–016**

The third basic system is called the *net settlement system*. In such a system, settlement is not intended to be carried out on a transaction by transaction   **28–017**

[9] See D. Humphrey, S. Sato, M. Tsurumi and J. Vesala, *The Evolution of Payments in Europe*, Japan, and the United States 16 (World Bank:1996).
[10] *ibid.*

basis. Instead, settlement occurs at given times during the day when payment orders of the participating banks are netted and the results communicated to those in debtor position. In such systems the credit that lubricates the system is extended by creditor banks to debtor banks rather than by the operator of the system. Each bank determines the maximum amount it will extend to each of its fellow participating banks. In order to guard against the effect of a failure of one of the participating banks, the rules may provide that each bank must maintain collateral to cover its position. Moreover, rules may provide in advance a procedure for dealing with such a contingency through loss sharing or otherwise. An example of such a system is CHIPS, which is operated by the New York Clearing House.

2. Comparative country experience

28–018   A number of studies have appeared on the payment systems in the Group of Ten Countries.[11] (The studies actually cover statistics in eleven countries).[12] An analysis of the figures in these studies[13] shows that *cash* is still the most important retail payment instrument for face-to-face transactions. While there may have been a long-term decline in the use of cash in the covered countries, it is not uniform and in some countries the use of cash has even risen. Thus, in currency GDP comparisons since 1990, the use of cash has risen markedly in Canada, the United States and in Japan, as well as in Australia, Germany, Italy and the United Kingdom. However, the average size of cash payments is low in value (below $10) and they account for less than five per cent of the total value of payments. It has been suggested that the continuing robust use of cash may reflect in part the growth of ATM networks. While these tend to reduce the amount of cash that a consumer must carry with him, they increase the availability of cash at the point of sale. Japan has the highest currency to GDP ratio among the countries surveyed at 12 per cent, while Switzerland is also high at about 8 per cent. Among the relatively low use countries are Australia, Canada, France, Sweden and the United Kingdom. In developed countries generally, cash transactions have been estimated to comprise from 75 per cent to 90 per cent of all transactions while cash settles an even greater proportion of transactions in developing countries.[14] Some investigators have suggested that the particularly high dependence on cash transactions in Japan may be related to the low incidence of violent crime in that country.

28–019   When paper-based instruments are considered, *cheques* and *giro* payments are the key instruments in use. (As has been noted above, giro systems are

---

[11] The latest study may be found in Statistics on Payment Systems in the Group of Ten Countries. It was prepared by the Committee on Payment and Settlement Systems of the central banks of the group of Ten countries and published by the Bank for International Settlements in February 2000. It contains statistics for 1998.

[12] The countries are Belgium, Canada, France, Germany, Italy, Japan, Netherlands, Sweden, Switzerland, United Kingdom and the United States.

[13] See Committee on Payment and Settlement Systems, Retail Payments in Selected Countries: A Comparative Study published by the Bank for International Settlements (1999)

[14] See D. Hancock and D. Humphrey, *Payment Transactions, Instruments, and Systems: A Survey, Journal of Banking and Finance 21 at 1578* (1998).

becoming electronic in many countries). Australia, Canada, France, the United Kingdom and the United States rely most heavily on cheques for retail payments. Credit transfers through giro systems are especially notable in Belgium, Germany, Japan, Netherlands, Sweden and Switzerland. Particularly remarkable is the extent of reliance on cheques in the United States where fully 74 per cent of non-cash payments in 1997 were cheque transactions. There has been some attempt to explain the particularly heavy reliance of the United States on cheques and the historical absence of giro systems in that country on the fact that its financial system has been based on many independent banks rather than on a centralised concentrated banking system which is characteristic of European countries, and the absence of a giro initiative from either the banks or the postal system.[15]

Payment card use is highest in Australia, Canada and the United Kingdom when it is compared as a percentage of the number of non-cash payments. (The rising use of debit cards in these countries as compared to the use of credit cards is also noteworthy. By way of example, debit card use in the United Kingdom has risen until it now exceeds the use of credit cards in that country). In continental Europe payment cards are used extensively in Belgium, France, the Netherlands and Switzerland. In these countries (with the possible exception of France for which the data is incomplete) debit card use exceeds credit card use. Credit cards are much used in the United States and Canada as well as in Australia, Japan and the United Kingdom. Only in Canada, Japan and the United States is credit card use significantly greater than debit card use.[16]

In the sphere of *wholesale payments*, the European Union has encouraged the establishment of *real-time gross settlement* systems in each of its members[17] and has followed suit with a transnational system (TARGET). TARGET (Trans-European Automated Real-time Gross-settlement Express Transfer) is a real-time gross settlement system for funds transfer in each of the 15 countries which links the component systems of these countries and serves as the payment mechanism of the European Central Bank. It is used for high value interbank payments. National central banks may grant intraday credit to participants up to the amount that participants will collateralise.

28–019

The cost of payment services is not insignificant. Some economists have estimated it as 5 per cent of the value of an average purchase and the total

28–020

---

[15] See D. Humphrey, L. Pulley and J. Vesala, *Cash, Paper, and Electronic Payments: Across-Country Analysis, Journal of Money, Credit, and Banking 916 at 926* (November 1996, Part 2): "Thus intensive check use is the logical outcome of limiting the concentration of the banking system in a geographically large country." It should be noted that the U.S. Postal Service has recently announced an e-payment plan called eBillPay that will let consumers receive and pay bills electronically through the Postal Service Website. If a payee does not accept electronic payments, the service will issue a cheque and send it to the payee in the mail. See "Postal Service Unveils e-Payment Program", Washington Post, E2, April 6, 2000.

[16] See Committee on Payment and Settlement Systems, Retail Payments in Selected Countries: a Comparative Study at 9.

[17] Alternative net settlement systems continue to exist in some member countries. Thus non-RTGS German and French systems and the Euro 1 system of the Euro Banking Association are net settlement systems. See Bertaux and Iyigun, The Launch of the Euro, Federal Reserve Bulletin 655 at 663 (1999).

cost of a country's payment systems may equal 3 per cent of the value of its gross domestic product. The cost of making payments electronically is substantially less than the cost of making them with paper-based systems. (In the United States this has led to legislation that requires the U.S. government to shift from payments by cheque to electronic forms such as direct credit of bank accounts through the ACH).

28–023   Some observers have suggested that a movement from paper-based systems to electronic systems is discernible in the statistics that have been collected. Nevertheless, if such a transition is taking place, it is not a universal and inevitable phenomenon. One reason for this that has been suggested is that certain payment systems are effectively subsidised and the consumer is unaware of the true cost of his transactions. Thus, in the United States, Canada and the United Kingdom, consumers are commonly given a choice of paying a transaction fee for each cheque or free service with the maintenance of a minimum chequeing account balance. Many consumers choose the latter. This permits them to issue as many cheques as they wish so that the marginal cost of issuing cheques appears to be nil (or at least is not readily calculable to the average drawer). Similarly, giro transaction expenses are said to be largely covered by debiting a payor's account one day before the value date on which the payment is to be made. Accordingly, the price to the consumer of a giro transfer appears to be lower than it otherwise is. The full cost of using credit cards is also obscured. The consumer is not charged a per-transaction price. Instead he pays an annual fee or interest on his unpaid balance while the merchants who accept the cards are charged a discount on the value of the transactions. In both the cheque and payment card situations (as well as in the case of deferred payment debit cards) the payor enjoys float, which is equivalent to an interest free loan. The result of all of this is said to obscure the real costs of the payment systems and skew consumer preference between the alternative instruments. If this were true, it would help to explain the halting progress that is being made from paper to electronic systems. However, other reasons are undoubtedly contributing factors. These include the features built into the various systems, particularly involving consumer protection, the familiarity of the consumer with the system that he habitually uses and other intangible factors, as well.[18]

.

3. Payment systems currently under development

28–024   There are a number of payment systems in various stages of development. In what follows, we will examine some of them and their salient features.

28–025   Many banks now offer some sort of *home banking facility*. This allows the bank customer to inquire about account balances and other information, to transfer funds between his accounts and to pay bills. The facility is offered in three ways: through telephone, personal computer (PC) or screen phone based systems. Telephone-based banking usually involves automatic voice

[18] See D. Humphrey, L. Pulley, and J. Vesala, *Cash , Paper , and Electronic Payments: A Cross-Country Analysis, Journal of Money, Credit, and Banking 915 at 932* (November 1996, Part 2):

response in which a customer, upon contacting the bank's number, is prompted for a personal identification number (PIN) and account number to access information concerning his account. In PC-based banking, banks set up their own private network or use a commercial online service (like America Online) or the Internet. The majority of these services in the United States are currently provided through bank-owned networks. The banks must also specify the software that will be used, which may be a proprietary system or a commercially available type (like Quicken). A password or other identification is required for a customer to access his accounts. With a screen phone the telephone apparatus projects a small image. It is through one of these devices that a bank customer can make home banking bill payments. Such a customer can instruct his bank (or an intermediary service provider) to pay a bill. He does this by indicating the amount of the bill, the date of payment, his account number and the intended payee's name and address. The bank (or the service provider) must then decide how to pay the payee. This may be done electronically or otherwise if the payee does not accept electronic payments. Thus the payment may take place by an ACH credit or the issuance of a cheque. If a cheque is used the bank (or service provider) prints and draws a cheque to the payee drawn on the customer's bank account and sends it on its way to the payee. Authorisation is, of course, needed from the customer to affix his signature to the cheque. In one variation the service provider's bank may initiate an ACH debit to the customer's account and a credit to the service provider's account. The service provider will then draw a cheque on its own bank account and send it to the payee.[19]

A number of payment systems have been proposed or are under develop- **28–026** ment to facilitate *electronic purchases over computer networks*. Several models may be described by way of example. In the On-Line Service Provider Model (OLS) a private network requires each customer to be authorised through a password and identification. Each customer pays a monthly fee for the service. If a customer wishes to purchase an item, he communicates to the OLS provider through his computer and modem and searches for the good that he wishes to purchase. He than completes an order form that requires his user identification and credit card information. This is sent direct to the merchant and the credit card payment is processed. The merchant then sends the good to the customer. The network uses encryption to safeguard the transmission of messages. If a customer does not wish to participate in an OLS, he may make purchases directly over the Internet. He may do this by transmitting credit card information to a merchant. This may be accomplished by sending such information in an unsecured mode. This practice risks interception by an unauthorised interloper and could result in loss to the customer. To forestall such a risk, the payment card companies have been developing encryption procedures to encrypt credit card information that is sent over the Internet. Another model payment system for Internet purchases is that of First Virtual. In this model, both the buyer and the seller must be registered with First Virtual. The consumer establishes his account by giving

---

[19] See Federal Reserve Bank of St. Louis Emerging Payments Primer: Home Banking Services (1996).

First Virtual his name, e-mail address and a codename. He is then telephoned by First Virtual and prompted to give his credit card information so that it may be stored in its computer. He may then buy goods over the Internet from vendors that indicate their participation in the First Virtual network. When the customer contacts the merchant, he is asked for the account codename so that the purchase can be reported to First Virtual. First Virtual then sends the customer e-mail asking for confirmation of the purchase. If it receives the customer's confirmation, First Virtual will charge the customer's credit card account having reference to the information stored on its computer. First Virtual encourages merchants to send the good to the customer before the customer's confirmation. The advantage of this model is said to be that once the customer's credit card information is stored in First Virtual's computer, it need not be sent by the customer for each purchase that he makes. By contrast, in the CyberCash model, the consumer's credit card information is encrypted, digitally signed and sent over the Internet to the merchant for each transaction. In this latter model, both customers and merchants are registered. Following the customer's choice of a good, the merchant sends a payment request message to the consumer. The consumer fills out a CyberCash application and CyberCash transmits the encrypted information to the merchant who sends it on to CyberCash. CyberCash then sends the data to the merchant's bank where the credit card information is processed and the issuing bank is requested to authorize the payment. After receiving authorisation from the issuing bank, CyberCash notifies the merchant who delivers the good.[20]

28–027   It should be noted that home banking and the systems that are under development to facilitate electronic purchases over computer networks that have just been described are not essentially new payment systems. They are rather what have been termed *access products* that allow consumers to use electronic means of communication to access conventional payment systems. The innovation that they embody is in the method of communication, *e.g.* through the use of a computer rather than a visit to a bank branch.[21] These products differ qualitatively from an entirely new type of payment system that is called electronic money (*e-money*).

28–028   *E-money* products are stored value, *i.e.* prepaid, in which a record of the value available to a consumer is stored in an electronic device in the possession of the consumer. There are two subclasses of e-money. The first consists of *prepaid (stored value) cards*, which are sometimes referred to as electronic purses. The second subclass consists of *prepaid software products* that use a computer network such as the Internet and give rise to what is sometimes referred to as digital cash. The cards are designed to facilitate low value payments made face to face. The computer software based systems are designed to make remote payments chiefly over the Internet. The schemes are being promoted primarily as substitutes for cash, although some believe that they may eventually make inroads on non-cash payment systems as well.

---

[20] See Federal Reserve Bank of St. Louis Emerging Payments Primer: Electronic Purchases Over Computer Networks (1996).
[21] See Bank for International Settlements, Implications for Central Banks of the Development of Electronic Money 1 (1996).

Stored value payment cards can be designed to be disposable or reloadable.   **28–029**
If reloadable, they can be augmented with additional value; if disposable,
they can be discarded once their value has been depleted. They can be
designed to pay only for certain services in a closed network such as a university setting or for limited purposes such as for public pay telephones, pho-
tocopy machines or urban mass transportation. Alternatively, they can be
designed to serve for payments with a general class of vendors of goods and
services. The cards are of two kinds: simpler cards that bear a magnetic stripe
and more complex ones (called smart cards) that embody a chip that is in
essence a microcomputer. While magnetic stripe cards are less expensive to
produce than smart cards, the life of a smart card is longer than that of a
magnetic stripe card and it is capable of carrying more information and serving a greater variety of purposes. Smart cards are also less subject to the risks
of counterfeiting or tampering. Some smart cards require the consumer to
enter a personal identification number (PIN) or sign a sales slip while others
dispense with these requirements. While some smart cards are designed to
allow customers to make transfers of value directly to other individuals who
have a compatible card, others limit the transfer to merchants. The smart
card was largely developed in France and has become widespread in a number of countries.[22]

Prepaid software products have been designed to facilitate purchases over   **28–030**
the Internet. Numerous products are in development in a number of countries and at the outset it was predicted that they would be accepted swiftly by
the public. In fact most are still undergoing trials and several of these systems
have been discontinued due to sluggish acceptance. One discontinued system,
DigiCash, may serve as an illustration of how a model might be designed. In
this system a new payment device called Ecash was developed for making
purchases over the Internet. To obtain Ecash, a customer first opened and
deposited money in an account in a bank that participated in the Ecash system. The customer was then entitled to withdraw funds in the form of Ecash
coins. These were provided by the bank in various denominations. The coins
were actually codes that the customer stored in his own computer. The customer could spend the coins by transmitting them over the Internet. After
receiving them, a merchant presented the coins to the issuing bank for verification and after verification, the bank would accept the coins and credit the
merchant's account with dollars. It should be noted that as with stored value
cards, such a system requires the customer to prepay their value. The value is
stored on the customer's home computer rather than on a payment card.[23]

E-money has been touted by its proponents as a replacement for cash. It   **28–031**
does enjoy certain benefits. Thus from the consumer's point of view, it may
eliminate physical security risks associated with visiting ATMs for cash. It
may facilitate budgeting and control, for example, of the amounts provided
for children to spend. From the merchant's standpoint, it may operate to

---

[22] See B. Good, Electronic Money 6–9 (Federal Reserve Bank of Cleveland Working Paper
97–16 (1997).
[23] See G. Maggs, New Payment Devices and General Principles of Payment Law, 72 Notre Dame
L. Rev. 753 at 759–760 ((1997). It should be noted that, due to slow acceptance, the DigiCash
system has been discontinued.

reduce the costs of handling cash including those associated with theft by employees. Nevertheless, merchants and consumers may have to install new equipment or software to handle the devices and their unfamiliarity with the risks and rights associated with these devices may make them wary of enthusiastic acceptance of the new systems. This leads to the critical mass problem: if not enough consumers and merchants join a particular system, the system will not catch on.[24]

28–032   There is little in the way of statutes or regulations that may be said to unambiguously cover e–money products in most countries. Accordingly there are many questions that have yet to be answered. Theft of a card or interception of electronic messages sent from a computer can raise the issue of who will suffer the loss. Similarly, if the issuer of the electronic money becomes insolvent what are the consequences to the holders of the electronic money? Who should bear the risk of malfunctions and how should expired or deactivated products be dealt with? What information should be disclosed to the users of these systems concerning their rules and should information concerning their use by the customers be anonymous or not? Until the answers to these and related issues are clarified, some observers have suggested that the potential for the products may not be fully realised.[25]

28–033   While the issues just mentioned affect the relationships between customers, merchants and issuers, another set of issues may affect central banks that issue the traditional cash that may be impacted by the new electronic money. One of these issues concerns the possible effects that electronic money may introduce on the ability of a central bank to implement monetary policy. If e–money substitutes for reservable deposits, the ability of central banks to set money market rates might be complicated to the extent that this rests on affecting bank reserves. Since e-money is more likely to substitute for cash than deposits, this effect is unlikely to result. However, it has been noted that cash is the largest part of central bank liabilities in many countries and that its counterpart is assets such as government securities. The interest earned on these assets constitutes revenue derived from seignorage. If e–money use became extensive, resulting in the shrinkage of the asset base and the resulting income to the central bank as issuer of the currency, then a central bank might have to seek other sources of revenue to support it.[26] Ultimately, the central bank might be forced to consider issuing electronic money of its own either in competition with or in substitution for that issued by private issuers. The issue is at the moment academic and no central bank is currently understood to be considering issuing its own electronic money.

28–034   Another issue that central banks have considered is how the phenomenon of electronic money may affect their responsibilities as regulatory supervisors. First, who should be allowed to be an issuer of electronic money? In the

---

[24] See Federal Reserve System, Report to the Congress on the Application of the Electronic Fund Transfer Act to Electronic Stored-Value Products 24 (1997).
[25] See W. Effross, Putting the Cards Before The Purse: Distinctions, Differences, and Dilemmas in the Regulation of Stored Value Card Systems, 65 University of Missouri –Kansas City Law Review 319 (1997); S. Hughes, A Case for Regulating Cyberpayments, 51 Administrative Law Review 809 (1999).
[26] See *Bank for International Settlements, Implications for Central Banks of the Development of Electronic Money* 7 (1996).

European Union, the European Monetary Institute issued a report in 1994 that concluded generally that only credit institutions should be allowed to issue multipurpose stored value cards.[27] In the United States the authorities have taken a different view and would not limit issuers to this category. If the category may thus be wider, questions may arise concerning the ability of the central bank to exercise proper supervision over the issuers. Different views have been expressed over whether deposit insurance should be applicable to the schemes if the issuers fail.[28] Again, the potential for systemic failure has been posed. Would the failure of one issuer lead to the failure of other issuers and the ultimate withdrawal of the public from the medium of electronic currency?

On the international aspects, if electronic money products will be designed to enable funds to be transferred across borders anonymously, questions may be raised concerning the potential misuse for money laundering. These concerns would be heightened if the systems now in development offer electronic money in more than one currency. Even putting aside concerns about possible criminal activities, other matters might need consideration. If the systems allow consumers to use electronic money to make payments to foreign merchants, while travelling or over the Internet, conflict of laws issues might arise in the event of disputes. If some countries adopt less than optimal supervision over issuers of electronic money, this might lead to the migration of issuers to a less regulated jurisdiction with the objective of issuing electronic money to consumers in another country that has stricter regulations applicable to its domestic issuers of electronic money.[29] **28–035**

4. The forecast

It has been said that experience is the only basis of prophecy for those who would be wise. Many who have attempted to predict the course of payment system developments have had to conclude that their predictions are at best premature. In what follows, we will only attempt to extrapolate from the current trends in order to arrive at a near term forecast. **28–036**

The use of *cash* in its traditional physical form is not likely to be replaced for the foreseeable future. Its use will continue in face to face transactions of relatively low values. The use of cash is a flexible means of payment that needs no sophisticated equipment or skills, is anonymous and has the force of legal tender to make it universally acceptable. It can be used to pay persons as well as businesses, needs no time for processing or collection and **28–037**

---

[27] Working Group on EU Payment Systems, Report to the Council of the European Monetary Institute on Prepaid Cards, European Monetary Institute (May 1994). The report did allow that some institutions that are not full credit institutions might be permitted to be card issuers subject to certain conditions.
[28] The U.S. Federal Deposit Insurance Corporation issued an opinion of its general counsel on the question of whether the funds or obligations that underlie stored value cards are deposits so as to qualify for deposit insurance under the Federal Deposit Insurance Act. The opinion seems to indicate that in most instances this would not be the case. See General Counsel's Opinion No. 8; Stored Value Cards and Other Electronic Systems, 61 Fed. Reg. 40,490 (August 2, 1996). See also Current Legal Issues Affecting Central Banks, Vol. 5 at page xx (IMF: 1998) (R. Effros, ed.)
[29] See Group of Ten, Electronic Money24–27 (1997).

therefore can be immediately re-spent. It has shown itself adaptable to changing technology so that it can be retrieved from ATMs and spent in automated vending machines. In the United States, by way of example, cash is currently used for about three-quarters of all transactions.

28–038   *Cheques* are also likely to continue to be favored by both persons and businesses .The public is familiar with the attendant rights and risks with cheque systems and the latter are bolstered by time-tested legal rules and supported institutionally by banks that find the operation of cheque systems profitable. Like cash, cheques require of the users little in the way of sophisticated equipment or skills and are eminently flexible. They can be used for large or small values and for remote payments or face-to-face transactions. They can be drawn to the order of individuals as well as merchants (unlike most payment cards that do not allow payment to individuals). In most developed countries (but not in the United States) there is a falling off in the use of cheques as inroads are made by newer non-cash payment systems, particularly payment cards. Moreover, in countries in which *giro* systems were well established, cheques never gained the prominence that they achieved in countries that lacked the giro. The progressive conversion of giro systems from paper to electronic versions together with the innate efficiency of the giro is likely to continue to assure its prevalence over the cheque in those countries where the giro is well established. However, the cheque is eminently adaptable to new technologies. A number of countries have overhauled their legal systems to make the cheque collection system more efficient. Thus the rules that require the physical presentment of a paper cheque to the drawee bank have been modified in some countries. In England, the Bills of Exchange Act of 1882 was amended in sections 74B and 74C to allow for truncation in 1996 and certain other European countries have been truncating cheque collection for some time.[30] The U.S. Uniform Commercial Code permits truncation and the Federal Reserve has been encouraging the practice as well as the related phenomenon of electronic cheque presentment. (In *electronic cheque presentment* a cheque is cleared and paid on the basis of information contained in an electronic file which substitutes for the actual paper cheque. If the cheque comes to rest in the collection process before it reaches the drawee bank, for example with the bank of deposit or an intermediary collecting bank, the process is called *cheque truncation*.)[31] A newer development involves test trials with *electronic cheques*. The U. S. Treasury Department has established a pilot project to be used to pay for obligations of the Defense Department to 50 vendors. The e-cheque is a computer document or file that can be processed by banks with only modest investment in new technology. It is an offline mechanism that does not completely eliminate float, but reduces it so that clearance and settlement can take place overnight. Under the system, the

---

[30] See J.P. Bouchon, Check Truncation Developments in France, World of Banking 13 (November-December 1983). See also A. Guest, *Checks and Check Collection in Current Legal Issues Affecting Central Banks*, vol. 5 at 177 (IMF: 1998) (R. Effros, ed.).
[31] See J. Stavins, A Comparison of Social Costs and Benefits of Paper Check Presentment and ECP with Truncation, New England Economic Survey 27–28 (July-August 1997). See also J. Kimball, Check *Collection for the 21st Century*, 31 Uniform Commercial Code Law Journal 3 (Summer 1998).

Department of Defense can generate an e-cheque, cryptographically sign it, encrypt it and send it via e-mail to the vendor. (E-cheques are not automatically encrypted but can be for transmission from the payor to the payee). Personal and small business accounts will sign and endorse e-cheques with an "electronic chequebook" which is a removable smart card that is not in a file on the computer hard disk of the payor where someone might misuse it to generate unauthorized electronic cheques. A PIN is necessary to activate the electronic chequebook so that a further measure of security is built into the system. The cheques are signed with digital signatures that are based on mathematical calculations to make them difficult to forge and yet allow them to be verified by the drawee bank. The e-cheque is said to be compatible with current cheque law (which generally requires a "writing"). Since electronic payments are less expensive than paper payments to process, it is believed that the e-cheque should realise substantial savings.[32]

The *ACH* system of direct debits and direct credits is growing rapidly. However, with its rules complicated and not well known, it has not realised its full potential. At present in the United States only about 45 per cent of payroll payments are currently made through the ACH and only about 8 per cent of consumer bill payments. The Debt Collection Improvement Act of 1996 requires the Federal Government to make most of its payments electronically and this is likely to increase the use of ACH transfers generated by the government. Additional transactions are likely to result from the growth of financial electronic data interchange between companies.[33] The cost of using the ACH system to make transfers is substantially less than the cost of using the traditional paper-based cheque payment system.

28–039

The use of *payment cards* is likely to continue to increase. As we have seen, in some countries credit cards are preferred over debit cards while in other countries this preference is reversed. It seems that in countries that have had a slow start with debit cards, use is accelerating. Payment cards are unlikely to replace cheque payments completely because they do not make payments to individuals. The consumer protection laws, regulations and codes of practice of the various countries have operated to assure the users as to the reliability, utility and safety of the cards.

28–040

A recent survey indicates that 50 countries have pilot projects involving *electronic money*. Most of these projects are *stored value card* systems.[34] The cards are widespread in Switzerland, the Netherlands, Hong Kong, Germany, Singapore, Belgium and Austria. In contrast, usage in the United States is confined to less than 1 per cent of the population. *Prepaid software products* are still largely in the development stage. Internet purchases for which they have been designed are largely settled with the use of credit cards

28–041

---

[32] See generally eCheck Q & A at http://www.e Check.org.
[33] Electronic data interchange (EDI) is a system used by companies to transmit purchase orders and corresponding shipping and invoicing information to one another electronically. When payments are integrated with this system , the result is called financial electronic data interchange. The payments are ACH payments. See K. Furst, W. Lang and D. Nolle, Technological Innovation in Banking and Payments: Industry Trends and Implications for Banks, 17 Quarterly Journal 23 at 26 (September 1998).
[34] See Remarks of E. Gramlich, Governor of the Federal Reserve Board, before the Electronic Payment Symposium, University of Michigan, September 17, 1999 at p. 5.

and it is unclear whether the public will perceive an advantage to using one of the experimental prepaid software products. These systems are not generally interoperable so that a consumer must choose between a number of alternative systems that have yet to prove their utility. Merchants, too, have not rushed to join the systems. Thus, the critical mass to make them popular and widespread is unlikely to be found soon for many of these systems.

28–042 *Wholesale electronic fund transfer* systems are largely in place in many of the developed countries and developing countries are in the process of adopting them as well. A consensus has developed in favour of *real time gross settlement* systems partly driven by considerations of prudence and protection of the central bank. However, in some of these countries, banks will continue to operate their own *net settlement* systems having regard to the fact that they tend to tie up less funds than RTGS systems.

CHAPTER 29

RECENT TRENDS IN EC PAYMENT SYSTEMS

Norbert Horn[1]

1. The relevant directives and recommendations on payment systems

1.1 Three directives and one recommendation

The full functioning of the internal market of the EC requires improved and   **29–001**
integrated payment systems. The EC has taken the following measures to this
end:

- Directive 97/5/EC on cross-border credit transfers[2]

---

[1] Norbert Horn is professor of Private and Commercial Law, Banking and International
Business Law and Legal Philosophy at the University of Cologne. He is Director of the Banking
Law Institute and of the Law Centre for European and International Cooperation (R.I.Z.) at the
University of Cologne.
[2] [1997] O.J. L43/25–31.

- Directive 98/26/EC on settlement finality in settlement systems[3]

- Directive 97/7/EC on the protection of consumers in respect of distance contracts[4]

- Commission Recommendation 97/489/EC on transactions by electronic payment instruments[5]

1.2 The context of the EC initiatives

29–002 Before we discuss the various directives and the recommendation, we should first have a look at the social, economic and legal context in which they are placed.

1.2.1 Different payment behaviour

29–003 In the USA, credit transfers as a mode of payment are rarely used in private or commercial transactions, with the exception of large sum transfers in inter-bank transactions or large enterprise transactions through Fedwire and CHIPS. The bulk of payments, specifically, more than 80 per cent of payments, are made by cheques, as shown in a 1987 survey by the Bank for International Settlement.[6] If we look at the European Union, payments by cheque still account for more than half of all payments in France (65.4 per cent), Great Britain (57 per cent), and Italy (52.5 per cent). In the use of credit transfers, the Netherlands leads (64.5 per cent), followed by Germany (54 per cent), Belgium (53.9 per cent) and Italy (44.6 per cent). In Switzerland and Sweden, credit transfers are the predominant method of payment. In Germany, payment through debit notes is the second most popular method of payment (36 per cent); in Japan, it was the preferred method of payment (50.8 per cent).

29–004   For inter-bank transactions and high value payments to and from big enterprises, credit transfers are the only globally adequate mode of payment. Accordingly, the development of a safe and harmonised inter-bank payment system was of paramount importance in preparing for the European Monetary Union. The Trans-European Automated Real-Time Gross Settlement Express Transfer System (TARGET) was developed for this purpose.[7] In addition to TARGET, the European Bank Federation has prepared an inter-bank payment system.

---

[3] [1998] O.J. L166/45–50.
[4] [1997] O.J. L144/19–27.
[5] [1997] O.J. L208/52–58.
[6] Bank für internationalen Zahlungsausgleich (Hrsg.), Zahlungsverkehrssysteme in elf entwickelten Ländern, 1989, p. 267.
[7] Schwolow, Internationale Entwicklungslinien im Recht der Auslandsüberweisung, 1999, at p. 219 *et seq.*

1.2.2 Other standardisation and harmonisation efforts

The three directives and the recommendation discussed below are not the   **29–005**
only efforts towards a better harmonisation of EU banking law relating to
payments. TARGET is another example of those initiatives. The European
Committee for Banking Standards (ECBS) has developed a standard form
"Electronic Data Interchange in Co-operation with UN–ECE, for Administration, Commerce and Transport" (EDIFACT). The processing of transactions through EDIFACT facilitates the communication between EDIFACT
users on an international level.[8]

There are numerous other initiatives to promote the harmonisation of the   **29–006**
law of European and international cross-border payments.[9] Some of them go
beyond the scope of the EU and are initiated by UNCITRAL, the most
important of which is a Model Law on International Credit Transfers of
May 15, 1992. This Model Law will be briefly discussed in the concluding
remarks.

2. The directive 97/5/EC on cross-border credit transfers

2.1 Goals and main Provisions of the directive

Directive 97/5/EC of the European Parliament and of the Council of   **29–007**
January 27, 1997 on cross-border credit transfers[10] was issued to enable
individuals and small and medium–sized enterprises to make credit transfers rapidly, reliably and cheaply from one part of the Community to
another.

The relatively low value payments made by such individuals and enter-   **29–008**
prises within the European Union have until recently met considerable obstacles and difficulties. In 1993 the EC Commission commissioned two studies
on remote (low value) cross-border payments; the studies identified the problems of long execution time, high costs, lack of transparency of the conditions, and double charging for the transaction.[11] These problems are not yet
resolved in practice. In May 2000, the Commission criticised the persistence
of high costs in cross-border credits within the EU In addition to addressing
the findings of the two studies, Directive 97/5/EC discusses the problems of
credit transfer non-completion and the customer's risk of monetary loss,
when it states:

> "... there should be an obligation upon institutions to refund in the event of a failure to
> successfully complete a credit transfer; ... the obligation to refund imposes a contingent
> liability on institutions which might, in the absence of any limit, have a prejudicial effect

---

[8] On EDIFACT, see de Busto (ed.), *Funds Transfer in International Banking—A Compendium on
Capital Adequacy, SWIFT, EDI, Bank's Liability and Payment Systems in the 1900s*, 1992, at
p. 53.
[9] Heinrich, Funds Transfers, Payments and Payment Systems—International Initiatives towards
Legal Harmonization, in: Norton, Reed and Walden (eds.), *Cross–border Electronic banking*,
1995, at p. 233 *et seq.*
[10] [1997] O.J. L43/25–31.
[11] COM (94) 436Intro. I; see also the report of the EC Commission on the studies carried out by
Retail Banking Research Ltd (RBR) in ZBB 1993, 275 *et seq.*

on solvency requirements; . . . the obligation to refund should therefore be applicable up to 12,500 ECU . . ."[12]

29–009 On these grounds, the Directive imposes a remarkable strict liability on banks, the famous "money back guarantee", as a sort of strict product liability for a bank service.

29–010 In short, Directive 97/5/EC regulates cross-border credit transfers within the EC Member States through the following requirements:

(a) greater transparency of conditions of such transfers through adequate information to the customer who wishes to make the money transfer ("originator") prior and subsequent to such transfer (Articles. 3 and 4);

(b) minimum obligations of banks regarding such credit transfers to observe time limits, to pay compensation in case of duty violations (Article 6), and to transfer the full amount without deduction of costs (Article 7);

(c) refund by banks of the amount to be transferred up to 12,500 euro (Article 8) in case of non-execution and the provision by Member States of adequate procedures for the settlement of disputes (Article 10).

29–011 Article 1 of the Directive confines its scope of application to cross-border credit transfers in the currencies of the Member States and the euro (ECU) up to the equivalent of 50,000 euro. The transformation of the directive into national law can therefore lead to the unpleasant situation that different rules apply to domestic credit transfers, to cross-border transfers to or from third countries, and even to transfer within the EU of an amount exceeding 50,000 euro. There are strong reasons for national legislatures to consider a new uniform regulation for all kinds of credit transfer that is in line with the Directive.

2.2 Transformation into German law

29–012 The German legislature has in fact decided to apply the Directive on a much broader scale than required by the Directive. The scope of the new German law on credit transfers is wider than that of the Directive. It also applies to transfers of over 50,000 euro and will, as of January 1 2001, apply equally to domestic transfers and transfers to countries outside the EU As a result, Germany will have a uniform regulation of all types of credit transfer. The German legislature, through a law enacted in August 1999, transformed the Directive into German law by inserting §§ 675 a and 676 a–676 g into the German Civil Code (BGB). This included a new concept of the credit transfer order (as a contract instead of a unilateral instruction), an extension of the responsibility of the bank to timely and effective execution, including a money-back guarantee of up to 12,500 euro, and the liability of the bank of

---

[12] Consideration (11).

the originator (*i.e.* the transferring customer) for other banks used in the execution of the credit transfer. The new law is not a complete regulation of all the legal aspects of credit transfers as developed by the courts and legal doctrine. In at least two respects, the new law deviates from existing legal practice. First, the instruction issued by the customer to the bank of origin for the execution of a credit transfer was traditionally seen as a unilateral instruction in the legal framework of a bank account contract, analysed as an agency contract or mandate.

Under the Directive and the new German law, each individual instruction by the customer (originator) to execute a credit transfer constitutes a contract on its own. This contract is concluded when the bank accepts or carries out such an instruction accompanied by the necessary information. The banks may hope that the new concept of an individual contract gives them more freedom to reject an instruction. This is, however, doubtful. Under the new law, the bank is obligated by the account contract (Girovertrag) to conclude such a credit transfer contract unless there are serious reasons to reject it, *e.g.* because the transfer is to be made to a country at war or with other troubles and the completion of the transfer cannot be expected or there is a risk of a loss of the sum to be transferred. Under the old legal approach, *i.e.* where the Bank customer has the right to give his bank a unilateral and binding instruction, the same exceptions were applicable. After all, the practical effects of the doctrinal differences are very small. **29–013**

Another important change is the liability of the bank for intermediary institutions. Such a liability was denied by the courts under the former law on the grounds that the intermediary bank is not an agent for the bank of the originator.[13] The bank of the originator was seen as entitled to substitute the intermediary bank as the new agent for the originator and was liable only as to the careful choice of an intermediary bank. Banks had tried to avoid even this limited liability in their general conditions of contract. The new law puts an end to this unjustified avoidance of liability. **29–014**

2.3 A brief remark on the transformation into British law

In England, the Directive was transferred into English law by the Cross Border Credit Transfer Regulations 1999.[14] The new individual contract concept of the credit transfer underlying the Directive was in line with the existing English position. During the regulation consultation procedure, the banking industry requested clarification that the banks are under no obligation to accept offers for credit transfers or to even offer the types of services covered by the Directive. There is in fact no obligation under the Directive to conclude such a contract. As to the time of conclusion, it is held that the contract is concluded when the Bank receives the necessary information and the funds for the credit transfer and expresses its will to execute the transfer. **29–015**

As the Directive only covers credit transfers of up to 50,000 euro and the U.K. has not joined the European Monetary Union, it had to be decided **29–016**

---

[13] BGH WM 1991, 797.
[14] S.I. No. 1876.

whether the scope of the U.K. Regulations should be dependent on the one-time calculation of the amount in stirling. In the end, the actual exchange rate change became determinative of whether a credit transfer in stirling is covered by the U.K. Regulations or not. In defining what constitutes a "cross border credit transfer", the Regulations adopt the narrow definition underlying Article 2 (f) of the Directive, covering only transfers which contain all necessary information. The transformation of the Directive into English law did not exceed the minimum amount required by the Directive. This approach not to establish a regulation for all credit transfers as in Germany but to remain within the minimum requirements of the Directives, was also adopted for most other points, including the information to be given by credit institutions to customers and the consequences of delay. Thus, the transformation of the directive into English law was not used as an opportunity to newly regulate the whole area of cross border transfers, but just added a new scheme for certain types of transfers covered by the Directive.

3. Other directives and the recommendation

3.1 Directive 98/26/EC on settlement finality

29–017   Directive 98/26/EC of the European Parliament and of the Council of May 19, 1998 on settlement finality in payment and securities settlement systems[15] copes with the important systemic risk inherent in payment systems that operate on the basis of several legal types of payment netting, in particular multilateral netting. The Directive aims at the reduction of legal risks and fosters participation in real time gross settlement systems. It also aims to minimize the disruption to a system caused by insolvency proceedings against a participant in that system.

29–018   The main systemic risk in payment systems is the disruption to the system caused by insolvency proceedings against one participant in the system. Through such a disruption, a payment transaction can be cut in half, leaving one performing participant in a short position, empty handed at the end of the day and even without recourse to collateral security. This risk is particularly great in those traditional netting systems, where the individual credit transfer is netted (or set off) in a first step and the resulting net positions are netted at the central Bank accounts in a second step. Modern real time gross settlement systems, in contrast, provide for the execution of credit transfers only when the funds are received and thus avoid the dangers of a short position. The directive also covers securities settlement systems. It obliges the Member States to modify their national insolvency laws and other laws to be in line with, among others, Article 3 of the Directive:

> "Transfer orders and netting shall be legally enforceable and, even in the event of insolvency proceedings against a participant, shall be binding on third parties, provided that transfer orders were entered into a system (*i.e.* payment system) before the moment of opening of such insolvency proceedings . . ."

---

[15] [1998] O.J. L166/45–50.

This Directive was transferred into German law by a law of December 8, **29–019**
1999.[16]

3.2 Directive on consumer distance contracts

Directive 97/7/EC of the European Parliament and of the Council of May **29–020**
20, 1997 on the protection of consumers in respect of distance contracts[17]
aims at protecting consumers against the specific risks of cross-border distance contracts. It has no general connection with payment systems. Its Article 8, however, contains an obligation on Member States to ensure that the
consumer is able to request cancellation of a payment, where fraudulent use
of his payment card has been made in connection with distance contracts,
and to demand to be recredited with the sums paid.

3.3 Recommendation on electronic payment instruments

The Commission Recommendation 97/489/EC of July 1997[18] concerning
transactions by electronic payment instruments and, in particular, the relationship between issuer and holder, covers transactions effected by electronic
payment instruments (payment cards, home and phone banking applications
etc.) It aims at ensuring transparency of transactions and sets out minimum
requirements concerning the obligations and liabilities of the parties concerned. It seeks to ensure a high level of consumer protection in the field of
electronic payment instruments.

29–021

4. Concluding remarks

As observed in the introduction, the endeavours within the European Union
to unify or harmonize the laws on cross-border payments and other financial
transactions cannot resolve the problems of such payments and transactions
to and from non-EU countries. Therefore, global solutions are needed. One
such solution is the UNCITRAL Model Law on International Credit Transfers of 15 May 1992. There are some similarities between the EC Directive
97/5/EC and the Model Law, e.g. with regard to the obligation of banks to
refund to their customers (originators) any funds received if the payment was
not completed (Art. 14). This reminds us that global solutions must be found
and the EC initiatives in this field cannot be more than a first step. The name
of the late Clive Schmitthoff is closely related with the establishing of UNCI-
TRAL. It is this kind of global vision, so typical for Clive Schmitthoff, that
should inspire us to work for global solutions.

---

[16] BGBl. I S. 2384. See also B.R. Drucks, 456/99 of August 13, 1999.
[17] [1997] O.J. L144/19–27.
[18] [1997] O.J. L208/52–58.

PART SEVEN

RESHAPING THE INTERNATIONAL INSOLVENCY PROCESS

CHAPTER 30

MANAGING DEFAULTING MULTINATIONALS WITHIN NAFTA

JAY LAWRENCE WESTBROOK[1]

1. Introduction

The last decade saw the remarkable achievement represented by the promul-   **30–001**
gation of the Model Law on Cross-Border Insolvency by UNCITRAL.[2] In
the new decade, the key emerging initiatives in international insolvency law
are found at the regional level. The most important, of course, is the EU
Insolvency Regulation (née Convention) of the European Union.[3] Perhaps
the second most advanced regional development is represented by the

---

[1] Benno C. Schmidt Chair of Business Law, School of Law, The University of Texas at Austin.
[2] UNCITRAL Model Law on Cross–Border Insolvency with Guide to Enactment, U.N. Sales
No. E.99.V.3 [hereinafter "Model Law"].
[3] The EU Regulation is virtually identical to the European Union Convention on Insolvency
Proceedings, Nov. 23, 1995, reprinted in 35 I.L.M. 1223 (1996) [hereinafter the "EU
Regulation"]. On that basis, this paper assumes that all of the provisions of the EU Regulation
that it discusses are identical to those in the Convention.

Transnational Insolvency Project of the American Law Institute. The ALI Project is designed to facilitate international co-operation in cases of general default by multinational enterprises within NAFTA.[4] At its May, 2000, annual meeting, the ALI approved the Project's final product, a Statement entitled *Principles of Cooperation in Transnational Insolvency Cases Among the Members of the North American Free Trade Agreement*.[5] This paper describes the Project and the Statement, compares the North American and European positions, and looks forward to the next steps in international co-operation in the insolvencies of multinational corporations.

2. The American Law Institute project

30–002   The American Law Institute is a private-sector law reform organisation. It follows two distinct approaches in its projects. In some of them, it describes existing law (for example, its famous "Restatements"), while in others it makes proposals for legislation (the most well-known is the Uniform Commercial Code). In both approaches, the Institute adopts the most advanced concepts emerging in the courts and the legal academy, so that even its statements of existing law adopt the best of the cases and statutes found among the various jurisdictions. It achieves this result by using reporters and advisors who are well-regarded experts in each field. The reporters propose texts which are discussed with a committee of advisors in a one or two day meeting. The texts are revised in light of the criticisms of the advisors and rediscussed. When a text has achieved a sufficient level of agreement, it is submitted to the Institute's Council and then to its membership. In that process it is often subject to further revision before final approval.

30–003   The Transnational Project partakes of both the Institute's approaches, stating existing law and recommending legislation. Its first goal was to maximise the progress in co-operation in international insolvencies under existing law in the three countries, by educating judges and lawyers about the laws of each of the three countries, about the fundamental principles underlying a transnational approach to the issues presented, and about the tools available for co-operation. However, it was intended from the start that the Project would also identify and recommend important reforms that could not be achieved without legislation or further international agreements. In particular, it was recognized that the promulgation of a Model Law by UNCITRAL (a Project begun about the same time) and its adoption by the NAFTA countries would help enormously in permitting important advances.[6] That

---

[4] The Project excludes bankruptcies of natural persons, leaving the thorny issues of public policy implicated by that type of proceedings, for another day.

[5] American Law Institute, Transnational Insolvency Project, Principles of Co-operation in Transnational Insolvency Cases Among the Members of the North American Free Trade Agreement (Tentative Draft April 14, 2000) (finally approved May 16, 2000) (hereinafter the "Statement").

[6] In particular, it was understood that a civil law country like Mexico would be far more able to co-operate if the express authority to co-operate, and the necessary principles of law governing co-operation, were enacted by its legislature. By adopting the Model Law, it has done so. To some extent, the common-law countries in NAFTA can co-operate more fully even before enacting the Model Law although its enactment would be highly beneficial in those countries as well.

hope has already been realised in part with the recent adoption of the Model Law as part of a comprehensive reform of Mexican bankruptcy law.[7]

Following its domestic tradition, the Institute appointed reporters and advisory committees for the Project in each of the three NAFTA jurisdictions.[8] The Project was divided into two phases. All of the reporters met with each advisory committee separately in Phase I of the Project. In Phase II, the reporters and all three advisory committees met in grand assembly.

30–004

Phase I was devoted to approval of international statements of the bankruptcy laws of each of the NAFTA countries. The advisory committee and reporters in each country produced their respective statements. What made Phase I unusual among comparative law activities was the fact that, after each statement had been initially approved by its advisory committee, it was then cross-examined, so to speak, by each of the other advisory committees and revised to address the questions raised by them, so that these statements truly speak to an international audience. All three have been completed and approved and are awaiting final translation.[9] These statements serve as useful and authoritative summaries of the insolvency laws of the three countries. It is hard to imagine that there could be successful international co-operation in insolvency matters without some understanding of the insolvency laws of the other affected jurisdictions. The country statements are helpful tools for bench and bar and may encourage more comparative study by legal scholars in the insolvency field. They also have served the indispensable purpose of educating all of the Project's reporters and advisors in the laws of the three jurisdictions.

30–005

3. Description of Phase II

With that background, the Project moved into Phase II. The goal of Phase II of the Project was to develop a set of agreed principles governing multinational bankruptcy cases and to offer useful approaches to managing such cases based on those principles. Once again, it has followed both of the Institute's traditional approaches. It gives lawyers and judges the tools for managing existing transnational cases by identifying the best approaches to be found in existing laws and practice. It also recommends legislation that is

30–006

---

[7] Ley de Concursos Mercantiles & de Reforma al Artículo 88 del la Ley Orgánica del Poder Judicial de la Federación, Diario Oficial May 12, 2000.
[8] Bruce Leonard and Jacob Ziegel served as reporters for Canada. Miguel Hernandez Romo and Carlos Sanchez-Mejorada were the Mexican reporters. I was the United States Reporter. Each country provided an advisory committee of well-regarded experts in bankruptcy and international law. The United States advisory committee included two distinguished experts from outside NAFTA, Diane Kempe, Esq. and Professor Ian Fletcher. In addition, a number of ALI members provided comments and assistance as members of a Members Consultative Group.
[9] See Transnational Insolvency Project, International Statement of United States Bankruptcy Law (Tentative Draft April 15, 1997) [hereinafter "U.S. Statement"]; Transnational Insolvency Project, International Statement of Canadian Bankruptcy Law (Tentative Draft April 15, 1998) [hereinafter "Canadian Statement"]; Transnational Insolvency Project, International Statement of Mexican Bankruptcy Law (Council Draft No.1 December 1, 1997) [hereinafter "Mexican Statement"]. All three statements will be updated and current upon final publication in 2001.

needed to advance beyond existing law. It is meant to apply to both liquidation and reorganisation (rescue) proceedings.

30–007   The statement is divided into three parts. The first is a series of General Principles that underlie both the best practices under present law and the recommended legislative reforms. The second part sets forth procedures that facilitate co-operation in multinational bankruptcy and are available without new legislation in the laws of the three countries (or, in some cases, under existing law in at least two of them). The third part consists of recommendations for lawmaking in the form of legislation or international agreement, although without setting forth specific texts.

30–008   Three central premises underlie the entire statement. First, the laws of the NAFTA countries reflect fundamentally similar purposes, although they differ considerably in method. Secondly, they all reflect a conviction that a single, unified proceeding is the only way in which the purposes of insolvency law can be fully achieved. Thirdly, because a unitary proceeding is often not possible in international cases at our current stage of legal development, the goal should be to use co-operation among national proceedings to come as close as possible to the same result as in a single transnational proceeding.

30–009   As to proceeding on the basis of existing law, it is understood, of course, that the courts of each country are bound by the laws of that country and therefore co-operation is constrained by the requirements of those laws. On the other hand, the notions of comity and of recognition of judgments, among other doctrines, provide a powerful basis for co-operative results. The statement identifies its approach as "modified universalism," understanding that term to embrace a worldwide approach to multinational insolvency, modified by the practical requirements of international co-operation and by the constraints imposed by domestic laws.

30–010   The Statement explicitly identifies the key benefits of an efficient international insolvency regime as follows:

- Maximising the value of the enterprise and its assets;

- Providing equality of treatment for creditors and other interested parties with similar legal rights;

- Preventing and undoing fraud; and

- Providing commercially predictable results and transparent legal procedures. [10]

30–011   On the other hand, the Statement identifies its own limits. Its focus is the process of co-operation rather than substantive outcomes. In that connection, it specifically identifies three important, but very difficult types of issues it does not attempt to resolve: the choice of ancillary versus parallel systems of co-operation, choice of law, and priorities in distribution. The Statement takes the position that the international system just emerging has

---

[10] Statement, *supra* n. 4, at 18. In so doing, it does not exclude other social and political values that may be served by insolvency laws in each country.

not yet reached the point of maturity at which resolution of these issues can be harmonized.[11]

3.1. General Principles

The General Principles follow from the central ideas mentioned above. The **30–012** General Principles can be divided into two categories, international perspective and procedure. General Principles I and V-VII deal with international perspective in an insolvency proceeding. General Principles I and V establish the goal of co-operation to maximise value and to share that value on a worldwide basis. The worldwide approach is supported by the ideas in Principle VI of national treatment of claimants and in Principle VII of adjustment of worldwide distributions to promote equality in each proceeding (for common lawyers, the "hotchpot" idea). General Principles II-IV are procedural. General Principles II and III encourage liberal and speedy recognition of foreign insolvencies and imposition of a sweeping moratorium to protect the interests of all concerned. Principle IV encourages maximum transparency and sharing of information for the benefit of all the proceedings involving the common debtor.

3.2. Procedural principles

3.2.1. Existing law

This section of the Statement adopts the best approaches available under **30–013** existing law. In various respects, of course, existing law may be untested, unclear, or even divided. Nonetheless, the Statement asserts that the suggested principles are those that the Institute, through its expert advisors from three nations, believes can and should be applied under existing law. In several cases, explicit note is made that a particular principle cannot be applied under existing law in one of the three countries. Most often such a note refers to Mexico and many of those caveats will be removed upon full analysis of the new Mexican law. Subject to the stated exceptions, judges and lawyers are encouraged to feel confident about applying the principles in this section without waiting for new legislation or new international agreements. While the Statement does not claim that every advisor to the Project agreed with application of its principles under existing law in every respect, it does state that the Statement represents a substantial consensus and that no principle was adopted in the face of substantial dissent by the experts of any one country. All of the Principles are accompanied by explanatory commentary and most have examples (labelled "Illustrations") as well.

3.2.2. Single and parallel proceedings

The Statement follows the Model Law in that its recommended procedures **30–014** for co-operation necessarily address two rather different situations: single proceedings and parallel proceedings. These two situations bear an approxi-

---

[11] Statement, *supra* n. 4, at 24–29.

mate relationship to the two different concepts of co-operation generally found in the world today: ancillary proceedings in aid of a "main" proceeding and parallel proceedings. The former approach involves something less than a full domestic insolvency. The ancillary court typically issues an injunction to protect assets and may oversee local operations in a reorganisation context. It may supervise distributions under a worldwide plan or it may turnover assets for distribution by the main or "home-country" court.

30–015   This approach is followed by several countries, including the United States and Australia.[12] By contrast, parallel proceedings involve full insolvency proceedings in each country where assets are found, but there may be co-operation among those proceedings in aid of a worldwide resolution.[13] Where a parallel system has some idea of deference to a main proceeding, it may be called a subsystem of "secondary insolvencies."[14] The EU Regulation may be put into this category. The Model Law is deliberately designed to work with either the single or the parallel approach.[15]

30–016   The NAFTA Project also accommodates both approaches. Mexico and the United States are more inclined toward the ancillary idea, while the Canadian statute favours a parallel structure. Although the ancillary idea fits more easily, and perhaps more efficiently, into a worldwide perspective, either can be used consistent with that perspective.[16] On the other hand, the Statement clearly encourages deference to a "main" proceeding, which is defined as the insolvency proceeding taking place at the centre of the debtor's main interests,[17] whether the "non-main" court follows the ancillary or the parallel approach.

30–017   To reflect the dual approaches, several of the ALI procedures address each situation separately. For example, Procedural Principle 3 describes issuance of a stay in aid of a foreign main proceeding, while Procedural Principle 5 deals with reconciliation of stays in parallel proceedings so as to avoid overlap and inconsistencies. Similarly, Procedural Principles 11–13 govern aid to administration of a debtor company in a single full proceeding, while Procedural Principles 14–21 address co-operative administration in multiple parallel proceedings. It is, of course, no accident that more procedures are required for parallel administrations.

3.2.3. A brief description of the procedural principles

30–018   The content of the procedural section is organized in 3 sections corresponding to the stages of an insolvency case: Initiation, Administration, and

---

[12] Australia: Corporations Act 1989, No. 109 of 1989, div. 9, sec. 581, 2 Austl. Acts 3119–20 (1989), amended by No. 210 of 1992, 4 Austl. Acts 4734 (1992); United States: 11 U.S.C. §304.
[13] Perhaps the most successful example of a parallel proceeding (although not pursuant to a "system") was the Maxwell case. In re Maxwell Communication Corporation, 93 F.3d 1036 (2d Cir. 1996) (United Kingdom and United States). See generally, Jay L. Westbrook, A Global Solution to MultiNational Default, Mich. Law Review (2000), 98, 2276. http://papers.ssrn.com/paper.taf?abstractid=259960.
[14] See Don Trautman, Jay L. Westbrook & Emmanuel Gaillard, Four Models for International Bankruptcy, 41 Am. J. Comp. L. 573 (1994) [hereinafter "Four Models"].
[15] See Model Law, *supra* n. 1, arts. 28–30.
[16] Statement, *supra* n. 4, at 34.
[17] Statement, *supra* n. 4, at 14. This definition conforms to that in the Model Law and the EU Regulation. See Model Law, supra note 1, art. 2(b); EU Regulation, *supra* n. 2, Art. 3(1).

Resolution. For the purposes of summary description, it can be redivided into five areas: Recognition and Stay; Court Access, Information and Communication; Administration and Claims; Corporate Groups; and Binding Effect of Plans.

3.2.3.1. Recognition and stay

Interestingly, in none of the three NAFTA countries is there a focus on "recognition" as such. All three most often simply grant certain kinds of relief to representatives of foreign proceedings upon a proper showing. The Statement, by contrast, follows the Model Law by introducing recognition as the central legal action,[18] with relief in the form of a broad moratorium to follow quickly after.[19] It emphasises the long history of co-operation among the three countries to justify virtually automatic recognition. The moratorium to be granted upon recognition is to be the equivalent of the moratorium the recognising court would grant in a similar type of proceeding under its own law and will generally bind creditors and the debtor. Fast and nearly automatic recognition and moratorium will ensure court control of assets and will permit continued operations in case of a reorganisation. In addition, a moratorium provides an invaluable opportunity for the debtor and key creditors to engage in serious discussions looking to a consensual reorganisation, by contrast to the melee often resulting from an ill-timed initiation of collection or insolvency proceedings by a single creditor. There is no one factor more important in international insolvency than a swift and comprehensive moratorium.

30–019

The court will then have the leisure to examine more closely any objections to recognition or to the scope of relief. The court may thereafter "lift" the moratorium on the grounds available under its local insolvency law or, under Principle 3, revoke recognition altogether in the event of fraud. Because the recognising court will be applying its own familiar insolvency law concerning the scope of the stay and grounds for lifting it, delay and confusion should be minimised.

30–020

Problems frequently arise in determining the territorial scope of an insolvency stay. Some friction has arisen between Canada and the United States in this regard. For example, where a debtor in a United States bankruptcy has property in Canada, a United States court is likely to take the position that a creditor subject to personal jurisdiction in the United States—like a big Canadian bank—is bound by the United States stay not to take collection actions as to that Canadian property. The Canadian bank is apt to feel the Americans are over-reaching, as usual.

30–021

Principles 4B, 5 and 6 address various aspects of this problem. In the example just given, under Principle 4B, if the Canadian courts recognise the United States proceeding and issue a stay equivalent to their domestic stay for the same sort of proceeding, the United States stay should be deemed not to apply to the Canadian property. Only the Canadian stay would control that property.[20]

30–022

---

[18] See Model Law, supra note 1, Art. 17; Procedural Principle 1, Statement, *supra* n. 4, at 47.
[19] Procedural Principle 4, Statement, *supra* n. 4, at 56.
[20] Statement at 65–66. The statement leaves open whether this result should follow automatically, as a matter of comity, or requires application to the court for an order to that effect. The principle may most often be useful as part of an agreed Protocol approved by both courts.

30–023   Having attempted to ensure that the courts of each relevant country will have gotten control of the debtor's assets for the collective benefit of the debtor's stakeholders worldwide, the Statement urges that a recognised foreign representative be granted control of local assets, as long as no local full insolvency proceeding is pending.[21] Indeed, if there is no unfair prejudice to local creditors, the Statement urges that the assets be permitted to be transferred out of the jurisdiction when that is appropriate.[22] This last provision is especially important in reorganizations, because an integrated multinational may well move assets across borders in the ordinary course of its business —as with an integrated production sequence between Mexico and the United States, for example.

30–024   The mirror image to granting control of assets is ensuring allowance of all legitimate claims. Where there are likely to be claims from another NAFTA country where no local full proceeding is pending, the court is urged to ensure adequate notice, including additional time for filing claims and, where appropriate, notice in the language of the other country.[23]

3.2.3.2. Court access, information, and communication

30–025   Another important consequence of recognition should be access to the courts of the recognising country (through licensed counsel, of course). The notion of access would embrace intervention in civil actions pending by or against the debtor, intervention in pending local insolvency proceedings, and initiation by the foreign representative of either civil actions or a domestic bankruptcy.[24] Access also includes an opportunity to use all of the devices available under local law to gather information about the debtor and its assets.[25] On the other hand, the information obligation flows both ways, because the foreign representative is obligated to furnish to the recognising court particulars of any other insolvency proceeding involving the same or a related debtor and to keep that information current.[26]

30–026   The section on Procedural Principles also addresses communication among administrators and courts. It strongly encourages such communication and urges direct communication (rather than through discursive orders, for example) to the maximum extent possible. It recommends the adoption of specific guidelines that are attached to the Statement as Appendix 2. These guidelines represent an innovative and important step in the development of "real time" communication in international insolvency cases. Among other things, the guidelines authorise video communications and encourage simultaneous hearings. The Statement also requires administrators to provide notice to their fellow administrators of important hearings and other matters to be resolved in their respective courts[27] and to seek co-operative agreements ("protocols") for the management of

---

[21] Procedural Principle 11, Statement, *supra* n. 4, at 82.
[22] Procedural Principle 12, Statement, *supra* n. 4, at 84.
[23] Procedural Principle 13, Statement, *supra* n. 4, at 87.
[24] Procedural Principle 7, Statement, *supra* n. 4, at 71.
[25] Procedural Principle 9, Statement, *supra* n. 4, at 79.
[26] Procedural Principle 8, Statement, *supra* n. 4, at 73.
[27] Procedural Principle 16, Statement at 94.

the case.[28] An Appendix likely to be of great practical use to the bar contains samples of recently successful protocols.[29]

3.2.3.3 Administration and claims

There are two Procedural Principles under the heading "Administration" that are especially important in reorganisation cases. One is that, when the main proceeding is an attempted reorganisation, the courts in the other proceedings should do their best to assist in the reorganisation effort before permitting liquidation in a non-main proceeding.[30] The second is a provision encouraging the courts to co-operate in approving the post-filing financing so often crucial to a reorganisation effort. Procedural Principle 19 specifically endorses the granting of priorities and security interest in connection with such financing. This provision is, of course, closely related to Procedural Principle 12 permitting asset transfer, because the effect of post-filing priorities will often be to permit the transfer of asset values among jurisdictions. For example, a United States court might be asked to approve a financing for a Mexican company in reorganisation by entering an order securing the financing with assets located in the United States. The funds might then be used in any of the NAFTA countries, or even in operations outside NAFTA. If the reorganisation ultimately failed, the value of the United States assets may be greatly reduced by the security interest, effectively transferring that value to other jurisdictions. Procedural Principle 19 would encourage the United States court nonetheless to approve such a financing after the usual consideration of the likeliho-od of success and the benefits and costs of the reorganisation effort, resisting any attempt to defeat the financing on purely parochial grounds.

30–027

At the heart of any insolvency system is the allowance and payment of claims. As mentioned above, in cases with no parallel proceedings, Procedural Principle 8 provides for special notices to foreign creditors. Where there are parallel proceedings, the Statement unfortunately does not go so far as to adopt the "universal cross filing" ("UCF") provision of the EU Regulation. That provision permits an administrator to file representative claims in other pending proceedings on behalf of all claimants in the administrator's proceeding. The result, which is that all claims can be asserted in all proceedings, is potentially of great importance in the movement to a universalist approach to transnational insolvency.[31] While the Statement does not include a UCF provision as such, it adopts two rules that come close to UCF. Procedural Principle 22 emphasises acceptance of claims-allowance decisions made in parallel proceedings in another country. The Illustration uses the example of a Canadian employee of a United States company. The allowance of the employee's claim as valid and the fixing

30–028

---

[28] Procedural Principle 15 (generally), Statement, supra n. 4, at 95; Procedural Principle 17 (as to coordinated sales of assets in different countries), Statement, *supra* n. 4, at 95; Procedural Principle 20 (as to avoidance actions), Statement, *supra* n. 4, at 100.

[29] Another practical aid is an Appendix setting forth the provisions of the Model Law.

[30] Procedural Principle 18, Statement, *supra* n. 4, at 97.

[31] See generally, Jay Lawrence Westbrook, *Universal Participation in Transnational Bankruptcies*, in Making Commercial Law, Essays in Honour of Roy Goode (Cranston ed. Clarendon Press 1997); Jay Lawrence Westbrook, *Universal Priorities*, 33 Texas Int'l L.J. 27 (1998).

of its amount by the Canadian court would be accepted as final in the United States main proceeding, although determination of its priority status under United States law would be subject to further factual and legal review in the United States proceeding.[32] In addition to this principle of acceptance (akin to *res judicata*), Procedural Principle 21 requires administrators to exchange full and complete information about claims filed in each parallel proceeding. The combination of these two principles takes the Statement right to the threshold of the UCF idea and certainly leaves it open for judges in any of the three NAFTA jurisdictions to go the one small step farther to universal cross filing.[33]

30–029   The Statement also addresses one aspect of priorities in distribution. It concedes from the start that the priorities contained in local law must, like all legal constraints, be enforced.[34] However, Procedural Principle 25 states that the priorities need not be enforced beyond what they would yield for their beneficiaries in a territorial system. Put another way, priorities are the creatures of a territorial system and should not be extended extraterritorially to give their beneficiaries more than they would have received from local assets in a purely territorial approach.[35]

3.2.3.4. Corporate groups

30–030   Corporate groups present difficult problems in every legal discipline, because of the tension between the importance of recognising the corporate form and the reality that these groups often operate as a single enterprise.[35] The Statement's approach, in Procedural Principles 23 and 24, is to encourage co-ordination and co-operation among proceedings involving affiliated debtors to the maximum extent consistent with honouring the corporate form under applicable law.[37]

3.2.3.5. Binding effect of plans

30–031   The Statement stops short of asserting that all creditors should be bound by a reorganisation plan approved in a main proceeding, although there is powerful precedent for such a result.[38] Instead, Procedural Principles 26 and 27 provide two independent bases for holding that a plan of reorganisation is

---

[32] Statement, *supra* n. 4, at 104–05.
[33] It is plausible that the failure to include UCF and certain other ideas in the Statement was the result of a relatively compressed period of development of Phase II, which was assembled with only two meetings of the multinational advisory committee, although the reporters met more often.
[34] Statement, *supra* n. 4, at 25.
[35] Procedural Principle 25, Statement, *supra* n. 4, at 116–18.
[36] Philip Blomberg, *The Law of Corporate Groups: Bankruptcy Law* xxxvi–vii (1985).
[37] A recent unpublished paper by one of my students highlights the advance of "enterprise liability," in derogation of the corporate form, in some courts in the United States, although not necessarily under that rubric. See, *e.g.*, *Simon v. Philip Morris, Inc.*, 86 F.Supp. 2d 95 (E.D.N.Y. 2000); but see *United States v. Philip Morris*, 116 F.Supp. 2d 116 (D.D.C. 2000).
[38] See, *e.g.*, *Canadian Southern Ry. Co. v. Gebhardt*, 109 U.S. 527 (1883) (enforcing Canadian reorganization plan as to debtor's bonds traded in New York); Decision of November 16, 1996, IX ZR 339/95 (Germany) (enforcing Norwegian reorganisation plan as to debtor's bonds issued at Frankfort) (translation on file with author); Decision of May 27, 1993, IX ZR 254/92 (Germany) (enforcing Swiss discharge), discussed in Christoph G. Paulus, A New German Decision on International Insolvency Law, 41 Am. J. Comp. L. 667 (1994).

binding on a party. The first is participation in the case by the creditor "in any way."[39] Participation specifically includes filing a claim in a case, voting on a plan, or accepting a distribution of money or property under a plan. Thus participation in a case can bind a creditor who would not otherwise be subject to the jurisdiction of the reorganisation court.

The second basis for binding a creditor is the existence of personal juris-   **30–032**
diction over the creditor in the country of the main proceeding where the plan was approved. That is, if in ordinary civil litigation there would be jurisdiction over the creditor in that country, then the plan is binding on the creditor even if it does not file a claim or otherwise participate, assuming it receives proper notice of the insolvency proceeding. The existence of jurisdiction over the creditor in the first instance is tested under the law of the main proceeding. However, in a subsequent action where the binding effect of the plan is asserted in another court, the second court is entitled to consider whether the asserted basis for jurisdiction meets international minimum standards or is "exorbitant." In the latter case, of course, the second court may decide to refuse binding effect.

3.3. Legislative recommendations

The final section provides recommendations for further action in the form of   **30–033**
parallel legislation or international agreement. It does not provide specific text for adoption. For the most part, this section recommends adoption of the Procedural Principles in the more complete and comprehensive form available through legislation. In addition, however, it recommends work toward a harmonised priority system among the three countries and development of an official mechanism for rapid authentication of judicial acts by fax or e-mail.

4. Comparison with EU regulation

A comprehensive comparison of the ALI Statement and the EU Regulation   **30–034**
is beyond the scope of this paper, but a few salient points may be mentioned. We must start with the fact that the EU Regulation will be an official and binding legal regime, while the Statement is merely advisory. On the other hand, the two have in common an attempt to achieve at a regional level a closer degree of co-operation than can reasonably be expected globally.

As noted above, the EU Regulation establishes a system of secondary   **30–035**
bankruptcies, a subgenre of the parallel-proceedings approach, with some deference to the country of the main proceeding. The Statement defines a main proceeding in the same way as the EU Regulation and accommodates a secondary bankruptcy system, but reflects some preference for an ancillary system.[40] Overall, the Statement promotes more deference to a main proceeding than does the EU Regulation.

---

[39] Procedural Principle 26, Statement, *supra* n. 4, at 123.
[40] Statement, *supra* n. 4, at 16, 119.

30–036   One key difference is that the EU Regulation establishes choice-of-law rules, while the Statement explicitly excludes those issues. The EU Regulation establishes the law of the country of the proceeding (*lex concursus*) as generally applicable.[41] This rule, and a number of stated exceptions, make very useful contributions to predictability. The Statement leaves these matters unresolved for the most part. Regrettably, as seen from North America, the rules chosen by the EU Regulation are territorial and relatively old-fashioned. Most importantly, the choices are with reference to each proceeding, main or secondary, so that the benefits of predictability and uniformity are largely limited to the happy circumstance where only one proceeding is filed with respect to a given debtor. Once multiple proceedings emerge, then each one generates its own set of choices, with little deference to the main, home-country proceeding.

30–037   Both the EU Regulation and the Statement defer to traditional situs rules with regard to secured creditors. The EU Regulation provides that, if the creditor's collateral is within the EU, but outside the country where a proceeding is brought, then it may be largely immune from the effects of that proceeding.[42] If the *situs* law does not restrain secured creditors in reorganisation cases, and the local assets are important to the reorganisation attempt, then the effect will often be to render the reorganisation impossible.[43] The Statement is like the EU Regulation in that secured creditors will not be stayed from exercising their security under the domestic law of the *situs* unless that law would permit a stay.

30–038   Despite its general disclaimer as to choice-of-law rules, however, the Statement does contain a subtle choice of law as to the general effects of the stay at commencement of a case and as to the powers of the foreign representative. That choice represents a fairly fundamental conceptual difference between the EU Regulation and the Statement. Where there is a single proceeding , the EU Regulation adopts the law of that proceeding as to both the effect of the stay and the powers given to the foreign representative in a recognizing country.[44] The Statement adopts the law of the recognising country as to the effect of its stay in its territory. Furthermore, the Statement is silent as to the extraterritorial effect of a stay against secured creditors, except where a proceeding has commenced and a stay has gone into effect in another territory. [45] Thus, for example, when there is a proceeding in Country A only, the EU regulation would apply the Country A stay throughout the EU By contrast, the Statement would apply the domestic forms of stay of A, B, and C to the collateral in each country. The State-

---

[41] Ian F. Fletcher, Insolvency in Private International Law: National and International Approaches 265 (1999) [hereinafter "Fletcher"].

[42] *Id.* at 269–73.

[43] See Legal Dept., International Monetary Fund, Orderly & Effective Insolvency Procedural Principles: Key Issues 30–31 (1999).

[44] See Fletcher, *supra* n. 40, at 269–70, 285.

[45] As noted above, the creditor may even be free of the extraterritorial effects of the stay in the main proceeding, if local court has issued a stay of the same sort it would issue in a case of the sort pending in the main jurisdiction. Thus the United States stay in a reorganisation would cease to have effect in Canada once the Canadian court had issued a stay equivalent to that arising in a Canadian reorganisation.

ment would, on the other hand, permit Country A to claim extraterritorial effect in the other two countries, unless a domestic stay came into effect, for example, in Country B, at which point the Country A stay would cease to operate as to collateral in B.

The resulting balances of cost and benefit may simply reflect the greater (and growing) sophistication of Europeans in comparative law. The obvious benefit of the EU rule is that it produces uniform relief across the Union, without the confusion and possibly conflicting requirements arising from different stays. The cost is that judges and lawyers in each affected country must acquaint themselves with the laws governing the insolvency proceeding and apply them in a foreign legal environment in which those laws were never designed to operate. Thus a British insolvency will make the British stay applicable in, say, Belgium, where the local lawyers will have to figure out what they can do under such a stay. By contrast, if a case is filed in New York, the Canadian lawyers will know the nature and effect of the stay resulting from recognition of the United States proceeding in Toronto, because the stay issued upon recognition will be the local one familiar to them. On the other hand, the Statement's rule may create considerable difficulty for a debtor or creditor trying to obey both the United States and Canadian stays, especially as to property (for example, accounts receivable) of questionable situs. If only one proceeding is pending, the British administrator and all the creditors in the EU case will know precisely which stay applies, subject to the list of specified exceptions. **30–039**

The EU Regulation surpasses the Statement in many respects. For example, recognition is automatic and imposition of a stay immediate. Already mentioned was the provision for universal cross filing or UCF. If properly exploited in parallel proceedings, it should permit virtually complete equality of distribution among general unsecured creditors under the EU Regulation, in principle an enormous step forward.[46] The Statement urges deference to a reorganisation attempt in a main proceeding, but the EU Regulation goes farther to permit a stay of secondary proceedings in favour of the main.[47] **30–040**

Nonetheless, the Statement can claim more ambition in some respects. One instance of both conceptual and practical importance is its attempt to make reorganisation plans binding across national borders. A more fundamental point is its embrace of a worldwide perspective and a worldwide sharing of value. **30–041**

5. Relationship with Model Law

The Statement urges the NAFTA nations to adopt the Model Law on Cross-Border Insolvency. One of them, Mexico, has already done so. Another, the United States, has been on the very verge of doing so for the past two years and is likely to do so in the near future. Optimists in Canada think it will do so as well. **30–042**

---

[46] See Universal Priorities, *supra* n. 30, text at n. 17.
[47] See Fletcher, *supra* n. 40, at 293.

30–043   In discussions with Europeans, however, there is sometimes a sense that adoption of the EU Regulation will be enough for now, relegating the Model Law to some indefinite future. The notable exception is the United Kingdom, where the pending insolvency legislation authorizes the adoption of a form of the Model Law. From a North American perspective, the postponement of the Model Law would be a great disappointment. As with the Brussels convention, the EU Regulation has several features that seem to make it a bit of a "club," with non-members distinctly second-class citizens.[48] For example, the *lex situs* rule protecting secured creditors is limited to EU members, so that a secured creditor with assets in, say, England, would be shielded from the stay of a French proceeding, while a United States creditor might not be, depending upon the French choice-of-law rule for application of a stay to a secured creditor.[49] The Statement applies more neutral rules and has an explicit disclaimer of unequal treatment for non-NAFTA countries.[50]

30–044   In the near future, we are certain to face an increasing number of insolvencies in which a multinational has assets and creditors in both NAFTA and EU countries, among others. It would be a great mistake were we to look only inward. Adoption of the Model Law by the EU countries (or, better still, by the EU as a whole) would ensure a high level of co-operation in trans-Atlantic insolvencies.

6. The next steps

30–045   Given the difficulty of the issues, the progress over the last five years has been remarkable. There may be a bit of a pause to catch breath. Nonetheless, it is not too soon to consider what might be the next steps in the process of improving the management of general financial defaults by multinational companies. There are many possibilities, including these:

(1)   *Further progress within regions.*

(a)   Within NAFTA, it would be enormously helpful to move forward with harmonisation in the treatment of tax and employment priorities. It might also be possible to make progress with regard to the other great bankruptcy priority, security interests, because the Mexican Republic has adopted a far-reaching reform in that regard as well.[51] The new Mexican law apparently moves some substantial distance closer to the regimes found in the United States and Canada under Article 9 of the Uniform Commercial Code and the Personal Property Securities Acts.

---

[48] See Four Models, *supra* n. 13.
[49] *c.f.* Fletcher, *supra* n. 40, at 270.
[50] Statement, *supra* n. 4, at 2, n. 3; 10. It should be noted these explicit statements were added at the original suggestion of Professor Ian Fletcher, who was an advisor to the ALI Project.
[51] *See Reforman, Adicionan Y Derogan Diversas Disposiciones De La Ley General De Titulos Y Operaciones De Credito, Del Cogigo De Comercio Y De La Ley De Instituciones De Credito,* Diario Oficial, p. 3, Tuesday May 23, 2000.

(b)   Within the EU, I wonder if it might be possible to consider new initiatives with regard to reorganisations, including a broad trans-EU moratorium applicable to all creditors in aid of a rescue attempt in the main proceeding, even if the moratorium were limited to a short period of time. As noted above, even a short moratorium can give parties an opportunity to reach agreements that are by definition superior to litigation.

(2)   *Global Infrastructure.*

Globally, it would be worthwhile to begin work on the infrastructure that will be necessary for the next phase of general advance. For example, it would be enormously useful to establish a central website that could be used to provide notices of insolvency proceedings any-where in the word, as well as information about such proceedings as they move forward. Such a site would be of great practical value and would also provide a storehouse of data for study by academics and policymakers. Such a site might be maintained by a private organisa-tion, like INSOL or the International Insolvency Institute, or by an international organisation like UNCITRAL or the OECD—Indeed, the new website of the World Bank—Global Insolvency Law Database (GILD)—might evolve into such a site.[52]

7. Conclusion

The problem of managing the general defaults of multinationals is one **30–046** important component of globalisation of trade and investment. We have seen gratifying progress in the last five years and can look forward to still greater achievements relatively soon. The globalisation of business failure requires no less.

---

[52] http://wbln0018.worldbank.org/legal/gild.

CHAPTER 31

UNCITRAL PROJECTS; INSOL INTERNATIONAL

R.W. HARMER BA, LLB
SENIOR VISITING FELLOW, CCLS
CONSULTANT TO BLAKE DAWSON WALDRON, AUSTRALIAN LAWYERS

1. Introduction

1.1 *An age of insolvency law revolution?*

It may be that history will record the last decade of the last century as an age **31–001**
of insolvency law revolution. Any such acclaim may fall far short of the
veneration or importance in which other revolutions are held and, indeed, it
cannot be said that the insolvency revolution, if that be what it is, is one that
has been accompanied by the type of radical overthrow or change normally
associated with such a thing. However, the sheer volume and extent of developments and initiatives in relation to insolvency law and related practices at
national, regional and global levels during the last decade would appear to
justify or support the view that there has been a revolution, albeit of a
different kind.

It may certainly be questioned whether, in the past, there has ever been **31–002**
such a degree of prominence, attention and concentration on insolvency law.
The evidence of this recent and continuing degree of activity is documented
by:

● the number of national endeavours to reform or create new insolvency
  laws;

● the endeavours of countries in trading blocks to reach consensus on
  regional co-operation and assistance in the development and application of insolvency laws; and

● the most concerted endeavours yet undertaken to provide global foundations to take account of cases of cross-border insolvency.

1.2 *Economic factors*

History tells us that a revolution cannot occur without the presence of some **31–003**
one or more underlying factors, sufficient to provoke development and
change. The insolvency law development of which we speak would not have
occurred but for a much belated appreciation and recognition that insolvency
and related laws are vital to economic development and stability. That appreciation and recognition has come from the occurrence of three, largely unrelated, economic causes or factors.

The first in time was the economic recession that affected many of the **31–004**
more developed economies early in the last decade. The nature of the economic cycle dictated that the boom of the late 1980s should be followed by
bust. Many corporations had borrowed extensively during the boom against
the soaring value of stock and real property. Those values dropped dramati-
cally with the crash. The inevitable result was widespread corporate collapse.

31–005   The second cause was the collapse of command economy practices and associated political ideologies in a large part of the world and the consequent process of economic transformation throughout the decade toward market-based economic practices. In the countries affected by this economic change the need has been for a full range of commercial laws, including an insolvency law.

31–006   The third was the regional economic crisis that affected many economies in the Asian region in the last years of the decade. The crisis exposed, amongst other things, the inadequacy of many of their commercial laws, particularly their insolvency and related laws.

1.3 Relevance and importance for trade and commerce

31–007   At a regional or global level the overall effect of these economic and histori-cal events in relation to insolvency law translates into the importance of such laws for international trade and commerce. It is, thus, highly significant that this Symposium should take, as its theme, law and trade and international business in this new century. The purpose of this paper is to present insol-vency law developments in this area.

First, however, it may be appropriate to briefly survey the overall develop-ments during the last decade. These may be best presented from national, regional and global perspectives.

2. Insolvency law developments in the last decade

2.1 At a national level

31–008   The major developments have been in relation to new or reformed formal insolvency law regimes; improvement in judicial and administration systems to handle insolvency cases; and the development of informal insolvency techniques and practices.

2.1.1 Formal insolvency law regimes

31–009   •   In the more developed economies there have been intensive endeavours at national level to develop or improve formal corporate "rescue" insol-vency techniques. This resulted in the introduction of formal corporate rescue laws in a number of countries, such as Australia, Canada, Argentina and Germany, and actual or proposed amendment or revi-sion of existing rescue laws in countries such as England, France, Spain and the USA.

•   In the economies affected by the shift to market economic practices there has been a need to establish insolvency law regimes to take account of economic based reforms associated with state-owned enter-prise sectors and the emergence of private enterprise sectors. Notable in this respect has been the emergence of new (sometimes "first ever") insolvency laws in many economies, including those of the former USSR, the People's Republic of China and in countries such as Vietnam, Mongolia and Laos.

- In the economies affected by the Asian economic crisis there have been widespread endeavours to improve the quality of their respective insolvency laws and their application. Thailand, Indonesia, Korea, Philippines and Japan provide the most notable examples.

One result of this concentration on the development and reform of national insolvency laws has been the extent to which insolvency law models practiced in other countries have been used or taken account of. Although this is capable of causing friction and misunderstanding (often expressed as a concern with so-called "globalisation"), a more positive result has come from the work of a number of international agencies to develop less intrusive and more politically acceptable and commercially justified guidelines or standards in relation to insolvency law regimes. That work is reviewed later in this paper. **31–010**

Hopefully, another possible effect has been to impress upon governments the need to maintain insolvency law regimes under constant review, in contrast to long gaps in time between sporadic, haphazard and, at times, impulsive reform. **31–011**

2.1.2 Informal insolvency techniques and practices

The last decade has also been notable for the development of informal insolvency techniques. This has been largely led by the banking and finance sectors in a number of countries in an endeavour to overcome defects in, supplement, or provide alternative techniques to formal insolvency law regimes. **31–012**

The main technique developed from these initiatives has come to be known as the informal corporate "work out". It has become widely practiced in a number of countries, such as the U.K., USA, Canada and Australia. More recently the technique has been applied to deal with widespread corporate failure in a number of the Asian economies that were affected by the economic crisis. Each of Korea, Thailand, Malaysia and Indonesia established agencies to encourage and develop informal corporate work outs. **31–013**

By comparison with the unregulated, banking sector led informal work out techniques practiced in countries such as England and USA, the practices in these Asian economies are markedly more structured and regulated. That has been necessary because of systemic problems arising from the effect of the crisis upon the banking and corporate sectors. **31–014**

However, and more importantly, the application of the informal technique in these Asian economies has been far more successful than the application of their respective formal insolvency laws (despite extensive reform and improvement to some of them). This is possibly due to cultural attitudes and influences. Regional studies (particularly those recently undertaken by the Asian Development Bank and OECD) have identified an aversion within the commercial community in these economies to confrontational/formal legal processes and a far greater acceptance of techniques that allow for informal structured negotiation. It is possible that in many of the Asian economies the introduction and development of the informal "work-out" technique may leave a greater lasting beneficial legacy than the improved formal insolvency law regimes. **31–015**

2.2 At a regional level

2.2.1 The European Union Regulation on insolvency proceedings

31–016   The economies of Europe that were first linked together as members of the European Economic Community and more recently as members of the European Union have long sought to reach agreement on cases of insolvency that involve cross-border issues within member states. Unfortunately, diplomatic disputes that have had nothing to do with insolvency have conspired to defeat and delay the most recent progress. The latest of these concerned the long-term running dispute between Britain and Spain over Gibraltar. However, thanks to diplomatic efforts it has been reported that an accommodation has been achieved that will allow the E U Insolvency Project to proceed to its conclusion after many decades of effort. Professor Ian Fletcher discusses the recently adopted Regulation in his paper.[1]

2.2.2 NAFTA insolvency project

31–017   The economies of the North American Free Trade Area have also sought to understand and bridge differences in national insolvency laws to make them more compatible and more easily applied in cases of insolvency that have transnational aspects to them. Professor Jay Westbrook comments upon that development in his paper.[2]

2.3 At a global level

31–018   The recession early in the last decade affected a considerable number of corporations that had assets and business interests in a number of countries. Although this was not a new phenomenon, the rapid increase in international trade and commerce had brought about a considerable growth in businesses with such international interests. However, very little had been done to meet the likely problems to be encountered by the financial failure of such international business organisations. The insolvency of a number of these enterprises exposed the difficulty and inadequacy of cross-border insolvency laws and practices.

31–019   The need to deal with the affairs of such an insolvent enterprise by reference to the insolvency law regimes of two or more countries also brought about a realisation of differences in standards between the regimes. That, coupled with the inadequacy of the insolvency law regimes of countries facing financial crisis, produced recognition that both domestic and international investment confidence is enhanced and encouraged by transparent and predictable insolvency law regimes.

Two major endeavours resulted from these effects.

---

[1] See *infra*, p. 496.
[2] See *supra*, p. 465.

2.3.1 The UNCITRAL Model Law

The first concerns the work of UNCITRAL on an international model law   **31–020**
for application in cases of cross-border insolvency. This affords a real
prospect of reaching international co-operation and assistance in cases of
cross-border insolvency. The prospect of implementation of the model law is
discussed later.

2.3.2 International insolvency law guidelines

The second endeavour concerns the work of a number of international agen-   **31–021**
cies in response to the realisation that trade and commerce is at the heart of
economic development and the fundamental requirement for a sound body
of commercial law to support that development. Insolvency law is a vital part
of a commercial law system. This has resulted in endeavours by the major
multilateral agencies to develop international guidelines toward acceptable
standards of insolvency law regimes and related areas. This is another area
that is likely to be pursued by UNCITRAL.

2.3.3 Other insolvency law related international endeavours

Other global or internationally related projects that have some indirect rele-   **31–022**
vance for insolvency laws should also be mentioned. These concern secured
transactions.

One such project is the work of UNCITRAL on a draft convention on   **31–023**
assignment of receivables in international trade. Part of this proposed
convention is concerned with the securitisation of receivables, which has
some relationship to the application of national insolvency laws.

Another project is the work of UNIDROIT on a draft convention con-   **31–024**
cerning international interests (which includes interests arising out of a
secured transaction) in mobile equipment (for example, aircraft and aircraft
equipment). It also has relevance to the application of insolvency laws.

Yet another project is the recent initiative of the Asian Development Bank   **31–025**
that urges the need for an integrated (or "tandem") approach to the development of insolvency and secured transaction laws.[3]

A further, prospective, initiative is that of the American Law Institute,   **31–026**
which may result in a project concerned with the development of model rules
or principles for both international and domestic secured transactions. This
will also involve considerations of insolvency law.

3. UNCITRAL and the Model Law on cross-border insolvency

The UNCITRAL model law on cross–border insolvency was formalised in   **31–027**
mid-1997, following some three years of concentrated effort. It has been the

---

[3] See "The Need for an *Integrated Approach to secured Transactions and Insolvency Law Reforms*", published in Law and Policy Reform at the Asian Development Bank, Vol. 1, Edition 2000).

subject of a number of papers and articles. It should not be necessary to refer to the content and detail of the model law in this paper. It might, however, be observed that, although the Model Law, both generally and with respect to particular of its provisions, has its critics, it has been generally acclaimed as a very important and valuable improvement in international insolvency law. The focus in this paper is on the adoption of the Model Law.

3.1 Progress toward enactment

31–028   A considerable momentum has been gathering toward the adoption of the Model Law by a number of countries. These include the USA, England, Canada, Australia, New Zealand and South Africa. In most of these countries legislation has been drafted or law reform or amendment projects are underway for the purpose of adoption and there is little doubt that the process of adoption and enactment will soon commence. The following is a summary of the position.

3.1.1 England

31–029   English judges and commentators have long claimed a "crying need" for an international insolvency convention. Although the Model Law falls short of a convention it is probably the next best thing. Toward that objective, an Insolvency Bill was introduced in the House of Lords on February 3, 2000 and enacted on November 30 as the Insolvency Act 2000. The Act provides for the adoption of the UNCITRAL model law by providing, in section 14, that:

> *"The Secretary of State may by regulations make any provision which he considers necessary or expedient for the purpose of giving effect, with or without modifications, to the Model Law on cross-border insolvency"*

The *"Model Law on cross-border insolvency"* is defined as meaning *"the model law contained in Annex I of the report of the 30th session of UNCITRAL"*.

3.1.2 USA

31–030   In the USA the Model Law has been faithfully adhered to in legislation that proposes a new Chapter 15 of the US Bankruptcy Code. The new chapter would deal solely with cross-border insolvency matters. The legislation to bring this about was originally conceived as "stand alone" but through some incomprehensible political mischief the legislation was later hijacked to form part of other legislation that had but a faint relevance to insolvency. This seemed to pave the way for debates over such things as liability for violence at abortion clinics and for tobacco related diseases. These quizzical excesses of the American political and legislative system leave most foreign observers glassy eyed. However, there is an assurance from most American commentators that eventually the American adoption of the Model Law will become part of its Bankruptcy Code.

3.1.3 New Zealand

The New Zealand Law Reform Commission published a report (*Cross-Border Insolvency, Report No. 52*) in February 1999. The report recommends that New Zealand adopt, with some minor alterations, the Model Law. There is, however, an element of a "wait and see" approach in the New Zealand attitude since the recommendation is not to enact without clear signs of enactment by the major trading partners of New Zealand (for example, Australia).   **31–031**

3.1.4 Australia

The responsible government Minister announced in November 1999 that the Australian government had commenced a review of its corporate insolvency legislation and that the review would include ". . . *the implementation of the UNCITRAL Model law on Cross–Border Insolvency* . . ." Legislation is anticipated during this year.   **31–032**

Australia provides an interesting example of a country that is currently reasonably well served by unilateral cross-border insolvency recognition and assistance provisions. Both its bankruptcy and corporate insolvency laws provide for recognition and assistance. In the case of a number of countries recognition is mandatory and in the others discretionary. This is, of course, "one way" legislation since, like the USA and England, Australia affords the reasonable prospect of recognition and assistance upon application from an overseas jurisdiction without requiring a corresponding mutuality in such a jurisdiction for recognition of a case of insolvency originating in Australia.   **31–033**

Notwithstanding that "one way" approach, Associate Professor Rosalind Mason, a leading Australian writer on international insolvency issues, has commented[4]:   **31–034**

> *'The Model Law has the potential to advance co-operation and co-ordination in Australian cross-border insolvencies. An important advantage is the ease of access for foreign representatives to local courts when time is often of the essence. . . . There are simplified procedures for recognition of foreign orders and foreign representatives, and the effects of such recognition are clarified.*
> *Given the effective way in which the existing provisions for co-operation between Australia and foreign courts in bankruptcy and corporate insolvency matters have operated, it is to be hoped, however, that the existing legislative provisions are amended to add extra avenues for recognition and co-operation rather than repealed and replaced with the Model Law."*

Associate Professor Mason has also, and quite justifiably, observed that:

- The Model Law does not address choice of law principles and the outcome of international insolvencies will continue to be uncertain; and

- There is also a question about the extent to which Australian courts will be willing to communicate directly with other courts.

---

[4] See "*Implications of the UNCITRAL Model Law for Australian Cross–Border Insolvencies*" in International Insolvency Review, (1999) Vol. 8, pp. 83–108 at 107.

3.1.5 South Africa

31–035 South Africa has also moved toward adoption, but with the possibility of a slight sting in the tail. It has been proposed that the legislation should only apply in respect of other jurisdictions that have similarly adopted the Model Law. This "*quid pro quo*" approach is somewhat further removed from the New Zealand "wait and see" approach. The South African attitude requires mutuality which, although discussed and debated, was expressly rejected by the member countries of UNCITRAL during the drafting of the Model Law. To make application of the Model Law conditional on a similar adoption by the country from which an application for recognition and assistance is made severely limits the "international" nature and substance of the law. Hopefully those who are pressing for this type of approach in South Africa might be persuaded otherwise. There is, of course, a real danger that if one country adopts this attitude, other countries will follow.

3.1.6 India

31–036 In India the government has recently appointed a committee on the law relating to the insolvency of companies. The issues to be examined by the committee include cross-border insolvency issues. Specifically the committee will address the following:

- "*What provision should be incorporated in the Insolvency Law for the protection of the interest of foreign creditors? Should the new law incorporate provisions of the Model Law of Cross-Border Insolvency?*

- *Are there other suggestions to expedite the process of winding up keeping in view the present development of international trade and commerce?*"

31–037 In most of the above countries there has been, for some time, an apparent willingness to endeavour to accommodate cross-border insolvency cases, difficult though it may have been under existing laws. There is thus a greater acceptance of the policies and aims of the Model Law and a corresponding positive view of the respective governments in those countries toward adoption. However, there are many other countries in which there is a need to radically change historical or political barriers and prohibitions against international recognition and assistance before there is any prospect of adoption and enactment of the Model Law.

3.2 Overcoming barriers to enactment

31–038 Despite that adoption and enactment of the Model Law may appear to reflect good sense and a commitment to encourage international trade and commerce, it may seem surprising that a number of the major Asian economies each have insolvency laws that prohibit international recognition and assistance. The following provide examples.

31–039 - In **Thailand**, section 177 of the Bankruptcy Act 1937 provides as follows:

"The receivership of assets or a bankruptcy action under this Act relates only to the assets of the debtor within the Kingdom.

The receivership of assets or a bankruptcy action under the laws of other countries has no effect as to the assets of a debtor in the Kingdom".

- In **Japan**, Article 3 of the Bankruptcy Law 1922 provides: **31–040**

"A bankruptcy adjudged in Japan shall be effective only with respect to the bankrupt's properties which exist in Japan.

A bankruptcy adjudged in a foreign country shall not be effective with respect to properties existing in Japan".

- In **Korea**, Article 3 of the Bankruptcy Act 1962 provides: **31–041**

"The bankruptcy shall be effective only to the bankrupt's property in Korea.

Any bankruptcy which is declared in a foreign country shall be ineffective to the property in Korea".

- In **Taiwan**, Article 4 of the Bankruptcy Law 1935 provides: **31–042**

"A composition reached abroad or a bankruptcy adjudicated abroad shall not take effect in respect of the properties which the debtor or bankrupt possesses within the domain of the Republic of China".

In part contrast, the Bankruptcy Acts (but not the Companies Acts) of both Singapore and Malaysia contain provisions for assistance and co-operation between those respective countries in cases of cross-border bankruptcy. For example, section 104 of the Bankruptcy Act 1967 (**Malaysia**) provides:

"(1) The High court and the officers thereof shall in all matters of bankruptcy and insolvency act in aid of and be auxiliary to the courts of the republic of Singapore . . . so long as the law thereof requires its courts to act in aid of and be auxiliary to the courts of Malaysia."

"(4). . . .where any person has been adjudged a bankrupt by a court of the Republic of Singapore, such property of such bankrupt situate in Malaysia as would, if he had been adjudged bankrupt in Malaysia, vest in the official receiver appointed by the Government of the Republic of Singapore, and all courts in Malaysia shall recognise the title of such Official Assignee to such property."

"(5) The production of an order of adjudication purporting to be certified under the seal of the court in the Republic of Singapore making the order. . . . shall be conclusive proof in all courts in Malaysia of the order having been duly made and of its date."

It seems clear that there will be a need for considerable co-operation and leadership in the Asian region to provide the momentum to overcome some of these barriers. Possibly the greatest hope lies with the recognition that these countries are part of an important economic region and that trade and commerce between them, and externally, might be assisted by the adoption of laws such as the UNCITRAL Model Law.

4. UNCITRAL and international insolvency law guides

31–043   It is not, as yet, possible to provide a more definitive or descriptive title to this latest proposed work of UNCITRAL. The precise objective is still to be identified. Some explanation of the origins of the work may be helpful.

4.1 Origins of the project

4.1.2 A proposal from Australia

31–044   Early in 1999 Australia, one of the member countries of UNCITRAL, presented a proposal to UNCITRAL on possible future work in the area of insolvency law. The proposal referred to recent regional and global financial crises and the work undertaken in international forums in response. It said that the resulting reports from those forums showed that strong insolvency and debtor-creditor regimes were an important means for preventing or limiting financial crises and for facilitating rapid and orderly workouts from excessive indebtedness. Australia, therefore, proposed that UNCITRAL consider the establishment of a working group with the development of a model law on corporate insolvency to foster and encourage the adoption of effective national corporate insolvency regimes.

4.1.3 The contributory work of international forums

31–045   As mentioned earlier in this paper, the work of multilateral agencies, notably the Asian Development Bank, OECD, the International Monetary Fund and the World Bank, has been extensive in relation to insolvency law in the economies of the former USSR, eastern Europe, PRC, Vietnam, Central and Latin America and Asia.

31–046   However, it was probably the effects of the Asian economic crisis that made it more apparent that there was a possible need for the development of some standards in relation to insolvency law regimes and in their application.

31–047   The onset of the Asian economic crisis (the date of which is generally recognised as around July 1997, when the currency of Thailand was devalued) exposed severe deficiencies in the insolvency law regimes of many Asian countries. These deficiencies, although reasonably detectable, had not, however, caused much, if any, effect on both domestic and foreign private investment in the region. The level of investment and general trade and commerce in many of the Asian economies was spectacular. Some were described as "economic miracles".

31–048   In many countries the effect of the crisis was devastating. The banking sector was almost paralysed by bad debts and foreign exchange liabilities. Investment funds poured out, back to their places of origin. The corporate sector, ultimately liable, awaited a huge shake out.

31–049   This is not the place to probe these effects and their resolution more fully, interesting and fascinating though they are, but it is the place to record that the effect of the crisis was probably the catalyst to prompt proposals for the development of insolvency law standards.

4.1.4 The work of the Asian Development Bank

The *Asian Development Bank (ADB)* was possibly the first international **31–050**
organisation to commence such a development. In mid-1998 it commenced a regional technical assistance on comparative insolvency law
reform in 11 Asian jurisdictions, ranging from Japan in the east to Pakistan
in the west.

The terms of reference of the project included that recommendations **31–051**
"suitable for the region" should be made to deal with corporate insolvency.
That necessarily involved the development of suitable standards to be
applied when both reviewing laws and practices in the 11 economies and in
making recommendations for reform. It should also be observed that the
comparative study of these 11 economies involved more than an examination
of their respective insolvency law regimes. It involved all debtor/creditor laws
and practices, including secured transactions, unsecured debt transactions,
secured property enforcement, debt recovery, formal insolvency law
regimes and their application and informal insolvency techniques and
their application.

Following that study a *Comparative Report* was published in October 1998. **31–052**
It contained an extensive number of proposed standards or practices for consideration in the formation and development of an insolvency law system.
Those proposals were to form part of the basis for the present UNCITRAL
initiative.

Following further study, research and public discussion, a final report con- **31–053**
taining over 30 "good practice standards" for insolvency law reform and
development was published in April 2000 (see "Insolvency Law Reforms in
the Asian and Pacific Region", published in *Law and Policy Reform at the
Asian Development Bank, Vol.1 Edition 2000*).

4.1.5 The work of the International Monetary Fund

The *International Monetary Fund (IMF)* published a report entitled *"Orderly* **31–054**
& Effective Insolvency Procedures" in April 1999. The foreword to the report
mentions that an effective insolvency law system:

- *"can play a major role in strengthening a country's economic and financial system"*;

- *"provides an important pillar of support for the domestic banking
  system"*;

- in economies in transition can *"play a critical role in addressing the
  problems of insolvent state-owned enterprises"*; and

- in the context of financial crises, can *"provide an important means of
  ensuring adequate private sector contribution to the resolution of such
  crises"*.

The IMF report then discusses and suggests the major policy choices to be **31–055**
addressed by countries when designing an insolvency law system. It states

that "the issues discussed are relevant to all countries, irrespective of the different stages of their development" and, whilst it does not seek to propose standards, it suggests "preferred" solutions.

The IMF Report was also used by UNCITRAL as a basis for discussion on its present initiative.

4.1.6 The work of the World Bank

31–056   The third international organisation into this field of endeavour has been the *World Bank (WB)*. In May 1999 it announced the commencement of an ambitious project "*on the development of standards and guidelines for sound insolvency systems*". The broad expectation is that these would "*serve as a benchmark to assess the state of insolvency systems in developing countries, as a tool to guide insolvency law reform, and as a means of increasing awareness in developing countries of the wider legal and economic context in which insolvency operates*'. The work of the World Bank is not due for completion until later this year, but much of its preliminary work has also been used by UNCITRAL as a basis for discussion.[5]

31–057   It is in those three endeavours that the geneses of the proposed project for UNCITRAL may be found. But, given the extent and the undoubted quality of the work of the three agencies, the question might be asked why or for what purpose should UNCITRAL also become involved?

4.1.7 Should UNCITRAL be involved and in what capacity?

31–058   On whether UNCITRAL should be involved, a consideration of three issues suggests that it should.

First, the issue of "coverage". Each of them, ADB, IMF and WB, has significant power and influence. Individually or co-operatively, it might be anticipated that they could influence or assist in the formulation and reform of insolvency laws according to the type of standards that they each support. But, and even assuming that to be so on a country by country, economy by economy assessment, none of those organisations may expect to cover the globe. Thus whilst their work in relation to individual countries or, even, a number of countries in a region, might bring about some desirable uniformity or internationalism in respect of insolvency laws, there would be obvious gaps. UNCITRAL has a more international coverage and influence.

31–059   Secondly, the issue of "perception". Despite the fact that many of the countries that are members (and/or shareholders) of the three international organisations are also members of UNCITRAL, the work of organisations such as ADB, IMF and WB is their own and the decisions and achievements they reach are those of the organisations themselves. On the other hand, decisions and achievements of organisations of the United Nations (such as UNCITRAL) are made by the member governments and not by the institution. Put somewhat bluntly, it may be that the three organisations do not

---

[5] See Gordon Johnson, "Towards International Standards on Insolvency: The catalytic role of the World Bank", Law in Transition 69–74 (Spring 2000).

represent the same influence or carry the same approbation that the United Nations or its various agencies might possess.

Thirdly, the issue of "consensus". It may not be expected that the three international agencies would necessarily agree on a statement or code of standards, whether described as "preferred", "best", "good" or howsoever. They have each had to pursue their respective agendas in response to their particular constituencies. Even though they might, if pressed to do so, reach common ground on such things, the question remains as to whether the fact that the three organisations had a common policy on those issues would add much to the weight, respect or influence with which such a policy might be treated? UNCITRAL might be better regarded as presenting a "united" view.   **31–060**

UNCITRAL presents itself as the preferable institution to promote the cause of the world wide insolvency law initiative.   **31–061**

4.1.8 The initial deliberations of UNCITRAL

Although there is much to commend that UNCITRAL might be the preferable organisation to undertake this work, even that raises the question of whether the work is something that should be done (whether it is likely to achieve anything) and, if so, the precise nature of that work. It was this that occupied the time of a working group of UNCITRAL on insolvency law in Vienna, 6–17 December 1999.   **31–062**

Understandably, there is some body of opinion that is highly sceptical of the nature of this work. It may be cogently argued that insolvency law regimes are best left to individual states and that, historically, there have been and remain so many differences between them on a range of issues that there can be no real prospect of bringing greater harmony or uniformity about by the urging of the application of common standards.   **31–063**

There is much to support that view, but it may also be submitted that support for the interests of contemporary economic, commercial and international business development would suggest otherwise. The development of internationally recognised standards in many areas of the law (such as intellectual property, arbitration, insurance) has demonstrated that commercial interests are more than capable of devising internationally acceptable legal standards in important areas of trade and commerce. In theory there is no reason why insolvency law should be an exception to this trend.   **31–064**

The issue of involvement leads, in turn, to the issue of defining exactly what might be done. The possibilities are somewhat infinite, but the more obvious may be presented as follows: **31–065**

● develop key objectives for an effective insolvency law;

● develop core features of an effective insolvency law;

● develop legislative guidelines of an effective insolvency law.

It is accepted that there is simply no purpose in producing a "Model Law" of insolvency. On the other hand there may be some good purpose in seeking to evaluate, consolidate and continue the work of the three international organisations with the aim of ultimately producing a statement of key objectives   **31–066**

31–067 and core features of insolvency regimes supported by a legislative guide toward the implementation of such objectives and features. Some of the latter might be represented as "model" legislative provisions if a high degree of consensus and support is achieved for them.

4.1.9 The recommendations for future work

31–068 That was the effective proposal or recommendation from the Working Group of UNCITRAL as a result of its deliberations during the 2 week session in Vienna in December 1999.
    The precise terms of the recommendation were as follows:

> *"The Working Group recommends that the Commission give it the mandate to prepare: a comprehensive statement of key objectives and core features for a strong insolvency, debtor creditor regime, including consideration of out-of-court restructuring; a legislative guide containing flexible approaches to the implementation of such objectives and features, including a discussion of the alternative approaches possible and the perceived benefits and detriments of such approaches. A legislative guide similar to that being prepared by the Commission for privately financed infrastructure projects would be useful and could contain model legislative provisions, where appropriate.*
> *Should the Commission decide to undertake the project, the Working Group should be mindful in carrying out this task of the work underway or already completed by other organisations, including the International Monetary Fund, the World Bank, the Asian Development Bank, the International Bar Association and INSOL International. The Working Group should seek their collaboration in order to benefit from the expertise these organisations can provide and to build on their efforts and should commence its work after receipt of the reports currently being prepared by the World bank and the Asian development Bank."*

31–069 The recommendation was considered at the plenary meeting of UNCITRAL in New York in June 2000. Subsequently, an international meeting in the form of a Global Insolvency Colloquium was arranged, to take place in Vienna early in December 2000. Hopefully it will be possible to create some precise and not too ambitious terms of reference to enable the member countries to make some positive progress. If UNCITRAL does embark on the project it may be assured of the willing assistance of the three international agencies. The prospect of these agencies working together and in concert, hopefully free from the immediate dictates of their respective constituencies, will achieve a desirable degree of co-operation and mutual involvement that is all too often absent.

5. The involvement of INSOL international

31–070 INSOL International was founded in 1981. It represents professional, insolvency-related member organisations throughout the world which, in turn, account for nearly 8,000 individual insolvency practitioners in 63 countries. The member organisations and the individuals they represent come from a variety of disciplines—ranging from law, accounting, the judiciary, academics, bankers and financiers to insurance.

31–071 INSOL is non-political and non-jurisdiction based. Its principal aim is to advance the development, knowledge and understanding of insolvency and related law and practice throughout the world. It does so by participating in regional and international endeavours and initiatives in respect of the law and practice of insolvency.

INSOL may properly claim to have provided the initial impetus for the **31–072** UNCITRAL Model Law project. It did so by focusing on the business and commercial needs for such a law and the importance of it for international trade and commerce. It looked to UNCITRAL as the obvious international forum to develop and progress the project. Once UNCITRAL had taken up the initiative, INSOL, as an invited non-government organisation participant, was actively involved in the development of the Model Law and remains active in continuing to support and encourage its enactment.

INSOL has also been invited and will continue to participate in the pro- **31–073** posed general insolvency law work of UNCITRAL. It is also involved in the UNIDROIT work on the proposed convention for international interests in mobile equipment, mentioned above.

INSOL will present its 6th World Congress in London in July, 2001.

6. Conclusion

There is every prospect that the early years of this 21st century will inherit **31–074** some substantive and long term benefits in insolvency law from the endeavours undertaken during the last years of the last century. As this paper has sought to make clear, these endeavours have been largely inspired by and relate to the importance of insolvency law and practice for trade and commerce at national, regional and global levels.

CHAPTER 32

INTERNATIONAL INSOLVENCY AT THE CROSSROADS—A CRITICAL APPRAISAL OF CURRENT TRENDS

PROFESSOR IAN F. FLETCHER
CENTRE FOR COMMERCIAL LAW STUDIES

1. Introduction

There is an ancient Greek proverb to the effect that:

When the gods wish to punish us, they usually begin by answering our prayers.

32–001 This distillation of the fruits of human experience is worth keeping in mind as we contemplate the current state of international insolvency, and the multiple initiatives which are in progress or contemplation, aimed at improving the processes by which cross-border cases are resolved. As one who has spent much time during the past quarter-century advocating the development of a system, or framework, of procedures to address these needs in a principled way, the author may well incur the charge of perversity by suggesting that we are now at risk of suffering from too much of a good thing.[1] Nevertheless,

---

[1] For a more detailed account of the author's studies in this area, see I.F. Fletcher, *Insolvency in Private International Law* (OUP, 1999).

there would seem to be a real possibility that duplication of effort, and dissipation of the limited human and material resources that are available for such a technically exacting task, could combine to deprive us of the long-anticipated fruits of the quest for the "Holy Grail". It is with this concern in mind that the present paper has been written.

The paper itself falls into two main parts. The first part anticipates the entry into force of the European Union Regulation on Insolvency Proceedings, and reviews its salient features with the aim of complementing the accounts of other contemporary developments in the companion papers presented at this session. The second part offers some reflections on the challenges that are posed by the near-simultaneous emergence of a plethora of initiatives in the field of international insolvency, presenting us with an embarrassment of riches that may prove to be both a boon and a bane.

32–002

2. Part I: A glimpse into the future—The EU Regulation and the wider world

2.1 Survey of current initiatives

The roll-call of international insolvency initiatives that are presently "in play" includes examples of both regional and global projects. These range from regionally-based projects such as those conducted under the auspices of the Council of Europe; the European Union; the North American Free Trade Agreement; and the Asian Development Bank, to globally-aligned ventures undertaken by the United Nations Commission on International Trade Law (UNCITRAL); the IMF; and the World Bank. The instrumental means of achieving these projects' respective purposes also exhibit a striking variation, from the "classic" form of multilateral convention founded upon the principle of reciprocal undertakings entered into among sovereign states; to the "uniform" or "Model" Law available for enactment at the discretion of states and without any formal pre-commitment on their part; to the formulation of statements of principles of co-operation, and guidelines representing "best practice", that are intended to inspire courts, legislators and practitioners to effect a progressive convergence of policy and practice in the international sphere. Standing some way apart from these is the latest product of the long-running EU insolvency saga, which now assumes the form of a Regulation and thus, having been adopted under the relevant legislative procedures of the EU as modified under the Amsterdam Treaty, will have the force of directly applicable law throughout the Union (with the exception of Denmark) without the need for any measures of implementation at state level. By this uniquely forceful system of supranational law the Member States of the European Union will become subject to a uniform code of rules covering jurisdiction, choice of law, and recognition and enforcement of judgments and orders in insolvency matters, to a degree never previously experienced in the realm of international insolvency. In view of these qualities, and in the light of the Regulation's adoption by the EU Council on May 29, 2000, it is appropriate to draw attention to some of its more notable features.

32–003

2.2 The EU Regulation on insolvency

32–004   Without in any way detracting from the achievements that have been depicted in the papers contributed by Professor Jay Westbrook and Ron Harmer, it may nevertheless be argued that the most remarkable adventure of all has been that experienced by the European Union, whose Protean efforts over more than three decades to conclude an insolvency convention for adoption by its steadily expanding membership seemed perpetually destined to collapse in failure. The chapter of accidents continued down to and including the ignominious events of 1995-96, when consummation was denied at the last minute due to the U.K.'s refusal to become a contracting party to the convention which it had actively helped to shape, and with whose terms it was fundamentally in agreement.[2]

32–005   Fortunately, after an uneasy hiatus of some three years following the technical lapse of the convention due to the U.K. failure to lodge its signature by the deadline of May 23, 1996, the project was rescued from limbo through a joint initiative by the German and Finnish republics, which successively held the presidency of the EU Council of Ministers during 1999. Still more remarkably, it was revived in the form of a regulation for adoption by the Council under the combined provisions of Articles 61(c), 65 and 67(1) of the EC Treaty as amended by the Treaty of Amsterdam. This development is of great importance, amounting to a transformation of the legal status and impact of the measure itself. As a convention concluded by the Member States of the EU, it would have been subject to substantial delay in implementation, due to the need for every state to complete the process of domestic adaptation prior to ratification (in the case of the Rome Convention on Contractual Obligations of June 19, 1980, these formalities had the effect of postponing that convention's entry into force until April 1, 1991). Now, as a regulation adopted by the Council in accordance with the law-making powers conferred by the Treaty, the measure has the force of directly applicable law according to the terms of Article 249 (previously numbered as Article 189). According to well established principles of supremacy of European Community/Union law—particularly where, as here, it is in the form of a regulation—the measure will take effect in all Member States on the date specified for entry into force (May 31, 2002) without the need for any legislative or administrative steps at national level. To the extent that any pre-existing provisions of national law are in conflict with the provisions of the Community measure, the former simply cease to be applicable and national courts are required to give effect to the latter. However, to avoid confusion that might ensue from reliance upon unamended provisions of domestic law that happen to be incompatible with the superimposed requirements of EU law, it would clearly be advisable for all states to undertake an assessment of any modifications in either law or administrative practice that are necessitated by this development. Provided that timely action is taken, the period of grace until 2002 should suffice for such adjustments to be made.

32–006   One curious consequence of the recasting of the former convention as a regulation is that it will be necessary for Denmark to make special arrange-

---

[2] The history of the EU project is related in greater detail in Fletcher, op. cit. supra n.1, pp. 246–256; 298–301.

ments to enable the regulation to apply there in a uniform way alongside the other 14 Member States. This is because the relevant provisions of the EC Treaty on which the measure is based are affected by the permanent "opt-out" negotiated by Denmark when the Amsterdam Treaty was concluded. Since Denmark had demonstrated its positive intentions towards the insolvency measure during the period when it was open for signature in the form of a convention, it is confidently expected that this anomaly can be taken care of by emulating the text of the Regulation and giving it the requisite effect in Danish law (possibly by means of a special convention concluded between Denmark and the other 14 states).

2.3 Outline - principal features of the EU Regulation

The Regulation contains provisions which affect each significant aspect of cross-border insolvency, namely the exercise of jurisdiction; the determination of the applicable law; the recognition and enforcement of proceedings in other Member States; and matters of special concern in the conduct of cross-border cases including the rights of creditors to participate effectively. Before exploring these matters in somewhat closer detail, an unusual aspect of the Regulation should be noted. The task of interpreting this legislative measure by courts and interested parties may have to be undertaken without the assistance of any officially sanctioned guide as to its intended meaning and effect. At the time of abandonment of the project for a convention after the events of May 1996 the planned Explanatory Report (under the authorship of M. Virgos and M.E. Schmit) had not been formally endorsed by the EU Council and thus far has not been officially published or released for general circulation. The Virgos-Schmit Report would in any case require further revision before being capable of serving as an authentic guide to interpretation of the Regulation as finally adopted, but there are apparently no plans to remedy this deficiency. The process of transformation from convention to regulation was carried out under a policy of non-interference with the substance of the text as finalised in 1995, and with just a limited number of exceptions this was achieved. Conscious of the need to address the more prominent issues of meaning and interpretation, the negotiators had recourse to the somewhat inelegant technique of supplementing the preambles and recitals that traditionally introduce legislation of this kind, with a series of preliminary recitals which are intended to furnish interpretative guidance on both the general approach to be followed and also on specific provisions and terminology. The final tally of Recitals is an astonishing 33 numbered paragraphs. These should be studied carefully by anyone who requires to gain as complete an understanding of the meaning and scope of the Regulation as can be derived from the currently authorised sources.

32–007

2.3.1 Subject matter

Article 1(1) provides that the Regulation shall apply to:

"collective insolvency proceedings which entail the partial or total divestment of a debtor and the appointment of a liquidator".

32–008   The wide scope of the above proposition is limited by the terms of Article 1(2), which declares that the Regulation shall not apply to "*insolvency proceedings concerning insurance undertakings, credit institutions, investment undertakings which provide services involving the holding of funds or securities for third parties, or to collective investment undertakings*". The excluded matters are generally the subject of special regulatory regimes, including provisions for insolvency procedures, maintained at national level and in several cases pursuant to harmonised provisions introduced by the EU through Directives. Further identification of the scope of the Regulation is provided by Article 2(a) in conjunction with Annex A: the definition of "Insolvency proceedings" is declared to indicate the collective proceedings which are listed in Annex A, which specifies the relevant proceedings for every one of the 14 states concerned. Thus, for the United Kingdom, the proceedings listed are:

- winding-up by or subject to the supervision of the court;

- creditors' voluntary winding-up (with confirmation by the court);

- administration;

- voluntary arrangements under insolvency legislation; and

- bankruptcy or sequestration.

32–009   It is noteworthy that all of the above procedures can be characterised as collective in nature, and involve the court in some way, even if the inauguration of the process is not in all instances dependent on an order of the court. However, these qualifying characteristics have precluded the listing of administrative receivership, or other forms of receivership, and these accordingly are outside the ambit of the Regulation.

2.3.2 Jurisdiction

32–010   The Regulation establishes a jurisdictional regime which controls the opening of all proceedings falling within its scope. The regime is carefully circumscribed, however: it only applies where insolvency proceedings are to be opened in relation to a debtor whose *centre of main interests* is situated within the territory of a Member State. In the case of such a debtor, proceedings can only be opened as and where permitted by the Regulation. Conversely, where the centre of the debtor's main interests is located outside the EU the Regulation does not apply, with the consequence that insolvency proceedings may be opened in any Member State whose laws permit this to be done in the circumstances of the case in question. This can include the exercise of so-called "long-arm" rules of jurisdiction over debtors with minimal contact with the forum. However, when proceedings are opened in circumstances that fall outside the jurisdictional scheme of the Regulation, it is necessarily the case that these cannot benefit from any of the further provisions of the Regulation, such as automatic recognition and effectiveness throughout the other Member States. It may be noted therefore that there is no requirement that states should totally abrogate any long-arm rules that may currently be found in their insolvency laws: all that is needed is an adjustment to the scope of application of these rules, so that they cannot be used as the basis for opening proceedings against a debtor whose centre of main interests lies in any of the other EU Member States.

The concept of the debtor's centre of main interests (hereafter referred to by the abbreviation "COMI") is indeed the key to the entire scheme of operation of this Regulation. Article 3 establishes a hierarchical structure of primary and subsidiary jurisdiction, with primacy being accorded to the proceedings opened in the COMI. A subsidiary competence is accorded under Articles 3(2) and (3) to the courts of any Member State in which the debtor possesses an establishment (as explained below). However, such proceedings are declared to be exclusively territorial, in the sense that their effects are restricted to assets of the debtor situated within the territory of the state of opening. Despite the paramount importance of the concept, however, there is no complete definition of COMI within the main provisions of the Regulation. Article 3(1) confines itself to establishing a presumption to the effect that: **32–011**

> "*In the case of a company or legal person, the place of the registered office shall be presumed to be the centre of its main interests **in the absence of proof to the contrary**". (emphasis added)

The presumption is thus a rebuttable one, and is limited to cases of legal, as opposed to natural, persons. No further guidance is provided as to the nature or degree of proof required to overcome the force of the presumption, although it may be inferred that it will be incumbent upon those who seek to have proceedings dismissed for want of jurisdiction to sustain the burden of convincing the court currently seized of the matter that the debtor's COMI is located in another Member State. Further insight into the intended meaning of COMI is supplied by Recital (13) to the Regulation, which states: **32–012**

> "*The 'centre of main interests' should correspond to the place where the debtor conducts the administration of his interests on a regular basis and is therefore ascertainable by third parties.*"

It can be seen therefore that transparency and objective ascertainability are to be given special emphasis in interpreting the COMI connecting factor. When faced with the need to determine the whereabouts of a debtor's COMI, a court should pay careful regard to the impression given to external parties as to the debtor's administration of its interests. It should not be permissible for the debtor—more particularly the management of a corporate debtor— to take advantage of some clandestine *modus operandi*, or of a peripatetic arrangement for conducting the control and management of operations, such that outsiders cannot readily identify any *locus* at which these functions are discharged "on a regular basis". The fundamental policy concern is that parties which have dealings with a debtor whereby they entrust it with their credit must be able to calculate the legal, as well as the financial, risks thereby assumed. Reasonable expectations, founded upon appearances for which the debtor is responsible, should be protected as far as possible.   **32–013**

Article 3(2) allocates a subsidiary jurisdictional competence to the courts of a Member State in whose territory the debtor possesses "an establishment". Although such proceedings, as already mentioned, are of territorial   **32–014** effect only, this can be of considerable significance in view of the legal consequences which ensue. In particular, the basic principle whereby the applicable law for most purposes is that of the state in which insolvency proceedings are opened, can create opportunities for interested parties to protect themselves against the full consequences of having their fate determined in accordance with the insolvency law of the state in which the debtor's COMI is located. By the same token, if it were too easily possible for such parties to bring about the opening of concurrent, territorial proceedings in relation to one and the same debtor, this could give rise to wasteful duplication of administrative expenses, resulting in loss of value for creditors generally. Such fragmentation would also undermine the integrity of the Regulation itself, which is designed as a response to the legal and commercial requirements of an integrated internal market operating under the fundamental principles and freedoms of the European Union. Accordingly, the definition of *Establishment* supplied by Article 2(h) is deliberately narrow. For the purposes of the Regulation, the term means:

> "*Any place of operations where the debtor carries out a non-transitory economic activity with human means and goods.*"

32–015   The above wording has the consequence that the mere presence of assets— however great or small their value might be—cannot be utilised as a basis for exercise of insolvency jurisdiction by the courts of one Member State in relation to a debtor whose COMI is located in another Member State, even though local rules of jurisdiction might otherwise have permitted this to take place. To justify the exercise of jurisdiction based on the presence of "an establishment", the court must be satisfied that the debtor maintains a "place of business" within the state in question. This will necessitate the court making a factual determination, based on appropriate evidence. It is submitted that the term "establishment" must be given an autonomous meaning in the context of the Regulation's application, for otherwise there could be considerable variation between national courts in their approach to this crucial jurisdictional concept. It may be anticipated that, as also in the case of the COMI concept, national courts will need to refer questions of interpretation to the European Court of Justice for the purpose of clarifying the meaning and scope of this key term in its application to particular patterns of facts. Although (as mentioned above) the status of the Virgos-Schmit Report is currently uncertain, the relevant passage in its paragraph 71 is worth quoting here:

> "A purely occasional place of operations cannot be classified as "an establishment". A certain stability is required. . . . The decisive factor is how the activity appears externally, and not the intention of the debtor."

32–16   *2.3.3 Recognition of Insolvency Proceedings*

The paramount practical need in any cross-border insolvency is that the duly-appointed office holder, as representative of the debtor's estate and of all collective interests associated with its administration, should be enabled to take swift and effective action to control and protect the assets of the estate in any foreign jurisdiction, as circumstances require. In many instances, the disparities between the laws of the relevant states, and the slow or inhospitable processes of the local laws of the *situs* of assets, may render it impractical for the office holder to attempt to assert the rights with which he is supposedly endowed by virtue of his original appointment. Although the Regulation cannot directly enhance the office holder's prospects of operating effectively outside the confines of the EU itself, the special cogency of EU law within the frontiers of the Union should ensure that the office holder is able to exercise his powers in the other Member States to a degree that is unprecedented in the history of international insolvency.

Article 16(1) establishes the principle of immediate and universal recognition of insolvency proceedings opened in accordance with the jurisdictional scheme of Article 3: the judgment opening the proceedings "shall be recognised in all other Member States *from the time that it becomes effective in the state of the opening of proceedings*" (emphasis added). Article 17(1) supplies the additional rule that the judgment opening the main proceedings under Article 3(1) shall, *with no further formalities*, produce the same effects in any other Member State as under the law of the state of opening of proceedings, except where the Regulation provides otherwise and as long as no secondary proceedings are opened in the other member state under Article 3(2).   **32–017**

A further, and crucially important, rule is contained in Article 18(1), which declares that the liquidator appointed by a court which has jurisdiction under Article 3(1) may exercise *all the powers conferred on him by the law of the state of opening of proceedings in another Member State*, as long as no secondary proceedings have been opened there nor any preservation measure to the contrary has been taken there pursuant to a request for opening of secondary proceedings in that state. Article 18(1) includes a specific provision to the effect that the liquidator is empowered to remove the debtor's assets from the territory of the member state in which they are situated (subject to Articles 5 and 7), but in exercising his powers he must comply with the law of the member state within whose territory he intends to take action (Article 18(3)).   **32–018**

To reinforce the aim of enabling the liquidator to take timely and effective action in other jurisdictions, Article 19 establishes a simple formality for providing proof of his appointment, by means of a certified copy of the original decision appointing him, or by any other certificate issued by the court which has jurisdiction. Translation can be required into an official language of the Member State in which the liquidator intends to act, but otherwise no legalisation or other formality shall be required. This is designed to eliminate the scope for imposing elaborate and expensive formalities in accordance with local procedures for granting recognition—as in the case of *exequatur* proceedings traditionally demanded in Civil Law countries—before the liquidator can claim standing to act there. Further diminution of the traditional scope for interposing barriers to recognition and enforcement of foreign judgments is effected by Article 26, which declares: **32–019**

> "*Any Member State may refuse to recognise insolvency proceedings opened in another member state or to enforce a judgment handed down in the context of such proceedings where the effects of such recognition or enforcement would be manifestly contrary to that state's public policy, in particular its fundamental principles or the constitutional rights and liberties of the individual.*"

32–020 The drafting of this provision is deliberately restrictive, so as to deny any scope for revision of insolvency judgments by the courts required to recognise and enforce them. Once it is confirmed that the judgment emanates from a court which claims jurisdiction under Article 3 of the Regulation, recognition can be refused only in the case where a grave violation of fundamental legal or constitutional principles would otherwise take place. The underlying intention is that the judicial and administrative authorities of the state in which the proceedings originally commence must take appropriate steps to ensure that jurisdictional propriety is maintained. This is likely to involve some modification of the domestic rules governing the exercise of insolvency jurisdiction, to require a more active vetting of the debtor's relevant circumstances including the lodging of active confirmation by the petitioner that the debtor's COMI - or failing that an establishment of the debtor - is situated within the territory of the state in question. Although these matters are not made the subject of any express requirement by the Regulation itself, they seem to be a necessary counterpart of the potent, extraterritorial effects to which it gives rise. Unless some kind of common standards - amounting to an agreed code of "best practice" - can be put in place, considerable economic damage could be inflicted through courts' inappropriate exercise of jurisdiction.

2.3.4 Uniform rules on choice of law

32–021 Although it has proved impracticable to undertake a harmonisation of the domestic laws of the EU Member States in relation to matters of insolvency, one of the principal achievements of the Regulation—and, it may be suggested, one of its chief claims to be an historic advance in the international governance of international insolvency—is that it imposes a unified code of choice of law rules for the cases falling within the ambit of its application. These rules, in conjunction with the mandatory regime of jurisdictional rules that will apply throughout the EU, will enable those who have dealings with a debtor whose COMI is within the EU, or which has one or more establishments located within the Union, to calculate with far greater precision the substantive legal provisions by which their rights will be determined in the event of the debtor's insolvency.

32–022 The choice of law provisions of the regulation are contained in Articles 4–15 inclusive. The general principle, as embodied in Article 4, is that the law applicable to insolvency proceedings and their effects shall be that of the Member State in which the proceedings are opened, save where there is contrary provision within the other provisions of the Regulation itself. The basic rule in favour of the *lex concursus* is by no means novel or controversial in itself: its significance in this context is that it articulates with considerable precision the matters which are destined to be governed by the law of the forum whenever insolvency proceedings are opened under the governance of the Regulation. Indeed, in addition to declaring that the *lex concursus* shall determine the conditions for the opening, conduct and closure of proceedings, Article 4(2) identifies no less than 13 matters which are referred to that same law. These include such significant issues as the determination of which assets form part of the estate; the conditions under which set-offs may be invoked; the process of distribution including the ranking of claims and the treatment of partially satisfied claims of creditors holding security or analogous rights; and the avoidance of antecedent transactions detrimental to the general body of creditors. Not only does this serve to emphasise the strategic importance of the venue of insolvency proceedings, from the standpoint of particular parties in interest, but it also imparts an additional significance to the further provisions within Articles 5-15, which introduce special exceptions to the general principle of determination according to the *lex concursus*. While it is not proposed to explore these provisions in detail in this paper,[3] they deserve close attention by those actively involved in international commercial activities, where much may depend on the ultimate determination of the law by which a transaction is governed. The list of matters which are the subject of special choice of law rules serves to emphasise the potential importance of these provisions of the Regulation. They concern: the rights of parties holding some form of security over property of the debtor (including holders of "floating" security over a fluctuating collection of assets) (Article 5); the right to claim set off (in certain cases where the *lex concursus* would otherwise not permit this) (Article 6); rights of unpaid sellers, and also rights of purchasers of assets, where the sale incorporates a reservation of title clause (Article 7); the effects of insolvency on a contract for the sale or leasing of immovable property (Article 8), or on the rights of the parties to a payment or settlement system or to a financial market (Article 9), or on employment contracts and relationships (Article 10); the effects of insolvency proceedings on the rights of the debtor in immovable property, a ship or an aircraft subject to some form of public registration (Article 11); effects upon intellectual property rights established by Community law (Article 12); special defences against avoidance of prior transactions afforded to the beneficiary under the law governing the transaction (Article 13); protection of third party purchasers for value of assets disposed of by the debtor after opening of insolvency proceedings (Article 14); and the effects of insolvency on lawsuits pending concerning an asset or right of which the debtor has been divested (Article 15).

2.3.5 Secondary insolvency proceedings

Chapter III of the Regulation is the product of a protracted quest to create **32–023** a workable compromise between the irreconcilable opposites of cross-border insolvency doctrine, namely universality and territoriality. In a world whose laws are so infinitely diverse in their approach to insolvency-related matters, the theoretical and logical attractions of there being a single set of proceedings bearing universal effects are confronted by the reality that such a process would in many instances disrupt the reasonable expectations of parties whose dealings with the insolvent debtor were conducted with reference to a different system of law. However, the converse theory of territoriality, which contemplates parallel sets of proceedings as dictated by the geographical disposition of the debtor's assets and interests, not only is open to criticism on

---

[3] See the detailed treatment in Fletcher, *op. cit. supra* n.1, at pp. 265–282.

grounds of its potential to bring about unequal treatment of creditors on account of the random (or, yet worse, the pre-calculated) disposition of assets at the moment of bankruptcy, but also is seen as a contradiction of the principles of freedom to engage in cross-frontier economic relationships that are the foundations of the European Union itself.

32–024   The pragmatic solution to the historic antithesis between the rival theories is the device of secondary insolvency proceedings. While sustaining the principle that accords primacy of effect to proceedings opened at the debtor's COMI in accordance with Article 3(1), the Regulation permits territorial proceedings to be subsequently opened under Article 3(2) and (3) with the status of secondary proceedings. As such proceedings can only be opened on the basis of the presence of an establishment of the debtor in the state in question, the fact that (as was previously explained) the definition of "establishment" has been so drawn as to require the existence of a place of business has the effect of curtailing the opportunities for parties to bring about the opening of such proceedings unless there is a sustained, business connection between the debtor and that state.

32–025   However, where circumstances permit the opening of secondary proceedings, the principal advantage is likely to be the substitution of the law of the Member State in which those proceedings are opened, in place of the law of the state of opening the main proceedings, for any purpose concerning the determination of applicable law (Article 28). This may enable parties whose claims would enjoy preferential status under the law of the state of secondary proceedings, but whose claims might not be similarly treated under the law of the main proceedings, to achieve a more favourable outcome from the distribution of such assets as can be collected in the state of secondary insolvency. However, the overarching principle of unity is reaffirmed by the terms of Article 32, which declares that any creditor may lodge his claim in the main proceeding and in any secondary proceeding, and that the liquidators in the respective proceedings are to engage in consolidated cross-filing of claims which have already been lodged in the proceedings for which they were appointed.[4] The inter-relationship between parallel proceedings may be complex, but the underlying aim of equality of treatment for creditors of equivalent status is confirmed by Article 20(2), which states that:

> "... a creditor who has in the course of insolvency proceedings obtained a dividend on his claim shall share in distributions made in other proceedings only where creditors of the same ranking or category have, in those other proceedings, obtained an equivalent dividend."

32–026   This restates the equitable proposition known as the *Hotchpot* rule, which has a long and honourable place in the U.K. tradition towards international and domestic insolvency matters. If somehow the process of liquidation of assets in the secondary proceedings results in the full satisfaction of all claims allowable in those proceedings, any surplus remaining is required by Article 35 to be transferred to the liquidator of the main proceedings. Thus, the notion of the essential unity of the debtor's estate is carefully maintained.

---

[4] This is the practice referred to by Professor Westbrook as "universal cross-filing". See his paper, *supra*, at p. ***.

2.3.6 Creditors' right to lodge claims

In Chapter IV of the Regulation (Articles 39–42) there are some useful, if   **32–027**
modest, provisions which should alleviate the practical disadvantages experienced by creditors when participating in proceedings which have commenced
in a foreign jurisdiction. Sometimes these disadvantages are the result of
directly discriminatory provisions of the *lex concursus*, whilst other forms of
disadvantage may simply be the consequence of differences of language or
procedure, or of the difficulties of long-distance communication.

The basic principle of equality of treatment of all creditors, regardless of   **32–028**
their state of residence or of business attachment, is proclaimed by Article 39
in the following terms:

> *"Any creditor who has his habitual residence, domicile or registered office in a member state*
> *other than the state of the opening of proceedings,* **including the tax authorities and social**
> **security authorities of member states**, *shall have the right to lodge claims in the insolvency*
> *proceedings in writing."* (emphasis added).

The striking feature of this provision is that it overrides, for the benefit of tax   **32–029**
and social security authorities of EU Member States, the long established
exclusionary rule of private international law whereby the courts of one state
will refuse to enforce, either directly or indirectly, the revenue or other public
laws of other sovereign states. One consequence of this rule, as exemplified
in the House of Lords decision in *Government of India v. Taylor*,[5] is that foreign revenue authorities are denied standing to lodge proof in insolvency
proceedings in the U.K. in respect of unpaid tax or social security liabilities
due from the debtor. Although this rule must henceforth be abrogated with
respect to claims by the public authorities of EU sister states, there is no
requirement that the rule be abandoned altogether in respect of revenue
claims of non-EU states. Moreover, the terms of Article 39 stop short of
imposing a requirement that foreign fiscal claims be accorded a priority of
ranking equal to that enjoyed by the domestic authorities of the state in
which the proceedings are taking place. It would seemingly suffice if foreign
revenue claims are included among the ordinary, unsecured debts under the
distributional process.

The provisions in Articles 40–42 are designed to place the liquidator under   **32–030**
a duty to give immediate notification of the opening of insolvency proceedings to all known creditors who have their habitual residence, domiciles or
registered offices in the other member states. It is to be hoped that this will
not give rise to any discriminatory treatment as against parties who happen
not to be linked with any Member State in one or more of the ways
prescribed.

Linguistic problems are an inescapable fact of life in international   **32–031**
insolvency. Practical considerations, and limited resources, preclude any
requirement which would make it mandatory for all communications from
the liquidator to be expressed in the recipient's preferred working language.
Articles 40 and 42 attempt a compromise by requiring the liquidator's

---

[5] [1955] A.C. 491.

notification to bear the heading "*Invitation to lodge claim. Time limits to be observed*" in all 12 official languages of the institutions of the EU, but the text of the notice itself need only be in one of the official languages of the state of opening of proceedings. A further concession is made to allow creditors to lodge their claim in one of the official languages of their country of habitual residence, domicile or registered office, but it is left open for the liquidator, at his discretion, to require the creditor to provide a translation into one of the official languages of the state of the opening of proceedings. Inevitably, the expense of complying with such a requirement would have to be borne by the creditor.

2.3.7 Interpretation by the Court of Justice

32–032   As an act of the Council of the EU, the Regulation falls within the scope of Article 234 (formerly numbered as 177) of the Treaty establishing the European Community. This provision confers on the European Court of Justice a jurisdiction to give preliminary rulings concerning the validity and interpretation of acts of the institutions of the Community. In most cases this jurisdiction can be invoked by any national court or tribunal, regardless of the level at which it functions in the national legal hierarchy. However, the Regulation on Insolvency Proceedings amounts to a special case, because it has been adopted pursuant to powers conferred under Title IV of the EC Treaty in its amended form (most recently amended by the Treaty of Amsterdam which entered into force in 1999). The jurisdiction of the ECJ to interpret measures falling into this category is subject to special restrictions imposed by Article 68 (formerly 73p). Article 68(1) permits a reference to be made by a national court only where a question on the interpretation of the Regulation is raised in a case pending before a court or tribunal of a member state against whose decisions there is no judicial remedy under national law. Therefore, only an appellate court of last resort is eligible to request a preliminary ruling from the ECJ. The terms of Article 68(1) declare it to be obligatory for such a national court to request a ruling if it considers that a decision on the question of interpretation is necessary to enable it to give judgment.

32–033   The practical consequence of the restricted facility for making a reference to the ECJ is that some quite crucial questions of interpretation are likely to be denied the benefit of that court's co-ordinating guidance for many years to come. The limited resources that are available in cases of insolvency are a severe constraint on the prospect of pursuing a point of interpretation to the highest appellate tier, in order to have the possibility of a reference to the ECJ. Moreover, the cumulative delays—especially at the Luxembourg stage of the proceedings—can impose unwelcome hardship on the parties affected. It must therefore be hoped that national courts of first instance, or at the initial level of appeal, will endeavour to approach the task of interpretation in a spirit of fidelity to the overarching purposes and principles of the Regulation, viewed in its entirety. By aspiring to emulate the interpretative techniques of the ECJ itself, national courts may play their part in ensuring the Regulation fulfils its intended purpose of enabling cross–border insolvency proceedings to operate efficiently and effectively, thereby contributing to the proper functioning of the EU internal market.

3. Part II: Managing the future of international insolvency: the choices before us

Between them, the papers presented at this session have demonstrated the extraordinary abundance of activity currently being directed at the goal of improving the functioning of international insolvency. Clearly, there is much that is to be welcomed about this "tidal surge" of energy targeted upon a field of considerable practical importance which has for so long been regarded as too obscure, and too technically intractable, to justify the allocation of the human and material resources required to bring about tangible enhancement of its international governance. For rather more than three decades, the twists and contortions of the EU saga seemed to many to furnish justification for both scepticism and pessimism: so many years of arduous labour, always seemingly doomed to be defeated by extraneous political factors at the eleventh hour. Yet suddenly, in the year 2000, we stand on the brink of an historic consummation of that ground-breaking project, which could lay the foundations for a future treatment of cross-border insolvency on an inter regional, and ultimately a global, basis. At the same time, a number of other projects in various quarters of the globe have either reached the point of completion, or are at a critical stage of evolution. As examples, the UNCITRAL Model Law of 1997 is beginning to receive the attention of law makers in a number of states around the world, and the first examples of its enactment into national law have already been reported.[6] With the recent completion of the American Law Institute's Transnational Insolvency Law Project, designed in the first instance to address the problems of insolvency of multinational enterprises operating within the three component states of NAFTA,[7] and the recent inauguration of a global initiative promoted by the World Bank,[8] there is lively debate concerning the ways in which international investment and commercial activity can best be assisted through the development of agreed standards and procedural arrangements covering both the domestic and the international aspects of insolvency.

32–034

In the face of such a miasmic swirl of activity, it is justifiable to think in terms of a metaphorical crossroads, with real and important choices to be made as to the future direction in which to advance. There are obvious perils in the form of the natural temptation to take advantage of the tidal flood of worldwide interest in this subject, after so many barren years, and to press ahead with several projects simultaneously for fear that the precious momentum may be lost. While such concerns are understandable, it is equally important that essential political and governmental support is not squandered through the generation of parallel projects which appear to duplicate each other—or which simply prove mutually incompatible or unworkable in practice. The requisite resources are most likely to be forthcoming if a convincing case can be assembled to show that the ultimate goal is the development of internationally standardised arrangements which are properly compatible

32–035

---

[6] See paper by Ron Harmer, chap. 31
[7] See paper by Professor Jay L. Westbrook, chap. 30
[8] See Gordon Johnson, "Towards International Standards on Insolvency: the catalytic role of the World Bank", in Law in Transition, 69–74 (Spring 2000).

with one another, while respecting the fact that fundamental differences of approach to insolvency are destined to remain in place for the foreseeable future. This calls for an acceptance of a realistic timetable for the accomplishment of even quite modest advances in cross-border co-operation between systems of opposing persuasion. Undue haste, or any attempt to provoke accelerated changes in policy on the pretext that "global market forces demand this", will be counter-productive. *Festina lente* should be the watchword.

3.1 The need for a co-ordinated strategy

32–036   But progress there must be, nevertheless. The exciting achievements of recent years have put in place the essential components for a properly planned, strategic approach to be formulated and entrusted to an appropriately constituted body, such as UNCITRAL, to execute in a progressive and balanced manner. As explained in Ron Harmer's paper, such a proposal has already been placed on the agenda of UNCITRAL and some progress towards a decision is anticipated during the year 2000.[9] If the proposal to renew the mandate of the Working Group is accepted in principle, the next phase of planning can begin. Sensibly, the involvement by invitation of a wider array of other agencies such as the IMF, the World Bank, and the ADB, and also non-governmental organisations such as INSOL International and the IBA, is anticipated. It is respectfully submitted that efforts should be made to involve other active players such as the EU in a representative capacity, and that a "round table" forum should be assembled at which to address the challenge of working towards an integrated framework of standards and procedures for insolvency matters that aspires to build bridges between legal traditions, and regional groupings of states, while at the same time the workings of the first wave of international arrangements can be monitored and evaluated.

32–037   While the difficulties of managing a vast and multilayered project of global aspiration can scarcely be underestimated, there are already some important factors that appear to justify a cautious optimism. For example, there has been a noticeable continuity of approach during the cycle of activity between 1980 and 2000 that has seen the evolution of the texts of, successively, the Istanbul Convention; the EU Convention/Regulation; the UNCITRAL Model Law; and the ALI-NAFTA Transnational Insolvency Project. These include conceptual innovations such as the "centre of main interests" and the "establishment" as connecting factors identifying different degrees of intensity in the relationship between the debtor and a particular jurisdiction; the pragmatic compromise that is the device known as "secondary bankruptcy" (capable of being identified with the concept of the "foreign non-main proceeding" for the purposes of the UNCITRAL Model Law); and the remarkable advances in judicial activism and cross-border co-operation that are confirmed and consolidated by the provisions in all four of the texts just mentioned. Also discernible is an emerging, standard vocabulary

---

[9] See paper by Ron Harmer, chap. 31

that infuses the language of these latter-day texts concerning the international governance of international insolvency. Provided that this apparent harmony of thought and provision is not displaced through divergent approaches to the interpretation of the texts in their respective spheres of application, there is a genuine prospect of a constructive global discourse being taken forward to the next, and subsequent, stages, with positive results.

CHAPTER 33

GLOBAL HARMONISATION OF INTELLECTUAL PROPERTY

RICHARD WILDER[1]

1. Evolution of intellectual property standards

The evolution of intellectual property at the international level can be   **33–001**
divided into three periods: the territorial international and global.[2] The territorial period is characterised by the principle of territoriality, "the principle that intellectual property rights do not extend beyond the territory of the
sovereign which has granted the rights in the first place."[3] The international
period culminated in the conclusion of the Paris and Berne Conventions and

[1] Director, Global Intellectual Property Issues Division, World Intellectual Property
Organisation. The views expressed in this paper are those of the author and should not be
imputed to WIPO or any of its Member States.
[2] See Dr. Peter Drahos, "The Universality of Intellectual Property Rights: Origins and
Development," Intellectual Property and Human Rights, WIPO Publication No.762, 1999.
[3] *Id.* at 16.

was characterised by states having agreed to some fundamental principles, the most important being national treatment. While the Paris, Berne and other treaties in the field of intellectual property characteristic of the international period did harmonise some norms in the field of intellectual property, the level of diversity allowed was great. In short, harmonisation was limited.

33–002   The current, global, period in the evolution of intellectual property is characterised by intellectual property being linked to trade. The high point—at least to date—was the conclusion of the Uruguay Round of trade negotiations in April 1994 in Marrakech. The conclusion of the Uruguay Round brought into existence the World Trade Organisation (WTO). All of the WTO members are bound by the provisions of the Agreement on Trade-Related Aspects of Intellectual Property (TRIPS Agreement).

33–003   The TRIPS Agreement contains a number of detailed obligations in the field of intellectual property. These standards will be the subject of another paper at this conference. What I will concentrate on is the evolving, generally negative, perception of the TRIPS Agreement and its implementation. Without implementation at the national level, the harmonising effect of the TRIPs Agreement that many anticipated will not be realised. For this discussion I will concentrate on the implementation of obligations concerning the fields of pharmaceuticals and biotechnology, as they are fields where the debate surrounding implementation of the TRIPs Agreement are the clearest.

2. The TRIPS Era

2.1 1999 WTO Seattle Ministerial: formal proposals

33–004   On January 1, 2000, developing country Members of the WTO were obliged to have fully implemented their obligations under the TRIPS Agreement.[4] At that time, globally enforceable intellectual property rights became available to the single largest number of rights owners having access to legal protection over their innovations and creativity in the history of the formal intellectual property system. As a consequence, new groups with specific needs and uses for intellectual property, including individuals and companies in developing countries, holders of traditional knowledge and countries rich in biological diversity, are being brought face to face, some for the first time, with existing or incipient national systems for exercise and management of intellectual property rights. The conflicts inherent in these new groups seriously addressing intellectual property are in evidence in some of the communications that were received by the General Council of the WTO from WTO Members in connection with preparations for the 1999 WTO Seattle Ministerial Conference. I would like to summarise some of those communications without commenting on them substantively. I make reference to them here only as a pedagogical device—they place into stark relief

---

[4] Some developing country Members of the WTO asked for an extension of the transition period allowed for developing countries provided for under Article 65 of the TRIPS Agreement. See Communication to the General Council of the WTO from Cuba, Dominican Republic, Egypt, and Honduras (WT/GC/W/209).

many of the issues in the field of intellectual property protection for biotechnology of interest to the new or emerging stakeholders. In addition, for background information, reference is made to relevant work in other fora, including WIPO.

Developed counties were clear in their communications to the General **33–005** Council of the WTO that the standards set in the TRIPS Agreement should not be lowered.[5] The Communication from the United States of America (WT/GC/W/115) agreed, going further in the area of biotechnology, specifically in respect of Article 27.3(b) of the TRIPS Agreement. The Communication—subsequently clarified by representatives of the Government of the United States of America—called for the elimination of the exclusion from patentability of plants and animals and the inclusion of key provisions of the UPOV agreement regarding plant variety protection in Article 27.3(b) of the TRIPS Agreement.

The positions taken by those developing countries that have issued com- **33–006** munications in respect of intellectual property and biotechnology.[6] Those positions fall into five areas: (i) requirement to mention biological source material and country of origin in patent applications, (ii) extend exceptions from patentability to address health concerns, in particular to exempt the essential drugs list of the World Health Organisation and to exempt from patentability microorganisms, (iii) ensure that obligations in the TRIPS Agreement are consistent with the Convention on Biological Diversity, (iv) establish protection that is applicable to the traditional knowledge of local and indigenous communities, and (v) improve ways and means to achieve the underlying goals of the TRIPS Agreement, including transfer and dissemination of technology.

2.1.1 Communications calling for the mention of biological source material and country of origin in patent applications

The Government of India, in a communication dated February 2, 1999 **33–007** (WT/GC/W/147), proposed a review of the TRIPS Agreement to "consider ways and means to operationalise the objective and principles in respect of transfer and dissemination of technology to developing countries, particularly the least developed amongst them." It was further stated that:

> The right of holders of traditional knowledge to share benefits arising out of such innovation cannot be over emphasised. This could be possible if commercial exploitation of such innovation is encouraged only on the condition that the innovators share the benefits through material transfer agreements/transfer of information agreements. A material transfer agreement would be necessary where the inventor wishes to use the biological material and a transfer of information agreement would be necessary where the inventor bases himself on indigenous our traditional knowledge. Such an obligation could be

---

[5] See, Communication from the European Communities (WT/GC/W/193) and Communication from Japan (WT/GC/W/242). Each of these proposals also calls for the TRIPS Agreement to be modified to choose one of the two competing systems for resolving who has a superior right to a patent: the first-to-invent or the first-to-file.
[6] I am aware that is inherently reductionistic to characterise the positions of any grouping of countries, including developing counties, as one. Thus, the matters raised by the countries identified here should not be viewed as being of universal applicability, even in the developing world.

incorporated through inclusion of provisions in Article 29 off the TRIPS Agreement requiring a clear mention of the biological source material and the country of origin. Article 29 deals with conditions on patent applicants. This part of the patent application should be open to full public scrutiny on filing of the application. This would permit countries with possible opposition claims to examine the application and state their claims well in time. At the same time domestic laws on biodiversity could ensure that the prior informed consent of the country of origin and the knowledge holder of the biological raw material meant for usage in a patentable invention would enable the signing of material transfer agreements or transfer of information agreements, as the case may be. Such a provision in the domestic law should be considered compatible with the TRIPS Agreement. The suggestion basically asks for further transparency in the form of additional information in patent applications, and an approach that allows a harmonious construction of the two international agreements.

33–008 Article 15 of the Convention on Biological Diversity (CBD) recognises that genetic resources, as a component of natural resources, are subject to the sovereign rights of States.[7] It follows that countries have the right to establish the conditions under which access to genetic resources is granted or facilitated. The CBD establishes that access to genetic resources shall be granted on mutually agreed terms and subject to prior informed consent of the Contracting Party providing such resources, unless otherwise determined by that Party.[8]

33–009 A number of regional and national laws have established to require that patent documents shall disclose the origin of the genetic resources used in the development of inventions as well as show that prior informed consent has

---

[7] Article 15 of the Convention on Biological Diversity (entitled "Access to Genetic Resources") reads as follows:

1. Recognizing the sovereign rights of States over their natural resources, the authority to determine access to genetic resources rests with the national governments and is subject to national legislation.

2. Each Contracting Party shall endeavor to create conditions to facilitate access to genetic resources for environmentally sound uses by other Contracting Parties and not to impose restrictions that run counter to the objectives of this Convention.

3. For the purpose of this Convention, the genetic resources being provided by a Contracting Party, as referred to in this Article and Articles 16 and 19, are only those that are provided by Contracting Parties that are countries of origin of such resources or by the Parties that have acquired the genetic resources in accordance with this Convention.

4. Access, where granted, shall be on mutually agreed terms and subject to the provisions of this Article.

5. Access to genetic resources shall be subject to prior informed consent of the Contracting Party providing such resources, unless otherwise determined by that Party.

6. Each Contracting Party shall endeavor to develop and carry out scientific research based on genetic resources provided by other Contracting Parties with the full participation of, and where possible in, such Contracting Parties.

7. Each Contracting Party shall take legislative, administrative or policy measures, as appropriate, and in accordance with Articles 16 and 19 and, where necessary, through the financial mechanism established by Articles 20 and 21 with the aim of sharing in a fair and equitable way the results of research and development and the benefits arising from the commercial and other utilisation of genetic resources with the Contracting Party providing such resources. Such sharing shall be upon mutually agreed terms.

[8] *Id*, Para. 5.

been obtained from the competent authorities and traditional knowledge holders. The stated purpose of such disclosures is to provide a mechanism to verify compliance with national laws and contracts concerning access to genetic resources and benefit sharing. The nature of these requirements and their implications have been studied in WIPO,[9] by the Executive Secretariat of the CBD,[10] the Secretariat of the Commission on Genetic Resources for Food and Agriculture (CGRFA).[11]

1.   Further work needs to be done to elaborate the role of intellectual property in this context. Indeed, the fifth Conference of the Parties on the Convention on Biological Diversity noted that an expert panel on the issue of access and benefit-sharing "was not able to come to any conclusions about the role of intellectual property rights in the implementation of access and benefit-sharing arrangements, and that the Panel developed a list of specific issues that require further study."[12] Part of the difficulty in coming to conclusions in this area is due to a failure to explore the issued raised in an interdisciplinary way to include representatives of the environmental and intellectual property communities. This failure has led to some missteps at the international level. For example, this issue was raised during the preparations of the Patent Law Treaty (PLT), which is the subject of a Diplomatic Conference taking place from May 11 until May 26, 2000. Raising the issue alone caused great concern as it had not been adequately prepared in an interdisciplinary way. Thus, at the opening of the PLT Diplomatic Conference, the Delegations concluded that the matter should not be raised at the PLT Diplomatic Conference. Instead, discussion was deferred but would be taken up in a format to be decided by the Director General of WIPO, in consultation with the Member States.[13] Indeed, the WIPO Working Group on Biotechnology,

---

[9] See "Intellectual Property and Genetic Resources—An Overview" (WIPO/IP/GR/00/2) and "Information Provided by WIPO Member States Concerning Special Provisions to Ensure the Recording of Some Contributions to Inventions" (WIPO/IP/GR/00/3/ Rev. 1).

[10] See "Access to Genetic Resources"(UNEP/CBD/COP/3/20), "Review of National, Regional and Sectoral Measures and Guidelines for the Implementation of Article 15" (UNEP/CBD/COP/4/23) and "Report of the Panel of Experts in Access and Benefit Sharing" (UNEP/CBD/COP/5/8).

[11] See "Revision of the International Undertaking on Plant Genetic Resources: Legal and Institutional Options" (CGRFA/8/9/99), "Report of the Chairman of the Commission on Genetic Resources for Food and Agriculture on the Status of Negotiations for the Revision of the International Undertaking on Plant Genetic Resources, in Harmony with the Convention on Biological Diversity"(CGRFA–8/99/13), "Composite Draft Text of the International Undertaking on Plant Genetic Resources—Incorporating the Chairman's Elements" (CGRFA 8/99/13 Annex), "Revision of the International Undertaking on Plant Genetic Resources—Consolidating Negotiating Text Resulting from the Deliberations during the Fifth Extraordinary Session of the Commission on Genetic Resources for Food and Agriculture" (CGRFA/IUND/CNT/Rev.1), and "Background and Documentation Provided by the International Association of Plant Breeders for the Protection of Plant Varieties (ASSINSEL)" (CGRFA–8/99/Inf. 9).

[12] UNEP/CBD/COP/5/WG.II/CRP.7 (May 22 2000).

[13] On May 11, 2000 the Director General read out the following statement to the Diplomatic Conference on the Patent Law Treaty:
"Following informal consultations conducted by the Director General concerning formalities in relation to the question of genetic resources, the following commitment was reached among the groups:

discussed further below, has identified this as a priority area for study and discussion within WIPO. The decisions of both the PLT Diplomatic Conference and the Working Group on Biotechnology are consistent with a decision taken at COP V where it was decided to further study the role of intellectual property rights on the implementation of the access and benefit-sharing arrangements and to do so in consultation with WIPO.[14]

2.1.2 Communications calling for an extension of exceptions from patentability

33–010   The Government of Venezuela (WT/GC/W/282) to the WTO General Council urged extension of "the list of exceptions to patentability in Article 27.3(b) of the TRIPS Agreement to include the list of essential drugs of the World Health Organisation, in order to develop the principles established in Article 8 of the Agreement." The communication from Kenya on behalf of the African Group (WT/GC/W/302) addressed the nature and scope of the review of Article 27.3(b) of the TRIPS Agreement and the timing of the implementation of the obligations under that Article. That communication also called for that review process to clarify the following three points in respect of exclusions from patentability:

1.   why the option of exclusion of patentability of plants and animals does not extend to micro-organisms as there is no scientific basis for the distinction;

2.   why the option of exclusion of patentability of "essentially biological processes" does not extend to "microbiological processes" as the latter are also biological processes; and

3.   that plants and animals as well as micro-organisms and all other living organisms and their parts cannot be patented, and that natural processes that produce plants, animals and other living organisms should also not be patentable.

2.1.3 Communications addressing the consistency between the TRIPS Agreement and the Convention on Biological Diversity

33–011   The Government of India, in a communication dated July 2, 1999 (WT/GC/W/225), stated the "the TRIPS Agreement is incompatible with the Convention on Bio-Diversity. There is first a need therefore to incorporate a provision that patents inconsistent with Article 15 of the CBD must not be

---

1.   No formal proposals or agreed statements will be submitted at the Diplomatic Conference. However, delegations can make any statement they wish for inclusion in the records.

2.   Member State discussions concerning genetic resources will continue at WIPO. The format of such discussions will be left to the Director General's discretion, in consultation with WIPO Member States."

[14]   UNEP/CBD/COP/5/WG.II/CRP.7 (May 22 2000).

granted." In a similar vein, the Government of Venezuela (WT/GC/W/282) stated that a review and possible renegotiation of the TRIPS Agreement should "[i]nclude the principles of the United Nations Convention on Biodiversity in the TRIPS Agreement, together with the Indian proposal (document WT/GC/W/225) to prohibit the granting of patents to those inventions made with foreign genetic material that are inconsistent with Article 15 of the CBD relating to the recognition of sovereignty and access to genetic resources." The communication from Kenya (WT/GC/W/302) proposed that the review process should seek to harmonise Article 27.3(b) with the provisions of the CBD and the International Undertaking, in which the conservation and sustainable use of biological diversity, the protection of the rights and knowledge of indigenous and local communities, and the promotion of farmers" rights, are fully taken into account.

2.1.4 Communications regarding the protection of traditional knowledge of local and indigenous communities

The Government of Venezuela (WT/GC/W/282) stated, in a communication **33–012** to the WTO General Council, that the TRIPS Agreement should be reviewed and possibly renegotiated to "[e]stablish on a mandatory basis within the TRIPS Agreement a system for the protection of intellectual property, with an ethical and economic content, applicable to the traditional knowledge of local and indigenous communities, together with recognition of the need to define the rights of collective holders."

In recent years, resurgent interest in tradition-based innovation and **33–013** creativity has given rise to legal, ethical, economic and social questions. Traditional knowledge arises as an issue in association with genetic resources under Article 8(j) of the CBD.[15] The language of Article 8(j) of the CBD suggests that its implementation requires three sorts of legislative action:

(a)   definition of standards concerning the availability, scope and use of rights (which could include intellectual property rights) in knowledge, innovations and practices of indigenous and local communities, as well as the establishment of measures concerning the enforcement of those rights;

(b)   promotion of wide application of such knowledge, innovations and practices with the approval and involvement of the holders of such knowledge; and

(c)   encouragement of the equitable sharing of the benefits arising from the utilisation of such knowledge, innovations and practices.

---

[15] Art. 8(j) of the CBD, which applies to *in situ* conservation of biological diversity, establishes that Contracting Parties "shall, as far as possible and as appropriate [. . .] [s]ubject to [their] national legislation, respect, preserve and maintain knowledge, innovations and practices of indigenous and local communities embodying traditional lifestyles relevant for the conservation and sustainable use of biological diversity and promote their wider application with the approval and involvement of the holders of such knowledge, innovations and practices and encourage the equitable sharing of the benefits arising from the utilisation of such knowledge, innovations and practices."

33–014   There are different views on how to address the first category of issues. Some would prefer to explore the possibility of using the existing mechanisms of intellectual property to protect traditional knowledge. Others would prefer to embark immediately on an exercise of developing a new, *sui generis* system of intellectual property protection, whereby the features of the existing mechanisms would be adapted to the particular characteristics of traditional knowledge. These differing views were expressed in the discussions leading up to the 1999 WTO Seattle Ministerial. In addition, this matter has been extensively discussed in WIPO,[16] in the context of the Convention on Biological Diversity[17] and by the Secretariat of the WTO.[18]

2.1.5 Communications regarding means to further the underlying goals of the TRIPS Agreement

33–015   The Government of India, in a communication dated February 2, 1999, to the WTO General Council (WT/GC/W/147), proposed a review of the TRIPS Agreement to "consider ways and means to operationalise the objectives and principles in respect of transfer and dissemination of technology to developing countries, particularly the least developed amongst them." That Government, in another communication dated July 2, 1999 (WT/GC/W/225), proposed, *inter alia*, that "Articles 7 and 8 of the TRIPS Agreement to be operationalised by providing for transfer of technology on fair and mutually advantageous terms."[19] In a similar vein, the Government of Venezuela (WT/GC/W/282) that a review and possible renegotiation of the TRIPS Agreement should "[e]xtend the incentives mentioned in Article 66.2 of the TRIPS Agreement in favour of developing country Members. Review the objectives and principles set out in Articles 7 and 8 of the TRIPS Agreement with the aim of making them effective and operational."

---

[16] See "Protection of Traditional Knowledge: A Global Intellectual Property Issue" (WIPO/RT/LDC/1/4), "Protection of Traditional Knowledge: A Global Intellectual Property Issue" (WIPO/IP/TK/RT/99/2), and "Intellectual Property and Genetic Resources—An Overview" (WIPO/IP/GR/00/2).

[17] See "Farmers" Rights and Rights of Similar Groups—The Rights of indigenous and local communities embodying traditional lifestyles: experience and potential for implementation of Art. 8(j) of the Convention on Biological Diversity" (UNEP/CBD/IC/2/14), "Knowledge, Innovations and Practices of Indigenous and Local Communities: Implementation of Art. 8(j)" (UNEP/CBD/COP/3/19), "The Relationship Between Intellectual property Rights and the Relevant Provisions of the Agreement on Trade-Related Aspects of Intellectual Property Rights (TRIPS Agreement) and the Convention on Biological Diversity" (UNEP/CBD/ISOC/5), "Legal and Other Appropriate Forms of Protection for the Knowledge, Innovations and Practices of Indigenous and Local Communities Embodying Traditional Lifestyles Relevant for the Conservation and Sustainable Use of Biological Diversity" (UNEP/CBD/WG8J/1/2).

[18] See "Environment and TRIPS" (WT/CTE/W/8 and W/8/Corr.1), "The Convention on Biological Diversity and the Agreement on Trade-Related Aspects of Intellectual Property Rights" (WT/CTE/W/50), "The Relationship Between the Convention on Biological Diversity (CBD) and the Agreement on Trade-Related Aspects of Intellectual Property Rights (TRIPS); with a focus on Art. 27.3(b)" (WT/CTE/W/125).

[19] Art. 7 of the TRIPS Agreement states:

> The protection and enforcement of intellectual property rights should contribute to the promotion of technological innovation and to the transfer and dissemination of technology to the mutual advantage of producers and users of technological knowledge and in a manner conducive to social and economic welfare, and to a balance of rights and obligations.

Matters regarding the transfer of technology in the context of the protec-   **33–016**
tion of biological diversity in connection with the CBD. Article 16 of the
CBD recognises that "access to and transfer of technology among Contracting Parties are essential elements for the attainment of the objectives" of the
Convention, namely the conservation and sustainable use of biological diversity for the benefit of present and future generations. In this vein, Contracting Parties undertake "to provide and/or facilitate access for and transfer to
other Contracting Parties of technologies that are relevant" to those objectives or that "make use of genetic resources and do not cause significant
damage to the environment." Accordingly, "access to and transfer of technology referred to [. . .] above to developing countries shall be provided
and/or facilitated under fair and most favourable terms, including on con-
cessional and preferential terms where mutually agreed." Where technology
is "subject to patents and other intellectual property rights, such access and
transfer shall be provided on terms which recognise and are consistent with
the adequate and effective protection of intellectual property rights."

Article 16 of the CBD stems from the acknowledgement that conservation   **33–017**
of biological diversity generates opportunity costs for biodiversity-rich countries that are not in control of the adequate and necessary technologies in
order to achieve the Convention's objectives. Article 16 establishes a legal
framework that seeks to reduce those costs, yet without undermining the
international intellectual property system. In this context, it is important to
note parallels between these provisions in the CBD and the TRIPS Agreement. In particular, Article 66(2) of the TRIPS Agreement provides that
developed countries shall establish incentives to enterprises and institutions
in their territories for the purposes of promoting and encouraging technology transfer to least-developed countries. Article 16(5) of the CBD mandates
Contracting Parties to the CBD to co-operate in order to ensure that patents
and other intellectual property rights are supportive and do not run counter
to the objectives of the CBD. This provision requires Parties to the CBD to
prevent the abusive use of intellectual property rights, which might impair
the attainment of the Convention's objectives. A parallel can be found
between Article 16(5) of the CBD and Articles 8 and 40 of the TRIPS Agreement, which contain principles and rules under which WTO Members may
control abusive practices by intellectual property rights holders.

As in the case of other matters arising under the CBD, means to promote   **33–018**
the transfer of technology relevant to the protection of biodiversity has been
studied in WIPO,[20] by the Executive Secretary of the CBD,[21] and Secretariat

---

Art. 8.2 of the TRIPS Agreement states:

> Appropriate measures, provided they are consistent with the provisions of the Agreement,
> may be needed to prevent the abuse of intellectual property rights by right holders or the
> resort to practices which unreasonably restrain trade or adversely affect the international
> transfer of technology.

[20] See "Intellectual Property and Genetic Resources—An Overview" (WIPO/IP/GR/00/2).
[21] See "Ways and Means to Promote and Facilitate Access to, and Transfer and Development of
Technology, Including Biotechnology," UNEP/CBD/SBSTTA/2/6, and "Promoting and
Facilitating Access to, and Transfer and Development of Technology," UNEP/CBD/COP/3/21).

of the WTO.[22] More work needs to be done that involves the Member States of both the CBD and the WTO, as well as the holders of rights in the technology and those desiring its transfer.

2.2 Discussions at the 1999 WTO Seattle Ministerial

33–019   What is implicit in the previous section of this paper is that while the conclusion of the TRIPS Agreement in the Uruguay Round of GATT negotiations may have been an end of international negotiations on a text, the work of implementation—the real heavy lifting—had just begun. The beginning of this "heavy lifting" comes at a time when all aspects of globalisation—including that involved in the broad adoption of standards of intellectual property protection—are under attack. Indeed, globalisation, including implementation of the standards under the TRIPS Agreement, has met with alarm if not outright rejection in many quarters. This anxiety about globalisation comes in the face of evidence that the globalised, rule-based trading system of today has brought unprecedented—albeit uneven—growth and prosperity. That anxiety was nowhere more evident than in the Streets of Seattle in late 1999.

33–020   The Seattle Ministerial of the WTO, which took place from November 30 until December 3, 1999, produced no results—the Ministerial having been suspended before any conclusions could be reached. There were, however, discussions of intellectual property issues—including issues that arise in the field of pharmaceuticals. These discussions proceeded from the communications to the WTO Council identified above. Again, while there were no results from the Seattle Ministerial, there was circulated, on December 3, 1999 an informal draft ministerial text which included the following relevant language regarding work proposed to be undertaken by the Council for TRIPS:

> Examine, in cooperation with other relevant intergovernmental organisations,[23] the scope for protection covering intellectual property issues relating to traditional knowledge and folklore under the TRIPS Agreement and other currently available legal means and practices, both national and international;
> In undertaking the review of the implementation of the Agreement provided for in its Article 71.1 and pursing the review of the provisions of Article 27.3(b), examine, on the basis of proposals by Members, ways of enhancing the extent to which the Agreement responds fully to its objectives and principles contained in its Preamble and its Articles 7 and 8 as well as to new international legal and technological developments and practices.

2.3 TRIPS Agreement: alarm and promise

33–021   The two faces of globalisation—alarm and promise—were certainly in evidence at the 1999 WTO Seattle Ministerial Conference. This was well captured in the following editorial:

> Advocates of globalisation are now increasingly inclined to accept that it creates losers as well as winners, and to concede that some provision must be made for its victims. Opponents are beginning to accept that globalisation has some benefits—a conclusion

---

[22] See "Factors Affecting Transfer of Environmentally-Sound Technology" (WT/CTE/W/22).
[23] It was understood that one of the "relevant intergovernmental organisations" referred to was WIPO.

hard to deny in the face of statistics showing huge gains in world prosperity and living standards during the wave of economic liberalisation over the past half-century.

We now, in fact, have the makings of a great political debate between the modern equivalents of the right and the left at the international level. On the right are those who believe that liberalisation[24] should continue because on balance it has done so much good and can do still more.

On the left are those who believe that something is going very wrong, that globalisation must only proceed, if at all, under a set of restrictive new rules on issues such as labor and environmental standards and human rights, as demanded by some of the demonstrators in Seattle.[25]

This political debate is also being played out in the field of intellectual property—to a certain extent in the field of electronic commerce, but most intensely in the fields of biotechnology and pharmaceuticals. Moreover, it is not being played out in a vacuum. Indeed, before the 1999 WTO Ministerial Conference in Seattle, the role of international trade rules in the field of health care was hotly debated. That debate continues.   **33–022**

For example, Medecins sans frontieres (MSF)—which won the Nobel Prize for Peace in 1999—had the following to say on patents for pharmaceuticals: **33–023**

> MSF is not questioning the importance of patents in stimulating research and development, but rather is insisting that a balance be founded between protecting intellectual property and assuring individuals" access to medicines. As it now stands a lucrative market for life-saving drugs simply does not exist in the developing world despite the fact that more than 90% of all deaths and suffering from infectious diseases occur there. Out of 1,233 new drugs brought onto the market worldwide between 1975 and 1997, only 13 were for tropical diseases. Market forces alone are not enough to address the need for affordable medicines or to stimulate research and development for neglected diseases.[26]

The World Health Organisation (WHO) has also made statements supportive of the need for intellectual property to encourage private investment in research and development. For example, WHO Director General, Dr. Gro Harlem Brundtland, has recently stated that "[t]o develop new drugs we need an innovative pharmaceutical industry, with appropriate incentives for innovation and protection of intellectual property rights. Experience demonstrates that protection of intellectual property rights goes hand-in-hand with successful research and development."[27]   **33–024**

---

[24] There has been some debate about whether the TRIPS Agreement is trade liberalising or protectionist. The TRIPS Agreement itself, in the Preamble, states the WTO Members desire that it "reduce distortions and impediments to international trade, and [take] into account the need to promote effective and adequate protection of intellectual property rights, and . . . ensure that measures and procedures to enforce intellectual property rights do not themselves become barriers to legitimate trade." Jagdish Bhagwati, Professor of Economics at Columbia University in New York was recently quoted as stating that the United States of America has "managed to push Western-style protectionism, like intellectual property rights and anti-dumping measures, under the guise of trade liberalisation. Non-trade issues should be left off the trade-liberalisation agenda." Reported by Shawn W. Crispin, Far Eastern Economic Review, February 17, 2000. As goods and services that are traded across international boundaries increasingly embody intellectual property rights, common standards, such as found in the TRIPS Agreement, will reduce friction and facilitate such trade. This is even more true where intellectual property rights themselves come increasingly to be licensed or traded internationally.

[25] Reginald Dale, *Globalisation Debate Getting Focused,* International Herald Tribune, January 14, 2000.

[26] see website: http://www.msf.org/advocacy/accessmed/press/1999/12/pr-seattle.htm

[27] Speech of WHO Director General, Dr. Gro Harlem Bruntland before the ad hoc Working Group on the Revised Drug Strategy, Geneva, October 13, 1998.

33–025   The WHO has also expressed a certain ambivalence, however, if not anxiety about intellectual property protection in the field of pharmaceuticals. For example, in a recent publication on the topic, the WHO stated that:

> [t]he major implications concerning access to drugs are linked with the strengthening of the monopoly of working conferred by a patent on its holder. By 2005 at the latest, all developing countries will have to grant legal protection by patents to pharmaceutical products. Such a monopoly situation could lead to an increase in drug prices. That is why developing countries that are WTO Members should make the fullest use of the periods of transition they have been granted to transcribe the provisions of the TRIPS Agreement into their domestic law. Member States have an obligation to integrate into their patent legislation the minimal standards established by the TRIPS Agreement (patents for 20 years, no differential treatment between nationals and foreigners, reversal of the burden of proof), but the Agreement leaves certain margins of freedom that can be used to limit the adverse effects on prices and access to technology.[28]

33–026   We are going through a period of rapid technological and social change, set against the backdrop of globalisation. The field of intellectual property—especially as it applies to pharmaceutical products—is not an exception in the level of anxiety that it generates. Given the increasingly interdisciplinary nature of discussions, there is no simple, one-dimensional response to eliminate the anxiety. Intellectual property alone is not a barrier to access to drugs, nor will intellectual property alone lead to the creation and widespread use of drugs in all countries and for all diseases. Similarly in discussions on the relationship between intellectual property and biodiversity, there is fear that the existence and exercise of intellectual property rights will narrow the focus of human activity to a few commercially viable plants or animals, squeezing out the rest. This "narrowing" of human activity would, it is argued, lead to unsustainable use of biodiversity and inequitable sharing of the benefits of such use. For example, there is a fear that developing countries will provide access to their genetic resources which would then be patented and commercialised by enterprises in developed countries without sharing of benefits. It is also argued that patents on genetic material will restrict the free flow of such material for use in research—in particular research by universities or not-for-profit entities. In the case of traditional knowledge, intellectual property is characterised as the tool used by multinational corporations to appropriate the knowledge of other, weaker parties and commercialise to their advantage and to the exclusion of the original holders.

33–027   The anxieties outlined above are, of course, stated in an overly simplistic way. Those who have participated in discussions on these issues in the World Health Assembly or the Conference of the Parties of the Convention on Biological Diversity know how complex they have become. Discussions in those fora on intellectual property and its role in the fields of health care or the protection of biological diversity, respectively, are often confused and

---

[28] Globalisation and Access to Drugs: Perspectives on the WTO/TRIPS Agreement, Health Economics and Drugs, DAP Series No. 7, *revised*, WHO/DAP.98.9, p. 39. In fact the number of developing and least-developed countries that excluded pharmaceutical products *per se* from patentability on January 1, 2000 was is relatively small, consisting of the following 16 countries: Angola, Argentina, Cuba, Egypt, Guatemala, India, Kuwait, Madagascar, Malawi, Morocco, Pakistan, Paraguay, Qatar, Tunisia, United Arab Emirates and Uruguay.

incomplete. The reason is that the constituencies at the national and international level that are affected by the outcome do not yet effectively communicate with one another. To put it bluntly, the health and environment people do not talk to the intellectual property people and vice versa. The nature of this problem, in the context of a discussion on intellectual property and human rights, was well stated as follows:

> The problem we face in the present time is that the institution of intellectual property has globalised without some set of shared understanding concerning the role that that institution is to play in the employment, health, education and culture of citizens around the world.[29]

What is needed is a more sensitive, nuanced approach that respects the value   **33–028**
of intellectual property, is cognizant of the social and economic aspirations of individual nations (including in the fields of biotechnology and health care), and leads to a focused, nation-specific, and results-oriented approach to implementing intellectual property systems at the national level. What I propose in the section that follows is a way forward that builds on a solid foundation—the development cooperation work of WIPO—and which moves forward in a rational, scientific and nationally-focused fashion. Without the "shared understanding" referred to by Professor Drahos the harmonisation of law and practice at the national level anticipated by the implementation of the TRIPS Agreement will not be accomplished—or accomplished only partially.

3. WIPO Responses—The medium-term

Any system—including that for the protection of intellectual property—   **33–029**
cannot long survive if it only serves (or is perceived to serve) the interests of only a few of its users. The task of all of us in the intellectual property community is to make the intellectual property system relevant to all. This has long been the basic work of WIPO, including work to make the system strong and relevant for all segments of industry, including the pharmaceutical and biotechnology industries while understanding and respecting the needs of our Member States and third parties, including consumers. WIPO will do this by continuing to build on the past work of WIPO to establish a strong foundation for the protection of intellectual property. Perhaps the best current example of this type of work is that in respect of biotechnology.

---

[29] Drahos, *op cit.*, p. 33. Professor Drahos goes on to say that "[l]inking intellectual property to human rights discourse is a crucial step in the project of articulating theories and policies that will guide us in the adjustment of existing intellectual property rights and the creation of new ones. Human rights in its present state of development offers us at least a common vocabulary with which to begin this project, even if, for the time being, not a common language." See also, Financial Times, April 24, 2000, p. 16 ("The complexity and closed nature of much international policymaking have intensified broader grassroots suspicion of globalisation, above all in the U.S. The phenomenon is blamed variously—and wrongly—for destroying jobs in rich economies, crippling poor ones, suppressing human rights and allowing big business to run rampant everywhere").

3.1 WIPO activities regarding biotechnology: traditional stakeholders

33–030   But for the added dimension of new and emerging stakeholders, the situation at present is similar to that in 1983 when the Assembly of the Paris Union for the Protection of Industrial Property instructed the WIPO Secretariat to "study the existing situation concerning the protection, by patents or by other means, of inventions in the field of biotechnology (including "genetic engineering') and possible means of providing for industrial property protection for such inventions, both at the national and international level." Thus was born the Committee of Experts on Biotechnological Inventions and Industrial Property (the Committee) which met four times from 1984 to 1988. Over that time, the Committee developed a series of "Revised Suggested Solutions Concerning Industrial Property Protection of Biotechnological Inventions" (suggested solutions). The last version of the Suggested Solutions was prepared by the WIPO Secretariat—on the basis of discussions by the Committee—and reported in WIPO Document BioT/CE/IV/3, which is attached as an Annex to this paper. The Suggested Solutions addressed questions concerning the availability of protection, scope of protection, and the deposit of microorganisms.

33–031   The questions and suggested solutions were developed, of course, within the context of the then-existing legal and technological framework. Since the final version of the suggested solutions, however, there have been a number of legal and technological developments in the field of intellectual property as it affects biotechnology. Moreover, there have been developments in diverse areas of international law and policy—such as in the protection of the environment and biodiversity and the protection of traditional biodiversity-related knowledge—which have had an affect on intellectual property protection for biotechnology. These developments give rise to a need to revisit past activities of WIPO and to co-ordinate and elaborate current and future activities to take into consideration the developments since 1988 and current realities.

33–032   A first step for that co-ordination and elaboration was foreseen in WIPO's 1998–99 Program and Budget. That Program and Budget called for the establishment of a "Working Group to study intellectual property aspects of biotechnology and of the implementation of the CBD (the Convention on Biological Diversity, 1992), including the potential role of the industrial property system in facilitating access to and transfer of related technology." That Working Group met on November 8 and 9, 1999 in Geneva and laid out an aggressive agenda for itself and the WIPO secretariat. I will identify the elements in that agenda in a moment, but first I want to draw attention to some items currently under discussion in WIPO.

33–033   Some of the issues in this field have been identified in the Program and Budget for 2000–01, including the study on the desirability and feasibility of a system for deposit in a data bank of DNA sequence listings, which deposit could be referred to in patent applications for disclosure purposes. The draft Program and Budget also calls for the "preparation of studies on important issues relating to the law of patents that might not yet be ready for consideration by the [Standing Committee on the Law of Patents], including certain practical questions relating to the patentability of biotechnological inventions." Examples can be readily found of practical questions, including questions set for discussion at this conference, including those relating to enabling disclosure, utility or industrial applicability and breadth of claims directed to inventions involving expressed sequence tags and single nucleotide polymorphisms.[30]

1. The Working Group on Biotechnology drew up an inventory of   **33–034**
    biotechnology issues connected with intellectual property to serve as a
    basis for the exchange of information and further study and work by
    WIPO (under the direction by the Member States of WIPO).[31] The
    issues identified fall within the following broad categories: legal stan-
    dards related to biotechnology, using intellectual property rights in
    biotechnological inventions, and administrative and procedural issues
    related to patent applications directed to biotechnological inventions.

3.2 New and emerging stakeholders

We must also be mindful of the needs of the new and emerging stakeholders   **33–035**
and their interests in intellectual property protection. When concerns are
raised in developing countries about traditional knowledge or biological
materials being appropriated without compensation, we in the intellectual
property community must take the concerns seriously. These concerns should
be taken seriously not because they raise political concerns about a threat to
the patent system. Rather, because the concerns are worthy of a response in
their own right. Indeed, by digging deeper we often find that the concerns
raise issues that are well known to traditional stakeholders in the intellectual
property system—adequacy of disclosure, enforcement of contracts, and
availability of prior art when searching patent applications. When concerns
are raised about the implications of intellectual property protection to health
care, we must respond. Not because we feel threatened, but because we need
to understand and then articulate how intellectual property can be made
relevant to and supportive of affordable health care in all countries. When
the new or emerging stakeholders contend that intellectual property and
systems of licensing and technology transfer are not working for them, we
cannot rely on a rote response. We must understand their concerns and
respond to them in a clear and focused manner.

WIPO has responded to many of these concerns in a concrete and pro-   **33–036**
ductive way. For example, during the 1998–99 biennium in the field of traditional knowledge WIPO was mandated by its Member States to "identify
and explore the intellectual property needs and expectations of new beneficiaries, including the holders of indigenous knowledge and innovations, in
order to promote the contribution of the intellectual property system to their
social, cultural and economic development."[32] Through a series of activities
over the biennium, including fact-finding missions, regional consultations,
and roundtable consultations, WIPO identified a number of needs in this

---

[30] Whether any of these questions are taken up at all and, if so, in what form is in the hands of the Member States of WIPO acting through the Standing Committee on the Law of Patents.
[31] WIPO/BIOT/WG/99/1.
[32] WIPO 1998–99 Program and Budget, Main Program 11.

area. To bring together the appropriate constituencies, WIPO conducted these activities with relevant stakeholders, including representatives of holders of traditional knowledge as well as those in the intellectual property field. The needs identified included further and more focused information on intellectual property protection as it applies to traditional knowledge, documentation of traditional knowledge, tests of the applicability of the existing intellectual property system to traditional knowledge, and tests of the applicability of customary laws to traditional knowledge and the relationship of such customary laws to the intellectual property system.

33–037   There are two hallmarks of the foregoing activities. First, they are based on a solid foundation—the work of WIPO over many years in the both development of norms in the field of intellectual property and in technical assistance and training in developing countries. Secondly, the activities have been inclusive. That is, they have been designed to include true stakeholders in the relevant debates. These hallmarks are further elaborated in the next and final section of this paper on solutions for the long term.

4. WIPO Solutions for the long-term

33–038   The work that WIPO has done in the field of traditional knowledge, which is also informed by years of development for co-operation experience, leads me to believe that the anxieties identified above cannot simply and quickly be allayed. Further, while the source of the anxiety may be global—the TRIPS Agreement for example—but the solutions depend on an inclusive, scientific, rigorous, and very local approach, having the following three elements:

> First, the discussion should take place at the country level. The work should be practical, scientific, and tailored to the needs of individual countries to implement international obligations (including under the TRIPS Agreement), ensure access to health care, and encourage and protect local investment and creative activity.

> Second, the discussion must include all stakeholders, including ministries responsible for health and intellectual property as well as the pharmaceutical companies (including generic drug companies), patients groups, and representatives of the medical community.

> Third, the discussion should proceed on the basis of an understanding of (i) the wide range of activities carried out by holders of intellectual property rights in a given country, (ii) the way in which those activities support needs of the government and people in that country, and (iii) the connection between those activities and intellectual property protection in that country.

33–039

Turning to the first element, I would recall that in respect of the TRIPS Agreement, WIPO has provided legislative advice to 95 developing countries and regional organisations by, *inter alia*, preparing 177 draft laws in the field of intellectual property. WIPO has also performed significant work in the areas of human resource development and infrastructure development. In each of these cases, the work was not done on the basis of a one-size-fits-all law or training program. Rather, all of our activities are tailored to meet the needs of each of our Member States. Such work is difficult and time-consuming. The result, however, is that the needs of our member states in the field of intellectual property are understood and addressed. When problems arise in connection with the application of intellectual property in other areas—such as access to pharmaceuticals or in respect of the protection of traditional knowledge or biodiversity—expertise in those areas has to be brought in. For example, in the field of pharmaceuticals, we are working now through a contact group that includes WHO and UNAIDS to ensure that our constituents at the national level in the field of intellectual property are working with their constituents at the national level in the field of health care. In the fields of traditional knowledge and protection of biodiversity WIPO works with a wide range of international intergovernmental and non-governmental organisations that bring the necessary expertise.

Turning to the second element, the type and scope of investments made by rights holders (primarily from industry) in developing countries are many and varied. The investments made by the pharmaceutical and biotechnology industries are typically presented in a one-dimensional way: industry needs patent protection to encourage private investment in research and development. While this is true, it ignores much of the investment of industry for which intellectual property protection is important. For example, companies will invest in the establishment of distribution mechanisms in a country in which they will introduce a new pharmaceutical product. Such mechanisms include infrastructure for physically moving the product into the market. In addition, they will include mechanisms for distributing information learned about the use or administration of a drug—including new indications or warnings. Absent trademark protection—if not an exclusive position in a market—there may insufficient incentives for making these types of investments. **33–040**

In a presentation at WIPO in June of last year, Mr. Maher Matalka, Secretary General of the Jordanian Association of Manufacturers of Pharmaceuticals & Medicinal Appliances, Amman, Jordan gave a presentation on "Industrial Property and the Pharmaceutical Industry— Opportunities and Challenges for Developing Countries." Mr. Matalka did express some of the anxiety that those in the pharmaceutical industry in Jordan were feeling as a consequence of the impending change to the patent law there. He did, however, indicate that with change come opportunities and identified several for industry in the Arab region. These opportunities identified a number of types of investments or investment vehicles important to industry for which intellectual property protection is important. Only one item on the list included research and development. These opportunities identified by Mr. Matalka included: **33–041**

- to seek new export markets by capitalising on high quality generic manufacturing,[33]

- to pursue contract manufacturing,

- to manufacture under license or joint venture,

- to establish clinical development programs, and

- to encourage local investment in research and development.

---

[33] In this respect Mr. Matalka identified a number of opportunities where the Jordanian industry could capitalise on its manufacturing and formulation expertise to produce for export products that were off patent. Matalka, Maher, *Industrial Property and the Pharmaceutical Industry— Opportunities and Challenges for Developing Countries,* WIPO Seminar on Intellectual Property and Economic Development (June 3, 1999). p. 8.

33–042 Finally, no process for the development and implementation of an intellectual property system can be complete without the involvement and acceptance by a broad range of stakeholders, including the governments concerned, industry, the medical community and patients.[34] This is consistent with the view taken by UNAIDS that addressing the issue of cost and availability of drugs, especially for the treatment of HIV/AIDS is possible but:

> only in collaboration with those companies who developed the drugs in the first place, because they would likely be best positioned to get into cost+ pricing efficiently. (Cost+ pricing factors in only the cost of raw materials, production facilities, labor and a fixed disclosed profit margin to produce the goods, not marketing or development costs).[35]

33–043 When crafting solutions we in the intellectual property community must be open to a greater range of influences that has been the case in the past. For example, when the issue is intellectual property protection in the field of pharmaceuticals, we must work with true stakeholders in the debate—patients groups, representatives of the medical community, the pharmaceutical and biotechnology industries, and relevant intergovernmental organisations, including WTO, WHO, UNAIDS, and UNCTAD.[36] In matters relating to

---

[34] The Chairman of the U.S. Senate Judiciary Committee, Orrin Hatch, has invited (in addition to the pharmaceutical industry) patient and consumer groups to meet with him to discuss pharmaceutical patent laws with a view to their possible revision "to facilitate the next generation of diagnostic tests and new lifesaving and life-improving treatments." *Congress Daily*, February 14, 1999.

[35] Perriens, J, *Compulsory Licensing and Access to HIV Drugs*, speech at Paris 1999 Conference on Community and Home Care for People with HIV Infection. Dr. Perriens identified several elements necessary to make access to cost-effective drugs a reality, including: (i) differential pricing, (ii) encouraging companies to pursue patents only in countries where they desire to recoup R&D expenses, (iii) provisions for compulsory licensing in national laws (in a manner consistent with the TRIPS Agreement), and (iv) advocacy for "a more equitable distribution of economic benefits." The second element identified by Dr. Perriens is a natural consequence of companies pursuing a rational patent strategy. That is, they will seek protection in countries where they have an investment to protect. The implementation of a compulsory licensing regime at the national level requires careful attention to legal and commercial realities. Such a regime must be consistent with international obligations under the Paris Convention and the TRIPS Agreement—a matter with which WIPO has a great deal of experience. In this connection not only the TRIPS Agreement itself, but also "TRIPS jurisprudence" is an important resource to determining what is possible and prudent at the national level. "TRIPS jurisprudence" includes panel reports and reports of the Appellate Body under the WTO Dispute Settlement Understanding. It also includes national laws of Members of the WTO that have been reviewed by the TRIPS Council and the questions and answers generated in that review process. Commercial realities dictate that a compulsory licensing regime be enacted to guard against potential abuse of patents by their holders, but not undermine the incentives offered by the exclusive rights under a patent to create, invest, and form long-term relations between the developers and consumers of technology.

[36] The members of the so-called "contact group" identified in the WHO document referred to on p. 14, *supra*. There is a growing awareness of the need to address the issue of intellectual property and access to pharmaceuticals in a cross-sectorial way. For example, in the United States of America, the Office of the U.S. Trade Representative (USTR) announced an arrangement with the Department of Health and Human Services (HHS) to "establish a process for analyzing and evaluating health issues that arise in the application of U.S. trade-related intellectual property law and policy. When a foreign government expresses concern that U.S. trade law related to intellectual property significantly impedes its ability to address a health crisis in that country, USTR will seek and give full weight to the advice of HHS regarding the health considerations involved. This process will permit the application of U.S. trade-related intellectual property law to remain sufficiently flexible to react to public health crisis brought to the attention of USTR. It will also ensure that the minimum standards of the WTO Agreement on Trade-Related Aspects of Intellectual Property Rights (TRIPS) are respected." USTR Press Release 99–97, December 1,

traditional knowledge, a key constituent is the community of holders of traditional knowledge. Resolving intellectual property problems that arise in areas as diverse as access to pharmaceuticals or the protection of biodiversity or traditional knowledge is not a simple task. Lasting solutions are not found in platitudes, slogans or simple answers, but in developing a shared and common understanding.

1999. Further, President Clinton, by Executive Order dated May 10, 2000 stated that "the United States shall not seek, through negotiation or otherwise, the revocation or revision of any intellectual property law or policy of a beneficiary sub-Saharan African country, as determined by the President, that regulates HIV/AIDS pharmaceuticals or medical technologies if the law or policy of that country: (1) promotes access to HIV/AIDS pharmaceuticals or medical technologies for affected populations in that country; and (2) provides adequate and effective intellectual property protection consistent with the Agreement on Trade-Related Aspects of Intellectual Property Rights (TRIPS Agreement) . . . " By letter dated May 16, 2000 Congressman Archer, Chairman of the Committee on Ways and Means of the U.S. House of Representatives expressed the concern to USTR Barchefsky that the Executive Order was "inconsistent with existing U.S. law on intellectual property rights protection."

CHAPTER 34

INTELLECTUAL PROPERTY IN THE MILLENNIUM
ROUND—THE TRIPS AGREEMENT AFTER SEATTLE

PROFESSOR MICHAEL BLAKENEY

1. Seattle and its Sequelae

34–001   At first blush, the failure of the Seattle Ministerial Conference appears to have been a major setback to proposals for significant updating of the WTO Agreement on Trade Related Aspects of Intellectual Property Rights (TRIPS). In particular, left on the table in Seattle were proposals for the incorporation into TRIPS of the WIPO Copyright Treaty and the WIPO Performances and Phonograms Treaty; proposals for the sui generis protection of plant varieties; the amplification of the protection of geographical indications; as well as the expansion of biotechnological patenting. WTO Member States also planned to discuss the non-violation provisions of Article 64(2) and (3).

34–002   However, the Seattle fiasco leaves intact the TRIPS Agreement as signed at Marrakesh in April 1994. This version of the Agreement contains its own built-in reform agenda. Article 71(1) obliges the Council for TRIPS to review the general implementation of TRIPS in the year 2000. Additionally, a number of Articles specifically provide for their review. Thus a number of the matters which were scheduled for discussion in Seattle will be dealt with in the normal course of events. Finally, the TRIPS Agreement left a number of intellectual property matters to national governments to determine, on the basis of domestic considerations. These include:

- the modalities employed to give effect to TRIPS obligations (for example, the nature of the "legal means" required to protect geographical indications—whether this is done by more general laws governing consumer protection, fair trading, unfair competition or passing off; or registration of GIs or use of the trade mark system);

- the nature of limited exceptions to copyright, patent, design and trade mark rights (for example, limited copying for educational purposes);

- the choice of registration or non-formality systems (such as for integrated circuit layout designs, and industrial designs);

- specific options noted in TRIPS: *e.g.* taking *ex officio* action on border controls; and

- whether to protect plant varieties by patent laws or by *sui generis* options.

The TRIPS Council will have the task of determining whether the implemen-   34–003
tation by individual countries of these obligations, substantially complies with TRIPs norms.

Also unaffected by Seattle is the on-going process of dispute resolution and the consequential interpretation of specific TRIPS provisions.

Over the next two years, the TRIPS Council is required to review the leg-   34–004
islation of developing county Members of the WTO, who were obliged to notify their intellectual property laws to the WTO under Article 63.2 of TRIPS. Hence the legislation of more than 70 Members of the WTO will have to be undertaken by the TRIPS Council. For example in June 2000 the Council will review the laws of Belize, China, Cyprus, El Salvador, Hong Kong, Indonesia, Israel, Korea, Macau, Malta, Mexico, Poland, Singapore and Trinidad and Tobago.

This paper will survey the principal reform and interpretative issues before the TRIPS Council, as well as the salient disputes which are under consideration.

2. *Sui Generis* protection of plant varieties

Article 27.3(b) of the TRIPS Agreement requires Members to "provide for   34–005
the protection of plant varieties either by patents or by an effective *sui generis* system or by any combination thereof." In the next sentence provision is made for "this subparagraph [to] be reviewed four years after the date of entry into force of the WTO Agreement."[1]

There is a vigorous debate on the sorts of sui generis systems which might comply with Article 27.3(b). The TRIPS provision makes no reference to the International Convention for the Protection of Plant Varieties (UPOV). This is considered to provide some leeway in the formulation of sui generis systems.[2] Furthermore, key elements for the shaping of sui generis systems are either unclear or not defined. First, there could be several ways to define the term plant variety. For granting protection under the traditional plant breeders right (PBR) system, plant varieties must meet the criteria of being distinct, uniform and stable (DUS). It has been suggested that "Uniformity" and "stability" could be replaced by the criterion of identifiability, allowing the inclusion of plant populations which are more heterogenous, thus taking into account the interests of

---

[1] *i.e.* by the end of 1999.
[2] For example, see "Various Systems for Sui Generis Rights Systems" (1998) No. 38 *Biotechnology and Development Monitor* 3.

local communities.[3] The scope of protection could be limited to cover only the reproductive parts of plants, or could be extended to include also harvested plant materials.

34–006   Secondly, the TRIPS Agreement does not prohibit the development of additional protection systems, nor does it prohibit the protection of additional subject matter to safeguard local knowledge systems and informal innovations as well as to prevent their illegal appropriation. Several elements could be added, such as community gene funds, the establishment of mediation procedures (public defender) for the protection of local interests or local registers. Darrell A. Posey and Graham Dutfield have conceived of Traditional Resource Rights (TRRs) as an approach to sui generis protection.[4] TRR are posited as "a process and framework to develop multiple, locally-appropriate systems and "solutions" that reflect the diversity of contexts where sui generis systems are required".[5] "Traditional resources" include tangible and intangible assets and attributes deemed to be of value (spiritual, aesthetic, cultural, economic) to indigenous and local communities.[6] TRRs are described as "an integrated rights concept that recognises the inextricable link between cultural and biological diversity" delineating a constellation of "overlapping and mutually supporting bundles of rights" which "can be used for protection, compensation and conservation".[7] TRRs are constructed around four processes:

(1) identifying "bundles of rights" expressed in moral and ethical principles; (2) recognising rapidly evolving "soft law" influenced by customary practice and legally non-binding instruments, declarations and covenants; (3) harmonising existing legally-binding international agreements . . . and (4) "equitising" to provide marginalised indigenous, traditional, and local communities with favourable conditions to influence all levels and aspects of policy planning and implementation.[8] Grounded in human rights discourse, TRRs are viewed as "more holistic than intellectual property rights".[9]

2.1 TRIPS Review

34–007   Article 27.3(b) provides for its review by 1999 by the TRIPS Council. The position taken by some industrialised nations was that the article should be modified, either to identify UPOV as the reference convention for the interpretation of the *sui generis* clause, or to delete the whole subparagraph

---

[3] Seiler, "*Sui Generis* Systems: Obligations and options for developing countries." Biotechnology and Development Monitor, (1998) No. 34, *Biotechnology and Development Monitor* 2.
[4] See the publications of the Programme for Traditional Resource Rights, The Oxford Centre for the Environment, Ethics and Society, Mansfield College, University of Oxford.
[5] D.A.Posey, *Traditional Resource Rights. International Instruments for Protection and Compensation for Indigenous Peoples and Local Communities*, Gland, IUCN, 1996, xiii.
[6] *ibid.*, 15.
[7] D.A. Posey and G. Dutfield, *Beyond Intellectual Property: Toward Traditional Resource Rights for Indigenous Peoples and Local Communities*, Ottawa, IDRC, 1996, 4.
[8] Posey, n.5 *supra.*
[9] L. Glowka, *A Guide to Designing Legal Frameworks to Determine Access to Genetic Resources*, Gland, IUCN, 1998, 39.

27.3.(b) entirely, leaving no more exceptions from patentability. This would ultimately correspond to the original objectives, pursued by the U.S. during the negotiations on the Uruguay Round.

The formulation and promulgation of TRIPS had occurred largely without the active participation of developing countries. Their principal negotiating position during the Uruguay Round was to question the relevance of intellectual property for the GATT, particularly as WIPO existed as the primary forum for intellectual property matters. As a consequence they had little contribution to make to the final text of the Agreement. Now that TRIPS exists as part of the legal landscape, groupings of developing countries have held a series of meeting to agree a negotiating position for the upcoming TRIPS and CBD reviews.   **34–008**

For example, the meeting of the Non-Aligned and Developing Countries at New Delhi on January 29–31, 1999 issued a Perambular Statement in which concern was expressed that the TRIPS Agreement failed to address the central objectives of the CBD, in particular the questions of access to genetic resources and the equitable sharing of benefits. The Statement also called for a regime to protect local and community knowledge and the knowledge systems of indigenous peoples.   **34–009**

The expansion of, or at the very least, the maintenance of the exceptions in Article 27.3(b) of TRIPS for the patenting of life forms was urged. The expansion was sought to extend to "micro-organisms, products and processes thereof". The definition of micro-organism was sought to be expanded to cover tissues, cells or cell-lines or DNA obtained from higher organisms, including human beings". The New Delhi meeting sought the expansion of the sui generis clause to :   **34–010**

(i)   ensure implementation of Article 8(j) of the CBD relating to indigenous and local communities;

(ii) ensure that full consideration of environmental and ethical concerns about IPRs on life forma are addressed;

(iii) allow the completion of a biosafety protocol that establishes minimum international standards for the environmental safety of releases of genetically modified organisms.

The meeting sought the removal of the word "effective" from Article 27.3(b) or by defining it such that national priority is paramount in the interpretation of the term, including: **34–011**

(i)   conservation and sustainable use of biodiversity;

(ii) promotion of traditional lifestyles;

(iii) promotion of food and health security;

(iv) ensuring equitable benefit sharing;

(v)   invoking the precautionary principle;

(vi) respecting the principles of equity and ethics.

34–012   The meeting recommended the insertion in Article 29, concerned with patenting, a specific requirement obliging the disclosure "of the genetic resources and the traditional knowledge used in inventions for which IPRs are claimed, the country and community of origin of these resources and knowledge and proof of consent having been sought of the relevant community and equitable benefit-sharing arrangements having been entered into with them, as required by the CBD".

34–013   Parallel recommendations were made in relation to the review of the CBD. Thus in relation to the access and benefit sharing provisions of the CBD, the New Delhi meeting urged: the "consideration of mechanisms such as certificates of origin, evidence of prior consent for access to genetic resources, evidence of prior approval of indigenous and local communities for access to traditional knowledge, and disclosure of this evidence in patent applications". Similar provisions were urged for the FAO Undertaking on Plant Genetic Resources.

34–014   In relation to national patent legislation in the countries of Southern Asia, the meeting recommended the exclusion from patentability of all life-forms, existing traditional/indigenous knowledge and products and processes "essentially derived from that knowledge".[10] It was recommended that patent applications should include:

(i)   disclosure of all places of origin in the material/knowledge used in the application;

(ii)   disclosure of all communities/persons of origin;

(iii)   proof of consent having been obtained from the community/persons of origin;

(iv)   proof of benefit-sharing arrangement having been entered into with the community/persons of origin . . .;

(v)   disclosure of any previous rejection of application, in the country or other jurisdictions;

(vi)   prior public notice in all relevant languages in the places or communities of origin.

34–015   The New Delhi meeting rejected the UPOV Convention as an adequate model for *sui generis* plant variety protection. It urged the adoption of alternative models, incorporating the same sort of provisions as it recommended for national patent laws, and recommended the inclusion of a comprehensive code of provisions protecting Farmers" Rights. The establishment of a gene fund, "derived from fees and other levies on plant breeding and the seed industry" was recommended, to be used to support *in situ* farmers" conservation. The consideration of new varieties for protection should include "an environmental and social impact assessment to ensure that they do not threaten agro-diversity and community rights".

---

[10] The European Patent Convention was suggested as a precedent for this legislation.

The New Delhi meeting also recommended the development of *sui generis* legislation to protect the folklore and traditional medical knowledge of indigenous persons and the compilation of a database, or registry of the knowledge wealth of a country. The Nairobi conference also addressed the interrelationship between the TRIPS Agreement and the CBD. Concern was expressed that Article 27.3(b) was being reviewed after such a short period of time since the creation of TRIPS. Developing countries were being obliged to introduce intellectual property laws by the end of 2000 to comply with TRIPS norms, in a situation where the norm concerning patenting and plant variety protection, was already under review. The hope was expressed that Article 27.3(b) could be revisited in later reviews, after developing countries had elaborated codes of best practice. The Nairobi Statement, issued by the conference, suggested that African countries in developing and adopting positions for the review of the article should give consideration to:

34–016

(i)   cross and linkages between different provisions of TRIPS and between TRIPS and other WTO agreements;

(ii) the need to avoid bilateral treaties on these matters;

(iii) the need for the WTO to acknowledge the importance of sustainable development in implementing the world's trade regime;

(iv) the need for countries to assert their sovereign rights over genetic resources and to protect and promote the rights of their traditional and local communities;

(v)   ensuring that the WTO takes account of the provisions of the CBD and the FAO Undertaking on Plant Genetic Resources.

Further regional co-operation and awareness raising on the review of Article 27.3(b) was urged.

A *Communication* was made to the WTO from Kenya, on behalf of the African Group, to assist the Preparations for the 1999 Ministerial Conference of the WTO. The Communication pointed out that as the deadline for implementation of the obligations by developing countries of the TRIPS Agreement was January 2000, the review would precede the implementation of obligations undertaken by developing countries. As developing countries would have had insufficient experience with the operation of the Agreement they would have had no prior opportunity to conduct impact assessment studies of implications resulting therefrom.

34–017

Furthermore, the Communication pointed out that the review would pre-empt the outcome of deliberations in other related fora such as CBD, UPOV, FAO, International Undertaking on Plant Genetic Resources, and the development of an OAU Model Law on Community Rights and Control of Access to Biological Resources. They proposed that an additional five years be allowed, prior to the review of Article 27.3(b).

34–018

The African group proposed that "after the sentence on plant variety protection in Article 27.3(b), a footnote should be inserted stating that any *sui generis* law for plant variety protection can provide for:

34–019

(i)   the protection of the innovations of indigenous and local farming communities in developing countries, consistent with the Convention on Biological Diversity and the International Undertaking on Plant Genetic Resources;

(ii)   the continuation of the traditional farming practices including the right to save, exchange and save seeds, and sell their harvest;

(iii)   preventing anti-competitive rights or practices which will threaten food sovereignty of people in developing countries, as is permitted by Article 31 of the TRIPS Agreement."

34–020   On July 25, 1999 a federation of Indigenous Peoples groups issued a statement for the purposes of the TRIPS review. The Statement commences with the observation that "Humankind is part of Mother Nature, we have created nothing and so we can in no way claim to be owners of what does not belong to us. But time and again, western legal property regimes have been imposed on us, contradicting our own cosmologies and values." It expresses concern that Article 27.3(b):

> "will further denigrate and undermine our rights to our cultural and intellectual heritage, our plant, animal, and even human genetic resources and discriminate against our indigenous ways of thinking and behaving.".

34–021   The Statement draws the distinction between private proprietorial rights and "Indigenous knowledge and cultural heritage [which] are collectively and accretionally evolved through generations . . . The inherent conflict between these two knowledge systems and the manner in which they are protected and used will cause further disintegration of our communal values and practices".

34–022   The Statement pleads for a legislative structure which "Builds upon the indigenous methods and customary laws protecting knowledge and heritage and biological resources" and which prevents the appropriation of traditional knowledge and integrates "the principle and practice of prior informed consent, of indigenous peoples" as communities or as collectivities".

34–023   With the interruption to the debate on Article 27.3(b), caused by the Seattle failure, the issue of *sui generis* systems of plant variety protection, has been taken up in other for a, for example, the May 2000 meeting of COP 5 and the contemporaneous negotiations on the International Understanding on Plant Genetic Resources.

34–024   This Statement was picked up by a submission of Cuba, Honduras, Paraguay and Venezuela to the TRIPS Council,[11] which stated that these countries "consider it fair to recognise the specific contribution of indigenous and tribal peoples and local communities to the cultural diversity and social and ecological harmony of mankind".

34–025   At the third session of the WIPO Standing Committee on the Law of Patents[12] the delegation of Colombia proposed the introduction into the Patent Law Treaty an Article which provided:

---

[11] *Proposal on the Protection of the Intellectual Property Rights of the Traditional Knowledge of Local and Indigenous Communities*, WT/GC/W/362, October 12, 1999.
[12] Held in Geneva from September, 6–14.

1.   All industrial protection shall guarantee the protection of the country's biological and genetic heritage. Consequently, the grant of patents or registrations that relate to elements of that heritage shall be subject to their having been acquired made legally.

2.   Every document shall specify the registration number of the contract affording access to genetic resources and a copy thereof whereby the products or processes for which protection is sought have been manufactured or developed from genetic resources, or products thereof, of which one of the member countries is the country of origin.

An informal meeting was held by WIPO in Geneva on April 17–18, 2000 to consider the issue of genetic and biological resources and the subject was addressed by parties to the Diplomatic Conference on the Patent Law Treaty, which WIPO convened the following month. At the same time, the issue was canvassed by the COP 5 meeting in Nairobi.   **34–026**

3. Geographical Indications

Article 24.2 of the TRIPS Agreement requires the TRIPS Council to monitor the operation of the scheme of protection for geographical indications, which is established under the Agreement and to conduct a review of them The Council is given a general power "to take such action as may be agreed to facilitate the operation and further the objectives" of the protection of geographical indications envisaged under the TRIPS Agreement.   **34–027**

In preparation for the Seattle Ministerial, the African Group of countries submitted that the system for the protection of geographical indications be extended to products other than wines and spirits, such as handicrafts and agricultural and food products.[13] An EC proposal, suggested a number of procedures to confer clarity in this area. It recommended the establishment of a registration system and the introduction of an opposition procedure. It also indicated a willingness to extend geographical indications to other products.[14]   **34–028**

Following Seattle, at the March 21, 2000 meeting of the Council for TRIPS, the Members of the Central European Free Trade Agreement (CEFTA), with Latvia and Estonia, also requested that geographical indications protection be extended to a broader range of goods. This was supported by a wide range of agricultural producing countries. The USA was opposed to this expansion of the geographical indications system and recommended that priority be given to concluding the current negotiations to set up a multilateral notification and registration system for geographical indications.   **34–029**

---

[13] *Communication to the General Council of the WTO by Kenya on behalf of the African Group of Countries*, WT/GC/W/302, August 6, 1999, 28.
[14] Berz, "TRIPS and Related Topics an EU Perspective', paper presented at Fordham University School of Law, 8th Annual Conference, April 17–18, 2000.

4. Non-violation

34–030   Article 64(2) of the TRIPS Agreement provides that non-violation and situation complaints described in Article XXIII, 1(a) and (b) did not apply to TRIPS disputes until January 1, 2000. Under these rules, a WTO Member may invoke the fact that any benefit is being "nullified or impaired" or that the attainment of any objective of the Agreement is being impeded as the result of (a) the application by another [Member] of any measure, whether or not it conflicts with the provisions of [the] Agreement, or (b) the existence of any other situation. The TRIPS negotiators were unable to agree on the nature and scope of the sorts of complaints which may fall within the rubric of non-violation.

34–031   The commonest category of non-violation complaint, likely to fall within TRIPS is those relating to tariffs.[15] are those which relate to competitive restraints in intellectual property licences and other technology transfer transactions.

5. Dispute settlement

34–032   The TRIPS Agreement has been a fertile source of disputes coming before the WTO's Disputes Settlement Body (DSB). At the time of the Seattle Ministerial there were a number of pending disputes., the resolution of which will refine the meaning of a number of TRIPS obligations.

34–033   Prior to Seattle, the Indian Government, on the complaint of the USA had been found by the Appellate Body, in January 1998, to be in breach of the provisions of the TRIPS Agreement in failing to establish a mechanism to receive black box patent applications in relation to pharmaceutical and agrochemical inventions. Such a mechanism would have preserved the filing date, novelty and priority of inventions until such time as Indian patent laws complied with the TRIPS obligation to provide for the patenting of chemical processes.

34–034   A panel report issued March 17, 2000 had found that the Canadian patent laws were deficient under TRIPS by permitting the manufacture and stockpiling of patented goods in anticipation of the expiry of a patent.

34–035   A number of disputes were settled prior to determination. Thus, pursuant to mutually agreed solutions: Japan amended its copyright law to provide for the protection of sound recordings in existence on the entry into force of TRIPS; Sweden amended its laws to provide for provisional relief in the form of Anton Piller orders; Pakistan introduced a black box style of protection for pharmaceutical patents; and Portugal introduced a 20-year patent term.

34–036   Since Seattle, a complaint by the EU concerning section 110(5) of the U.S. Copyright Act, in relation to public performances, was sustained in part. A number of cases are pending. These concern pharmaceutical and agricultural patents and a number of aspects of copyright. As each of these is determined, further clarity of the TRIPS norms will be attained.

---

[15] See Evans, "A Preliminary Excursion into TRIPS and Non-violation Complaints" paper presented at Fordham University School of Law, 8th Annual Conference, April 17-18, 2000.